England and the Spanish Armada

The Necessary Quarrel

England and the Spanish Armada

The Necessary Quarrel

James McDermott

Yale University Press
New Haven and London

For information about this and other Yale University Press publications, please contact:
U.S. Office: sales.press@yale.edu yalebooks.com
Europe Office: sales@yaleup.co.uk www.yalebooks.co.uk

Designed by Sandy Chapman

Printed in Great Britain by Biddles Ltd, King's Lynn

Library of Congress Cataloging-in-Publication Data

McDermott, James, 1956–
A necessary quarrel : England and the Spanish Armada / James McDermott.
p. cm.
Includes bibliographical references.
ISBN 0-300-10698-X (cl : alk. paper)
1. Armada, 1588. 2. Great Britain--History, Naval--Tudors, 1485–1603.
3. Great Britain--Foreign relations--Spain. 4. Spain--Foreign relations--Great Britain. 5. Spain--History, Naval--16th century. I. Title.
DA360.M225 2005   942.05'5--dc22

2004021246

A catalogue record for this book is available from the British Library
10 9 8 7 6 5 4 3 2 1

Published with assistance from the foundation established in memory of Oliver Baty Cunningham of the Class of 1917, Yale College.

'... *what care then I say, my Lords, ought we to have in so holie, so juste, so honourable, so profitable and so necessarie a quarell to joyne together, to foresee the daungers, to provide for them, and to set up our rests either nowe or never to be able to withstaunde them?'*

Sir Chris. Hatton's address to the House of Lords, 4 Feb. 1589

Contents

List of Illustrations   viii
Note on Editorial Policy   ix
Introduction   x

PART ONE

ONE   *The Two* Barbaras   3
TWO   *The Rise of the Privateer*   13
THREE   *Mid-Tudor Malaise*   31
FOUR   *Gloriana*   47
FIVE   *The First Cold War*   64
SIX   *God's Englishmen*   92

PART TWO

SEVEN   *Non Sufficit Orbis, 1574–1584*   117
EIGHT   *Failing Brinkmanship*   146
NINE   *Military Preparations, 1587–1588*   171
TEN   *Awaiting an Enemy*   191
ELEVEN   *In Defence of Ourselves*   209
TWELVE   *The Happy Hour*   228
THIRTEEN   *Portland and Wight*   249
FOURTEEN   *Gravelines and the North Sea*   265
FIFTEEN   *A Contrary Success*   279
SIXTEEN   *England's Garland*   303

Abbreviations   329
Notes   330
Bibliography   385
Index   397

List of Illustrations

1. Elizabeth I: the 'armada portrait' by George Gower. By kind permission of His Grace the Duke of Bedford and the Trustees of the Bedford Estates.

2. Philip II, by Alonso Sanchez Coello. Glasgow Museums and Art Galleries.

3. Sir Francis Walsingham, by John de Critz. National Portrait Gallery, London.

4. Alexander Farnese, Duke of Parma, by O. Vaenius. Royal Museum of Fine Arts of Belgium, Brussels.

5. William Cecil, 1st Baron Burghley. Bodleian Library, University of Oxford, Poole Portrait 38.

6. Charles Howard, 2nd Baron Effingham, Lord Admiral of England by Daniel Mytens; a late portrait. National Maritime Museum.

7. Robert Dudley, Earl of Leicester, English School, sixteenth century. From the Collection at Parham Park, West Sussex.

8. Sir John Hawkins, English school, sixteenth century. National Maritime Museum.

9. Lord Henry Seymour, attrib. Federigo Zucchero. From the Collection at Parham Park, West Sussex.

10. Bowls on Plymouth Hoe, by John Seymour Lucas. National Maritime Museum, London.

11. The opposing fleets engaged, English school, sixteenth century. National Maritime Museum, London.

12. The fight off Portland Bill and aftermath, one of a series of narrative charts by Augustine Ryther, after Robert Adams. National Maritime Museum, London.

13. The armada campaign, English school, sixteenth century. By kind permission of the Society of Apothecaries, London.

14. Calais: the fireships advance, Netherlandish school, sixteenth century. National Maritime Museum, London.

15. The course of the armada, by Augustine Ryther, after Robert Adams. National Maritime Museum, London.

16. The Somerset House Conference, 1604. Attrib. de la Cruz Pantoja. National Maritime Museum.

Note on Editorial Policy

Quotations from contemporary sources are presented with original spelling, punctuation and grammar unchanged, though elisions are expanded and presented in parentheses. Where drawn from secondary sources, quotations modernized by previous editors are so identified in the accompanying endnotes. As the present work is largely concerned with English actions and motives, and the material cited overwhelmingly of English origin, dates are presented 'old style', according to the Julian calendar. Dates cited by non-English sources in the 'new' or Gregorian style after 1582 are distinguished as (NS).

As in previous works, the author has utilized the term Englishmen throughout to identify a race, not a gender. In mitigation of this unsatisfactory device, it is almost certainly the case that contemporary 'Englishmen' of both sexes considered the term to be neither inappropriate nor demeaning. It is also clear that the woman who looms most prominently in this book would have allowed no alternative claim to the status of foremost Englishman of her day.

Introduction

The struggle between Elizabethan England and Habsburg Spain has long been considered a defining episode in the story of the emerging nation-states of Western Europe. To many generations of Englishmen, it was an engagement their forefathers entered into almost guiltlessly and in which they were sustained by the abundant energies of a nascent sense of identity, the leadership of an iconic sovereign, and, of course, the benevolent hand of providence. It was the first, inspiring episode in England's essentially defensive journey to empire; the founding weave in a reluctantly assumed mantle of greatness. Like the later struggles against Napoleonic Europe and Nazism, it was a conflict that could not be shirked if an independent English polity were to endure.

This reassuring world-view has been undermined, if not entirely supplanted, by the revisions of modern research, but the inexorable nature of the slide to war, predicated upon remorseless political and religious frictions, remains an axiom of armada historiography. The protagonists' views of the world and its Creator were irreconcilable; too many powerful figures on either side of the confessional divide – princes, politicians and polemicists – believed that the defining battle between good and evil awaited only the appointment of champions to wage it. Upon that logic, the path to conflict was sketched out and engraved from the moment that Elizabeth – an heretical bastard in the eyes of the greater part of Europe – ascended her throne. Yet the path had few unequivocal signposts. Almost twenty years passed between the duke of Alba's descent upon the Low Countries (to many of Elizabeth's councillors the beginning of the feared Protestant apocalypse) and the execution of Mary Stuart, which finally pushed Philip into setting a definitive timetable for his 'enterprise of England'. During that period, the growing enmity of England and Spain was interrupted by lateral and often contradictory pressures, checked by the reluctance of its principal players to proceed further, and, until the eleventh hour, fuelled principally by the ambitions and actions of parties for whom the diplomatic process was at most a distant annoyance. In light of these often confounding truths, the conflict that ensued was less evidently a fated one.

The seeds of the possibility of conflict were, however, sown many years before its likelihood became apparent. In 1493, a Spaniard, Alexander VI, promulgated the bull *Inter Caetera*, which divided the New World between Castile and Portugal: nations whose intrepid explorations had begun to open up previously unknown regions. What constituted the 'Indies' would not be clear for some decades, of course, and the matter of boundaries was necessarily to remain rather open-ended. Papal pen drew an arbitrary north–south line of demarcation one hundred leagues further into the Atlantic than the westernmost limit of the Christian world, the Azores. All as yet un-pacified heathen territories in the hemisphere to the west of that line fell by right of future conquest and possession to Castile; those to the east, to Portugal. By this gift, Alexander intended that the new territories would be held as papal fiefdoms, ensuring that their formerly disadvantaged indigenous peoples would be brought into the light of salvation upon strictly prescribed terms. Given that Castilian and Portuguese ships were the only European vessels penetrating the non-European world at the time (the occasional Genoese and even English adventurer excepted), the terms of this division were largely uncontroversial, particularly as it had been determined by the unchallenged master of a united western Christendom. It could not have been anticipated that the same unity would shatter within the lifetimes of many who, however distantly, witnessed Alexander's grant – and that it would do so just when its disproportionate benefits were becoming manifestly clear.

In the year following *Inter Caetera*, Alexander conferred upon Isabella of Castile and Ferdinand of Aragon the title 'Catholic Kings', rewarding both their conquest of Granada, the last remnant of the Iberian Caliphate, and their intended crusade to carry the faith – and Spanish power – into North Africa. While the honorific had few temporal implications, its pretensions further cemented what was to become a century-long partnership of papal and Spanish power. In its early phase a pragmatic foil to French ambitions for the Italian pensinsula, the alliance, despite its many trials and testings, would be devoted increasingly to the preservation of orthodoxy against the rising tide of spiritual reformation. Although ostensibly unrelated to the pope's earlier bull, the assumption of this exemplary duty to preserve the True Faith was understood – particularly in the eyes of one subsequent, Habsburg monarch – as a quid pro quo for the near-miraculous acquisition of a vast and profitable empire. To challenge one was to deny the other, as Spain's future enemies well understood.

A decade later, Alexander's successor and erstwhile bitter rival, Julius II, granted a dispensation to the English King Henry VII's only surviving son, allowing him to marry his dead brother's widow, Katherine, daughter of Ferdinand and Isabella.[1] Despite its consanguineous taint, the arrangement had the blessing of all the interested parties. Castile, Aragon and England had every reason – Valois France – to maintain their recent blood-pact, and Katherine's own wishes were rendered inconsequential by the urgent pressure placed upon her by her parents' envoy to accept the new arrangement. Had this makeshift political match not taken place, and prince Henry taken instead a younger, more fertile consort (such as his father's former choice for him, Katherine's neice Eleanor), his subsequent break with Rome almost certainly would not have occurred, in which case any tender young English reformation must have faced the wrath of a ruthless, orthodox monarch and his equally Catholic heirs. As both marriage and break did occur, however, two of Henry VIII's three legitimate children were to be educated by Protestant tutors, ensuring the survival of the Act of Supremacy beyond the King's death. If *Inter Caetera* opened a first path to distant conflict, the disappointments of Henry's first marriage guided English feet toward it.

Yet these events provided only a foundation for future antagonisms. Mutual fear of France, and the strong economic linkages forged by the Habsburg inheritance of the overlordship of the Low Countries, made Anglo-Imperial friendship almost mandatory. The urge to preserve it proved enduring at a political level, even allowing for the vacillating diplomatic moods of Henry VIII and his son Edward VI's strongly Protestant reformation. Later, the staunchly orthodox Philip II would support his heretical sister-in-law's regime – albeit with strong moral reservations – during its fragile early years. She, in turn, was never to exhibit the slightest desire to lead or participate in any effort to roll back the boundaries of Catholic Europe. On these fundamental grounds alone, an amity that had already proved robust might have weathered the spiritual and economic upheavals that swept Europe – had princes alone, even in an autocratic age, been capable of determining the fate of nations.

That was to prove impossible, however. As shall be discussed, neither the Habsburg nor Tudor monarchies were able to insulate themselves from the impact of forces that they – indeed, all existing sixteenth-century power structures – were ill-prepared to meet. Throughout this period, 'Spanish' strategy was, ostensibly, what Charles v and then Philip ii declared it to be. Inevitably, this was moulded as much by political necessity as intention; but there emerged no element in the formulation of Spanish foreign policy that could be regarded as independent of the will of the Crown. Nevertheless, burdened by its imperial 'over-stretch' and the challenges of growing local nationalist sentiments and unorthodox ideologies, the most effective military power in Western Europe fought what would prove to be little more than a fifty-year holding action, and, by its own measure, failed.

The Habsburgs' Tudor cousins enjoyed a far more modest and homogeneous patrimony, yet the resources they commanded were not nearly sufficient to allow the royal prerogative to be wielded unsupported (or unhindered) by faction. 'The Monarch of Englands, King or Queene, hath absolutelie in his power the authoritie of warre and peace, to defie what Prince it shall please him, and to bid him warre, and againe to reconcile himselfe and enter into league or truce with him at his pleasure ...'[2] Few contemporary Englishmen refuted this principle, but managing it in the face of conflicting realities proved difficult. Henry viii, the epitome of the strong-willed, even ruthless Renaissance prince, squandered his nation's wealth in pursuing a European status that was all too easily faced down by the mightier Valois and Habsburg monarchies. Thereafter, the tidal waves of spiritual confusion, economic upheaval and military enervation that marked the later years of his rule had repercussions that survived the dynasty itself. All his successors came to the throne with the enthusiastic support of a vast majority of their subjects; all soon experienced the invisible limits of their rule. Edward's vi's policies were determined largely by the vacillating ambitions of powerful favourites; Mary Tudor's by counter-reforming fervour and unrequited adoration. Elizabeth was, ostensibly, her own woman, but for all her undoubted strength of will she depended overwhelmingly upon the loyalty and self-interest of her nobility, the personal faculties of her officers of state, and, above all, the affection of subjects whose priorities rarely corresponded with her own. With no army to speak of, and a navy that, although strong, burdened the Exchequer inordinately, the pursuit of war or peace increasingly devolved upon private initiative and resources. Given that troublesome necessity, English foreign 'policy' cannot be said to have reflected the royal will alone.

The obvious disparities in power and constituency enjoyed by the governments of Habsburg Spain and Elizabethan England, and the impact of an increasingly assertive Counter-Reformation, have made their contest seem strikingly unequal. The vastly disproportionate resources commanded by Philip II, and the tendency – then as now – to regard the theopathic nature of his kingship as indistinguishable from an aggressive imperialism, have encouraged a perception of England's 'Spanish' strategy as both defensive and cautiously implemented. The Spanish King's tyrannical mode of government was apparent to many non-Spanish Europeans (and to all Protestants among their number), as was the suffering of those who challenged or failed to acknowledge his sovereign authority. The necessity of resistance to his perceived ambitions, subsequently validated by the seemingly God-given deliverance of 1588, became as incontrovertible to future generations of Englishmen as did the 'black legend' of Spain's belligerency and moral degeneracy. Yet as this work will show, the apparently reactive policies of Elizabeth's government were often counter-responses to Philip's attempts to end increasingly bold assaults by Englishmen upon his assets, dominions and sovereign prerogatives. Much of the momentum towards alienation and then open enmity, it will be suggested, derived from English – but not Tudor – ambitions. Where those ambitions began, how they developed and the manner in which they came to be rationalized as moral imperatives are no less part of the history of the armada campaign than the battle itself.

To the present work, the Spanish 'story' of the approach to war is contextual rather than central. In recent years, the researches of scholars in the archives at Simancas and elsewhere have vastly increased our understanding of the pressures and motives that drove Philip II, his regional governors and the men who carried the great fleet of 1588 to English shores. The many excellent pieces resulting from these efforts will be cited as and where necessary, but the present author intends wherever possible to view the 'Spaniard' as did contemporary Englishmen, because their perspective – in many ways a self-consciously limiting one – had a fundamental impact upon the events that brought conflict closer. At the beginning of the sixteenth century, relatively few Englishmen had laid eyes upon a Castilian, much less enjoyed the opportunity to develop a distaste for him. At its close, when English merchants had been expelled from the Iberian Peninsula and their former entrepôts in the Low Countries, even fewer opportunities existed for some form of habitual contact between the two races that might have corrected the preconceptions and prejudices nurtured in the intervening decades. During those years, Englishmen briefly had suffered a Spanish King and – worse – his entourage; but this incited their enduring hatred of foreigners rather than any degree of constructive engagement. Subsequent attempts by a small number of their compatriots to access the profits of the New World brought violent confrontation and added little to English understanding of the cultures they attempted to penetrate. Emergent religious identity contributed to, and in turn was hugely influenced by, this creeping alienation. The process culminated in a perfect metaphor: the glancing, fractured nature of the armada battle itself. The two fleets met, clashed and parted; and had the *Rosario* escaped the supremely opportunistic Drake, the *San Salvador* the freak accident that crippled her and the *San Pedro Mayor* an unexpected Devon reef, hardly a single Spaniard would have been glimpsed by the men of the English fleet as more than a distant figure upon a poop-deck. Not until the modern era would a 'war' be fought again at such a remove, yet this was regarded by contemporary Englishmen as an intensely personal battle for the body and soul of the nation. A dispassionate examination of how a near-unknown enemy had seized such a dark place in the English psyche requires that one view much of him through a similar glass.

Tracking this slow-burning process is often difficult, because contemporary perceptions were not necessarily those that hindsight has assumed. For decades, the cumulative effect of spiritual, economic and political divergences loosened once-strong bonds of mutual self-interest; but this was movement on a near-tectonic scale, visible to few who did not actively seek, or expect, confrontation. One might identify certain moments at which a faint track became a furrow, others at which a dozen possible outcomes became a stark choice of advance or withdrawal. To lay peculiar emphasis upon any, however, would be to discount the ambiguities and misapprehensions that dogged contemporary political relations. Even in the modern age, the march to war is often more about misconception than calculation. At a time when reports from amateurish, partial or ill-informed diplomats travelled across Europe at a maximum velocity of twenty miles a day, suspicions, hearsay and outdated 'intelligence' informed the commitments of princes. With the intercourse of nations dependent upon such fraught raw materials, long-term strategic goals lay at the mercy of the moment.

Those outside government were of course infinitely less well-informed than their rulers. No mass media yet existed; no reliable means of disseminating information that might have leavened prejudice with a thin layer of perspective. Proclamations initiating foreign policy decisions often came no less as news to a domestic audience than to the rival power they aimed at, while the far-off events that invited such initiatives often acquired a thick patina of embellishment or exoneration before entering the public consciousness. For Englishmen, the history of their own times was a straightforward catalogue of other nations' perfidies – the loss of Calais to Henry II in 1557, John Hawkins's bloody repulse by the *flota* of Spain at San Juan de Ulúa eleven years later, Philip's increasingly interventionist policy towards English and Irish Catholics and the collateral but threatening atrocities inflicted upon European Protestants. The fact that none of these events contributed directly to the outbreak of war is immaterial; all increasingly agitated a public mood to make the possibility of conflict more acceptable.

The Anglo-Spanish War neither began nor ended with the armada campaign, but its brief fury represented to Englishmen a moment of release, invigoration and renewal. They venerated it as the 'War of 21 July', because everything that came before was nervous, dangerous indecision, and almost all that followed an anti-climactic haze of unfulfilled strategies and creeping economic hardship. Despite the enormity of the ostensible prize for which the protagonists clashed in 1588, the larger, eighteen-year conflict was largely a distracting episode in the developing destinies of England and Spain. It was a war that could not be won, only lost. Elizabeth and Philip, had they believed themselves to possess the choice, would have avoided it as happily as they would each other's company. They were unable to do so for many reasons, but above all because one of them presided over a nation whose shifting awareness, both of itself and of its place in the world, was only peripherally influenced by government. This trend had no single face and few obviously common values; its motors – social, economic, religious – were as diffuse as the concept of identity itself. But its heterogeneous and often conflicting imperatives found a powerful focus in fear: fear of the prospect of cultural extinction that the rising wave of Habsburg power seemed to presage. Before that spectre, too many of Elizabeth's subjects came to regard the avoidance of confrontation as inhibiting, and, eventually, fatal. In a sense, what resulted may be regarded as the first people's war. How it became so is the subject of this work.

PART ONE

A little Infant . . . demaunded of them whither they were those that should comme to devide the worlde with the Emperour? And as they aunswered yea, he tooke vp his shirte behinde and shewed them his buttocks, sayenge vnto them, drawe your Lyne throughe the middest of this place . . .[1]

The Two Barbaras

And I see that the preciousnesse of these things is measured after the distance that is betweene us, and the things that we have appetite unto.[2]

On 7 March 1540, the English ship *Barbara*, owned by the London merchants John Chaundelor and Richard Glasier and commanded by one John Phillips, departed Portsmouth Haven. She had a complement of approximately one hundred mariners and merchant-factors, including a number of Frenchmen. Their commission, sealed by the Mayor of Southampton, stipulated that they 'shulde do no robery but folowe ther vyage like honest men'. The following day, three Frenchmen and an Englishman – possibly disheartened by this restrictive clause – had second thoughts about their employment and abandoned the expedition at Calshot Point in the Solent. Chaundelor and Glasier, who had accompanied their ship to this point, also departed, to make their way back to Portsmouth. The *Barbara* sailed on to Falmouth, where she took in victals and water before passing out into the Atlantic Ocean. Her intended destination was Pernambuco, on the coast of Brazil.[3]

On Good Friday, off Cape St Vincent, the 'honest men' of the *Barbara* sighted a number of ships, including a Biscayan salt bark. Using their ship's boat they promptly boarded the bark and transferred her crew to a nearby Portuguese carrack (whose cargoes they pillaged before departing). The seizure was later justified by one of the English captors as a necessary measure to provide for the safeguard of their lives and the profits of their owners against the hazards of the coming voyage, rather than – as it may have appeared to the bark's unfortunate crew – a blatant act of piracy. Thus safeguarded, the expedition passed on to the Canary Islands, guided either by one or more of its French participants – pilots and adventurers who, like many of their countrymen, had been following Iberian ships into the Atlantic since the commencement of the Valois–Habsburg struggle in 1521 – or by their own, very recently acquired expertise.[4] In those waters, another raiding party was despatched from the *Barbara* to board and ransack a Portuguese vessel returning from the Barbary coast (Phillips later claimed to have forced his men to hand back their plunder, although he retained and distributed a quantity of gold coins among them). The following day, now off the island of Gomera, they attempted to hail a Spanish ship, and fired upon her when her crew sensibly decided to flee. This was the *Barbara's* final encounter in African waters. Making her westward trans-Atlantic passage without incident, she came next to the island of Fernando de Noronha, near Cape Roque, and from there passed on to the coast of Brazil, making landfall on 4 May.

It seems that the Englishmen's intention in coming to this region – the only peaceful aim of their voyage – was to obtain 'brazil', a redwood whose extract provided much-prized dye for European clothes. Contact was made almost immediately with friendly locals, who told them that such bounty was to be found only to the north, in the country of the dreaded 'Kenny-balles'. Discounting the implicit warning, Phillips and his men promptly set their course northwards. Two days later, their luck failed them. The *Barbara's* hull was breached upon a reef as the relatively deep-draughted vessel moved into a shallow bay in the search for amenable suppliers. She remained there for a month (despite her French passengers' complaint that the choice of anchorage was suicidally poor), while her pinnace and the captured bark were sent to reconnoitre the coastline further to the north. At first, contacts with the indigenous people were fruitful. Trading their own and previously stolen wares, the expedition acquired some three to four tons of cotton wool and fresh victuals. However, the arrival at their shore camp of a Portuguese official, guided by a Frenchman and a party of less obliging locals, marked the end of productive trading. Not unreasonably, the official demanded to know what business the interlopers had upon Portuguese territory. When they refused to give an adequate explanation or remove themselves, their own Frenchmen, sensing trouble looming, defected. These were chased into the bush by a party of nine Englishmen, who, with one exception, were slain in an ambush by the native levies. The survivor, Richard Everton, claimed later to have watched from undergrowth as the corpses of his compatriots were dismembered and eaten.

Following this encounter, the Portuguese official ordered his subordinates to deal with the main group of interlopers. In the next two days, they made a series of attempts to capture the English vessels, but were repeatedly scattered by ordnance and small arms fire. Wearying of this unprofitable persecution, and by now convinced that there was little chance of recovering any of their shipmates alive, Phillips and his men decided to leave the area. With nine of their number dead and their French allies fled, however, too few mariners remained to man both ships during the return passage to England. The survivors stripped out and burned their Biscayan prize (of only some forty tons burden, she was too small to carry the survivors home) and put to sea in the *Barbara*, which was still leaking badly. They set their course northwards once more – towards the Spanish Caribbean, hoping to 'safeguard' themselves with more reliable transportation.

Regrettably, the first Spanish ship they sighted was well-armed, and more than capable of defending herself. She gave the *Barbara* volleys from both her broadsides before retiring, causing further damage to the English ship's already-weak hull. A few hours later, off Hispaniola, the Englishmen sighted another Spanish vessel and hailed her to ask directions to a safe harbour. Curiously, she also was named *Barbara*: the *Santa Barbara*, commanded by a man who put far too much faith in strangers' promises. At the offer of a share of the English vessel's cargoes, he agreed to accompany her to a nearby lagoon, where she was driven aground. His men assisted her mariners in stripping out her valuable fittings and cargo, after which he was politely informed that his own vessel was requisitioned. He and most of his crew were abandoned on the shoreline of the lagoon with a sufficient proportion of victuals and a request to report the Englishmen's fair dealings to his superiors.

With the *Santa Barbara's* master and pilot forcibly conscripted, her new owners set a course for home. However, unfavourable weather, lack of understanding of the Gulf Stream's location and a lack of fresh water made their return passage a protracted ordeal. Disease and malnutrition killed some of the crew and incapacitated most of the remainder during the eleven weeks in which they struggled to re-cross the Atlantic. Of the original complement of ninety-four Englishmen, it was claimed that only thirteen healthy men brought the ship into Dartmouth in August 1540, although they and most of their frailer brethren managed to shift themselves and flee before the mayor of the town arrived to detain them for interrogation by

Admiralty officials. Only a few unfortunates were arrested and taken to London in chains.

The uncharacteristically prompt arrest of the *Santa Barbara* was made after urgent representations from the Emperor Charles v's envoy in London, Eustace Chapuys. His concern was not for the fabric of the ship, her cargoes or her kidnapped master or pilot, but for her charts. Spanish ocean-going vessels carried far more accurate plots than the rudimentary versions available to Englishmen, and Chapuys wanted to secure what might have become a template for a new generation of English charts before it could be copied. Given the tardiness of the English legal process, he was probably too late. Examination of the *Barbara's* crew in the Court of Admiralty did not commence until 20 November, and it was three weeks later still when its judges first heard testimony (from John Wood, her master's mate) of 'a very excellent goodly carde' that had been taken out of the *Santa Barbara* by the mariner Edward Gremell. Officers of the Court retired swiftly to Gremell's lodgings at St Katherine's Dock and seized the man, but there is no evidence that they found the chart, or any part of the expedition's booty.

The fate of Gremell and his companions is unknown. The statements made by these men were preliminary depositions, not evidence given in trial proceedings. It is not known whether those proceedings took place subsequently, although the *Santa Barbara* was, it seems, returned to her legal owners. The entire episode might have remained lost to posterity, were it not for Henry viii's recent reorganization of procedures to try and punish felonies committed on the seas. Until that year, 1540, cases of piracy could be heard variously under common law in King's and Common Benches, Assize, Port or Admiralty Courts, and under civil law before the Chancellor, Privy Council or Parliament. The potential for jurisdictional mayhem and the ineffectual application of the letter of the law – whatever that might be, precisely – was considerable. Henry's reforms brought all crimes at sea under the jurisdiction of common law, to be tried by the Judge of the Admiralty and one or more common law judges.[5] It is in the period immediately following this reformation that formal records of examinations of, and proceedings against, acts of piracy commence. Even so, those for early years are fragmentary. The frequency of offences remains hard to determine, although the system's overhaul indicates that a problem was already apparent. During a dinner they shared on 2 January 1541, the Lord Admiral, John Russell, hinted to Chapuys that if tried and found guilty the men of the *Barbara* might be executed.[6] Examples are not often made, or threatened, unless an audience exists to appreciate them.

If there was an audience, what circumstances had gathered it? At a political level, relations between England and the Empire were becoming relatively cordial once more after several fraught years. Henry's break with Rome and his dissolution of the monastic foundations had been provocative to all Catholic monarchs (although not, to Charles, as much as Henry's shameful treatment of his aunt, Catherine of Aragon). Briefly, during 1538/9, the truce between France and the Empire, and the pope's belated excommunication of Henry, brought the threat of a Valois–Habsburg crusade against England. However, neither Charles nor Francis had any real intention of exposing his back to the other. With the eclipse and fall of Thomas Cromwell, and the corresponding rise in influence of Bishop Gardiner and the duke of Norfolk, Charles came to believe – correctly – that there was a point beyond which the Henrician Reformation would not proceed. Even before this hopeful development, it was apparent to the Emperor that the alienation of Papacy and England was more about political authority than dogma; in any case, the man whose own troops had sacked the Eternal City only thirteen years earlier was hardly qualified to represent himself as God's avenging hand. Keeping Henry as an occasional resource in the over-arching conflict against France was, for Charles, a far higher priority than forcibly re-establishing the Christian commonwealth in England.

However, while not seeking the English King's overthrow, the Emperor was only too happy to pick at the vulnerable edges of the Henrician Reformation, particularly at the more objectionable strands it had acquired during Cromwell's tenure. Henry's supremely capricious nature made him difficult to influence; yet there were at hand certain means of persuasion that fell short of the threat of war. To assist in the process of nudging him back towards political quiescence and orthodoxy, Charles applied himself to the only English constituency over whom he enjoyed any substantial degree of influence – the Anglo-Spanish merchants.

Theirs was a vulnerable, if profitable occupation. For centuries, English consumers had relied upon foreign suppliers to provide products to which their own countrymen had no direct access. Wines, sugar, oils, nuts, exotic fruits and spices were all in strong demand among those fortunate elements of English society who did not live at subsistence level. The first of these commodities apart, high-value imports had long been carried predominantly in the ships of other nations. From the mid-fifteenth century, the monopoly enjoyed by foreign carriers loosened somewhat as more enterprising Englishmen – many from Bristol – set out their own vessels with the intention of reducing their intermediate costs. Tentatively, as English-carried

trade with the Iberian peninsula expanded, some English voyagers entered
the Mediterranean; others, as shall be discussed, followed the established
Portuguese trade routes and either interloped upon, or participated in, the
existing traffic in goods. However, these initiatives remained exposed to the
risks of natural disaster, ignorance of the markets they sought and interception by those who enjoyed their benefits already.

In contrast, the relatively safe and extremely profitable Low Countries'
trade, through which English half-finished clothes were exchanged for cash
and/or a plethora of manufactured commodities, exerted a powerful and
still-growing attraction upon English merchants' capital. This attraction in
turn was only the principal component in a larger, centralizing process.
What was known in England as the 'Anglo-Burgundian' intercourse (the
dukes of Burgundy had been overlords of the heterogeneous territories of
the Netherlands until 1477) was now in fact an Anglo-Habsburg relationship. As the family's shrewd matrimonial alliances brought more of Europe
within its patrimony, a greater proportion of English overseas trade, whether
speculative or well-established, had fallen within the dynasty's sphere of
control. *Magnus Intercursus*, the comprehensive commercial treaty that
would govern trading conditions between England and the Low Countries
for more than half a century, was concluded in February 1496 between
Henry VII and the Habsburg Philip 'the Handsome'. In 1499, the Portuguese
Crown established its northern European entrepôt at Antwerp, bringing
much of the precious ivory, spices and gold trade to a city in which English
capital was already heavily committed.[7] By 1516, all the Iberian and
Mediterranean lands formerly ruled by Isabella and Ferdinand had been
added to the patrimony of Philip's son, Charles, himself now overlord of
the 'Burgundian' inheritance. Importantly, these consolidations occurred
during years when new, potentially vast non-European markets, denied to
non-Iberians by *Inter Caetera* and its secular tweak, the Treaty of Tordesillas, were being exploited for the first time. If English merchants wished to
secure the world's exotic produce, they had little option but to do so within
a world-order laid out largely to Habsburg specifications.

With powerful economic incentives to toe an Imperial line, English merchants could be expected to respond promptly to disruptive pressures. Since
Henry's initial break with Rome some six years earlier, Englishmen in Spain
had been subjected infrequently to examination by the Inquisition for
alleged expressions of non-conformity and the possession of heretical tracts.
From 1538 (a year, not coincidentally, in which Henry was actively seeking
an alliance with the German Protestant Schmalkalden League to counter the

feared Catholic 'crusade' against England), the Holy Office began systematically to harass members of the Anglo-Spanish trading community. Yet if
these men were a tempting and accessible tool with which to influence their
King's policies, they were also an ill-judged one. They had long been
extremely industrious and law-abiding guests of Charles's Iberian subjects,
having traded directly with Castile and the 'old possessions' – her Atlantic
islands – since the early days of Iberian expansion into the oceans. When,
from the beginning of the sixteenth-century, restrictions were placed upon
access to Spain's conquests in the New World, they had acquiesced to the
fait accompli of Tordesillas, and worked industriously within the straitjacket
of regulation and limited access that crown policy rigorously enforced.
Probably, they were the closest friends of Spain that England ever produced.

The vast majority of them were also staunchly Catholic still, even several
years into the Henrician Reformation. However, they shared a peculiar vulnerability. Although spiritually conventional, they recognized – as did all
Englishmen – Henry's right to determine what constituted 'orthodoxy'. This
was not a matter of choice, but of a compulsion provided by the Act of
Supremacy – as their Spanish hosts were well aware. Yet this passive acceptance of what was an incontrovertibly heretical device to anyone acknowledging the transcendent rights of the Papacy gave the Inquisition a perfect
excuse to harass individuals whenever denunciations – made by Spaniards
with entirely earthly grudges – occurred. The usual technique employed by
the accuser was to urge an Englishman (before sufficient witnesses) to
denounce his king as a heretic. The victim's failure to do so – and this was
by no means the inevitable response – was faithfully reported to officers of
the Inquisition. In some cases, initial proceedings were followed by confiscation of the merchant's goods and chattels, with the offender sentenced to
compulsory attendance at mass, garbed as a penitent. In others, obdurate
Englishmen were subject to imprisonment and torture, and in one extreme
instance it seems that the intractable party was burned at the stake.[8]

The level and intensity of persecution should not be overstated, nor its
effect upon the hearts and minds of Englishmen. Wielding his Six Articles,
their own king was doing far worse to his domestic 'heretics' during these
years than anything the Inquisition had yet attempted; and although some
Anglo-Spanish traders permanently departed Spain as a result of these
unwelcome attentions, most remained.[9] The sole corporate response of the
merchants of the Spanish Company was to vote increased powers to their
governor, William Ostriche, to negotiate the release of members taken by
the Inquisition. Otherwise, it was business as usual. However, if the trade

itself weathered the squalls of persecution (which appear to have lessened after 1541, when wider political circumstances caused Charles to rein in the Holy Office), the attitude of those who conducted it was subtly altered. In acknowledging, however reluctantly, Spanish claims for rights of possession and exploitation of the known and as-yet unknown New World, they had regarded themselves as parties to an unspoken agreement. The quid pro quo – to be allowed to proceed in their trade unmolested – had been dishonoured. It was one thing to be unable to access new foreign markets directly; to be excluded *and* persecuted at political whim invited a rationale for resistance.

In the short term, the mistreatment of English merchants provided reason enough for a small minority to seek some form of redress. However, the seeds of a far more fundamental grievance – the conviction that Iberian hegemony over large swathes of the world was against natural justice – had been fertilized by these clashes. It was a modest, first contribution to an eventual corpus of moral, spiritual and economic antipathies that would allow Englishmen to justify their resistance to a world order that heavily favoured Habsburg ambitions. England and Spain would remain natural allies at a political level still, and continue to do so for as long as France represented a threat to both. But a psychological shift from amity had begun. Whatever the best interests of their sovereigns, a few, and then many Englishmen would come to regard the Anglo-Spanish relationship as not only immaterial but undesirable. Ominously, their number would include some who, formerly, had every reason to prolong it.

Was it a coincidence that the first known English voyages to the Spanish New World – a solitary, shadowy venture apart – commenced in the years in which Anglo-Iberian merchants were being systematically harassed for the first time?[10] The speed with which individual adventurers and small syndicates began to intrude where they were most definitely unwanted suggests that the urge was waiting upon the excuse. Already, the less heavily defended Portuguese American possessions were the subject of sustained English interest. The elder William Hawkins had visited Brazil upon at least two, and possibly three occasions in the previous decade; by 1540, a group of Southampton merchants – including one Robert Reneger, whose history does not end here – was said 'ordinarily and usually' to visit its coasts. Another of their number, a man named Pudsey, made what he claimed to be his second voyage to the region in that year. Near the principal Portuguese settlement of Bahia he built a fortified redoubt: a clear statement of future intent that would neither seek nor require the goodwill of his hosts.[11] The precise ambitions of Pudsey and his like-minded compatriots are unclear, but the implications of their daring and potentially ruinous attempts to access the forbidden fruits of Iberian enterprise were obvious, then as now. In all contemporary European societies, the right to wage war or otherwise to confront the pretensions of another state was the prerogative of the sovereign power alone. What *Inter Caetera* and Tordesillas had bestowed upon the Crowns of Spain and Portugal was not a matter for commoners to debate, much less oppose. Yet the un-franchised citizens of an increasingly second-rank power had begun, if obliquely, to test the limits of an imperial dynamic that had swept across unimaginably vast distances with God-given ease. The challenge could not be ignored. Whatever Henry VIII and Charles V – and their respective successors – imagined the parameters of their relationship to be, lesser men were redefining them.

And what of the *Barbara*? Hers was claimed to be a trading mission, but to a land where direct trade was forbidden by papal bull and right of prior conquest. Unsure of their welcome, her crew had not waited to test it but readily anticipated their hosts' ill-will with acts of piracy en route. For centuries, Englishmen had taken to the seas to commit similar depredations against the traffic of many nations – even their own. In peacetime, they were regarded as pirates; during times of war or international tension their status modified somewhat, when naval resources had to be supplemented by those of 'voluntaries', licenced by the Crown. Often, such commissions were taken up also by legitimate merchants, authorized to recoup losses suffered by them upon the seas, but who similarly failed to resist the temptation to extend their depredations beyond the strict remit they had been granted. Opportunities and temptations, arising far from the restraining hand of authority, did not often go begging. Yet there is no clear evidence that prior to 1540, those merchants who had always been the principal victims of pirates were themselves setting out commercial voyages whose ostensible aims were expected – or suspected priorily – to be supplemented by casual acts of robbery along the way.

Eventually, profits from depredations against foreign vessels, for centuries the recourse of lawless men or wartime necessity, would come to be regarded as be a near-legitimate element of England's seaborne 'trade'. As they did so, the boundaries between the motives of merchant and freebooter would fade to indistinction. With the voyage of the two *Barbara*s, we have a first sight of that creative blending of enterprise and banditry, industry and duplicity. We cannot say that similar incidents had not occurred prior to 1540, only that the recorded history of the semi-piratical ventures exemplified by Francis Drake, John Hawkins and their imitators emerges here, in the shadowy ambitions of messrs Chaundelor, Glasier and Phillips.

TWO

The Rise of the English Privateer

wee . . . are moste infamous for our outeragious, common, and daily piracies.[1]

Our perception of the English privateer commences with his Elizabethan incarnation, but the trade of the 'likedealer' or 'voluntary' was already venerable by the mid-sixteenth century.[2] The earliest extant reference to letters of marque or reprisal dates from almost three hundred years earlier, when Edward I issued a proclamation halting the execution of existing commissions allowing the seizure of Castilian cargoes (a retaliation against the King of Castile's policy of decapitating mariners from English-ruled Bayonne caught in his ports).[3] Almost certainly, there had been earlier occasions upon which such commissions were issued, and there would be many more subsequently, but their underlying rationale was consistent. For half a millennium following the Norman conquest, the domains of English kings were linked – or sundered – by the English Channel, making the matter of its control an acute concern. The seas were vast, however, and not easily policed. Few monarchs prior to Henry VIII possessed large, well-maintained naval forces, which made the requisitioning of privately owned shipping an inescapable element of maritime policy. In certain cases this could mean a near-permanent contribution to policing the seas. The Cinque Ports of Kent, for example, were noted in the Domesday Book as having an already long-standing responsibility for the protection of traffic passing through the eastern Channel. Usually, however, substantial non-naval resources were called upon only during wartime, to contribute to operations against an enemy with significant maritime capabilities. At its most basic, the role of privately armed vessels was to render sea routes dangerous for the enemy's civilian trade; but in the long periods during which the English 'navy' was almost non-existent, they also provided the only readily available means of carrying an English army to the Continent (or, with luck, of halting an enemy attempting the same passage in the opposite direction). It was a further advantage that such ships could return to their habitual employment – fishing or the transportation of merchandise – as soon as a threat diminished, keeping disruption to England's seaborne trade to a minimum. Finally, it need hardly be said that as the impressment or commissioning of privately owned vessels was a relatively cheap option, it was the preferred one. War has always been the most expensive occupation of nations; means by which it may be waged at someone else's risk and expense tend to be self-recommending.

That economy, however, depended upon how private vessels were utilized. Hiring them directly saved the costs of construction and maintenance of their fabric, but as with the King's own ships, merchantmen brought into naval service needed to be victualled and their mariners paid – usually from the royal purse. To that extent, they did not add appreciably to the resources that might be put to sea without extraordinary capital expenditure. The privateer's vessel, in contrast, required only an advance investment of the price of the ink, paper and seal that produced her letters of marque (and these were usually recouped in the clerks' fees). All other costs necessary to put her upon the seas were met out of sight and concern of the Exchequer; thereafter, the burden of her upkeep, repairs and crews' wages fell entirely upon the enemy, providing a double benefit that successive kings found hard to resist.

From its early days, privateering was regulated in theory and, inconsistently, in practice. The process of obtaining letters of marque or reprisal required recourse to the Chancery or, later, the Admiralty Court. In the case of individual applications, proof of losses suffered by the appellant was required before he could secure a licence to obtain restitution through seizures. When it became politically expedient to authorize the large-scale issue of commissions, however, the definition of what constituted a loss or grievance necessarily became a fluid one. At such times, reprisals might avenge the 'loss' of a king's initiative in his dealings with another prince, or merely anticipate identical measures from a looming enemy. Nevertheless, the legal process was usually observed with some care. Letters commissioning privateers typically stated the amount of restitution to be sought and the period over which their writ was valid. Most carried also a clause forbidding depredations against neutral shipping or that of the King's allies. Increasingly, it became the practice of courts to take bonds from appellants before they put to sea – the only realistic means by which the courts might encourage restraint from a distance.

Predictably, the process was tested to breaking point during times of open warfare, when law and practice had to serve the moment. During Edward I's Gascony campaign, even Englishmen who had murdered their own countrymen upon the seas – for example, the crew of the *Rose* of Harwich who had mutinied, killed their employers and stolen the ship and her cargoes – could obtain hastily drafted amnesties in return for service. These devices were unreliable on the whole (they were often dishonoured when the return of peace made the use of such reprobates unnecessary), but the mutual insincerity with which they were offered and accepted made them no less an indispensable tool of monarchs anxious to shore up their inadequate resources with those of a willing private sector.[4]

The collateral disadvantages of the system were often significant. Habitual pirates, hoping to lose themselves in the crowd of voluntaries, invariably put to sea without bothering the courts beforehand, and even those who had followed the legal process and obtained commissions to harry an enemy often interpreted their terms too liberally. The slightest ambiguity upon a question of the ultimate ownership of spoils – a favourite claim in Admiralty proceedings was that a seized neutral vessel carried 'coloured' wares, belonging to an enemy but misidentified in the ship's manifest as being those of a friendly power – ensured that the lawful owners' chances of restitution were minimal.[5] Bonds, even involving relatively large sums, rarely exercised a restraining influence where opportunities for plunder far outweighed the risk of forfeiture.

In unpoliced seas, so evident were these opportunities that even the more trustworthy elements within England's maritime communities fell prey to temptation. In 1299, the men of Cinque Ports, ordered to make restitution of spoils taken in a fight against French ships, petitioned their sovereign with a hardly veiled threat: 'And let the King's council be well assured that if wrong or grievance be done to them in any way against justice, they will forthwith forsake their wives and children and all they possess, and go to make their profit upon the sea wheresoever they think they will be able to acquire it'.[6] Ample precedent existed to give the warning credibility. Several of the Cinque Ports had sustained a long commercial rivalry with Great

Yarmouth that upon occasion had degenerated into mutual acts of piracy and murder; one of them, Rye, had a home-grown freebooting industry whose indiscrimination drew frequent attention from the Crown.[7] Men who were less exercised by the burdens of duty and custom did not announce their intentions so obligingly, or willingly follow either the timetable or priorities of their governments. Most wars fought by English kings were followed by peaces in which the same kings were obliged to open their purses and dispense compensation to injured parties. In 1354, Edward III issued a statute providing redress to foreign merchants whose vessels had been despoiled by Englishmen sailing under his commissions. 'In the years between 1399 and 1404 an unofficial pirates' war was waged in which unlicenced English ships preyed indiscriminately upon Flemish and English vessels alike, unchallenged by the as yet insecure administration of Henry IV. In the relatively lawless period immediately following the end of the Wars of the Roses, Edward IV was similarly embarrassed by the activities of his West Country subjects (specifically their seizures of Spanish ships), and found it necessary to compensate the injured parties by waiving all customs duties upon those wares they managed to bring safely into England. In 1484, his brother Richard III was obliged to prevent *any* armed ship leaving an English port without first securing pledges that it would not attack vessels of nations previously – but not presently – at war with England. The proscription was largely unheeded. Six years later, Henry VII issued a proclamation against what appear to have been precisely the same offenders, still busy upon their 'divers and monifold spoliations and robberies'.[8] These were only some of the more notable occasions of official discomfiture. Almost every conflict involving the passage of men and materials across English seas, or the breakdown of effective government at home, involved large-scale depredations against innocent parties. It is a testament to the enduring value of 'voluntaries' that no king ever baulked at the anticipated cost, post-conflict, of utilizing their energies.

Although statistics for the years prior to 1540 are sparse and unreliable, logic and the available evidence suggests that the pattern of such depredations followed the political cycle closely. Encouraged by official sanction during wartime, opportunities to plunder other men's cargoes brought to the seas many men who, in other circumstances, might have found profits in less violent pursuits. Conversely, the restoration of good relations between England and her maritime neighbours saw measures more industriously applied against those who refused to observe their princes' peace. As with highway robbery, however, it was not possible to control or discourage the more determined offenders. Privateering and piracy, as shall be discussed, were legally distinct activities that shared a common rationale. Each was fed and encouraged by the other: pirates made the most effective privateers, and newly redundant 'likedealers' often replenished the gene pool of piracy. The courts of all nations with coastlines were occupied in peacetime with the pleas of foreign merchants whose goods had failed to reach their ports of sale. England's own Court of Admiralty was first convened (at some time between 1340 and 1347) principally to address problems of adjudging spoil claims regarding foreign cargoes – cargoes that were not, on the whole, those of Edward III's French enemies.[9]

As enduring as the problem was, however, its potential to subvert the peace of nations was limited. The very indiscrimination with which male-factors plied their trade at sea encouraged governments to regard them more as a pestilential visitation than a *casus belli*. Occasionally, diplomatic protests were made and embargoes (or counter-embargoes) imposed; but the activities of semi-condoned pirates could not, alone, persuade princes to risk the expensive corrective of renewed warfare. Frequent confusion regarding the precise identities and location of the guilty parties, and the unwilling-ness of their victims to prolong economic or diplomatic counter-measures (which, inevitably, hurt their own interests also), meant that efforts to cure the problem were at best sporadic and half-hearted. Like endemic disease, depredations were regarded as an unpleasant permanence in contemporary seas. Efforts were made to alleviate its worst symptoms; compensation soothed their inevitable failures.

In western Europe this historic reality, unsatisfactory but manageable, modified considerably during the middle years of the sixteenth century. The causes were complicated and the process itself was, inevitably, obscure, but the perceptions and motives that drove men to 'privateering' – in the loosest sense of the term – were increasingly freed from effective political influence. The trend was apparent in almost every maritime region, although it was not experienced uniformly. The decades long Valois–Habsburg conflict was to create a near-permanent need (and opportunity) for French privateers to infest the sea-lanes across which much of the enemy's trade passed. With the collapse of royal authority in the French maritime regions and the effec-tive dissolution of the King's navy following the outbreak of the wars of religion in the 1560s, the expertise nurtured by this tradition became an indispensable – and largely uncontrollable – element of the rival factions' military resources. Further north, the labrynthine coastlines and shallow inlets of the Low Countries had long sheltered a particularly savage breed of pirate who preyed indiscriminately upon passing sea trade. The gradual breakdown of civil authority and growing political and ideological resistance to Habsburg authority in the Seventeen Provinces recruited many to his profession; in that company, an incorrigible plunderer was raised to the station of patriotic hero – the Sea Beggar. In Scotland and England, the process was more complicated, owing its impetus to the often blurred interaction of free enterprise, political calculation (and miscalculation) and a growing, if often insincere spiritual dimension. Only in Spain, where a strongly regulated maritime tradition, effective regional policing and widespread state-requisitioning of shipping resources discouraged the wrong sort of private initiative did an endemic privateering culture fail to take deep root. Those of other nations were, however, more than content to fill that void.

One of the dangers in charting the English contribution to this diffuse process is to anticipate rationales that, eventually, were to underpin the efforts of its most persistent elements. We have seen the appearance, during the years 1538–40, of the first fault-lines in the Anglo-Habsburg relationship that were not expressed at a purely political level. Tales of religious persecution filtering back to the quaysides of English towns, and the retaliatory seizures of Iberian vessels by 'merchant' voyagers, generated real grievances, both in England and Spain, that the diplomatic process could not address adequately. Even so, without further substantial grounds for contention there is little reason to suppose that the majority of those who considered themselves wronged would not have found satisfaction within the traditional mechanisms of protest, embargo and restitution. The conduct of trade, even when complicated by confessional disruptions, was too rewarding to forego readily; it would remain so until incentives to seek a sustainable alternative to the status quo became more apparent to a wider constituency than the career-pirate. Traditionally, it had been war and/or the breakdown of political authority that had both allowed and made apparent those incentives. It is particularly ironic, therefore, that during the 1540s it was precisely the opposite condition – a period of cordial relations between England and the Empire – that tempted many Englishmen into activities that would severely test the 'old amity'.

On 11 February 1543, Henry VIII commenced his third French war. Predictably, he did not communicate this fact to the French King, Francis I, choosing rather to wait until he was ready to proceed with some chance of victory. Success depended upon the close alliance he and Charles V concluded on the same day, committing each monarch to raising an army of 42,000 men and placing it on French soil by June 1544. The gathering of

England's share of this vast commitment began almost immediately and continued, slowly, through the year. At the same time, a major new building and purchasing programme for the Navy Royal was initiated which, with a number of pressed prizes, was to provide a further twenty-one vessels during the next two years.[10] Notwithstanding Henry's ready debasement of his kingdom's coinage, the extraction of forced 'loans' from his wealthier subjects and heavy subsidies from parliament, the wholesale alienation of lands seized from dissolved monastic foundations and the bulk-sale of lead stripped from the roofs of their conventual buildings, his treasury was swiftly emptied by these obligations.[11] Early English efforts to destabilize the as-yet unsuspecting enemy were therefore modest. A small squadron of four armed merchantmen of Newcastle was sent out in February 1543 to seize Scottish and French ships north of the Humber, but this appears to have been a retaliatory measure for earlier depredations against English vessels. Two further squadrons, based in the Downs and western Channel, were despatched in the following month. These were at best perfunctory measures, and the squadrons' habitual misidentification of friend as foe – to the extent that one of the captains in the Downs was pointedly ordered by the Privy Council to 'behave himselff in suche a sorte as itt myght nott appere that his Grace wer in hostilitie wyth all the worlde' – offset even such small advantage they might otherwise have delivered.[12]

Already nearing bankruptcy under the burden of her commitments, England finally declared war upon France on 2 August 1543. The course of this, Henry's final and least glorious military venture, is well known and needs only brief mention here. His failure to attempt (much less to achieve) the objectives agreed with his ally, and Charles's own campaign difficulties, led to the Emperor's abandonment of the war and conclusion of peace with France by the treaty of Crépy on 18 September 1544. Having forsaken his ally, Charles rubbed salt into the wound thereafter by offering his services as a mediator between the English King and Francis I.

Henry (whose own diplomatic treacheries were legion) was outraged by this betrayal, which left the English forces in France perilously exposed. The Dauphin (the future Henri II), taking advantage of the premature evacuation of Boulogne by Henry's generals, ranged the English 'pale' around Calais with fifty thousand troops while the bulk of the English army embarked in near-panic from the town itself. At the same time, well-coordinated French depredations against English ships made communications between England and her vestigial continental possessions extremely insecure. Moved partly by the same panic that had gripped his army, and by his indiscriminate anger against France, the Emperor and anyone else that had, or had seemed, to frustrate his grand design, Henry responded to these checks precipitously. On 20 December 1544, a proclamation was issued to his 'loving faithfull and obedient subjectes inhabiting upon the sea coasts, using trafique by see, and divers others . . . to prepare and esquipp sundry shipps and vessells att their owne costs and charges to the sea for the annoyaunce of his Majesties' enemies . . .'[13]

The chronicler Edward Halle considered this to be a traditional device: '. . . this yere was open warre proclamed with Fraunce, and lycence geuen to the Kynges subiectes to seaze vpon the Frenchemen and their goodes as in lyke cases before had been accustomed'.[14] In a narrow sense he was correct. There had often been an element of indiscrimination built into previous grants or commissions authorizing privateering activity. Since the middle of the twelfth century, the men of the Cinque ports had been allowed to retain a proportion of all spoils taken in seizures from specified enemies; in 1294, the men of the Isle d'Oleron obtained similar rights. Over a century later, Henry vi was obliged by penury and political chaos to permit a form of institutionalized piracy, barely camouflaged by the official licensing of surrogates to appoint their own admirals and keep the seas with their privately raised squadrons – the only means by which some form of royal authority could be maintained off-shore at that time.[15] But the terms of even these notably wide remits had been limited to named beneficiaries, or officers of the crown, or certain coastal communities as recompense for their quasi-official service. The new proclamation effectively dispensed with any such limiting devices. It sought rather to mobilize the entire English sea-going community (and any who might care to join it) in a campaign of undirected and unlimited warfare against the commercial traffic of the King's enemies.[16]

The proclamation had several further striking characteristics, none of which suggested that Henry intended to limit the side-effects of his policy. It explicitly exempted Englishmen who sailed under its writ from any obligation to give bonds for their good behaviour, or of any requirement to provide proofs of prior losses. And having equipped their ships, put to sea and seized their prizes, they were favoured by a further immunity – from the troublesome need to prove that their own spoils were 'good prize'. Nor were any proscriptions made regarding non-belligerents or friends of England. The King's enemies – France and Scotland – were named; otherwise, the sole discriminatory clause in the entire document required only that Englishmen did not attack other Englishmen or those foreigners who had specifically obtained the King's safe-conduct.

This was a dangerously arbitrary instrument, shaped by frustration (at the thin political rewards of the earl of Hertford's expensive Scottish campaign that year), spite (Charles's 'betrayal' of Crépy), desperate government penury (the 1544 campaign had drained the Treasury by £650,000, rather than the budgeted £250,000[17]) and false lessons drawn from damage done to English seaborne trade by Scottish and French privateers during the preceding two years. Its principal, near-immediate effect was to encourage a host of new, unwanted confrontations without either lessening existing strategic exposures or providing returns to government that were nearly commensurate with its risks. With temptation waved in the face of a nation as an act of policy, the painfully constructed mechanisms Henry had established only six years earlier to quell piracy were rendered wholly ineffective.

If the proclamation permitted Englishmen to act indiscriminately upon the seas, the peace of Crépy gave them both motive and opportunity. The restored commercial relationship between France and the Empire enabled Flemish and Spanish shippers to carry French goods in their holds once more. To what extent they did so is impossible to judge accurately, but English privateers very quickly came to assume that every vessel they sighted was in league with their King's enemies, and, therefore, an enemy also (as the Imperial envoy Van Der Delft observed some months later: 'apparently the English mean to seize everything at sea as French').[18] By January 1545, Henry's call to his 'loving faithfull and obedient subjectes' had encouraged large-scale depredations against neutral vessels – mainly those of Charles's subjects, who were said to have lost cargoes valued at 150,000 ducats since Henry's French war commenced.[19] Even when their ships escaped the wrath of the freebooters at sea, recourse to any English port invited seizure by officials upon suspicion that they carried victuals and munitions bound for France (a Spanish herring fleet, stayed at Dover, became the source of considerable dispute upon this pretext).[20] Imperial envoys reported to Charles a situation so untenable that his Flemish subjects were demanding outright war with England as preferable to this 'peacetime' persecution of their trade.[21]

Equally spectacular retaliation was inevitable, and on 5 January Charles ordered the detention of all English ships and goods in Low Countries' ports. These, like most of the spoils of Henry's policy, were the chattels of lawful traders, not of privateers or pirates. While the Emperor intended his measure only as a temporary restraint rather than outright confiscation, it generated an acute sense of grievance among the English merchant adventurers who spent half their lives at the Antwerp mart. These men readily acknowledged (and often suffered) the depredations of their compatriots, but appear to have believed that their own King was doing all he could to alleviate the plight of Charles's wronged subjects. One of their number, the London draper Otwell Johnson, declared it 'a strange kind of restraint in mine opinion, and to last so long, after the King's Majesty hath so gently used th'Emperor's subjects here that could complain of any loss, for to the uttermost denier they have been recompensed for all their loss, not escaping so much as a ship tankard'.[22]

Johnson's opinion was woefully ill-informed. There were still claims awaiting examination from plaintiffs whose cargoes had been pillaged by Englishmen even before the French war commenced, and they headed a rapidly growing queue.[23] Already intractable, Henry reacted to Charles's embargo by seizing all the Flemish ships and cargoes he caught in English ports, citing once more their alleged succour of the French enemy. For several months thereafter, his representatives and those of the Emperor conducted painful negotiations on the letter and spirit of each monarch's treaty obligations to the other. In the meantime, very little spoil was released. Eventually, on 6 April in Vienna, a preliminary agreement was grudgingly endorsed that provided for a general release and commitment by each party to prevent similar incidents in future. Unfortunately, at the moment when peace seemed about to break out, word came from Spain of a new outrage.

This was the Reneger 'incident' – the most famous act of piracy during the period – whose outcome graphically illustrated Henry's ready manipulation of the letter of his existing maritime treaties. In March, Robert Reneger, Anglo-Spanish merchant and alleged Brazilian trader, was cruising off Cape St Vincent with a small, privately financed flotilla.[24] There, he seized the ship *San Salvador*, returning to Spain from Hispaniola. For years, Reneger and his fellow Southampton adventurers had been involved in a private war against merchants from ports in northern France, with each despoiling the others' cargoes at sea. Lately, Reneger had been getting the worst of these exchanges, and during 1543 had taken up letters of reprisal (which, unlike the later general proclamation, had been granted bearing relatively restrictive terms of redress) in an effort to recoup his losses. However, having failed to make the expected returns from that source, he had widened arbitrarily the remit of his commission to include less well-armed prey. Later, examined before the Privy Council (to whom he had promptly despatched a report of his actions at Cape St Vincent to pre-empt any less favourable version of events), Reneger stated that his seizure of the *San Salvador* had been a reprisal for the detention of one of his vessels at San Lucar. Part of the Spanish ship's cargo was bullion to the value of some £4,300; much of this, he claimed, had been laden clandestinely by the ship's master rather than be registered for the Spanish Crown's use, and was not, therefore, to be considered the lawful property of its shipper.

Although evidence given in response by Spanish witnesses in the Admiralty Court was at best inept, nothing in Reneger's testimony provided any justification for his offence, which, furthermore, specifically contravened the letter of a clause in the Anglo-Imperial treaty of February 1543 protecting the subjects of both parties from depredations permitted under letters of marque.[25] While the Emperor himself did not react overtly to this outrage, his son Philip, regent in Spain, ordered the seizure of all English ships in Spanish ports pending restitution of the *San Salvador* and her cargo. Henry reacted by refusing to ratify the recent agreement regarding the mutual embargoes in England and the Low Countries. Charles observed that he had not authorized his son's actions and, somewhat optimistically, asked the English King not to conflate two separate issues. Henry, still consumed by the Emperor's 'betrayal' of Crépy, sulked throughout a succession of interviews with Chapuys – whom he openly accused upon at least one occasion of being a liar – while industriously lying about his own actions and intentions. In April, as Charles began to release English ships in the Low Countries, Henry, allegedly annoyed by Reneger's insolent actions, claimed to have recalled all privateers and prohibited them from returning to sea. This was untrue (though in the following month, men of Bristol, having shown particular enthusiasm for seizing Flemish and Spanish vessels, were allowed to return to sea only 'upon bonde not to moleste themperoure's subjectes'). In July, when Charles offered to release all English property in Spain if Reneger's spoils were returned, Henry claimed that he had ordered their restitution already. Again, this was untrue.[26] In fact, he later made the release of Reneger's booty conditional upon the prior lifting of Philip's embargo. The stand-off continued into the reign of Edward VI. Eventually, having made only a token restitution of part of the *San Salvador*'s bounty, Reneger was permitted to keep the bulk of his prize – less that portion already accepted and spent by the King – and became a minor, if transient celebrity at Court thereafter.

The episode demonstrated the capacity of sixteenth-century diplomacy to confound its intentions. Both Charles and Philip misread Henry's wounded pride and assumed that their embargoes (which contravened both the letter and spirit of the 1543 Anglo-Imperial treaty as baldly as the English King's actions) would draw their usual, and logical, response. Henry, in turn, considered the treaty's first rupture – Charles's peace with France – as one that invalidated the whole (at least, with regard to his own actions). Each party probably regarded the matter in the personal light that characterized princely relations, and believed it to be capable of resolution given the timely surrender of the other. But far removed from the rarefied atmosphere of sovereign rights and expectations, the repercussions of the 1544 proclamation were assuming an independent momentum. Englishmen absolved of any obligation to justify themselves before an Admiralty Court either before or after their seizures could not be expected to honour unspoken proscriptions; nor did they attempt to do so. Encouraged by a perception that carte blanche had been given to an entire generation of existing and would-be privateers to wage war upon their own terms, and justified by simmering (if largely disingenuous) resentments regarding Crépy and the habitual treatment of Anglo-Spanish traders, the scale of their depredations increased far beyond the anticipation or intention of government.

The policy's architects – other than Henry himself, who seemed quite indifferent – quickly came to regret its indiscrimination. At the beginning of 1546, the Lord Admiral Viscount Lisle (who was by no means averse to financing privateers on his own behalf) complained to the King's secretary, William Paget: 'Every Spaniard, Portugall or Fleming that comes from the South is robbed by our adventurers, some calling themselves Scots and some with vizors . . .'[27] By April, bombarded by complaints from English as well as foreign merchants, the Privy Council directed that all privateers entering West Country ports should be prevented from returning to sea 'tyll further advertisment' (this was a full year after Henry claimed to have imposed the measure).[28] Unfortunately, many were ranging widely by now, far from the grasp of Admiralty officials. In the same month, three English vessels entered the Basque harbour of Munguia in broad daylight and plundered a heavily laden Spanish merchantman.[29] From Portugal, the Spanish ambassador Lope Hurtado de Mendoza wrote to Prince Philip in somewhat vague outrage: 'Armed English ships are doing as much damage as they can, which is a lot. It is said they have captured I know not how many ships loaded with grain bound for Lisbon.' The Prior and merchants of Burgos, addressing a petition to Philip, suggested that the plate ships were especially vulnerable 'for the English and French dare to plunder everything they come across'.[30] Testimony provided to the Admiralty Court by some of the unfortunate victims of these outrages indicated that their English tormentors were treating Henry's ostensible allies every bit as savagely as they might his French enemies. In May 1546, the Spanish crew of the *Barbara* of Lequetia, boarded by Topsham men off Baltimore in Ireland, alleged that their captors twisted bowstrings around their genitals to encourage them to reveal the location of hidden parcels of goods – a technique that became something of a tradition among English pirates and privateers.[31]

If depredations by enterprising individuals were not burden enough for Charles's subjects, Henry's navy participated enthusiastically in the carnage during 1546. A powerful English fleet of some fifty vessels was assigned to guarding the passage of the annual wool fleet to Calais against French privateers. Upon that short navigation, elements detached themselves at will to plunder passing trade. Their efforts were so successful that the city of Antwerp addressed a formal petition to the Privy Council, claiming that between February and April, goods to the value of 35,000 Flemish crowns had been seized: 'Not a ship is allowed to pass without the English pillaging something from her . . . the persons despoiled . . . are mostly Spaniards.' Another report suggested that these incidents were also used to press hapless Flemish mariners into the English King's service.[32]

The Admiralty Court was not staffed to deal with the volume of complaints it received from injured foreign merchants, and its efforts to redress English outrages were extremely selective. The Anglo-Flemish trade was too valuable for either Henry or Charles to sacrifice upon points of treaty or principle, and there is evidence that from the latter part of 1545 seized Flemish cargoes that could be shown definitively not to have been bound for France were sometimes restored to their owners (provided that they had not been sold off immediately). But Spaniards, having no greater leverage than the relatively modest volume of the Anglo-Spanish trade to encourage their fair treatment in English courts, fared less well. In their case, the only occasions upon which restitution was made with reasonable despatch occurred when the Imperial ambassador in London made particularly strong representations on individual cases, or where Spanish merchants arrogated the responsibilities of Admiralty officials and personally tracked down their persecutors in English ports.[33]

One of the most industrious of these men seems to have been one Pedro de Villa Nova, a factor representing other Spanish merchants, who obtained letters from the Privy Council to the mayors, sheriffs and bailiffs of all the southern maritime counties, demanding that they assist him in finding the despoilers of his employers' ship *Trinity*. The Herculean nature of his task indicates something of the practical effects of Henry's 1544 proclamation. Leaving Southampton on her return voyage to Spain, *Trinity* had been 'sundrye tymes upon divers coastes . . . robbed and spoyled of more then three partes of her ladeng ... Months later, it had been determined that vessels of Dartmouth and Rye, and a pinnace belonging to Sir Richard Worseley, Captain of the Isle of Wight, had all (and separately) taken their share of the *Trinity*'s cargoes as she struggled to leave the deadly waters of the Solent. Worn out by his exertions, Villa Nova died during this epic quest to trace the stolen cargoes; but his persistence was rewarded by at least partial success, which is probably all that his principals had expected.[34] Indeed, such were the fading hopes of appellants to the Admiralty Court during this period that they seem to have exhibited a degree of gratitude when they managed to recover even a proportion of their goods. In October 1545, two Spaniards acting on behalf of another group of injured subjects of the Emperor appealed against seizures made by another *Trinity*: the *Trinity of Totnes*. Her owners had applied the standard defence: that part of the cargoes of vessels taken by her had been French, and therefore 'good' prize. The Spaniards proved this to be false. Nevertheless, when pressed by the Privy Council they agreed that some of the spoils should be retained by the perpetrators 'in recompense of their travailles, costes and charges that they have susteyned for the safeguarde of the other goodes of the saide Spanyardes'. The thieves were being compensated, in effect, for the costs of warehousing their stolen goods.[35]

Given the significant increase in the scale and incidence of English depredations, it will be apparent that the troublesome 'men of warre' whom the Council attempted belatedly to rein in now comprised a much wider constituency than the career pirate. The latter was heavily engaged of course, supplied and abetted by the south coast ports whose profits from trade had always been supplemented by less commercial activities. The men of Dartmouth, Plymouth and Totnes were not only active upon the seas but proved adept also at abstracting goods from the ships of foreigners coming to anchor in their harbours (doubtless relieved at having run the gauntlet of Channel despoilers unscathed). The mayor of Plymouth, Thomas Clowter, ordered by the Council to take custody of goods abstracted from two Spanish ships by William Hawkins, was imprisoned with him in July 1545 for 'fencing' the spoils in question. His counterpart at Lynn, John Mokkesand, narrowly escaped the same fate after steadfastly refusing to hand over to Admiralty officials a local pirate, William Peere. The bailiff of Newport in the Isle of Wight, Thomas James, was part-owner of a ship that spoiled another Spanish vessel (with indomitable optimism, the latter's owner applied to the freebooting Sir Richard Worseley to assist him in obtaining restitution). Port authorities at Poole, Southampton, Shoreham,

Hastings and Rye also collaborated with local pirates as a matter of course and ignored Council orders to arrest the goods concerned.[36]

These alliances long predated the growth of organized piracy during the 1540s, but they were supplemented and strengthened by a growing mercantile element, particularly from among the Anglo-Spanish community, creating several of the collaborations that had seemed remarkable only half a decade earlier with the voyage of the *Barbara*.[37] Undoubtedly, a number of merchants had seen an easier path to profit than in the plying of their legitimate businesses; but the majority, having attempted to find satisfaction for seizures and losses through representations to the English and Spanish governments, had discovered that self-help was the only sure help (as a later Lord Admiral would observe: 'My Lord, assure your selfe yf men have not justis they wyll be pyrates'[38]). Merchants of Bristol and Southampton, whose cities' resources for many years past had assisted in the suppression of piracy in the southern Irish Sea, the Soundings and Channel, led this trend as, many years earlier, they had the establishment of the trade to Spain. Knowing the waters of the Andalusian and Basque coasts intimately, they became no less efficient despoilers than their disreputable compatriots. Naturally, the outrage they had expressed previously in respect of their own, pillaged goods was not now reflected in any discriminatory policy towards their new victims. The indistinct 'colour' of cargoes – even those of their countrymen carried in non-English ships – brought more than one of them to the Admiralty Court to justify their depredations before their fellow merchants and compatriots.[39]

Habitual pirates had ancient motives, their new merchant allies more recent grievances, but they were joined also by men motivated almost entirely by the speculative opportunities inherent in the 1544 proclamation, and some were dangerously close to the regime. The voyages of Reneger himself – an erstwhile merchant who had almost wholly abjured his former career even before his famous 'incident' – appear to have been at least partly financed by Thomas Wriothesley, earl of Southampton (it was only following his patron's fall from power in 1547 that Reneger was coerced into restoring a proportion of his booty).[40] Thomas Wyndham, a Norfolk soldier, mariner, habitual freebooter and, from 1547, Master of the Ordnance at the Tower, seized a Spanish vessel in January 1545 whilst in command of the ship *Magdelene Russell* – the personal property of Lord Russell, Lord Privy Seal and Lisle's predecessor as Lord Admiral. In this instance, with Russell's involvement generally known, the seizure was sufficiently embarrassing to move the Privy Council to action. Wyndham was ordered to make restitution of as much of some £500 of identified spoil as he could recover from those with whom he had shared it – including £85 9s. 5d. from Russell. The Lord Privy Seal, however, disagreed with the judgement and resisted it (three months after the ruling, Van Der Delft wrote to Cardinal Granvelle that restitution still had not occurred).[41]

At the very pinnacle of the burgeoning privateering industry presided Henry VIII's former brother-in-law, Thomas Seymour, an enthusiastic sponsor of licenced voluntaries and outright pirates alike. In May 1546, one of his ships, commanded by Robert Bruse, took a Dutch ship laden with Spanish goods and disposed of them in open auction at Ilfracombe. This was a first, modest token of what would become a catalogue of felonies committed in Seymour's name. Appointed Lisle's successor as Lord Admiral a matter of days after Henry's death, he used his Scillies fiefdom to establish an entire infrastructure for the conduct of piracy. Ships passing to and from Ireland on their lawful business were waylaid and either plundered outright or made to pay bribes to allow them to pass unmolested. Seymour's estate in the islands was a veritable warehouse for stolen goods and ransom fees, from which he distributed largesse to his followers (excepting those spoils that became the subject of Council orders for restitution and had to be swiftly removed to safe locations elsewhere). When an occasional official effort was made to clear the seas of freebooters, he sent his own ships out to intercept the 'pirate-takers', re-plundered them of their recovered spoils, and gaoled their crews; informing his own captains in the meantime that any orders from the Council to assist in policing duties were to be ignored. In effect, until Seymour's arraignment in 1549 (at which testimony regarding his piratical activities helped usher him swiftly towards the scaffold), the Admiralty functioned less as an instrument of government policy than as an independent ministry for freebooters.[42]

What is notable is that this huge expansion in lawlessness at sea had been barely slowed (much less reversed) by the restoration of peaceful relations between England and France following the Treaty of Ardres, 8 June 1546. Receiving word of its ratification, Charles had written to his son in Seville, directing him to refrain from retaliating further to English depredations until Henry's 'peace' policy could be discerned.[43] He was being typically prudent, but optimistic also. The 1544 proclamation had opened a Pandora's box that would not be closed again in the sixteenth century. Periods of relatively strong amity between England and the Habsburg possessions would be re-established, and bring further attempts to curb depredations at sea. Some of these would be effective, if only briefly. Anglo-Spanish merchants, although still suffering sporadic ill-treatment from the Inquisition, would for many years forsake their association with privateers after suffering almost as many losses as their Spanish counterparts. Without letters of reprisal or more general commissions from their prince, many of those who intended robbery or worse became necessarily more circumspect. The same conditions of peace also brought relative economic prosperity, and the temptation to risk such exposure diminished accordingly. Yet if there remained distinct cycles of privateering and piratical activity, the conditions that determined their scale and impact were changing in two important respects. First, Henry VIII's three legitimate children would in turn commit English seaborne forces to a succession of wars during the following sixteen years whose demands would significantly undermine the mechanisms that, in more tranquil times, discouraged piracy and diverted its resources. Second, the reservoir from which the privateering and piracy industries drew their strength no longer comprised only the economically depressed or wronged coastal community, leavened by a scattering of itinerant wastrels, outcasts and adventurous gentlemen seeking an easy fortune. Henry had called upon such men, but upon 'divers others' also. As demonstrated, the characters and motives of those who answered his summons were as disparate as he might have wished – perhaps more so. In an age of rigid social boundaries, thieves had begun to associate with lords, adventurers with Lord Admirals, law-abiding citizens with those for whom the letter of the law was usually a summons. Overriding their instinctive antipathies was a common interest in a new enemy: one who was rich, growing richer, and who – unlike the Frenchman – did not appear willing to fight back except through embargo (of someone else's property), diplomatic representation and legal process. Their subsequent experience, and the benefits they derived from it, percolated into those parts of English society for whom the seas – and the foreigners upon them – had been at most a distant prospect.

With such profoundly profitable reasons to confront the Spaniard, it is inevitable that justifications for doing so would become increasingly prevalent. At the highest level, they eventually would serve a geo-political struggle excited by growing confessional divergences. Their common underpinning, however, was a more fundamental human imperative. The brutal practice of war has always demanded the demonization of a present enemy. Its consequences are extreme but brief, and usually do not survive the outbreak of peace and the blurring of what was once unpleasantly expedient. But men who took their livings from others' ships made and sustained their own wars – with foes of their choice, not that of the government requisitioning their energies. Without peace upon the seas, antipathies generated by the exigencies of conflict would loose much of their natural transience.

Henry died six months after concluding peace with France. As he did so, the time-tested means of curbing the activities of English freebooters were becoming ineffective. Their King had gambled the prudent legacies of his father and the windfall of the monastic dissolutions upon a final lunge at a European reputation, and had lost – or rather, the English nation had lost. The town of Boulogne had been added to the tiny splinter of England's remaining continental 'empire' (although only for eight years, under the terms of the Treaty of Ardres), and a hardly defensible English Pale extended a few miles down the French coast. These achievements had cost some two million pounds in the short-term, and, an as yet unsuspected corollary, the virtual exhaustion of English economic and military power for years to come. During the next decade England shrank in stature from a would-be major power to a nervous pawn in the vast Valois–Habsburg struggle. Iron-ically, her very existence as an independent power would rely upon the good offices of an Emperor whose subjects were becoming the prey of choice to a growing number of Englishmen: men for whom proclamations and the shortening arm of an under-funded Navy Royal no longer represented an adequate deterrent. As avarice and contempt for authority urged on the bolder entrepreneurs within English society, growing fears of domination – physical and cultural – encouraged their compatriots' island parochialism into new and potentially virulent channels of awareness. The turbulence of Henry's final years had provided only a first taste of the tumult to come.

THREE

Mid-Tudor Malaise

What assurance can we haue but that when we haue lifted them into the chaire of state, wee shall not be compelled to be their footmen? If our prince were a man and should marry an inheretrix of England, wee should happily haue no cause to feare, but that he would maintaine the liberty of his natiue country, but being a woman and desired in marriage of a King of England, vnder whose power and custody she must abide, how shall we be able against his minde either to benefit or preserue us . . . ?[1]

The perception of a 'mid-Tudor crisis' colours our view of the eventful period between Henry VIII's last years and the stabilization of Elizabeth's reign, though recent commentators have tended to dismiss this as an over-simplification of a complex, unsettled phase in sixteenth-century English history. Despite the near-concurrent onset of confessional upheavals, eco-nomic recessions and sporadic social disorders that had their roots in either or both, the mechanisms of state functioned adequately and the majority of Englishmen continued to live in peace.[2] Nevertheless, there were areas in which government almost entirely failed its constituents. The regimes of Edward VI and Mary, struggling with their father's poisonous religious legacy, were unable to provide any definitive solution that did not alienate a significant minority of their subjects. Their economic policies also fell short of the onerous challenges they faced, although Mary, attempting to implement much-needed structural reforms, managed at least to pay off her foreign borrowings (largely by transforming them into domestic debt).[3]

Repeated debasements of the coinage fuelled massive inflation of basic commodity prices; the vital Low Countries' cloth trade fluctuated dramatically after a boom that had endured for almost half a century; a succession of bad harvests exacerbated the already miserable lot of the rural poor, whose copyhold rents had been rising as steadily as their incomes plunged. That there was no overarching 'crisis' as such would have been thin comfort to many, perhaps most, Englishmen obliged to suffer its symptoms. Rose-tinted memory told them that a uniformly happy bygone age had given way to uncertain and potentially disastrous times.

English foreign policy, trailing still those clouds of ersatz glory gathered expensively by Henry, also proved unequal to its unrealistic expectations. During Edward's reign, Scotland successfully fought off the duke of Somerset's premature dream of a united 'British' state, and Boulogne was forcibly regained by France. Within four years following these debacles, Mary, having bound herself to her Spanish husband's wider strategic ambitions, relinquished the last of her nation's venerable continental possessions when Calais, a town that Englishmen had come to regard as 'theirs' no less than Norwich, fell to the French King's armies. England's march from empire had been a long journey. For more than a century, internal dynastic feuds, enervating and distracting, had pulled her Kings' preoccupations away from the once-profitable pastime of ruining France. Now, in the middle years of the sixteenth century, the process came to its inglorious conclusion. Elizabeth, who was to be welcomed by her people as much for not being Mary as for any personal quality, acquired a throne uniquely unburdened by foreign territories (unless the uneasily occupied 'kingdom' of Ireland could be so regarded). Not since the Anglo-Saxon era could an English monarch have been described so aptly as such.

While these failures occurred in a period in which Anglo-Imperial diplomatic relations were on the whole stable, their impact laid much ground for future grievances. From the moment of Edward VI's accession, Charles V had adopted a cautious and pragmatic English policy. As a staunch Catholic, it was to him – literally – an article of faith that Mary was Henry's immediate heir; however, her refusal to consider challenging Edward's claim to the throne, and the young King's obvious legitimacy in the eyes of a majority of Englishmen, resigned the Emperor to the fait accompli of his untroubled accession. The increasingly heretical leanings of the new government were of course anathema to him; but at some personal cost he did not allow this to undermine Anglo-Imperial relations (although briefly he threatened war when Edward rubbed salt into the wound by preventing Mary from attending mass). This was not an enlightened policy, but one of necessity. The progress of the Council of Trent, and the related struggle against German Protestantism, consumed Charles's diplomatic attention and military resources during the first years of Edward's reign. The further complication of a resurgent Valois threat to the Empire from 1551 made continuing friendship with England vital, even when the duke of Northumberland's alliance with radical English Protestants and his brief, abject search for an Anglo-French rapprochement exhausted the Emperor's reserves of goodwill.

Other, existing points of contention further tested Charles's patience. As already seen, he had forbidden further retaliation against the activities of English privateers and pirates following Henry VIII's death.[4] Logic suggested that a new regime, anxious to ensure Imperial friendship during its vulnerable early days, would have a strong incentive to address the issue. Edward's government had other priorities, however. The problem of lawlessness at sea was appreciated, but after making an initial, token gesture, the Privy Council either ignored or actively abetted the freebooting industry. On 25 September 1547, a proclamation, lamenting 'the great piracies and robberies daly doone by . . . sundrie Englishemen, pirates uppon the seas', directed that no one should put to sea without first providing sureties.[5] The first and final general proscription against piracy during the reign, it was largely ineffective. A year later, even this lukewarm initiative was tacitly abandoned when new orders were issued to the incorrigible Lord Admiral Seymour regarding privately owned ships appointed to go to sea. It was to be declared publicly that the vessels sailed only against Scots, pirates and other of the King's enemies. Secretly, however, they were to be allowed to attack the French Newfoundland fishing fleet and any other French vessel in retaliation for recent French seizures of English crayers. The privateers were to give the pretext either that they had been robbed previously by Frenchmen or that their victims were suspected of secretly supplying the Scots.[6] The same retaliatory spirit also moved the Council to reprieve several pirates previously condemned for assaulting French ships during peacetime, among the more notorious – and most fortunate – of whom were the crew of the ship *Leonard* who, two years earlier, had captured a French herring boat and gratuitously drowned her entire complement of fourteen mariners and a ship's boy.[7]

Predictably, these surreptitious nods from officialdom were interpreted with far greater latitude than had been intended. With unconscionable optimism, the Council had instructed Seymour that the names of all ships sailing under commission should be recorded and all seized French cargoes inventoried, to be made available for restitution should some accommodation be reached regarding prior English losses. Under the less than rigorous stewardship of the Lord Admiral, however, the majority of those sailing under commission made little effort to confine themselves to French cargoes, much less provide written evidence of their spoils. Seymour, sharing little of the Council's concern to limit the collateral effects of their strategy, dispensed his commissions with no discernible discretion. To Devon shipowners alone, he granted twenty-one licences; they included a small but portentous syndicate comprising the Ralegh family of East Budleigh – already adept pirates, notwithstanding their patriarch Walter's employment as vice-admiral of Devon – and their relatives by marriage, the Drakes of Littleham.[8] Taking advantage of their government's new anti-French policy, they set out a vessel in 1549 that promptly took a Spanish ship laden with Flemish goods. There is no evidence her owner ever received restitution or compensation.[9]

Following Seymour's execution and his brother Somerset's fall from power, some effort was made to ameliorate the worst effects of official policy, with varying results. Seymour's successor Lord Clinton set out a squadron that took some forty English and Scottish pirate vessels during the winter of 1550/51 – the most effective campaign of the reign. In contrast, an expedition of just two ships despatched less than a year later under the command of Sir William Tyrell and William Holstocke generated far more problems than prizes. On 22 September, the Privy Council noted that 'their folkes have so serched the maryners of their hoyes by them lately stayed that they have taken awaye their clothes, stripped them and made havock of their beire, etc'. Six days later, it became necessary to send them another warning 'not to doo any violent act or any other wayes wrong . . . themperour's subjectes'. In 1552, a better-disciplined fleet of three vessels under Richard Bethell pursued the 'notorious pirates' Henry Stranguishe and Peter Killigrew, whose industry off Cornwall and Brittany had made the western Channel a parlous navigation for merchantmen. Both managed to escape to Brest, from which repeated representations to the French Court subsequently failed to prise them.[10]

Setting out ships was expensive, and the government also offered bounties to private citizens of up to £100 for the capture and conviction of pirates. Those taken appear to have been treated harshly, but the infrequency of executions suggests few arrests were made.[11] Their brief efforts exhausted, the Privy Council, aware that the problem had hardly been dented, adopted a policy of pretending that it did not exist. There was probably very little else it could do, given that the taint of implication continued to be evident throughout the chain of English authority. Men with the right connections could avoid punishment for the most brutal crimes, even when perpetrated against other Englishmen. In 1547, one Richard Holbrooke, formerly of Rye, attacked and sank a Rye fishing boat in what appears to have been a revenge attack, drowning her crew of twelve. Convicted of murder and piracy, he was pardoned 'without fee or fine' on 16 March 1549, only three weeks after Seymour, the patron saint of pirates, had been arraigned.[12] Clearly, the former Lord Admiral was not the only sustainer of Holbrooke's profession in government.

When the victims of English piracy were foreigners, the chances of the legal process passing beyond preliminary proceedings were slight. The Imperial ambassador in London, Jehan Scheyfve, bombarding the Council with complaints of seizures of ships belonging to the Emperor's subjects (including one in which Clinton himself was heavily involved), ranted in frustration at the quiet, obfuscating tactics he met with. Told that he should trust to the 'good and prompt justice' of the Admiralty Court, he responded with asperity: 'I told them that it worked out otherwise in practise, and as for promptness, I have never seen anything approaching it, for since my arrival I had not heard of a single sentence being given, in spite of all my solicitations and utterances.' A few months later, by now familiar with the workings of the Privy Council, Scheyfve's anger had subsided to a weary cynicism. Reporting to the Queen Dowager, Charles's regent in the Netherlands, on his efforts to secure the councillors' commitment to curbing English depredations, he merely observed that Privy Councillors: 'professed themselves to be greatly astonished at the account of the said pirates' doings, as if entirely ignorant of such occurrences.'[13] In fact, they were perfectly well aware of these 'doings', as Patent Rolls for the period, recording their stream of pardons to Englishmen who had despoiled the vessels of friendly nations, make abundantly clear.[14]

The furore created by these incidents diverted diplomatic attention from another emerging English maritime activity that – even more than the worst depredations of freebooters – carried the seeds of potentially devastating confrontations. As the contraction of England's once-mighty French dominion ran its final, humiliating course, new expansionary pressures, entirely unconnected with regal ambitions, marked her engagement with a far wider world. Beginning in the year 1550, when merchant adventurers watched their profits plunge at the Antwerp Mart during a short but acute recession, they and their peers began actively to seek new suppliers and outlets for their wares. These were not to be isolated intrusions into established markets, such as Southampton's Brazilian adventures had been, but sustained efforts to redress England's reliance upon its preponderant Low Countries' trade. From 1551, English ships financed principally by Anglo-Spanish merchants began to visit the Moroccan Atlantic coast, seeking to access directly the sugar, dates, almonds and other luxury comestibles that Portugal vainly argued to lie within her sole right of exploitation. Within ten years, the trade had become an habitual one, with English merchants maintaining resident factors at the port of Safi.[15] From 1553, the longer and more perilous passage to the Guinea and Benin coasts was made sporadically by English ships, meeting with much firmer Portuguese opposition, but also – when successful – the fabulous rewards of gold and spices. In that year also, Sir Hugh Willoughby and Richard Chancellor, financed by a wide cross-section of London merchants and noblemen, set out to find a navigable north-eastern passage to the Far East that would entirely circumvent known sea routes and, hopefully, offer a far shorter navigation than that made by Portuguese Moluccan traders. They were unsuccessful – Willoughby terminally so – but two years later England had secured a formal trading relationship with Muscovy. It was a first staging post on the elusive journey to the fabulous entrepôts of the East: a goal made ever more desirable by the growing disruptions to existing foreign markets.

There were few impediments to these embryonic activities during Edward VI's reign, when the duke of Northumberland – an avid promoter of expansionary schemes – shielded them from the protests and subterfuges of the Portuguese King.[16] Nor did Mary's reign bring any significant interruption to the developing trades, although both her husband, Philip, and the Portuguese ambassador in London, Lopes de Sousa, made several attempts to abort the Guinea voyages. In 1555, efforts to stay one expedition resulted in compensation being paid to its backers by the government. A petition, drawn up by the disappointed merchants and presented to the Privy Council, protested the fundamental injustice of restraint: 'we be merchauntes, who by the commone usage of the worlde do use traficque in all places of the worlde . . . as we be appoynted by the auctoritie of the place wherunto we cumme.' In other words, without prior right of conquest – and whatever was claimed provisionally by gift of papal bull or bilateral treaty – Englishmen should not be prevented from trading with willing clients. The argument was a powerful one, and its justice was acknowledged (if tacitly) by the Council. In the following year, several orders to Admiralty officials and mayors of English ports, staying ships intending to 'further trafique in . . . Gynney', were careful to infer that some alternative licence might subsequently be granted to their owners.[17]

English efforts to avoid Spanish-claimed territories in the initial stage of the search for new markets reflected the appreciation that the New World possessions of Charles (and, from 1555, Philip II) would be defended aggressively. By the same token, Portugal's relative weakness militarily made her claims much less respectable in English eyes. Yet in challenging the Portuguese half-hold over the trade of the Barbary and Guinea coasts, Englishmen were definitively rejecting the claimed prerogatives of Spain no less than those of her neighbour, because they were built upon precisely the same foundation. If the entirety of the unknown world were reserved for future exploitation by the Iberian nations, all English voyages into that world would by definition be both intrusions and challenges.

To some extent, the predominantly peaceful nature of early English reconnaissances obscured their full implication. In the short term only the Muscovy trade (which lay outside the ambit both of *Inter Caetera* and Tordesillas) acquired the corporate identity that indicated a degree of persistence. Most who invested in these early ventures, moreover, had largely 'respectable' motives, seeking a profit without generating occasions of conflict that might render subsequent voyages problematic (witness the large number of merchants' factors who sailed – and often died – in the voyages). However, there was not such a pool of English talent that the organizers of these dangerous enterprises could be overly fastidious in their choice of men to command them. These proved to be an eclectic mix of gentlemen-adventurers, adept navigators, honest merchants and near-professional pirates. Most confined their attentions to the letter of their instructions; some, like the erstwhile freebooter Thomas Wyndham, founder of the English Barbary and Guinea trades, did their best to supplement their expected trading revenues with the spoil of prizes taken en route.[18] Wyndham himself became an early victim of the perils of long-range voyaging, but the experiences of men such as him were disseminated no less swiftly than intelligence on the prospects for peaceful trade. In less than a decade, syndicated schemes to exploit sea routes to new marketplaces would be followed by far more aggressive (and aggressively implemented) projects in which trade formed only one element of the search for profits.

We are anticipating events, however. Despite the tensions generated by English depredations in the Channel, and the portentous but as-yet obscure implications of Englishmen's interest in distant markets, Anglo-Imperial relations weathered the tempestuous reign of Edward and emerged into seemingly calm waters with the young King's premature death, the fall of Northumberland, Mary Tudor's accession and her subsequent betrothal and marriage to Charles's son, Philip. At a stroke, the Emperor had added significantly to the resources that could be brought to bear against Valois France, with the destinies of England and the Empire – or at least, that part which might be secured for Charles's heir – bound in the same manner as so many of the Habsburg dominions.

Once more, however, diplomacy functioned and reality confounded it. Mary's accession had been welcomed wholeheartedly by the majority of her subjects. Despite possessing no army to support her cause in the days following Edward's death, she easily defeated the stratagems of Northumberland (who controlled the only effective English military forces), and crushed the unfortunate Jane Grey's timid lunge at the throne. The state and form of religion, a fundamental issue both for Mary and her dead half-brother, had proved to be of remarkably little importance to the English nation as a whole. What did exercise its collective consciousness, however, and very greatly, was how she intended to govern her new realm.

Fear of 'strangers' had long been embedded within the English psyche, particularly of those who lived among Englishmen in any number. The Evil May Day riots of 1517, perhaps its most spectacular manifestation, reflected a near-timeless distaste for aliens who came to England to take local jobs, homes and womenfolk. When they were not threatening, individual foreigners could be pleasantly surprised at the warmth of their welcome. In 1560, Levinus Lemnius, a Dutch physician travelling in England, was struck above all by his hosts' 'incredible curtesie and frendliness in speache and affability'. Conversely, those who, however inadvertently, made Englishmen aware of their own inadequacies were swiftly punished, as the Duke of Wurtemburg's entourage discovered many years later: '. . . they care little for foreigners, but scoff and laugh at them; and moreover one dare not oppose them, else the street-boys and apprentices collect together in great crowds and strike to the right and left of them unmercifully without regard to person . . .'[19] Late in 1553, a striking outbreak of this enduring phenomenon was prompted by the new Queen's intention to contract a Habsburg marriage. Although the match had been gestating for some months and was commonly spoken of (and argued about) at Court, news of it came as a thunderbolt to most Englishmen. Almost overnight, the entire nation seemed to unite in outraged, fearful protest, even if the marriage's implications for the nation's spiritual identity concerned only a tiny minority. Many (and probably most) of the signatories to a parliamentary petition begging the Queen not to take a Spanish husband were Catholics. A large number of those who supported an alternative suitor, Edward Courteney, Earl of Devon, were Protestants for whom their candidate's unwavering Catholicism was a trifle lighter than air. A government commission was established hastily whose sole purpose was to reconcile the unpleasant reality of this match to the nation. The safeguards it proposed in the wedding treaty, which severely limited Philip's rights as king-consort, were largely mistrusted.[20] To many Englishmen, it remained almost axiomatic that their proposed King's entourage would come as conquerors and ravishers of wives and daughters, not as a wedding party.[21]

The timing of the match undoubtedly fuelled the anxieties of Mary's subjects. The several political and economic crises of the early 1550s were giving Englishmen a keen appreciation of their relative weakness as a nation, and of the powerful threats they faced. Yet if fears of resurgent French military power – by far the most obvious and pressing threat to England – were strong, they proved not nearly so traumatic as the prospect of a Habsburg King dragging England into his father's vast, polygynous empire and, worse, filling the lucrative sinecures of government with his countrymen.[22] Almost as soon as arrangements for the marriage commenced, so too did a web of conspiracies – several of which depended upon a degree of French naval intervention – to prevent it. All were unsuccessful, but their abettors and sympathizers were neither neutralized nor placated by the subsequent failure of Philip to conform to their worst expectations.

In 1554, in the aftermath of 'Wyatt's rebellion' – the fragmented and inchoate series of uprisings named after its only near-successful component – many disaffected Englishmen fled the country. Those who left on a point of religion did so with their families, settling in Protestant states in Germany or the Swiss Cantons to await another turn in the bewildering progress of England's spiritual odyssey. Others with more earthly motives – that is, most of the failed plotters – went to France and promptly offered their ships and services to Henri II.[23] This reflected no new-found affection for his nation or affinity with her people, but rather a shifting of English partialities to accommodate a new *bête noire* – the Spaniard. Men who had departed England precipitously with neither vessels of their own nor money to buy one could expect generous assistance from their new host, who was only too pleased to nurture a new front in his war against the extended Habsburg dominions. He offered subsidies and ships to fit out their expeditions, and provided safe haven – 'safe as Jerusalem' – against occasional policing measures by the English Admiralty.[24] To note only the more persistent of their

number, the Killigrew brothers and Henry Stranguishe (all implicated with
Sir Peter Carew in the late rebellion), Richard Cole (during the previous
reign an unwilling resident of the Tower of London on piracy charges) and
the erstwhile Calais-based pirates Humphrey and John Thompson, formed
or resurrected alliances with French rovers and haunted the English coast,
preying indifferently upon Spanish, Flemish, Irish, French and, inevitably,
English vessels.[25] Following the failure of Sir Henry Dudley's (1556) conspiracy, they were joined – or rejoined – by a further wave of English exiles,
many of whom were perfectly willing to exchange political principle for
gainful employment at sea.[26]

With the incremental effect of this new influx of politically motivated
outlaws upon an existing problem (and the corresponding harm to the trade
of the subjects of her husband and father-in-law), it was inevitable that Mary
would attempt to deal with piracy more robustly than had her half-brother's
government. No pardon was granted to any convicted pirate in the first
three years of her reign, in stark contrast to the liberality with which her
half-brother's regime had dispensed them.[27] However, having ridden anti-
Spanish feeling in England, many of the freebooters ranging the Channel
in borrowed or French-financed vessels retained the sympathy of their compatriots. The Queen did not remain entirely insensitive to this. Her subsequent discretionary treatment of captured felons indicates that an iron-fist
policy against career pirates alternated with genuine attempts to rehabilitate
many of the former rebels who had taken to the seas from necessity.

The matter of timing, however, was critical in this process. In June 1556,
seven ships were despatched from Portsmouth under William Tyrell to intercept and apprehend any freebooter he encountered. Perhaps sensing the lack
of equivocation in his mistress's instructions, Tyrell improved greatly upon
his efforts of the previous reign. Within a month, a first batch of 'robars of
the see' had been interrogated at Portsmouth, tried and sentenced in
London, and six of their number hanged at the low watermark at Wapping
Stairs. In July of the same year, the Killigrew brothers and Henry Stranguishe, sailing in a rebel fleet of some ten sail, were intercepted and captured off Plymouth before they could flee to their Brest sanctuary.[28] In their
case, however, the extreme penalty was not imposed. It was their good
fortune that concurrent attempts to place the English navy upon a war
footing (following the discovery of French connivance in the Dudley plot)
generated an urgent demand for experienced seamen of any character or
history. By July of the following year, Peter Killigrew had seamlessly abandoned his former patrons to command the ship *Jerfalcon* in a Narrow Seas

squadron under Sir William Woodhouse; Humphrey and John Thompson commanded the *Salamander* and *Greyhound* respectively in Sir John Clere's squadron; while Henry Stranguishe was named in 1558 as one of eight 'gentilman of the west' to be appointed as captains of ships.[29] Similarly, a significant number of former insurgents (from both the Wyatt and Dudley conspiracies) were to serve in Philip's 1557 St Quentin campaign, having seized the double opportunity of royal clemency and a chance of enrichment at the expense of their old keeper, Henri II. Nevertheless, there was a limit to the pragmatic accommodations Mary was inclined to make. With a certain hard-headedness her half-sister Elizabeth would later emulate, she coldly sifted her resources, retained the best of a tainted crop and discarded the detritus. Twenty-four men taken with Stranguishe and the Killigrews were hanged at Southampton in September, while another batch of seven unwanted pirates tested the water at Wapping on 6 April the following year.[30]

The necessities (and shifting prejudices) of war had encouraged this limited reconciliation between exiled English conspirators and their Queen, and in a sense, their absence from England had assisted the process. Among her more faithful subjects at home, proximity to Philip's entourage and its numerous camp-followers had turned conceptual dislike into voluble detestation. Had these courtiers been his father's men – and, therefore, natives of the Low Countries – the English reaction doubtless would have been similar.[31] But being Philip's companions and officers they were Spaniards. From the moment they set foot on English soil, their hosts – principally Londoners – regarded them much as a pampered child would a new sibling. Writing to the Emperor at the beginning of September, the Imperial envoy Simon Renard offered an early glimpse of looming trouble:

> The foreigners, they complain, are making Englishmen feel strangers in their own homes, and have taken to managing everything since they landed . . . They proclaim loudly that they see they are going to be enslaved, for the Queen is a Spanish woman at heart and thinks nothing of Englishmen, but only of Spaniards and bishops.[32]

Even before Philip's entry into London on 18 August 1554, the Court of the Mercers' Company (whose hall, like that of the other guilds, had been requisitioned as secure accommodation for the bridegroom's entourage) was obliged to issue a warning to its members to cease insulting, mocking and picking fights with their newly arrived guests. These, it should be recalled, were relatively urbane men whose business was habitually conducted with foreigners; like their ruder compatriots, however, they had swiftly convinced themselves that the Spaniards had come to 'make Englishmen worse than conies'.[33]

Unwisely, Philip made little attempt initially to calm the anxieties of his new subjects. His efforts to set up a court in parallel, staffed exclusively by his countrymen, gave rise to rumours that all matters of English state were being discussed in Castilian.[34] Eventually, a compromise was reached on this delicate issue, and a nominal English presence imposed upon the new King's immediate entourage. However, a far more serious 'threat' – his attempt to have his kingship sanctified by coronation rather than by the restrictive letter of a marriage treaty – resurrected his new subjects' fears that Mary would be an obedient wife first and queen last. Thus confirmed in their prejudices, Englishmen rebuffed all subsequent efforts by the king-consort to win their affection. Individual occasions of friction between Londoners and Spaniards occurred almost daily in the first year of the royal marriage, and even otherwise sober commentators vastly amplified both the threat and scale of the Spanish presence. The anonymous author of the *Chronicle of Queen Jane . . . and Mary* ('a resident of the Tower') stated with unabashed hyperbole that 'ther was so many Spanyerdes in London that a man shoulde have mett in the stretes for one Inglisheman above iiii Spanyerdes, to the great discomfort of the Inglishe nation'. The same author assiduously reported rumours of the arrival of six thousand Spanish courtiers (the true figure was closer to two thousand), and that a Spanish friar was to be made Archbishop of Canterbury.[35] Rumours of plots to slaughter all Spaniards in England were reported by ambassador Noailles to his master, Henry II, in September or October 1554, and every member of Philip's Westminster entourage crept in fear of his life for several weeks thereafter. In November, a design to assassinate Philip himself was foiled and it was later confessed by one of the unfortunate plotters, when his co-conspirators lost their nerve at the deadly moment. Briefly, the Queen's imagined pregnancy eased tensions when it seemed that an heir – to be raised in England as an Englishman or woman according to the marriage treaty – would preserve the nation from outright Spanish domination.[36] However, when the child proved illusory, Englishmen's hatred for their putative oppressors reasserted itself, and was further strengthened by the regime's developing religious policy.

The condemnation and burning of unrepentant heretics commenced in February 1555, providing spectacles that most Englishmen found extremely distasteful, and for more than just their barbarity. These 'martyrdoms' were very quickly, and widely, regarded as the initiative of Philip and his friars, notwithstanding the reality of the King's pragmatic attempts to moderate the pace at which his wife reversed her half-brother's reformation. Those present at the fires convinced themselves and others that they saw only the Spanish Inquisition at work, when what they witnessed was the ultimate sanction of their own venerable English laws against Lollard heresies, re-activated – by a unanimous vote of both houses of parliament – at the end of 1554.[37]

Undoubtedly, there was some foundation to the less febrile English fears, and not all Spaniards who came to England were innocent of accusations laid against them. Their undoubtedly tender pride wounded by a frigid reception and the natives' readily expressed antipathies, a number of them went out of their way to find trouble. Others, confirmed in their prior assumptions of English barbarity and boorishness, made little secret of their own contempt for their loud, unwashed hosts (the anonymous Spanish author of a letter 'to a gentleman of Salamanca' admitted that hostility, if fuelled by English provocations, was mutual: 'We Spaniards move among the English as if they were animals, trying not to notice them . . .'[38]). More seriously, the future of an independent English nation had hardly been assured by the convoluted terms of the marriage treaty, and in any case diplomatic covenants had a habit of being overtaken by events. Pamphleteers could cite the example of other 'dowry' states of the Habsburg dominions that were now little more than satrapies of an increasingly overbearing polity – one in which Spaniards were likely to have an ever-greater role.[39] The warnings of these English jeremiahs were partially vindicated in 1557 when Mary took the disastrous decision to declare war upon France. There was little good reason for it, other than to fulfil old Anglo-Imperial treaty obligations to defend the Low Countries. The apparent *casus belli* – Henri II's alleged involvement in Thomas Stafford's pitiful 'invasion' and capture of Scarborough castle – was implausible, even to contemporary observers.[40] Most informed Englishmen assumed correctly that Mary's abject need to please her indifferent husband was the principal reason for their participation in a war they could neither afford nor profit from.[41] At its conclusion, the now-widowed Philip's perfunctory defence and subsequent abandonment of English interests at the conference of Cateau-Cambrésis would strengthen the perception that they had been duped by Habsburg ambitions. In the succeeding decades, the loss of Calais grew to tragic dimensions in the mythology of injustices perpetrated against England. In 1568, the poet George Ferrers, prefacing his account of the fall of the town, would write indignantly:

For if ought were won by the having of St Quentin,[42] England got nothing at all; for the gain thereof came only to King PHILIP: but the loss of Calais, Hammes, and Guisnes, with all the country on that side of the sea, which followed soon after, was such a buffet to England as had not happened in more than an hundred years before; and a dishonour wherewith this realm shall be blotted until GOD shall give power to redubbe it . . .[43]

As late as 1598, when England had been at war with Spain for more than a decade, Lord Burghley would list the irrevocable acknowledgement of the half-century-old loss of Calais (now in Habsburg hands) as one of the principal disadvantages of seeking peace.[44] By this time of course, Philip's king-consortship was little more than a distant memory; nevertheless, the wound opened by the loss of Calais provided a defining core around which Englishmen's recollections of their Spanish 'captivity' coalesced, encouraging them to lament the manner of Philip's departure no less than they had feared the prospect of his arrival.

The four fraught years of an Anglo-Spanish monarchy in England ended with Mary's death in November 1558. She was mourned by few; not, as Foxe insisted, because of her harsh brand of papistry, but for the apparent ascendancy of the Spanish half of her psyche.[45] Yet the intensity of her subjects' reactions to her Spanish marriage was fundamentally disingenuous, notwithstanding the fears upon which their hostility was grounded. At the start of Mary's reign, Wyatt and his fellow conspirators had sought to prevent the match in order to preserve the Royal Supremacy and keep the pope out of English affairs, and had risked the extreme price of failure.[46] But the motives of the far greater number of Englishmen who had failed to rise in support of the rebels, yet who expressed their hatred of the marriage with no less enthusiasm, bear little close scrutiny.

Throughout these years, the overwhelming physical threat to English interests came from France. The vestiges of English continental power lay increasingly exposed to Valois ambitions, the seas between England and her vital Low Countries markets to French freebooters. Yet voices raised against these very real dangers were lost in the tumult that greeted the arrival and brief English 'rule' of Mary's husband, Philip. Clearly, what the English Channel could not keep at bay exercised an inordinate impact upon Englishmen. The perceived cultural threat posed by the Spanish invasion ensured that Mary's reign swiftly occupied a place of dark legend, its evils enjoying a clutch of insincere moral underpinnings. The most enduring of these conflated England's Spanish 'subjection' and the Queen's sanguinary religious policy. An article of faith to the leading Protestant propagandists of the following reign, it was eventually to occupy no less secure a place in the English psyche than the tragedy of Hastings and triumph of embryonic democracy at Runnymede.

Yet the linkage was deceitful, and known to be so by those who promoted it most strongly. The prospect of a reversal of the Edwardian reformation – with its inevitable human cost – had been a matter of indifference to a majority of Englishmen until Mary had announced her matrimonial plans. Those who feared the personal implications of spiritual upheaval had plotted, fled, conformed or prepared themselves for martyrdom. They had constituted a small minority even in London, where Protestant activism was most pronounced and its repercussions most visible. In all, rebellious refugees, godly exiles and the Marian martyrs probably numbered no more than two thousand in a nation of some three to four million.[47] Many more had preserved their Protestant convictions silently and hoped for better days to come, but there is little evidence that the most spiritually disaffected Englishmen led, or even fed, the widespread fear of Spanish cultural infection. To take a single, prominent example: two of the leading non-conforming activists in the City, the substantial London merchants Thomas Lok and Anthony Hickman, ran an underground 'railway' for English Protestants fleeing to Geneva until they were arrested and interrogated – by other Englishmen – for their persistent failure to attend Mass. Released at his promise to conform, Hickman swiftly fled abroad, though in doing so he was obliged temporarily to abandon his pregnant wife, Lok's half-sister, Rose. Lok was also freed, but failing to persuade his own wife – Hickman's sister, Mary – to join the exodus, he remained in London, where, in 'feare of further trouble to fashion himself outwardly to the popish religion', he and his entire family died during an outbreak of plague.[48] Yet however heavily the implications of the Queen's counter-reforming policies fell upon Lok and Hickman, neither appears to have held adverse opinions regarding her husband and his countrymen. Both continued to do much business with Spaniards during these years, and stood apart from the general furore regarding their presence in England.[49] It can not be said how many of their colleagues did, or felt, likewise, but it is clear that the greater number of their fellow citizens who happily mocked, incited and assaulted their Spanish guests had previously welcomed reconciliation with Rome with some enthusiasm. Unlike Lok, they had troubled little to fashion themselves to the 'popish religion', outwardly or otherwise.[50]

Clearly, their enthusiasm for the regime's religious policy waned considerably as persecutions began, but there was not much, if any, association of faith and foreigners in contemporary English minds. The awareness of Protestantism as a defining element of 'Englishness' was not, as yet, remotely apparent. It was not the religious predilections of Spaniards that Marian Englishmen despised, but their alien-ness and the preference they were believed to enjoy. There was greater reason to fear their King's political priorities and the impact they might have upon England, but even so, it seems improbable that the potential subjugation of national resources to Habsburg policy could have excited the concern of more than a small minority of well-informed and educated Englishmen. For the rest, few had seen a Spaniard before 1554; fewer still could rationalize the extreme dislike that the prospect of one encouraged.

It was observed by many contemporary 'strangers' that Englishmen hated foreigners, and there can be little doubt that the trait was tested to its limits during the years of Philip's marriage to Mary. When that brief alliance ended, those few Spaniards who had not left England with their King in 1557 departed, freed from the yolk of cohabitation with a nation that appeared to define itself by whom and what it was not. Even at the quayside, anxious to be freed from their self-imposed exile, they were manhandled and mocked by their former compatriots.[51] What they left behind, swiftly to become embedded in the English psyche, was a deeply felt resentment of Spanish arrogance (teased by the suspicion that it might be justified), fear of Spain's growing wealth and the power it brought, and a sense that England's relationship with the Habsburg dominions created dependencies that its indisputable advantages could not outweigh. The final humiliation – the loss of the last sliver of England's historic presence on French soil – merely completed the dismantlement of the fond illusion of Tudor England as the third leg of a European power-triumvirate. For many Englishmen, the effect of that understanding, if inconsistently felt, was cathartic. At the moment at which sixteenth-century England achieved its closest political linkage with European affairs, her people began a new and robust phase in the long process of their psychological withdrawal into an 'English' world. How its nature and boundaries were to be defined was not yet clear, but envy, insecurity and a will to emulate that which they so readily despised provided an impetus that even royal authority would find difficult to channel.

FOUR

Gloriana

O sweete Virgin! O blessed Ladie! O glorious Queene! O noble Elizabeth! . . . Beholde, you Englishmen, behold your naturall Prince, the offspring of your kinges, the image of their nature, the peer of their virtue, the onelie reminder of so manie worthies, the flower of all prince-hoode and royaltie, the miracle of nature, the glorie of womanhoode, the paterne of all godlinesse and vertue, the modile of perfection, the wonder of the world, the Phenix of our time, the honour of England.[1]

The final, implausible disposition of Henry VIII's political testament was realized on 17 November 1558, when his youngest daughter became Queen of England. As with most peaceful accessions, the inauguration of the 'Elizabethan age' brought few immediate tokens of change beyond the expected rotation of Privy Councillors, court intimates and their trappings. Nevertheless, more so than any of her Tudor predecessors, Elizabeth came to the throne as the embodiment of her people's hopes for something other than the recent past. She was extremely sensitive to this mood, and from the earliest days of her reign she became the Visible Queen: playing to a cult of personality speedily erected by poets, pamphleteers and polemicists to consecrate their release from the twin tyrannies of papistry and foreign courtiers. To requisition her subjects' affections so strongly was a prudent act of policy, given that she had inherited a nation of potentially divisive loyalties; but she intended also to avert the fears that Mary's matrimonial intentions had excited. What happy fate had delivered to the English nation, no husband – an inconvenience that everyone, including the Queen herself, must have anticipated in 1558 – could be allowed to diminish or threaten. Even had the lessons of her half-sister's reign been insufficiently obvious in that respect, Elizabeth was utterly convinced of her greater ability to rule than any man she may choose merely to secure the Tudor succession.

Physically personable, apparently (though not actually) modest and ruled by neither hated favourite nor Spanish husband, the new Queen met all the preconditions of those who were ready, even anxious, to love her. During the previous reign, her courage and steadfastness in adversity, and her grave and dignified demeanour before the near-hysterical accusations of her sister, had excited much popular sympathy and a sense that she had shared something of her subjects' tribulations. Her Protestant leanings were well known, but her refusal to acknowledge faction or entertain extreme spiritual prejudices attracted few of the instinctive enemies who had tested the early years of her siblings' reigns. Elizabeth's greatest handicap was her sex; her greatest strength the knowledge that the mass of the English people cried out for stability and an end to constant revolution. Although she was tainted by bastardy (that is, if Mary's reign had not itself been illegitimate), this appeared to matter little to a nation that had become accustomed to a logically impossible order of succession. What statute determined, Englishmen on the whole regarded as something to be taken as gospel. The principle was one of the few reasonably secure legacies of the Henrician Reformation.[2]

This instinctive conservatism accorded with the genius of their new sovereign, particularly upon the spiritual debate. The precise nature of Elizabeth's personal faith was, and remained, a mystery to her closest advisers, but it was expressed most practically in the search for an accommodation that would put the maximum number of Englishmen in churches, content with – or compliant in – the form of their worship. The character of that accommodation was, however, unclear in 1558. It was obvious that Roman Catholicism could allow no degree of relativism, nor even the possibility of Elizabeth's legitimacy as monarch. Inevitably, therefore, any middle-ground of uniformity must necessarily ignore the aspirations of England's Catholics, except where minor preferences of ritual coincided with the Queen's personal tastes. Conversely, only a relatively few of her councillors believed that a return to the *status quo ante* of her half-brother's reign was either desirable or practical. Radical Protestantism, though partly re-legitimized and nurtured by a constant stream of returning Marian exiles, failed to strengthen its hold upon more than a small minority of Englishmen in the opening months or even years of Elizabeth's reign. A balance was needed that did not alienate too great a constituency at either side of the spiritual divide. The challenge for government was to bring about change without disruption; consensus with a minimum of alienation.

Driving this cautious policy of engagement was uncertainty. The Queen's self-appointed mentor Sir Nicholas Throckmorton had urged her 'to have a good eye that there be no innovations, no tumults or breach of orders', and with this at least she seems to have been in full agreement.[3] It is still debated whether the Act of Uniformity – pushed, or supported strongly by a core of Protestant parliamentarians – had more radical features than she favoured initially. In time, its provisions would have near-incalculable implications for the development of English spiritual life, but there is no evidence that they met with any immediate enthusiasm.[4] To the contrary, the act's passage was smoothed greatly by the moral exhaustion and confusion that a Submission of the Clergy; Restraints of Appeals and Annates; acts regarding Dispensations, Supremacy, Treason and Chantries; a Dissolution; Ten Articles; Six Articles; two English Prayer Books; two (Edwardian) Acts of Uniformity; Forty-Two Articles; and Mary's subsequent efforts to reverse or expunge most of them had wrought upon the nation. Intending to impose clarity and conformity, this barrage of compulsion had ensured instead that almost no one had a clear understanding of where the English 'reformation' would, or could, come to rest. Few, indeed, could even begin to guess what percentage of Englishmen still cleaved to the old ways, how many followed a variant of the new, and what number accepted passively whatever happened to be the doctrine of the moment.[5] At the height of the Edwardian Reformation, the near-agnostic Sir William Paget (surely an impartial voice), had observed that Protestantism was not 'printed in the stomachs of eleven of twelve parts of the realm', and little had happened in the intervening period to encourage it further.[6] Even those who most wished to see the triumph of a rigorous, radical faith (and who had every reason to argue its progress) held gloomy views of their effectiveness to date.[7] Conversely, while Mary's subsequent efforts to expunge 'heresy' had halted its growth and kept the uncommitted within what might broadly be defined as conformity, not many had been enthused, much less willingly reconverted, by her brand of orthodoxy. Perhaps the only positive effect of the preceding twenty years of reformation and counter-reformation had been to make most Englishmen believe that it was better to have a single religion, and that someone else should decide which one.

In the secular sphere, Elizabeth was again fortunate in the timing of her accession. Appalling harvests in 1555 and 1556 had been followed by two years of relative plenty, and inflation – particularly of all-important food prices – was slowing appreciably. A severe outbreak of plague that had brought further misery to many of the larger English towns during the final months of Mary's reign became dormant once more during the winter: an expected development, certainly, but one that was seen also as a harbinger of better times to come (ironically, London was only half a decade from the worst pestilential visitation it was ever to suffer).[8] Nevertheless, Elizabeth was by no means so secure that she was able to throw off the past quite as readily as her subjects. None of the underlying problems that England had come to suffer in the previous decade had been resolved by the fact of her succession. The country was poor, cursed with a horribly tainted coinage, bereft of the great resources of France (the nation Englishmen had most reason to fear) and, it seemed, set to sink further from that apparent state of glory wantonly promised by the Queen's father. If there was any degree of optimism for more than the mere fact of a new reign, it grew principally from the temporary remission of the agues that had marked its predecessor.

From a happier, victorious age, Camden and other commentators proclaimed that God and events had conspired to give Englishmen 'a most prosperous and auspicious beginning' in 1558.[9] Yet the correspondence of William Cecil, the Queen's new secretary of state, makes it clear that he and his colleagues were of one mind with other 'rich, wise, and honestly disposed' Elizabethans in being fearful, careful and doubtful that year.[10] The nation had passed precipitously between confessional poles, its rural classes had been obliged to accept economic hardship much as they did bad weather, and – the new government's most immediate concern – it retained few plausible pretensions as a major European power. When, in a first flush of defiance, Elizabeth refused to countenance the English Peace Commissioners' acceptance of the loss of Calais, her Treasurer of the Chamber, Sir John Mason, told her bluntly that the nation could afford no more wars.[11] From Brussels, the Lord Admiral Clinton (sacked but re-instated during the previous reign) unintentionally confirmed the poverty of English martial resources when he listed the smaller northern French ports that might, even now, be seized with minimum effort as bargaining counters for Calais, given that its recapture was plainly impossible. Of other news, his best was that the navy would be ready within a month to face a potential seaborne threat against England; his worst, that the threat might be upon them already. Obligingly, Philip II had passed on to him a rumour that the duke of Vendôme was preparing to take an army into Scotland to relieve the Queen

Dowager, Mary of Guise, in her struggle against the self-styled 'Lords of the Congregation'. If successful, that powerful military instrument would be ideally located to enforce her daughter Mary Stuart's claim to the English throne thereafter.[12] It was a gloomy prognosis. Paget, manoeuvred out of an expected seat in the new Privy Council, reminded his rival Cecil (whom he already suspected of a more aggressive posture towards the old Habsburg alliance) of what he hoped had become an axiom of English foreign policy – the necessity of keeping the Spanish King as a good ally, rather than allowing France and Spain between them to 'make a Piedmont' of England.[13]

It was sound advice at a time when England's ability to defend herself was at best questionable, but foreign perils did not press quite as imminently as Paget and others feared. The mightier Valois and Habsburg regimes had been suffering almost total war-exhaustion for several months prior to Elizabeth's accession. Henri II had achieved his overwhelming 'English' objective – the recovery of Calais – but having also lost Italy to acquire Metz, he was unwilling to do more than consolidate his paltry gains. His enemy, the supposedly victorious Philip II, bereaved of a father and wife almost simultaneously, bankrupted and technically at war with the Papacy as well as France, needed his English ally – even one ruled by a heretical Queen – should the peace negotiations at Cercamp fail. Not being over-optimistic of English enthusiasm for maintaining their one-sided alliance, he hurriedly checked the detail of existing Anglo-Imperial treaties to ensure that his wife's inconvenient death would not invalidate their terms. He also attempted to consolidate his formerly cordial relationship with the princess Elizabeth by authorizing the payment of bribes – termed 'pensions' – to Cecil, Robert Dudley and the earl of Bedford (all leading Protestants), and to the new Lord Chamberlain, William Howard, one of the English representatives at the Cercamp negotiations and Elizabeth's oldest male friend. Otherwise, he scrupulously supported England's interests during peace negotiations, even pressing for the return of Calais (in English hands the town had been a significant buffer against Valois expansion towards his Low Countries) until French obduracy on the issue threatened to paralyse all progress. Finally, he resorted to the traditional Habsburg device of offering himself to the new Queen as a potential husband, though half-heartedly and principally to forestall a Protestant recovery in England.[14]

Elizabeth's reign commenced, therefore, with that rarest of blessings: a general desire for peace. The fears of all parties that the negotiations at Cercamp would fail virtually guaranteed their success. With the Treaty of Cateau-Cambrésis in March 1559, Valois and Habsburg ambitions

disengaged after a half-century of bloody convergence, while England, clinging to her old ally's coat-tails, obtained an unlikely face-saving arrangement
whereby the French agreed to surrender Calais in eight years' time, provided
that peace between the two nations endured in the meantime. It was
miserable compensation for entering an unwanted war solely at the behest
of an unpopular, foreign king, but as a second-rank power England was
obliged to take what fell from the table.

The peace, however, was almost immediately shaken, from England's perspective, by new and threatening portents. A collateral initiative of Cateau-
Cambrésis – Philip's betrothal to the French King's daughter – hinted at an
unhealthy degree of rapprochement between the two most powerful (and mil-
itantly Catholic) dynasties in Europe. The implications of this were still being
absorbed when Henri II's untimely death at their wedding feast, and the accession of his son, Francis II, brought a new and potentially fatal threat to the
new English regime. Mary Stuart, now Queen both of France and Scotland,
had in many eyes a far better claim to the throne of England than its present
incumbent. Mary's uncle, Françoise, duc de Guise, had recently demonstrated
a talent, and appetite, for beating Englishmen in the field. He also controlled
the most effective French military forces, the royal artillery train and, with
his brother Charles, Cardinal of Lorraine, the mind of the pliable new French
King. One of Guise's immediate priorities was to secure his niece's Scottish
kingdom against the revolt of its fractious, heretical nobility. Fortunately,
inept French attempts to relieve Mary of Guise's besieged Scottish regency
administration rescued an equally inept English land campaign to thwart
them. A model naval operation conducted by William Winter, Surveyor of
the Navy, prevented any reinforcement of the initial French expedition,
and the death of the Queen Dowager in July delivered total victory to the
Lords of the Congregation and their English allies.[15] The subsequent
Treaty of Edinburgh removed French troops from Scottish soil – forever, as
it transpired – and ensured that the only substantial 'Scottish' threat to
Elizabeth's throne would derive in future from the person of Mary Stuart
herself, rather than from her increasingly divided nation.

By the latter part of 1560, England was without discernible external
threats to her security; indeed, one commentator has suggested that in
the period immediately following the treaties of Cateau-Cambrésis and
Edinburgh she was as completely at peace as at any time during the entire
sixteenth century.[16] However, any promising vista of future tranquillity was
illusory. The necessities that had urged the peace of Cateau-Cambrésis upon
its signatories were ripe with the potential for new and far greater discords

than princely ambition alone might have generated – most threateningly, where matters of religion pressed. Under the terms of their treaty, both Henri and Philip had committed themselves to extirpating heresy within their respective domains. Neither monarch, however, was to enjoy the freedom, – nor, in Henri's case, the time – to address that goal. Partial success was, of course, no success; the history of previous internal crusades had shown that compromise from weakness gave the worst possible message to the heretical and orthodox alike. Only in England, where the relatively smooth imposition of the Act of Uniformity, Thirty-Nine Articles and Book of Common Prayer reflected a general weariness for dogma and doctrine (and fear of their familiar consequences), did it seem, briefly, that a 'mixed' population might be able to draw back from the worst implications of sectarianism. Across the Channel, that disengagement proved impossible.

Following the conspiracy (or 'Tumult') of Amboise in 1560, during which the Guise faction's military forces slaughtered hundreds of its Protestant enemies, France faltered for almost two years upon the brink of civil war. Superficially, the process was driven by the ambitions of her noble houses, but it was marked out almost precisely upon the widening confessional divide. During this dangerous period, the potential for conflict was vastly enhanced by the unlucky mortality of the French Royal House. The death of Henri II had exacerbated the potential for conflict by placing royal authority entirely into the hands of the Guise, to the dismay and resentment of the Bourbon party. That of his son Francis at the close of 1560, and the subsequent regency of Catherine de'Medici, reversed this balance of power; but gave the now-excluded Guise faction every reason to anticipate the storm that was closing upon France. From March 1562, when internecine conflict commenced with the sectarian massacre at Vassy, England's timeless enemy was in a poor position to injure anyone other than herself.

For Philip II's part, an acceptable peace with France had been his overwhelming priority, but it was not driven by financial embarrassment alone. Like his Valois counterpart, he was increasingly exercised by domestic problems, particularly within the Iberian portion of his patrimony. He was at heart a Castilian, who longed for a homeland he had not seen in six years: a homeland that had been stricken by poor harvests, threats of rebellion and, worst of all, apparent outbreaks of heresy on its northern borders. Against this latter threat, more stringent proscriptions were introduced hurriedly in 1559, and the Holy Office, over-burdened with its increased duties, needed a royal authority in attendance to support – and hopefully increase – its own.

Abroad, a new (or, rather, a resurgent) challenge to Philip's Mediterranean interests emerged just as the Valois threat receded. Before departing the Low Countries in August 1559, he gave his blessing to a joint Spanish–Italian expedition to seize Tripoli. Its disastrous failure (with the deaths of some 12,000 Christian troops at Mostaganem) triggered a new, decade-long phase in the struggle against the Ottoman Empire for control of the entire western Mediterranean. In the face of that and his Iberian preoccupations, the Spanish King was eager – too eager – to place the government of the Low Countries into the hands of a surrogate administration.[17]

The retreat from dynastic confrontation in north-western Europe was therefore followed almost immediately by the retreat of direct royal authority from the region, with its corresponding reliance upon local (and locally concerned) officials. In that partial vacuum, men whose ambitions could neither be directed by diplomatic conventions nor limited by national boundaries found new room for manoeuvre. In France, the first phase of the Wars of Religion saw Huguenot and Catholic forces achieve and lose brief ascendancies while each proclaimed their loyalties to a crown whose writ increasingly failed to run beyond its core patrimonies. Large parts of the country fell under the effective control of Protestants, particularly in the south, where their influence and doctrines threatened to spill over into Philip's Catalonian territories. In the north, where Guise forces were largely successful in crushing their heretical opponents, Huguenot refugees from Picardy fled into Artois, Hainault and Flanders: provinces that had been painstakingly, (if incompletely,) cleared of heresy during the 1540s. There, they proselytized, and, with like-minded Netherlanders, swiftly established an underground network of churches – the spiritual focus, eventually, for disaffections that triggered the long revolt against Habsburg authority.

Elizabeth soon discovered that her own pragmatism and an English Channel could not fully absorb the shockwaves of these tectonic movements. Being a 'heretic', her diplomatic priorities were always given the worse possible interpretation in Catholic Europe. Her early intervention in France's civil war in support of the Huguenot forces was not so much motivated by spiritual considerations as uncharacteristic optimism – at the prospect of recovering Calais – and fear of the implications for England of an outright Guisarde victory.[18] Yet although the adventure was short-lived (Protestant Frenchmen quickly decided that even the Guise were preferable to Englishmen), it had far deeper repercussions than its military failures. Elizabeth received a swift and profoundly useful object-lesson on what English resources could achieve, but much of Catholic Europe saw her brief French adventure – and her support of the Lords of the Congregation in Scotland – as proof that she was becoming an active element in the resistance to the Counter-Reformation. As she would discover upon numerous occasions during her reign, being determined not to be regarded as a Protestant champion was one thing; to persuade others was much more difficult. Even where self-interest urged extreme circumspection (and for Elizabeth, it rarely did otherwise), it proved impossible to isolate secular concerns from their spiritual implications. England's economic relationship with the Low Countries provided a salutary early example of this unwelcome association.

When Philip departed Brussels in August 1559, he appointed as regent his half-sister Margaret of Parma, with detailed instructions on policy and a Council of State, dominated by the bishop of Arras (later Cardinal), Antoine Perrenot de Granvelle, whose priorities closely reflected those of their sovereign. Unlike his father, Charles, Philip intended to ignore the patchwork local rights and obligations with which his variegated overlordship of the Seventeen Provinces was burdened. Whatever his subjects might believe of their relationship with their sovereign, he was determined to govern them as he would a unitary state, particularly with regard to financial and religious policies. The struggle between royal authority and local privileges had commenced even before his departure, with clashes regarding individual states' rights to impose taxes and the brooding presence of three thousand Spanish soldiers who remained in the Low Countries following the conclusion of peace with France. Tensions were exacerbated by Granvelle's overhaul of the Provinces' archaic episcopal system, which established new bishoprics on a linguistic rather than the old patrimonial basis, and allowed for the permanent functioning of the Inquisition throughout their jurisdictions.[19]

Initially, the momentum of resistance to Philip's regency government came almost exclusively from the great houses of Orange-Nassau, Lannoy, Ligne, Egmont and Bronkhorst, and the many lesser noblemen whose anachronistic dignities had been carefully pampered by their previous overlords. Eventually, they were to succeed in removing both Granvelle and the *tercios*, and place themselves in the posts vacated by the cardinal and his patronees. But while most would seek little more than to reassert their own authority within the framework of Margaret's government, they could not ignore, as Granvelle undoubtedly could, local grievances against the spiritual and economic policies she implemented on behalf of Philip.[20] It was this less exalted but much vaster constituency – which, like its English counterpart a few years earlier, increasingly feared cultural submersion beneath a Spanish 'occupation' – that was to provide the engine of resistance to Habsburg sovereignty.

Physically distant from the Seventeen Provinces, Philip was obliged to rely upon often-belated reports from servants whose priorities increasingly were not his own. The element of insecurity this encouraged was heightened by his suspicion that England, the one nation enjoying a near-symbiotic relationship with the Low Countries, was actively assisting the corruption of his authority there. His fears were not entirely groundless. Elizabeth's accession had brought an immediate reversal of the tide of human traffic fleeing religious persecution. Englishmen joyfully returning from their self-imposed Marian exile were accompanied or followed by Calvinist refugees from the Low Countries. These were not always made welcome (especially by the Queen, who regarded extreme forms of Protestantism with little more warmth than Catholicism),[21] but the exodus exacerbated both the Regency government's frustration and its sense that the Elizabeth's personal heresy had a strongly political element.

Increasingly, this perception was to colour the 'English' policy of Philip and his successive governors in the Low Countries; yet Elizabeth had as much interest as Philip in preserving tranquillity there. The health of England's relationship with Antwerp, particularly the unimpeded conduct of trade across the English Channel, was a vital factor in her efforts to rebuild the English economy. The *Magnus Intercursus* (or 'Great Intercourse'), the comprehensive trade treaty first negotiated by Henry VII and the Duke of Burgundy, remained the cornerstone of England's overseas cloths trade. The loans that Elizabeth raised in Antwerp's money markets – the first was arranged on the day after her succession – enabled her government to function without calling parliament more than she wished (which was very infrequently indeed).[22] She had every reason, therefore, to ensure that the old Anglo-Burgundian amity continued with the minimum of disruption. However, the very scale and importance of commerce between England and the Low Countries made it an obvious stick to wave when either party wished to secure some advantage or concession from the other. Existing grievances regarding trade and its restraints provided work enough for Elizabeth's government from the beginning of her reign; but the impact of new political tensions, and the absence of direct royal authority in the Low Countries, both aggravated these contentions and encouraged confrontation where compromises were both obvious and available.

New customs duties upon a range of English goods had been introduced with the publication of a revised book of rates in May 1558. This, of course, had been the previous regime's initiative, but when the impositions on exported English cloths quadrupled overnight the new Queen reaped both its profits and the outrage of foreign merchants. Worse, the rises were discriminative, with domestic cloth exporters paying less than half the 'stranger's' rate (it was a further barb to foreigners that Englishmen who exported their cloths in non-English vessels also paid the higher duties).[23] The issue was an immediate source of diplomatic tension between London and Brussels, although its repercussions were muted while the vital settlement between the Valois, Habsburg and Tudor regimes was being negotiated at Cercamp. The outbreak of peace, however, re-exposed the wound – and at a time when a much thornier problem was beginning to undermine Anglo-Habsburg relations once more.

Inevitably, the French war of 1557/8 had encouraged a new surge in privateering activity. This had been sanctioned on the English side by Philip and Mary's proclamation of June 1557, a device that was little less restrictive than Henry VIII's notorious 1544 exemplar. In one of the first proclamations of her own reign, Elizabeth attempted to undo its worst effects, noting the abuses committed by those 'going unto the seas (as well under licence as without) by color and pretense to repress, apprehend and annoy the enemy . . .'[24] Given the Queen's thin resources, early efforts to curb the problem were necessarily reactive, although by 1562, there was a distinct, if very limited attempt to encourage English privateers to regard their French war commissions as expired. In July of that year, admiral William Woodhouse was at sea with a squadron of four ships, and captured a number of the more persistent offenders.

Unfortunately, new political expediencies once more confounded the best intentions of government. England's Huguenot alliance and the onset of war with Guisarde France that year required every proven resource to be mobilized. Having just imprisoned as many freebooters as Woodhouse and others could lay their hands on, the Queen urgently instructed the vice-admirals of the maritime counties to send to the fleet all 'rovers' in their custody.[25] One of those who seized the opportunity was the irrepressible Henry Stranguishe. Having tried his hand at legitimate naval command during the previous reign, he had since reverted to despoiling Iberian vessels, and, allegedly, planning to sack Madeira. At least two complaints against him were put to the Queen by Philip II himself via his envoys, Count Feria and Alonso de la Quadra. Elizabeth had responded by promising to capture and execute Stranguishe even if it cost her £10,000. He and his men were soon taken and committed to the Tower (being 'cast all to suffer', according to the London diarist Henry Machyn). Clearly, however, Elizabeth had overstated her intended revenge almost as much as her resources.[26] Now, pressed into royal service once more and commanding the ship *Fleur de Luce*, Stranguishe died bravely while attempting to force the royalist blockade of the Seine and relieve Huguenot Rouen. In an ironic postscript to a career that had redeemed itself at the last, his surviving mariners were hanged as pirates by Constable Montmorency on the grounds that Elizabeth had omitted to declare war formally.[27]

To supplement English naval operations, a new proclamation was issued, inviting Englishmen to repair to the seas in their own ships to assault Catholic France's seaborne trade. Despite its relatively restrictive terms, the initiative was to launch a new phase in indiscriminate private warfare against merchant traffic.[28] Within weeks, Hanseatic and Flemish merchants were busy petitioning the Privy Council to complain of the Admiralty Court's time-tested indifference to assaults upon their persons and chattels.[29] Even more numerous, however, were complaints from Spanish shipowners, who appear to have suffered the backlash from a resurgent English grievance.

A new phase in the activities of the Inquisition – responding to the threat of heretical pollution seeping into Spain from Huguenot Languedoc – affected Anglo-Spanish merchants still semi-resident in Spanish ports. While not directed overtly as during their brief persecution twenty years earlier, it was inevitable that the community (among whom a much larger number were acknowledged Protestants than at the time of the Reneger incident) should be targeted by an organization that was coming to suspect all racial or social deviations from an Iberian 'norm' as indications of heresy. No one was immune from its attentions. The new English ambassador, Sir Thomas Chaloner, arriving at Philip's court in January 1562, had his books seized by the Inquisition and his servants quarantined in lodgings three leagues from his own (though even this ordeal paled before that of his immediate predecessor, Sir Thomas Chamberlayn, whose personal cook was seized and tried as a heretic).[30] In this intimidating atmosphere, Chaloner's first duty was to plead the case of a group of Bristol merchants arrested at Seville upon the suspicion of heresy.[31] As always, Philip, a dutiful servant of the Inquisition, listened politely to Chaloner's entreaties but refused to interfere in any way in the activities of the Holy Office.

Reports of English merchants' mistreatment at the hands of Spanish inquisitors, filtering back to their home ports, reawakened the often-counterfeit outrage that had fuelled the rash of English assaults upon Iberian vessels some twenty years earlier.[32] Once more, many privateers and outright pirates took it upon themselves to redress wrongs that they themselves had not suffered in the least degree. Ships leaving or entering Basque ports, having no nearby naval contingents to come to their assistance, were particularly popular targets. By mid-1563, Chaloner was claiming to Cecil that some four hundred commissioned English vessels with up to 25,000 mariners were at sea.[33] That it was he who raised the matter suggests that their attentions were disproportionately directed towards Philip's Iberian subjects. A catalogue of complaints, submitted in the latter part of the year, tempted the Spanish King to take direct reprisals rather than waste his efforts in further diplomatic representations. His resolve was strengthened in November when an English fleet of eight ships brazenly violated Spanish neutrality to attack a French ship as it lay at anchor at Gibraltar. They were chased and half their number taken by Spanish galleys under the command of Albaro de Bazán, Marquis of Santa Cruz (later Philip's Captain-General of the Ocean Seas). Following brief proceedings, every English mariner was condemned to servitude in the galleys.[34] Having taken this robust first step, Philip decided to attack the problem in its entirety. In January 1564, all English ships in Basque ports, whether merchantman or privateer, were seized and their crews thrown into prison.[35]

This crisis was mirrored by developments in Philip's northern territories. As security for the cost of assisting the Huguenot armies, English troops had been permitted to occupy Le Havre ('Newhaven' to its new tenants). The port provided an excellent base from which English privateers quickly launched assaults on seaborne traffic shadowing the French coast as it entered or departed the Narrow Seas. Ships evading these predators faced a further screen of despoilers, haunting the waters around Jersey and Guernsey, who were almost entirely immune to the attentions of either the English or French governments.[36] Philip's administration in the Low Countries was no longer at war with Catholic France, and, as twenty years earlier following the peace of Crépy, renewed trade between the two powers gave privateers with anti-French commissions the right (in their eyes) to stop and search neutral vessels suspected of carrying 'coloured' cargoes. Most neutral traffic in the Channel was, of course, that of Philip's Netherlander or Spanish subjects. Many had troubled themselves to secure official letters of safe conduct from the Admiralty – letters almost uniformly disregarded by English privateers, who much preferred to strip vessels without first checking the 'colour' of their cargoes.

Englishmen were not the only offenders, but it was becoming harder to distinguish the national identities of individuals in the crowded seas off the

northern coast of France. Scottish and French privateers had already transferred their former national loyalties to the confessional struggles that
had erupted with the coming of peace between Spain and France. The
imminent failure of the Huguenot cause during 1562 accelerated the process,
causing many French Protestants to put to sea to attempt there what Guise
armies were preventing on land – the beginning of a long and vital tradition in the French wars of religion. During the following twelve months,
many of these men, who had formerly enjoyed a working relationship with
the English exiles of Mary's reign, shared the occupation of Le Havre with
their temporary landlords, and privateers sailing from the port often carried
a polyglot crew of like-minded despoilers.[37] Even the English government,
usually not too sensitive to such activities (until diplomatic representations
became particularly strident), seems to have appreciated their extent and
implication. As early as 3 March 1563, Cecil wrote to the earl of Sussex,
urging him to drastic action: 'My Lord, this matter of resort of pyratts, or
if ye will so call them, our adventurers, that dayly robb the Spaniards and
Flemings, and make port sayle in that realme, is a matter of a great long
consequence. For God's sake I require you to employe some care therin, that
some might be apprehended and executed.'[38]

　　Three months earlier, Margaret had sent to England an envoy, Christophe
d'Assonleville, bearing a list of grievances. He was to complain of manifold
English piracies and perceived abuses of the *Magnus Intercursus* (particularly
the arbitrary customs increases), and ask for, but not demand, redress.
D'Assonleville misinterpreted the warm welcome he received in London as
an implicit acknowledgement of the weakness of the English position, and
wrote to Margaret suggesting that Elizabeth, particularly with her French
war proceeding so badly, could not afford to have the Low Countries' trade
further disrupted.[39] His report inclined Margaret and Granvelle to favour
some form of embargo to achieve concessions, for which the Regent sought
Philip's authorization. Already angered by depredations against his Basque
subjects, the King agreed that limited sanctions should be imposed upon
some English goods (but not the all-important cloth and wool imports).
However, in November 1563, before his instructions reached Margaret, the
ports of the Low Countries were closed to all English shipping. Ostensibly
this was a temporary reaction to rumours of plague in England; in reality,
it was a deliberate ploy by Margaret and Granvelle (anticipating that Philip's
instructions would be more robust than they proved) to force Elizabeth into
compliance.

　　To the extent that the English cloth fleet could not depart the Thames,
and not a penny could be raised by Thomas Gresham on the Antwerp

exchange to service his sovereign's debts, Margaret's strategy looked, initially, to be successful. Elizabeth, unnerved also by reports of Philip's seizure of English ships in Spain, quickly promised to take more stringent measures to curtail piracy in the Narrow Seas and Channel, and also proposed a commission to consider the outstanding claims of Netherlanders that had languished for months in the Admiralty Court. Her Privy Council sent urgent letters to the vice-admirals of the maritime shires, demanding action in respect of the 'dayly complayntes that are made by the subjectes of the King of Spayn . . . for the spoyles of them uppon the seas commytted by such as pretend to make warre agaynst the French . . .' (another admission that the English government had been perfectly aware of the problem and its mitigations for some time).[40] Finally, the Queen urged that an international conference be convened to settle all grievances regarding perceived and actual restraints of trade.[41]

Encouraged to the wrong conclusions by these conciliatory signals, Margaret prevaricated and even extended the total embargo beyond Candlemas 1564, the date of cessation announced originally. In this she was supported strongly once more by Granvelle, who had come to regard English discomfiture as a weapon that might even bring internal revolt against Elizabeth, remove a heretical queen and end the succour given to Calvinist refugees in England. Both Regent and Cardinal were hugely optimistic of their own position. The extension of the embargo infuriated Elizabeth, who in the meantime had received word from Flanders and her neighbouring provinces that cloth-workers there had been severely affected by the growing shortage of English wool.[42] The news did not incline her to further concessions. She had already secured agreement from her Merchant Adventurers that, if absolutely necessary, they might establish an alternative mart for their cloths at Emden, within sight of the Netherlands but on the German bank of the Ems estuary. However, they demanded a precondition for their removal: a counter-embargo to preserve their monopoly rights against interlopers who might wish to fill the vacuum at Antwerp during their absence. The Queen acceded to this. In March 1564, she conflated two entirely separate issues by threatening to suspend all imports from and trade with the Low Countries until Margaret's embargo was lifted *and* English ships and mariners seized in Spain two months earlier had been released.[43]

The linkage was disingenuous. Margaret had neither responsibility for nor power to resolve the stay of shipping in Spanish ports; nor were communications between the Low Countries and Spain sufficiently swift to provide any satisfaction on the matter. Elizabeth was perfectly aware of this. She fully intended her own embargo to proceed as an object lesson to the Regent that the benefits of the cloth trade were not one-sided – that the Antwerp mart itself was not necessarily indispensable to England.[44] It proved to be a portentous step, though not in the manner the Queen had anticipated. Starved of its English raw materials, the Flemish cloth-trade ground swiftly to a halt, and unemployed cloth-workers, their sufferings magnified by a vicious winter and failed harvest, flooded into churches and marketplaces to hear the rabble-rousing oratory of Calvinist preachers. As they did so, the mutual interests that had bound the historic relationship of the people of the Seventeen Provinces and their overlord began to unravel. Most of the aggrieved wanted only food and jobs; their haranguers wanted to build the City of God on Earth; Philip wanted – demanded – a restoration of order and orthodoxy that could be achieved only by force. Should local efforts fail, this would of course mean Spanish force.

In years to come, Elizabeth would repeatedly and strongly express a desire to see the restoration of the freedoms, privileges and responsibilities that had made the Low Countries an exemplar of financial and mercantile increase for more than a century past. Yet in 1564, hers was one of the principal contributions to a conflagration beyond the ability of good intentions to dampen. This was a pivotal moment in Philip's developing attitude towards England. As a reward for having (in his own eyes) regarded Elizabeth's heresy and her succour of like-minded Netherlanders with considerable restraint, he was being repaid with ever-bolder assaults upon his prerogative to govern the Low Countries as he wished. The recovery of civil and religious conformity there would become one of his most obsessive and expensive goals; its frustration a commensurate engine of resentment. The identification of England with that frustration had commenced. The King of Spain was wrong to consider Elizabeth's policy, then or later, as being either consciously antagonistic or the principal sustainer of his subjects' continuing insurrection. Yet it was easier to believe this than acknowledge that, as in France, across lands that had for centuries been the battlegrounds of Kings, the preoccupations of priests and hungry peasants had begun to impede the exercise of sovereign authority. For any monarch this would have been unpalatable; for Philip II, who regarded himself rather more the instrument of God's will than any pope, it was inconceivable.

Elizabeth had taken a conscious political decision to test the trading relationship between England and the Low Countries. This had been a short-term reaction to measures against her own policies and the activities of her unruly subjects, but in another sense she had initiated a disengagement that eventually would make Anglo-Spanish amity an irrelevance. This was not in itself sufficient cause for outright enmity; England had no official expansionist ambitions (other than for its Irish domains), and for as long as Philip had more pressing enemies he had little reason to make new ones or wantonly throw off old friends. The mutual embargoes would be lifted quickly as both he and Elizabeth weighed the utility of confrontation against its cost to their exchequers. As early as April 1564, the Queen had established a commission intended to deal summarily with any English pirates caught at sea or upon land; in August, Philip, appraised of English efforts by his new envoy in London, the almost-anglophile Don Guzman de Silva released all but a few of his English prisoners and ships. By the beginning of 1565, English merchant adventurers were flocking back to Antwerp with their government's blessing.[45] But none of this signalled a resumption of 'normal' relations. Trade had been one of the two time-tested pillars of the Habsburg relationship with England. The other – a mutual fear of Valois ambitions – had been undermined significantly by the descent of France into near-constant strife. What remained was shakier than before, and would rely upon whatever self-interest determined was better than conflict.

For both monarchs, the financial burden of war would remain a powerful disincentive. Yet neither could prevent their sincere efforts to maintain a profitable state of tranquillity from being confounded by three rapidly developing imperatives. The impact of the first of these – the strengthening appeal of the reformed religion throughout north-western Europe – ensured that many low-born men and women would increasingly regard neither priests nor kings as necessary mediators, much less arbiters. Their priorities, incapable of being bound by pragmatic considerations, were to compromise and eventually fracture the secular relationships between England and the Low Countries. The second – nascent nationalism – was no less immune to rational intervention, although it drew both strength and identity from parochial appropriations of the first. The last – private enterprise – may have appeared to be the least problematic to governments struggling with heresy, counter-reformations and the breakdown of old political loyalties. Yet a slow metamorphosis of one strand of this acquisitive urge – from semi-condoned banditry at sea to near-legitimate predation – was to create tensions that would reflect and in turn influence at least one nation's developing view of itself and its God. Thereafter, Philip would be given every reason to regard war with England as not only unavoidable but utterly necessary.

FIVE

The First Cold War

The Perills ar many, great, and imminent[1]

During the 1560s, the first cracks in the Anglo-Spanish relationship resulted from pressures placed upon the mutual interests that had built the 'ancient amity'. For both England and Spain, these were overwhelmingly the Low Countries' trade, the tranquillity of the seas that transported it and the potential Valois threat to both. Direct commercial intercourse between the two nations, if profitable, was a relatively inconsequential aspect of the relationship. Its disruption by the Holy Office and English freebooters was an occasional source of contention, but usually reflected or contributed to the impact of larger grievances elsewhere. The very conduct of the trade, however, gradually exposed a far more fundamental confrontation of philosophies – one whose implications would fuel a principal element of subsequent English 'resistance' to expanding Spanish power.

The Treaty of Tordesillas had divided the unknown world between Spain and Portugal at a time when other European nations' interest in oceanic voyaging was minimal. As that situation changed, so the treaty's assumptions became ever more hopeful. By sixteenth-century norms, territories conquered by a regime were regarded broadly as legitimate acquisitions of war (even if other regimes coveted, and eventually intended to gain control of, the same territories). Far less acceptable, however, was any policy that excluded friendly nations from accessing the wealth of those conquered lands through the legitimate conduct of trade – the 'commone usage of the worlde'.[2] Propagandists for economic expansion, particularly in England, would argue increasingly that if this fundamental right was denied, the validity of other rights – even those established by papal bull, treaty or conquest – could be challenged with equal legitimacy. In respect of Spain's New World monopolies, the nature of that challenge remained diffuse for many years, but the long collision course between Spanish assumptions and the ambitions of foreign interlopers may be said to have been first plotted on 20 January 1503, the day Queen Isabella of Castile established the Casa de Contratación, or House of Trade, in Seville.

From its initial base in the Ataranzanas (the city arsenal), and thereafter from a modest room in the Alcazar palace, the Casa organized and directed all commercial intercourse between Spain and her new possessions in the Americas. At the time of its foundation, those territories constituted little more than the coastal regions of Cuba, Hispaniola (Haiti) and the Islas Lucayas (Bahamas). Later, when the larger part of the American landmass south of the Rio Grande had fallen under Spanish occupation, the same small body continued to provide the mechanisms through which Spain's trans-Atlantic commercial system functioned.

The Casa's inception marked the end of a brief period of relatively liberal conditions in which any subject of Castile or León had been permitted to emigrate to, or trade (almost) freely with, the new territories. From 1503, all vessels passing to and from the Americas were obliged to register, load and discharge their cargoes at the Casa's warehouses in Seville, but the growing difficulty in carrying larger ships up the silting Guadalquivir River brought a reluctant concession whereby outgoing vessels were permitted to lade at Cadiz and certain other, nominated ports. Control of incoming traffic, however, remained the exclusive prerogative of Seville. Other towns and cities within the patrimony of the Crown of Castile were permitted to enjoy the fruits of this trade, but only through sales to, and purchases from, Crown agents or licensees. No less than foreigners, they were forbidden to trade directly with the New World.[3]

Almost from the start, the arrangement hampered much of what it was intended to achieve. Its narrow bureaucracy was an effective bottle-neck, preventing any individual initiatives that might have relieved the near-perennial under-supplying of Spanish colonists (though clandestine shipments of unregistered wares in official vessels provided an early and persistent source of irritation to the Crown).[4] Many of Castile's best oceanic mariners and her most plentiful supply of seagoing vessels – those of the ports of the northern coast – were effectively excluded from participation in the new trade unless they submitted to the Casa's onerous licensing system. In the first years of colonial occupation, New World settlers were dependent upon the Spanish government for almost all of their livestock, non-subsistence foodstuffs and manufactured supplies. These arrived infrequently, and, until the late 1520s, in single ships or 'fleets' of two or three vessels. It was never enough. The exploitation of the fabulous gold and silver reserves of the Americas constituted the overwhelming priority of the Spanish Crown; the well-being of those who colonized the lands from which they were derived remained a secondary consideration.

In peacetime, the complaints of the colonists were heartfelt; when war or persistent piratical activity interrupted such supplies as they had come to expect, they were pitiful. As already seen, French assaults upon Spanish shipping in the Atlantic and Caribbean were almost as venerable as Spain's interest in the New World. The Spanish Crown responded to the threat with the organization of convoys – *flotas* – that were to become the principal (if elusive) targets of later generations of English and Dutch privateers.[5] However, while the systemization of communications with the New World brought a measure of protection for the ships themselves, it provided little incremental benefit to those who awaited them in the colonies. During the final phase of the Valois–Habsburg struggle, increasingly well-organized French depredations made the Spanish Caribbean settlements almost unviable (ironically, it may have been the colonists' persistent clandestine trade with Portuguese interlopers, putting in at Hispaniola and her neighbouring islands, that prevented several towns from being abandoned as untenable). In 1543, Cartagena was sacked; the following year came the turn of Santiago de Cuba. In 1555, the Huguenot commander Jacques de Sores led a raiding party of two hundred men that seized Havana. Following a breakdown in a truce negotiated between Sores and the local Spanish authorities, the French leader massacred his prisoners and fired the city before leaving. A few weeks later, another group of his compatriots returned to loot the ruins and the nearby villages in which Havana's population had taken refuge.[6]

For the Spanish Crown, the vulnerability of the New World settlements was an intractable problem, given the crippling logistical price of providing adequate protection. Threats to the *flotas*, in contrast, were entirely unacceptable. Following the onset of the French wars of religion, the Huguenot admiral Gaspard de Coligny authorized the establishment of a permanent French presence in Florida, whose *raison d'être* would be the interception of Spanish fleets as they passed through the Florida Channel. Conceived and led by a Le Havre pilot, Jean Ribault, the colony was established in 1562 but evacuated and repatriated within a year, following a mutiny by its hard-pressed settlers. When Ribault's home port of Le Havre fell to Guisarde forces in 1564, he fled to London to press for an Anglo-French expedition to establish a second colony. Initially, Elizabeth was interested in his proposal, but subsequently demurred (to the Spanish ambassador she later claimed brazenly that she had considered the proposal only because she believed Florida to be a French, rather than a Spanish discovery). Without English support, Ribault returned to reinforce a second, purely French Florida colony established by Réne de Laudonnière, only to be killed in 1565 with most of his fellows fighting a Spanish expeditionary force, led by Pedro Menéndez de Avilés, that had been charged with its extermination.[7]

Protestant Europe, ignoring the entirely predatory nature of the French Florida project (and the fact that Ribault and his men had been searching for Menéndez with precisely the same intention when they clashed), added the outrage to its growing corpus of Spanish depravities. Yet under the impact of this and other French assaults, Philip had little choice but to adopt salutary measures to protect Spain's vital Atlantic highway. His colonies' resources – even under the effective supervision of men such as Menéndez – were never sufficient to cover more than the most pressing of several dangers of the moment. Punitive operations were inevitable, therefore, as was an increasingly rigorous policy towards any form of interloping by non-Spaniards. At sea, meanwhile, Philip instigated a wholesale reorganization of the *flota* system, including the creation of a 'Guard of the Indies' – a fleet of twelve small galleons – to accompany and protect the precious convoys through the dangerous navigations at the extremities of their Atlantic passage.[8]

Again, while the sea routes between Spain and her possessions were made marginally safer by these measures, the Spanish colonists shared little of the benefit. Stories of their enduring weakness and inability (or reluctance) to enforce the Casa's restrictive regime circulated from French ports into Protestant Europe, while tales of their woes percolated through the colonial system itself. Clearly, opportunities existed either to alleviate or add to their sufferings; to seize any, however, would be to assault either the Spanish Crown's commercial interests or its sovereign prerogatives. By the early 1560s, the promise (and potential dangers) of these opportunities had gripped at least one Englishman, the Plymouth mariner John Hawkins. Son of William, the pioneering Guinea/Brazil trader, and with prior connections both among French privateers and the Spanish mercantile community in the Canaries,

Hawkins decided to test the limits of Spain's determination to maintain her monopolies.[9] In 1562, he secured the backing of a consortium of rich London merchants and officers of the English naval administration to expand the embryonic Guinea trade into a three-cornered enterprise. Given Portugal's increasingly ineffectual defence of her markets, he proposed that it would be relatively easy (and inexpensive) to acquire black slaves and carry them to the Spanish Caribbean, where labour-starved colonists would pay a premium – in coin, spices and other high-value commodities – for field and plantation workers. For his financial backers it had a further attraction in being an almost wide-open market. To date, even the enterprising and ruthless French interlopers in the Caribbean had regarded the traffic in human beings as too abominable to contemplate. An Englishman's example would soon blunt their sensitivities, however.

The four slaving voyages led or organized by Hawkins between 1562 and 1568 represented a significant development in English maritime enterprise.[10] In a narrow sense they revived a family experiment initiated by his father over thirty years earlier; but their motives and rationales also presaged those of almost every one of the English New World projects that Philip would come to regard as fundamental attacks upon his authority. Indubitably beneficial to hard-pressed Spanish colonists, they were also impossible to countenance if the assumptions upon which Spain enjoyed her new empire were not to be entirely undermined.

In 1562, Hawkins's first expedition, of three small vessels, one hundred English mariners and a renegade Spanish pilot, captured or bartered several hundred slaves in the Sierra Leone region. Passing on to Hispaniola, Hawkins extracted a licence to trade there from a local official – who later claimed to have been outnumbered and outgunned into submission, but who probably colluded with the English interlopers – and disposed of his cargoes at a considerable profit. Its margin was depressed somewhat by Hawkins's decision to send a proportion of his acquisitions via Seville – possibly to test Philip's resolve in the face of a mutually beneficial arrangement. However, the expedition returned to England with a sufficient return upon expenditure to incline the Queen, the Lord Admiral and the earls of Leicester and Pembroke to join Hawkins's original backers in financing a further voyage.[11]

The Queen's overt involvement in his project was uncharacteristically provocative. She may have intended it in part as a measured 'incentive' to unblock concurrent negotiations regarding the Low Countries' embargo and the detention of English ships in Spanish ports, but there can be little doubt that the principal attraction was monetary. The loss of customs income to the embargo that summer had been heavy, and her Exchequer – never overly sensitive to the sources of its replenishment – was still struggling both to settle outstanding debts from the previous reign and cover some £750,000 of military expenditure commissioned since her accession.[12] Like her merchants and adventurers, Elizabeth had every reason to be receptive to new money-making opportunities, even at a potentially large political cost.

Despite several attempts by Philip's envoy in London to prevent it (and urgent discouragement from Sir Thomas Chaloner in Seville, who had borne the brunt of the Spanish King's anger at news of Hawkins's first voyage), the next expedition departed England in October 1564.[13] This comprised four ships, including the ageing naval vessel *Jesus of Lubeck*, which stood as part of the Queen's investment. As in the previous year, Hawkins obtained hundreds of slaves on the Sierra Leone coast (although not without loss of a number of his men). From there he sailed to the coast of Venezuela rather than to Hispaniola, but was rebuffed by local officials who evacuated the settlement of La Margarita as he approached. Further west, at Burburata, the townspeople requested that he wait until they received their governor's permission to trade. Initially, Hawkins agreed to this, but here and at Rio de la Hacha, delays and arguments regarding the local duties he should pay on his purchases exposed the limits to which he was prepared to maintain the fiction of legitimate enterprise. Trade duly proceeded on his terms, following thinly veiled threats to seize what he was not permitted to barter.

Before returning to England, Hawkins's ships moved northwards to visit Laudonnière's Florida colony, which by that time was in dire need of resupply. The visit was premeditated; Hawkins had been involved briefly with Ribault's projected Anglo-French colonial scheme and remained interested in reconnoitring the area to test its potential. The Spanish envoy de Silva learned of the visit and had reported it to Philip while the expedition was still at sea. Following Hawkins's return, de Silva invited him to dinner at his residence and asked about the colony. He was assured that it had been evacuated in one of the English expedition's ships, sold by Hawkins to the desperate French colonists. The lie, soon discovered, added to Spanish suspicions of Anglo-French complicity to render the Atlantic sea routes unviable.[14]

The second slaving voyage realized a profit of approximately sixty per cent for its investors, and plans for a further expedition commenced almost immediately.[15] Once more, de Silva worked hard to prevent it. He secured a promise from the Queen to forbid Hawkins's departure from England,

and she duly pretended to honour it. During his temporary 'detention', however, Hawkins managed to despatch three of his own ships under the command of a kinsman, John Lovell. Lovell acquired slaves in West Africa, and attempted to follow precisely his employer's itinerary of the previous year. However, without sufficient men and guns to 'persuade' the inhabitants of La Margarita and Burburata to trade once more, and being short-changed in the sale of slaves at Rio de la Hacha, the expedition proved unprofitable. The only notable feature of the voyage (and that to future generations alone) was the presence therein of Hawkins's young cousin, Francis Drake.[16] Otherwise, Lovell's brief collaboration with a notorious French privateer, Jean Bontemps (reported in detail by Philip's officials at Rio de la Hacha), only further obscured the difference between English trade and French depredations in the Spanish King's eyes.[17]

Meanwhile, Hawkins proceeded with preparations for his third slaving voyage. By the middle of 1567, the Spanish envoy knew that these were far advanced, and that at least two, and possibly four, of the Queen's ships were to be employed. Repeated assurances from both Elizabeth and Cecil (the latter gave his formal oath, according to de Silva) that the ships were not going to visit any part of Philip's territories were received with some scepticism, though both the Spanish King and his envoy continued to express their gratitude that the Queen was sensitive to their concerns.[18]

That the expedition was allowed to sail thereafter represented a significant testing of the diplomatic temperature by Elizabeth. News of the extermination of the French Florida colony had now reached England, providing confirmation – were it needed – that Philip was determined to defend his rights aggressively. Yet far from being deterred by this example, Hawkins planned the scale of his new voyage – six ships, including two heavily armed naval vessels – to meet head-on any threat of confrontation. During several audiences with the Queen in the weeks prior to Hawkins's departure, de Silva made it clear that no licences provided by culpable or intimidated colonial officials would legitimize activities that she had already promised would not occur. Despite these urgent warnings, there was an increasingly obvious lack of care to disguise the expedition's aims, and at worse an insolent pretence. On Hawkins's part, this amounted almost to provocation. Eight days before he sailed, a small Flemish fleet flying Habsburg pennants entered Plymouth's Cattewater and attempted to anchor near Hawkins's vessels. Without cause, he fired upon them to force their withdrawal to Eastwater. Later questioned by the Flemish admiral Baron de Wachen with a degree of politeness he hardly deserved, the Englishman claimed boldly that he did not know what the destination of his coming expedition was to be, as the Queen had not yet revealed it to him.[19]

Hawkins sailed at the beginning of September 1567. At each stage of this latest voyage, he showed himself ready to act more aggressively than in previous years. Following the now-habitual visit to the West African coast to acquire human trading wares, he moved on to the Venezuelan coast. At La Margarita, the expedition acquired victuals without resistance from the governor and townspeople; at Burburata trade was similarly unrestricted, despite the town having acquired a new, supposedly less obliging administration. The ports of Rio de la Hacha and Santa Marta were less welcoming; both had to be seized by force before trade could be imposed (though the latter outrage was prearranged with the town's governor), and at Cartagena, the principal city of Terra Firme, the English fleet was repulsed under fire. Nevertheless, having managed by this time to sell the bulk of his cargoes, Hawkins was ready to return to England. Before he could re-enter the Atlantic, however, the parlous condition of his flagship *Jesus* had to be addressed. Moving northwards into the Gulf of Mexico, he decided to make for the roadstead of Vera Cruz, San Juan de Ulúa, where he intended to repair and re-caulk her hull.

The expedition's encounter there with the *flota* of New Spain has become an iconic episode in England's seafaring history. The allegedly treacherous assault by Philip's viceroy Don Martin Enriquez, Hawkins's heroic resistance and destruction of two Spanish warships, Drake's flight (his desertion, according to Hawkins) in the *Judith*, the abandonment of many Englishmen upon the Isthmus coast and their subsequent ordeal in Spain, and the epic homeward voyage of the *Minion* all contributed then and later to English perceptions of Spanish iniquity. Yet Hawkins and his men had reaped the logical consequences of an enterprise that had tested the resolve of the Spanish government and colonial administration to breaking point. The lip-service paid to a legal process, and Hawkins's repeated claim to be a loyal servant of the Spanish King, had been entirely insincere. The world knew perfectly well how Philip regarded his New World dominions and their exploitation; to pretend that the assumptions underpinning the painfully constructed trade between Spain and the Spanish New World were open to re-interpretation by individual adventurers invited a swift and condign reaction. Enriquez, a senior colonial official (one of the uncommonly dutiful variety), had some six million ducats' worth of bullion in his ships' holds when he encountered Hawkins at San Juan de Ulúa. It is hard to imagine any responsible commander failing to assume the worst of his uninvited and unexpected guest. Nevertheless, his 'unexampled perfidy' has been no less a point of faith to successive English historians than it was to Hawkins's contemporaries.[20]

The failure of the fourth and largest slaving voyage (Hawkins barely covered the costs of the expedition's outfitting) ended this phase in English interest in the West Indies. It had been too ambitious, and, in the face of the Spanish King's determination to maintain his prerogatives, too likely to generate problems out of any proportion to its potential profits. As a collateral achievement, the intrusions of Hawkins and other Englishmen into the Portuguese African trade led, in 1568, to the suspension of all commerce between England and Portugal, with mutual embargoes of shipping and goods.[21] More ominously, the episode exacerbated yet another developing confrontation between the Tudor and Habsburg regimes.

Given the project's potential to generate such commotions, it is still not entirely clear why Elizabeth permitted Hawkins to depart England in 1567. She had been made amply aware that Philip did not distinguish between English 'trading' expeditions to the Caribbean and continuing French depredations, particularly when it became evident that Englishmen were joining French privateers, aiding their colonists, or, possibly, attempting to supersede them in both activities. The sixty per cent return on the second voyage could hardly have been considered ample reward for risking the King of Spain's friendship – unless the value of that friendship had been rendered questionable already. Elizabeth often responded laterally to unwelcome developments, as the circumstances of her 1564 Low Countries' embargo indicate. Such gestures made telling points without necessarily inviting the kind of direct confrontation for which England was ill-prepared. It is probable that she used the 1568 slaving voyage in the same spirit. To Hawkins, his enterprise had been the all-absorbing occupation of a half-decade; to the Queen, it was at most a tangential device to influence far more pressing concerns.

The first, and, to an extent, second slaving voyages had departed during periods of tension between England and Spain. While both Elizabeth and Philip variously made decisions to escalate or reduce confrontation, they were responding to events over whose underlying causes they enjoyed only limited influence. Ostensibly, concession and counter-concession at a diplomatic level had restored something of the normal conditions of trade between England and the Low Countries after 1564. Their future preservation, however, depended upon the ability of both monarchs to manage their policies with sufficient detachment from their subjects' priorities. This proved impossible. Little more than a year after the return of the merchant adventurers to their Antwerp mart, a chain of events commenced that would tie both Elizabeth and Philip to increasingly reactive measures.

In summer 1566, the 'iconoclastic fury' swept outwards from the south-western provinces of the Low Countries. A small group of Calvinist *provo-cateurs*, manipulating a far larger number of Netherlanders with almost entirely secular grievances, created widespread civil disorder and brought effective government to a standstill. The concessions subsequently forced upon Philip's regent Margaret (particularly that of freedom of worship in all areas where Protestantism was already established) were wholly unacceptable to the Spanish King. Driven on in part by Margaret's exaggerated claims for the number of heretical seditionists she faced, but also by the impulsion of an indecisive man driven finally to action, Philip determined to re-impose a definitive measure of orthodoxy and obedience upon his troublesome Low Countries.[22] Despite Margaret's subsequent success in quelling the 'fury' (with small yet effective forces, she had successfully reasserted royal author-ity in every major town in the southern provinces within a year), he began and continued to assemble a striking response to this assault upon his sov-ereign authority. On 3 August 1567 – a fateful day in European history – the relentless Duke of Alba led ten thousand Spanish troops into the Low Countries, tasked with crushing a revolt that no longer existed and expung-ing its heretical elements.

The event tipped the whole balance of power, and tension, in north-western Europe. Elizabeth, like her predecessors, wanted to keep the eastern shores of the Narrow Seas free from direct occupation by an inimical power. For most of the period since England's removal as a significant player in the region, the struggle between the Valois monarchy and the expanding Hab-sburg patrimonies had provided a de facto balance of power that suited English policy very well. Now, however, Philip's ambitions for his Low Countries could no longer be influenced by the potential threat of inter-ference from the French Crown. To the contrary, by exciting Huguenot sus-picions of a secret Guise–Habsburg pact, Alba's passage along the 'Spanish Road' through Savoy, Franch-Compté and Lorraine triggered the outbreak of second phase of the French civil wars. For Elizabeth, the old spectre of French domination of the Low Countries and Narrow Seas was being replaced by a Spanish equivalent that was militarily more effective and far more interested in fighting heresy – including, potentially, her own. Within two months of his arrival, Alba had begun to validate the worst fears of his intended victims. Even before Margaret, offended by his arrogation of

almost all of her powers, resigned as regent in November, he had arrested
several leading noblemen and city officials, dismissed many of her spiritually suspect German mercenaries and made it manifestly clear that ancient
local privileges and recent grievances would be ignored equally. It was also
apparent that he would rely exclusively upon Spaniards or loyal Walloon
placemen to discharge his policies – most ominously, in the establishment
and operation of the Council of Troubles, a tribunal that incorporated the
most oppressive characteristics of tyrannical secular government and the
Holy Office.

Alba's captain-generalcy of the Low Countries was intended to be a short-
term holding operation until Philip could return to take personal charge of
government there (rumours that a large Spanish fleet was being prepared to
bring him through the Narrow Seas tested the English government's nerve
throughout the summer of 1567);[23] but that opportunity was never to come.
The regime was therefore increasingly one of military occupation rather than
restored sovereign authority. For many of those obliged to suffer the consequences of his rule, Alba's arrival marked the moment at which their
overlord proved himself to be a foreign despot. Sustained and incited by
a massive immigration of Protestant refugees from the south, the northern
provinces – Gelderland, Zealand, Holland, Utrecht, Friesland, Ommelanden
and Drenthe – would soon commence their long, squabbling journey to
independence. For their southern neighbours, loyalty to a particular form
of god and government would, eventually, preserve Habsburg authority, if
at huge cost in lives and property. Yet even here, amongst the disintegrat-
ing fabric of town life, Philip was losing a further constituency – the English
cloth merchant.

The iconoclastic fury and its collateral civil disorders had erupted too late
in 1566 to prevent the merchant adventurers from disposing of that season's
cloth exports. However, their Queen's finances were badly affected by the
suspension of the Antwerp Bourse and temporary disappearance of her
habitual moneylenders. The latter problem became considerably less temporary following Alba's arrival, when many of the Netherlander merchants
to whom her agent Thomas Gresham usually turned for loans decided to
seek new and quieter environs in the north or abroad. The urgency with
which Elizabeth now sought a source of loans elsewhere went some way to
encouraging her mercantile community to address their own arrangements
during this 'brablinge time'.[24] As early as January 1567 they were rumoured
to be negotiating terms with representatives from Hamburg to relocate their
mart in or near the city. On 19 July, formal heads of agreement were

exchanged between the Merchant Adventurers' Company and the Hanse town's civic government.[25] This was as yet a legal entitlement rather than a binding commitment, but from September, further impetus was provided by the first verified reports of Alba's persecutions, brought by Protestant Netherlanders seeking English sanctuary.[26] More mundane, but even more decisive, was a looming threat that the province of Brabant might finally match English customs duties with her own, thus obliging English merchants to compete upon a level playing field. Most disturbing of all was the lesson drawn from the ordeal of certain prominent Netherlander merchants, arraigned for their part in the previous year's disturbances. Cast into prison, their goods and properties forfeited, the sufferings of these men exercised their English associates tremendously – particularly as their outstanding debts for English cloths were now unpayable.[27] Even the most conservatively minded among England's merchants were gradually acquiring powerful incentives to consider innovation.

It is against this backdrop of failing royal credit facilities, growing impediments to the English cloth trade, and, above all, the presence of the Duke of Alba in the Low Countries that Elizabeth's provocative patronage of Hawkins's last slaving voyage should be viewed. She had a horror of anticipating events; but losing all initiative in the face of a tide of unpleasant developments was less acceptable than the risks of reminding Philip that she was his equal, not a client-queen. No less than her former brother-in-law, however, the Queen appeared to misunderstand the complexity and interaction of the crises she believed herself to be addressing. In an otherwise amicable milieu, the diplomatic repercussions of Hawkins's expedition would have required a deft touch; but the wider political situation in western Europe, already turbulent, deteriorated markedly during 1567/8. As Alba implemented his master's policies, the stream of Calvinist refugees fleeing to England and Germany became a torrent. At the same time, their more martial compatriots from the coastal communities of Holland and Zeeland were putting to sea and coalescing into fleets of 'Sea Beggars'. These men – habitual criminals, heretics, entrepreneurs and outraged minor members of the Seventeen Provinces' disinherited nobility, committing themselves in treaty with William of Orange to harry Alba's supply lines – were joined by many like-minded Englishmen when Elizabeth, pushed by Cecil and others to provide succour to their failing Huguenot brethren, issued her own commissions permitting reprisals against French Catholic vessels.[28]

To this volatile *mélange*, Mary Stuart's flight to England in May added a potentially fatal dimension. It opened a wound in the English succession question and presented Elizabeth with uncomfortable choices, none of which would serve her interests. As Cecil pungently observed, they could neither send Mary back to possible execution at the hands of her rebellious subjects (or, worse, to be reconciled with them) nor onward to France to re-create a familial version of the 'auld alliance' with her Guise uncles.[29] By default, therefore, she became Elizabeth's problem: potential heir to the English throne and a figure-head for English Catholics (or rather, for their would-be sustainers abroad), about whom resistance to the fragile religious settlement might gather. With Mary's arrival in England, Elizabeth's virginally weak grip upon the English throne acquired a European context.

Across the channel, localized crises swiftly coalesced, giving each a dangerous international relevance. In June, Huguenot fears of extinction, fuelled by their catastrophic defeat at St Valéry, mirrored those of William of Orange following Alba's mass execution of Netherlander noblemen and his subsequent annihilation of the Orangist army at Jemmigen. In mutual desperation, French and Netherlander rebels signed a formal defensive treaty in August. From that moment, English aid to the Huguenots – upon whatever self-limiting rationale – was bundled inextricably with the wider anti-Catholic struggle. By the same token, the papacy and Spanish Crown came increasingly to see Catholic reverses not as the result of local circumstances, but of the machinations of a supra-national Protestant conspiracy – of which Elizabeth, as the senior prince, could hardly avoid being regarded as de facto leader.

As opportunities for misinterpretation of motives and intentions developed, the diplomatic channels between England and Spain almost ceased to function. Since the expulsion from the Spanish Court of the allegedly indiscreet English envoy John Man in March 1568, Elizabeth had no one to put her case in her words to Philip.[30] In September, however, she gained a new and spectacularly ill-disposed Spanish envoy to Whitehall, Don Guerau de Spes, who was only too willing to put to his master the worst possible interpretation of her actions. Before the end of the year, he was corresponding secretly with Mary Stuart and encouraging a quarrel that took England and Spain briefly to the brink of war.

In November, closely pursued by Huguenot privateers, four Genoese ships carrying much-needed funds to pay Alba's soldiers sought sanctuary in Plymouth harbour. Within days, this potentially happy reminder of the benefits of Anglo-Spanish amity mutated seamlessly into minor misunderstanding and then major stand-off without any testing of possible compromises. The specie carried in these vessels (valued at some £85,000) had not been assigned legally to Alba as yet.[31] As Elizabeth considered how to deal with the situation, John Hawkins's brother William arrived at Court, bringing advance news of the debacle at San Juan de Ulúa and the loss of all profits accruing from the voyage.[32] Piqued by this, and urged on by Cecil, she gave serious thought to the option of borrowing the Genoese windfall herself. Brazen though the step would be, it was not intrinsically dishonest. In fact, its anxious owners were only too pleased to lend their money to someone with a far healthier credit history than any servant of the Spanish King (and to be relieved of the problem of how to carry it into the Low Countries). However, Philip and his impecunious captain-general, given de Spes's version of Elizabeth's motives, saw this latest incident as a coldly judged escalation of the same aggressive English policy that provided financing for interlopers, asylum for Calvinist refugees and safe havens for Sea Beggars. On 29 December 1568, even before the Queen announced her definitive decision to retain the bullion, Alba reacted to de Spes's urgings – if reluctantly – by staying English ships and property in Low Countries' ports and crowding their unfortunate merchant-owners into gaol.[33] Elizabeth retaliated promptly, and massively. She ordered the seizure of chattels belonging to Spaniards and Flemings in England (though not their persons, as was urged by the Lord Mayor of London and a gaggle of outraged English merchants), imposed a ban upon trade with any territory under Philip's authority, authorized the interception of Spanish vessels entering the Channel, and, for good measure, placed the malevolent de Spes under house arrest.[34]

Four years earlier, the Queen had carefully paced her provocations. Now, the readiness with which she retaliated against Alba's measures (knowing that they could not have been sanctioned personally by Philip in the brief time available) indicates how far circumstances had changed during the intervening period. Though she considered herself dependent still upon the Antwerp financial markets, Thomas Gresham's ability to raise loans there had already been disrupted by civil unrest and the regency government's counter-measures. Her Exchequer, furthermore, was in such a rare state of surplus at the end of 1568 (owing in part to a recent large-scale farming-out of customs) that the Genoese funds she had appropriated were not spent but only cosseted in the Tower.[35] As for her cloth merchants, they had their piece of Hamburg paper, which although untested was valid for a further seven years, offering an alternative venue for their mart that Alba's sanguinary administration was doing its utmost to make more attractive. Trade, like finance, was ready to go elsewhere if necessary.

These circumstances undoubtedly encouraged Elizabeth to consider bolder responses to Habsburg 'provocations'; in isolation, however, they could not have provided sufficient incentive to risk abandoning the old Anglo-Burgundian relationship so precipitously. It has been suggested that Alba's (even more precipitous) embargo was entirely unexpected by the English government; that until she heard of his drastic initiative, the Queen had intended only to detain temporarily the monies from the pay-ships, whatever she led the Spanish envoy to believe.[36] Yet her vigorous response to Alba hints at more than indignation. There was a growing sense of urgency – of panic, almost – in the face of crises that seemed to have descended upon England in batches. Barely a month after the latest confrontation developed, Cecil (whose advice had done much to precipitate it) gave voice to this mood in a long memorandum on the state of the realm.[37] A manifest of what he regarded as the nation's ills, it ranged over the several evils of civil disobedience, religious indifference, England's martial inadequacies and the Scottish Queen problem. Above all, Cecil was exercised by what he termed 'the Conspyration of the Pope and the two Monarchees' (Guise-dominated Valois and Habsburg): a potentially fatal alliance of powers whose purpose, invigorated by the Council of Trent, threatened the existence not only of Elizabeth's regime but of an independent English nation.

There was little that was new in this survey, but Cecil's recommendations marked a radical departure from the policy of cautious engagement that both he and the Queen had favoured since England's painful extraction from the French war of 1562/3. He was now suggesting that circumstances favourable to England's potential and actual enemies in Catholic Europe made foreign intervention in English affairs far more likely than in the past. The threat was so imminent, he argued (nodding anxiously towards Alba), that doing nothing was no longer an option. Among more prudent measures – the summoning of musters on a more regular basis, addressing defects of armaments, training, shortage of horses, decay of fortifications and, of course, bringing the navy to readiness – he now pressed also for a 'Conjunction with all Princes Protestants' and the abandonment of trade with Flanders and other dominions of Philip II.

It is difficult to overstate the significance of this document. Cecil was proposing the reversal not only of the tenor but of the underlying assumptions of English foreign policy. Since the beginning of the French wars of religion, the historic balance of power in western Europe had shifted. As in 1558, when Elizabeth came to the throne, a Spanish army was in the

Low Countries; now, however, it was seen by Englishmen not as a welcome foil to the traditional, overarching threat from Valois France, but as the instrument of a resurgent, repressive orthodoxy that no more recognized the sanctity of national boundaries than the sectaries it sought to destroy. In 1568, the danger it posed to England was not – or did not appear to be – speculative. In Antwerp and elsewhere, rumours had been circulating almost from the moment of Alba's arrival that many of his soldiers believed their next task would be to deal with the English 'problem'.[38] To hinder the duke's regime would therefore not only assist the failing Orangist cause but might well preserve England also. Denying his soldiers their pay was a first step, and a profitable one; but the memorandum's arguments were an explicit demand that the Queen go much further.

Cecil's world-view was that of a poorly travelled statesman with fundamental antipathies towards Catholic Europe who gave too much credence to evidence, no matter how doubtful, of designs against England. His analysis addressed many genuine concerns, but it was coloured by fears of a threat that was by no means inexorable in 1569: of a net he believed to be cast already by the 'shaven priest at Roome that occupyeth the place of Antechrist'.[39] Throughout Protestant-controlled Europe, great significance had been placed upon the (as-yet unknown) substance of conversations held four years earlier between Alba, Catherine de' Medici and her daughter (Philip's Queen) Elizabeth of Valois during their conference at Bayonne. To Cecil and others who persuaded themselves that they had been the matter under discussion there, the event had inaugurated a long-feared combination of Catholic malice whose purpose must be inimical to the reformed religion.[40] The logic underpinning their conviction could not allow that Alba's 'pacification' of the Low Countries was an end in itself.

However illusory the conspiracy feared by Cecil, the initiatives he proposed to check its advances went far to create facts from fears. Like Elizabeth, he longed above all for the removal of Spanish troops from the Low Countries and a return to stable, even cordial, relations with Philip and his subjects. Yet he and his sovereign underestimated both the growing divergence of English and Spanish preoccupations and the potential effect of measures intended to address it. The threat that England might abandon her Low Countries markets had, traditionally, proved a severe and effective one. In encouraging his sovereign to retaliate so robustly against Alba's embargo (which the duke regretted almost from the moment he imposed it, as the English government was aware), Cecil anticipated a collapse of Habsburg obduracy similar to that five years earlier.[41] It was a fundamental miscalculation. Philip, like Elizabeth, had already begun to regard the historic Anglo-Burgundian amity as less than irreplaceable. As the fight against heresy and anarchy in the Low Countries absorbed more of his resources, the traditional benefits of peace exercised a progressively weaker influence upon his policies. Although no conscious decision was made to sacrifice the commercial well-being of the Seventeen Provinces as a collateral price of victory (certainly not by Alba, who desperately needed every penny he could squeeze from his unwilling subjects), the Spanish King's preoccupations allowed no possibility of a middle-ground that might salve both sovereign ire and local grievance. Without English merchants at Antwerp there could be no substantial economic grounding to the 'ancient amity'; without the lure of a profitable, stable relationship with England, what Philip was coming to see as Elizabeth's wilful provocations – her theft of 'his' monies and succour of those who rejected his sovereign rights – could no longer be mitigated by pragmatic considerations. In fact, pragmatism was increasingly to establish quite different priorities, most of which spoke to that most dangerous side of Philip's nature – his orthodoxy.

More than a decade after the accession of his former sister-in-law, Philip was finally abandoning any hope that she might renounce her Protestantism and bring England back to the fold voluntarily. The matter became more pressing as the likelihood of her bearing an heir receded (she was now thirty-six years old). Imminently extinct dynasties were both threats and opportunities, as the example of the Portuguese Royal House would prove little more than a decade hence. On the point of religion alone, the cautious Philip may not have considered active measures to force the English succession question. In recent months, however, he had acquired several subsidiary grievances against Elizabeth that hugely enhanced the perceived advantages of some form of intervention in England's domestic affairs.

His inclination to consider more aggressive measures was further encouraged by a marked increase in English intransigence as the year turned. Elizabeth, sustained by forced loans secured domestically against future Privy Seal income, and by embargo seizures that had more than compensated for the loss of customs revenues, acceded to Cecil's anxious advice and began negotiations for a defensive alliance with German Protestants.[42] Part of the treasure Philip had lost to England in November 1568 was provisionally allocated as subsidies to this end and to support the Huguenot leader, Henri, Prince of Condé's armies in the field: assignments that, when he learned of them, must have rubbed a great deal of salt into the Spanish King's wounds.[43] Another large point of contention – John Hawkins –

returned to England in the *Minion* in January 1569. News of the true extent of his losses at San Juan de Ulúa, assiduously reported in pamphlet form within weeks of his return, caused a predictable surge of popular English fury at Spanish perfidy that accorded neatly with the Queen's claims for Philip's duplicity.[44] English seafarers seeking to express their sense of outrage in the traditional manner found themselves spoiled for a choice of ready employer. Admiral Coligny's brother, Odet, Cardinal de Châtillon, had been in London since the previous year, recruiting mariners for a fleet of privateers (he had arrived on English soil the same day as de Spes).[45] By the end of January its fifty sail – manned, it was said, by more Englishmen than Frenchmen – had begun to prey upon the seaborne trade of 'Catholic' merchants of any nationality. Their plight deepened in February, when William of Orange offered his own commissions to Englishmen willing to supplement the efforts of the Sea Beggars.

Within months, the tentative alliances of freebooters first apparent during the Anglo-French war of 1562/3 re-emerged as a truly international force. From bases in northern France, Holland, Zeeland and southern England, fleets of privateers increasingly identified with the cause of Protestant resistance assaulted ships in the Channel traffic with an ecumenical disregard for their crews' spiritual convictions. Very soon, seaborne trade between Spain, France and the Low Countries slowed to a trickle of fraught dashes between friendly ports. The freebooters' enthusiasm and industry was such that even the English wine and cloth fleets had to be provided with armed escorts to deflect the temptation their cargoes excited.[46] This embarrassing collateral risk was compensated, however, by the swift growth of trade between English ports and the Huguenot hinterland, encouraged in part by the parallel movement of spoils of war. It must have been a further frustration to Philip that much of this traffic was in Spanish goods brought into France and sold on, thereby allowing Anglo-Spanish merchants to side-step the stay of their normal trade with the Iberian Peninsula.[47]

This was war by any other name. Adding to existing points of contention, it brought a significant shift in Philip's perspective which mirrored that of Cecil's, and upon similar logic. In January, spurred on by de Spes's outlandishly inaccurate claims for Elizabeth's domestic unpopularity and the corresponding fragility of her regime, he was in secret communication with Mary Stuart via his ambassador to France, Don Francés de Álava. He committed himself to assist her claim to the English throne 'as much as lies within my power' (she had promised that with his help, Mass would be heard again throughout England within three months), and sent word to

Alba to examine the possibility of an invasion of England directly from the Low Countries. This, if feasible, was to assist the planned uprising of the earls of Northumberland and Westmorland, whose intentions had been communicated to the Spanish court by January at the latest.[48]

These were dramatic initiatives – the proofs, it seemed, of Cecil's worst expectations; yet Philip was still far from making a rationally considered commitment to overthrow Elizabeth's regime. It was rather that the belligerence of English policy towards Spain during these months had provoked his 'messianic vision' (one might as accurately term it an hallucination) to override his habitual circumspection.[49] Prey to this intemperance of mind, he was more than usually receptive to transient possibilities that might have benefited his strategic interests at minimal cost, diplomatically and monetarily. The great latitude that he allowed Alba – 'If you think the chance will be lost by again waiting to consult me, you may at once take the steps you may consider advisable in conformity with this, my desire and intention, which would certainly give me great pleasure' – hints at a hurried lunge at opportunities made suddenly apparent. Even now, however, that lunge was tentative.[50] Possibly aware of how reluctant Alba would be to seize the 'chance', Philip also made it clear elsewhere that Spanish assistance would only be forthcoming once Elizabeth was dead and the duke of Norfolk firmly in control of her orphaned administration – in other words, to assist in stabilizing a new and favourable situation, not to destroy the present status quo.[51] The prospect of a Guisarde puppet ruler in England – even a staunchly Catholic one – was hardly something that Philip could consider with equanimity; indeed, it was one of the feared consequences that had informed his protective policy towards Elizabeth since her accession. That he was now apparently committing himself to that end (albeit with the same romantic unreality that allowed him to believe that John Hawkins and a fair proportion of the Navy Royal also stood ready to restore Catholicism in England) illustrates the degree to which he believed alternative options were being removed.[52]

With a failing English presence at Antwerp – the cloth fleet would make its inaugural voyage to Hamburg in May – and his own subjects' maritime trade almost extinguished by the Sea Beggars and their allies, Philip could no longer employ commercial leverage to achieve his aims even had he wished to do so. Furthermore, without adequate diplomatic channels in place, England and Spain had not enjoyed the means even to talk to each other for many months. To the Spanish King, his only other recourse short of the threat of outright war was to emulate recent English escalations. His decision to support disaffected Catholic Englishmen (and, from 1570, Irishmen) was spurred by concern for their spiritual welfare; the more immediate incitement, however, was Elizabeth's aid to Netherlander Protestants and her increasingly overt support for the privateering war against his subjects' trade. This was not perceived by the Queen, of course, who shared little of Cecil's apocalyptic vision and whose reaction to Philip's incursions was one of hurt puzzlement. Commenting upon his rumoured promise of assistance to the rumoured Irish 'invasion' of the renegade English Catholic, Sir Thomas Stukeley, she complained:

> We cannot but finde it straunge that either he or any such fugitives moving matters of attempt as rebells should either be allowed or hearkened vnto; for whatsoever hath been conceiued that any person of any degree, being the King of Spaine's subjects, coming into our realme of late years, as many have done for safetie of their lives for matters of their consciences (as we always vnderstood), yet we do assure this of our honour, that there was never person of any degree, that did motion unto us any matter offensive to the King or his Low Countries . . . that was ever allowed by us, or any such motion, or that ever received reward, or comfort therein, but was rejected'.[53]

With her southern ports full of Sea Beggars even as she wrote, this was a remarkably bare-faced claim. It was also self-deluding. Until Elizabeth allowed Englishmen to serve with the rebels in the Low Countries, commenced her (albeit infrequent) subsidies to keep their armies in being and gave safe haven to men who had made the Narrow Seas a near-impossible navigation for Spanish ships, Philip had exhibited little interest in fomenting or encouraging domestic plots in England or her Irish possessions. The Catholic world conspiracy predicted by Cecil and other Protestant luminaries was and remained a wraith, despite the persistence of their fears (and Philip's often-expressed longing for the restoration of orthodoxy throughout Europe).[54] Yet largely as a consequence of the aggressive policies they had proposed to defeat its designs, the Spanish King's reservations regarding confrontation with Elizabeth had begun to unravel.

The crises that commenced in 1569 had fundamentally more serious implications than those of earlier quarrels between England and Spain. The religious disharmonies and emergent nationalist feelings that characterized the civil conflicts in the Low Countries and France offered Philip and Elizabeth little scope for the pragmatic manoeuvres that had marked their previous confrontations. Each felt threatened by the other's perceived successes – Philip by Elizabeth's apparent assumption of an active role as Protestant champion, she by Alba's sanguinary campaign in the Low Countries and his suspected ambitions for England. Both assumed greater forces to be plotting their destruction than actually existed. To the threat of these spectres their reactions were less considered; less capable of abandonment or reversal without significant loss of face. Although both monarchs sincerely wished to avoid war, the points of confrontation they had created or allowed to develop might easily have triggered subsidiary clashes that would have made open conflict inevitable. What prevented this was a combination of unflustered political acumen – most notably on the part of Alba, who considered any English adventure prior to the subjugation of the Seventeen Provinces as both intolerably expensive and risky – and the pressure of crises that Philip was obliged to address elsewhere. Faced almost simultaneously with the Morisco rebellion, the most serious domestic upheaval of his reign, and the climax of his naval confrontation with the Ottoman Empire, he was far more concerned to prise Englishmen out of the Netherlands and off the seas than to seek a definitive solution to what he was beginning to regard as his 'English problem'.

Nevertheless, Elizabeth's regime did not emerge unscathed by the events of these years. In entering the sink of Europe's confessional struggle the Queen had broken one of her own cardinal rules. Identification with active Protestant resistance to the Counter-Reformation was not now something she could avoid, and the repercussions rebounded swiftly into domestic politics. In hindsight, it is too easy to regard Englishmen's growing awareness of their peculiar identity as a seamless, relatively inclusive process. In fact it was anything but that, as shall be discussed in the following chapter. Policies that deliberately alienated Spain and other Catholic powers had many enemies within England, whose motives were variously as honourable or self-serving as Cecil's. Many of his closest colleagues in Council, leading officers of state, had come to resent his growing ascendancy and where they believed it was leading. The increasingly robust foreign policy he proposed was a catalyst in uniting in opposition those, like the duke of Norfolk, who regarded it as suicidal, and others, including the earl of Leicester, who harboured more personal motives. Yet if their brief, surreptitious alliance to promote Mary Stuart's right to be named as Elizabeth's eventual successor was ostensibly an anti-Cecil strategy, it was symptomatic also of the enduring sense of insecurity that an heirless throne engendered.

Whether England was to seek some form of reconciliation or eternal enmity with Catholic Europe was not yet entirely a dead question to contemporary Englishmen. Should Elizabeth's periodic sickliness prove fatal before the succession was arranged, the matter of the nation's future religious character might be thrown wide open once more, with appalling consequences. Norfolk was no less 'sound' in his Protestantism than Leicester (who for all his patronage of Puritan interests had inherited much of his father's elasticity of principle), but the willingness of them and others to contemplate the same solution to the succession question as Philip, albeit without Elizabeth's forcible removal, illustrates the widespread uncertainty regarding England's ultimate destiny in 1569. The only near-unanimous belief in government was that there had to be an end to the ambiguity of the nation's relationship with her powerful neighbours. Cecil believed himself to be addressing that problem. At least some of his political opponents considered him to be pouring oil upon the flames.

Their fears reflected a strong concern for the delicate health of Anglo-Protestantism. Cecil's own opinion of the nation's spiritual life – 'weakned by Coldness in the trew Service of God; by Increase of the Nombre and Corrage of Baptists, and of Derydors of Relligion; and lastly by the Increase of Nombres of Irreligious and Epicures' – exercised him at least as much as Alba's *tercios*.[55] To formulate a policy that dragged this domestic malaise into unavoidable proximity, even linkage, with confessional turmoil abroad may have struck an impartial observer as unwise. It certainly challenged another of Elizabeth's fundamental principles – that of never seeking to confront problems that may otherwise drift on serenely. From the moment Cecil commenced the construction of his defences against foreign domination and internal apathy, a series of blows struck at the edifice of the Elizabethan settlement. In successive years from 1569, the Northern Rising, Pius v's excommunication of Elizabeth and the Ridolfi plot prised open or highlighted divides that the Act of Uniformity had supposedly bridged. While none of these unwelcome developments could be said to have been incited by Cecil's strategy, all drew sustenance from the problems it exposed – not least, that of what English Catholics were obliged to render to God and Caesar.

Elizabeth's policies bought a little time for the failing Protestant cause in the Low Countries and France at the price of inviting threats to her regime that she had long determined to avoid. She quickly came to appreciate this, and upon at least one occasion berated her council for persuading her to follow their advice.[56] English foreign policy had been locked into other, faith-driven agendas in a manner that even the pietistical Philip would have considered imprudent (for his part, he refused to allow Pius's bull of excommunication to be published in Spain, recognizing the damage it would do to the English Catholic cause). Abroad, the Queen was becoming an unwitting rallying figure for rebels and intransigent sectaries – breeds she instinctively loathed. Domestically, her government had conspired with the papacy to remove the delicate balance between public conformity and private conscience that had achieved the least problematic co-habitation the Reformation had yet witnessed.

This was a significant surrender of political initiative and had consequences that outlasted all the individual upheavals facing England in the years 1568–72. The coordinated threat to the nation feared by Cecil did not materialize. There was a complex political crisis, certainly, but the Queen and her principal secretary, having done much to precipitate it, worked hard to make it something more thereafter. Conspiracies almost always loom larger than their true likeness, and in facing down an imagined behemoth, the English government had commenced a series of policies that would deliver anything but the restoration of tranquillity that Elizabeth persistently held to be her overwhelming goal. At sea, a generation of English privateers was already in emotional as well as economic consortship with the Protestant 'resistance' to the Counter-Reformation. On land, their compatriots' already pronounced jingoism was being buttressed by an aggressive anxiety for the future, which, while reflecting the attitude of Elizabeth and her ministers at a particular moment, could not easily be tempered, much less reversed, by subsequent turns in the political cycle.

The beginning of 1572 saw the nadir of Anglo-Spanish relations to date. At the same time, however, cold-war weariness was increasingly evident in English counsels. After a brief, unusual state of budgetary surplus, Exchequer revenues had been badly affected by the extended embargoes; customs dues on cloth exports had progressively fallen to little more than 50 per cent of their pre-crisis levels, owing in no small part to evasion by many merchant adventurers, who, homesick for their old Antwerp mart, were clandestinely shipping their wares into the Low Countries once more.[57] Politically, the Queen had been shocked, and certainly made to feel insecure, by revelations of Norfolk's involvement in the Ridolfi plot and its instigator's claims of Europe-wide support. Alba's gathering of fleets in 1570 (to escort Anne of Austria, Philip's bride-to-be, into Spain) and 1571 (to counter the growing depredations of the Sea Beggars) had been watched nervously from London, and rumours of their diversion to Scotland or the north of England were rife.[58] Above all, negotiations for a defensive alliance with the French Crown – a major preoccupation of her government in the previous months – had stalled on points of religion and the reluctance of the duc d'Anjou (the future Henri III) to marry Elizabeth. That last-ditch surety gone, her government embarked upon a minor diplomatic offensive to reduce the gratuitous number of enemies England had acquired in recent years.

On 1 January, heads of agreement were concluded with the King of Portugal's envoy, providing for the mutual release of all vessels and goods seized since 1568, and – an important concession – the prohibition of English traffic to the African coast south of Cape Verde. These were formally ratified in a treaty of 2 February (although full economic relations between England and Portugal did not resume until 1576).[59] In the same month, Elizabeth began to consider seriously the conciliatory feelers that Alba had been extending for more than a year past. The duke, through his negotiator in London, M. de Sweveghem, had repeatedly made it clear that he regarded the continuing embargo and Elizabeth's support for the Sea Beggars as the only substantial issues of contention, and urged the complete restoration of commercial relations between England and the Low Countries. Prompted by the prospect of his vanishing Exchequer receipts, Cecil (now ennobled as Baron Burghley) opened a further channel of communication to Alba in March via the London-based Spanish merchant Antonio de Guaras, through whom he expressed his own hopes for a resumption of good relations.[60]

In the same month, Elizabeth expelled the Sea Beggars from English ports. For almost a year past, their habit of assaulting English and Hanse vessels as enthusiastically as those of their enemies – 'to the sclandour of the realme and impeachement of the haunt and trafficque of merchaundize' – had progressively undermined any political advantage she had once discerned in their protection.[61] As a placatory gesture to both Alba and Philip, the expulsion was somewhat compromised by the Beggers' subsequent capture of Brielle and Flushing, which resurrected a revolt that had all but died – and, vitally, secured the rebels' seaboard flank.[62] But there is evidence also that the Privy Council began to do more than pay lip service to its latest (1569) proclamation enforcing penalties against home-grown piracy. Admittedly, the impetus for this was a wound to English, not Spanish, dignity. In January, the earl of Worcester was sent to France to discuss Elizabeth's mooted betrothal to Anjou's younger brother, the duc d'Alençon. At sea off Boulogne, his ship was taken by Anglo-French pirates and his

personal baggage ransacked.[63] Though only one among many similar depredations encouraged by the English government's self-induced myopia, it was
an insult to the Queen's authority that could not be overlooked. Within a
fortnight, the redoubtable William Holstocke, Comptroller of the Navy, was
at sea with three ships 'for the repressinge of those pirates and sea rovers
which haunteth her Majestie's narrowe seas and streames, disquietinge the
publicke trafique, course, and trade of merchandizes'.[64] The force was a
modest one, but Holstocke had a record of enthusiasm for this sort of task
and is said to have seized or recovered thirty-six ships within six weeks.[65]
His efforts were supplemented by those of several former, and future,
privateers, commissioned to equip, man and set out vessels for the same
purpose. Among these were John Hawkins, George Winter, Sir Henry
Radcliffe (captain of Portsmouth and brother of the earl of Sussex) and
Edward Horsey, captain of the Isle of Wight and, formerly, the Sea Beggars'
most obliging host. Other, lesser recidivists employed included the incorrigible Martin Frobisher, who was released from close confinement in the
Marshalsea to hunt down his former colleagues.[66]

These measures undoubtedly represented a genuine effort on the government's part to ease what had become one of the principal wounds in the
Anglo-Habsburg relationship; but the background against which they were
implemented made a mockery of its intentions. Even as Hawkins made
ready to put to sea to suppress piracy in the Channel, he and George
Winter's brother William (hero of the 1559 naval campaign in Scotland) were
discreetly financing preparations for Francis Drake's second freebooting
expedition to the Panama Isthmus.[67] In April, as Elizabeth indicated that
she would be willing to lift her embargo in return for a reciprocal gesture
on Alba's part, she was also entertaining three hundred enthusiastic English
volunteers at Greenwich, most of them veterans of former Irish and Scottish campaigns: the first tranche of England's 'unofficial' assistance to the
Netherlander rebels at Flushing.[68] However she herself perceived the role of
these men, she was soon made aware of Philip's feelings. On 24 June, an
unnamed English correspondent wrote to Burghley from the Spanish Court:

> The King ys enformed, that yf yt had not bene for the Quenes Grace of
> *England*, *Flanders* had not rebelled agaynst the Dewke of Alba; for he
> wrytithe, that there be many Ynglyshemen come into the Lowe Coun-
> tres, of whose coming, bothe the Quene and her Council doo wel knowe,
> and so that hathe bene writtin unto him out of Inglande, by those that
> doo know that wel enou; whiche Letters be sent hether to the King to
> see; so that the King ys veri angry wythe the Quenes Grace, and as I have

harde say of those whiche doo wel knowe, that he hathe sworne, that he wyl be revengid in suche sorte, as bothe the Quene and Ingland shal repent that ever they did medil in any of hys Countres . . .'[69]

Ironically, Elizabeth, in the middle of one of her mood-swings, now feared the resurgence of French influence in the Low Countries as Alba's cash-starved administration faltered. A further contingent of English volunteers despatched there in July were intended to counter growing Huguenot influence over the Sea Beggars and, hopefully, prevent a French occupation of Flushing (though hasty instructions followed, demanding that their leader, Sir Humphrey Gilbert, should advertise that he and his men had departed England 'without either licence or knowledge of Her Majestie').[70] In a memorandum to the Queen and Council, Burghley went so far as to propose that the 'good and honorable end' for England would be to support Alba with English military resources against any French invasion (Huguenot or otherwise) under obligations set out in still-binding Anglo-Imperial treaties.[71] Such byzantine subtleties of English foreign policy were wholly lost on Philip, however. At a moment when England and Spain were feeling their way tentatively towards some form of rapprochement, this escalation of English involvement in the most sensitive sphere of his sovereign concerns was badly timed. To what extent was made terribly clear within weeks.

In Paris, beginning on St Bartholemew's Day, 24 August, and continuing for three days thereafter, a Guise-led attempt upon the life of the Huguenot leader, Admiral Coligny, escalated into the slaughter of almost the entire Huguenot leadership, their families and followers, who had gathered in the city to attend the wedding of Margaret of Valois and Henri, King of Navarre. Fearing the implications of Huguenot aid to the rebel Netherlanders, and the growth of Coligny's influence over her son, Charles IX, Catherine de' Medici had priorily agreed to the initial objective of the plot. The scale of killing, however, went far beyond what she – and even Henry of Guise – had anticipated or desired, and the murders did not stop at the outskirts of the French capital. In the following weeks, approximately 3,000 more Huguenots were killed in a dozen cities throughout France as local nobles saw their chance to re-establish their former political ascendancy and mobs, fired by sectarian frenzy and avarice, enthusiastically surrendered to their basest instincts. From this onslaught, the surviving Huguenot aristocracy and its forces, abjuring all obligations of loyalty to the French Crown, retreated into their fortified towns – La Rochelle, Montauban, Nimes, Sancerre – and prepared for a war of extermination.

The prospect of this butchery – premeditated, sanctioned (albeit reluctantly) by the French Crown and perpetrated enthusiastically by ordinary men and women – had a profound impact upon Protestant Europe. Shocking as it had been in itself, however, the episode was regarded less as an isolated example of internecine hatred than the first taste of Rome's coming 'final solution' to heresy: a sixteenth-century mirror of the Albigensian crusade that would requisition some of the most effective military resources in Europe. In England, its immediate political effect was to render impossible the long-discussed alliance with the French monarchy. In a wider sense, the massacre fundamentally validated the worst fears of Protestant Englishmen that the threat to their reformed religion was not capable of being negotiated away. The public reaction in England was one of unfeigned horror, and drastic responses were demanded. Even the Bishop of London, the otherwise peaceable Edmund Grindal, urged immediate crisis measures, including the restraint of all English Catholics, a ring of Protestant bodyguards to be thrown about Elizabeth's person, and, most practically, 'forthwith to cutte of the Scottishe Quene's heade: *ipsa est nostri fundi calamitas*' (she is the foundation of our ruin).[72]

The renewed sense of urgency with which Elizabeth's government now pursued an Anglo-Spanish rapprochement appeared to reflect a new and hopeful policy of conciliation. However, a subtle shift in the regime's underlying assumptions had commenced. In years to come, efforts to preserve peace with Spain would reflect little hope that a former state of amity could be recaptured (whatever the Queen claimed to the contrary), but rather the belief that England needed time to redress a balance of power that was tipping ever more steeply in favour both of the imperial ambitions of Philip II and the seemingly genocidal aims of the papacy.

Burghley had feared this trend for some years past, but the wider shift in perception delivered also a shift in the emphasis of resistance. In Paris, Francis Walsingham, English ambassador to the French Court and the Huguenots' best friend in English government, had witnessed the St Bartholomew's Day carnage close to hand and barely escaped with his life. His home, crowded with Englishmen and women who had fled there for sanctuary (including the earl of Leicester's nephew, Philip Sydney), was attacked by a Parisian mob despite the presence of a royal guard posted outside.[73] In the months following the massacre, Walsingham, convinced that he had witnessed the preamble to a Europe-wide confrontation, collected the names of every murdered woman and child with almost obsessive care and passed the gory list to his Privy Council masters.[74] Later, as the Queen's principal

Secretary of State, he would become the mouthpiece of a generation of Englishmen who regarded it as inconceivable that motives nurtured in Rome and Madrid could be anything but unswervingly malevolent. For several years past, his mentor Burghley had struggled to implement a strategy against England's many perceived perils in the face of resistance from those who considered it too aggressive. The braking influence he was to exercise in years to come was not so much a reversal of that policy as a measure of how far the debate had moved – from resisting the tide of post-Tridentine Catholicism to meeting its threat head-on.

In May 1573, the embargoes upon traffic between England and Philip's Low Countries were lifted by mutual consent. In the following year, the final, brief era of peaceful Anglo-Spanish relations in the sixteenth century was inaugurated officially by the Treaty of Bristol.[75] In the first flush of goodwill that followed, Catholic Englishmen were expelled from the Low Countries by Philip and their seminary at Douai closed. In turn, Elizabeth recalled the English companies (though she continued to allow individual English volunteers to serve in forces raised by the states of Holland and Zeeland), closely limited her financial aid to the rebels and forbade any English voyages 'below the equinoctiall' (the celestial equator).[76] Yet despite the sincerity both of Elizabeth and Philip in wishing for a resumption of good relations, neither would abandon the commitments that had nurtured their several confrontations. She was unable to forsake the Protestant cause in the Netherlands and France; he would not, under any circumstances, consider an accommodation with the heretical subjects of his – or any other – territories. Even the old lynchpin of their self-interested amity, the Antwerp mart, had become an irrelevance. What the years of Alba's stern occupation had not entirely disrupted was finally strangled by the Sea Beggars' permanent blockade of the city's artery, the Scheldt estuary. Soon, its venerable and once-dominant entrepôt would be extinguished entirely. In England, a re-armament process was commencing with a building and renovation programme to reverse the Navy Royal's ten-year decay.[77] Out in the Atlantic, the plate fleets continued to bring to Spain the means of financing an aggressive Catholic counter-assault against Protestantism – the wealth of a continent that Englishmen, Huguenot Frenchmen and rebel Netherlanders regarded as anything but Spanish domain. To an impartial observer in 1574, the truce that had been negotiated bore no promise of future tranquillity.

SIX

God's Englishmen

With brinishe teares, with sobbing sighes,
I, Englande, plunge in paine,
To see and heare such secret sectes
Amongst my people raine.[1]

If the crises of the years 1568–72 had not fundamentally altered the world-view of the Tudor regime, they had accelerated its fears. More so than at any time since Elizabeth's accession, it had become apparent that the uneasy co-existence of England and her major Catholic neighbours could not be expected to endure. This was already an article of faith to some of her principal advisers. To them and their like-minded godly constituents, the English Reformation was as yet a delicate, newly bedded plant, its survival dependent upon the tender care that the Queen and her regime alone could provide. As English foreign policy was increasingly shaped by – and subsumed into – the wider European struggle for the soul of Christianity, these men argued with ever greater force that the external threat to their 'true' religion and monarch was both enhanced and abetted by the survival of domestic Catholicism. Intensifying efforts to discourage, neutralize and, ultimately, remove the enemy within affected more than the lives and freedoms of English Catholics, however. Their portrayal as an intrinsically foreign and subversive intrusion into the commonwealth (rather than the remnant of an ancient domestic mainstream) was fundamentally to influence an emerging sense of self-awareness among the majority of those who, indifferently or otherwise, accepted the English religious settlement.[2]

The doctrinal and cultural implications of the several English Reformations were pervasive, notwithstanding the regime's attempts to manipulate their form and pace. It would be absurd, therefore, to suggest that attitudes towards English Catholics were solely driven by an agenda set in Whitehall, any more than Catholic fears of Protestant advances were shaped exclusively in the Roman Curia. This was, after all, a vast upheaval that in its myriad forms represented a fundamental challenge to the very concept of politically ordained spirituality. Yet nowhere in Europe – not even in Catholic Spain – was the state so structurally bound to the 'state' of religion as in England. Statute, as has been discussed, provided both the mechanisms and conditions through which Englishmen worshipped. In all sixteenth-century Christian states, non-conformity had profound political as well as spiritual implications; in England, it was a de facto assault upon the ineluctable premise by which government defined every aspect of its authority.

From 1569, the domestic 'threat' to Elizabeth's regime assumed a far darker relevance. Ostensibly, the dangers perceived in Sir William Cecil's memorial of that year had been traditional preoccupations of government. There was nothing novel in 'conspyrations' involving the pope and monarchs with more earthly ambitions; since the eleventh century, would-be invaders of England had often secured papal acquiescence – even approval – for their conquests. Within living memory, Francis i and Charles v had pledged themselves to overthrow Henry viii and restore the pope's authority in England; in a purely military sense, that forbidding (if brief) alliance had represented a greater danger even than Alba's putative threat to English Protestantism. Yet to Cecil and his contemporaries, their own day wore a face that that previous generations had not known. Throughout Europe, the struggle to re-impose papal authority, or, conversely, to nurture a more primitive form of Christian commonwealth increasingly obsessed governments. It did so not because princes were becoming more solicitous of their subjects' spiritual welfare, but because the ramifications of divergence from orthodoxy (whatever that was held to be, locally) were becoming ever more starkly apparent. Since the Reformation commenced, England herself had experienced fleeting but salutary reminders of what the wrong sort of zealotry could inflict upon society; but they had been as nothing compared with the unfolding prospect across the English Channel. Barely over the horizon lay ample proof that spiritual imperatives were immune to the restraints of political and civic obligation alike. Frenchmen slaughtered

Frenchmen, Netherlanders enthusiastically put their rebel compatriots to the sword; there was no reason to believe that England's own dissenters were any more likely to place temporal loyalties above that owed to God:

> What tumults Antichrist hath raised up in France, in Germanie, in Spaine, and in Flanders, who is there thorow out all Europe which knoweth not? And in England, what hath he practiced and wrought even in this present yeare that we write these thinges, I would to God it were as ready to be avoyded, as it is easye to remember it.[3]

But what was the nature of this dire threat to England's tranquillity? By the end of the 1560s the government of the Catholic Church in England was extinct; in the parishes, however, a significant, if variable, degree of affection for the Roman rite remained. The struggle to remove 'popish' images, fixtures and practices from churches continued even twelve years after Elizabeth's succession. Battles to impose or resist the requirements of the Act of Uniformity threw up innumerable parochial vendettas whose endurance reflected the ineffectuality (or lack of enthusiasm) of local officials charged with the implementation of legislation.[4] Yet the nature and extent of English Catholic dissent remains difficult to gauge, because notwithstanding the violent contribution of a small number of activists, it was largely a subdued, even a sullenly passive phenomenon. There is little evidence of any significant desire for a wholesale restoration of the Marian church, although a longing for old certainties – for a world of ritual that had endured, seemingly unchanging, for longer than the English polity itself – remained strong. A very few self-exiled English Catholics hoped for a politically imposed counter-reformation that, without significant domestic military support, would require foreign assistance. In contrast, the mass of their co-religionists who remained in England seem only to have entertained an increasingly fond hope that the spinning wheel of England's spiritual journey had not yet come to a final rest.

In the traditionalist (and remote) northern counties, some had responded to Pius v's demand that they did not attend divine service, and chose instead to make their own, surreptitious arrangements. Elsewhere, many of their brethren – including a significant number of clerics – acquiesced unenthusiastically to the Act of Uniformity on the principle that 'it is safest to do in religion as most do'.[5] For several years this was not unacceptable to Elizabeth. As long as Englishmen paid their dues, however unwillingly, to the authority of the state in religious matters, she was not inclined to search their souls gratuitously. Yet that accommodation was built upon the most fragile premise: that rational self-interest would or could override spiritual loyalties. To many of the Queen's councillors this was unthinkable. They could hardly imagine, much less accept, that most English Catholics were able to consider themselves as such while simultaneously abjuring the pope's political pretensions (a very real quality, in fact, that had greatly aided Henry VIII's original break with Rome). Cecil himself regarded any appearance of tranquillity on their part necessarily to presage some great attempt upon the present settlement:

> In this meane tyme, all the papistes in england shalbe solicited not to styrr, but to confirme there faction with comefort; to gather mony, and to be redy to styrr at one instant when some forrayn force, shall be redy to assayle this realme or Ireland. When the matter is brought to these terms that the papistes shall have the upper hand, then it will be to late to seke to withstand it . . .[6]

As early as 1562, this had been his analysis of the internal dangers facing England. These dangers had not materialized, and England's 'papistes' had remained largely quiescent. Yet the thesis, like all hanging prophecies, was not undermined by non-events. Seven years later (and only months after Cecil warned of the 'many, great and imminent' perils facing England), the outbreak of the Northern Rising marked the beginning of the end of the hopeful engagement of regime and Catholic residue. This was a revolt of a small group of politically disaffected conservative nobles and gentry, protesting that if they themselves did not bring about a reform of the present state of religion in England, others – that is, Philip or his servant Alba – might, 'to the great hazarding of the state of our country'.[7] Their cause received sympathy, but very little practical support, from the northern Catholics in whose name the rebels ostensibly marched. In fact, the rank and file of those who joined the revolt (some five to six thousand of whom a significant number appear to have been coerced) brought with them a complex mix of economic, social and spiritual grievances, leavened by a last-gasp outpouring of feudal loyalty.[8] Nevertheless, the apparent popularity of the rising, and rumours of Alba's intention to provide succour to the rebels' cause, shook the government.[9] Like the Pilgrimage of Grace and the Western Risings, the revolt appeared to be a fundamental assault both upon the reformed religion and the Tudor regime, rather than a diffuse expression of pent-up resentments that would require little force and/or concession to dissipate.

Pius v reinforced that perception within six months following the end of the revolt with his bull *Regnans in Excelsis*, which excommunicated Elizabeth. Though its terms stopped short of demanding that Catholics should rebel against her authority (obtusely, it stipulated that they should not consider themselves obliged to obey her, nor regard any oath to her as binding), its promulgation highlighted the international implications of domestic conformity and begged a question of English Catholic loyalties that would have been far better unasked.[10] While it was inconceivable that Elizabeth's government could ignore the challenge, there was some uncertainty on how it might be met effectively, and, initially at least, a degree of circumspection was evident. Less than a month after an ill-advised (and swiftly executed) Catholic Englishman pinned a copy of the bull to the Bishop of London's palace door, the Queen had her very reasonable demands of dissenters read out in the Star Chamber:

> Wherefore her majesty would have all her loving subjects to understand, that, as long as they shall openly continue in the observation of her laws, and shall not wilfully and manifestly break them by their open actions, her majesty's meaning is, not to have any of them molested by any inquisition or examination of their consciences in causes of religion; but will accept and entreat them as her good and obedient subjects.[11]

In the following year's parliamentary debate on a bill to introduce compulsory attendance at common prayer and the taking of communion, the member for Warwick, Edward Aglionby, expanded elegantly upon the principle governing this pragmatic policy: 'there should be no humane, positive lawe to inforce conscience, which is not discernable in this world . . . the conscience of man is internall, invisible, and not in the power of the greatest monarch . . .'.[12] What he argued for, and what the Queen demanded, was obedience, not an inward conformity that God alone could police. How that might be achieved in the face of papal obduracy was, surprisingly, considered at some length. Commissioners appointed by the Queen were charged with questioning leading English Catholics on what they understood to be the bull's demands of them. They discovered that many were anxious to interpret it as anything rather than an obligation upon individual consciences. The imperatives of their faith recognized Mary Stuart's claim to the English throne to be superior to that of Elizabeth; nevertheless, most were, and remained, content to observe the maxim, later expressed by one of the Queen's own councillors, 'we are bound to obey good princes. God doth correct by ill princes.'[13]

Yet doubts regarding the innate loyalties of 'roman' Englishmen, intensified by the Northern Rising, were never to subside. Though not as momentous a threat to the regime as it had seemed, the severity of government's response indicates that it had been profoundly shaken.[14] In the aftermath of the Rising, a brutal object lesson was delivered to northern England. Between Newcastle and Wetherby, in every town, village or hamlet that had supplied men for the rebel army (no matter how unknowingly), one of these malfeasants was strung up – a provincial mirror of the 'heads upon the gate' tradition that for centuries had provided Londoners with a lesson in civic obedience. Faced now with an even more palpable line in the sand etched by papal toe, the government's initially cautious attitude towards English Catholicism gave way to a more relentless policy. When Parliament was recalled in 1571, every member was obliged to swear the oath acknowledging the Royal Supremacy before taking his seat – a requirement that effectively delivered England's first exclusively Protestant legislature. Once sitting, neither house showed much taste for moderation on the matter of religion, despite the occasional cautionary contribution by men such as the enlightened Aglionby. Their principal piece of business, the Treasons Act, did not contradict the letter of Elizabeth's previous statement of toleration; but its terms were so constrictive that it effectively forced English Catholics either to renounce the pope's authority – political and spiritual – or deny the totality of the Queen's sovereign rights. In doing so, it closed the circle that papal inflexibility had begun to describe. During the next two decades, as political assassinations, domestic plots and the growing external threat to the nation shaped a siege mentality in government, the politicization of individual conscience proceeded apace. Further legislation made treasonable the re-conversion of Protestants to Catholicism and the very presence of foreign-trained English priests upon their mother soil. By the year of the Armada campaign, a number of unfortunates were going to the scaffold merely for having given assistance to those priests who chose to remain or return.[15]

This increasingly rigorous reaction to the threat of internal dissension (however ephemeral) had profound implications. An overwhelmingly loyal constituency was presented with the same hard, irreconcilable choices that Elizabeth's father had offered to them in 1534, and with similar consequences. Those few English-born Catholics whose fervour made any form of accommodation with the regime unthinkable were driven abroad. For the majority of their co-religionists, the promise of increasingly heavy fines and outright violence against their persons expunged the narrow but precious lee-way of semi-conformity that had allowed duty to be discharged both to monarch and God for a decade past. As it did so, the catacomb mentality of the early martyrs reasserted itself in English Catholic life. Recusancy – deliberate absenteeism from the decreed forms of public worship – was an inescapable consequence of the pope's refusal to sanction 'church-papistry'; its growth, however, was nurtured greatly in this new spirit of persecution.[16] The seminarians of Douai and Rheims, whose missionary activities in England would exercise Burghley, Walsingham and other leading Protestants profoundly from the early 1570s, were to have at best an insignificant effect upon the political loyalties of English Catholics. Nevertheless, their pastoral task was assisted hugely by the growing needs of a constituency whose spiritual beliefs were bringing unprecedented social exclusion.[17]

Official fears of internal dissension were greatly enhanced by the perception that the English reformed religion was not yet sufficiently cohesive to withstand the forces of the Counter-Reformation. A necessary compromise between its many incompatible elements, the Elizabethan Church had an imposed unity of observance but not of belief. As Cecil later lamented to his Queen 'amongst your protestant subjects, in whom consisteth all your force, strength, and power, there is so great a heart-burning and division . . . .'.[18] Fratricidal clashes regarding the government of the church, and, on a more prosaic level, the use of altar, chalice, cap and surplice (the 'filthy popish ragg'), had already split its natural leadership, alienating radicals who regarded the existing form of established religion as an 'unhappy compound of popery and the gospel'.[19] The reaction against this half-reformation saw the first stirrings of domestic Presbyterianism and outright Separatism, and the desertion – in spirit if not in body – of many of the most highly committed Protestants from the mainstream of church life.

For the vast majority of those who remained, arcane points of ritual and doctrine were irrelevances and they treated them as such. Observant yet hardly enthused, many had come instinctively to regard themselves as of the 'new religion' (a term that devout Protestants loathed), without knowing what that entailed, precisely. Their devotions, being compulsory by law, were discharged largely in the manner of other civic obligations: duty was done, often reluctantly, without any unnecessary attention paid to the detail. The Puritan minister and polemicist George Gifford railed at this large, unengaged congregation, condemning the breed as 'cold statute Protestants . . . they care not what religion come: they are like naked men, fit and ready for any coate almost that may be put upon them' (comprehensively, he dismissed them also as 'mass gospellers' for their former acquiescence during Mary's counter-reformation).[20] This lack of enthusiasm was a matter of enduring concern for government. A sixteenth-century Catholic state might survive widespread indifference if most of its subjects continued, mutely, to accept the truth of the apostolic succession. The early Protestant state, in contrast, defined itself in reaction to a powerful, threatening status quo. Without the buttress of an enthused, observant and socially cohesive majority, true reformation, and the state itself, was regarded as unviable. The strength and persistence of government attempts to frighten its constituency into some consistent degree of anti-Catholic self-awareness reflected this.

Cecil and others may have overstated the stubborn streak of ennui they perceived among contemporary Englishmen, but correcting it proved difficult. The majority of them did not become noticeably more 'godly' during this period, or more susceptible to dogmatic interventions, and one should question therefore whether they responded readily to official efforts to demonize their Catholic neighbours. This has not been evident to some historians, who have regarded the spread of the reformed religion in England as reflecting a surge in popular piety, which, inevitably, amplified and focused antipathies towards the 'old' religion. At least one commentator has stated explicitly that anti-Catholicism was central to the Elizabethan mind.[21] This is undeniably true, if one speaks only of the minds of Protestant polemicists and their parliamentarian allies (many were both); but if their intended audience was of the same mind, these men consistently deluded themselves as to the scale of the task before them. It may be argued with equal force that the efforts of Bradford, Wadsworth, Bale, Jewel, Foxe, Gifford and others to expose the roman 'antichrist' were persistent precisely because their enthusiasm received little immediate reward. Some of their works – particularly those of Foxe – were to have an enduring influence, yet the Elizabethan age did not have a constant, immutable character.[22] The approach of war transformed the popular perception of what constituted the 'enemy'; thereafter, its outbreak and subsequent longevity fostered a greater sense both of common cause and, inescapably, of what was inimical to that cause. Until conflict with the mightiest military power in Europe became at least a probability, however, a majority of Englishmen almost certainly did not regard their non-conforming compatriots in the same light as foreign Catholics – or, more pertinently, as foreigners who happened to be Catholics also.

Burdened by the long hindsight of a recognizable and enduring Protestant England, it is tempting to see the output of Elizabethan polemicists, pamphleteers and balladeers as reflecting rather than seeking to manipulate the prejudices of their public. Yet to regard the volume of propagandist literature emerging from 1570 as a token either of its effectiveness or popularity is simplistic. Almost nothing was published in England without prior government scrutiny, and much was the result of active official promotion.[23] The results were not engaging. As in any age, works addressing the state of religion tended to be either exhortative or cautionary: abusive of their targets and reverential towards their exemplars. Pius's bull of excommunication generated a host of ballads of the quality of *The braineles blessing of the bull*:

> O Sathans sonne! O pope puft vp with pryde!
> What makes thee clayme the clowdes where God doth dwel,
> When thou art knowne the glorious greedie guyde
> That leades in pompe poore seelye soules to hell?
> The pumpe of ship hath not so fowle a smell
> As hath the smoke and fume that flames from thee;
> O graceless grace, O rotten hollow tree![24]

Its anonymous author at least had wielded a vocabulary. More general blasts against popery, such as the (1566) *Song against the Mass*, seemed designed for a nursery readership:

> Lament I doe
> Here to see nowe,
> The joyes that some be in,
> Wyshyng for Masse,
> I say, alas!
> The cloke of filthy sin![25]

Easily memorized, such vituperative sentiments probably enjoyed fleeting popularity (although there is no reason to believe that the 'message' of a song or ditty was any more readily absorbed then than now). Attempts to advertise the political implications of non-conformity, in contrast, tended to levels of allegorical density and sycophancy that would have deflated the most sympathetic audience:

> When heapes of heauie hap had fild my harte right full,
> And sorrow set forth pensiuenes, my ioyes away to pull,
> I raunged then the woods, I romde the fields aboute,

A thousand sighes I set at large, to seeke their passage out;
And walkyng in a dompe, or rather in dispaire,
I cast my weeping eye aside, I saw a fielde full faire;
And lokyng vpwarde then I spied a mount therein,
Which Flora had, euen for her life, dect as you haue not seen . . .[26]

The hopes invested in 'Flora' were far greater than those that a mere prince might command. To her nervous officers of state, the Queen's health and well-being were becoming those of the nation itself, and the implications of her loss were consequently profound. Following an accidental discharge of shot near her person in 1578 (which winged an unlucky court servant nearby), William Elderton penned *A newe ballad declaryng the daungerous shootyng of the gunne at the Courte*. Its warnings of 'what might have been' might have been penned by Burghley himself:

And tolde again, if that mishap had happened on her grace,
The staie of true religion. How perlous were the case:
Which might have turnde to bloody warres, of strange and forreign
    foes,
Alas! How we might have been accurste, our comforte so to loose.[27]

Unless contemporary Englishmen were entirely malleable, it is hard to believe that these and other, equally clumsy efforts were sufficient in themselves to mobilize what the regime regarded to be a necessary intolerance. That they were often promoted from the pulpit – the one place where government was guaranteed a massive, captive audience – seems telling.[28] Again, one might ask whether such single-minded industry satisfied a general hunger for the message or addressed an abiding resistance to it.

Propaganda, to be successful, requires a measure of credibility. The government's case was compromised by its use of unswervingly partial servants who were known to be such. During Edward VI's reign, Cecil had been one of three official censors appointed to examine all English-language works prior to publication. Though he soon relinquished this office, he maintained a close interest in the activities of printers and book licencees, many of whom owed their profits to his patronage. William Seres, a poet and balladeer responsible for *An Answere to the Proclamation of the Rebels in the North* (1569) was a former servant of Cecil's who enjoyed monopoly publishing rights for the publication of primers and psalters (he was also, in 1559, joint-publisher of one of the earliest vituperative histories of Mary

Tudor's reign, the *Epitome of Cronicles, etc.*).[29] In 1570/1 he became Master
of the Stationers' Company – the government-regulated organization
through which all printed matter published in England was registered.
Stationers' Hall itself was built on Cecil's own land, sold to the company
via Seres and another proxy.[30] From the 1570s, Sir Francis Walsingham,
Cecil's assistant-caretaker of the regime's propaganda machinery, was equally
assiduous in channelling government patronage towards a select group of
polemicists. The parliamentarian Thomas Norton, son-in-law of Thomas
Cranmer and a prolific pamphleteer (author of *To the Quenes Maiesties Poor
Deceiued Subjects, A Bull Graunted by the Pope to Dr Harding & Other* and
A Warning Agaynst the Dangerous Practises of Papists) was, predictably, an
energetic loather of every token of Catholicism. But he was also Walsingham's sometime employee and, later, an official censor who tended to worry
more about the regime even than its own officers of state.[31] Norton, like
Seres, Elderton and virtually every minister of the established Church, laid
unremitting emphasis upon absolute obedience to the sovereign authority
and the principle that rebellion was an act against God as much as the state.
It would not have required a cynical world-view to regard such voices as
being those of officialdom in mufti.

The means by which their words were disseminated further emphasized
government's control of the process. Much propagandist literature passed
through the hands of a small number of London printers – men such as
Alexander Lacy (Little Britain), William Howe (Fleet Street) and John Allde
(Poultry), whose bread-and-butter output consisted of ribald and scurrilous
ballads for popular consumption, but who also, with a relatively few other
presses, functioned as near-official stationers for the distribution of godly
and political works. Other, less openly patronized journeymen produced
pieces that exhibited an almost uncanny uniformity in lauding the present
regime and urging good Englishmen to root out the canker in their midst.
The quality of their works was extremely variable, but their aim was true
to the point of monotony. They were intended to instruct, rather than
to entertain; to be an influence upon, not a reflection of, the elusive
'Elizabethan mind'.

Even an accessible and attractive message, moreover, would have required
efficient circulation to be widely effective, and this was not an age of mass
readership. The government's assiduous use of the pulpit for everything from
homilies upon civic obedience to anti-papal doggerel reflected the fact that
relatively few Englishman, even if literate, enjoyed the leisure to indulge
their learning (hence the high proportion of women among the 'godly'

element of the middle-classes). The market was shaped by this. The halfpenny ballad sheet, hawked around the countryside by peddlers, was the
medium that most effectively penetrated popular culture, but it is unlikely
that it was capable of providing both populist entertainment and adequate
instruction. For all but a small minority of more substantial works, print
runs were not large, nor did most receive more than a single edition.[32] Foxe's
Actes and Monuments was first printed in 1563. It then took seven years to
receive a second edition, six years for a third and a further seven years for
a fourth. Yet this was a work that had been strongly promoted by government in the meantime and placed compulsorily in all offices of state,
grammar schools, city orphanages, company halls, Bishops' palaces,
deaneries, cathedrals, universities and many parish churches (all, significantly, were establishments in which tuition proceeded formally, not at the
whim of the reader). Private purchases of the relatively expensive, four-
volume piece were not likely to have been significant, even had copies been
readily available. Twenty years after its first publication, the *Actes* remained
'little to be accepted' according to the moralist Philip Stubbes, who observed
that Englishmen strongly preferred 'pamphlets of scurrility and bawdry', and
Foxe himself expressed similar fears in the final edition of the *Actes* produced during his lifetime.[33] Lesser, cheaper works tempted those with the
funds to buy more than bread, meat and small beer, but the browsing,
informed patron of booksellers was an emergent, almost wholly middle-class
phenomenon, and seems to have remained an exception even among his or
her peers: 'for fashion's sake merchants have Bibles, which they never peruse;
for fashion's sake some women buy Scripture books, that they may be
thought to be well disposed.'[34]

Other than from the ballad sheet, most non-godly Elizabethan Englishmen
received instruction by means of relatively simple visual images (biblical
scenes or quotations from the psalms, hung in ale-houses and inns) or
spoken word – and, almost invariably, in public. Ever-present 'improving'
images, particularly those adorning temples of inebriation, would have lost
their impact over time, eventually moving the spirit no more than would a
beer-mat in our own day. In the case of oral exhortation, the effectiveness of
the message depended greatly upon the voice that proclaimed it, and standards varied hugely from parish to parish. If, in a later age, when active participation in religious life was far more prevalent, a relatively assiduous
church-goer like Samuel Pepys could happily sleep or leer at female parishioners throughout bad or tedious sermons, it seems hardly credible that his
ancestors – 'Derydors of Relligion . . . Irreligious and Epicures' – were any

more closely engaged by tepid gospellers proclaiming that which they were obliged by law to proclaim.[35]

What Cecil and his peers observed with frustration was a persistent secularist tendency within a statutorily observant society. The business of ecclesiastical courts throughout this period was devoted largely to punishing the behaviour of those who, having attended divine service in accordance with the law, behaved in God's House much as they might in an ale-house.[36] Even Colchester, a notable bastion of 'godly' folk ruled by a radically Protestant town government, is calculated to have comprised a population of whom one-third were so terminally indifferent to the state of religion as to express no saving sentiment in their wills (the proportion had been less than one in ten in the years prior to the break with Rome).[37] Almost certainly, apathy was even more prevalent elsewhere. Having been singed by the flames of two reformations and a sanguinary counter-reformation, it would be surprising if a majority of Englishmen had remained as enthusiastic upon any point of dogma as polemicists may have wished. Their physical environment – one in which the stone tombs of saints were requisitioned as horse troughs, the fabric of friaries reconstructed as rich men's houses and knights' effigies set upon hill-tops as landmarks – bore too many reminders of recent upheavals for more of the same to be sought gratuitously. Belief in God was not synonymous with piety: all accepted the truth of His Word, but only a minority enthused about the particular means by which it was acknowledged.[38] In such a milieu, the wilder anti-popery of contemporary propagandist literature may have entertained; it did not, as yet, strike an anxious note among the many unengaged.[39]

Contradicting the claims of the state and its more godly collaborators, the average 'cold-statute Protestant' had the evidence of his own eyes. The vast, brooding fifth column of which he was warned – Stubbes's 'sedicious Vipers, and Pythonicall Hydraes' and Audley's 'traytours, rebels and papisticall enemies' – bore little resemblance to an element within society that had long sought to avoid attention except when proclaiming loyalty to Queen and country as robustly as he.[40] These apparently dangerous folk lived among their conforming countrymen still and were mostly known to them, yet there were few popular expressions of anti-Catholic sentiment, much less the internecine conflicts that characterized continental civic life wherever two forms of the same faith collided. So-called 'church papists' were self-confessed quiet-lifers, and even recusants, their faith newly invigorated by clandestine missionary activity, and they do not seem to have made a significant negative impact upon the public consciousness during years in which they were intensely preoccupying government. In the depth of the complex Anglo-Spanish crisis of 1568–72, when one might assume anti-Catholic feeling to have been excited by the Northern Rising, Ridolfi plot and rumoured Spanish assistance to both, it is still possible to discern a marked anti-sectarian mood. One John Brabant, a rich clothier of Farnham, attending a scripture group among the town's godly in December of the latter year, heard some of those present revile 'ranke papists'. Brabant, not a Catholic (though 'more endued to welthe, than well-affected to religion', according to the outraged Bishop of Winchester, who reported the incident to Burghley), sternly admonished his neighbours, reminding them of the obvious truth that there were good papists as well as evil Protestants.[41]

This was not a lone voice, nor unrepresentative of men and women who otherwise regarded themselves as staunchly loyal to their Queen and government. The regime's difficulty lay in overcoming this innate resistance to active spiritual engagement: in instilling fear of, and contempt for, the excesses of popery while simultaneously imposing increasingly stringent measures to preserve conformity of religion at home. Without achieving that engagement, the process of containing the domestic 'threat' – when pressed to its inescapable conclusion – became self-defeating. Most of those who witnessed the ordeal of the first Catholic missionaries to mount an English scaffold were impressed rather than repelled by their demeanour; indeed, by recreating recognizable modern tableaux of the passion and death of Jesus himself, government provided condemned priests with excellent opportunities to further their missions in England. One of their number, John Boste, proclaimed as much from his own scaffold: 'My head and quarters will preach every day on your gates and walls the truth of the Catholic faith', and in a very limited sense he was correct. Catholic 'martyrs' provided strong icons of conviction and fortitude for their orphaned flocks, and several spontaneous conversions were reported – encouraged, no doubt, by the same cathartic shock that had made the Roman circus such an effective recruiting ground.[42]

Elizabeth was not unaware of this. Probably more so than most of her councillors, she was anxious to give condemned seminary priests every opportunity to convince her that their spiritual and political loyalties were distinct qualities, though the questions posed of them were so tightly framed in this respect that any meaningful repudiation of the pope's temporal authority – short of denying Catholicism itself – was impossible.[43] Cecil, again with the divisive state of English Protestantism in mind, brooded upon the effects of policies he had encouraged. As he later admitted:

I account, that putting them to death doth no ways lessen them, since we find by experience, that it worketh no such effect, but, like Hydra's heads, upon cutting off one, seven grow up, persecution being accounted as the badge of the church; and, therefore, they should never have the honour to take any pretence of martyrdom in England, where the fulness of blood, and greatness of heart, is such, that they will even, for shameful things, go bravely to death . . .[44]

He referred to the seminarians' flock, not to the priests themselves, but as the latter were Englishmen also the distinction was largely irrelevant to those who witnessed their martyrdom. Salutary proof of the phenomenon was first provided by the trial and execution of the Jesuit Edmund Campion, who, in his previous incarnation as a brilliant young Oxford scholar of Divinity, had won the patronage both of Cecil and Leicester. Campion was not only saintly, but, worse, highly articulate. His ordeal proved to be one of the government's rare public relations blunders, and Burghley himself was obliged to join the pamphleteering profession in 1583 to defend the near-indefensible charge of treason against Campion with his *Execution of Justice in England*. A piece appended to this work excused the practice of torture upon Campion in particular and Catholic priests in general on the basis that it did not do that much damage to its recipient.[45] Unsurprisingly, the argument largely failed to convince. The extreme violence meted out to seminary priests, Jesuits and their sustainers remained unpopular with Englishmen, whose embryonic Protestant 'identity' embraced (if sometimes insincerely) an abhorrence of cruelty inflicted in the name of God.[46] Ironically, their revulsion presented Catholic propagandists, who fully endorsed the remorseless papal line on heresy and heretics, with an unexpected weapon. In his *True, Sincere, and Modest defense of English Catholics* (a direct rebuttal of *The Execution of Justice in England*), England's future cardinal-elect William Allen dismissed as irrelevant Cecil's proposition that the present suffering of Catholics was insignificant compared with that inflicted upon the Marian 'martyrs':

The difference is in these points: you profess to put none to death for religion. You have no laws to put any man to death for his faith. You have purposely repealed by a special statute made in the first year and Parliament of this Queen's reign all former laws of the realm for burning heretics, which smelleth of something that I need not here express. You have provided at the same time that nothing shall be deemed or adjudged heresy but by your Parliament and Convocation. You have not yet set down by any new law what is heresy or who is an heretic. Therefore you can neither adjudge of our doctrine as heresy or who is an heretic. Nor have you any law left whereby to execute us. And so, to put any of us to death for religion is against justice, law, and your own profession and doctrine.[47]

Such sophistries may offend the modern eye, but Allen's was an effective argument against a regime that regarded statute as the only regulator of the form and practice of religion. The tribulations of Catholic priests – one brief, intense period of persecution aside[48] – may have been less in scale than those endured by their Marian predecessors, but it is difficult to believe that the men and women who witnessed their ordeals judged them relatively. What they saw, in every meaningful sense, was the same cruelty for which Foxe and others excoriated the Holy Office, and from which, supposedly, Englishmen had been delivered by the triumph of the reformed church. Undoubtedly, the message was diluted by the spectacle.

Government's task in attempting to engage a coherent spirit of vigilance was also made more difficult by the latent jingoism of their audience, who tended to believe that English Catholics were Englishmen first and only papists thereafter (witness Burghley's grudging tribute to their 'fulness of blood, and greatness of heart'). That attitude slowly decayed in the face of sustained propagandist activity, but it survived for some years following the beginning of the government's assault upon recusancy and attempts to end entirely the practice of the Catholic rite in England. It survived the intrusion of government into the privacy of the home and the rise of the private informer, the removal of Catholics from public office, and the first imprisonments of Catholics for being Catholics, rather than for any specific transgression of English law.[49] As late as September 1586, by which time the Spanish threat to England was incontrovertible, London apprentices – the praetorian guard of unthinking prejudice – remained far more interested in wreaking a reprise of the Evil May Day riots upon their refugee French Huguenot and Dutch Calvinist neighbours than against the English Catholics in their midst.[50] Only when the regime managed fully to inculcate its own sense of trepidation did a majority of Englishmen come to regard the statutory persecution of English Catholics as an inescapable price of their own freedom.

In contrast to the difficulty with which the government demonized the enemy within, the casting of foreign Catholics in the worst possible light met with little public scepticism. The proof of claims made against them was, to most Englishmen, self-evident. They had heard, or perhaps read in translation, the lurid anti-Spanish propaganda of Las Casas and Montanus (the latter's damning description of the workings of the Inquisition struck a particularly receptive chord). They recalled the interval during which they had endured a Spanish King, and, probably, more Smithfield fires than had ever been lit. They were also aware, if from second- or third-hand sources, of the ordeals of Anglo-Spanish merchants taken by the Inquisition, and of Hawkins's mariners, captured after the clash at San Juan de Ulúa and condemned to a living death in Habsburg dungeons or galleys. What they had lacked to date was compelling proof that it was Spaniards' Catholicism, rather than just their Spanish-ness, that made them so abhorrent: that their own, peculiarly English identity could be preserved only in resistance to a doctrine that was a defining component of foreign ill-will.

The government's conflation of foreign threat and English Catholic malevolence therefore leaned heavily upon the credible evidence it could muster for the former. Early efforts to portray the Northern Rising and Ridolfi plot as international Catholic conspiracies failed to excite the popular imagination, not least because of their feeble success and the palpable failure of foreign parties to materialize (though government persisted in its claims that the duke of Medinaceli had been poised to lead an army of six thousand men into England to support Ridolfi's scheme).[51] Nevertheless, there was ready precedent to indicate what Englishmen might expect following a successful foreign invasion, and this was advertised widely. In 1570, Foxe, possibly at Cecil's urging, hurriedly included a section on victims of the Spanish Inquisition in his second edition of *Actes and Monuments*.[52] Two years later, almost before the blood had dried on the streets of Paris, an English translation of Ernest Varamund's lengthy account of the St Bartholemew's Day massacre – 'the wicked and strange murder of Godly persons' – was published in London and Scotland.[53]

On the worst aspects of Spanish attempts to pacify the Low Countries there was, if anything, too much information available, and care was needed to sift out unhelpful material. In 1574, Burghley was presented with 'The Expedition in Holland', a series of detailed and perceptive military intelligences by the gentleman-soldier Walter Morgan.[54] These dealt factually not only with Spanish deeds but those also of the rebel Netherlanders and their English allies. Accounts of Spanish atrocities at Rotterdam, Naarden and Haarlem alternated with descriptions of the great courage and elan of Alba's troops. English mercenaries' ineffectuality and, sometimes, panic was described in morose detail, as was the Sea Beggars' merciless treatment of the Catholic population of Gorcum. The manuscript was withheld from publication in England.

Fortunately, a stream of less impartial material issued from Protestant propagandists in the Low Countries and France, supplemented by the efforts of Englishmen who were more aware than Morgan of what was expected. These works had two principal themes: the bestial actions of Spanish troops as individuals and the broader quality of Philip's tyrannical rule, which in God's eyes absolved his Netherlander subjects of their obligations as such. The government took particular care to disseminate literature concerning the more spectacular atrocities. The sometime-soldier and poet George Gascoigne, having entered the Low Countries with Walsingham's blessing to search out evidence of Spanish cruelties, was present in Antwerp on 4 November 1576 when mutinous Spanish troops stormed and sacked the city. His anonymously presented account of the ensuing massacre was completed before 25 November and, as a printed pamphlet, was circulating in London by the end of the month.[55]

Occasionally, political necessity dictated a volte-face. In June 1578, during one of Elizabeth's occasional furies at what she perceived to be the Netherlander rebels' intransigence, Walsingham and Lord Thomas Cobham travelled as ambassadors to the Low Countries to attempt to reconcile them to Don John of Austria – Philip's half-brother and, since 1576, Governor-General there. To publicize the issues they confronted, Thomas Churchyard – soldier, scribbler and agent of Walsingham – was encouraged to publish his *Lamentable and pitifull Description, of the woefull warres in Flaunders*, a full-length catalogue of the depredations suffered by Netherlanders from the reign of Charles v to the then-present. Far from being an inflammatory piece, Churchyard's work reflected the government's conciliatory initiative. Reasonably impartial upon events, it provided a protracted justification of official English policy towards the Low Countries in which Elizabeth was portrayed as an honest broker. Criticism of Spanish behaviour was kept to a minimum and emphasis placed on the (erroneous) point that Englishmen who previously had gone to the Low Countries to fight for the rebels had done so secretly and against their sovereign's wishes. Recalling the recently massacred citizens of Antwerp, Churchyard merely spoke of their poor judgement at throwing themselves upon the mercy of their despoilers, 'whyche are not ignorant in the vsage of victorie, nor over-mercifull till they finde themselves Maisters of the fielde . . .'.[56]

This lull in the pamphlet war was brief. As the perception of growing Spanish power insinuated itself into English consciousness, the tenor of reportage became increasingly strident. Whereas in 1576 even a thinly disguised government agent such as George Gascoigne might still observe that no Spaniards of quality had been involved in the sack of Antwerp (and, indeed, could not help but praise the perpetrators' 'order and valour' when storming the city), later commentators had fewer scruples. Even the most erudite Englishmen, who might otherwise have admired the achievements of the Iberian nations over the previous century, lost no opportunity to recall the depravities and cruelties of the enemy they were creating. That the subtlety of the message might not be lost, Richard Hakluyt commenced a chapter in his *Discourse of Western Planting* with the proposition:

> That the Spaniardes haue exercised moste outragious and more then Turkishe cruelties in all the west Indies, whereby they are euery where there becomme moste odious vnto them whoe woulde ioyne with vs or any other moste willinglye to shake of their moste intollerable yoke, and haue begonne to doo yt already in diuers places where they were lordes heretofore.[57]

John Hooker, dedicating his 1586 edition of 'The Irish Historie . . . by Giraldus Cambrensis' to Walter Ralegh, referred to the Spaniards' 'cruel immanitie, contrarie to all naturall humanitie' (a judgement that might have summed up Ralegh's own record in Ireland admirably).[58] Elsewhere, the uncommitted reader may have been swayed, or confused, by revelations that the average Spaniard was simultaneously an accomplished ravisher of womenfolk and a slave to sodomy.[59] As the slide towards open war accelerated, any semblance of proportion or perspective was abandoned in popular English literature, and a truly demonic enemy was fashioned, with no claim for his bestial nature left untested. Even as the sea battle raged eastwards up the Channel in 1588, Thomas Deloney was scribbling his famously febrile ditty upon the several sorts of whips with which the would-be invaders had equipped themselves in pleasant anticipation of their conquests:

> One sorte of whips they had for men
> So smarting fierce and fell:
> As like could neuer be deuisde
> By any deuill in hell.
> The strings whereof with wyerie knots,
> Like rowels they did frame,
> That euery stroke might teare the flesh
> They layd on with the same,

And pluck the spreading sinewes from
The hardned bloudie bone,
To prick and pearce each tender veine,
Within the bodie knowne.
And not to leaue one crooked ribbe,
On any side vnseene:
Nor yet to leaue a lump of flesh
The head and foot betweene.[60]

It need hardly be said that to Deloney's equally forensic description of the whips intended for use upon English womenfolk was added a Puritan's relish of the rapine that would precede the main business. Sold by the sign of the Black Raven in Paternoster Row, the ballad was handy source-material for harangues at St Paul's Cross, a few yards distant.

Propagandist works that addressed the average Englishman's xenophobia were far more digestible than blasts regarding the putative threat from English Catholics. It was inevitable, however, that as the perceived external threat magnified during the 1580s, even the most cynical among them began to look askance at their own papists. Preaching at the beginning of the decade, William Fisher had posed a simple question to his congregation: 'Al our bold Recusants, al our quondam priests, al our harpers upon a change, all our lookers for a golden daye, all our private whisperers, and subtile surmisers whiche we have in Englande, what els are they but the Popes souldiers?'[61] In 1580, this was a voice struggling still to engage the public ear, but successive plots against the Queen (all of them assiduously encouraged, thwarted and later advertised by Walsingham via his tame pamphleteers, broadsiders and balladeers) appeared to identify an ever more palpable brotherhood of domestic dissenter and foreign tyrant. Their earliest precursor, the Ridolfi plot, had been little more than the sickly child of a self-deluding Florentine banker and malevolent Spanish envoy, morally (but not practically) supported by Philip II. But those of Francis Throckmorton (1583) and Anthony Babington (1586) were fundamentally more threatening. Throckmorton, a besotted servant of Mary Stuart, was shown to have plotted with the Spanish ambassador for a Guise-led invasion of England. Helpfully, he revealed under torture that several English Catholic nobles and gentlemen were implicated, including Henry Percy, brother of the Northern Rising's executed leader.[62]

Even more damaging to the reputation of English Catholics was Babington's plot. He and his co-conspirators planned to begin their rising by assassinating the Queen, and thereafter to lead an army of Englishmen loyal to Rome, hopefully supported by foreign troops, to place Mary Stuart on the emptied throne. Babington had been a leading light in English Catholic circles for several years past, and had actively assisted the Jesuit mission to England. It was difficult, therefore, to dismiss him as a peripheral malcontent. His chief ally in the plot (indeed, the instigator of the plan to kill Elizabeth) was a priest, John Ballard – proof, so it seemed, of government's insistence that the seminarians' mission to England was a military, not a spiritual movement:

Was euer seene such wicked troopes,
Of traytors in this land,
Against the pretious woord of truthe,
And their good Queene to stand?
But heer beholde the rage of Rome,
The fruits of Popish plants;
Beholde and se their wicked woorks,
Which all good meaning wants[63]

That any degree of popular English Catholic support for Babington's scheme was lacking no longer mattered. The growing desperation of exiled Catholic polemicists, tormented by the same enduring patriotism of their co-religionists that the English government signally failed to acknowledge, found expression in increasingly virulent assaults upon the regime. In his *Copie of a Letter Concerning the Yielding Up of Daventrie* (1587) and *Admonition to the Nobility and People of England and Ireland* (1588), William Allen abandoned any conciliatory pretensions and explicitly urged his putative English constituency to put conscience before earthly loyalties and rise up against their Queen. In doing so, he presented Elizabeth's government with seemingly indisputable evidence that plotters' treasons and Catholic dissent were indistinguishable components of an ill-disposed whole. However unjust, Stubbes's sweeping indictment – 'all papists are traitors in their harts, how soever otherwise they beare the world in hand' – had been gifted a telling credibility.[64]

By this time, there was hardly need to reiterate the external element of the threat. As shall be discussed, the growth of direct Anglo-Spanish confrontations in the Low Countries and New World, the vast increase in Spanish military power from 1580 and its occasional rumoured support of

Irish rebellions all served to remind Englishmen that a successful domestic plot against the regime would not want for foreign assistance. The unpleasantness of the dark 'abroad' was already well understood. In contrast, the venerable threat of a vague conjunction of papal ambition and recusant longing had long failed to move a largely indifferent audience. But when that conjunction seemed likely to be facilitated by fleets of whip-wielding Spanish rapists, the average Englishman's attention became fully engaged. The unifying element in the government's sophisticated equation – that which identified the Counter-Reformation's crusading imperative and Philip II's temporal ambitions as synonymous – had never been problematic. Every utterance of the papal curia confirmed it, to the Spanish King's enduring irritation.

There was no single, discernible moment at which the 'cold statute Protestant' Englishman became aware of an emerging spiritual self, but its nature is reasonably clear. Unlike that of his more godly neighbours, it was not defined upon dogmatic principles (the subtleties of which would have befuddled him), but upon the identification of Anglo-Protestantism as a blurred yet intrinsic element of his Englishness. This perception, like all tribalisms, derived its strength from an antithesis – that Catholicism was a fundamentally alien creed. Elizabeth's ministers struggled to impress this truth upon the nation for more than two decades prior to the outbreak of hostilities with Spain. Their efforts were influenced at various times by prudent anxiety or exaggerated fear of foreign interventions, but above all by the nervousness with which the Tudor regime regarded its own masses. When, in 1569, northern English Catholics had burned the Book of Common Prayer in the churches briefly 'liberated' during the Northern Rising, their government had seen this not as part of an unthinking reprisal for decades of iconoclasm and desecration, but as an assault upon an instrument of state, and, therefore, upon the state itself. All subsequent evidence of traitorous activity by individual Catholic conspirators was assumed to reflect the nature of the species and proclaimed as such – not least by Burghley:

Multitudes of such as are yet obedient subjects, will, by these secret persuasions, and by example of others that are their superiors, as lords of the realm in honour, or as their landlords, or as persons of great esteem for their auntienty, or for great house-keeping, decline from their inward love of her Majesty, and yield their hearts and devotions to such persons as they shall be persuaded are right heirs in this crown. And so shall they

be in no small multitudes ready, upon any occasion offered, by the only
show of any outward force, to rebel suddenly and put in hazard the good
estate of her majesty and the realm.[65]

After twenty-eight years of largely tranquil rule, this was a regime that
remained ill at ease with its constituency. Its enduring overestimation of the
threat from English Catholics (nearly all of whom would rally unquestion-
ingly to Elizabeth's cause in 1588) was mirrored by an equally persistent
underestimation of the loyalties of England's 'irreligious' majority. On the
eve of the armada campaign, when the Queen's Lord Admiral and cousin
Charles Howard urged her 'For the love of Jesus Chryste, madam, awake
thorowghly and see the velynous tresons round about you agaynst your
majeste and your Relme', the mind of a majority of her servants in government was laid bare.[66] Their promotion of the 1584 Bond of Association,
and its provision of a huge bodyguard for the Queen during the armada
year, reflected a profound fear that she was neither safe from many of her
own subjects nor able to rely upon the loyalties of the remainder. The reality
– of an overwhelming affection for Elizabeth's person – was rarely and
imperfectly understood. Even she, though in other ways acutely sensitive to
the iconic nature of her relationship with her people, was infected by this
misapprehension. Faced with the wraith of the enemy within, she allowed
policy to be enacted that ensured the alienation of many Englishmen from
that broad church her Act of Uniformity had sought to build. Ironically,
both her ideas about civil obedience and her personal faith closely matched
the partialities of the vast majority of her subjects – including those who
regarded themselves as 'catholic' only in their fondness for, and loyalty to,
the old forms of worship. But too many of the men upon whom she relied
regarded the Elizabethan settlement as a reformation half-completed, a half-
open door through which the Roman antichrist was all too likely to be
thrust by his Spanish servant. Remarkably, their anxieties found expression
in a strategy that succeeded in uniting the nation in fear of foreign aggres-
sors while further splintering it in the name of God.

From foreine foes, O Lord! Her keepe,
and enemies at home,
from fained friends and trayterous hearts
preserve her, Lord, alone[67]

PART TWO

I fear not all his threatenings; his great preparations and mighty forces do not stir me; for, though he come against me, with a greater power than ever was, his invincible navy, I doubt not (God assisting me, upon whom I always trust) but that I shall be able to defeat and overthrow him. I have great advantage against him, for my cause is just.[1]

SEVEN

Non Sufficit Orbis, 1574–1584

If God be on my side, why doth this Popish wonder
Seek to affright me with his beastly thunder?
Why doth this new-born giant seek to ride
Above the clouds, with his prodigious pride?[2]

On 12 July 1580, the Catholic Anglo-Spanish merchant and part-time intelligencer Roger Bodenham wrote from Sanlucar de Barrameda to the Principal Secretary of the Privy Council, Dr Thomas Wilson. He suggested that Wilson and his fellow councillors might make an easy profit by using their own money to finance grain shipments to Spain, the harvest there having failed once more (Wilson, who many years earlier had been seized and tortured by the Inquisition, presumably wore his sectarian prejudices lightly).[3] Bodenham was not so hopeful of Spanish misfortunes elsewhere, however. Reporting the progress of Philip's on-going subjugation of Portugal, he observed gloomily: 'It will be the greatest conquest that ever Spain made since the conquest of the Indias. This is without comparison . . .'.[4]

The death of the ageing Cardinal-King Henry in the previous January had marked the extinction of the Portuguese royal house of Avis, an event anticipated in every court in Europe, and dreaded in most, since his succession two years earlier. Philip II, himself half-Portuguese through his mother Isabella, had possibly the firmest claim to the succession. However, despite extensive prior bribery, he was able to purchase the loyalties of a decimated Portuguese nobility only (its finest bloodstock having died with

Henry's predecessor, Sebastian 1, at the battle of Alcazarquivir in 1578). Most of the remainder of Portugal's population, loathing the prospect of domination by Spain, favoured the claims of Dom António of Avis, Prior of Cato and illegitimate nephew of the late King. Dom António duly made his bid, and it proved as fragile as had been expected. One of the Fugger bankers' many intelligencers, writing from Lisbon, put it tartly, but spoke most of Europe's mind when he wrote: 'The Portuguese . . . refuse point-blank to become Spanish, though I should like to know what they are going to do about resisting'.[5] On 18 June, the duke of Alba crossed the Portuguese border with some 47,000 troops; less than three months later, all resistance ended at Coimbra. Dom António fled his country, and only a number of Azorean islands continued to proclaim their loyalty to him thereafter. On 12 September, Philip was crowned King of Portugal in Lisbon.

His accession brought an immediate and stupendous expansion of Spanish power. 'Uniting the kingdoms of Spain and Portugal will make Your Majesty the greatest king in the world' wrote Philip's chaplain Hernando de Castillo; 'because if the Romans were able to rule the world simply by ruling the Mediterranean, what of the man who rules the Atlantic and Pacific oceans, since they surround the world?'[6] It was hardly a fanciful analogy. In less than a year the Spanish King had acquired a near-stranglehold upon Europe's incredibly lucrative spice trade, and a potent instrument of war – the Portuguese navy – had been added to his existing, predominantly Mediterranean-based naval forces. Moreover, the silver mines at Potosí were reaching near-maximum production at this time. In the five years following Spain's absorption of the Portuguese possessions, imports of Spanish New World bullion would rise to more than double the quantity of just a decade earlier. Philip was acquiring both the apparatus and, potentially, the finances to deal with his most persistent political problems.[7]

In England, many would have concurred with de Castillo's logic, and feared its implications. By the Treaty of Bristol, the Tudor and Habsburg regimes had attempted to patch their relationship into some semblance of their former amity. Yet, as discussed earlier, the pact skirted rather than addressed the principal points of contention that had undermined the relationship. Neither Elizabeth nor Philip wanted war; neither was prepared, or able, to make the compromises that would ensure peace. Despite removing the bulk of English volunteers from the Low Countries, Elizabeth continued to provide moral support and infrequent subsidies to the Netherlander rebels while proclaiming herself a disinterested party, wishing only for a settlement that would preserve both ancient liberties and princely authority. For his part, Philip, never able to force a definitive pacification upon the Seventeen Provinces, lost most of the remaining goodwill of his subjects there when his unpaid troops mutinied – upon four occasions between 1572 and 1576 – and relieved their frustrations in widespread pillage, rape and murder. Heavy reverses in the Mediterranean – the loss of Tunis and its fortress, La Goleta, and the rapid recovery of Ottoman naval forces after Lepanto – inclined him briefly, *in extremis*, to consider granting important concessions in the Low Countries. He tentatively authorized the recognition of the authority of the States-General (the council representing the individual provinces of the Netherlands) and the withdrawal of Spanish troops from the region, though rebel leaders and heretics were still to be pursued and punished. However, the shockwaves from the final and worst mutiny of his soldiers in November 1576 overtook this hopeful initiative. The man who carried Philip's proposals to the Netherlands – his half-brother and new regent Don John of Austria, hero of Lepanto – faced the outrage of a united aristocracy and States-General without an effective military force or, equally importantly, the means to pay one. He was obliged to accept the fait accompli of the 'Pacification of Ghent', submitting to much of what the Spanish King had been prepared, reluctantly, to concede. The humiliation could not be allowed to stand. Although a year would elapse before the tide turned once more in Philip's favour, neither he nor Don John had the slightest intention of allowing the Netherlander nobility to dictate the terms of the future relationship between the overlord of the Seventeen Provinces and his subjects.

Across the Channel, English hopes for a negotiated settlement between Philip and his rebellious subjects rose as Spanish fortunes sank. They were soon dashed, however, and rumours regarding Don John's interest in English affairs resurrected something of the trepidation that had marked the period of Alba's governorship. From 1575, renewed papal ambitions to reverse the English reformation (goaded in part by the petition of the English Catholic exile Sir Francis Englefield to Gregory XIII) identified him as the likely leader of a putative papal–Spanish–Genoese crusade to that end.[8] Don John himself, even in the depths of his difficulties in the Low Countries, enthused about the project, which aimed to place Mary Stuart on the English throne and marry her thereafter to Philip's nominee (whom Don John readily identified as himself, whatever the Spanish King intended).[9] The new regent was rendered largely powerless by the absence of Spanish troops from the Low Countries during his first year of office, but their return in 1577, led by Alexander Farnese, son of Margaret of Parma and the greatest general of his day, ended any hopes that the potential threat to Elizabeth's regime had dissipated. In January 1578, Don John and Farnese swiftly reasserted Habsburg authority in the southern Low Countries with the crushing victory of Gembloux, near Namur. Thereafter, even Don John's untimely death from plague could not deflect a growing conviction within a powerful clique in English government – led by Leicester and Walsingham – that William of Orange must be supported at all costs. The survival of the rebel cause, they argued with increasing vehemence, was less a fraternal duty than a vital element of England's home defence. Even the cautious Burghley, horrified at the growing pressures that dragged England towards an open alliance with the rebels, was obliged to admit: 'The nearer their end, the nearer is the peril come to England'.[10]

Had there been no other issue to poison Anglo-Spanish relations, this continuing English engagement with the Netherlander revolt would have made their preservation almost impossible. The restoration of Philip's authority in the Low Countries was the principal non-Iberian concern of his later reign; its drain upon his resources a major cause of his several bankruptcies. Elizabeth consistently maintained – probably truthfully – that she, too, wished to see Habsburg rule re-established throughout the Seventeen Provinces, though with local privileges safeguarded and all Spanish military forces removed permanently. That, however, would require concessions that neither Philip nor the rebels were capable of making, which left English policy attempting to track the fickle gusts of fate that swept the struggle for the 'cockpit of Europe'. This was appreciated by none of the parties involved – particularly the Spanish King, whose rancour at Elizabeth's on-off engagement could not be salved by efforts to alleviate tensions elsewhere. In another of his Spanish reports, Roger Bodenham gave Burghley a prophetic glimpse of where two irreconcilable ambitions were heading:

> I find that great is the hatred that grows between all nations for matters of religion; therefore Spain being, as you know, governed altogether by the spirituality, and the King being thereto most earnestly bent, he gives the more occasion to their pretence. You know what is to be looked for at their hands, considering how far we are from them in opinion of religion . . . the loss of the Low Country is also a great grief to them, which they say is only by the aid that England has given . . .[11]

Bodenham's government was as aware as he that its policies had the capacity to drag England towards a war it could not as yet fight. In the seemingly contradictory strategy that Elizabeth pursued in the years

following the Treaty of Bristol, there was a thread of consistency that recognized this. Abandonment of the Netherlander rebels was inconceivable (if,
at times, only just so), despite their drifting loyalties, unhealthy Calvinist
associations, their blockade of the Scheldt estuary and 'taxation' of English
ships attempting to pass to Antwerp, and their intransigence in negotiations
with Philip. Spanish plans for their extinction therefore had to be impeded,
but not at the cost of an outright confrontation from which neither England
nor Spain could retreat. Already, the English government had been made
aware that Spain could collect sufficient naval resources west of the Pillars
of Hercules to pose a strategic threat to England. Early in 1574, Philip had
ordered the concentration of a large fleet at Santander, commanded by Pedro
Menéndez de Avilés (nemesis of the French Florida colony nine years
earlier); its purpose to sweep the Sea Beggars from the seas and destroy their
bases in Holland and Zeeland. According to Antonio de Guaras, a Spanish
merchant and intelligencer long resident in London, the prospect of this
armada operating in the Narrow Seas and English Channel caused great
anxiety to Elizabeth and her councillors.[12] They feared, not without cause,
that at least part of its considerable strength (wildly exaggerated at some
350 sail) might be diverted to assist the renegade Stukeley in supporting the
earl of Desmond's rebellion in Munster.[13] To face that threat, the entire
effective strength of the Navy Royal – a mere twenty-four vessels – was
'scrambled' in May and June, and levies hurriedly mustered throughout
the kingdom.[14]

The danger posed by the Spanish fleet proved to be ephemeral (plague,
and the logistical problems of equipping a fleet of 233 vessels of all sizes,
overwhelmed Philip's officers at Santander), but the lesson could not have
been lost upon Elizabeth's government that impeding Spanish advances
would require an extremely deft touch, if England were not to reap consequences she might not survive. Six years later, amidst the heightened sense
of urgency that followed the 1580 Union of the Crowns, the Queen would
make the point explicitly: '. . . we think it good for the King of Spain to be
impeached both in Portugal and his Islands and also in the Low Countries,
whereto we shall be ready to give such indirect assistance as shall not at once
be a cause of war'.[15] In the intervening period, the same policy (if as-yet
unspoken) simultaneously ignored or encouraged tacitly the occasional long-
range raid upon Spain's New World silver routes and voluntary service in
rebel armies whilst seeking to inhibit other causes of Anglo-Spanish friction.

This balance was extremely difficult to manage, particularly on occasions
when Elizabeth, knowingly or otherwise, surrendered initiative to men
whose own sense of circumspection was at best minimal. Her proscription

regarding English voyages south of the equator was obeyed for three years following the Treaty of Bristol; unfortunately, Philip's most tender preoccupations – and those most vulnerable to English interference – lay to the north of that boundary. Already, John Hawkins's slaving voyages had generated serious diplomatic tensions because they seemed to represent a new, more persistent strategy to undermine Spain's monopoly rights in the Caribbean. During the next decade, further English incursions followed. They were organized almost exclusively by men who had been employed in those earlier expeditions and who now returned to exploit, revenge or seek compensation for their former experiences. Some were at least partly financed by Hawkins, though none went under licence, or with permission, from the Crown. The only other consistent characteristic of these ventures was that they had wholly piratical intentions; otherwise, their fortunes varied extremely. Francis Drake, following two poorly executed raids in 1570 and 1571, stumbled upon a bullion train near Nombre de Dios during his third expedition in 1572–3 and returned to England a wealthy man. Gilbert Horseley, with twenty-five men, fought and tortured his way far into Nicaragua during 1575 and gathered considerable plunder (most of his fifteen surviving comrades were arrested by Admiralty officials upon their return; none appears to have been prosecuted subsequently). Others, such as John Noble (1574), Andrew Barker (1576) and John Oxenham (1576/7) met with more effective Spanish resistance and catastrophic failure, paying with their own lives and those of all but a handful of their men.[16]

These were idiosyncratic incursions, small in scale and necessarily underpinned by brief, makeshift alliances with French corsairs and *cimarrones* (escaped Negro slaves organized into bandit communities in the Panama jungle). Even under torture, Englishmen captured by local authorities always denied that they had official sanction. Understandably, neither their inquisitors nor Philip himself regarded this as proof of official English disinterest.[17] Barker's voyage was known to have been financed in part by Elizabeth's favourite, Leicester, while Drake's unfortunate habit of shouting 'victory to the Queen of England' as he led assaults upon Spanish colonial settlements was reported assiduously by his sharp-eared victims.[18] If these raids, limited in scale and ambition, were not comparable with the earlier, near-apocalyptic Huguenot assaults upon the major Spanish Caribbean settlements, the vigour and effectiveness of the colonial authorities' response indicate that they were taken very seriously. A Spanish strategy of force and, remarkably, concession gradually neutralized the threat from the *cimarrones* and deprived English interlopers of their irreplaceable sustainers in the harsh climate of the Panama Isthmus. Without succour even from their own government (which agreed, if half-heartedly, the justice of Philip's complaints), most of the survivors of these incursions saw little future in their particular strand of maritime enterprise. As the memory of Hawkins's defeat, and profits, faded, his imitators began to look elsewhere for less heavily guarded opportunities. By 1577 the Caribbean had been cleared of Englishmen. Their successors would not return in strength until open war commenced in the following decade.

As one opportunity closed off, however, another, far more promising prospect opened. Also in 1577, Drake departed England on the latest campaign in his private war against Spain. His opaque intentions were financed by several of the most prominent men in government and by the Queen herself, whose patronage explicitly shattered her previous 'below the equinoctiall' prohibition. Other than vastly enhancing Drake's already considerable reputation, this voyage – his famous circumnavigation – was graphically to expose the vulnerability of Spain's Pacific possessions to a determined assault. The full implications of the project would not become apparent for many months, but the stream of intelligences that flowed into Spain from the cities along Drake's route – Santiago, Lima, Panama, Guatemala – indicated that something new and devastating had descended upon what previously had been regarded as the more secure regions of Philip's empire. In isolation, Drake's voyage would have constituted a major source of future contention between the crowns of England and Spain. As it was, his glorious progress, and the vast profits that accumulated in its wake, provided a fundamental spur to developing English ambitions that no degree of official discouragement could temper.

Meanwhile, Elizabeth's government, torn between temptation and its consequences, attempted to balance its toleration of spectacular far-horizon depredations by discouraging those in home-waters, which hurt English trade almost as severely as that of Philip's subjects. Yet official attempts to end lawlessness at sea (by 1575, Elizabeth's government had issued fully nine proclamations intended to suppress piracy) had long proved ineffectual.[19] Years of near-endemic civil war in France and the Low Countries had encouraged conditions that offered both sanctuary and constantly recurring opportunities to professional freebooters. Englishmen now habitually sailed under commissions issued by the Huguenot leadership or William of Orange, which their government recognized or prohibited as the diplomatic cycle dictated. Others disdained to seek out real commissions and assumed the benefits of imaginary ones – a number of creative individuals even claimed to be sailing under Habsburg letters of marque in order to access the holds of rebel Netherlander ships 'legitimately'.[20] When circumstance turned unfavourably against them (a proclamation of 26 October 1575 forbade English mariners to serve foreign princes 'in these troublesome times of civil wars'), freebooters had ample recourse to ports where English law could not touch them.[21] In a string of havens along the Channel's southern and eastern shores, they rested, repaired their ships and sat out their government's brief enthusiasm for quiet seas; when official efforts flagged, they returned swiftly to the Irish, Welsh and West Country ports that had become entrepôts for a near-formal industry. From 1574 the re-establishment and growth of commercial traffic between England and Spain provided even greater opportunities for career-pirates. Some of the bolder of the breed, enticed by the return of rich Iberian cargoes to English inshore waters, scoured the Thames estuary just a few miles from the centre of government, preying upon vessels passing to and from London.[22]

Statistics regarding these incidents are incomplete and unreliable, but there was something close to a unanimous conviction among monarch, statesmen and the mercantile community that a crisis had been reached. A draft proclamation for the suppression of piracy, speculatively attributed to 1580 (but which, given its context, is far more likely to have been drawn up during 1577), lamented 'the unbridled licentious outrageousness of pirates and rovers which at this day commit more spoils and robberies on all sides one upon the other than hath been heard of in former times...'.[23]

With a virtual war being waged upon the seaborne trade of friends, neutrals and potential foes alike, Elizabeth made the only substantial effort of her reign – indeed, of any Tudor reign – to attack the institutions of piracy at root and branch. In March 1577 a semi-permanent tribunal system was convened in Cardiff where sixty suspected pirates and their abettors were examined before local juries. In the following month further juries were sworn in at Wareham and Melcombe Regis to hear cases against many suspected pirates detained in nearby Weymouth gaol. In September the system was extended massively, with commissioners appointed in every maritime county to apprehend and try the 'maintainers' of piracy – the large, shadowy constituency that received and sold on spoils. The volume of correspondence to and from the Council indicates that the business became one of the principal concerns of government towards the end of 1577 and the following spring. During March and April 1578 commissioners for seventeen counties submitted their detailed proceedings to the Council, as their deputies, appointed to a series of ports and havens around the English coast, worked to prevent the resurgence of piracy following the prosecution of those taken and arraigned.[24]

The detail of these reports indicates that good intentions were hampered by officers whose relationship with their prey was, to say the least, ambiguous. The Council's original exhortation to their appointees – that 'you doe assemble yourselves and proceede to severe examination without respecte of persones' – was often interpreted with less than zeal, even by those close to government.[25] The earl of Bedford, newly appointed Lord Lieutenant of Dorset, Devon and Cornwall (counties in which piracy and its attendant infrastructures were more an honoured tradition than an occupation), reported of his proceedings that he could 'find no great matter' to be pursued. The commissioners for Denbighshire made the rather remarkable claim that there were absolutely no landing places or havens in their county, and therefore there could be no abettors of pirates. Those of Kent and West Sussex tried a little harder; in their first year's tribunals each county managed to prosecute just one person for aiding pirates while releasing all others previously detained on suspicion of the same offence. In many cases elsewhere, local juries heard damning evidence against offenders and then promptly acquitted them. Yet despite these checks, the Council pushed hard to see its initiative succeed. The abetting culture that allowed piracy to flourish in the coastal regions was examined to its innermost recesses, and for once it was not just the inferior sort who found themselves under examination. The Lord Admiral himself – often an enthusiastic financier of privateering voyages – was obliged to hand over his secretary, Gilbert Peppit, for examination by the Judge of the Admiralty on a charge of aiding pirates. He was exonerated subsequently.[26]

The results of this sustained and expensive initiative were disappointing. Only a few dozen felons appear to have been convicted; most were fined, a few – recidivists or those who had committed murder in the course of their depredations – hanged, but the incidence of cases in the Admiralty Court did not noticeably decrease thereafter.[27] There was an arbitrary quality to many proceedings that reflected more than the vacillating efforts of local officers and government's desire not to extinguish entirely the gene pool of seamanship that freebooting provided. Piracy, as discussed, had always been a pervasive element in the culture and economy of the English maritime counties. Juries sworn to hear evidence were often obstructive because their communities were the principal beneficiaries of the defendants' industry. Members of prominent local families appointed to oversee proceedings were often deeply compromised by long-standing relationships with those they prosecuted. Following preliminary investigations by the Somerset deputy commissioners, the deputy vice-admiral of Bristol, John Dye, was summoned by the Privy Council to answer charges that he habitually took bribes to release and support pirates. The mayor of Dartmouth, John Plomleigh, was fined £100 for regularly abetting his town's notorious maintenance of the piracy trade.[28] At Falmouth, the relationship between local crime and its supposed prosecutors was graphically illustrated once more by that pernicious dynasty of Arwennack, the Killigrews. Sir Henry Killigrew – diplomat, Exchequer teller, Burghley's brother-in-law and a leading figure in the Council's assault upon piracy – had been appointed commissioner for the collection and delivery of fines from proceedings in western and Welsh counties. Though his own mother famously had been tried many years earlier for a murder committed during a piratical raid she had led personally, Sir Henry had thrown off the poisonous legacy of his bloodline to build a career on talent and principle.[29] Of the funds he secured upon his official duties during summer 1577, however, at least £50 came from the pocket of his elder brother, the incorrigible Peter, prosecuted (more than twenty years after being named by the Privy Council as a 'notorious' pirate) for receiving stolen goods from a new generation of despoilers.[30]

By the 1570s such ambiguous or openly illicit relationships were no longer peculiar to coastal communities. In an age of near-constant civil and confessional conflict into which Englishmen had been drawn by conviction, circumstance and avarice, cargoes appropriated from the holds of other nations' vessels had come to represent an ever greater proportion of England's 'imports'. As they did so, the palpable benefits derived from piracy spread inland to benefit all levels of English society. As the complex linkages between licensed depredation and banditry created ambiguities in the legal process, so the fruits of their industry fostered a corresponding greyness in public morality. Put bluntly, the theft of aliens' property could be excused or justified by too many extenuations to be considered in the same light as highway robbery, its domestic equivalent.

To cite the example of just one port, Southampton, it is evident that the process was becoming an acknowledged permanence in English life. During the early 1570s the officers and men of Calshot Castle, a royal fortress guarding the entrance to Southampton Water, habitually fired upon merchant vessels anchored beneath their walls – including those of their compatriots – to encourage them to part with a 'token' of their cargoes (the castle itself, it was observed by one ship's master invited there to discuss his own wares, was a veritable warehouse of stolen wines and Spanish wool).[31] Offended parties who appealed to the authorities at Southampton for restitution were not likely to receive the sort of satisfaction they may have expected. During the previous decade, the town had pioneered a system of brokerage of stolen goods that served not only the freebooters and their potential customers but also their victims, who could negotiate a price for recovery of their property. The brokers secured their percentage-based fees unhampered by official discouragement, and the income generated from this activity paid for the refurbishment of Southampton's slipways and jetties (something that customs dues from the town's failing legitimate trade could no longer provide). This was not merely a case of making the best of a regrettable fact of life. By institutionalizing an ad hoc practice that had prevailed since the early days of piracy, a municipal government, fully accountable to the Crown, was acknowledging the legitimacy of the industry itself. Later, when the system had become more widespread, the Spanish ambassador Bernadino de Mendoza would warn his King of its damaging attractions:

> . . . the merchants send powers to their agents resident here to recover the goods. For this purpose and their own gain they come to terms with the pirates, the owners despairing of any other course. This is a direct incentive to the pirates, because when your Majesty's representatives request that the pirates should be punished, they are told there is no one to complain of them, as they have come to terms.[32]

The indistinct relationships between local law officer, community, plunderer and even government made any consistency in the application of policy impossible. Personal circumstance appears to have counted for far more than legislation, polluting the system to a point that bordered upon the farcical. On 13 November 1580, Clinton Atkinson, a some-time merchant of London held in Exeter gaol under sentence of death for piracy, was reprieved at the plea of the Spanish Company, whose wares he had extracted from an Italian ship seized off Cape Palos. The following day, however, before word of his reprieve could be carried to Exeter, he had escaped – allegedly with the connivance of the gaoler and the town's mayor (the latter had already given at least two favourable testimonials regarding the condemned man's character). The much-beloved Atkinson prudently disappeared thereafter, only to re-emerge a year later, suing in the Admiralty Court for a share of proceeds from the sale of his vessel. This brazen initiative backfired and earned him a brief stay in the Marshalsea, but by 1582 he was free and at sea once more under the commission of the Portuguese Pretender, busily despoiling (Scottish) vessels and torturing their crews.[33]

Atkinson was by no means uniquely fortunate in his choice of associates. In 1578 Thomas Halfpenny, a 'rover' taken at sea by Edward Fenton's *Judith* as she returned to England from Frobisher's third Baffin Island expedition, was quietly set free at Tilbury – having been provided with the *Judith*'s boat – by Frobisher's cousin, Alexander Creake. Three years later, two condemned pirates being taken in chains from Arundel to London were allowed to escape into Horsley woods by the local constable charged with escorting them through his 'beat'.[34] Local contacts were occasionally unhelpful, however. Philip Boyte, one of Clinton Atkinson's confederates in 1580, was seized and examined at Weymouth by the town's mayor. He defended himself manfully against the charge of stealing Spanish wares with the rather novel assertion that he had understood the Queen to be already at open war with Spain. Unfortunately for Boyte, Hugh Randall, a former pirate and associate, was persuaded to take the stand also, and used the opportunity either to settle old scores or prove his newly respectable credentials. In November Boyte was hanged at Wapping Stairs almost at the same moment that Atkinson was fleeing Exeter gaol, while Randall went on to become vice-admiral of Devon and bailiff – later mayor – of Weymouth, though not before suffering further imprisonments for receiving stolen goods and threatening murder upon another rival.[35] Facing this systemic corruption, government was obliged sometimes to override its own mechanisms; in 1582 the Admiralty Court's authority to try cases of piracy was suspended, and, for three years thereafter, the Council supervised directly the application of criminal law in maritime cases.[36]

Given that the government's initiative against piracy had minimal implications for its victims (fines levied against offenders were retained by the state, not dispensed as compensation), its strenuous efforts had no appreciable effect diplomatically. When Mendoza reported to Philip in August 1579 that English acts of piracy against Spanish ships were now a daily occurrence, he omitted to give any credit for attempts during the previous two years to discourage them.[37] Conversely, he continued to report every snippet of intelligence (and rumour) regarding new English long-range voyages, all of which he alleged to have the aim of plundering the traffic of the Indies.[38] Drake's on-going voyage was, of course, a continuing source of intense interest – and irritation – to Philip. Mendoza faithfully passed on all news of its progress, and accurately identified members of the Council as Drake's principal supporters. His account of their response to Anglo-Spanish merchants fearing reprisals from Philip reads as what it was – a well-rehearsed alibi: 'The Council replied that Drake had gone on a voyage of discovery, and that if he had plundered it was not their fault, nor did they think his Majesty would seize English property in consequence'.[39] It was the same hopeful refrain that Philip had heard previously regarding Hawkins's slaving voyages, and persuaded him likewise.

Elizabeth genuinely wished to curb a problem that had come to harm English trade as much as that of foreign nations with whom she was 'in amitie'. To regard it as entirely unconnected with more distant offences, however, was disingenuous. Subsequent generations have regarded the awesome achievement of Drake's circumnavigation as a significant milestone upon the road to Anglo-Spanish conflict, but it is doubtful whether Philip regarded it as other than a stunning example of the same curse that afflicted his subjects' Caribbean and European seaborne trades. On this, no less than on the intractable matter of the Low Countries, there was a fundamental divergence of attitude between London and Madrid. Elizabeth's search for a suitably non-disastrous 'impeachment' of Spanish power was based upon the assumption that the state of nervous tension that had characterized Anglo-Spanish relations for twenty years past remained constant, capable of manipulation according to rules and dictates of diplomacy that Philip, no less than she, observed. A growing party within her government disagreed. To these 'hawks', their own motives and actions were grounded in preservation of self and faith, and those of the Spanish King in an overweening ambition to encompass the world in a Habsburg vice that, if successful, would subvert nationhood and the reformed religion. Their view was not yet in the ascendant, but in its dismissal of the possibility of compromise it more accurately judged the mind, if not the motives, of their instinctive enemy.

Given the fundamental dissonances that were coming to permeate the Anglo-Spanish relationship, time was on the side of the anti-conciliation party. Certainly, their convictions appealed more to the prejudices of a majority of their compatriots, who readily absorbed the most partial interpretations of Spanish actions and policies. To a dispassionate observer, Philip's loose alliance with the newly constituted, Guise-led Catholic League in France was no less a reluctant exercise in realpolitik than Elizabeth's support for the Netherlander rebels. Yet it was perceived in England as a token of purely aggressive intent, unleavened by any legitimate concern for the fate of the Spanish King's co-religionists. Similarly, his lukewarm assistance to Irish rebels was as intentionally coercive as the English government's acquiescence to (or active support of) attempts to redirect his New World silver. It too, however, was regarded as an element of that ephemeral 'conspyration' of papacy and Catholic powers to expunge the Protestant faith. This logic, which refused to acknowledge the contribution of English actions to Spanish policy, was self-nurturing. It ensured that Philip's every initiative or reaction was greeted with hurt misapprehension and a strengthening resolve to resist a power that was seen not only as dangerously unchecked, but morally reprehensible.

The events of 1580 brought a marked acceleration of this process of alienation. It would be difficult to overstate the anxiety with which Elizabeth and her councillors witnessed Spain's near-effortless assimilation of the Portuguese empire. It came, furthermore, at a time when the long-feared Catholic conspiracy against England seemed to be gathering pace. Since the beginning of the year, rumours of renewed papal 'crusades' and putative invasions had been rife. In January, new musters were ordered in the maritime counties to provide for defence of the coasts, and twenty ships of the Navy Royal prepared for three months' sea-service 'for all attempts of any forrayne power'.[40] Fears generated by the Vatican's contribution to the Catholic offensive were swiftly dampened by its reality – the ineffectual James Fitzmaurice's Irish expedition. But the participation of a number of Spaniards in his pitifully small force created a disproportionate furore. Despite Philip's continuing strong resistance to fronting or assisting the projects of successive popes against England, the perception among Englishmen was that Spain and Rome were already in unshakeable alliance. If even the well-travelled and perceptive Thomas Wilson could claim confidently to Burghley 'the king [Philip] doth all in the pope's name', it was not likely that evidence to the contrary would be given weight in the Privy Council.[41]

News of the Union of Crowns (at a time, moreover, when France had succumbed to the seventh active phase of her civil wars and could offer no brake upon Spanish ambitions in western Europe) added to this growing sense of encirclement. The perceived danger intensified during August, when a predominantly Italian force of mercenaries was permitted by Philip to concentrate at Corunna, prior to being conveyed to Ireland in locally hired ships. Intelligences flowing into England during the summer months all emphasized the Spanish nature of this 'second wave'.[42] It proved to be no more effective than Fitzmaurice's poor effort, but growing English fears of a Spanish presence in Ireland prompted the cold-blooded slaughter of the mercenaries following their surrender at Smerwick fort three months later – a disgraceful episode lauded by Sir Walter Mildmay in parliament as a 'notable service of a noble capteyne and valiaunt souldiers'.[43] Though their Spanish-born commander, immediately before his own execution, denied that Philip's involvement in the project was more than peripheral, his very presence there seemed to shout the contrary.

Again, Englishmen did not see these growing pressures as being in any way the fruits of their compatriots' interference in the Low Countries and depredations in the Narrow Seas, or of Drake's activities in the Spanish Pacific. They were rather symptoms of the same insatiable strategy that had swallowed Portugal, joined Spanish ambitions to those of the Guise and now stood upon the shores of Flanders, awaiting a favourable moment to cross the Channel and expunge the last major Protestant state in western Europe. As the reach of this imagined monster lengthened, the urge to slash out at its tentacles infected the deliberations of Elizabeth's councillors and encouraged them to consider ripostes that would have seemed unconscionably hazardous only a few years earlier. Even the Queen herself, usually mistrustful of the apocalyptic world-view of her more aggressive advisers, became convinced that Philip had to be reminded of the limits of his power.

In September, Drake's *Golden Hind* docked at Plymouth, ending an epic three-year circumnavigation: 'The Spaniard digged out sweete honeye from the golden Mines, and Sir Francis Drake fetched it home to be tasted in England'.[44] The Queen's personal taste was valued at some £140,000; half her council (including Burghley) wanted this and the remainder of Drake's vast bounty seized and returned to Spain. Those who did not – Leicester, Hatton and Walsingham, the three leading proponents of a more aggressive anti-Spanish policy – had been major investors in Drake's voyage. The personal cost to them of placating Philip, even had they wished it, was clearly insupportable.[45] Elizabeth agreed. Pretence was made of an official investigation in which the value of Drake's booty was established at a minuscule figure, and a new, exciting opportunity was made manifest to a generation of would-be venture capitalists. Drake's return from Nombre de Dios nine years earlier had excited similar attention, but political pressure then had been sufficient to discourage most of his imitators. Now, far from being deterred, the same constituency observed their monarch very publicly receiving a series of trinkets from the nation's foremost bandit. At a New Year's Day reception the Queen wore his jewels in plain sight of ambassador Mendoza. Even more provocatively, she visited the *Golden Hind* two months later to knight Drake and accept a further scoop of jewels from his hands.[46] The message – that contempt for her sovereign authority carried a price – could not have been made more explicit.

Yet in blatantly endorsing Drake's feats, Elizabeth had so mocked Philip's own authority that the message read less as a caution than a slap in the face. Perhaps she sensed something of this, as her government's search for methods to check his growing power acquired some urgency. On 25 January 1581, in the same parliamentary speech in which he waxed fulsomely upon the recent massacre at Smerwick, Mildmay recalled the history of Catholic plots and strategems against the nation, and primed his audience for more to come: 'seing o(u)r enemyes sleepe not, It behoveth vs also not to be careles, as though all were past, but rather to thinke, that there is but a peece of the storme over, and that the greater part of the Tempest remayneth behinde and is like to fall vpon vs . . . '.[47] The process of determining an appropriate strategy to face this looming threat, however, revealed much of the continuing struggle between peace and war parties both in government and society. When news of Philip's victorious progress through Portugal had first reached England, Walsingham's former Paris secretary, Richard Hakluyt, had hurriedly provided his mentor with a pamphlet in which he urged the English seizure and fortification of the Brazilian settlement of San Vicente and the Straits of Magellan, the latter to be 'colonised' (presumably will-ingly) by groups of *cimmarones* transplanted from the happier climes of the Panama Isthmus. He also urged concurrent attempts to discover a north-east passage to the Far East to compensate for the likely loss of English access to Portugal's former colonial markets.[48] Walsingham himself framed, or encouraged, a proposal to establish a permanent corporation, to trade 'beyonde the equynoctiall line'.[49] Ostensibly, this was a purely commercial venture, but it proposed also the establishment of an English equivalent to the Casa de Contratacion of Seville, the instrument by which rules gov-erning the exploitation of the Spanish New World were rigorously enforced. An English version could only be intended to enforce similarly exclusive measures, which implied that *Inter Caetera* and the Treaty of Tordesillas were considered in England to be not so much dead letters as red rags. Further-more, the document proposed Francis Drake as governor of the company of adventurers, an incendiary and hugely inappropriate choice for a com-mercial enterprise – though perfectly appropriate for a proto-East India Company that would be expected to establish, and defend, its claims robustly.

The Queen did not agree to, or even acknowledge officially, these pro-posals. Striking at the heart of the Spanish empire to expropriate its assets, or establishing fortified bases along Spanish sea routes, undoubtedly would have represented those 'causes for war' she wished to avoid. An alternative scheme (first reported to Philip by Mendoza in December 1580) envisaged a straightforward reprise of Drake's former visit to the Pacific, but provided with far greater resources. Drake, with ten ships, was to rendezvous with a smaller fleet, commanded by Henry Knollis, in the Moluccas; en route, he might seize any Spanish or Portuguese ships and property he encountered. Mendoza believed Leicester's to be the project's moving spirit, with Walsingham, Drake, Hawkins, Frobisher, John Winter and Richard Bingham involved also.[50] Again, the scheme was much too provocative for the Queen's tastes. If interloping directly upon existing Spanish trade was unacceptable, assaulting it during the course of an expedition whose scale palpably required official sanction – and, probably, participation – was doubly so.

Confronting the King of Spain was not necessarily difficult; doing so without inviting war was proving more problematic. Intelligences from Europe, furthermore, suggested that efforts to disguise English policy might need to be made with more subtlety than previously. As Lord Thomas Cobham reported laconically to Walsingham from Paris in February 1581:

> An English papist has written from Rome to the Bishop of Glasgow that there are three things which are marvelled at. One is that the King of Spain is not privy to the going of those Spaniards who went into Ireland; the other, that the Queen of England was not privy to the Englishmen who went into Flanders; the third, that the Pope is not privy to the bull which is now printed and set forth against the Queen of England.[51]

The only apparent room for English manoeuvre short of further outright provocation lay in offering some form of support to the exiled Dom António, now actively seeking assistance for his forlorn claim to the throne of Avis. The governing council of Terceira had declared its continuing recognition of the Portuguese Pretender's claims; if the island could be secured on his behalf, the sea routes between Spain and her colonies might be rendered extremely vulnerable. Each year, a substantial part of Spain's wealth – the precious metals, jewels and spices carried in the Terra Firme *galleones*, New Spain *flotas* and Goan carracks – would be obliged to run the gauntlet of hostile, acquisitive seaborne forces operating out of the fortified Terceiran port of Angra. With the economic underpinnings of his over-mighty ambitions thus threatened, even Philip might then be inched towards a more accommodating foreign policy. Not incidentally, England might also be vastly enriched in the process.

This aim solidified into a scheme, its logic owing much to John Hawkins's earlier strategic musings, known as the First Enterprise.[52] A development of the plan previously reported by Mendoza, it proposed that a powerful squadron of English ships commanded by Drake should occupy Terceira in Dom António's name and remain there throughout 1581, poised to intercept the incoming plate fleets. Should Drake miss that profitable rendezvous, he was to sail to the Spanish Caribbean and plunder its coastal settlements.[53] Again, Leicester, supported by Walsingham and Drake, appears to have been the proposal's principal mover. If anything, it was even more provocative than his previous recommendations, but it had at least the threadbare imprimatur of Dom António's authority, with the Pretender's banner raised above the English ships that would implement it.

Elizabeth was extremely wary. She made her permission for the project contingent upon financial support from Henri III and the active participation of substantial French military forces; a putative alliance that effectively reversed the traditional bias of English foreign policy. Indeed, such was her fear of Spain's newly enhanced power that even the prospect of outright French sovereignty over the Low Countries (offered to Francis, duke of Anjou by the States-General in September 1580 and accepted by him four months later) no longer loomed as the catastrophe that English governments had sought for centuries to prevent. Henri III responded to her urgent advances with a promise of all the military assistance she could wish for – if she would first marry Anjou, her on-off suitor. Walsingham, sent hurriedly to France to argue for something – anything – short of matrimony, could not push the French King into accepting a more realistic arrangement. In August 1581, while this cumbersome diplomatic ballet proceeded, Philip succinctly and economically extinguished the last, faint spark of Elizabeth's enthusiasm for the First Enterprise. He informed her, via Mendoza, that any military support for Dom António, no matter how it was dressed, would bring war between England and Spain: 'This is so important that I need not urge it further upon you'. The threat, arriving with word of the marquis of Santa Cruz's annihilation of a Franco-Portuguese fleet in waters between the Azorean islands of Terceira and San Miguel, had a telling resonance. A few days later, discreet orders were sent to Southampton, where the ships and supplies for the enterprise had been expensively gathered, to sell off the expedition's stores, including a pristine set of Portuguese flags, for whatever price could be secured.[54]

Leicester and his associates had probably been expecting this. A 'Second Enterprise' had been mooted at the same time as the First, involving an

English expedition to Calicut to divert Portugal's spice traffic into English hands (though with some proportion of its profits reserved for Dom António). A relatively mild proposal, this, too, fell through when the ex-Prior of Crato, tired of English prevarications, refused to participate and went off to seek further French support. However, the spirit of the scheme appealed strongly to the Queen, Burghley and the mercantile elements, who, provisionally, had committed themselves to some form of enterprise. It was felt that a supportable distinction might be made between the possessions Spain had won by right of conquest and those she had inherited by the Union of Crowns. The Portuguese trade to the spice islands had been graphically exposed by Drake as one that did not enjoy, and could not enforce, a monopoly. Like the Guinea trade (Portugal's claims over which the Queen herself had lucidly deconstructed almost twenty years earlier),[55] it was no more than a barter arrangement between independent states, each of which had the freedom and right to treat with competitors, should they choose to do so. Philip may respond angrily to such interloping; he could hardly regard it as cause for war.

Significantly, however, it was Leicester who took charge of arrangements for this supposedly non-predatory scheme, and with some enthusiasm. He donated as his personal venture the largest ship in the fleet previously assembled for the abandoned First Enterprise, the *Galleon Oughtred* (built and still part-owned by the merchant Henry Oughtred and now re-named *Galleon Leicester*). Other major investors were Drake, Walsingham, Hatton, the earls of Pembroke and Shrewsbury, Lord Admiral Lincoln, Sir Thomas Heneage and Sir Edward Horsey, none of whom could be regarded as instinctive pacifists. The Muscovy Company had a significant investment also, however, and immediately busied itself in thwarting an expected coup that might substitute a more aggressive agenda. Its merchants, aided by Burghley (who appointed three of their number to supervise much of the organization of the voyage), were successful initially. The proposed commander of the voyage, the belligerent Martin Frobisher, was replaced by Edward Fenton, his former lieutenant in the north-west voyages. Furthermore, the final instructions for the expedition directed that the voyagers:

> neither going, tarying abroad, not returning, you doe spoile or take anything fro[m] any of then Queenes Maiesties friends or allies, or any christians, without paying iustly for [th]e same, nor that you use any maner of violence or force against any such, except in your owne defence ... deale altogether in this voiage like good and honest merchants, traffiquing

and exchanging ware for ware, with all curtesie to [th]e nations you shall deale with. . . .[56]

Such exhortations could be effective only if there was a will to obey them on the voyagers' part, and as subsequent events indicate, many of the officers who accompanied Fenton had about as much interest in dealing 'like good and honest merchants' as had their precursors in the *Barbara*. A number had accompanied Drake on his circumnavigation; more looked to that voyage as an exemplar for future English ventures. The merchant-factors who accompanied them were powerless to prevent the factiousness that overwhelmed the expedition once at sea. Had Fenton's weak and paranoid leadership, an incompetent, egomaniacal pilot and their near-permanently drunken mariners not brought its disintegration long before the English ships reached the Pacific, the impact upon Anglo-Spanish relations would have mirrored or even exceeded Drake's best efforts.[57]

Like the French naval attempt to seize the Azores for Dom António in the same year, the English response to the Union of the Crowns failed abjectly. Spain, faced by a militarily ineffectual England and prostrate France, appeared to be almost wholly ascendant. Only in the Netherlands did there seem to remain some opportunity to slow the progress of Spanish arms, yet during 1582 Farnese worked brilliantly upon the antipathy of Flemish population towards their newly elected 'sovereign' Anjou. By bribing key Walloon nobles with prodigious abandon and manipulating their fears of French domination, he secured their reluctant agreement to bringing Spanish troops back into the southern Provinces.[58] Early in the following year, Anjou's authority effectively collapsed following his abortive attempt to seize Antwerp. He fled, and a few months later ignominiously abandoned his Low Countries' ambitions entirely.

With the spice trade untouched, plate fleets unmolested and Elizabeth's on-off flirtation with Anjou soured by his military failures, diplomatic blunders and bottomless appetite for subsidies, the English government had little return upon its recent efforts. However, the impact of these failures upon already-worsening relations with Spain was not nearly as marked as that which followed the re-deployment of another instrument of English foreign policy – the privateer. Though baulking at the financial and political costs of providing substantive assistance to Dom António directly, the Queen had allowed her subjects to take up his commissions to harry the seaborne traffic of the 'usurper' Philip. Hundreds of Englishmen took advantage of this new sanction, led by their freebooting aristocracy. Drake, disappointed in his grander collaborations with Leicester, set out two vessels during 1582 under the Pretender's commission. Leicester himself set out the *Galleon Leicester* with his new partner Henry Oughtred, having obtained a commission as a prior condition of their investment in the abortive Moluccan voyage.[59] The enterprising Fenners, former Guinea freebooters, also put to sea in the *Galleon Fenner* under similar license and immediately assisted their sponsor's cause by targeting the vessels of his would-be subjects.[60] Meanwhile, the Hawkins dynasty used the Pretender's commission to resurrect one of its own cherished projects. The ageing but intrepid William Hawkins, sixty-three-year-old brother of John, received letters patent authorizing him to reconnoitre and trade upon the coasts of Africa and America.[61] It is likely that this referred to Portuguese possessions or trading areas which, like the Spice Islands, were now considered to be fair game for English interlopers. Yet as the record of Hawkins's voyage shows, a reprise of his brother's attempts to open up the Spanish colonial trade was a primary motive also. With a fleet of seven ships he called first at the Cape Verde island of Santiago, from which he was repulsed with many fatalities (the inhabitants suspected his ships of having been part of the now-extinct Franco-Portuguese fleet that had sacked their island in the previous year[62]). He touched upon the coast of Portuguese Brazil thereafter, but by the beginning of June 1583, he was pearl fishing at La Margarita off the Venezuelan coast. A little near-legitimate trade was conducted with colonists, though its meagre profits were overshadowed by that from the seizure of a Spanish ship, later reported missing from that year's *flota*. The author of the report, Mendoza, estimated Hawkins's total haul from his voyage to be worth some 800,000 crowns.[63]

Ostensibly, Elizabeth's sanctioning of Dom António's commissions was the traditional makeshift response of a cash-starved regime. Yet if it seemed little more than a reprise of her blessing upon earlier 'foreign' employments, when English privateers had served Condé and Coligny in the 1560s and William of Orange in the 1570s, this initiative had far greater potential to undermine Anglo-Spanish relations. The Union of the Crowns, and English reactions to it, effectively gave a global perspective to a European power struggle of formerly conventional characteristics. To Philip, the activities of Hawkins, Drake and Oxenham in the Spanish New World had been individualistic irruptions. While acutely provocative and costly to confound, sufficient ambiguity had remained regarding their relationship to official English policy to deflect the worst diplomatic consequences. From 1580, however, by permitting her subjects to serve the Portuguese Pretender, Elizabeth effectively thrust the sanctioned English privateer into the oceans, and in a manner that extended more than the geography of confrontation. Privateers sailing under Dom António's commissions were redressing, in effect, the Spanish King's confiscation of a nation and empire. How their spoils might be valued against such a monumental 'loss' was not touched upon by the English government: a lack of restraint that hinted at something very much like open-ended war against Spanish seaborne trade. In European waters, its immediate effect was to render inconsequential every official measure taken against organized English piracy since 1577. In a wider sense, Philip was being told that he could have the Treaty of Tordesillas or Portugal, but not both. It was a broad and very clear line drawn in the sand, even if not intended as such by the Queen who traced it.

This widening physical reach of English privateers seeded an even more portentous challenge to Philip's empire. Following William Hawkins's brief visit to his island in summer 1583, the governor of Puerto Rico had reported to Philip that the Englishmen's intention had been to seek out a suitable site for permanent settlement. The accusation was unfounded; but even as he wrote, English colonial ambitions, for years obscured by (and clogged in) the mire of Elizabeth's lunatic Irish 'policy', or disguised among the many motives that informed the typical English voyage of reconnaissance, were clarifying. In the previous year, Richard Hakluyt had published his *Divers Voyages*. An explicit urging of colonial plantation, it called upon past experience (Ribault's account of the French Florida colony), present anticipation (his cousin the elder Richard Hakluyt's notes on founding colonial settlements) and, most provocatively, a recollection of prior explorations to justify future English claims to North American soil. Within a year it was followed by Christopher Carleill's *Discourse* and Sir George Peckham's *True Reporte*, both of which provided a mixture of incentive and patriotic exhortation to would-be investors in English New World plantations.

The common inspiration for these works, Sir Humphrey Gilbert's 1578 letters patent, provided (among much else) that 'he . . . his heires and assignes and every or any of them shall have hould occupie and enjoye to him his heires and assignes and every of them forever all the soyle of such landes countries and territories soe to be discovered'.[64] Gilbert's intentions for his first voyage under this patent – an abortive 1578 expedition – were shrouded in ambiguity. He may have intended to attack Spanish possessions in the Caribbean, though a preliminary reconnaissance of regions in which a colony might be founded was equally likely. Most probably, he would have attempted both. By 1582, however, his aims had focused considerably. In the space of twelve months, he assigned a vast acreage of virgin North

American soil to his would-be colonists, including eight-and-a-half million acres to a group of Catholic investors – a potential solution to (and removal of) the recusant problem of which Walsingham was particularly support-ive.[65] At least two voyages were mooted for the following twelve months, to plant separate colonies of Englishmen in the ill-understood but inviting ter-ritories first reconnoitred by a Portuguese pilot, Simon Fernandez, during a brief but remarkable voyage in 1580.[66] Gilbert's death at sea, and Peckham's subsequent failure to attract sufficient support for his Catholic colony, ended this first phase of English plans for American settlement, but the torch was picked up immediately by Gilbert's energetic half-brother, Walter Ralegh.

As the Queen's rising favourite, Ralegh experienced little difficulty in securing backing for his enterprise. Only a few weeks following his acqui-sition of a preliminary patent in March 1584, he was able to despatch two ships, guided by the estimable Fernandez, to search out a suitable site for settlement. Marking a course to take them sufficiently north of Florida to prevent early Spanish interference, they sighted and explored the Carolina Banks in July.[67] The area was promising, but further investment was needed to plant a colony there. A remarkably vigorous effort was then launched to interest Englishmen in this new and inviting prospect. Recalled from Paris by Walsingham, Richard Hakluyt drafted his *Discourse of Western Planting* for the Queen's attention, specifically to urge her blessing upon the project (though its arguments were framed to promote any and all English colonial activity). Meanwhile, Ralegh presented a bill to parliament to have his rights to the newly discovered lands confirmed. The bill was withdrawn sub-sequently, but his project received much useful publicity in the process and secured the participation of Ralegh's cousin, Sir Richard Grenville (a member of the parliamentary committee that considered the bill) and Thomas Cavendish, MP for Shaftesbury and soon to be the second Englishman to circumnavigate the world.

The least momentous aspect of Ralegh's subsequent project, the succes-sive Roanoke colonies planted near Cape Hatteras on the Carolina Banks, was to be its utter failure. Conversely, the influence of this and other schemes upon Philip's eventual decision to attempt an invasion of England can hardly be overstated. The rationales and motives of the English planting movement grew directly from privateering activity, and this was apparent – perhaps too apparent – to the Spanish King.[68] Every snippet of information, gossip and hearsay reported from London by the industrious Mendoza strengthened his conviction that English intrusions into Spanish spheres of interest were becoming dangerously persistent. Some of these numerous intelligences – a scheme of Gilbert's to seize and fortify Cuba, the rumoured voyage under Martin Frobisher to follow Fenton into the Pacific, and the latter's reported intention to conquer the Spice Islands – were wholly inaccurate, but their impact was profound nevertheless.[69] As early as 1577 – the year in which Oxenham had proclaimed his intention to conquer the Panama Isthmus, Frobisher had been mining New World 'gold' in Baffin Island (and, ostensibly, seeking the elusive 'Strait of Anian' into the Pacific) and Drake had embarked upon his secretive but undoubtedly provocative voyage – Philip had begun to discern a web, rather than individual filigrees, of English ambitions for his possessions.[70] If there were some foundation to his suspicions, new English attempts to establish colonies in territories claimed by Spain (whether or not yet explored or exploited) would appear to be the culmination, rather than the genesis, of a trend. A successfully planted settlement, intended to support long-range privateering raids – as Spanish commentators unanimously assumed Ralegh's project to be – offered a frightening vision of a Spanish Empire sundered at will by men possessing the greatest of all incentives to pursue their trade energetically. And however much Philip misunderstood Elizabeth's own motives in permitting these plantation projects, those of her subjects who most energetically backed them were perfectly transparent. Within the doggerel verses that relieved the arguments of Peckham's *True Reporte* lay a strong hint (attributed to Sir William Pelham, Lieutenant of the Ordnance Office at the Tower) of what the Spanish King already suspected to be official English intent:

> Our forren neighbours bordering hard at hand,
> Have found it true, to many thousands gaine:
> And are enricht by this abounding land,
> While pent at home, like sluggards we remaine.
> But though they have, to satisfie their will
> Inough is left, our cofers yet to fill.[71]

If a starker warning were needed, Hakluyt and his sponsor Walsingham openly exulted at whose expense England would claim her place at the trough:

> Yf you touche him [Philip] in the Indies, you touche the apple of his eye, for take away his treasure which is his *nervus belli*, and which he hath almoste oute of his west Indies, his olde bandes of souldiers will

soone be disolved, his purposes defeated, his power and strength diminished, his pride abated, and his tyranie vtterly suppressed.[72]

The Queen had no intention of ruining Philip, but her own priorities neither drove nor limited the intentions of colonial propagandists. Portentously, their schemes provided rationales that drew together the diffuse strands of English maritime enterprise into intuitive proximity, rather than the brief, uneasy alliances that had underwritten previous projects. Colonization, it was proposed, would bring the Word of God – the true Word, not an abhorrent Roman variety – to indigenous peoples who would be natural allies in England's struggle against the oppressive ambitions of the Spaniard. To civilize rude cultures was not only virtuous, but economically advantageous. Men who wore loincloths had little use for merchandizes, but those who sought to emulate their wealthy masters would provide vast new markets for English goods. As the elder Richard Hakluyt, recalling Spain's spectacular example, reminded potential investors in the Virginia experiment, 'Trafficke easily followeth conquest'.[73] King Philip and the bankers who kept him solvent would be denied their treasure fleets, savages would find salvation and Englishmen would grow rich not only upon spoil but in the conduct of new, lawful trades. It was a profoundly attractive justification for empire, at the direct expense of an existing one.

All manifestations of a coordinated English colonial policy (however modest or unrealistic) were therefore intolerable to Philip. For decades, the Spanish Florida settlements had existed for the sole purpose of denying the North American coast to European interlopers intending such stratagems. Thus, 'Virginia', like the French Florida experiment some twenty years earlier, was a threat that the Spanish King neither would nor could allow to develop. Ignorance of the colony's exact location, and the developing pace of events elsewhere, prevented any immediate Spanish reaction, but the extermination of this first permanent English intrusion into North America was intended from the moment of its establishment.[74]

However, to deal piecemeal with this and any future settlements would be futile, if England were now embarked upon an expansionary programme. Philip may have been unaware of the venerable Arab observation 'a fool swat flies before the swamp is drained', but the message was self-evident. The more that Englishmen made forays into his empire, the clearer the only possible remedy became. He was wrong to believe that either these experiments or more forthright depredations against his possessions constituted any overall strategy of Elizabeth's government (no matter how much her more hawkish councillors may have wished it), but the consequences of that mis-understanding – and of her failure in turn to understand the potential impli-cations of her subjects' ambitions – brought a momentum that created facts from fears. As early as August 1583, Santa Cruz was urging his sovereign to capitalize upon the striking naval victory at Terceira with an invasion of England. Philip dismissed his plea, but nevertheless evinced some interest in a similar, Guise-led scheme by requesting strategic appraisals of the task both from Santa Cruz and Farnese. He also set himself to studying the history of domestic plots against Elizabeth.[75] For almost two years more he would waver, but each new word of English schemes for settlement would strengthen the logic expressed in the succinct, cold observation of the junta of Contaduría Mayor: 'the barbarous foreigners . . . spread themselves over the earth in search of rich and fertile lands where they can settle. It is greatly to be feared that so long as the queen is alive they may extend still further the plundering of the Indies.'[76]

Ironically, colonies did not excite Elizabeth nearly as much as they did the prophets of English 'plantation'. They promised much expenditure and poor returns for years following their establishment, and her patentees usually secured spectacular terms for their exploitation only because she had such little faith in their ultimate viability. These schemes, and the aggres-sive, shorter-term expeditions that occasionally provided spectacular gains for their investors, were to her useful, occasionally profitable but above all collateral devices to divert Philip from his remorseless campaign in the Low Countries and his growing interest in English recusants. She seems not to have been aware that to the Spanish King, English interference in the Seventeen Provinces, transatlantic raids against his possessions and attempts to found North American colonies were indistinguishable components of a single, growing threat – the rise of an aggressive Protestant state that appeared to be defining itself by resistance to legitimate Spanish interests. In that light, tentative colonial experiments and Elizabeth's other 'impeach-ments' were the cement that gradually strengthened Philip's resolve, after years of prevarication, to expunge the entirety of the problem.

As he allowed himself to be convinced by argument and circumstance, the Spanish King's responses in turn strengthened the arguments of those powerful Englishmen whose determination to seek a reckoning with Spain had been maturing for almost a decade. Among the cabal of Puritan sym-pathizers in the Privy Council, the strongest backer of the English planting movement was Walsingham: spymaster-general, near-victim of the St Bartholemew's Day slaughter and enthusiastic hounder of domestic papists.

Peckham, a staunch Catholic, called him 'my principall patron'. Hakluyt later dedicated the first edition of the *Principall Navigations* to him: 'whereas I acknowledge in all dutifull sort how honorably both by your letter and speech I haue bene animated in this and other my travels'.[77] Simon Fernandez, the Portuguese pilot whose skills had marked the path for English settlers, had been Walsingham's man before he was Gilbert's, and Christopher Carleill, who wrote his *Discourse* to sway cautious London merchants into backing the planting movement in the face of Spanish hostility, was his step-son.

Unlike his own mentor Burghley, who, for all his loathing of popery had long sought to avoid conflict with the dreaded 'conspyration' of ill-willed foreign princes, Walsingham had never believed in the possibility of recon-ciling Spanish rights with English ambitions (or vice versa). Almost from the moment he replaced Burghley as Elizabeth's principal secretary, his goal in Council was to persuade the Queen that the present peace was an ill-judged deferral of the inevitable. Any reservations he expressed regarding confrontation – and he rarely sounded a circumspect note – were grounded in matters of timing, not of principle. In 1571, even before his near-death encounter with a Guise-roused Parisian mob, he had written to his ally Leicester to justify the Queen's interference in the Low Countries: 'that she may (as heretofore she hath done) take profit of others troubles; for surely ... their peace will be the beginning of our wars'.[78] As Spain grew remorse-lessly more powerful, the logic of time and place reversed. Walsingham was one of the first of Elizabeth's councillors to argue that England's ability to resist Philip's ambitions was dissipating. His support of aggressive projects to confront Spain from 1580 was therefore motivated not only by a desire to 'impeach' Philip's advances (as Elizabeth and Burghley intended), but also to push the Spanish King into a reaction that would end all prevarication. His patronage of colonial projects was characteristic of this aim. An English New World counter-balance to Spain's economic power was of course a worthwhile goal in itself, but the more immediate attraction of overseas expansion lay in its potential to end forcibly the present state of dangerous equivocation.

To Walsingham and his like-minded colleagues, the years 1583–4 brought a further, fundamental shift in the possibilities and dangers facing the English nation. Overtly, both England and Spain drew back from direct confrontation. Elizabeth ordered the cancellation of commissions provided by Dom António to individual Englishmen, while the Spanish King, rejecting both Santa Cruz's urgings for a decisive move against England and the latest papal plans for a Catholic liberation of Scotland, confined his 'English' activities to permitting Mendoza to encourage the conspirator Frances Throckmorton in London. This apparent return to the low-level cold war tactics of more than a decade earlier was illusory, however. Though as yet uncommitted to a specific plan or timetable, Philip had come to believe that that an all-out war with England would be better fought than avoided – a reversal of his policy, occasional impulsive episodes aside, for a quarter of a century past. For her part, Elizabeth continued to hope that peace might somehow be maintained, but Walsingham and his peers were turning the English mind-set to the necessity of joining the Netherlander rebels in open war against their Habsburg master. In doing so, their efforts went far to fulfilling the prophecy. In 1584, the Queen's principal secretary of state not only broke Throckmorton's plot but accomplished the ejection of Mendoza and his embassy from England, brought Mary Stuart a significant step closer to the scaffold and, as previously noted, further impressed upon his compatriots the image of Catholicism as not only un-English but an engine of foreign-inspired subversion that must be confronted if the nation were to survive. The psychological preconditions for conflict, more dangerous than any single provocation, were falling into place.

As Spanish and English relations became more strained, the deaths of the duke of Anjou and William of Orange in the space of a single month during summer 1584 drove the final nail into the coffin of the 'ancient amity'. From a Spanish perspective, the events promised both short-term political advantage and near-disastrous implications for the future. With the Valois line now facing extinction upon the death of Henri III, the Bourbon, and Protestant, Henri of Navarre became heir-presumptive to the French throne. To Philip, this was an unthinkable inheritance. On the final day of 1584, the loose alliance of convenience that he and the Guisardes had maintained since 1577 was formalized in a secret compact, the Treaty of Joinville. Ostensibly, this committed Spain to supporting the Catholic League's struggle against Henri and his allies, but its wider effect was to slot the most viable military force in France into Spain's strategic resources and removed the possibility of a French check to Philip's pacification of the Low Countries. There, the assassination of William (at the prompting, if not the active connivance, of the Spanish King), and Farnese's remorselessly effective campaign of that year, were knife-thrusts at the heart of the rebel cause. Yet the very success of Habsburg policies, further unbalancing the strategic equilibrium in western Europe, re-invigorated the influence of those who argued that Philip's ambitions were escaping any pragmatic limitation. The States-

General were a full year from offering the sovereignty of the Low Countries to Elizabeth, but she was finally, reluctantly allowing herself to be persuaded that with the death of the great Stadtholder, only her overt assistance to the rebels could prevent Philip's definitive re-conquest of his Seventeen Provinces. Princely non-ambitions, the depredations of commoners and mutual misunderstandings regarding both had brought the monarchs of England and Spain to the brink of open war. The precipice now beckoned.

EIGHT

Failing Brinkmanship

Awake now, therefore, my countrymen; pluck up your spirits, ye that have courage in you: advance yourselves, which have so long lain in security.[1]

The eighteen-year conflict now recalled as the first Anglo-Spanish War commenced at eight o'clock in the morning of 14 September 1585, when Sir Francis Drake departed Plymouth with twenty-five ships (including two of the Queen's vessels), eight pinnaces and the implicit permission of his usually circumspect sovereign to intercept the *flotas* and despoil the cities of the Spanish Caribbean.[2] This was the first outright English aggression, but Elizabeth had cast her die a month earlier in signing the long-negotiated treaty of Nonsuch, by which she committed an army of some 7,400 men to the Low Countries to support the rebel Netherlanders' war against their own sovereign.[3] These measures undoubtedly represented a victory for those of her councillors who had long urged a more aggressive policy towards Spain. What is remarkable is that the Queen herself did not yet regard as exhausted her search for 'impeachments' that would not also be causes for war.

The chronology of cause and effect that brought Elizabeth to this point has been examined at great length, though much of the process remains elusive. Clearly, she made decisions prior to these commitments whose implications strongly hint at a growing acceptance that war was impending. It would be wrong, however, to regard each or any of them as firm tokens of intent, or to assume that the eventual nature of any project or undertaking reflected its original purpose. The aggressive schemes promoted by enterprising Englishmen during these years all required royal assent and/or material assistance; few were allowed to proceed without major alterations to serve the foreign policy or crisis management objective of the moment, and official involvement usually brought a strong dose of circumspection to the mix. Elizabeth's famously vacillatory nature, her hatred of anticipating unpleasant developments by her own actions, ensured that this was a less march than an often-confused drift to outright conflict with Spain.

These first overt challenges to Philip's sovereignty were, however, unequivocal. Despite her keen sense of self-preservation, the Queen agreed or acquiesced to actions that were almost incapable of providing returns commensurate with their risks. Drake's expedition offered some hope of plunder (hopefully of the magnitude that had marked his previous foray into the Spanish New World), but with the indelible seal of government approval upon a military adventure that could be interpreted only as a declaration of open war. England's official entry into the bog of the Low Countries' rebellion – without the Valois alliance that Elizabeth had long held to be a prerequisite of overt involvement – offered only an infinitely greater promise of the financial and political wounds that had marked her last European adventure, the French war of 1562–3.

These potentially fatal undertakings reflected a sea change in England's 'Spanish' policy. Even so, it is difficult to identify a single cataclysmic cause or event that made unavoidable what, previously, had been unthinkable. They seem rather to have been the end-consequence of fears, slowly intensifying, that opportunities to check Philip's ambitions were fading – of a sense of confrontation looming that might otherwise, and fatally, take place upon his terms alone. Following the death of William of Orange, Catherine de' Medici assiduously passed on her opinion, via the French ambassador in London, that the Spanish King would complete his subjection of the Low Countries in short order and turn upon France and England thereafter.[4] Already, revelations of the depth of Philip's involvement in the Throckmorton plot and its subsidiary Guise-led papal 'crusade' against England seemed to support this stark interpretation of his designs, and had excited a brief but intense war-scare during the early months of 1584. Hurriedly, Burghley drafted plans for the summoning of musters, the strengthening of defences at likely landing places (particularly those of Dover harbour), the readying of the navy, a stay upon large merchant ships in port and – a stark admission of Exchequer poverty – the calling of a new Parliament within two months.[5]

The state of the Navy Royal – England's only substantial means of defence – was of particular concern. The so-called Ellesmere survey, its findings presented in January 1584, concluded that a majority of the Queen's ships were 'in servisable state for eny sodaine service'.[6] The trouble was that there were not yet nearly enough of them. Following improvements to correct several years of relative neglect during the reign of Edward vi (a programme of restoration, ironically, that had been initiated at the urging of England's then king-consort, Philip), Elizabeth had inherited from her half-sister Mary a navy of some thirty-seven vessels. Of these, twenty-one had been identified as fully seaworthy in 1559.[7] A flurry of construction work and acquisitions during the early years of the new Queen's reign had added several vessels to the fleet (including four very large capital ships, known as the 'great ships of the Navy'), but more had been de-commissioned in the meantime owing to age and/or severe degeneration of their fabric.

Predictably thereafter, the pattern of financing for the navy tracked a succession of perceived foreign threats to the nation. The hiatus in activity in the mid-1560s reflected the disappearance of an effective French navy, and absence, as yet, of a significant Spanish equivalent capable of operating offensively outside the Mediterranean. The diplomatic crises of 1568–72 encouraged a new spate of construction, some purchases of private vessels converted for naval use and 'bounty' payments to private citizens building merchant ships in excess of 100 tons, though during the same years further de-commissioning of older vessels took place.[8] Again, this process slowed following the Treaty of Bristol in 1574 and resumption of reasonably steady relations with Spain. From 1577 rising tensions once more concentrated minds, but principally upon a programme of repair and updating of older-fashioned vessels, rather than major acquisitions or new construction. By the time of the Ellesmere survey the strength of the navy remained at the twenty-four ships established as the optimum 'proportion' as long ago as 1559.[9] The debate upon what might be considered a sufficient shield in that year, however, could hardly have anticipated an enemy wielding the combined naval strengths of Spain and Portugal. With only some fifteen capital ships of more than 250 tons burden, the Navy Royal was not yet nearly in proper condition to meet a threat of that magnitude.

Insofar as there was any consistency in English policy during the months following the 1584 survey, it was driven by government's understanding of its present military incapacity. In June, John Hawkins presented yet another of the strategic plans he had come to regard as his gifts to the nation. It proposed a coordinated privateering war against Philip's plate and fishing fleets in which Huguenot and Dutch ships would join their English counter-parts, with concurrent efforts to encourage revolts in the Portuguese colonies acquired by Spain in 1580. The plan was wide-ranging in its ambitions – at least one modern commentator has commented upon its boldness – yet its most notable characteristic was a strong element of circumspection (by now Hawkins was fully attuned, or resigned, to his monarch's sensitivies).[10] It relied not upon official commitment of ships and men, but the resources of enthusiastic individuals who would set out their own vessels under com-missions issued by Dom António – again, with the express purpose of dis-inclining Philip to regard this as an English aggression. In effect, Hawkins was arguing for more of what had failed so far to interrupt Spain's New World traffic in the slightest degree. While his scheme recognized present English weaknesses and in part sought to address them ('Our own people, as gunners (of which we have but few) would be made expert, and grow in number . . . our idle people would growe to be goode men of war, bothe by land and sea'), its deeper significance lay not in any short-term practical merit but in the unwitting acknowledgement that the Elizabethan state would never have the resources to manage an offensive war without heavy private commitment.[11]

Philip's stark warning to Elizabeth of August 1581 remained sufficiently clear to make the implementation of Hawkins's proposal unlikely.[12] However, the near-collapse of rebel resistance in the face of Farnese's advances (his seizure of almost all the ports on the Flemish coast was par-ticularly menacing to English observers) and William of Orange's shocking, untimely death reinforced the sense of imminent catastrophe. Holding strategies that relied upon illicit alliances with pretenders or *cimarrones* in New World adventures were not likely to halt a momentum that had brought Spain, and militant Catholicism, to the brink of European domi-nation. On 10 October 1584, Elizabeth's councillors assembled in an historic conference. Its purpose, outlined by Burghley in a typically comprehensive discussion document, was to re-examine the fundamental relationship between England and the Netherlander rebels, and, by inference, their overlord. Amidst the unswervingly pessimistic assessments of the nation's present readiness that emerged from the day's discussions, one explicit con-clusion – long argued by Walsingham and rejected by the Queen – stood out prominently: that it would be wiser to fight a war with the rebels as useful allies, rather than await their extermination and stand alone there-after: 'if her Majesty shall not take them into her defence, then what shall she do or provide for her own surety against the King of Spain's malice and forces, which he shall offer against this realm, when he hath subdued Holland and Zeeland?'[13]

The question introduced an element of immediacy into their counsels, given that Philip's foremost general was now at the gates of Antwerp, poised to complete the pacification of the southern Provinces. However, the minuted decisions of the meeting indicate that the process of committing English aid to the rebels was to be a slow one, and demand much of its recipients. It was concluded that the States should seek French military assistance in the first instance, and ask for overt English support only if this did not materialize. In the latter eventuality they were to present their requirements to Elizabeth, but if an English army were to be committed thereafter the rebels were to relinquish the ports of Flushing, Brielle and Middelburg (the 'cautionary towns') as security for its campaign expenses. They were also to provide a detailed schedule of what financial and military resources each rebel province would contribute to the conflict. If the 'hawks' in Council had won their argument on 10 October, the hands of the Queen and her Lord Treasurer nevertheless lay heavily upon the outcome.

The only other commitment arising from these deliberations was ostensibly timelier. Tentatively, Elizabeth authorized a project to exploit Drake's previous visit to the Moluccas, though upon a scale far exceeding both his 1577–80 voyage and Fenton's farcical follow-up. This (or a similar) proposal was first made some months earlier (Hawkins referred to it in his July missive, when he suggested that the voyage might shelter beneath Dom António's obliging writ), but details of the intended project were committed to paper only in November 1584. Endorsed as 'The charge of the navy of the Moluccas', the plan anticipated a fleet of fifteen ships and barks with twenty pinnaces costing some £40,000 to set forth.[14] The Queen was named as the leading investor, with Leicester, Drake, Sir Christopher Hatton and the Hawkins and Ralegh brothers contributing smaller amounts. Others may have been involved, but no mercantile interests were stated explicitly; nor, apparently, was provision made for the expedition to carry goods to trade for spices or other commodities. This, and plans for a significant complement of soldiers to accompany the voyage, has inclined some commentators to regard the project as intending widespread depredations or even conquest.[15] This may have been the case, though there is no way of knowing whether the schedule was a preliminary draft, a fragmentary summary of a broader scheme or merely one of several proposals then under consideration. What is clear, however, is that the project in any form represented a dangerous escalation in English provocations. Part of the Queen's investment was to consist of naval vessels to carry the expedition, which would have made her collusion glaringly obvious to Philip. Acutely aware of this, Elizabeth did not allow the scheme to proceed further in the months that followed her initial disbursements to Drake.

Nevertheless, the signals coming from her court were no longer as ambiguous as formerly. On 18 December, Ralegh's plantation bill had its third reading and was passed by the Commons. The following day it went to the Lords.[16] On 6 January, Elizabeth knighted him, and, some weeks later, presented him with his patent as Governor and Lord of 'Virginia' (his name for the territories to be settled). This sealed also her own commitment, for the first time, to challenge overtly Spain's claims for sole rights over the New World's bounty. The fleet that Ralegh assembled to take possession of his new lands was not such as to avoid or otherwise disguise this fateful confrontation. Under the overall command of Richard Grenville, its seven ships, carrying some three hundred soldiers, departed Plymouth on 9 April. Rather than making directly for 'Virginia', the ships set a course for Puerto Rico, where Grenville laid out and strongly fortified an encampment: 'with trenches, huts erected and a smithy; and all in as great perfection as though they had purposed to remain there ten years' as the governor there reported to Philip.[17] Before leaving the island, Grenville seized two Spanish ships and sold them back to local colonists. Moving on to Hispaniola, he traded amicably with the population of the town of Isabella, purchasing many commodities for the Virginia colony before being entertained with a feast and a bullfight. By mid-June, the expedition had reached Roanoke Island. The colony was established, a fortress constructed, and during the expedition's return passage a rich prize was seized off Bermuda: a ship that had become separated from that year's *flota*. The project had not only fulfilled its principal initial objective but generated an early profit for Ralegh's investors.[18]

In October, Grenville's ships returned from the New World to a new world. An English army stood upon the soil of Spain (if very briefly), while the vanguard of another awaited reinforcements at Middelburg before marching out in defence of the Netherlander rebels (though Antwerp, the city they had been despatched to preserve from the King of Spain's 'malice and forces', had already fallen to Farnese's army). Long-term equivocation in English government had ended. Given the impetus of events that amplified the boot-tread of approaching Spanish *tercios* Elizabeth and her councillors now anticipated the confrontation that English foreign policy had worked for decades to avoid.

By 22 March 1585 (some three weeks before Grenville's expedition departed Plymouth), Walsingham had received word of the supposedly secret Treaty of Joinville.[19] Though no one in England was yet aware of its provisions (none of which hinted, in fact, at any 'English' ambitions), it was obvious that the two most militarily effective powers inimical to the reformed religion were now in firm alliance. Rumours had also been reaching England since the previous autumn that Philip planned a new, overtly Spanish-led invasion of Ireland, for which the fruits of his three-year galleon-building programme were ear-marked.[20] English fears of foreign interventions were already roused, therefore, when, on 8 June, the ship *Primrose* came into London, bringing a captive Spanish official and word that Philip had ordered the seizure of all foreign vessels in Iberian ports. The *Primrose* had been the only English ship to escape the embargo, fighting her way out of the port of Portugalete on the Basque coast. The official and his three assistants, seized by her crew while attempting to detain her, carried with them a copy of the *cédula* authorizing their action. The episode, and ambiguous information gleaned during the interrogation of the captured Spaniards (none of whom were remotely privy to their King's intentions), added significantly to existing English anxieties.

Philip's embargo has been regarded by some historians as a defining moment in the slide to war.[21] The same commentators have assumed – as did contemporary Englishmen – that it had been imposed to secure sufficient shipping to attempt an invasion of the rebel provinces, followed by a descent upon England. This was not the case, although the Spanish King's precise motives are still not entirely clear. Equally strong arguments have been made to suggest that he was attempting to strangle the rebels' seaborne trade at its Spanish terminus and starve them into quiescence, or that he was securing sufficient shipping to meet Drake's expected attempt on the *flotas* (intelligence regarding the assembling expedition had reached Madrid during March).[22] It may be that the inclusion of English vessels in the embargo was partly a response to Elizabeth's stay upon English trade with the Low Countries, imposed in April to impede the stream of supplies to Farnese's army. What is incontrovertible is that the seizures generated repercussions out of all proportion to any short-term advantage derived by Philip. Anglo-Spanish merchants – perhaps his last group of friends in England – were particularly incensed by the assault upon their trade. For years their community had suffered increasingly onerous attention from the Holy Office, whose criteria for imposing the most severe penalties appeared to be growing ever more arbitrary.[23] This, undoubtedly, had loosened loyalties to their host (though by now such treatment was regarded as almost an immutable a condition of trading with Spain as her customs duties), but the impact of the new embargo far eclipsed that of mere religious persecution. In May 1585, ninety-two of their vessels lay in Spanish ports, many at the express invitation of the King, with cargoes of English wheat to make good the shortfall from poor harvests in the previous year.[24] All save the intrepid *Primrose* were impounded, their factors and sailors imprisoned, and, in some cases where 'evidence' of heretical impulses was discovered, handed over to the Inquisition. The claims their owners made for redress were enormous (if almost certainly exaggerated), with London merchants alone reporting losses to the value of £39,100 in vessels and cargoes.[25]

The Admiralty Court readily obliged their pleas. Letters of reprisal were drafted, and while the Privy Council issued regulations governing their writ, it appears that all petitioners, whether victim or entrepreneur sensing a rare business opportunity, were required only to give an oath, rather than proof, regarding prior losses.[26] The seas were soon full of voluntaries (though at least one group of shipowners, the Fenner family, must have been considerably irritated by the timing of this development; their principal privateer, *Galleon Fenner*, suspected of being employed 'pirateously', had been seized by Admiralty officials only days before the flood of new licences ended any official efforts to deter privateers).[27] From Paris on 22 September, Elizabeth's cousin and ambassador Sir Edward Stafford passed on a note from Mendoza that calculated that twenty-seven major ships had been taken by English privateers in less than two months.[28] The tally might have been higher had not the Queen followed her Low Countries' embargo with a stay upon Spanish shipping resting in English ports, which, with the earlier restraint, largely removed Spanish and Flemish vessels from England's coastal waters.

The licensing of voluntaries in June 1585 marked a watershed in the history of the sixteenth-century English privateer. The traditional trade-off between the need for cheap, swiftly organized naval resources and the protracted diplomatic problems they created had defined successive English governments' maritime policies. The marked increase in the incidence, scale and daring of depredations since the 1540s had been met by sporadic official attempts to slow or reverse the trend, though never to extinguish it. The results had been predictable. By 1584, even the partisan Richard Hakluyt was obliged to admit, if tacitly, the justice of hundreds of foreign complaints against his countrymen: 'wee . . . are moste infamous for our outeragious, common, and daily piracies', and proposed that the diversion of their energies would be a principal advantage of a vigorous English colonial programme.[29]

From June 1585, however, all such criticisms and concerns became irrelevant. When the Court of Admiralty issued letters of reprisal in that month, it did so to a nation, not a profession. To the names of such privateering dynasties as Hawkins, Drake, Vaughan, Killigrew and Fenner were joined those of great mercantile families – Cordell, Watts, Smith, Pullison and Stokes – whose wealth had been built upon lawful trade with the regions that were now being denied by embargo and seizure. Possessing the resources to set out greater squadrons than their compatriots had yet envisaged, they became not so much an auxiliary resource with which to reinforce the Navy Royal as its private arm. Gradually, former Anglo-Spanish merchants would assume the role of predominant persecutors of that trade to which they had formerly devoted their professional lives.[30] At the same time, their impact on the rebalancing of England's traditional overseas trade was immense. The export of half-finished English cloths continued (albeit with significant interruptions), but a growing proportion of the luxury comestibles and manufactured goods for which previously they had been exchanged were now brought home in the holds of captured foreign vessels. In the first two-and-a-half years of unrestricted English privateering activity, it was estimated by one impartial observer that losses to a value of some six million ducats were suffered by Spanish merchantmen at the hands of English freebooters.[31] Iberian merchant fleets would shrink to near-extinction in the face of this massive assault upon their trade and fabric; those of England would expand enormously. A nation that had been the backward producer of half-finished goods was to become a re-exporter of high-value products at the direct expense of its enemy. England was not yet able to win far-flung wars, but her more enterprising subjects could make them pay for themselves.

There were casualties, of course. It was inevitable that as the number of English privateers upon the seas increased dramatically, so too did occasions upon which their liberal interpretation of 'enemy' cargoes generated fury among England's remaining friends. Merchants of the Hanse towns, Denmark, the rebel Low Countries and northern France were to fill the Admiralty Court with pleas for restitution of stolen wares for years to come. Given the best will of government (and from May 1585 the system was presided over by Charles Howard, the most enthusiastic privateering Lord Admiral since the days of Thomas Seymour), there was no possibility of satisfying more than a small minority of these appellants. In the turmoil of war, furthermore, what actually constituted justice was by no means readily apparent. The continuing trade, including that in war materials, between many Dutch merchants and their Spanish persecutors, and of Catholic and

Protestant Frenchmen who often collaborated to transport their wares in the same vessels, ensured that the 'colour' of prize cargoes was often a dull grey.[32] Nor were English privateers alone on the seas. As the Anglo-Spanish war crawled on, the cargoes of English merchants in turn would become ever more vulnerable to the Catholic privateers of Dunkirk and northern France (and to 'friendly' Sea Beggars and Huguenots), and the justice they received in foreign courts was for the most part no better than that which the Admiralty Court dispensed. Nevertheless, the activities of English privateers – among them, investing or participating directly, almost all of Elizabeth's principal seamen and courtiers – became the main business of a generation of European envoys to Elizabeth's court.[33] Their indiscrimination generated its own momentum of counter-reprisal, strengthening the already firm domestic conviction that England stood alone against the world and enriching some Englishmen while beggaring many others. The endemic problems of privateering did not disappear after 1585; they merely lost themselves in the fortunate maelstrom of a war that sucked in the greater part of western Europe.

Another casualty of outright conflict between England and Spain was the embryonic English colonial movement. A few visionaries continued to argue for plantations that in time would bring into being a British empire; but the commercial justifications put forward by Gilbert, Halkuyt, Ralegh and others paled before the present opportunities for plunder. Walsingham, the colonialists' greatest friend in government, finally had a war against Catholic Europe and lost any real enthusiasm for planting his recusants abroad. Ralegh's personal commitment to his pet project ensured that the Roanoke experiment would stagger on, but it is significant that following the disappearance of his second colony sometime during 1588, the next English attempts to establish permanent settlements in the New World would occur only in the next century, following the conclusion of peace with Spain.

Yet as profound as the implications of the June proclamation would prove, it was not, nor was it intended to be, a particularly innovatory measure. The issuing of letters of reprisal was a traditional, and expected, first response to a foreign embargo. But to a government that had little intelligence regarding Philip's true intentions, his seizure of English shipping in May 1585 seemed far more threatening than the economic spats that such actions usually presaged. In the first flush of this acute anxiety, the now-venerable warnings of a Catholic world-conspiracy from Elizabeth's 'hawks' acquired a telling credibility. Still brooding upon the Treaty of Joinville, Walsingham in particular was gloomily triumphant: 'This late arrest . . .

cannot but be interpretid as a manifest argument of secreat intelligence and mutual concurrency lykely to be betwin the French and the Spaniard for the ruyne and ouerthrow of the professours of the Ghospell'.[34] Moved by their fears (if for her throne, rather their brand of religion), the Queen provisionally agreed to a swathe of aggressive measures. On 20 June, at Walsingham's suggestion, she provided a commission to Drake's cousin, Bernard, who had been outfitting a supply expedition for the Roanoke colony, to seek out and seize as many vessels of the Spanish Newfoundland fishing fleet as possible – a task he performed with great enthusiasm and success.[35] Far more portentously, she agreed also to resurrect Drake's project, moribund since the early part of the year. This was not, however, to be the Moluccan voyage mooted originally. Shrouded in ambiguity (Elizabeth's correspondence referred only to 'special service to be by him executed'), his new orders were never to be explicitly stated, even years later.[36] As always, this vagueness was intended to allow government to mitigate its involvement in whatever overtly aggressive acts the expedition might perpetrate, or at least to claim that Drake had exceeded his brief. Yet the time for such obfuscations had passed, whatever the Queen believed.

On 14 September 1585, after much prevarication on Elizabeth's part, Drake sailed from Plymouth with an expedition whose heterogeneity graphically confirmed that it was a regime, not an enterprising freebooter, that now made war upon the Spanish empire. Walsingham's step-son Christopher Carleill commanded a ship; the Treasurer of the Household's son and namesake, Francis Knollys (also Leicester's brother-in-law) was Drake's rear-admiral. Sir William Winter, surveyor of the Queen ships, provided both a son and a ship, the *Sea Dragon*; while Lord Admiral Howard and the earl of Shrewsbury sent their ships (*White Lion* and *Bark Talbot* respectively) but kept their sons at home. Leicester provided his *Galleon Leicester*, only slightly less powerful a warship than Drake's flagship, *Elizabeth Bonaventure*. Martin Frobisher, temporarily out of pocket for ships but keen to reverse his declining fortunes, sailed as the expedition's vice admiral in the redoubtable *Primrose*. His wealthier colleague, John Hawkins, was too busy upgrading the Navy Royal to adventure his person in the expedition, but he and his family provided six vessels (if we include an apparent part-stake in the *Primrose*).[37] Whatever limiting orders these men took with them, there could be little doubt in the Spanish King's mind that they sailed with the wholehearted blessing and support of their mistress.

The voyage proved to be a freebooting effort upon a massive scale, its aim to plunder Spain's bullion lifeline as it crossed the Atlantic or gathered at its New World marshalling points. Its secondary, complementary objectives were the hindrance of Philip's ability to finance his Low Countries' war and the strengthening in turn of England's resources to ease a looming commitment that the Queen, Burghley and everyone else in government expected to be expensive.[38] Some weeks before Drake sailed, a delegation from the States of Holland and Zeeland arrived in England to negotiate the terms of England's assistance for their cause. Even more so than Elizabeth's newly belligerent naval policy, her defensive pact with Philip's subjects had massive implications. Clearly, both she and her government appreciated this. There was no alternative claim for sovereignty – *pace* the obliging Dom António – upon which English interference in the Low Countries might be justified. By standards that the Queen no less than Philip held to be inalienable, the rebel's government was a war-council of renegades whose rebellion, however validated by circumstance, struck at the roots of political, even social, order. Yet on 12 August, several days after she had heard of Philip's release of all English ships in his ports, Elizabeth proceeded to sign the heads of treaty with the States' representatives. It is obvious, therefore, that she had committed herself to providing overt English assistance even before the Spanish embargo was imposed – as early as March, in fact, when Henri III, cowed by the threat of Joinville, had informed her that he would neither authorize nor support any further Low Countries' adventures.

Three months after concluding the Treaty of Nonsuch, Elizabeth's formal defence of her actions – 'A Declaration of the causes moving the Queene of England to give aid to the defence . . . of the Lowe Countries' – would be published simultaneously in England, France, Italy and the rebel provinces of the Low Countries. It was a history – as she saw it – of her involvement in the quarrel to date, a catalogue of Spanish plots against her person and a manifestation of Philip's failures in his duties as the rebels' sovereign lord. Once more, she declared herself a disinterested party, anxious only for a return to an imaginary golden age in which the citizens of the Low Countries would enjoy the religious freedom and ancient liberties that a distant, weak sovereign authority had engendered.[39] In other words (the implication was not subtle), she intended to save Philip from the consequences of his own bad overlordship.

The moment marked the final abandonment of Elizabeth's heartfelt aim of distancing herself from European entanglements. For years, she had dispensed small parcels of aid to Netherlander rebels without allowing herself to be clutched by the hands that snatched at them, and had taken much advice on the perils of any greater involvement.[40] As the rebel cause faltered before Farnese's remorseless campaigns, however, her government's trepidation grew to the point at which any eventuality, no matter how unthinkable a few years earlier, had to be considered. How far the debate had moved may be gauged from the tenor of Burghley's final briefing-paper prior to Nonsuch. The past master of constructive non-engagement had reached the extremity of counselling strongly against the Queen accepting the rebels' offer of outright sovereignty over their provinces – a gift that would have represented a de facto English annexation of Philip's territories:

> The perpetuall quarrell w[hi]ch Soveraignetie will breede betwene the Crowne of England and the pretended heires of the howse of Burgondie, which maye bee the rate of longe bloudie warres: whereas Protection draweth on but a warre determinable: . . . by the death of the K. of Spaine euerie daye looked for . . . by some amiable compossition: or . . . by an honorable victorie.[41]

If the Lord Treasurer put an over-optimistic case for the fruits of protectorship, it was only because it represented the lesser of several evils he had sought to avoid for two decades past. In fact, England's intervention in the Low Countries during the next two years was to incite a situation very much akin to that feared 'perpetuall quarrell', with or without the Queen's acceptance of sovereignty. It would prove also to be a model of ineptitude. Direct English assistance to the rebels, whether in the form of grudgingly given subsidies, ad hoc volunteer arrangements or the despatch of small armies, was never sufficient to impede Spanish military operations nearly as effectively as they demolished Philip's final reservations regarding an early assault upon England, and Leicester's campaign represented the nadir of even this pale record. Though of less than a year's duration, it went far to vindicate the alleged alternative strategy of a member of the Council (possibly Burghley himself, in a last-ditch attempt to stave off the inevitable), who suggested it might be more prudent to remain out of the Low Countries altogether, commit the saved resources to the Navy Royal and trained bands and make England effectively impregnable to Spanish attack.[42]

Despite his principal role in forging an open alliance with the rebels, Leicester's own martial experience had commenced and ended at the battle of St Quentin almost thirty years earlier (during which his brother Henry's valiant death had redeemed the stain of their father's treasons).[43] In 1585, the earl's only qualifications for command were his name – an effective recruitment device – and a purse hopefully deep enough to absorb the expected failure of Elizabeth to pay her soldiers before they starved. Prior to his arrival in the Low Countries he enjoyed a popular reputation among the rebels, but his regal behaviour once among them, and his partisan support of Calvinist elements against the broader-based 'Orangists', ensured that an alliance cemented by the deepest need would come close to dissolving into factiousness and mutual recrimination. The lack of any clear timetable of intervention, or explicit goals for which the English forces were being committed, made his task one that even a far more talented commander could not have discharged successfully. True to her nature, the Queen allowed him too much discretion, and then, following his unauthorized acceptance of sovereignty on her behalf, none whatsoever.[44] Forced thereafter to rely upon instructions that, if they arrived at all, usually contradicted those immediately preceding them, Leicester's main efforts were devoted to recovering his sovereign's favour in the face of Court intrigues and self-inflicted checks, and to wresting sufficient funds to keep his army in being. The latter problem was particularly acute. On the rare occasions when Exchequer funds were provided in a remotely timely manner, the earl himself embezzled a fair proportion to cover his increasingly parlous finances while his captains cheerfully stole much of what remained. At the end of this inglorious chain of fraud and duplicity, the common soldiers soon resembled scarecrows, and either threatened loudly to emulate their mutinous Spanish counterparts or held their tongues and deserted in droves.[45]

Nor were the expertise and opinions of the earl's professional subordinates of much practical value, given his aversion to heeding the advice of his social inferiors. His entourage was a court-in-exile, not a military administration; his army – even unfed – was usually willing enough to fight but remained archaic in equipment, tactics and organization. Under the circumstances, it is a miracle that some military action occurred, and even with the presence of several competent senior soldiers – Willoughby, Norreys, Sackville – the English forces managed only to slow the rate of Farnese's advance marginally. Antwerp had surrendered eleven days before the first tranche of the relieving force (2,500 men under Norreys) disembarked at Middelburg in August 1585. Thereafter, a series of inconclusive skirmishes punctuated a sporadic campaign, few of them nearly so bloody as the confrontations between the English commanders themselves. Only at Zutphen, a year hence, would the embryonic English army find glory, if at the cost of one of England's finest minds, and, indirectly, the slow decline and deaths of two of her leaders.[46] Even this limited victory was to prove ephemeral. Five months after Spanish forces evacuated the area, starving, unpaid troops under Sir William Stanley and Rowland Yorke – respectively, Leicester's appointees as governors of the liberated strongholds of Deventer and Zutphen – would betray the towns to Farnese (by now duke of Parma) for cash and supplies.

They at least would see some form of profit. The burden of all this upon the Exchequer, in contrast, was crippling. About half of the Queen's ordinary revenues disappeared into the maw of her Low Countries' commitment in each of the three years prior to the Armada campaign. After an initial alarm, Parma probably regarded Elizabeth's descent into the morass as tactically useful. With devastating understatement, he wrote to his master 'she is . . . by no means fond of expense', and surmised that the experience might well swiftly induce war-weariness in England. This was a rare flash of over-optimism on his part, but in other ways English intervention was of considerable political value to Philip (even if he was unable fully to appreciate the favour). The incursion provided him with the first substantial justification for any future 'enterprise of England', diverted much-needed funds from where they may have bought substantial benefits – the English navy – and, as shall be discussed, placed great financial pressures upon the government at a time when the threat of domestic disorder was higher than at any time since the 1550s.[47] Unlike Drake's West Indies raid (which, though ultimately unprofitable, dealt a heavy blow to the Spanish King's prestige), Leicester's campaign was almost uniformly damaging to English interests.

During the fateful year 1585, Elizabeth's government had responded with uncharacteristic decisiveness to what had been seen as a gathering threat to England in particular and to the reformed faith in general. However, the measures authorized by the Queen, driven by a mistaken perception of the imminence of that threat, were neither proportionate nor well-judged. Fear that time was on the side of her enemy encouraged a reaction that made conflict far more likely, in that its principal effect was to strengthen Philip's determination to seek confrontation. His involvement in the Throckmorton plot and his assumed implication in the assassination of William of Orange had genuinely alarmed Elizabeth and her councillors, but the logic underpinning their chosen responses remains elusive. The crisis of the rebel cause in the Low Countries following the death of Orange demanded that England provide more substantial support than previously, yet the commitment of an army, modest in size yet far too large to be other than an outright challenge to Philip's sovereignty, utterly confounded the Queen's long-proclaimed intention of reconciling rebels with ruler. And while the Treaty of Joinville had opened up a new prospect of the perennially feared

Catholic crusade against Protestantism, there was little sound reason to encourage a decisive confrontation in 1585. The most immediate source of contention – the May embargo – had been resolved before the Queen decided to allow Drake's expedition and the Low Countries' campaign to proceed. Yet with the former she legitimized large-scale depredations against a nation with which she was not, in her own mind, at war. With the latter, she became fully embroiled in a conflict whose resolution lay far beyond her power to effect.

Elizabeth's more aggressive councillors took it for granted that Philip intended, and had intended for some years past, to turn upon England once the Low Countries were subdued. It was perhaps the fundamental assumption in the interventionists' argument. However, the logic that proclaimed 'their peace will be the beginning of our wars' managed both to overestimate Philip's strategic lucidity and dangerously discount the development of his resources in recent years. With the long-term Ottoman threat to his Mediterranean possessions in abeyance, and his acquisition of a much enlarged fleet (partly inherited but supplemented by an energetic building programme), there was no reason to believe that the Spanish King was bound to frame his English policy as circumspectly as in previous years.[48] All hinged upon his perception of what was expedient. By the summer of 1585, the rebellious northern provinces of his Low Countries seemed to be upon the threshold of defeat – one that would be definitive, it was felt increasingly in the Escorial, if England could be removed from the equation. It is clear, therefore, how far Whitehall was pushing policy in Madrid during these months. As late as August, Philip rejected yet another plea from the pope that he initiate an English enterprise, arguing that such a project would be both unconscionably expensive and lacking in reality. Two months later, however, an English army had arrived at Middelburg and Drake had descended upon Spain's Galician coast, prior to sweeping out into the Atlantic to attack the precious economic lifeline that kept the Spanish King's armies in the field. Philip had no clear understanding of Elizabeth's goals (her own councillors were not significantly more enlightened), but evidently, the time and lee-way for measured responses was past. On 24 October (NS) he wrote to Sixtus, finally committing his own resources to assist the Holy See's ambitions for the recovery of England.[49] Far from slowing, diverting or confounding his plans for an English 'solution', the policies long urged by Walsingham, Leicester, Hatton and others were the catalyst that triggered them.

Having made the commitment, however, there was little that the Spanish King could achieve in the short term. The coasts of Spain herself could not be defended adequately against Drake's attentions, much less the plate fleets upon whose cargoes the financing of any 'enterprise of England' would depend utterly. Moreover, the swarm of English privateers released under commission in the previous June were now ranging far more widely than the Channel and Western Approaches. Outraged Anglo-Spanish merchants provided funds and shipping for Drake's expedition, but they also equipped their own vessels to return to the Spanish coast to despoil those of their former trading partners. None of these incursions was major, initially; at most, two or three vessels sailed in consortship together, though their numbers were significant in total. Yet against even these scattered forces Philip had no effective response, until the disaster of the armada campaign necessitated an urgent (and massively expensive) reorganization of his convoy system. Nor could he provide much comfort to the cities of Santo Domingo and Cartagena, seized and sacked by Drake for the promise – illusory as it would prove – of their fabulous wealth, or to the fort of San Augustin, destroyed by the same English forces for the safeguard of the English Virginia plantation. All these depredations, word of which spread sensationally through a Europe starved of news of Spanish reverses, could be met only by silent promises of future redress.

Drake's fleet returned to England in July 1586. His nation was Protestant still, its shores not defiled by Spanish or Guisarde boot, nor polluted by the bishop of Rome's 'malignant Synagogues of Satan'.[50] In the Low Countries, Leicester's campaign had not succeeded in souring Parma's fortunes appreciably, but neither had it brought the duke's wrath down upon the English army, much less upon England herself. To the extent that Elizabeth had provided a momentary check to Spanish advances, it appeared as though her gamble had succeeded. Yet news from Europe was unsettling. Since the previous December, rumours of gathering Spanish preparations against England had circulated at Court, 'givinge some hot alarme, but forgotten in a day or two, after the olde manner' as the new Lord Admiral, Charles Howard, complained to Leicester.[51] These, and the occasional Spanish 'brag', reporting claims of mighty fleets being assembled at Lisbon and Cadiz, were hardly reliable intelligence. However, in April, owing to the efforts of Sir Anthony Standen, Walsingham's agent at the court of the Grand Duke of Tuscany, the Queen received a copy of a disturbing document just weeks after Philip himself read it.[52] This was the marquis of Santa Cruz's invasion plan, envisaging a colossal seaborne assault that the English Navy Royal, even with its merchantman levies, would have been ill-equipped to prevent.

Santa Cruz's proposals were brutally realistic of the task. He envisaged a campaign launched directly from Spain, rather than relying upon a fortuitous conjunction of an invasion fleet and Spanish forces based in the Low Countries. Two hundred and six warships would escort and protect an army of more than sixty thousand men, carried in a vast assortment of craft (including two hundred landing-barges). Yet even this mighty host would not risk a direct descent upon England, but rather land in Ireland, expunge English rule there and cross the Irish Sea thereafter only if Elizabeth refused to come to terms.[53] The scale of the plan, and its anticipated cost (almost 4 million ducats for pay and victuals alone), probably inclined the Queen and Council to consider it as much of a dead letter as did Philip himself. That such a document had been drafted at all, however, only confirmed in English minds that the long-expected enterprise was being actively discussed at the Spanish Court. It was a timely perception. In the same month that Drake returned to England, Philip committed himself to a more modest but definite invasion plan that utilized elements of Santa Cruz's scheme and an alternative proposed by Parma – an assault upon England by 30,000 Spanish troops carried directly from Flanders.[54]

Almost simultaneously, Walsingham obtained his first copies of Mary Stuart's correspondence with the Catholic conspirator Anthony Babington, who had asked her blessing upon a scheme to invite a French or Spanish invasion of England (to be preceded by the assassination of Elizabeth). John Hawkins, outfitting five naval vessels and thirteen armed merchantmen at Plymouth – another attempt upon one of the *flotas* or the Goan carracks – was detained there following reports that a Catholic League fleet assembling at Rouen might be intended for English shores.[55] In August, further details of Babington's plot emerged following his arrest, including the revelation that Mary intended to name Philip as successor to her claim upon the English throne against that of her son, James, should he – as expected – refuse to renounce his Protestant faith. To most members of Elizabeth's government, this was all striking evidence that the various, long-perceived strands of malice that threatened their security – papal plot, Guise vengeance and Spanish ambition – had finally coalesced into a single, coordinated push to expunge the English 'problem'.

The Scottish Queen was put on trial on 14 October, and the prorogued parliament of 1584 dissolved so that a new one could be summoned hurriedly. Whatever Elizabeth's own plans for her troublesome cousin, her Lords and Commons, carefully primed by a series of speeches by leading Privy Councillors, were near-unanimous in their condemnation of 'this wicked and filthie woman'. On 3 November, Sir Walter Mildmay presented the House with a forensic survey of the Scottish Queen's crimes and concluded ominously 'it remayneth now to consider what is to be done'. The following day Job Throckmorton, the incendiary member for Warwick, rose to provide a rather more febrile summary of Mary's career and to steel his colleagues to the ruthless course their sovereign might yet resist:

> The yssue then of the whole is that we be all joynte suteres to her Majestie that Jezabel may lyve no longer to persecute the prophets of God, nor to attempt still in this maner the vyneyarde of Naboth by bloudde; that so the land may be purged, the wrath of God pacified, and her Majestie's dayes prolongued in peace to the comfort of us and our posteritye . . .[56]

One week later, both Houses presented a petition, carefully screened and corrected by Burghley, to Elizabeth. Their plea was for Mary's 'juste and spedye executyon'; the Queen heard them and gave a gracious undertaking to refer to God for guidance.[57] Yet despite this and her subsequent prevarications, the journey that began with the arraignment of the Scottish Queen could have only one ending. Putting her cousin to death would be one of those decisive actions that Elizabeth always tried to avoid. It was, after all, a near-blasphemy in a world that regarded princes as God-appointed, and would give England's enemies excellent justification for pursuing their aims with even greater vigour. But Mary Stuart had become the hinge upon which every real and imagined stratagem against the English regime pressed. The language deployed against her in parliament, if colourful ('daughter of sedition, the mother of rebellion, the nurce of impietie, the handmaide of iniquitie, the sister of unshamefastenesse . . .'), reflected the widespread loathing that both her person and history excited among Englishmen.[58] Eighteen years had passed since she had fled her own kingdom and thrown herself upon Elizabeth's mercy. During that time, she had failed utterly to build a meaningful domestic constituency for her claims to the English throne, even among the Catholics whose devotion she and her supporters abroad assumed to be hers by right. Revelations of her implication in successive plots to seize what she would never be offered only strengthened the antipathy of her intended subjects. Even before her collusion in the Babington scheme was revealed, the patriotic 'Bond of Association' (the device under which she was eventually tried) had implicitly provided for her execution should Elizabeth be murdered.[59] Only the Queen herself, with the implications for her own sovereign sanctity in mind, was less than wholeheartedly enthusiastic for Mary's death. Yet every intelligence from abroad seemed to reinforce the wisdom of those, like Job Throckmorton, who regarded any show of mercy as 'a verie dreadfull and perillous presidente'.

As Mary slowly approached the scaffold, more specific word of armada preparations began to arrive in England. From Paris, late in September, Stafford passed on to Walsingham reports that a concentration of vessels had commenced at Lisbon; while from Rome and Venice came word that papal preparations for a crusade against Geneva might encompass also an early solution to the English problem. Ominously, this latter possibility was said to await only the commitment of Spain.[60] Such intelligences were necessarily second- or third-hand, and the projects to which they referred did not, as yet, appear to be so far advanced that their threat was imminent. However, if a final spur were required to transform ambition into commitment, it was provided now by the act that most of the Queen's advisors regarded as the surest safeguard of her throne.

Twelve years earlier, in the aftermath of the Ridolfi plot, Elizabeth had sent quiet word to the Scottish regent, the earl of Mar, offering to send Mary back to Scotland if he would undertake to execute her discreetly.[61] Unfortunately, the earl died before he could make up his mind to oblige his illustrious petitioner. Now, once more, she attempted to remove a persistent problem in what Englishmen regarded as the Continental manner. At her urging, Walsingham tried and failed to persuade Sir Amias Paulet, Mary's gaoler at Fortheringay Castle, to murder his charge.[62] The deed, if it were to be done, would have to be owned publicly. On 8 February 1587, therefore, in the semi-official presence of the earls of Shrewsbury and Kent, the Scottish Queen's head was hewn clumsily from her shoulders. Having authorized the sentence with a great show of reluctance and damned those among her faithful councillors who conspired to implement it (her secretary William Davison was sent to the Tower, Burghley was banished from Court and Walsingham prudently exiled himself to his bed at Barn Elms with a bout of a recurring urinary infection), Elizabeth played the part of one whose hands remained unstained by the deed. She may even have convinced herself of her innocence, but that part of Europe that most exercised her government thought otherwise.

Much of Catholic France, Mary's former realm, went into deep, angry mourning at news of her murder. At Notre Dame, the brothers Guise held grand obsequies for their dead niece, during which Henri III slipped a helpful note to Stafford, suggesting that he might wish to avoid the mob's wrath by hiding in his embassy for a few days. At Rouen, a city that for generations had relied heavily upon its trade with London, rioters seized English ships and destroyed their cargoes. In Catholic churches throughout the country, incendiary sermons demanded a holy war against Elizabeth's regime.[63] In Rome, meanwhile, the pope gave a cardinal's hat to William Allen, the putative interim governor of England following her conquest, and pledged more than a million ducats to support Philip's great enterprise. In the Escorial, the Spanish King received first word of Mary's execution from Mendoza's Paris despatches. He wept for the new Catholic martyr, authorized a solemn requiem mass (after taking detailed advice from his confessor and theologians on the protocols of martyrdom) and trawled through a small forest of family trees to justify his new claim to the English throne.[64] Only from Scotland was there reasonably good news for Elizabeth and her regicidal government. After a fraught few weeks during which James VI refused to receive the envoy of his mother's murderer (and made several 'secret' threats to avenge her death), he decided to believe the Queen's protestations of revulsion for the deed – having been assured privily that his own claims to her throne, when she vacated it, remained intact – and continue to pocket his English subsidies.[65]

The execution of a fellow sovereign was a politically seismic event, as Elizabeth had anticipated – an irrevocable challenge to Catholic Europe to move against England, or, finally, to accept her loss. Given that his personal claim to Elizabeth's throne was now widely known, there could be little doubt that Philip at least would rise to it. Ten days after he received word of Mary's execution, orders flooded out from the Escorial to all parts of his Iberian and Mediterranean possessions, demanding that the resources he had earmarked for the assembling fleet at Lisbon be provided as soon as possible to allow the Marquis of Santa Cruz to put to sea before summer. He also sent word to his Guise allies, triggering the duke of Aumale's Picardy offensive to secure ports on the southern coast of the Narrow Seas in which the armada might rest and re-provision.[66] It was time, as Philip's secretary Idiáquez observed to the duke of Medina Sidonia, to put the Englishman's house 'to the torch'.[67]

For once, Elizabeth anticipated her most powerful enemy's intentions and moved swiftly to forestall them. Fortunately, the means to do this were readily available. In the previous December, a consortium of leading London merchants had outfitted a powerful fleet of eleven armed merchantmen, with the optimistic intention of intercepting the outgoing East Indies carracks as they departed Lisbon. Almost all of the investors and captains in the enterprise had been Anglo-Iberian traders; many had lost money, goods and even employees to Spanish embargoes or the activities of the Holy Office.[68] This, the first large-scale 'private' reprisal against Spain since the 1585 embargo, did not proceed as planned, however. Having readily obtained an Admiralty licence, the expedition was detained in the Thames, and, on 18 March 1587, amalgamated with a naval fleet of seven vessels (including the Lord Admiral's ship *White Lion*). Sir Francis Drake, recently disappointed in efforts to secure either English or Netherlander finance for a new expedition to be set out under Dom António's flag, received instead a commission from the Queen to 'impeach the joining together of the King of Spain's fleet'. Taking advantage of Burghley's temporary disgrace and absence from court, Walsingham and Leicester had persuaded Elizabeth to strike before she was struck.[69]

Following frantic preparations, Drake sailed from Plymouth on 2 April 1587. Seven days later, a countermanding order from the Council reached the port, requiring that he only seize shipping at sea and not enter into any ports belonging to the King of Spain 'or do any act of hostility upon the land'.[70] It is difficult to judge whether this was indeed a change of heart – rather feebly explained in the order by an apparent stay of armada preparations by Philip – or an equally unconvincing alibi to detach the Queen from responsibility for anything Drake might do upon the Spanish coast.[71] If Elizabeth was indeed wavering (a trait with which her councillors were intimately familiar), it was upon very little evidence that the threat to England had diminished. Before Drake sailed, word came from Portugal that three hundred ships had been stayed in southern Spanish ports, that the cargoes of all Dutch and Hanse provisions vessels coming into Lisbon were being requisitioned, and that all corn laden in 'Easterlings' (Baltic merchantmen) were ordered to discharge their cargoes into the King's warehouses at Lisbon by 10 March (NS).[72] Whatever the Queen's foremost despoiler of Spanish property might take upon himself to wreak, it could hardly be an over-reaction to such preparations.

Drake was absent from England for less than three months, but during that time he added spectacularly to an already awesome reputation. Three days after departing Plymouth, he was already off Cape Finesterre. Eleven days later, struggling through gales, his fleet stood off the Tagus estuary, hub of Philip's armada preparations. This was not, however, its goal. The English warships passed on to the south, and, on 19 April, arrived before the bay of Cadiz.

Drake's two-day sojourn at Cadiz has been minutely examined, and requires only brief mention here. Though the prompt arrival of the Duke of Medina Sidonia with eight thousand troops prevented the English raiders from disembarking and seizing the towns of Cadiz, Puerto Santa Maria and Puerto Real, the impunity with which they fought, seized, stripped and burned Spanish shipping in the bay and inner harbour sent a salutary message to the supposedly invincible fleet gathering at Lisbon. In the confines of Cadiz harbour, eight Spanish galleys that attempted repeatedly to engage the English galleons were massively outgunned and proved almost entirely ineffectual, and Philip's 'standing' naval power – certainly that part not acquired from Portugal with the Union of Crowns – consisted very substantially of galleys still. It was a validation of a growing suspicion, fostered by previous encounters in the Mediterranean between English Levanters and the Habsburg-controlled galleys of Sicily and Naples, that the latter were intrinsically disadvantaged against weatherly sailing ships: 'We now have had the experience of Galley fights, wherin I can assure you that onely foure of her Maiesties shippes, will make no account of xx. Gallies, so as they were alone and not driven to gard others . . .'[73] Santa Cruz's original plan for the invasion of England had allocated fully fifty galleys to the Spanish fleet; the armada of 1588 would be accompanied by just four, and even these would be forced by high seas to turn back to Spain before reaching the English Channel. Yet despite their increasingly apparent limitations, galleys had a potentially decisive ability to protect the short, fraught passage of troops moving between ship and shore. Without their presence in the fleet that would carry Philip's great enterprise to England, 'God's obvious design' might well unravel in the surf.[74]

The destruction of some twenty-four Spanish ships at Cadiz was humiliating for Philip, but did not seriously undermine his armada preparations. However, Drake's subsequent occupation of Sagres, though only of short duration, undoubtedly went far to fulfilling his brief to 'impeach' the invasion fleet's concentration. With a powerful, predatory English force waiting to pounce upon passing sea-traffic, those elements of the armada that had not yet concentrated at Lisbon – the Andalusian squadron, four Neopolitan galleases, eight other Italian warships and almost thirty transports – did not dare to move westwards through the Pillars of Hercules.[75] An enterprise that Philip had optimistically intended to depart within weeks remained fragmented and vulnerable to further damage at the hands of Drake and his countrymen. This dislocation of the armada's schedule was to have profound consequences.

The daring and success of Drake's raid astonished Europe. In Florence, it was said that all of Spain was terrified of him; from Paris, Stafford reported

jibes, allegedly made by Sixtus v, that Philip was 'a coward that had suffered his nose to be held in the Low Countries by a woman, braved and
spoiled at his own nose in Spain by a mariner'; at Seville, the Venetian
ambassador wrote to the Doge and Senate 'This woman has shown the
world how they can strike at the Spaniard in Flanders, in the Indies,
and in his own house'. From Paris, Mendoza reported to Philip that
Catherine de' Medici was openly delighted to hear of the ease with
which his ships had been burned or taken.[76] Elizabeth herself was more
delighted with Drake's subsequent capture, during his fleet's brief sweep
westwards to the Azores, of the Goan carrack *São Felipe*, whose cargoes
would more than recoup expenditure on the Cadiz expedition. Otherwise,
satisfaction in England at the raid's startling success was muted. Preparations observed off the Tagus estuary and in Cadiz harbour suggested that
the various pessimistic intelligences received at the English Court in recent
months had been broadly accurate. When Drake returned home at the
end of June, he brought treasure and glory, but above all a sense that
armada arrangements were not only enormous in scale, but possibly nearing
completion.[77]

With Mary's death, Elizabeth had expunged the principal remaining
'domestic' threat to her regime; with Drake's brilliant Cadiz raid, she secured
a half-victory over her gathering enemy and a sizeable profit (though the
failure to provide sufficient means to keep the English fleet at sea beyond
June, and the premature return to England of its merchantmen contingent,
ensured that the expedition's full potential to damage Philip's preparations
was not realised). Conversely, she had united much of Catholic Europe in
revulsion for her regime and ceded to the Spanish King an invaluable moral
justification for his intended enterprise against England. There was no sense
that the Cadiz raid had been decisive; no indication that the enterprise of
England would not proceed as soon as Philip could gather his scattered
forces. Drake's voyage, spectacularly bold as it may have appeared to contemporary eyes, was the last large-scale commitment Elizabeth could permit
before her own fleet's concentration commenced. Indeed, as the 'climac-
terical year of the world' approached, England's resources and manpower
were pulled back into her borders to await the storm.[78] Subsidies to Protestant forces in the Low Countries and Germany were almost halted, most of
Leicester's troops were brought home to save money and provide a stiffening
to the trained bands, and all English merchant shipping was stayed in its
home ports. With the destruction of the factious and unruly German Protestant army at Auneau in December, only the rebel Netherlanders (as the cities

and towns of Flanders fell, this was becoming increasingly a 'Dutch' rebellion) stood with their English allies against the combined might of Philip, Parma and the Guise dynasty. And even they had ceased to trust Elizabeth in the least degree.

Far away from the gathering fleets that would decide the struggle for western Europe, a final effort was being made to resurrect something of the good old days in which Philip had been far too busy to deal with English provocations. On 9 December, the Queen's ambassador to the Ottoman Porte, William Harborne, addressed a letter to the Sultan:

> It is now the intention of the Spaniard relying on the help of the Pope and of all idolatrous princes to utterly destroy her and afterwards when no other obstacle shall remain in Christendom the Spaniard will direct his invincible strength to the destruction of thee and thy empire . . . But if your highness at the same time with my Sovereign, wisely and bravely, without delay, will now wage war at sea . . . the proud Spaniard and the lying Pope with their followers will not only have the cup of promised victory dashed from their lips but will receive the punishment in their own person due to their rashness.[79]

The true Christian conscience of western Europe was to be preserved, apparently, by the sacrifice of its papist Mediterranean portion. Though Harborne failed to secure a promise of active support, Philip's aims, in turn, were frustrated by his own envoys' failure to secure a formal renewal of the 1577 naval truce between Spain and the Ottoman Empire: a disappointment owing in no small part to the Englishman's efforts. In the following months, a rumour reached the Escorial of a secret Anglo-Ottoman defensive alliance. This was to have little practical effect on the nature and scale of armada preparations (the only resources that Philip might otherwise have spared for 'English' operations were his Mediterranean galleys, whose use therein had already been largely discounted). Even so, Elizabeth's refusal to pay that portion of Harborne's expenses that the Turkey Company refused to meet following his return to England in December 1588 constituted one of her less forgivable economies.[80]

NINE

Military Preparations, 1587–1588

Be vigilant, sleepe not in sin,
Lest that thy foe do enter in:
Keep sure thy trench, prepare thy shot
Watch wel, so shal no foil be got.[1]

Spanish losses of ships and material to Drake's raid at Cadiz had been heavy, and the impact upon Spanish morale was significant. As noted, however, its principal immediate effect was collateral, in preventing the early gathering of resources at Lisbon. Uncertainty regarding English intentions following the raid also brought a large part of Santa Cruz's existing concentration of ships out into the Atlantic, to protect the incoming *flota* and its vital cargoes from the threat of interception.[2] The time consumed by this unwanted duty made Philip's summer 1587 invasion timetable impossible to achieve, and this dislocation had further, possibly crucial repercussions. The ageing Santa Cruz, weakened by the burden of his sea duties, returned to Lisbon at the end of September as much in need of rest and repair as his battered ships. His incapacity aggravated the already acute logistical difficulties in provisioning the vast Spanish fleet, slowing and then paralysing preparations in the weeks that followed. Philip, meanwhile, having been seduced by Parma's now-optimistic assessment of the chances of carrying his invasion barges across the Channel intact, lost much of his natural prudence and pestered his admiral with increasingly curt demands that he put to sea.[3]

Although Santa Cruz's original plan for an invasion of England had been over-ambitious of Spanish resources, he had been shrewd in appreciating the magnitude of the task before him. Now he displayed similar prudence in resisting temptation, urgings and blunt commands to seek his destiny in a bruised, under-provisioned fleet. Parma's inability to make more than preliminary preparations for a Channel crossing during the following months proved the wisdom of the marquis's circumspection, but he had won his last battle. During one of many inspections of his Lisbon fleet, he was fatally exposed to the same virulent strain of typhus that was decimating his mariners in their cramped, unsanitary quarters. Philip's foremost sea commander died early in February 1588, and with him went the final, slim prospect of any English enterprise meeting its ambitious objectives. Another man was to sweep away the administrative paralysis of Santa Cruz's last days, but the old admiral's martial abilities, and his laudable habit of ignoring his King's instructions when his own better judgement dictated, were qualities that would be sorely missed during the coming campaign. His replacement, the duke of Medina Sidonia, would prove far too dutiful a servant to depart from the detail of a restrictive brief that held little prospect of success. Nevertheless, with his appointment the hiatus in preparations for the great enterprise came to an end. With a master bureaucrat in charge, they proceeded thereafter at a pace that even the Spanish King could hardly fault.

These delays were of inestimable value to England, although the degree to which Philip's intended schedule had been interrupted was not apparent for several months. The stream of advices, advertisements and intelligences from Spain and elsewhere that poured into the country during the summer of 1587 indicated that an invasion was not only in active preparation still but possibly imminent.[4] In July, Walsingham received word from Sir Thomas Leighton in Guernsey, reporting the claims of his Breton merchant contacts that a hundred Spanish ships carrying 15,000 troops would depart Lisbon within the month. A few weeks later, an eyewitness at Lisbon sent word that fifty-seven ships and 10,000 men were assembling to join Santa Cruz's squadron when it returned with the *flota*.[5] On 18 September, Leighton again wrote to Walsingham to warn that someone close to Mendoza in Paris had heard that the armada was at sea already – though bound for Scotland – and carrying between 15,000 and 18,000 soldiers.[6] From Elsinore in Denmark, Thomas Tuncker sent word to his employer, the London mercer William Watson, warning of fleets of Hanse vessels carrying supplies of anchors, cables, tackle, dried fish, cheese and butter to Lisbon 'of a wonderfull quantitie'.[7] In Paris, meanwhile, Sir Edward Stafford obtained and sent on to London an anonymous Spanish proposal for an invasion of

England. Marked for Philip's attention, it anticipated a fleet of 171 vessels carrying 38,000 troops that would seek to defeat an English fleet at sea before landing, fortifying a beach-head and advancing upon London. The author of this piece must have touched a raw nerve in his unanticipated audience when he pointed out that such an operation need expect no interference from French or German Protestant forces.[8]

Swept by this flurry of ominous information, the Privy Council might usefully have thrown itself into frantic preparations to meet the invasion. This was far from the case, however. Almost six months earlier, during the heightened sense of emergency that followed the execution of Mary Stuart, letters had been sent out to the Lord Lieutenants of the maritime counties ordering the muster and training of their levies, with ordnance and shot to be distributed from the Tower for their use.[9] Lack of subsequent reference to these orders (other than in the complaints of those required to discharge them) suggests that little more was attempted in the subsequent months. A major Privy Council meeting of 3 October was the first occasion upon which war preparations were considered in depth. Its agenda, drafted by Burghley, indicated how much remained to be done. Only now, a quarter of a year after Drake's return from Cadiz, did Queen's councillors sit down to address such matters as the registration of recusants, detention of all merchant shipping in port, the securing of Ireland's south coast against an anticipated landing there, new efforts to muster and train the shire levies and, not least, to ensure 'that the Queen's whole Navy be put in readiness'.[10]

This apparent lack of urgency might be considered reckless in the face of the greatest crisis of Elizabeth's reign. As usual, however, stratagems and good intentions waited upon the same matter – money. Although defence of the realm itself was the overwhelming priority, most of the Queen's resources were already committed to the outworks of her foreign policy. In 1585, when overt English aid to the Netherlander rebels commenced, the agreed military undertaking had been costed at precisely £12,526 per month (which the States-General were obliged, but for many years failed, to refund).[11] An unprecedented obligation, it proved inadequate from the start. Planned expenditure was far exceeded during the first year of campaigning, with the English occupation of Flushing, Brielle and Middelburg alone draining the Exchequer by more than £20,000.[12] The budget for 1587, in addition to having to meet that shortfall, was burdened further by measures to counter Parma's descent upon Sluys in June of that year. The manoeuvre represented a severe threat to Flushing (standing directly across the Scheldt estuary) and could not be ignored whatever other priorities pressed. Having previously resisted Dutch pleas for further subsidies, Elizabeth was now obliged to commit an incremental £35,000 and 3,000 of her troops to meet an assault that, if successful, would give Parma an ideal invasion assembly port and control of the Scheldt estuary.[13] The only resource she could afford to squander was the relief force's commander, the earl of Leicester, though the instructions she gave him – to browbeat the States-General into giving him direct control of their war resources or to appeal directly to the individual provinces for the same – ensured that the fruits of his doubtful military talents would be fully complemented by abject diplomatic failure.[14] As for the hapless earl's personal 'table', such was Elizabeth's acute sense of her own poverty by now (and of Leicester's profligacy) that his anticipated personal expenses of £6,000 were only loaned to him, to be repaid within two years. For even this pale benevolence, he was obliged to offer up as security the rights to future income generated by his wine and alienations patents.[15] The Queen's frugality proved to be well-judged. Leicester's subsequent success in waging unremitting war against the States-General that autumn, while allowing Parma to take Sluys unopposed, proved to be almost as useful to Philip as Santa Cruz's exhausting yet vital preservation of the incoming silver ships.

With these and smaller subsidies to keep Huguenot and German Protestant armies in the field, demands upon the Exchequer far outstripped its income – from land revenues, parliamentary grants, privy seal loans and forced 'contributions' from recusants – long before the onset of a fighting war. Consequently, England's relatively small fiscal reserves were heavily depleted. From its historically high balance of £299,000 at Michaelmas 1584, Burghley's carefully hoarded contingencies fund – the 'chested treasure' – evaporated rapidly, standing at just £154,000 by December 1587.[16] In the six months from Michaelmas 1587 to Lady Day 1588, extraordinary expenditure met from the 'Receipt' would come to a massive £96,770.[17] By the latter date, the Lord Treasurer – for whom this seepage was a matter of acute concern – calculated that during the previous three years almost £600,000 of English specie had been poured into the Netherlands campaign and other foreign subsidies to achieve what looked very much like nothing.[18]

Moreover, these unprecedented calls upon Elizabeth's purse occurred against the background of the deepest economic recession of her reign to date. The principal source of England's overseas earnings – the exportation of cloths – had been almost curtailed by the wartime loss of many of her foreign customers. As the towns of Flanders fell to Parma, so the once-vast Low Countries market shrivelled; by 1587 only Middelburg remained, loyal to her English merchants but deep in the midst of a war zone (with Parma's approach to Sluys, the town's position was becoming ever more precarious).

More seriously, since April 1585, when the citizens of Nijmegen declared for their lawful sovereign, Parma had controlled both banks of the Rhine estuary. English cloth merchants had been denied access thereafter to many of their principal buyers in northern Germany, making pointless the long-urged establishment of a new staple in Holland (a constant goal of the rebels). Emden might have provided an alternative venue as it had in 1564 during Elizabeth's first economic 'spat' with the regency of the Netherlands, but England's erstwhile rebel allies were closely blockading the Ems estuary against friend and foe alike.[19] By the end of 1586, unemployment in England's cloth-producing regions was growing perceptibly. Again, it was Burghley who felt the pain most keenly. Writing to Walsingham on 26 May 1587, he lamented (with a degree of hyperbole) that although Blackwell Hall and its Westminster equivalent, the *George*, were full of that year's stock of cloths brought in from the country, not one had yet been sold.[20] And if that were not worry enough for a man whose preoccupations were nailed to the nation's balance sheet, the poor harvests of 1586–7 had caused the price of corn briefly to treble, bringing small but portentous hunger riots in Somerset and Gloucestershire. Encouraged by malnourishment among the poor, plague returned to many of England's provincial towns during 1587, increasing the base death-rate in some localities by up to thirty per cent. Paradoxically, prices continued to rise, belying the logical interaction between high mortality and deflationary pressures – conditions that had augured the breakdown of civil authority in Flanders two decades earlier.[21]

With all of these concerns pressing upon her, the Queen had little option but to delay the onset of war expenditure for as long as possible. She even vetoed an early proposal for the restraint of leading recusants, because – alleged Burghley – the cost of its implementation might be as high as 200 marks.[22] Inevitably, the same pressures encouraged her to regard any peace initiative, no matter how illusory, as worth pursuing with vigour. The miserable failure of Leicester's campaign in particular (which had requisitioned a large proportion of her most experienced soldiers to little purpose) inclined her to seek some form of accommodation with Parma, rather than encourage an expensive conflict that might even now, she believed, be averted. By the latter months of 1587 the duke's successes had given him little incentive to seek peace; nevertheless, he played shrewdly upon pacifist tendencies at the English court. Urged on by her most persistent peacemonger, the Comptroller of her Household, Sir James Crofts, Elizabeth agreed to initiate an unofficial dialogue that had augured intermittently since December 1585, though the futility of any hopes of achieving a workable compromise was already obvious.[23] The terms regarded by the Queen as mandatory – freedom of worship for Philip's Netherlander subjects and their inclusion in any treaty agreed between England and the regency government – were known to be utterly unobtainable. Stafford, moreover, had already sent word of Philip's admission – to Henri III's envoy at Madrid – that his agreement to the peace negotiations had been given only 'to winne tyme and to abuse the Quene of England'.[24] Nevertheless, the faintest prospect of peace tempted Elizabeth to risk alienating her Netherlander allies, who saw her threatened contact with Parma as a prelude to their abandonment. Negotiations regarding negotiations dragged on through the winter of 1587/8, delicately manipulated by the duke's representatives to prolong English uncertainties and rebel ire. In the meantime, Parma's own preparations for a descent upon England were quietly advanced by the widening and deepening of canals leading to Sluys, to facilitate the concentration of his invasion barges there.[25]

However misplaced, Elizabeth's hopes for a negotiated resolution to Anglo-Spanish enmity did not deteriorate into outright naivety. Even as she invested her hopes in Parma's pragmatism, the buttressing of England's own defences commenced. The state of the government's finances made this a selective process but clearly, the highest priority was her navy. Here, too, expenditure, if only a fraction of that which Philip was lavishing upon his fleet, had been greatly expanding during 1587 but much of this was devoted to outfitting the Cadiz raid. The cost of victuals and pay for the expedition's mariners alone came to some £9,700; adding to this the 'ordinary' and 'extraordinary' expenditure upon her other ships, the previous year's entire naval budget was exceeded even before extensive preparations to meet the armada commenced.[26] On the credit side of the ledger, the spoils from the *São Felipe*, Drake's principal prize in 1587, would eventually realize over £108,000 (of which the Queen's share was a useful £46,672); but the figure had not been established, much less made available, when expenditure to meet the threat of invasion commenced. Indeed, the agenda of the 3 October Privy Council meeting indicated that the profit or loss from Drake's 1585/6 West Indies raid had yet to be calculated to Burghley's satisfaction.[27]

The Navy Royal, hopefully the instrument of England's salvation, was by 1587 more powerful than it had been for some decades past, but areas of concern remained. Following a burst of shipbuilding and acquisitions during the previous three years, it now consisted of some thirty-four vessels, of which twelve were of less than 250 tons burden.[28] The potential of the newer, race- or raze-built vessels, constructed since 1572, has hugely exercised generations of naval historians, who have discerned a revolutionary process in ship design and construction during Hawkins's stewardship as Treasurer of the Navy.[29] These warships – built or re-built with only vestigial remnants of the fore- and aft-castles that had made the traditional naval vessel a cumbersome, floating fortress, undoubtedly represented a significant improvement over their precursors. Shallower draughted, with an increased keel-to-beam ratio that allowed more weatherly handling and a greater weight of ordnance to tonnage, these were the best fighting ships – that is, as gun- rather than boarding-platforms – in any western Navy. Yet only ten of them – the *Ark Royal* (formerly Walter Ralegh's pride and joy, *Ark Ralegh*), *Revenge*, *Dreadnought*, *Nonpareil* (the old *Philip and Mary*, entirely rebuilt in 1584), *Golden Lion* (rebuilt 1582), *Vanguard*, *Rainbow*, *Foresight*, *Antelope* and *Swiftsure* – were capable of carrying significant armament, and even these modern vessels, the pride of the Navy Royal, varied in performance and quality of construction.[30] There was no standard raze-built design as such; each had been a test-bed, in effect, for the developing ideas and techniques of one of a number of shipwrights (though not, probably, of Hawkins himself, whose vital administrative input to the process has often been expanded by commentators to encompass its entirety).[31] To speak of a new 'type' of vessel is somewhat misleading, therefore. The *Rainbow* and *Vanguard*, for example, were particularly shallow-draughted vessels (of only twelve and thirteen feet respectively), built specifically for operations off the shoal-infested coasts of the Narrow Seas. When fully armed – both were allocated a relatively high weight of ordnance relative to tonnage – they were said to be unstable in rougher seas (Lord Henry Seymour observed of the *Rainbow*, his command in 1588, 'My summer shippe, alwaies ordayned for the Narrow Seas, will neuer be able to go throughe with the Northern, Irishe, or Spanishe seas, without great harm and spoyle of our owne people by sicknesse.'[32]). The deeper draughted *Swiftsure* and *Dreadnought*, though contemporaneous – both were built in the royal shipyards during 1573 – had notably dissimilar keel-to-beam proportions, which again suggests an element of experimentation.[33] As with the application of any 'new' science, moreover, the results were not uniformly successful, and modifications to hull-design undertaken during these years may have outstripped the limits of contemporary shipbuilding technology. Most of the major warships built or rebuilt by Peter Pett and Matthew Baker in the mid 1580s – *Swallow*, *Antelope*, *Nonpareil*, *Rainbow*, *Vanguard* – exceeded (in some cases by a notable margin) the 3:1 keel-to-beam proportion later declared both by William Borough and the anonymous author of the (*c.* 1620) *Treatise on Shipbuilding* as optimum.[34] However, from 1587, Richard Chapman, the third of England's triumvirate of great shipwrights, began to construct major vessels (including *Ark Ralegh*) with a more conservative proportion – one closer to that employed in earlier decades than to their immediate predecessors. He also deepened their draught relative to beam.[35] Both developments suggest a growing realization that the superbly weatherly qualities of the most radical ship designs came at the expense of stability.

The skills that built these vessels, furthermore, were not always applied consistently. It was an occasional habit of each of the principal shipwrights, when not accusing Hawkins of cost-paring and embezzlement, to damn his professional colleagues for incompetence, graft and/or plagiarism.[36] Undoubtedly, much of this was motivated by jealousy and flagrant career-positioning, but there is some evidence also of neglect. The use of cheaper, unseasoned timber continued in the royal shipyards until at least 1580; the *Swiftsure*, *Dreadnought* and *Revenge* were all cursed by their own fabric in this respect, and required unusually heavy maintenance throughout their working lives. When, much later, Sir Richard Hawkins described the *Revenge* as 'the unfortunatest ship the late Queenes Maiestie had during her raigne', he may have been referring to more than the manner of her destruction.[37]

Such variations in principle, faults in design and outright poor workmanship did not render any of these vessels remotely ineffective, as shall be discussed. Undoubtedly, they were superior in almost every respect to the vast majority of the ships they would face in the coming campaign (most of which were archaic in design, or, if otherwise, rendered so by the addition of further superstructures at Lisbon to facilitate boarding operations). Nevertheless, their flaws were real, and should be assessed in the perspective of their age. If English tactical philosophy regarding the use of ships in battle was innovative, the complementary improvements in ship design during these years constituted at most an evolutionary, not a revolutionary process.

The remainder of the English navy in 1587 consisted of four very large, sturdy, recently improved but still outmoded galleons – the 'great ships' *Triumph*, *Elizabeth Jonas*, *White Bear* and *Victory* – and a collection of smaller vessels of widely varying performance, few of which would be capable of engaging the principal vessels of the armada.[38] Elizabeth's navy, while superior even to that impressive creation of her father, had always been envisaged as an instrument for the defence of home waters against an enemy with similar or smaller resources. It had not been anticipated – not, at least, until after the union of the Crowns of Portugal and Spain in 1580 – that the danger might be of another order of magnitude.

In autumn 1587, moreover, it was claimed that the Navy Royal was as yet unfit to meet the threat from Spain and the Low Countries. According to Pett and Baker, reporting on 12 October in response to questions raised by the Privy Council nine days earlier, all the naval vessels that had taken part in the Cadiz raid, other than the mutinous *Golden Lion*, were in need of some measure of repair.[39] Of their sisters, three of the four 'great ships' were said to require structural work (all but the *Victory* being 'much decayed' in their timbers), whilst a further five vessels were considered unready for prolonged service without prior work. A significant proportion of the nation's defences therefore had to be withdrawn from even the possibility of active service at a time when accurate news of armada preparations was almost entirely lacking – an exposure that reinforced Elizabeth's already strong sense of circumspection. The only substantial naval operation she permitted during the winter months comprised a small squadron of seven vessels, *Foresight*, *Tremontana*, *Tiger*, *Scout*, *Achates*, *Charles* and *Moon* (reinforced in October by the *Rainbow* and *Bull*), under the command of Martin Frobisher.[40] His brief was to patrol the Narrow Seas 'in warlike manner', to intercept the passing trade of Spain and the Netherlands, impair communications between Philip and Parma and secure information on the armada's progress. With only a month's refit during sea service from 18 August to 23 January 1588, and no ships available to rotate in their duties, the qualities of these vessels were severely tested.[41]

The pessimistic tenor of the shipwrights' report suggested that they faced a protracted struggle to make the fleet seaworthy, yet most of the Queen's ships were brought to battle-readiness within two months. All the major vessels that had been identified as in need of repair in the October report were declared fit for sea duties on 9 December by the Surveyor and the Controller of the Ships, Sir William Winter and William Holstocke. Their declaration was timely in more than one sense: it signalled also the end of a long-running feud within the navy establishment, perhaps the most vendetta-prone organization in sixteenth- and seventeenth-century English government. After years of attempting to sabotage Hawkins's 'bargains' – in reprisal for the Treasurer's damning criticisms of his own performance as Surveyor of the Ships – Winter put his signature to a declaration that his colleague had not only fulfilled his side of the arrangement but also 'expended a far greater sum in carpentry upon her Majesty's ships than he hath in any way allowance for'.[42] The Queen's ships were fully manned by

22 December. Two days earlier, Lord Admiral Charles Howard had received his commission to command the fleet in the coming campaign. In his first report, he was able to reassure Burghley that as soon as he could take in his sea victuals, 'all things will be in a readiness'. What Philip had laboured for over eighteen months to prepare, Elizabeth could counter, apparently, in a matter of weeks.

The metamorphosis was not as striking as it appeared. England's naval establishment enjoyed several significant structural advantages over that of its imminent foe (not least in being an 'establishment'). If rudimentary by modern standards, it was a homogeneous organization, possessing a mature, centralized – if constantly bickering – administration, dedicated shipyards at Deptford and Woolwich (Philip had no similar facilities in Spanish ports) and a significant ability to expand during times of crisis. Above all, the master shipwrights were intimately familiar with the vessels they maintained, most of which had been their own creations. In their October report, furthermore, Pett and Baker had reported not upon defects discovered during the course of an urgently ordered inspection, but upon those monitored and allocated for repair long in advance. Much, if not most of the work noted subsequently by Winter and Holstocke as completed had been in hand already in October as part of the normal maintenance schedule, not a frantic programme of pre-campaign renovation. It is also clear that the shipwrights' report had been deliberately over-critical of the ships they examined. Both men detested John Hawkins, who had overall responsibility for maintaining the Queen's ships and who, in turn, rarely failed to blame the shipwrights for shortcomings of work carried out under his 'second bargain' with the Crown.[43] Yet even as they offered the worst possible opinion of the ships' condition, Pett and Baker nevertheless had admitted that most were fit for present, if limited service. The ships of the Queen's Navy Royal had faults, but there was nothing that could not be fixed – or patched – in relatively short order.

Part of the reason for their relatively sound condition was the lack of prolonged wear and tear upon their fabric. Service was a far more prevalent destroyer of ships than warfare, and the Queen's principal vessels, unlike those of her adversary, were not employed near-constantly at sea. Drake had been given two of her ships for his West Indies raid; his Cadiz expedition took six. Only one vessel, the *Elizabeth Bonaventure*, participated in both campaigns. In 1586, Hawkins had sailed to the coast of Portugal with five naval vessels and a number of armed merchantmen; but failing entirely in his attempt to intercept a *flota*, this had been little more than a gentle testing of their fabric.[44] These were the only occasions in which any of the largest of the Queen's ships are known to have been at sea during the years 1585–7 (ten naval vessels were reported by Mendoza to have been made ready to sail from the Thames in June 1587 to reinforce Drake off the coast of Spain, but none sailed subsequently).[45] At other times, most vessels of the Navy Royal were docked at Woolwich and Deptford or moored at Chatham under the supervision of the shipwrights. In the months prior to the assembly of Howard's forces, only Frobisher's squadron suffered notable sea duties, and he commanded relatively new ships.[46] With few exceptions, therefore, it seems that the necessary work carried out by the Queen's shipwrights in the two months following their October report involved re-rigging and re-fitting, rather than the more significant graving, caulking and timber replacement that formed their habitual peacetime function.[47] This is evidenced by the reservations they expressed regarding at least five of the largest ships (not identified), which were said to have departed the dockyards following repairs without having been grounded for hull inspection.[48]

As efficient as its preparation had been, however, the fleet that assembled in January 1588 was only the core of what would be needed to defend England. By the beginning of that month, twenty-three privately owned vessels had been appointed to serve at the Queen's expense.[49] Most were merchantmen (and, in some cases, occasional privateers), allocated to join Drake's squadron of six naval vessels at Plymouth. Among them were ships owned by the earl of Leicester (*Galleon Leicester*), Walter Ralegh (*Roebuck*) and the Fenner family (*Bark Fenner*). The great London companies also contributed a number of significant vessels. Members of the Turkey Company, whose investments in the dangerous eastern Mediterranean were protected by well-armed merchantmen, provided at least six ships. These included the *Merchant Royal* and *Edward Bonaventure* (owned by the wealthy London mercer Thomas Cordell), which had proved themselves at Cadiz and elsewhere and were almost as powerfully armed as naval vessels of equivalent tonnage.[50] With even these fine ships, however, the entire English fleet at the turn of the year comprised only some fifty-five to sixty vessels of all sizes: a painfully thin sea wall between Philip and his ambitions for England.

*   *   *

If the Navy Royal was as yet unready to face the full might of the expected Spanish invasion fleet, the English 'army' – the second, final line of the nation's defences – was and remained burdened by profound systemic disadvantages. England had no professional land formations other than the principal permanent garrisons at Berwick and Dover and those formations in Ireland and the Netherlands that could be considered a 'standing' resource only by reason of their protracted employment. The bulwark of England's seas obviated the need to maintain large, expensive armies except in times of crisis. Inevitably, the quality of what then was assembled could not be pre-determined.

Since 1573, the English shire militias had been distinguished by the level of training they received. The general muster had long been an infrequent concentration of each county's 'substantial honest men' aged between sixteen and sixty (though the destitute and simple-minded usually turned out in unrepresentative numbers), who brought their archaic weapons to a prede-termined location on holidays or 'convenient' working days to perform a somewhat perfunctory series of exercises. Typically, the first day of the muster was devoted to marksmanship, the second to drilling. The men then disbanded and returned to their homes without any provision being made for their rudimentary skills to be tested or improved until the next muster.[51] Representing an English tradition of home defence that stretched back to the days of the Anglo-Saxon fyrd, the general muster's rationale had been rendered almost obsolete by the onward march of military science and the rise of small, professional continental armies. The special (or 'particular') muster, to be called by local captains several times each year, was an inno-vation of the early 1570s, conceived to address this failing.[52] Gradually, the practice enabled the identification and segregation of 'strong, lustie, able men, fytte for the warres', who were to be instructed in the use of modern weapons.[53] Their formations became known as trained bands; their purpose to fill the void opened by the demise of the great English feudal magnates' private armies.

It was the quality of the trained bands that constituted the principal concern of government, rather than the militia of the general muster (who in the months prior to the armada campaign were assigned to crossroad-guarding, beacon-watches and vagabond-chasing). There was certainly cause for worry. Martial expertise, where it existed, was largely disseminated as an individual, rather than group experience. The Low Countries had been an invaluable training ground for some Englishmen (by 1587 government had a list of 200 men fit to be captains of trained bands), though many of their comrades in arms disqualified themselves from home employment by their Catholicism (the greater number of 'Englishmen' serving in the Netherlands in 1587 were said to be Irishmen), or in lacking the qualities of sobriety and steadiness of temperament demanded by government. The lessons learned campaigning as part of a distinct English 'army', moreover, were not easily absorbed by local shire-men statutorily obliged to meet together upon only ten days per year – a requirement by no means met by all bands in every year. Even when they did gather, training was often extremely cursory. In 1586, for example, the Privy Council noted that footmen of the bands of Lancashire, Cheshire, Derbyshire and Staffordshire had been enrolled but not trained owing to unseasonable weather (a common complaint), and their horse troopers viewed but supplied with neither cassocks nor captains.[54] The experience of veterans was equally prized by government, of course, which did not hesitate to remove them once more when new foreign service was required, making an already inconsistent system even less satisfactory. The 'strong, lustie and able' quality of the levies, moreover, was an ambition rather than reality. While government repeatedly stressed the need for good men, unemployable or masterless wanderers tended to find the paltry daily wages more attractive than did their more respectable neighbours (whose wholesale conscription into the bands, incidentally, compromised the economic well-being of their districts). The results were predictable. For every shining report of men 'so well sorted and chosen both for able bodies and comlye p(er)sonages . . . that I assure Yo[u]r Lordshippes yt dothe exceede anie contrey that I ever came in' (Somerset), there were sour admissions that some trained bands were 'utterly untrained by any man of experience' (Sussex), or that apparently 'able' men were incompetent, unruly or had promptly absconded with their newly provided weapons (Kent). Nor were the bands always at their determined strength – whatever, after long wrangling, that was agreed to be. It was a venerable habit of captains in the Low Countries when not embezzling the wages of their men to leave gaps in their ranks created by death or disablement, certify the full number to their paymasters and pocket the surplus funds. The tradition translated readily back to the domestic bands.[55]

Exacerbating the problem of variable standards, the quasi-standing military structure, grafted uncomfortably upon local hierarchies, encouraged near-permanent jostling for pre-eminence among the bands' leaders. Despite the implication of the list of able 'captains' mentioned above, it was government's policy to ensure that a captaincy was usually within the gift of a local notable family, bestowed upon one of their number who very rarely possessed first-hand military experience. These men relied greatly upon the skills of the local muster-masters, into whose role government increasingly directed their Low Countries veterans.[56] Whenever the taint of incompetence demanded the removal of a captain, local influence quickly mobilized to attempt to have the order rescinded; when local vendettas threw up false accusations of the same, the effective business of training local bands could be paralysed for months.[57]

The provision and quality of material resources was no less inconsistent than that of the men who wielded them. Though favoured with better weapons than those supplied to the general musters, the bands were by no means the English equivalent of the professional armies of the continent. Even by 1587, the musket, corslet and harquebus had only partially replaced England's venerable weapons of mass destruction, the longbow and bill. Familiarity with the pike, a vital instrument in continental formations, was largely the preserve of the gentlemen in the bands, a badge of social exclusivity that further ensured that necessary reforms were only slowly affected. Training in the use of artillery was almost non-existent except in bands specifically assigned to defend the most likely invasion sites. Shot and powder were too expensive to allow more than a basic degree of gunnery competence, even among the few chosen to master that difficult art (in 1586 it was decreed that a mere four or five men in each of the inland counties should be trained as artillerymen), and no bands, with the possible exception of the Isle of Wight companies, seem ever to have ever received more than a nominal allocation of ordnance from Whitehall. That appointed in March 1587 for the vulnerable coasts of southern England, for example, had comprised just two sacres (five-pounders), two minions (four-pounders) and two falcons (three-pounders) for each maritime county.[58]

An even more fundamental brake upon improvements to the form and efficiency of existing forces lay in the provision for their upkeep, which fell entirely upon local communities. The muster wages that manned the bands, the weapons that armed them and the horses that carried their lancers were levied upon the rateable worth of a district's citizens (different rates applied in almost every shire). The signal beacons that sat upon hills or disfigured the fine lines of church towers and steeples were maintained from municipal funds, and their watchmen were paid 8d per day from the same purse. With few exceptions, the cost of fortifications of ports, beaches, inlets and ancient inland towns and cities was also borne by those who benefited from their protection, not by the government that demanded their erection and maintenance. This devolution of almost every aspect of the cost of war was intended to ease the burden placed upon the Exchequer; in reality, it encouraged an endemic culture of evasion that even a state of national crisis would not discourage.

Following the disappointing results of the March 1587 muster (in the opinion of Lord Hunsdon, Lord Lieutenant of the Isle of Wight, 'so badly chosen and worse furnished . . . I had rather have none'), the Privy Council sent out new orders in October to the Lords Lieutenant of the shires, to commence regular training of their able men 'for the withstandinge of all soddaine attempts that maie be made uppon anie part of her Majesties dominions'.[59] If the inference of an imminent threat was intended to gal-vanize the countryside, Elizabeth's councillors were to be sorely disap-pointed. Again, the resources assumed in their calculations, based upon local asset values, were far more substantial on paper than in fact. Constables of the hundreds, charged with collecting levy payments, consistently returned less than the assessed figures. Most deputy Lords Lieutenant asked for rebates upon their constituents' commitments or reductions in appointed numbers, and submitted hopeful pleas for financial assistance from the Crown to equip their bands. To a degree this was expected; but the unprece-dented scale of mobilization graphically revealed the extent to which the system had been manipulated at local level. With all the shires' able men summoned at the same time, it became obvious that the long-standing prac-tice of training in divisions upon separate days had allowed the local Great and Good to buy and pool small quantities of equipment, which they bor-rowed in rotation to provide as 'their' due obligation when necessary.[60] If the militias themselves could not be considered a national resource, such tricks were already reassuringly widespread. In Northamptonshire, which government regarded as something of a shining example to its sister shires, a full muster of November 1586 had managed to scrape together a total of eighty-eight calivers for the provision of 2,063 men. The reaction to this pitiful showing of the local Lord Lieutenant, Sir Christopher Hatton, had been to lobby his fellow Privy Councillors, successfully, for a marked reduc-tion in his county's arms quota.[61]

It was known already that particular difficulty would be experienced in finding sufficient suitable horses for the shires' mounted troops. Measures first introduced during the reign of Henry VIII had sought to ensure a reli-able supply of semi-wild horses, bred and maintained upon common land at the shire's expense. The widespread failure to implement the law – despite a major initiative as recently as 1580, when Privy Councillors had been made personally responsible for their Lieutenancies' horse-stocks – led the Queen's commissioners to conclude in 1585 'theyr be at this present verye fewe or no horses kept uppon anye common . . . wherby the breed of horses is greatlye decayed . . .'.[62] Little was done to correct this situation thereafter, which meant that gentlemen assessed in 1587 to supply horses had to do so from their own stables. Understandably, few were willing to send off their £15 geldings, the pride of careful husbandry, to be ridden pell-mell at Spanish artillery by half-trained levies. Accusations that some (perhaps many) were providing coach-horses and nags in lieu of more suitable mounts were investigated by the Council immediately following the end of the campaign, and the practice was unwittingly confirmed by the diplomat Sir Horatio Palavicino, who later threatened to do the same to meet his own (1592) assessed quota of six horses.[63]

Local gentry were not the only evaders. The clergy, that eager vanguard of resistance to popery and its damnable accretions, proved equally resistant to emptying its pockets for the defence of the nation. Even immediately prior to the commencement of the 1588 campaign, the Privy Council was obliged to name and shame the entire breed, lamenting its clamour for exemption 'although they have good and sufficient livinges'. Certificates eventually supplied by seventeen dioceses committed them to raising a total of 4,444 soldiers for the Queen's personal protection, but few of these materialized before the end of the campaign. Only the bishops of London, Salisbury, Lichfield and Coventry showed any enthusiasm for meeting their obligations, and pledged more than their assessed number of men.[64]

If wealth determined the degree to which a man was obliged to contribute to the gathering war effort, its absence often paralysed an already painful process. From Portsmouth in November, the earl of Sussex complained bitterly of the near universal opposition he had encountered from the rural poor when attempting to arm his trained bands: 'I have found neither armour, weapon, nor shott, nor men, accordinge to my expectacon . . . Your Honors wolde thinke these speeches to be strange, if you shold heare them, the meaner and poorer sort, to saie he that wold not sell horse and carte to defende his prince, countrye, famile, and children'.[65] With the salutary choice of starving in freedom or suffering a Spanish boot upon its collective throat, the 'meaner sort' appears to have had a keener strategic appreciation than Sussex may have wished.

The same problems encountered in arming the trained bands hampered the adequate fortification of the most vulnerable potential landing sites. The nation's entire coastline had been surveyed and mapped in the years 1583–5 (Burghley kept a full set of charts, which he annotated minutely), and the result, a 'list of dilapidations', had since been addressed, with varying results.[66] The defences of Portsmouth, for example, had been strengthened as early as 1582 with a new set of ramparts – raised partly at government expense – that Walter Ralegh, surveying in the following year, declared inadequate and had demolished (much to the Queen's fury). Dover, by contrast, fortified strongly during the years 1584–7, was virtually immune to seaborne assault.[67] Between these extremes, dozens of potential landing sites enjoyed widely different levels of protection, ranging from new circuits of walls with bastions (Great Yarmouth), to low banks of earth, hurriedly excavated by local labour and planted with spikes on their forward faces (much of the exposed Sussex coastline between Brighthelmstowe and Shoreham). Booms, usually fashioned from small vessels lashed together and fortified with chains, were the preferred method of securing river mouths and inlets. However, as the human defence of these potential invasion sites was the sole responsibility of the maritime counties' trained bands and militias, money expended upon one facet of local defence almost invariably took from another, and much necessary work was deferred. As late as 1587, for example, it was noted that a breach in the coastal defences at Bletchington Hill, made by the French admiral Claude d'Annebaut's raiding party forty-three years earlier, remained un-repaired.[68]

As the deputy Lords-Lieutenant and their officers began the onerous task of assembling and assessing the trained bands in October, a commission, chaired by Burghley in the absence of Walsingham (incapacitated by an eye infection), was convened to plan and coordinate the nation's home defence.[69] Upon it sat some of England's most competent soldiers – Sir John Norreys, Sir Francis Knollis, Sir Thomas Leighton and Lord Grey de Wilton – whose brief was to consider not only the training and disposition of militias but the fundamental assumptions upon which they were utilized. As with any body that requisitioned the opinions of strong-willed (and often bull-headed) 'experts', its early efforts were not entirely productive. Burghley complained to Walsingham that having broached measures for improvements with Leighton and Walter Ralegh (who joined the commission at the beginning of November), 'I find their Answers so slight, as for my Part I mind no more to deal in the Commission, but to yield my Authority up to her Majesty . . .'.[70]

Perhaps the threat of losing Burghley's facilitating skills galvanized his colleagues. Norreys in particular took advantage of a growing intimacy with the Lord Treasurer to side-step the committee and pass on his recommendations directly. Within weeks, substantial measures to improve the quality and disposition of England's 'army' were evolving. Special sub-commissioners were appointed for the maritime counties to assess the state of static defences and their needs, the Council demanding 'the presente [i.e.

immediate] certyfinge backe unto their Lordships what defectes were founde'.[71] Norreys's particular brief was to increase the number of men in the trained bands without diluting their quality. In November, it was directed that levies assigned to the protection of the Queen's person should commence training in London (the comfort of their presence would be offset somewhat by its expense: once out of their home shires, responsibility for the upkeep of the bands fell upon government).[72] To provide these forces with a core of expertise, 1,200 seasoned soldiers were brought back from the Low Countries, to the further resentment of the States-General. Norreys used some of these to stiffen the City's muster as this came up to its full assessed strength of 10,000 men – 'in better sorte then they had ben afore tymes' – though it seems that of the London contingent, some 4,000 were armed but remained untrained. Elsewhere, local captains were instructed to drill their bands more frequently, and have them ready to mobilize by April at the latest.[73]

In the provinces, measures to improve the bands' quality continued to be hampered by local rivalries and the efforts of deputy Lords Lieutenant to transfer the burden of costs to government. Ultimately, they were unsuccessful, but the Privy Council did its best to provide alternative solutions that did not burden the Exchequer. Recusants with an annual income in excess of £100 were required to meet double or even treble the 'loyal' rate for supplying light horse and arms; and their personal weapons, once confiscated, were distributed to the trained bands. Ironically, the response of many recusants in supplying arms and horses during an earlier enforced levy had been so enthusiastic – in contrast to that of their tight-pursed Protestant neighbours – that the Queen had been moved to offer to commute the recurring penalties for non-attendance at church in return for 'some reasonable compensation' paid annually.[74] A more fundamental reform was the Council's removal of much of the ability of the deputy Lords Lieutenant to hamper (or misinterpret) government orders by imposing a new, higher authority over the shires. In April, Norreys, Leighton, Sir Thomas Morgan and Sir Richard Grenville were each appointed to oversee military preparations in jurisdictions comprising several counties ('whereby the confusion likely to ensue may be avoided' as the Council tactfully put it), and authorized to report their findings and recommendations directly to London.[75]

Very real improvements to the organization and drilling of many of the counties' trained bands resulted from these measures in the months prior to the 1588 campaign, though the most enthusiastic comments made by those charged with the task almost certainly exaggerated their scale.[76] In June, fulsome thanks from the Queen to the Lords Lieutenant, praising their efforts and the response of her subjects, prefaced a request that the previously certified provision of weapons and horses be exceeded – a tacit admission, perhaps, that shortages persisted.[77] It remains difficult, moreover, to assess the precise military value of the instrument shaped by the efforts of Burghley, Norreys and their fellow commissioners. At the end of 1587 it had been calculated that the realm could mobilize some 45,000 trained foot and 3,000 light cavalry, with a further 130,000 militia available in the general musters.[78] These numbers increased in the following months as deputy Lords Lieutenant improved upon their formerly laggardly efforts; yet it was not so much an 'army' that was being forged as a series of concentrations that might prove capable of inflicting sufficient attrition upon a very real army – Parma's – to render its goals impossible. It was only at this eleventh hour, furthermore, that archaic, and potentially disastrous, assumptions regarding the bands' employment were addressed. A vital reform was the abandonment of the venerable imperative to secure every inch of coastline from Wales to the Wash – one that the Britons who had confronted Caesar's legions may have acknowledged. In April, it was directed instead that troops should concentrate at the likeliest bridgeheads for an invasion force carried in a fleet of large, deep-draughted vessels – Yarmouth, Harwich, Sheppey, Portsmouth and Wight, Poole, Plymouth, Falmouth, Milford Haven and Anglesey (the reform brought predictable complaints from several deputy Lords Lieutenant, who feared for the coastlines left denuded of adequate cover).[79] It was proposed also that if the enemy should succeed in landing his forces intact, a main battle should be avoided until an English 'grosse armye' could be gathered in their path.[80]

These were sound measures, but extempory. Any English concentration, even if effected successfully at the right location, would comprise men who (at other than company level) would be meeting as an 'army' for the first time just prior to facing a formidable enemy. And while the old parochialism of the shire levies had been partially addressed in the months prior to the campaign, significant loyalties to local commanders – even among the relatively urbane City bands – remained regrettably intact, as Leicester observed to Walsingham in July 1588.[81] The potential effectiveness of the bands was further compromised by continuing indecision regarding the number of men to be diverted to protect the Queen's person. Extant documents indicate how this provision grew enormously as the campaign drew nearer and government's nerves frayed. In March, 28,900 trained foot, 371 lancers and 2,114 light horse, supported by 36 pieces of ordnance, were allocated to the defence of Whitehall. By July, according to one source, this proposed bodyguard had grown to a staggering 45,000 men – 41,000 foot and 4,000 horse – which, unless comprising largely useless 'general' muster forces, would have denuded all other formations of their most effective men and allowed Parma to advance upon London almost unmolested.[82] The lack of clarity regarding these deployments reflected the larger uncertainties of preparing for a war on English soil. The commissioners and Lords Lieutenant who laboured in the months prior to the campaign had too little time, too few resources and almost no 'professional' corps of officers from which to create a truly national militia.[83] The forces that gathered to face the Spanish army were by no means insignificant either in training or (potential) numbers, but whether they were sufficient – or sufficiently well-organized – to defend their nation adequately is a question that has not been answered definitively, even four hundred years later.[84]

TEN

Awaiting an Enemy

With God's assistance, they shall be so sought out and encountered withall in such sort, as I hope will qualifie their malicious and long pretended practises.[1]

The experienced soldiers who laboured to improve England's home defences knew that they were creating an instrument that, barring calamity, would not be employed. The Navy Royal remained their overwhelming hope as it did the nation's, and the priority given to its preparation reflected this. However, the process of creating and maintaining a battle fleet was not simply a matter of gathering and repairing ships, pressing mariners to man them and then setting out the result to meet its destiny upon the high seas. Timing was as much a concern as organization; by the end of 1587, the first tentative steps to effect a concentration had been taken, but as yet there was no sign of the armada, nor any firm understanding of when it might be expected. Unlike its rudimentary, land-locked sister service, the Navy Royal and its auxiliaries could rely neither upon local levies nor papists' pockets for funding. The Ottoman Empire aside, no sixteenth-century state had the resources to maintain such a force at readiness for more than a few weeks at a time. Until it could be determined that the Spanish fleet was prepared to sail imminently, Elizabeth's government had every incentive to reduce its military expenditure as much as possible without leaving the English coastline parlously exposed.

The quality of intelligence from overseas – the ailing Walsingham's particular concern – was of paramount importance, therefore, in determining how and when the individual elements of England's naval forces should be brought together. Inevitably, this was extremely variable, and 'news' provided by a number of agents during these months was contradictory. In spring 1587, Walsingham had sent to Venice two of his sometime employees, John Wroth and Stephen Powle (Walter Ralegh's roommate from his Middle Temple student days), where Europe's most efficient diplomatic service provided the Doge and Senate with the best intelligence from Madrid, Rome and elsewhere.[2] In November, Wroth was able to pass on broadly accurate news of the damage inflicted upon Santa Cruz's fleet by its extended Atlantic duties (although the quality of his earlier intelligence had been poor).[3] A month later, Powle confirmed that the armada's preparations had been suspended. Within a further two weeks, however, he was reporting rumours that the Spanish fleet had already departed Lisbon. Other advertisements received from Spain and Venice during January suggested variously that the armada was not nearly ready to sail; that the state of its ships was deteriorating rapidly; that Philip longed for peace with England, and, most incredibly, that the Porte (presumably at William Harborne's urging) had despatched a fleet of galleys to invade inland Spain via her principal rivers.[4]

Among this flood of partially accurate and entirely misleading intelligences, much importance has since been placed upon a single note, sent by Sir Edward Stafford to Walsingham in January, which reported that Philip had decided to disband his fleet entirely. This was of course untrue, but given that it was seemingly corroborated by other information arriving in London almost simultaneously (particularly that which dwelt upon the epidemic sweeping through the Spanish ships at Lisbon) it seems unjust to assume that in this instance Stafford was earning his secret Spanish pension.[5] His brother-in-law Howard reacted to the intelligence with frank incredulity, but Walsingham's opinion is unrecorded (and in his weakened state even he was not entirely immune to peace-longings during these months).[6] It is probable, moreover, that Parma's subtle playing of English hopes to avert war increased the sense of confusion in government counsels. On several occasions during November and December 1587, Burghley received Parma's assurances, via the Italian merchant and part-time diplomat Andreas de Looe, that he longed for peace. More specifically, the duke repeatedly gave his promise to write to Spain to halt his master's naval preparations as soon as the Queen despatched her peace commissioners to treat with him at Bergen.[7] Warm words of potential reconciliation from Europe's foremost general would not, alone, have removed English fears (in December, de Looe also reported to Burghley a widespread rumour that Parma's barges were intended for an English invasion),[8] but the cumulative effect of these and other intelligences gleaned from Walsingham's agents – most of which suggested that the immediate prospect of an invasion might be receding – reinforced Elizabeth's determination to eke out her dwindling resources.

That urge had been increasing as winter drew on. The cost of bringing together an unprecedentedly large fleet had been underestimated by all in government, and the error had unpleasant consequences. As early as 22 December (the day after receiving his commission), Howard had written to Burghley to inform him that his mariners were already making inroads into their sea victuals, and asked that the entire warrant lately voted for the supply of the Navy be paid at once.[9] Should the fleet put to sea, its active service in winter seas would inflict further attrition upon the shrinking 'chested treasure', though the same conditions made the armada's early despatch less likely. The cost-to-risk equation was therefore being monitored carefully by the Queen and her Lord Treasurer as the year turned. By 5 January, Burghley had begun to assess the relative costs of a navy maintained at full or half complement. The potential savings of a partial demobilization – predictably, of almost half the expenditure incurred by a fully manned fleet – were too great to forego. With her ships only just commencing their concentration, the Queen ordered their complements to be halved and the redundant mariners paid off, though initial orders regarding deployments were to be implemented. Howard was to remain at Queenborough with sixteen of his ships while Drake would continue to assemble his mixed squadron at Plymouth. Only Sir Henry Palmer, having taken over the guard of the Narrow Seas from Frobisher and therefore on active service, was to maintain a full complement in his small fleet of nine ships.[10]

What followed was an English mirror of the Spanish lacuna, if not as protracted or chaotic. For most of January, little further work was done. Drake arrived at Plymouth in the middle of the month, and his squadron grew slowly thereafter to its ordained strength of thirty ships. He was not, however, permitted to use them. Despite his repeated pleas that he be allowed to sail and carry the war to the enemy (and his later allegation that Elizabeth had reneged upon his original instructions to do just that), he was able to despatch only two of his barks – *Makeshift* and *Spy* – and a number of Plymouth pinnaces to reconnoitre the coasts of Spain and Portugal (their fortunate captains each received bounties of six shillings for their troubles).[11] Otherwise, he was employed in supervising further necessary repairs to his vessels and organizing occasionally fatal gunnery practises on Plymouth Hoe.[12]

Drake's frustrations were echoed at Queenborough, where Howard, incessantly inspecting his half-empty ships for want of more useful occupation, grew increasingly agitated. Coordinating his correspondence with that of Hawkins (both wrote to Walsingham on 1 February upon matters too similar to be coincidental), he complained of the dangers of inaction and of the difficulty in re-manning his fleet, should, as he predicted, the negotiations with Parma come to nothing. For his part, Hawkins, after reminding the Queen's secretary (had he needed it) that papistry was synonymous with servitude, poverty and slavery, once more urged an end to prevarication and the commencement of full-blooded hostilities against Spain. Appealing to one of Walsingham's particular prejudices, he suggested that a fighting war would bring together the English people and undermine the effectiveness of Jesuit proselytisers.[13]

However much Walsingham himself concurred with his correspondents' warnings (and we may be sure that he was assiduous in passing them on to his Queen), Elizabeth refused to give way to calls for immediate re-mobilization. Perceptibly thereafter, letters from Howard, Hawkins, Drake, Lord Henry Seymour and others moved from the reiteration of reasons for aggressive strategies to providing evidence that the war was already upon them. The acquisition of intelligence was, of course, one of the primary duties of the sea-commanders, but the manner in which plentiful (if not always accurate) evidence of Spanish difficulties was filtered out of their reports to Walsingham suggests a degree of collusion. On 11 February, Howard repeated rumours of a concentration of Guise forces near Dunkirk, and, on 29 February, sent on French intelligence from Spain that the armada would be ready to sail on 25 March. Several days later, Thomas Fenner wrote to Walsingham with detailed (though wildly inflated) figures for ships, men and supplies gathered at Lisbon. Via Howard again, on 9/10 March, the Queen's secretary received letters intercepted by Frobisher's squadron discussing the armada's probable date of departure.[14]

At the same time, Walsingham's own agents in Europe were able to confirm that preparations at Lisbon continued. On 1 March, the much-mistrusted Stafford sent urgent word from Paris that the Spanish fleet would be at sea in little more than a fortnight. This was seemingly confirmed by the Huguenot crew of a Dieppe vessel lately returned from Portugal, who had heard that the Spanish fleet was due to sail within eight days of their own departure on 14 March. A distracting note was sounded by Stephen Powle from Venice at the end of the month; he had heard from Lisbon that the armada was to sail on 20 March, but against Algiers, not England. While discounting this rumour, his own view was that Philip's offensive posture was no more than a 'brag' to deter Drake from any further operations against Spain.[15] Clearly, none of this information was accurate, but collectively it provided a useful momentum to keep the fleet's re-mobilization in mind, if not in hand.

Even when feeling her penury most painfully, the Queen had never intended that her ships should be incapable of sailing at relatively short notice. The protection given by winter seas, and news of disorders at Lisbon, had been gratefully seized upon; neither blessing was expected to last, however. As early as 5 February, only seventeen days after Hawkins had discharged half the fleet's mariners, instructions had been sent to James Quarles, Surveyor-General of the Victuals, that the ships under Howard's command at Queenborough (but not the four 'great ships') would be at full complement from 15 March and should be victualled for a month thereafter.[16] This would at least place the core of the English fleet in readiness, yet the leisurely timetable hints at the reluctance with which Burghley looked forward to spending another £3,188 of his 'chested treasure' to facilitate it. In the event, Howard and Hawkins appear to have assisted the Lord Treasurer's schedule considerably. Even while providing intelligences regarding enemy movements they had been urging the Queen to allow an interim, partial re-mobilization. With her permission, they sent the four 'great ships' back to Chatham on 15 February with only ship-keeping crews aboard them.[17] This released sufficient mariners to fully man eight of the Navy Royal's more modern ships and a number of pinnaces. Howard's calculation of six weeks' pay for these and the men of the Narrow Seas squadron was, unremarkably, very similar to Burghley's own, though his expedition in presenting the bill a month early may have been rather less in tune with the Lord Treasurer's aims.[18]

Almost as soon as his ships were up to strength, Howard put to sea. His eight ships, six pinnaces and a ketch were in the Downs on 21 February, all in such fettle that he swore they were fit to pass on to the River Plate and back.[19] On 1 March the wind veered westerly, allowing the fleet to cross the Channel to Cape Gris-Nez and tracked the coastline north-eastwards thereafter as far as Flushing. Howard had already announced his intention of visiting the town to put heart into those rebels of Arnemuiden and Campvere who had declared for the Queen (and, implicitly, against their Stadholder, Prince Maurice), and to calm the nerves of Flushing's English governor, Sir William Russell, to whom the brooding prospect of a Spanish army on the opposite bank of the Scheldt estuary had given considerable anxiety.[20]

The Lord Admiral and his ships were back in Margate roads by 10 March, but his brief visit to Flushing had been a minor triumph of public relations. A consummate diplomat, he was lionized by the burghers of Middelburg, Arnemuiden and Campvere, provided a timely demonstration of English sea power to Parma's forces at Sluys, and dealt delicately with the Stadtholder Maurice, whose quarrel with his anglophile subordinate Sonoy was threatening to splinter the Anglo-Dutch alliance. Most importantly, Howard had given his own men a taste of fleet action and a first sight of their great, unknown enemy.

The Lord Admiral's other signal service during his days at Flushing was to intercept the latest news brought out of Lisbon. His report of 10 March to Walsingham, gleaned from a packet of letters addressed to Parma, anticipated the departure of an armada of 210 sail from Lisbon just ten days' hence. This seemingly cast-iron corroboration of earlier rumours from Europe triggered the full re-mobilization of all elements of the English fleet, notwithstanding Burghley's continuing industry in attempting to pare its costs (on 12 March he had before him an anonymous, lunatic proposal to replace the English mariners' beloved beef ration with fish).[21] On 22 March, Hawkins and Quarles issued a calculation of costs to bring Drake's squadron and the four 'great ships' to full complement.[22] It was a painful bill – more than £12,500 – but by this time new and novel measures had been put in hand to supplement the Exchequer's vanishing treasure.

As already noted, the government had made strenuous efforts via pamphlets, ballads, tracts and pulpits to keep the twin threats of foreign invasion and domestic dissension firmly in English minds. The process had been aided considerably by the same flood of intelligences and advertisements that had stimulated war preparations, supplemented by less verifiable but equally terrifying prognostications for the year 1588 which had been in circulation (though not, until very recently, in mind) since 1569:

> When after Christ's birth there be expired
> Of hundreds, fifteene yeeres eighty and eight,
> Then comes the time of dangers to be feared,
> And all mankind with dolors it shall fright:
> For if the world in that yeere doe not fall,
> If sea and land then perish ne decaie:
> Yet Empires all and kingdomes alter shall,
> And man to ease himselfe shall have no way.[23]

With such alarums playing upon the public mood, judging and manipulating it required a delicate hand. In July, on the eve of battle, Burghley and Hatton hurriedly summoned the Home Counties' justices of the peace to Whitehall, to lecture them upon the fleet's readiness, the Queen's disappointment at the failure of peace negotiations with Parma, and the 'Luciferian authority' underpinning Cardinal Allen's increasingly strident exhortations to English Catholics.[24] Clearly, the calming message was intended to percolate down to a constituency that had now fully absorbed the frightening detail of looming papist world-conspiracies. If, however, officially sanctioned scaremongering occasionally over-reached its aims, it had at least one positive effect. A Spanish descent upon England had come to be regarded as a national, rather than a dynastic threat.

Sixteenth-century princes were expected to fight wars from their own pockets, supplemented by unpopular 'extraordinary' levies and occasional grants from parliament (which usually demanded some heavy quid pro quo). Elizabeth, as noted, enjoyed the fruits of a system that pushed much of the cost of maintaining domestic militias upon her (largely unwilling) subjects, but that was the limit of her good fortune. For every other element of the nation's home defence and for all of her foreign wars, there was only the Exchequer, which had been heavily burdened for almost three years. As the crisis loomed, her most obvious recourse was to her parliament once more, but that particular well had run dry. Those called in 1585 and 1586 had voted two fifteenth and tenth subsidies that produced some £90,000 in 1586 and £56,000 during the following year.[25] To test her MPs' generosity still further would have been unfeasible (and distracting, at a time of national emergency). Foreign loans, the other traditional source of short-term financing, had been denied by the fall of the Antwerp money markets, and recent attempts to find alternative sources, even dangling a usurious rate of interest, had come to nothing.[26] All normal channels of funding were denied to government, therefore, precisely when they were most needed. Yet if the very existence of the nation was threatened, it became the duty of all the Queen's subjects – even those already burdened with the provision of arms and mounts for the trained bands – to meet that threat. Burghley now prepared to attack his persistent deficit in ways that reflected the equally unusual 'national' emergency that pressed. During the last week of January, privy seals poured into the counties, requiring loans from private citizens based upon their assessed wealth ('which we have and mynde alwayes to repaye' as the pro-forma loan notes stated reassuringly).[27] This was a patriotic fund in effect, which eventually realized almost £75,000 from 2,416 named individuals. The citizens of London were not called upon for this subsidy (Burghley was simultaneously begging an 'easy' loan of £30,000 from the wealthier among them), but members of the guilds and city companies voluntarily provided almost £52,000 by private subscription, in addition to the City's prior contributions to the fleet.[28]

This windfall would assist in feeding mariners and repairing ships, but the need for more of both became pressing as reports of the preparations at Lisbon began to over-estimate the scale of the armada. Even a full-strength navy with voluntaries had produced a fleet of less than one hundred ships of all sizes to date.[29] The largest vessels of the English fleet – the four 'great ships' – lay at Chatham still, awaiting crews and new masts (on 10 March, Howard proclaimed them fit for nothing in that state but the defence of Chatham church).[30] If even the lowest estimate of the armada's strength were correct, this was far from an adequate bulwark against the twin threats from Lisbon and the Low Countries. Another appeal for voluntaries might produce more vessels, but their mariners would require feeding, and the rudimentary naval establishment was already stretched almost beyond endurance by existing demands upon its resources.[31] The next, and final, sweep of Burghley's comprehensive trawl through the nation's resources was therefore one that relied little upon voluntary contributions or even patriotic funds. As the hour of England's destiny approached, a degree of coercion became necessary.

Plans to reinforce the navy other than from the royal purse had been in hand for several years. Since 1582, the Privy Council had possessed data on the number, types and location of privately owned English vessels that might, in times of emergency, be drafted into royal service. A survey conducted by the then Lord Admiral, the earl of Lincoln (formerly Baron Clinton), had established that England's ports harboured 177 vessels of 100 tons or more, 74 of 80–100 tons, and 1,383 smaller craft. To man them, the same ports could provide 1,488 trained masters and almost 15,000 mariners (including 957 'wherrymen').[32] Clearly, no more than a fraction of this vast total could be requisitioned if needed; nevertheless, it ensured that the Council would plan their campaign with known resources.

The general stay upon private vessels in English ports, authorized during the previous October, had remained in force. This was not a popular measure; nor was it universally obeyed. John Watts, the London cloth-magnate and enthusiastic financier of privateering expeditions, managed to obtain bonds from the Admiralty – possibly by bribing an official – to set out four vessels, on or around 8 March, for a raiding voyage to the West Indies.[33] Sir Walter Ralegh was not so lucky. While busy organizing Devon's home defences, he attempted also to facilitate his cousin Grenville's departure from England with a fleet of eight ships for the relief of the second Roanoke colony (which Bernard Drake, diverted to attack the Spanish New-foundland fleet in the previous year, had failed to re-provision).[34] Apprised of his plans, the Council swiftly sent orders that Grenville should instead send his vessels to reinforce Drake's Plymouth squadron. Grenville's some-what transparent attempt to evade this order by offering to maintain his fleet as a separate squadron off the Scillies was brusquely rejected. At a cost of a lost English colony, Drake's squadron was usefully supplemented by several fighting ships, including the *Galleon Dudley* (250 tons) and *Virgin God Save Her* (200 tons).[35] Three weeks later, a far more significant rein-forcement of the fleet commenced, when an uncompensated ship levy was proclaimed and orders issued to forty named English ports and towns to provide a total of forty-nine ships and twenty pinnaces – armed, furnished and victualled at local expense.[36]

A torrent of pained demurrals, echoing those of the Lords Lieutenant regarding their trained bands, swiftly reminded the Privy Council of the out-ports' poverty, or of their existing commitments of men and ships. Only Lyme Regis, Weymouth and, with reservations, Exeter immediately under-took to provide at least part of their quota, though as their respective mayors made clear in letters to the Council, they had been beggared by the great decay of their peacetime trade. Other ports pleaded to be re-assessed or excused entirely. London alone, required initially to assume a dispropor-tionately light burden of just eight ships and two pinnaces, exceeded expec-tations and validated its role as the cradle of English patriotism. Meeting on 3 April, the Common Council of the City arbitrarily doubled its own quota, promising '16 of the greatest and best merchaunte ships for warre that can be founde within the River of Thames.'[37] By the close of the cam-paign, London's levy contribution was to rise to thirty ships and pinnaces, of which ten were vessels of 200 tons or more.[38]

Elsewhere, the struggle to secure these uncompensated levies was pro-tracted, and required constant pressure from the Privy Council. The pleas of a fortunate few ports – Poole's was a particularly melancholy effort – were accepted and absolution followed: 'it is thought convenyent they shalbe spared for this present and eased of their burden'.[39] In other cases, local ani-mosities were kindled when the levied ports demanded that their neighbours assist with the burden, and helpfully identified them by name. On 16 April, the bailiffs of Colchester complained that the neighbouring Essex towns of Coggeshall, Dedham and East Bergholt were refusing to make any contribution. Two weeks later, Exeter's mayor and council reported poor success in meeting their allocation and asked that the burden be spread among towns and parishes within twelve miles of their city. This and similar initiatives simply multiplied the incidents of complaints to government. When the mayor of Gloucester was told that he and his fellow citizens should assume part of Bristol's burden by furnishing one ship, he complained of his own town's poverty (the pernicious decay of sea trade once more). He was then ordered to require assistance from Tewkesbury. When this was not forthcoming, the Privy Council exhibited remarkable optimism in ordering the citizens of Gloucester to try their neighbour once more: 'wherein their Lordships doubte not but that the towne of Tewxbury will shewe them selves willing to contrybute with you in all reasonable manner, consideringe it is for the defence of the Realme'.[40]

A further difficulty lay in obtaining levy ships that were remotely suitable for duties in a war fleet. The Cinque Ports, for example, still possessed many vessels despite the silting of their estuaries and decay of their trade. However, most of these were crayers, lighters or river boats, useful for smuggling arms into the continent (an activity that continued well beyond the outbreak of hostilities between England and Spain) but not capable of any modification that might produce a useful man-of-war. Assessed to provide a total of twelve ships, the Ports' levy was revised to just five following representations to the Council on 5 April, and most of these, armed with small pieces of municipal ordnance, had to be hired from elsewhere. The town of Rye at least managed to provide an appropriate vessel; using their venerably ambiguous connections, her burghers secured a French privateer, the 80-ton *Guillaume*.[41]

The levies were instructed to join one of the several divisions of the fleet by 25 April. Not surprisingly, the deadline was met by no more than a handful of out ports. A large proportion of their vessels that found their way into the fleet, being near useless in battle, were assigned to Lord Henry Seymour's Downs squadron for reconnaissance duties. In many cases, it would appear that the ports' protestations of poverty were corroborated in that their ships' victuals, once exhausted, were not replenished thereafter from home. Several vessels were dismissed before the campaign commenced for this reason; others, better provided, would nevertheless suffer considerable privation following the battle, when responsibility for their crews' welfare was generally evaded.[42] Dragooned into the fleet at a moment of crisis, the levies were to add little or nothing to its fighting abilities, place a significant burden upon its resources, and contribute greatly to its Lord Admiral's preoccupations. Like their land-bound equivalent, the formations of the general muster, they were intended to reassure the nation, not frighten an invader.

*   *   *

Between April and June, the number of English ships in service steadily increased, but achieving some sort of parity with the enemy was only half the task. As yet, the fleet remained fragmented; its divisions intended to cover several potential threats. At Plymouth, Drake would be the first to sight and engage the armada as it entered the Channel. What might then be done with his force of some thirty to forty ships against the host of Spain might make for a decent obituary notice but surely little else, despite boasts (most famously iterated by Howard himself) that one English ship was the equal of five or more of the enemy.[43] Yet for several weeks Drake himself seems to have resisted any consolidation of the fleet under the direct authority of Howard. It was rather his intention, expressed several times in letters to the Queen and Privy Council, to use his squadron, reinforced with as many ships as possible but under his sole command, to break up the armada as it assembled off the coast of Portugal or Spain.[44] Only when it became apparent that he would not get his way did he begin to urge the full concentration of the fleet. In the meantime, it was predominantly Howard, aided by intelligences that consistently overstated the size of the armada (one placed it at 'between four and five hundred sail'), who begged the Queen to allow him to bring the entire fleet together.[45]

This had not been his original priority. Like many of the Queen's closest advisors Howard had regarded the threat from Parma's *tercios*, disembarking at some point on the east coast of England or Scotland, to represent a more imminent danger than that posed by the armada itself.[46] Even immediately prior to the battle, he was still warning Elizabeth not to trust the empty promises of her peace commissioners, and with good reason.[47] However, as Seymour's squadron came up to full strength and Parma's chances of making a successful, unaided Channel crossing diminished, Howard's preoccupations adjusted. He became convinced that only a fully concentrated English fleet could confound the increasingly likely strategy of the enemy – a conjunction of the two dukes' forces. In arguing this case, he appears to have taken advantage of his close personal relationship with the Queen to bypass potential dissent within the Council. On 13 April, he wrote to Burghley 'it weer fit I shuld make your Lordship acquaynted with her Majesty's resolusion touchyng the sarvis on the seas . . .'. Four days later, to the same correspondent, he stated explicitly 'It is nowe determined that I shall goe westward with the greateste parte of her Majesties shippes, wherof I have thought good to advertise your Lordship.'[48] The tenor of his correspondence infers that this was a decision to which not even the Lord Treasurer was privy in advance – possibly because of the arguments he might raise against it. Even now, however, doubts remained regarding the wisdom of placing almost all of England's naval strength in one place. On 29 April, Howard drafted a memorandum on the ships to be taken westwards and those to remain with Seymour; but it was not until 10 May – probably following further, urgent representations by the Lord Admiral and his senior commanders, most of whom were present at court three days earlier – that a resolution of the entire Privy Council authorized this.[49]

With his instructions safely endorsed, Howard moved swiftly. The four 'great ships' had been made fully fit for sea duties by 21 April (at Chatham that day, Lord Sheffield, John Hawkins, Sir Robert Southwell and Martin Frobisher took command respectively of the *Bear*, *Victory*, *Elizabeth Jonas* and *Triumph*).[50] The entire English fleet other than Drake's squadron assembled in Margate road between 13 and 15 May. Further vessels were allocated to Seymour's coastal squadron – in the case of the out port levies, those victualled for the shortest period – to a total of some twenty-nine sail.[51] When these arrangements had been completed, Seymour formally relinquished command of the *Elizabeth Bonaventure* to George Raymond and transferred to his new flagship, the *Rainbow*.[52] The reorganized fleet took in further victuals and awaited a favourable wind, which arrived on 21 May. With some thirty-eight ships and a number of pinnaces, the Lord Admiral took 'a pleasant gale', and arrived before Plymouth on the morning of 23 May.[53]

Drake, forewarned of his arrival, came out of Plymouth Sound with his entire force – with recent voluntary and 'levy' additions this had grown to approximately sixty vessels – to affect a grand liaison in the Channel. There is no indication that Howard had either requested or authorized this time- and resource-wasting encounter, but Drake appears to have been making a point. By sailing out to meet and escort his Lord Admiral, he invoked a sense of ritual that suggested (and was probably meant to suggest) that he subordinated himself as an act of will, not of compliance. That a commoner – of whatever talents – assumed a right to consent rather than submit to the Queen's commission was a remarkable demonstration of Drake's indomitable self-regard (or, as his biographer Ubaldino suggested, 'an example of singular self-mastery'), but Howard bore the gesture with good grace and took care not to stand too highly upon his own, indubitably superior authority. With a great show of formality, he conferred the station of vice-admiral of the combined fleet upon Drake, and of rear admiral upon John Hawkins.[54]

Following his arrival at Plymouth, Howard intended to pause only for two days to re-fill his ships' water-casks before putting to sea to seek the enemy.[55] The wind, however, had not yet become a Protestant breeze, and the English fleet was to remain embayed for almost a month. Repeatedly, the Lord Admiral would attempt to set out at least some of his ships; a few would manage to beat their way westwards to the mouth of the Channel, but strong, contrary winds made it impossible to maintain station there. Indeed, they threatened to drive the vessels far to the east – away both from the expected enemy and their sister ships.[56] Unable to depart Plymouth, the combined fleet swiftly began to experience the problem faced by all warhosts – that of finding adequate forage.

The partial demobilization of January had been dictated above all by the difficulty of maintaining the Queen's ships in readiness to meet an enemy who did not then appear. The policy of half-manning had relieved the pressure upon stores somewhat, but Howard, Hawkins, Drake and others had constantly argued for a more satisfactory system of supplying their ships than the prevailing month-by-month arrangement, which made the fleet extremely vulnerable to the timing of the enemy's movements. On April 8 (while its various formations remained splintered), Howard had outlined a worst case to Burghley. His latest intelligence at that time indicated that the armada would be at sea by 15 May. Were this information correct, he pointed out that the timing of the campaign might be such that his ships would sail to meet the enemy with just three days' victuals in their holds. 'Yf it be [fit] to be so', he wrote, 'it pasethe my reson.'[57]

His warning was timely, but other, cash-consuming priorities made an effective reformation of the victualling impossible in the months prior to the campaign. The implications of this failure became fully evident with the fleet's final concentration, when what had been a nagging worry developed into a crisis. There were now over eight thousand mariners at Plymouth (in addition to soldiers and gentlemen-volunteers), more than doubling the peacetime population of the town. The West Country as a whole could not nearly support the burden of feeding them, no matter how timely the provision of Exchequer funds. The bulk of resources therefore had to come from London still, a distance of almost three hundred miles through unseasonably high seas and unhelpful south-westerly gales. To provide a reasonable margin of safety, a significant overlap of supplies needed to be organized. This proved beyond the abilities of the victualling establishment. As they departed the Downs on 22 May, Howard's ships carried less than four weeks' sea-stores. Previously, the Lord Admiral had received Surveyor Quarles's assurance that ten victualling boats would follow the fleet to Plymouth within eight days. By 28 May, Howard had been told that these would not now be arriving until 1 June at the very earliest – and, given Quarles's alleged difficulties in finding mariners to man his boats, it was likely to be long after that. With at most 18 days' victuals remaining, and the latest word being that the armada would be out within seven days (for once, an entirely accurate word), the English fleet was already in danger of being starved into defeat.[58]

Quarles's assistant, Marmaduke Darell, who had been with Drake at Plymouth since January, worked energetically in his mariners' interests. In April, he had rubbed salt into the wound of Grenville's recent disappointment by sacking the remnants of his small fleet for its substantial store of victuals (intended for the mouths of the unfortunate Roanoke colonists) and distributing them among Drake's ships.[59] Two months later, as stocks of food dwindled once more, there were no similarly convenient means to provide for what had become a far larger fleet. Scouring the Devon countryside, Darell managed to secure fresh provisions to a value of £900 – just six days' supply. Inadequacies both in quantity and quality of victuals had serious repercussions. Disease had first been noticed in some of the ships at the end of March, at which time the Privy Council hurriedly appointed more physicians to prevent an epidemic.[60] Then, the affliction had affected a relatively small concentration; in June, it reawakened in the midst of a sizeable proportion of the nation's ablest seamen. Prior to the commencement of the campaign, almost a thousand men would be discharged from the English ships, necessitating a large-scale (and extremely unpopular) impressment of substitutes from West Country ports. Inevitably, these were not as well-trained – particularly in the handling and use of ordnance – as their diseased predecessors. Many were not even professional mariners, only unfortunates who happened to live too close to the sea and the press gang's beat; yet however much they lacked of the seaman's craft, they made equally robust inroads into the fleet's dwindling stores.[61] The problem was eased somewhat on 23 June, when fifteen London boats finally arrived at Plymouth carrying a further month's victuals. Unfortunately, these brought no indication that their successor convoys would be any timelier.[62]

Howard's composure was not improved by this creeping prospect of starvation, as his correspondence makes clear: 'We thinke it shuld be marvaylled at how we keepe our men from runninge away, for the worste men in the fleete knoweth for how longe we are vitelled . . . God sende us a winde to put us owt; for go we will, though we starve.' He continued to profess his utmost confidence in his ships, his men and their impending victory, but his enthusiasm was forced. Being of a family whose relationship to the Tudors had long been intimate (and occasionally homicidal), no one was more sensitive to how much of England's political identity and strength was invested in the person of the Queen, or to the consequences of her death or capture. His present impotence raised that awareness to near-panic. On 22 June, he urged Walsingham to strengthen the guard for the protection of Elizabeth's person to a minimum of 10,000 to 12,000 men. Given his present inactivity, he saw no better use for his own 6,000 but that they be despatched to London to gather around her. Six months earlier, his 'fidelity, prudence, zeal, experience, circumspection, industry and diligence' had brought him unprecedented power to defend his cousin and her estate; now, commanding the greatest fleet in English maritime history, he was reduced to considering the unthinkable – that it might not be used. The Lord Admiral's principal officers, blessed with only a single responsibility, constantly urged him to take the first favourable wind and seek the armada at the 'Groyne' (Corunna). Their single-mindedness hints at secret fears that their commander, a professional courtier with no previous experience of battle, lacked the will to confront the enemy. If so, they were misplaced. The prospect of the death of a regime for lack of supplies, and the immortal infamy of his part in that demise, had made a warrior of Howard already.[63]

To the east, Seymour's resolve was being tested no less than that of his admiral. A rumour that Parma's *tercios* had broken camp and were making for the sea sent his Downs squadron eastwards across the Channel once more on 4 June.[64] For three days, he covered the Scheldt estuary until the Privy Council, upon new information, redirected him to provide support for the rebel port of Ostend, upon which Parma was now expected to descend.[65] However, by the end of the month the duke's putative goal had come full circle. The Isles of Thanet and Sheppey were now feared to be the destination of the duke's army of invasion; belatedly, Sir John Norreys was sent to organize defensive works there, while Seymour was confined to the Downs once more, still with no inkling of the movements or intentions of the greatest army in Europe.[66]

To add to the pain of the English commanders' enforced leisure, definitive news that the armada was at sea had reached England by 15 June at the latest.[67] Thereafter, the imminence of crisis generated numerous visions of ghostly elements of the Spanish fleet, though a report from a Mousehole bark, sighting on 19 June a number of Spanish ships driven as far north as the Scillies by the storms that had sent their sisters scurrying into Corunna, was 'good' intelligence, confirmed as such by the Lord Admiral's own scouting pinnaces. By 27 June, such was the expectation of invasion that all shire levies were placed upon one hour's notice to march to their allocated concentration points. Fortunately, however, they were no longer likely to constitute a forlorn front-line against the coming invaders.

Four days earlier, the welcome easterly wind that had carried the victualling ships into Plymouth eased Howard's several torments. To Walsingham, he had previously written: 'I wyll not tarry one hower after our vytells do come to us, and yf the wynd wyll sarve us . . .'. On the afternoon of 23 June, as his men hurriedly distributed fresh stores around the fleet, he scrawled a further series of letters. To the Queen herself he provided the small comfort of rumours that the armada had been scattered by storms, but found a moment also to lament once more the 'velynous treasons' that enveloped her. In the day's first note to Walsingham, he begged him to ensure that the Queen trust no more to 'Judase's kyses' (the peace negotiations), and post-scripted: 'Sir, God wylling I wyll cut my sayll within this three hower'. Some minutes later, scrawling a further note to answer new letters from the Queen's secretary, his timetable had shortened to two hours.[68]

The English ships, their decks littered still with unstowed victuals, were at sea by sunset. After weeks of idleness, agues and growing despondency, Howard had drawn England's sword swiftly and was eager to use it. Yet again, however, the moment of decision evaded him. Despite his increasingly urgent pleas – reinforced by the expert opinion of his subordinates – to seek the enemy upon the coast of Spain, Elizabeth was adamant that he should await firm news of the armada before committing himself. As Walsingham reminded him in despatches of 6 June, he was permitted only 'to ply up and down in some indyfferent place betwene the coast of Spain and this realme'.[69] During the next two-and-a-half weeks, the English fleet would cruise between the Scillies and French coast, labouring against winds, tides and impossibly contradictory orders, seeking some sign or news of the Spanish fleet.[70] When the weather allowed, Howard deployed his ships as a thin screen through which, hopefully, the armada could not pass unseen. Upon his western flank, near the Scillies, Hawkins commanded approximately twenty vessels, covering any attempt by Medina Sidonia to make for Ireland or the Welsh coast. In the centre, Howard's own formation spread out across the 'sleeve' – the mouth of the Channel. Drake, with a similar squadron to that of Hawkins, lay off Ushant to monitor shipping movements along the French coast. Their intelligence allowed no more decisive manoeuvre. As he fled Plymouth on 23 June, the Lord Admiral had received word from 'a sure fellow' that the armada might rendezvous with and embark Guise's Leaguer army prior to its descent upon Flanders and then England. Otherwise, there was silence, and empty seas. In more than a fortnight's ceaseless searching, not a single confirmed sighting of a Spanish vessel was made. 'Whatsoever hathe bin made of the Sleeve, in is another manner of thinge then it was taken for' lamented an increasingly frustrated Howard; 'we finde it, by experience and dailie observation, to be an hundrethe myles over; a large rowme for men to looke unto.'[71] Through that 'large room', it seemed all too likely that an intact armada might proceed unnoticed.

This perplexing failure to sight the enemy fleet convinced Drake in particular that it must have been driven back to Spain by the recent squalls. Accordingly, during the flag officers' daily councils he pressed ever more urgently that the English ships should search out and destroy its scattered elements before they could reform.[72] Howard had no authority to sanction this or any other divergence from instructions that had been framed to stifle excessive initiative, but now he requisitioned the weather to give him the leeway his Queen had refused. To maintain his extended station upon unseasonably high seas was becoming difficult. Previously, in acceding reluctantly to Elizabeth's restrictive orders, he had disingenuously begged God not to make the wind force him towards Spain against his mistress's will; on 5 July, it began to do just that. News brought to the fleet by English mariners out of La Rochelle on 7 July, confirming that elements of the armada lay scattered in several harbours across northern Spain, was a further goad. Off Ushant that day, following a brief conference with his principal lieutenants, Howard surrendered to the wind and their pleas, and the entire English fleet moved southwards.[73]

Two days later, it returned hurriedly. Before any of Howard's ships were in sight of the northern Spanish coast, the wind veered strongly southerly once more, dashing hopes for a pre-emptive encounter with a weak, disorganized enemy. At the least, the Lord Admiral had hoped to seize several Spanish fishing boats and obtain definitive word of the armada's location and condition; without a single such encounter, he was dangerously exposed. To have attempted to remain in Biscay, fighting a wind that could bring the armada swiftly northwards, would have been imprudent in the extreme – and, moreover, utterly against both the spirit and letter of the Queen's wishes (though Elizabeth would exhibit great perversity some days later in criticizing Howard for not seeking his foe with sufficient eagerness).[74] There was also a growing problem of disease among his ships' crews, and the victuals in several of his smaller 'levy' vessels were almost exhausted after just fourteen days' sea duty. By 12 July, the English fleet was snug once more in Cattewater and Plymouth Sound.

At the moment it anchored, however, the principal ships of the armada were warping out of Corunna. The entire expedition was far smaller than Englishmen had come to fear and expect – in fact, only 101 major vessels, many of them armed merchantmen, supported by some thirty to thirty-five patches, zabras and pinnaces. Before it sighted English shores it would lose the company of its only four galleys (forced by high seas, and, in one case, a mutiny among her convict oarsmen, to turn back) and the *Santa Ana*, flagship of its Biscayan squadron, which would make for the French coast after losing a mast. But between them, the remaining Spanish ships carried 18,000 soldiers and the expectation, unrealistic though it would prove, of accompanying a further 26,000 of Parma's finest troops into England 'to satisfye ther ragyng myndes of revendg'.[75] They sailed, it was said, in confident expectation of a miracle. They would be overthrown, it was countered, by God's miraculous favour. Double-booked, the Lord of Hosts prepared to rectify the defects of military planning.

1. (above) Elizabeth I: the 'armada portrait', by George Gower.

2. (left) Philip II, by Alonso Sanchez Coello.

3. Sir Francis Walsingham, by John de Critz.

4. Alexander Farnese, Duke of Parma, by O. Vaenius.

5. William Cecil, 1st Baron Burghley.

6. Charles Howard, 2nd Baron Effingham, Lord Admiral of England by Daniel Mytens; a late portrait.

7. Robert Dudley, Earl of Leicester, English school, sixteenth century.

8. Sir John Hawkins, English school, sixteenth century.

9. Lord Henry Seymour, attributed to Federigo Zucchero.

10. Bowls on Plymouth Hoe, by John Seymour Lucas. The Drake legend triumphant: Howard hovers anxiously, the senior captains cluelessly; all wait upon England's saviour.

11.   The opposing fleets engaged, English school, sixteenth century. A gorgeous, highly stylized interpretation. In the centre foreground is one of the armada's four Neopolitan galleasses, complete with friars and a jester.

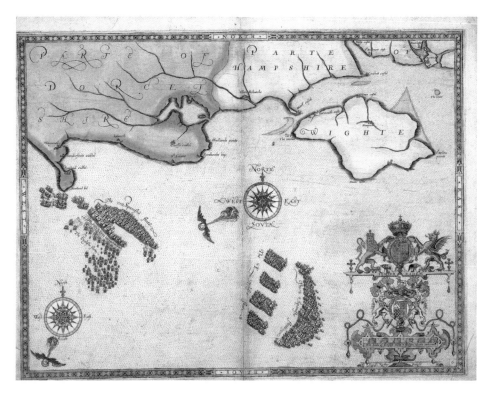

12.   The fight off Portland Bill and aftermath, one of a series of narrative charts by Robert Adams. In the first encounter only a few of the leading English ships engage the enemy: an accurate recollection. Thereafter the English fleet, chasing the reformed armada, has been reorganized into four distinct squadrons.

13.   The armada campaign, English school, sixteenth century. A romantic compendium; Elizabeth and her armies watch the battle from an impossibly mountainous and highly fortified English shore (a warning to future would-be invaders?).

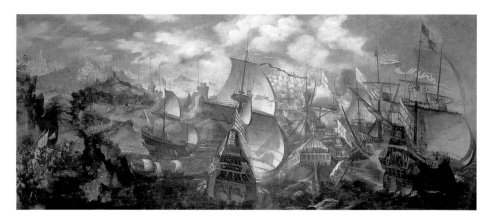

14. Calais: the fireships advance, Netherlandish school, sixteenth century. The tableau conflates several events. In the left foreground English and Spanish galleons exchange fire at point-blank range. The disparity in their respective sizes is vastly exaggerated.

15. The course of the armada, by Augustine Ryther, after Robert Adams. Had the retreating Spanish ships indeed taken this circumspect route around Scotland and Ireland, many more might have made their home ports.

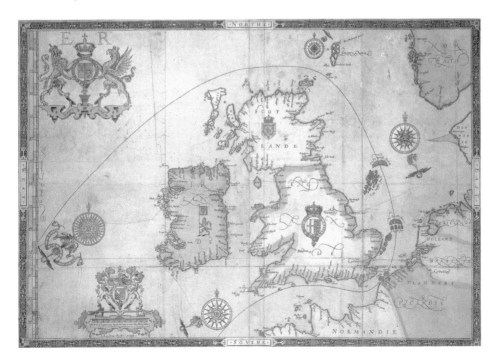

16.   The Somerset House Conference, 1604, attributed to de la Cruz Pantoja. The Spanish delegation of six sits to the left, their five English counterparts to the right, Charles Howard at the rear.

ELEVEN

In Defence of Ourselves

It is then most necessarie, howsoever you consider of it, by all lawes of nature and of nations, of God and of man, this defence that we are driven unto. It is holie, iust, honourable, and necessarie.[1]

On the morning of 19 July, approximately ninety English ships lay at anchor in Plymouth Sound, awaiting word of the approach of the Spanish fleet.[2] They, and the vessels that would join them in the coming days, were a match for any seaborne force that Philip II could set against England – provided, of course, that they could find their enemy. The qualification was all-important. Burghley, the officers of Marine Causes and their unsung subordinates had laboured hard upon the practicalities of bringing this vast fleet into existence, but its ultimate fitness for the coming battle was hardly in doubt. The principal concern of government was the possibility that the encounter might not take place – that Philip's invasion force(s) might avoid it entirely and descend upon England unmolested.

The formulation of a war strategy by the Queen and her council had been a tortuous process. It evolved slowly, bending and reversing with the receipt of intelligence from Europe and the seas, and had not yet come to full maturity when the first shots of the campaign were exchanged. Our understanding of its dynamics has been greatly influenced, and to some extent tainted, by the work of the first great armada historian, Julian Corbett. Corbett was in no doubt as to whom England owed her greatest debt. It was Sir Francis Drake alone who realized the need to wage aggressive war; Drake who stood against the prevaricators, penny-pinchers and outright traitors (poor Sir James Croft and his fellow 'appeasers' once more); Drake who single-handedly turned the minds of his colleagues, superiors and, eventually, his sovereign from a craven defensive posture to wholehearted endorsement of his personal strategy of total war against Philip and his minions. The principal flaw in this thesis (one that has been adopted in varying degrees by many subsequent commentators[3]) is that it relies entirely upon Drake's own version of events, as related to, and propagated by, the Florentine Petruccio Ubaldino – a third-hand account, in effect, so wholly credited by Corbett that he referred baldly to the English strategy as 'Drake's plan of campaign'.[4]

Extant correspondence suggests that Drake was indeed the most persistent advocate of a strategy that would carry the war to the enemy, but there was little novelty in what he proposed. His cousin and mentor John Hawkins had been devising belligerent naval projects against Philip's possessions and forces since 1572. His latest proposal, despatched to Walsingham at the beginning of February 1588, urged a 'determined and resolute war' involving a permanent, rotating squadron upon the coast of Spain and Portugal which anticipated Drake's famous exhortation to the Privy Council by some two months.[5] Almost simultaneously, Thomas Fenner petitioned Burghley with a similar, if more modest proposal to equip a squadron of thirty sail to strike at the gathering armada's seaborne supply lines.[6] Ubaldino's *Narrative* later suggested that Hawkins, Fenner and other members of the Lord Admiral's informal council of war at Plymouth were persuaded by the force and logic of Drake's arguments, yet their own proposals predated the first gathering of this group. In any case, the aggressive predilections of Howard's advisors – soldiers, past and future freebooters and young noblemen in search of a reputation – make any inference of hesitancy highly implausible. The idea of waging an offensive war was not new; nor was it remotely controversial to contemporary Englishmen. Even the unwarlike Burghley had previously drafted a long and detailed proposal that envisaged at least half the English fleet sailing to intercept the Spanish ships as they assembled at sea.[7] If Drake had a peculiar contribution, it was to regard the offensive as the *only* proper strategy, with neither consideration of, nor provision to address, the implications of its failure.

The faith of Corbett and others in Drake's vision has encouraged much speculation upon what might have been achieved had he reprised the previous year's raid, with far greater forces, before the Spanish fleet could put to sea. Yet the lessons of Cadiz were hardly applicable to Lisbon. For Drake to have assaulted the greater number of Philip's ships while most exposed to damage, he would have been obliged to take his squadron far into the Tagus river: a manoeuvre he was reluctant to attempt both in 1587 and 1589 without supporting land forces, and with good reason. Its estuary was riddled with sand bars (several of the armada's larger ships would need to be towed carefully over these by galleys as they departed Lisbon); its course was defended by major fortresses at St Julian, Torres Viejo and Belém and by numerous shore batteries between; and in February 1588 (even before Medina Sidonia brought their complement to full strength) it hosted thousands of Spanish troops, all of whom might have descended enthusiastically upon an English fleet which, in the confines of the river, would not have had the luxury of standing off from the enemy.[8] Drake was well aware of these hazards, and actually urged something quite different in the early months of 1588 – that his fleet should patrol the Portuguese Atlantic coast and engage the armada piecemeal as it emerged from the Tagus. However, his proposal was hardly less dismissive of realities than an outright assault upon Lisbon. Its success would have relied upon Spanish acquiescence to an enemy that must surely have been observed beforehand (and even the otherwise aggressive Santa Cruz had happily ignored Drake's taunts to come out and meet him in battle the previous year). It would have required also that the English fleet remain on active service far from friendly English shores for up to several months – a feat demanding mastery of winter gales and, more problematically, of Elizabeth's victualling establishment.

More fundamentally, this and other speculations rely heavily upon our subsequent understanding of Philip's resources and intentions. In the minds of the Queen, her councillors and their intelligencers abroad, there was no single, immutable threat. As it developed, the government's strategy was – could only be – formulated upon such information as became available. This, as already observed, was fragmented and contradictory.[9] To an impartial observer, the Privy Council's early plans to meet the coming dangers might be regarded variously as incoherent or optimistic, particularly in their efforts to address all possible eventualities. But it was fear rather than over-confidence that informed the decisions of Elizabeth's principal advisers. If they worked with a single, consistent assumption, it was that any substantial misreading of the enemy's intentions and movements would be irredeemable. If they were cautious in committing themselves to a definitive course, it was because they fully recognized the cost of getting it wrong.

The process of identifying every permutation of a likely Spanish war strategy had been underway for some years. The earliest example of a clearly defined counter-strategy had been drafted by Burghley in 1584, when Philip's involvement in the Thockmorton plot and Parma's spectacular gains in the Low Countries suggested that some move against England might be gathering momentum.[10] The contrast between his assumptions then and his strategic assessment of February 1588 reveals a growing confidence in the ability of an English fleet to carry the battle to the enemy. It did not, however, reflect any belief that the war – as opposed to a single encounter – could be won on the offensive. Unlike Drake (and, to a lesser extent, Hawkins), Burghley did not plan for the knock-out blow. Rather, he foresaw that England's best hope lay in making war too onerous – that is, too expensive – for Philip to seek wantonly. Nevertheless, between 1584 and 1588 there seems to have been an important shift in his perception of how it might be fought.

The 1584 strategic summary had been outlined at a time when the memory of the naval battle of Terceira remained fresh. The spectacular outcome of that clash suggested that the consolidation of Spanish and Portuguese naval forces had created an overwhelmingly powerful instrument of war. Should this be turned against England in the near-future, Burghley proposed that the tactical response be wholly reactive. The English fleet would be divided into three squadrons, based upon the Scillies, Isle of Wight and the Downs. If the attacking force moved eastwards into the Channel, Ireland might be discounted as its objective; at that point, the Scilly squadron would fall back to reinforce its sister squadron off Wight. If the eastward passage of the Spanish fleet continued, the south coast of England might also be regarded as 'safe', and the entire English fleet would then consolidate in the Downs to defend the likeliest enemy objective – the Thames estuary and London. Though Spanish land forces in the Low Countries were not considered likely to be utilized directly at this time, the intention to retain a third of the fleet in the Downs throughout the posited campaign suggests that English hopes for continuing rebel resistance were not high.

Four years later, a state of war existed between England and Spain. English self-confidence had been restored – perhaps too much so – by Drake's West Indies and Cadiz raids, and Spanish naval power was no longer regarded as significantly superior to that which the Queen could mobilize in response. In fact, the Privy Council's deliberations were now based upon the assumption that English naval strength (that is, the Navy Royal, armed English voluntaries and levies, supported by the Dutch naval contingent due under the terms of the Treaty of Nonsuch) was at an historic apogee. It was believed that any Spanish attempt to disembark an army on England soil could be thwarted by these forces – provided that they could concentrate in time and place to meet it. The problem, of course, was effecting that concentration. While English naval strength had grown during the period, so too had the enemy's disposable resources. The Netherlander rebels had survived the setbacks of Parma's earlier campaigns, but the duke still wielded the initiative. His forces were now known to be an element of Spain's strategy for England, which meant that some division of English defences was unavoidable until his precise intentions could be divined. Most early intelligences from Spain could not be accurate about the size of the gathering armada, but before the end of 1587 Walsingham knew of the safe return of the *flota* with sixteen million ducats' value in bullion, and of a mooted papal loan of a further three to four millions.[11] Finances were not anticipated to be a limiting factor, therefore. The committee that considered Burghley's latest appraisal prudently assumed the worst: that should Philip move against England, he had the ability to mount two or more attacks simultaneously to fragment or distract the English response.

The committee comprised Burghley himself, Walsingham, Leicester, Hatton and the Queen's Latin secretary, John Wooley.[12] The 'hawks' were in a majority, therefore, and proposals to counter the enemy's intentions appear to reflect this (not least, they seem to have encouraged Drake to persuade himself that he was about to be unleashed). A vaguely stated demonstration towards Spain was discussed, as was another attempt to seize a plate fleet in the Azores, perhaps amalgamated with a project to assist Don António to land in Portugal and raise a rebellion there. Yet these proposals, however tactically aggressive, shared a common, essentially defensive aim: to divert or splinter the armada's strength, thus diluting the potency of its descent upon England. Burghley himself thought this goal sufficiently vital as to be worth the diversion of Drake's squadron to the Azores throughout the coming campaign, where its presence would, he believed, distract the greatest number of Spanish warships from English shores.[13]

Moreover, while the committee saw merit in each of these proposals, it recognized also their common, potentially disastrous flaw. All required that Philip await the English onslaught and deploy his own forces precisely in the manner expected of him. Should he choose rather to despatch his armada northwards at a time when most of the English navy lay outside the Channel and its approaches, or Parma break through whatever thin screen of English ships could be spared for home defence, the trained bands and general musters might well experience a fatal testing. Such possibilities –

Elizabeth's overwhelming concern during the months prior to the campaign – had strongly coloured the official instructions provided to Howard on 15 December 1587.[14] These had anticipated the worst: a dual-pronged assault launched simultaneously, with the armada sailing directly from Portuguese and Spanish ports against Ireland or Scotland while Parma's troops descended upon the British east coast anywhere between the Downs and Scotland (in fact, a fairly accurate assumption of Philip's original aims for the aborted 1587 campaign). In the face of such a strategy, Drake's squadron, based at Plymouth, was to await the former thrust by plying 'up and down between out realm of Ireland and the Isle of Scilly and Ushant'; meanwhile, Howard's concentration of ships would cover the Narrow Seas and intercept any attempt from the Low Countries.[15] The shallow-drafted vessels of Lord Henry Seymour's squadron would cover the treacherous waters off Flanders, hopefully to prevent, or at least to provide early warning of, Parma's embarkation. At this point, the Queen's attitude to placing almost all her forces in one location was unequivocal. Only if Howard received 'certain advertisement' that the approaching armada was too powerful for Drake's squadron alone to defeat, or that it would attempt to effect a liaison with Parma's army prior to a combined descent upon England, was Howard either to send some of his vessels to reinforce his vice admiral or combine their fleets to meet the Spanish advance. Flexibility was the paramount consideration. Absent that certain advertisement (and it remained frustratingly absent), we may be sure that Elizabeth considered an all-or-nothing pre-emptive strike southwards to be as prudent as anchoring the entire English fleet in ranks across the mouth of the Thames estuary.[16] Drake may not have agreed, but the fate of his nation could not be wagered upon how well his famous luck held.

Clearly, however, attempts to cover all possible permutations of Philip's strategy were not realistic, given the resources available to Howard. They became even less so once circumstance dictated that the English fleet concentrate at Plymouth. Yet the Queen's reluctance to commit to a single, decisive plan of campaign persisted even then. It did so because the threats to England, rather than focus as the campaign approached, appeared to splinter and multiply. By the end of May 1588, her most optimistic peace commissioners in the Low Countries had lost any hope that Parma was negotiating in good faith.[17] The prospect of more than a single assault upon England, which appeared to have receded slightly since the beginning of the year, now strengthened once more. Indeed, the threat was greater because distractions that may have deterred or at least diluted Philip's English adventure were dissipating. In April, Frederick II, King of Denmark, died, leaving a minor to succeed to his throne. His eleven-year reign had marked a high point in Anglo-Danish relations; with his death, the Protestant cause in Europe lost a notable figurehead and also, possibly, the services of a not-inconsequential navy and control of the Øresund, through which vital supplies of Baltic hemp, pitch and timber were carried to Spain. Upon an even more critical shore, Elizabeth's protracted peace negotiations with Parma had infuriated the States-General, notwithstanding her repeated assurances that any peace which abandoned the rebels to Philip's mercies was not acceptable to her.[18] With Leicester's earlier diplomatic blunders, they pushed Holland and Zeeland almost to the point of reneging upon their treaty obligation to provide naval support for their seemingly faithless allies. Thus, Howard was obliged to reinforce Seymour's squadron significantly before departing with the rest of his fleet to Plymouth to reassure himself and his Queen that Parma's *tercios* would be blockaded adequately.[19]

In France also, the Queen's policy had fallen apart. For months, she had made a priority of pushing Henri III away from the Catholic League and closer to Navarre (the unacceptable alternative was to continue paying subsidies to her Huguenot ally). In April, however, Henri of Guise, directing the siege of Boulogne on behalf of his Spanish paymaster, broke off and hurried to Paris to ride the mob's fury against the King. The 'Day of the Barricades' ended royal authority in the city and marked the nadir of Henri III's reign. With his abject submission to the League on 19 May, the Huguenot cause was thrown back once more upon securing its continuing existence, and Elizabeth had lost – if temporarily – the effective support of an ally whom Burghley had described as 'the hinge of her security'.[20]

Fortunately for England, none of these apparent failures brought a corresponding rise in Spanish fortunes. Denmark maintained her friendly neutrality (helped in part by Elizabeth's hasty promise to the new King to do something about English depredations against his long-suffering subjects' vessels[21]); the Dutch cromsters were to play a vital role in blockading Parma's forces (if for entirely self-interested reasons), and, despite the personal triumph of Guise in Paris, the ports of Boulogne and Dieppe kept their gates closed to Leaguer forces, thereby denying adequate deep-water havens in which the armada might otherwise have awaited its rendezvous with Parma in safety. Nevertheless, perception was everything. Burghley's hoped-for 'conjunction with all Princes Protestant' had proved an expensive chimaera. The Netherlander rebels apart (and they could offer little that was not needed to defend their own cause), England effectively stood alone, awaiting one of the greatest invasion fleets in the history of naval warfare.

At this desperate juncture, the temptation to set out a major new expedition that might, as in the previous year, snatch the initiative from Philip must have been strong. Almost frantically, Drake was urging a descent upon Spain, supported by – or in concurrence with – almost all the senior English sea commanders. Yet to know, much less confound, the timetables both of Philip's new admiral Medina Sidonia and Parma was beyond England's rudimentary intelligence resources. Elizabeth's continuing resistance to pleas from the fleet, and her infamously vague direction to Howard to 'ply up and down in some indifferent place' in the Channel, were not symptoms of inner confusion or strategic naivety, but of a reluctance to share her sea commanders' faith in their own instincts. The brief, profitless foray southwards that Howard made with his entire fleet between 7–9 July validated this wariness. The Lord Admiral had finally received reasonably firm intelligence that the armada lay at Corunna. This, undoubtedly, was the best opportunity to do serious damage to the enemy while it remained far from England's shores. Even now, however, the vagaries of weather offered equal odds on an easy victory or devastating defeat. The English fleet, with its superbly weatherly galleons, was unable to reach the northern coast of Spain in the face of contrary winds; a failure that had obvious and urgent implications to Howard and his subordinates. Had Medina Sidonia chosen to warp out of Corunna harbour on the southerlies that drove the English ships back towards the Channel (rather than spend a further three days completing his repairs and re-victualling), he might have been passed the enemy unawares and ranged the English coast with only Seymour's small force between the armada and the Thames estuary.[22] Fortunately, the fog of war drifted equally thickly over Spanish and English awareness.

*   *   *

At Plymouth, on 19 July, that fog had not yet dispersed, but a happy blend of caution, half-useful intelligence and good fortune had already provided Howard with a decisive advantage. The concentration of the greater part of the English fleet in the West Country virtually extinguished any possibility that Medina Sidonia's ships might pass eastwards up the Channel unchallenged – the vital pre-requisite for Philip's cumbersome plan to have any chance of success. Consequently, unless the English commanders allowed their enemy to close, board and overwhelm their ships in engagement (which, as shall be discussed, they were sensibly loath to do), the grand liaison of Spanish naval forces and Parma's *tercios* would have to be effected under the guns of a substantially intact English fleet: a manoeuvre that at least one of the dukes regarded as suicidal. In a sense, therefore, the 'Spanish' wing of the invasion of England entered the Channel already defeated in its objectives, though no one could know that as yet.[23] Each side was aware of its own weaknesses but could only guess at those of the other; neither had a clear plan of campaign, because the nature of the coming conflict was beyond contemporary experience.

On Howard's part, that ignorance was aggravated by the novelty of the instrument with which he was expected to deliver his nation. Far-sighted naval planning and a fair amount of timely improvisation had provided England with the most powerful fleet to ride in English waters since the days of the Saxon sailor-king Edgar. And if the scale of this weapon was striking, its nature was entirely unprecedented. Unlike the major English war fleets of previous reigns, this was not an army afloat. The ships transported soldiers as protection from boarding parties, not as an offensive arm to decide a battle at sea or upon foreign soil. Their mariners were not auxiliaries, but the means by which an instrument of war would be wielded. In effect, the battle philosophy of this fleet reversed the traditional etiquette of naval warfare; an innovation encouraged by England's relative weakness as a military power, the vulnerability of her long, accessible coastline and the growing expertise of a small section of her population in the art of using ships to fight other ships. That expertise was enhanced, as previously noted, by evolutionary developments that had made the best English ships far more weatherly than the higher-charged vessels of their enemy. It was further aided by the deployment of the four-wheeled naval gun carriage, a profoundly important device whose ordnance, unlike that mounted upon the two-wheeled, long-trailed field carriages still supplied to Spanish warships, could be brought inboard rapidly and reloaded after discharging their shot. This was by no means a recent advance; the *Mary Rose* had gone to the bottom of the Solent in 1545 with a fine collection of guns mounted in similar carriages. For more than forty years, therefore, English gunners had been developing skills that allowed the relatively rapid employment of their ordnance in battle (subject, of course, to the limitations of contemporary gun-casting technology). Their Spanish enemy, wedded still to the tactic of closing with and boarding an enemy (one that had delivered overwhelming victory at Lepanto and Terceira), regarded ships' ordnance primarily as a useful preliminary tool to disorient and scatter their foe, rather than to inflict traumatic damage upon the vessels they assaulted. The coming clash of these opposing philosophies would illustrate starkly the efficacy of fire-power used to its full potential.

The margin of English superiority can be overstated, however. Some commentators have regarded the English fleet of 1588 as a new and decisive weapon in the nation's developing maritime tradition. In doing so, they have rightly placed much emphasis upon the relative quality of ships and ordnance (and the individual skills of mariners and gunners) while passing over a profound limitation governing their effective employment – the inexperience of all English captains and crews in fighting en masse. Despite reasonable claims to be Western Europe's foremost naval power, England had been obliged to prove the point upon remarkably few occasions. It had been almost half a century since the entire Navy Royal had come out to challenge Francis 1's abortive 'invasion' of England; an encounter that had revealed little more than that neither protagonist had much idea of how to fight a sea battle. Since that time, English ships had been used aggressively in numerous clashes, but none involving significant formations. Even Francis Drake, the very exemplar of the English 'sea dog', was a near-novice in the art of fleet engagements. His only relevant experience had occurred at San Juan de Ulúa at the outset of his career, and at Cadiz, where several galleys had repeatedly been fought off by the superior fire-power of English galleons. Upon both occasions, coordinated manoeuvre under sail had played very little part in the fighting. Otherwise, his martial experience consisted of a number of successful amphibious assaults upon immovable fortifications (Santiago, Santo Domingo, Cartagena and St Augustin), small-scale land campaigns in the Panama Isthmus and some very profitable engagements against individual plate-ships. Drake the opportunist of genius was famous throughout Europe; Drake the ineffectual and divisive commander of large-scale forces would be a revelation of the coming years. His old mentor Hawkins, another erstwhile sea fighter, had given something of a drubbing to the Spanish fleet at San Juan de Ulúa before losing six of his expedition's eight ships, but that engagement between embayed or anchored vessels had occurred fully a generation earlier, and provided few lessons for the approaching battle.

Men like Martin Frobisher, Robert Crosse, and the Fenner family had similarly fought their way into the fleet; but their hard-won experience was hardly apposite for a battle in which they would be expected to maintain formation and stand off, rather than close with and pillage their enemy at the first opportunity.[24] The aggressive spirit and elan that they and many others shared were extremely valuable qualities in a sea fight; nevertheless, the ruggedly individualistic career-privateer was not ideal raw material from which a disciplined cadre of naval officers might be forged. Of all the commanders of English vessels in 1588, only Sir William Winter had directed naval campaigns in a real sense, and even his experiences – the most recent during 1562/3 – were not remotely comparable with the coming clashes.

Opportunities to correct this endemic failing were singularly lacking in the weeks and months prior to the campaign, even had the will existed to attempt it. Of the men commanding the major warships, only those in the principal merchantmen had enjoyed more than a few months' acquaintance with their current ships and crews. Yet the extensive manoeuvres that might have gone some way to addressing this failing were curtailed, like the fleet's victualling arrangements and Howard's ability to seek out his enemy, by the remarkably unseasonable weather that scoured the Channel during the spring and summer of 1588. As a result, when the fleets met on 21 July, Howard's men (other than those who had accompanied his small fleet to Flushing four months earlier) brought to the battle only twenty-two days' experience of handling ships in mass formation.[25] Like the trained bands of the intended 'grosse army' that would form a last-ditch line between Parma's *tercios* and their Queen, they did not in any way comprise an integrated instrument of war.

This was an age, furthermore, in which no sophisticated system of fleet signalling existed to allow prior tactical decisions to be adapted or corrected during an engagement, or to inform the Lord Admiral and his subordinates of what was occurring beyond their line of sight. In an encounter that would involve almost 300 vessels, clashing repeatedly over several days across an unprecedentedly vast area of sea, lack of effective communications would further test the elementary formation-fighting skills of the English captains and posed severe problems for Howard. What in the present day is thought of as a 'battle' in fact consisted of a series of discreet actions, forced by rel- atively few of the best and most competently commanded fighting ships acting in concert, while the greater number of their sister vessels attempted little more than to 'make a show', as Winter later alleged.[26] This is not something that sits easily with the modern perception of England's armada heroes, but they, no less than the armies of 1914, approached a clash for which the theory and manuals had yet to be written.

With no experience of, or need for, large-scale fleet actions, there had been no incentive for Englishmen to develop the mechanisms that would permit them. Accordingly, the command organization of the 1588 fleet was near-archaic. On 23 May, Howard had conferred vice and rear admiralships upon Drake and Hawkins, yet how their authority would be exercised within the fleet is unclear. Although the English force was now substantially that which would face the armada, the only evident instrument for disposing of its many elements was the informal advisory council that Howard convened for the first time at Plymouth. Other than himself and his two flag-officers, this comprised rank amateurs (his cousin Lord Thomas Howard and nephew Edmund, Lord Sheffield, both in their mid-twenties and new-comers to naval command), two highly experienced sea captains, Martin Frobisher and Thomas Fenner, and a veteran of the Low Countries' land campaign, Sir Roger Williams. The evidence of surviving correspondence suggests that this body discussed the strategy of the campaign in some detail – particularly the means by which the Queen might be persuaded to allow them to attack the armada off the coast of Spain – but their similar discussion of tactical matters is lost to us. There are no extant fighting instructions for the 1588 fleet – nor, indeed, for any Elizabethan naval campaign, though directions for a provisional (and rudimentary) fighting formation decreed by Frobisher for his third Baffin Island expedition survive.[27] Little is known, therefore, of the assumptions made by Howard and his senior officers regarding the nature of the battle they expected to fight.

Their tactical intentions are fairly clear, however. Given that Medina Sidonia had to be prevented from effecting a liaison with Parma or disembarking his own troops independently, Howard had to seize the initiative and hold it with unremitting attacks upon the enemy formations that would cripple or even destroy them. To do this he had to take and keep the weather gauge. Placing ships to windward, rather than engaging from leeward where the enemy held the initiative (and whose sails, in higher-charged vessels, might create a local calm), was by 1588 an habitual manoeuvre employed by English fighting ships, though in rough seas this could make the employment of lower gun tiers difficult.[28] It is evident also that Howard and his commanders made a prior decision to engage the enemy in line-ahead formation to keep the English rate of fire consistent (this order of engagement should not be confused with the far more sophisticated formation-breaking 'line-of-battle' manoeuvre first conceived by seventeenth-century sea commanders and brought to near-perfection by the Nelsonian Royal Navy).[29] And even Philip II assumed that the English ships would attempt to avoid boarding actions and use their advantages of superior handling and ordnance to pound the heavily manned Spanish vessels.[30]

These intentions, however, provide little insight into the command arrangements that would allow them to be used in battle. In contrast to the minutely agreed dispositions of their Spanish enemy, the sole indication that English fleet deployments were considered or agreed prior to the first clash on 21 July 1588 is found in a document drawn up sometime after 18 June.[31] This shows what appears to be a preliminary order in which the most powerful of the Queen's ships were to be disposed in ranks, three abreast, each leading a merchantman and a pinnace. Five such waves were followed by a deeper rank of fifteen ships (though still deployed three abreast), led by a single navy vessel.

Revenge (vice admiral)	*Ark Royal* (admiral)	*Elizabeth Bonaventure*
Minion of Plymouth	*Galleon Leicester*	*Bark Talbot*
Charles	*Disdain*	*Bark Young*
Golden Lion	*White Bear*	*Nonpareil*
Margaret & John	*Minion of Bristol*	*Thomas of Plymouth*
Advice	*Larke*	*Elizabeth Drake*
Hope	*Elizabeth Jonas*	*Dreadnought*
Brave of London	*Hopewell of London*	*Golden Noble*
Hind of Exeter	*Hart of Dartmouthe*	*Golden Hind*
Swiftsure	*Triumph*	*Foresight*
Bark Burr	*Galleon Dudley*	*Mayflower of London*
Diamond	*Chance*	*Passport*
Mary Rose	*Victory* (rear admiral)	*Swallow*
Spark of Plymouth	*Tiger of Plymouth*	*Tiger of London*
Delight	*Moon*	*Unity*
Bark St Leger	*Ayde*	*Hope of Plymouth*
Bartholemew	*Merchant Royal*	*Royal Defence*
Red Lion of London	*Hercules of London*	*Golden Ryall*
Ascension of London	*Edward Bonaventure*	*Centurion of London*
Minion of London	*Toby of London*	*Frances of London*

A further forty English ships, not identified individually in the document, were 'appointed at sea in winges to deale with straglers'.

This arrangement dispersed the best ships throughout the fleet (though giving weight to the leading ranks). Each principal naval vessel was matched with a lesser merchantman, the smaller naval vessels with larger merchantmen, and every grouping supported by a pinnace to facilitate communication between the elements of the fleet.[32] That such a deployment could not be expected to survive the first exchange of fire intact suggests that it is merely an allocation of ships in relation to each other – an order to integrate the naval and voluntary elements of the English fleet. In the event, Howard's precipitous departure from Plymouth, his urgent efforts to seize the weather gauge, and the nature of his initial engagement with the armada suggests that it was never attempted. Nevertheless, the disposition of the fleet into three squadrons of roughly equal strength – possibly a conscious emulation of L'Isle's similar deployment of the English forces in July 1545 – hints at intended operational divisions once battle commenced.[33] The Lord Admiral's central column contained the largest vessels (and the least handy – all four 'great ships' followed the *Ark Royal*), while the outer columns, with a greater percentage of modern, raze-built ships, would presumably react more quickly in manoeuvring to turn the enemy's flank or maintain contact with the core. What is significant in this order is that none of Howard's principal captains (the ungovernable Drake apart) were yet appointed to lead substantial sub-divisions within the fleet. During the opening stages of the battle, it seems that the Lord Admiral wanted his best men close to hand, rather than elsewhere amidst a conflict whose form could not yet be anticipated.

It need hardly be said that a commander needs to see and judge the enemy's formations before any definitive plan of battle can be established.[34] Again, however, Howard's preliminary (or mooted) dispositions, more redolent of a medieval war host than a recognizably 'modern' navy, reflected both the extemporary quality of the English fleet in 1588 and the primitive character of contemporary English naval command. The fighting core of the fleet – the Navy Royal – was as yet a collection of vessels supported by a victualling and building/repair establishment. In the absence of a standing officer corps, it was not – could not be – a service. As early as 1574, the Privy Council had drawn up a list of 'Sundrie gentlemen' suitable to take charge of the Queen's ships during wartime. This was updated at the beginning of 1586 with a new list of seventy-six men 'fit to command ships' in an expanded English fleet.[35] In the intervening years, death and circumstance had removed some names and added others, yet one characteristic of the list remained constant: none of the men named therein was a professional naval officer in the modern sense. A very few might be regarded as what their Stuart successors would disparagingly term 'tarpaulins' (low-born men who had been apprenticed and risen to command upon a fighting ship's deck), though the sixteenth-century Navy Royal could not provide the continuity of service that would comprise a career.[36] A few others – Sir William Winter and William Borough, for example – had served the establishment for so long that any qualification of their role seems obtuse. But the same financial and political constraints that made the maintenance of a standing navy impossible ensured that active naval command, even for the officers of Marine Causes, was an infrequent duty. Many others named in the 'fit to command' list had great experience in commanding individual ships both in private voyages (privateering and trading) and quasi-naval operations. Some, like Drake, Hawkins, Frobisher and their former subordinates, had extended England's reach in the oceans in a series of spectacular (if not always successful) voyages. Others named in the list had not participated in any form of sea battle prior to their appointment in 1588. Their only universal quality was the natural authority that would allow them to direct the true professionals – the 'other ranks' of career mariners ranging from master to ship's boy.[37]

Presiding over this kaleidoscope of talents was the Lord Admiral himself, the man to whom Elizabeth had entrusted the future of her regime and of the Protestant faith in England. Like those other members of his extended family who had avoided a Tudor scaffold, Charles Howard had been a loyal and largely unassuming presence at court. His present appointment was purely political (the office was invariably held by one of the realm's principal peers), yet there is much evidence that he was a fortunate choice. Apparently well-versed in much of the minutiae of pilotage and even the mundane craft of setting sails, he was also to exhibit a flair for administrative work and a strong concern for the welfare of the common men in his charge – far too much so for the tastes of his sovereign, who regarded such tenderness as an expensive indulgence.[38] He was receptive, furthermore, to advice from men of greater practical experience than he, though careful always to prevent their enthusiasms from reflecting poorly upon his own, fiercely guarded reputation. Unknowingly, Elizabeth and Philip shared a taste in admirals. Like Medina Sidonia, Howard was the safe choice: competent, courtly and acutely sensitive to the responsibility he discharged. He inspired loyalty without love, effort without incontinent sacrifice. Most importantly, he applied a grandee's tact and sensitivity in handling his subordinates' tender egos. With Drake as his second-in-command, this was an invaluable quality.

True to his instincts and the age's nepotic conventions, Howard had surrounded himself with the most loyal men available – his kin. In addition to his nephew Lord Sheffield and cousin Lord Thomas Howard (commanders of the *White Bear* and *Golden Lion* respectively), Howard's son Charles was appointed to command the Lord Admiral's own battle-tried *White Lion*; one of his sons-in-law, Sir Robert Southwell, commanded the *Elizabeth Jonas*; another, Richard Leveson (subsequently, like Lord Thomas Howard, a distinguished naval commander), served as a volunteer in the *Ark Royal*. A cousin, Nicholas Gorges (a naval veteran of Leicester's Low Countries campaign and brother of Arthur Gorges, future author of several important expositions on fleet tactics), was given charge of the levanter *Susan Parnell* and appointed Admiral of the merchant coasters charged with carrying victuals and munitions to the fleet.[39] When struck down by illness, he would be replaced by another cousin, Thomas Knyvet. Finally, Sir Henry Seymour, commanding the squadron with the vital duty of keeping Parma firmly in port, was the step-son of Howard's sister, Frances.

The Lord Admiral's immediate subordinate, Drake, had also brought in his known men, though theirs was a less familial relationship. Each of the Queen's ships appointed to his Plymouth command was commanded by a trusted acquaintance. The Fenners of Chichester – Thomas (*Nonpareil*), William (*Ayde*) and Edward (*Swiftsure*) – had long shared both Drake's company and his taste for acquiring Iberian assets. Thomas had been Drake's flag captain in the West Indies Raid and rear admiral of the fleet at Cadiz, while his kinsmen had a decades' long record of semi-piratical voyages to the Azores, Cape Verde Islands, Guinea and the Caribbean.[40] Another old acquaintance, Robert Crosse (*Hope*), rear admiral of Drake's squadron at Plymouth until the concentration of the fleet, had sailed both in the West Indies and Cadiz expeditions.[41] Commanding the larger merchant ships under Drake were yet another Fenner, George (*Galleon Leicester*), and further veterans of the circumnavigation (William Hawkins, *Griffin*), the West Indies Raid (Henry Whyte, *Bark Talbot*; James Erisey, *Galleon Dudley*) and Cadiz expedition (Henry Spindelow, *Thomas Drake*; Humphrey Sydenham, *Unity*; Ambrose Manington, *Bark Manington*; William Poole, *Bark Bond*).[42] The clique of levanters that joined Drake's squadron enjoyed the informal leadership of another former colleague, Robert Flicke (*Merchant Royal*), who had exercised similar authority over the London merchantmen in the Cadiz expedition and would do so again in the 1591/2 Atlantic expeditions.

John Hawkins did not inspire the personal devotion that Drake's record attracted, but his own family's contribution was substantial nevertheless. His nephew William had been with Drake's squadron since January, as had one of Hawkins's own vessels, the *Bark Bond*; his only son, Richard, commanded the Queen's ship *Swallow*, and his brother-in-law Edward Fenton (no doubt anxious to redeem a reputation ruined by the farcical 1582 Moluccas voyage) had the important if ageing naval ship *Mary Rose*. Another brother-in-law, Benjamin Gonson, while not commanding a vessel in the campaign, later earned a vignette alongside the principal captains of the fleet in Howard's commemorative 'armada tapestries' for his sterling service as Clerk of the Ships (succeeding William Borough in that post). Finally, Hawkins's elder brother William (mayor of Plymouth in 1588) made an inestimable contribution to the fleet's maintenance, manning and victualling both before and during the battle.

The numerous privateers, gentlemen of fortune, merchant-adventurers and minor captain-owners who joined their own, less renowned talents to this august gathering were an island nation's obvious recourse. But even that rich vein was fully tapped by the needs of the huge English fleet. Consequently, the supply of 'men fit to command the Queen's ships' had been augmented by several individuals who may have expected to have seen the last of active service long before 1588. Besides Hawkins, almost all the officers of Marine Causes were at sea. Of them, only Christopher Baker, Keeper of the Queen Stores at Chatham and now commander of the *Foresight*, was of what we might regard as 'fighting' age. His colleague William Holstocke, the Comptroller of the Ships, was too frail for active service and remained on shore (an officer of Marine Causes since the establishment's foundation in 1546, he had been named as 'fit to command' as recently as 1586),[43] but the sexagenarian Surveyor of the Ships, Sir William Winter, was given command of the powerful *Vanguard*, one of the principal ships of the Queen's navy (his son and namesake commanded the merchant ship *Minion*). Holstocke's acting-successor, the erstwhile navigator William Borough, lay under something of a cloud following his ship's mutiny and defection during Drake's Cadiz expedition, but was appointed to command the *Bonavolia*, the Navy Royal's only galley (her lack of sea-worthiness confined her to the Thames and Medway during the ten days' battle: a lone, last-ditch foil to any Spanish break-through).[44] Yet even this venerable pool of talents was not to provide the oldest captain appointed to serve in the coming campaign. Since his inclusion in the 1586 list, death or infirmity had disqualified from service Clement Paston, a seventy-three-year-old veteran of the battle of Pinkie, but another 'fit' man, George Beeston, emerged from comfortable retirement on his Cheshire estate to take command of one of the best of the Queen's ships, the *Dreadnought*. Variously stated to be either sixty-eight or eighty-nine years old in 1588, Beeston had been present in the English army during Henry VIII's Boulogne campaign forty-four years earlier, and had fought in Scotland at the battle of Musselburgh in 1547. His last naval command prior to the armada campaign had been as 'admiral of all ships at sea' during the 1562–3 Le Havre expedition.[45] This old man's inclusion in the command list, remarkable to the modern observer, was to be justified handsomely by his contribution in the coming campaign, when his furious assault upon every Spanish vessel that came into range of his guns would be mentioned in despatches and earn him a knighthood.

How should we regard these strikingly disparate guardians of a nation's continuing existence? It would be prudent not to diminish their stature by overstating it. Whether of immortal memory, proud recollection or near absolute anonymity, the Englishmen who manned the fleet during the armada campaign represented no recognizable naval tradition. Nor were they the instigators of one. The fortunes of the English 'navy' would rise and fall several times more before a recognizable entity, enduring and evolving, emerged. In 1588, the likeness of a naval community was formed momentarily from a galaxy of widely dissimilar experiences and backgrounds, joined together in a vital purpose: a first manifestation of the 'nation in arms' egalitarianism that Englishmen since have evoked during their moments of greatest crisis. Whether that quality has ever been more real than fondly imagined is debatable; but those who manned the English fleet had little uncertainty regarding the 'great discovered strength' of their association.[46] That strength lay not only in the excellence of their ships, gunners or mariners, but in a shared perception: of the destiny of a fortunate nation being not only preserved but forged anew in resistance to tyranny. Their cause – liberty, identity and religion – could not be diminished by uncomfortable truths: that they had no greater freedoms than the men they would soon face (other, perhaps, than the unfortunates who manned the oars of the Neopolitan galleasses); that their government and compatriots had been culpable of inciting the enemy to the point where continuing acquiescence would have damned him as ineffectual in the eyes of Europe; that the 'true and sincere religion of Christe' they defended was as willing to preserve itself by coercion as the Roman edifice at which it tilted.[47] If any tradition was being forged here, it was one that future English navies would serve, not exemplify – a rationale for empire, the indivisible identification of God's will and English interests:

> They for the greediness of a kingdom, for despite they bear to our religion, for vain-glory, pride, and presumption, for maintenance of the pope's kingdom; against God, against his word and truth, against our

blessed Queen, against all reason, conscience, and humanity, do offer all this violence unto us. And we, on the other side, in defence of ourselves, our native country, our annointed prince, our holy religion, our own Jesus Christ, his holy word and sacraments, against very antichrist, and all the pillars of his church, and against those that have cursed and indicted the kingdom, do withstand the injury done unto us.[48]

TWELVE

The Happy Hour

In happy hower
Our foes we did discry,
All under saile with gallant winde
As they came passing by.[1]

At approximately 3pm on 19 July 1588, the bark *Golden Hind* came into Plymouth harbour under full sail, bringing urgent word of the approach of a great formation of ships, sighted off the Lizard. Her hurried passage was assisted by a flood tide and south-westerly wind; conditions that prevented the English fleet from retracing her course for several hours thereafter. According to legend, the *Golden Hind*'s captain, Thomas Fleming (a kinsman of John Hawkins), found the English fleet's senior commanders playing bowls on Plymouth Hoe. Whether this heroic tableau actually greeted Fleming's eyes has been the subject of much otiose debate, but it is unlikely that any of the players – even Drake, the consummate self-publicist – wished to 'finish the game' after his interruption. Many of the English ships were still re-provisioning following their recent sea duties (several would leave Plymouth up to two days after the main body of the fleet); and a large number of their mariners were billeted on shore to minimize the effects of the shipboard epidemics of recent weeks.[2] Needing desperately to depart upon the next ebb-tide, Howard and his immediate subordinates were unlikely to have had either leisure or inclination to turn an eye to posterity.

Most of the ships were made ready for sea during the following hours. By nightfall, Howard's *Ark Royal* and six other vessels had emerged from Plymouth Sound and lay off Rame Head, awaiting their sisters.[3] At first light on the morning of 20 July, a further fifty to sixty ships had joined them. Only partially assembled still, the English fleet raised sail and set a tacking course alternatively south and north-westerly, attempting to beat westward against prevailing winds. Through heavy rain, the leading elements of the armada were in sight to the west at about 3pm, by now athwart Fowey.[4] Rather than allow the advantage of the weather gauge to his enemy, Howard made the bold decision to lead his fleet directly southwards and then north once more to place it behind the advancing Spanish ships. This he had achieved by dawn on 21 July (though his manoeuvre was almost frustrated, if unwittingly, by Medina Sidonia's decision to lie at anchor during several of the intervening hours). The appearance of the English fleet to the rear of the armada the following morning disconcerted the Spanish Admiral, who had assumed that most of his enemy's ships lay to the east still (an hour earlier, he had sighted a small group of vessels beating westwards beyond the armada's inshore flank, and had mistaken these for the English vanguard).[5] Immediately, he had his own fleet come about in its *en lúnula* (crescent moon) formation of a long, shallow curve with two trailing wings, its deeper centre containing the main 'battle' of fighting ships.[6] At approximately 9am, Howard sent his own pinnace *Disdain* forward to 'give defiance' to the enemy, and launched the first assault. The English fleet divided to assault the extremities of the Spanish formation, the Lord Admiral himself leading a squadron of English vessels against the left *cuerno* (horn), while his vice and rear admirals closed upon its opposite wing.

One English eyewitness, Captain Henry Whyte of the *Bark Talbot*, described this first clash as 'more coldly done then became value of our nation and the credit of the englishe navye.'[7] He inferred faint-heartedness, but Howard and his lieutenants had good reason to be circumspect. Before them was a disciplined formation of some 130 vessels, spread across a wide front, that refused to conform to English expectations. Medina Sidonia's orders were to defend himself, but otherwise to avoid an outright sea battle. His primary task was to carry troops to a rendezvous and guard the combined expedition's passage across the Channel thereafter – to invade a kingdom, not maul a navy.[8] Having received his opponent's first challenge, the Spanish Admiral awaited the English thrusts in the manner of a counter-puncher, hoping to draw individual ships into the grasp of his fleet's formation and overwhelm them there. Howard, in turn, had no intention of conforming to Spanish hopes. Should the wings of the armada envelop the English fleet, almost every tactical advantage enjoyed by his ships would be neutralized. Accordingly, his efforts (as in subsequent days) were devoted to turning the Spanish fleet's formations in upon themselves – in effect, to drive the enemy vessels into dangerous proximity to each other, where the guns of the English ships could do the most damage. The uniform Spanish response was to seek to entice the English captains into the sort of ship-to-ship duels that would both neutralize the larger assault and improve the chances of grappling. These tactics gave much employment to individual 'shepherds', the relatively few powerful warships in the armada whose principal role was to defend its slower troop-carriers and hulks. To the extent that this form of encounter played precisely to the instincts and prior experience of most of the English fleet's senior officers it was a largely successful ploy, as the first day's action illustrated.

Conforming to their instructions, the ships following the *Ark Royal* advanced in a rough line-ahead formation, discharging first their bow-chasers and then broadside armament as they came to bear upon the outermost vessels of the enemy fleet. Each attacking ship then luffed to keep the weather gauge, refusing her opponents' invitation to close, and retired to reload her guns (no contemporary navy developed the skills to reload ordnance under fire).[9] Bearing down upon the armada's opposite wing, however, Howard's flag-officers attempted only briefly the same coordinated manoeuvre before abandoning any pretence of a fleet action in favour of a prolonged assault upon a single ship: Juan Martínez de Recalde's *San Juan de Portugal, almiranta* of the Biscayan squadron. The line-ahead approach of Drake's *Revenge*, Hawkins's *Victory* and Frobisher's *Triumph* was rather a queue of eager individualists, all hoping to deliver the *coup de grâce* to one of the armada's principal vessels.

The action was wholly unsuccessful. Although her sister ships drifted eastwards away from the clash, the *San Juan* was neither cut out by her opponents nor seriously damaged. Repeated volleys from some of the most powerfully armed vessels in the English fleet parted the *San Juan's* rigging and caused some significant but repairable damage to her fore- and main-masts.[10] Her human casualties were equally light. After two hours of daring the English ships to close with her, the *San Juan* finally received support from other vessels of the Biscayan squadron, at which the English right-wing withdrew. Meanwhile, frustrated by the tardiness of Recalde's squadron in supporting its flagship, Medina Sidonia had brought the *San Martín* and her escorts to her aid. This developed into a counter-feint – again, with the intention of drawing some of the retiring English vessels into boarding range. However, failing to tempt the enemy, the Spanish Admiral withdrew to rejoin his centre. All fighting had ceased by 2pm. The English fleet merely shadowed the armada thereafter, though scoring two important, if inadvertent successes some hours later when the rear magazine of the *San Salvador* (*almiranta* of the *Guipúzcoan* squadron) exploded with great loss of life, and the *Nuestra Señora del Rosario* (*capitana* of the *Andalusian* squadron) lost her bow-sprit in a collision with a sister vessel, *San Catalina*. The burning *San Salvador* was nursed into the body of the Spanish formation; other Spanish vessels attempted (unsuccessfully in a rising squall) to secure tow-lines to the *Rosario* while the *San Martín* rode guard for her. Neither operation was interrupted by further English assaults. Importantly, however, the two damaged vessels together carried more than ten per cent of the armada's total weight of heavy ordnance, making their subsequent loss a severe blow to morale within the Spanish fleet.[11]

For Howard and his commanders the day's experience had been salutary. Standing off and out-gunning an enemy was becoming an instinctive method of sea fighting to the merchant captains in the fleet, particularly those of Levanters obliged to run the gauntlet of Habsburg galleys and Barbary corsairs on their perilous trade routes. Their privateering compatriots, in contrast, habitually used ordnance, as did their Spanish enemy, as a brief prelude to boarding vessels and overwhelming their crews (though with a different end in mind). Nevertheless, during the first closely pressed actions the most hot-headed among them had maintained a prudent distance from the heavily manned Spanish ships, relying instead upon the greater range of their own guns to silence those of the enemy. Unfortunately, the tactic did not appear to be working.

Contemporary English ships' ordnance was superior in almost all respects – range, mounting and, in the case of iron pieces, casting – to that carried by the armada, but modern characterization of guns exceeding nine-pound calibre as 'ship-smashers' seems optimistic in light of their effect.[12] The theoretical and effective firing ranges of sixteenth-century ordnance were very different quantities. English culverins (seventeen-pounders) and demi-culverins (nine-pounders) had a maximum range of some 2,000 to 2,500 paces; yet in the coming days they would prove unable to inflict structural damage upon the Spanish ships except when delivering their shot at the effective firing-range of hand-held weapons – that is, well within their ostensible 'point-blank' range of about 300 paces. In total, the vessels of the Navy Royal carried only some fifty to sixty of the larger calibre demi-cannon (thirty-pounder) types whose shot was capable of causing more traumatic damage to hulls, and even these had to be employed at extreme close-range to be effective.[13] It is likely that very few, if any, of the merchantmen in the fleet were armed with this type of weapon. Without achieving the proverbial lucky shot (usually to a powder magazine), no contemporary English ship carried enough or sufficiently powerful guns to fulfil that 'destroyer' role they have since been assigned.

Undoubtedly, there had been a significant increase in weight of ordnance carried in the major English warships since 1570 as theories on their role in battle developed.[14] But the same gradual improvements to fighting-ship architecture that had delivered greater manoeuvrability and speed also placed very finite limits upon the number of heavy guns that English ships could carry safely. In absolute terms, the vessels carrying the most (and heaviest) ordnance in the 1588 fleet were the 'great ships', but their relative unhandiness – bulk being a vital requisite for the burden they assumed – negated much of the advantage of their armament. Relative to tonnage, the most heavily armed ship in the fleet was probably the *Vanguard* (with Seymour's squadron in the Downs), which, in later centuries, would have been classed as a fifth-rate.[15] Even in the years immediately following the armada campaign, when urgent efforts were being made to absorb its lessons, new vessels constructed for the Navy Royal would remain lightly armed by later standards. One of the most powerful of their number, *Warspite* (built in 1596), is the only contemporary vessel for which precise information is available not only of weight but also disposition of her ordnance. She carried just ten 'heavy' guns on each of her broadsides: six culverins and four demi-culverins (though with eight more pieces of these calibres as bow and stern chasers).[16] For all the attention being devoted to the advancement of naval gunnery and warship design in late sixteenth-century England, this was the beginning, not the culmination, of a process. The complex and inter-related improvements to ship design and gun technology needed to develop true 'destroyers' of enemy vessels were to be the achievement of the following centuries.

To the Englishmen present during the initial clash of 21 July 1588, the sum of their efforts provided an unpleasant revelation. For years, many of them – merchantman and privateer alike – had employed ordnance at sea as a means of disheartening an enemy sufficiently to make him surrender or break off an attack. In 1568, Hawkins had managed to destroy two Spanish ships with gunfire, but one of these kills had been the result of a fortuitous shot upon a powder magazine; the other of a fire that had swept uncontrolled between decks. English experience of sea 'warfare' – that is, the intentional destruction of major enemy vessels at sea – was virtually non-existent. This day, 21 July 1588, provided a first lesson in that art, and its outcome hinted at much work yet to do. Unstinting in their gunnery (Recalde later claimed that 300 rounds of shot had been fired at the *San Juan* alone), the English ships had failed to damage significantly any enemy vessel, much less sink one. Until, some days later, they began to move into almost suicidal proximity with their enemy (thus radically re-interpreting the accepted meaning of point-blank), the principal response of Howard and his commanders to the seemingly negligible effect of their guns was to increase their rate of fire. Undoubtedly, this inflicted more damage upon the human enemy (if not the structures that sheltered them), but it had a dangerous consequence. By the first evening of the battle, several of the most powerful English ships had seriously depleted their stocks of powder and shot.

The same relatively narrow- and shallow-hulled architecture that limited the weight of a ship's ordnance also reduced storage space, one of the reasons why the standard shot issue for the English ships was limited to approxi-mately thirty rounds per gun (and why the perennial problem of inadequate victualling was not merely a matter of finance).[17] By the end of the first day's fighting, the trade-off was looking unacceptably risky. An obviously unwelcome side-effect of English gunnery skills, which allowed a rate of fire of up to ten times that of their Spanish opponents, was that ships' stocks of munitions dwindled rapidly. Each demi-cannon required some twenty pounds of powder to discharge a single round-shot, a culverin twelve pounds and a demi-culverin eight pounds.[18] If Recalde's estimate of the weight of shot thrown as his *San Juan* was accurate, at least one full last (2,400 pounds) of English gunpowder had been expended to dishevel her rigging.

Without sufficient soldiers to risk, or defend against, boarding actions, Howard dare not allow his guns to fall silent long enough for the enemy to seize an initiative that could not be retrieved. The armada, as every man in the English fleet was aware, was not an instrument of sea warfare per se but the bearer of an invasion army that must, at some point, attempt a landing. Lacking any understanding of Philip's unworkable strategy, the common English view credited him with a more prudent plan than he possessed. Whether or not Medina Sidonia intended a liaison with Parma prior to the invasion, it was considered improbable that the Spanish admiral would press on into the Narrow Seas without first securing a bridgehead on the English south coast where his fleet and soldiers might be resupplied from Spain or northern France.[19] The armada was now east of Plymouth, which made that landfall almost impossible to recover. The next potential disembarkation points for its troops were Torbay, Lyme or Portland harbours. Given a fortunate combination of wind and tide, a landing might be attempted at one of these sites as early as the following day. If the English ships were present, it must surely fail – but only if they had adequate means to press their attack. In his despatches to Walsingham that evening, the Lord Admiral did not understate the problem: 'Sir, for the love of God and our country, let us have with some spe[e]d some great shot sent us of all bignes . . . and some powder with it'.[20]

The Privy Council reacted swiftly, though the transfer of munitions, even along the short supply lines enjoyed by the English fleet, proved problematic. Four lasts of powder (9,600 pounds) were despatched from the Tower on 22 July, but this would not have reached the fleet by the following day, when the second major engagement took place. From Plymouth, William Hawkins hurriedly sent out what powder and shot remained in the town, and the mayors of a string of small ports on the south coast, urged on by the Privy Council, did likewise. The irascible earl of Sussex, Lord Lieutenant of Hampshire, was particularly industrious during the following days, and any spare munitions to be found in (or brought to) Portsmouth and Southampton went to the fleet promptly.[21] His first recourse was to the earl of Cumberland's small privateering squadron, currently anchored in Portsmouth harbour. Previously, the Council had directed that its vessels be sent to join the fleet, but Cumberland argued that they were not yet fit for sea duty. Sussex was then told to strip out their munitions and despatch them to Howard's ships.[22]

This and other stopgap measures – not least, two unexpected windfalls on 22 July – would prove invaluable, but in themselves they would be sufficient only to make good the large quantities of shot and powder expended by the fleet's best fighting ships on 21 July, not that which was understood (all too belatedly) to be required for the coming clashes. The next major replenishment from the Tower's stores would not reach the fleet until 26 or 27 July.[23] In the meantime, there remained sufficient munitions for a further battle, perhaps two (if powder and shot carried within the fleet were to be redistributed efficiently); but as the campaign progressed towards the Narrow Seas without a decisive action, the struggle to keep the fleet adequately supplied with the means to stop its enemy would become the critical issue to Howard and his commanders.

On the evening of the first day's battle, moreover, the Lord Admiral's anxieties were fuelled by more than the matter of munitions. The armada, moving seamlessly into its defensive posture, had given an impressive demonstration of the mass formation discipline – honed over decades of Atlantic convoy duties and clashes against the Turks – that was as yet an ambition of its English enemy. The skills of the Spanish mariners, and the *San Juan*'s formidable resistance to her attackers, hinted also at a fighting prowess that belied the apparent lessons of Cadiz. A sense of anti-climax seems to have pervaded the English fleet, and extant references to the first day's fighting are subdued. Hawkins played down his own efforts in referring to the first encounter as 'some smale fight'.[24] Drake, writing to Seymour that evening to warn of what bore down upon him, observed perceptively that only half the Spanish vessels appeared to be warships; but like Hawkins he passed over the ineffectuality of English guns against Spanish hulls in dismissing the first day's action as a negligible encounter. Their sangfroid was disingenuous. Almost certainly, they and many of their colleagues had expected their first action to be the decisive clash, rather than an inconclusive skirmish that left the enemy largely intact and a day's sailing closer to its unknown goal.[25] Drake's reassurance to Seymour – 'what his Lordship & the rest here fallowing him maie doe, shalbe surelie performed' – was a strangely restrained comment from a man who had been seeking this encounter for the greater part of his adult life.[26] His conviction that the Spanish fleet could be beaten remained undiminished, but the means by which he and his compatriots would achieve this were less obvious than only a few hours previously.

Drake's own battle was about to improve significantly, however. At a council of war that afternoon the *Revenge* had been appointed to lead the fleet by a stern light during the coming night. Instead of discharging this vital duty, she temporarily deserted her station, and, indeed, the rest of the fleet, to do a little lucrative business. Subsequently dogged by complaints regarding his conduct (particularly from Martin Frobisher, whose forensic description of the damage he intended to inflict upon his vice admiral entertained the fleet for weeks to come), Drake was at pains to defend his role in the capture of the galleon *Nuestra Señora del Rosario*.[27] Yet his version of events is hardly credible. The indisputable facts are that one of the London merchantmen in the fleet, the *Margaret and John*, came upon the *Rosario* some five miles to seaward of the main body of the English fleet in the early evening of 21 July. Since losing her bowsprit that afternoon, the *Rosario* had suffered a further collision within the densely packed armada formations that badly damaged her foremast. This collapsed soon afterwards despite frenzied attempts by her crew to make running repairs. Initially, as already noted, Medina Sidonia seems to have tried to keep the near helpless vessel within his fleet, but as the remainder of the armada drew away to the east, he allowed himself to be dissuaded from this by his lieutenant, Diego Flores de Valdés – cousin, and bitter rival, of the *Rosario's* commander, Pedro de Valdés. Effectively abandoned, the *Rosario* was beyond recovery by her own fleet when the *Margaret and John* encountered her.

The merchantman gave the Spanish vessel a single broadside volley, but quickly withdrew to rejoin the English fleet when the *Rosario's* heavier ordnance returned fire. At first light the following morning, however, Don Pedro and his men (among them a significant number of Spain's young noblemen, accompanying the armada for reputation and glory's sake) found themselves only three cables' length from Drake's *Revenge* and the *Roebuck*. Called upon to surrender, Valdés made only a brief pretence of defiance before meekly accepting a summons to the *Revenge* to hear what terms he might expect. Within an hour he had yielded the *Rosario*, the first English prize of the battle, with forty-six largely unused guns, 2,000 invaluable rounds of shot, 350 soldiers, two English traitors (several others had fled the *Rosario* in a ship's boat when their predicament became apparent) and, not least, 50,000 ducats intended to reward the victorious Spanish forces.[28]

Whether dictated by a collapse of her mariners' morale at the armada's 'desertion', dread of their fearsome opponent or Valdés's spiteful desire to teach his admiral and cousin a sharp (if self-injuring) lesson, the *Rosario's* astonishingly craven surrender added greatly to Drake's invincible reputation. It also brought near-disaster for England. Throughout the night, Howard, still imagining the *Revenge* to be guarding the sea ahead of him, closed blithely with the armada in the company of just two other English vessels. The remainder of his ships, seeing no guiding lantern before them, more prudently reduced sail to await its re-appearance or new instructions. In doing so, they unwittingly distanced themselves from their flagship. At first light, as Drake received Valdés with courtly condescension, his Lord Admiral was desperately attempting to put space between the *Ark Royal* and approximately 130 Spanish ships. Other than the *Bear* and *Mary Rose* immediately to his stern, the only sight he had of the remainder of his own fleet was an occasional masthead to the east. The second day's battle did not occur. The armada sailed on, untroubled by an enemy that required almost twelve hours to recover its formation, though the badly damaged *San Salvador*, which Medina Sidonia had ordered to be scuttled, drifted into English hands that afternoon with fifty seriously wounded mariners – inexplicably, they had not been evacuated the previous day – and a further 2,246 rounds of heavy shot.[29] By evening, the Spanish fleet had passed almost as far eastwards as the mid point of Lyme Bay.[30]

In defending his actions, Drake later claimed to have sighted some unfamiliar vessels to the southeast during the night, and had broken formation to investigate. Discovering them to be German merchantmen, he was attempting to rejoin the fleet when he encountered the *Rosario*. Yet even if this implausible version of events was true in all respects, his was the last vessel that should have abandoned its station. It is far more likely he had been doing what came naturally, even instinctively, in chasing a prize that had begged to be taken. It was precisely what half the captains in the fleet would have done (and what, on past experience, they knew their Queen would have wished them to do), had they known of the *Rosario*'s predicament. Frobisher's loud complaint that Drake had deserted his fleet was argued with irreproachable logic, but it was envy alone that fuelled his rage. Whether Howard was more sympathetic – to the deed, if not the doer – is hard to judge. His diplomat's tact and the fleet's need of Drake's talents made it unthinkable that he should overtly criticize his subordinate's actions. Had the battle not proceeded so happily for England, however, it is equally unlikely that Drake would have escaped serious censure. His scrupulous service during the remainder of the campaign suggests that he was aware of this.

* * *

News of the *Rosario*'s capture, carried to London from Dartmouth (into which the *Roebuck* had escorted Drake's prize), was the first small glimmer of light in an otherwise gloomy vista. The coming of the armada may have been a moment of release for Howard and his men, but their government's already acute anxiety for the nation's safety was exacerbated by growing horror at the price of ensuring it. As the battle at sea commenced, the Council took its final, cost-free war measure. Orders were sent to the Archbishop of Canterbury to instruct his bishops and ministers to exhort their flocks: 'to joyne in publyke prayers to Almighty God, the giver of victoryes, to assiste us against the mallyce of our ennemyes'.[31] Yet it was all too apparent – particularly to Burghley, obsessed by the shrinkage to his 'chested treasure' and with a new pile of urgent bills before him – that victory would not be given but bought, and expensively. Hawkins's latest estimate for sea-wages came to £19,570 (though the Lord Treasurer, checking Hawkins's arithmetic, concluded morosely that he had really meant £21,209), with a supplementary demand for £1,854 for Lord Seymour's mariners. The victuallers Quarles and Darell had added a new invoice for £6,000 to their previous, as-yet unpaid claim for £7,000. Rubbing salt into Burghley's wounds, the Office of the Ordnance also took the opportunity to present – once more – its outstanding bill for £8,049.[32] It was enough to prompt him to the immortal (and uncharacteristic) observation, scribbled into the margin of his summary of costs: 'I marvell that wher so many are dead on the seas the paye is not dead with them'. As he admitted to Walsingham in the note that accompanied this depressing schedule, his callousness was incited in part by the prospect of more to come: 'I shall but fill my lettre with more melancholy matter, if I shuld remember what mor mony must be had to paye 5,000 footmen and 1,000 horses for defence of the enemy landing in Essex'.[33]

The enemy landing was, of course, what the fleets of Howard and Seymour were at sea to prevent, but their success could not be assumed. On 19 July, as Captain Fleming's *Golden Hind* hurriedly approached Plymouth with word of the armada's approach, the Spanish ships had been sighted also by soldiers on the Lizard peninsula. With the beacon they lit there, England's comprehensive early-warning system was triggered and the long-planned concentration of land forces commenced. Within hours, the 2,000 foot, 140 light horse and 16 lancers of the Cornish trained bands began their eastward march along the coastline, joined by their comrades from Devon and Somerset as they advanced (their passage was occasionally hampered by over-officious general muster-men, appointed to guard cross-roads and other faintly strategic points).[34] By 22 July, several thousand troops – an enthusiastic horde, if not quite an army – were shadowing the course of the sea battle eastwards, their venerable opposition to operating beyond their home shires readily abandoned.[35] Unfortunately, their timely example had a limited impact elsewhere. Far ahead of them, true to the embryonic English military tradition, the leaders of the troops upon which Parma's *tercios* might soon descend were not speaking to each other.

Ostensibly, the nexus of English military preparations was the fortified encampment at West Tilbury on the north bank of the Thames, twenty-six miles east of London Bridge, where the earl of Leicester – Lieutenant and Captain-General of all English land forces – held court. His relationship with the principal soldiers of the realm (particularly the difficult Sir John Norreys) had already been poisoned by their service in the Low Countries, where, as has been discussed, the earl made little attempt to secure their advice and even less to show them the respect their experience demanded.[36] Norreys himself had reported to his commander at the beginning of July but had since crossed into Kent and stayed there, despite repeated demands from the earl that he return to present regular reports.[37] In fact, Norreys had neither the time nor inclination to indulge his titular commander. Since April, he had enjoyed independent charge of the training and disposition of all mobile forces in the maritime counties between Dorset and Norfolk, a role that gave him, not Leicester (who appears to have had no input to the military preparations in the months prior to the campaign), the principal responsibility for moulding England's tactical response to Parma.[38] If the implications of this appointment had been conveyed to the earl, it had been done in such a way as not to wound his tender pride. He continued to consider himself supreme commander of land forces; his immediate subordinates regarded him as a troublesome irrelevance. Such frictions were not confined to England's 'general staff', however. In turn, Norreys's authority was continually tested by his subordinates in the shires, most notably when he attempted to ride rough-shod over assumed local privileges and long-cherished practices. It required a stream of sternly supportive directives from the Privy Council to allow him to effect his innovations in the face of sullen, and often outspoken, resistance from men who believed both in their own prowess and the necessity of meeting the enemy in the surf.[39]

As Norreys perambulated frantically, very little happened at Tilbury. Leicester and his armed camp shared a doubtful quality: neither was the rational choice for the job they had been allocated. The earl's qualifications for high command were his rank, his Queen's misplaced affection and an increasingly fragile self-belief in his military genius. Tilbury's only aptness for defence was the hill upon which Leicester's camp sat and a small shore fortification, which, with a mirror installation at Gravesend on the opposite bank of the Thames, had been erected in 1539 by Henry VIII. They entertained tiny garrisons and a few guns, while, two miles downstream at Tilbury Ness, an unarmed blockhouse (slightingly referred to as 'old' even in 1588) threatened very little.[40] Together, these works constituted the outer, near-forgotten perimeter of the Capital's defences. As the campaign opened, a boom was being constructed hurriedly between the Tilbury–Gravesend blockhouses to impede any river-borne thrust towards the capital. All ordnance in Upnor Castle was requisitioned to reinforce the bulwarks' shore defences, while its garrison was set to heavy labour repairing the Gravesend 'fort'. A few miles upstream, the maritime communities of Limehouse and Ratcliffe were ordered by the Privy Council to hand over their chains and anchors to one of the bulwark's overseers, the master shipwright Peter Pett, to help strengthen and bind it. Their widespread failure to do so swiftly brought another order – to Sir Owen Hopton, Lieutenant of the Tower, to track down and imprison the 'disobedyent' citizenry.[41]

Though primarily an obstacle to enemy ships, the construction between Tilbury and Gravesend was also intended to carry a bridge (hardly begun, much less completed, as the sea battle commenced) to enable troops to be moved swiftly from Kent to Essex, or, more likely, in the opposite direction. The same logic that demanded this facility challenged the very purpose of the Tilbury camp. Should Parma cross the Channel in his vulnerable barges, it was probable that he would choose the shortest crossing – to one of the ports on Kent's east coast – and disembark his troops as quickly as possible, rather than press towards London via the closely watched Thames or the longer sea- and land-route via Essex. This should have been, and probably was, apparent to most of those involved in planning the 'Parma' leg of their strategy; though as late as 23 July Elizabeth continued, stubbornly, to regard Essex as his likely goal.[42] As has been discussed, large forces had been allocated initially to cover the county's principal landing places (Harwich, the best large harbour in Essex, was to be defended if necessary by up to 17,000 troops), but few of these had been provided subsequently, in contrast to the considerable preparations south of the Thames.[43] Tilbury's remained the closest substantial force available to hamper an Essex landing, yet it sat some fifty miles from Harwich, much too distant to prevent Parma from seizing the port and breaking out of his bridgehead before any English counter-attack could materialize.

In fact, Elizabeth's subsequent, highly publicized visit to Tilbury has given spurious relevance to what was almost certainly intended as a subsidiary element of England's defences. Despite possessing a glittering title and being allocated a total of 22,000 men and 872 horse,[44] Leicester was not intended to operate independently of other formations in any battle foreseen by those who appointed his concentration. Nor was he authorized to make any decisions regarding those other formations. On the one occasion he made a substantial effort to discharge the duties of a fighting general (some days before 17 July he visited and inspected the Hertfordshire and Essex musters),

Elizabeth speedily despatched Sir Thomas Heneage – who seems to have built a career out of reporting her displeasure to the earl – to reprimand him for making himself unavailable should she require his comforting presence at Court.[45]

By 25 July, the earl had 4,000 infantry at Tilbury, with some locally raised light horse in support.[46] In the following five days, this force would increase in number to some 16,500 troops of all arms (arriving with 'cheerefull countenances, couragious wordes and gestures, dauncing and leaping wheresoever they came' as one commentator claimed implausibly), but thereafter his efforts would be devoted almost exclusively to the business of feeding them, not planning their deployment as an army.[47] The entire encampment, far from being the centre of arrangements for resisting a Spanish invasion, appears to have functioned with the urgent efficiency of a reserve depot. Victuallers, summoned to the earl's presence, ignored his instructions, as had his captains; shipwrights, charged with building the Thames bulwark and camp defences, continually pestered him for funds he was not quite sure were his responsibility to find, and troublesome noblemen and courtiers appeared uninvited to demand roles worthy of their exalted rank. Among the latter, the utterly unemployable Edward de Vere, earl of Oxford, arrived on 28 July – presumably not too incapacitated by the recent death of his neglected wife, Burghley's daughter – and stormed away again on 1 August after being offered command of a mere detachment of troops to cover Harwich – 'though a place of great trust and great danger' as Leicester wrote plaintively to Walsingham.[48] If not quite a backwater, the Tilbury camp was at best a near chaotic outwork of the nation's defences.

In placing Leicester's contingent there, it is likely that the Privy Council, even the Queen herself, wished to provide the earl with a role commensurate with his long-exalted status without exposing his men to the consequences of his leadership. From his Netherlands campaigns, he had earned a reputation for avoiding battle with Parma (most recently during his abortive 'relief' of Sluys). This had been dictated partly by their respective resources, but also by Leicester's awe of the duke's genius and fear of his soldiers' prowess. While it was intended that English forces present at the *tercios'* disembarkation should fight only a delaying action, it was not the intention of the Council that they should retreat indefinitely thereafter. In a subtle manner, it seems that England was being preserved from the talents of Elizabeth's favourite until her forces were fully gathered.[49]

In contrast, there was no equivocation regarding Norreys's appointment. A far superior organizer and leader of troops, and the only English general to have (very nearly) defeated Habsburg troops in battle, he was given the vital task of delaying Parma's forces until England's 'grosse armye' could be concentrated in their path.[50] He had given particular attention to drilling a small but well-disciplined force of Low Countries veterans, with which, in the weeks prior to the armada campaign, he had attempted to integrate the Kentish trained bands (4,000 foot, 1,100 pioneers and 700 horse).[51] Based at Sandwich and Shornecliff, with a reserve at Canterbury, these forces, insufficient to deny a Spanish landing, were intended to fall back slowly and concentrate near Ashford, making every mile of Parma's advance thereafter an arduous march, with English cavalry harrying foraging parties as the main body of Norreys's force dispersed livestock, destroyed means of transportation and burned crops as they retreated.[52] As Parma's *tercios* pushed this screen back towards the capital, Leicester would move his forces tangentially to join with Lord Hunsdon, 'Lieutenant-General for defence of her Majesty's person', and, on paper at least, the operational commander of the greatest number of trained troops.[53] Their combined force of some 45,000 men would absorb Norreys's retreating contingent and await the hopefully weakened invaders on the outskirts of the city. Whether they and Norreys could have dealt a decisive check to Parma's *tercios* there remains debatable; but there can be little question of where the greatest responsibility lay.

Such massive dispositions would be very expensive to maintain (hence Burghley's 'melancholy'), and given the government's already vast commitments with respect to the Navy Royal and her auxiliaries, the summoning of the trained bands was left until the very last moment. That moment, even at the close of the second day of confrontation between the English and Spanish fleets, had not yet arrived. The levies of the southern maritime counties were marching eastwards, and those in Kent awaited their coming.[54] Most of London's own, 10,000-strong contribution lay within a mile or two of the expected site of a last-ditch battle (a thousand of these were redirected to Gravesend on 23 July);[55] but the majority of their provincial compatriots who had been assigned to the capital, or to the encampment at Tilbury, remained in their home counties still: gathered, ready to march, and largely idle. The Privy Council had received no intelligence that Parma's *tercios* were moving as yet towards one or more of their likely concentration ports. At the very least, it was believed that their passage across the Narrow Seas, disembarkation and fighting progress to London allowed some two weeks in which to activate the greater part of England's land defences. This leeway was invaluable in allowing Burghley to preserve the remnants of his 'chested treasure', and he took full advantage of it. Orders sent out to the shires even after the armada arrived off the English coast directed that the trained bands should arrive in London no earlier than 6 August, and in some cases four days later.[56] Given the distances involved, a successful concentration – had it been necessary – would have required a degree of good fortune. Contingents with a relatively short march were able to meet their deadlines (the Northamptonshire levies were at Islington by 5 August), but those of more distant shires – the Worcestershire and Leicestershire bands had also been allocated to the defence of London – were to begin and end their campaign on the road.[57]

Until the trained bands arrived, Elizabeth's personal shield against the vengeance of Catholic Europe was a minimal, if enthusiastic, bodyguard assembled at St James's Palace in the days immediately prior to the first clash of fleets. 'Voluntary' contributions of light horse and foot from the entourages and estates of court officials had produced a core of some 1,500 to 2,000 men, probably all relatively well-trained. Those required from the kingdom's foremost magnates are more difficult to assess. Leicester appears to have taken his own men to Tilbury; his dignity requiring (as it always did) a substantial entourage. Those of other noblemen had in many cases been allocated already to their home shires' trained bands. These had to be extracted and re-assigned, making them a double-counted (and probably absent) resource.[58] In total, it is unlikely that as many as 5,000 men had been assembled to protect the Queen's person by 22 July.[59]

The organization of this force, and the manner of its deployment around St James's Palace, presaged the apocalyptic atmosphere of 1940, when Churchill and the more ambulatory members of his cabinet would vow to fight every inch of the panzers' advance through Whitehall. Under Lord Hunsdon's overall command, the earl of Essex was appointed general of such cavalry as could be assembled (he had been appointed to a similar role at Tilbury in the previous month, but was now recalled); Sir Robert Constable (a veteran of the Scottish wars) utilized his expertise as Master of the Tower Ordnance to command the gunners of the Queen's bodyguard; and Sir Francis Knollis the younger became Colonel-General of the Palace Foot (re-assigned from his initial role as Master of the Tilbury ordnance). Theirs at least would be a martial presence. More doubtful were the contributions of Burghley's son, Sir Robert Cecil, as Constable's immediate superior, and of Leicester's nemesis Sir Thomas Heneage, seamlessly raised from his role as Vice-Chamberlain and Treasurer of the Chamber to that of Treasurer at Wars, charged with dispensing sufficient funds to keep the final line of . London's defence from going home prematurely. The enemy within – fifth-columnists who might seek to aid Parma's thrust into London – were the roving brief of the butcher of Smerwick, Lord Grey de Wilton, authorized by the Council to 'slay, destroy and put to execution of death such and so many of them as you shall think meet by your good discretion to be put to death, by any manner of ways, to the terror of all other offenders'.[60]

With a huge papist counter-offensive looming upon its several horizons, government's fears for English Catholic loyalties had intensified in the weeks prior to the campaign, notwithstanding extensive measures to contain the threat. Already, counties with large dissenting minorities had not been required to despatch their levies to concentration points, but to use them to secure their own borders.[61] Lancashire in particular was considered a potential hot-bed of subversion; her commissioners, when first mustering their resources in 1587, had been ordered to ensure that 'none suspected in religion have the chardge of any nomber of soldiaurs' (though the generally miserable quality of the county's troops would have made their subversion irrelevant).[62] The personal weapons of recusants had been confiscated in 1586, 1587 and, as noted, once more in 1588, and the arrest of seminary priests accelerated as the campaign commenced. Few were reassured, however, that the danger had been neutralized. Indeed, the English Catholic 'menace' that the regime had long attempted to impress upon the nation was by now fully appreciated. 'We are now in peril of goodes, liberty, life, by our enemies the Span(iards), and at home papistes in multitudes ready to come uppon us unawares', the minister of Westerfield, Richard Rogers, confided fearfully to his diary, before organizing a mass fast among his parishioners to speed their local trained band on its way.[63] The Privy Council itself was as certain as ever of the menace posed by its dissenters: 'It is . . . certaine that such as should meane to invade the Realme woulde neuer attempt the same but vppon hope which the fugatiues and rebells ofer to give . . . that are knowen to be recusauntes . . .'; and it was widely believed in the north-west that Sir William Stanley, betrayer of Deventer and now a fighting pensioner of Philip II, would invade Anglesey at the head of a mixed Anglo-Spanish host while the nation's land-forces were occupied with Parma's thrust in the south.[64]

Before this fearsome, multi-faceted threat, mere disarmament of its domestic arm was hardly an adequate safeguard. At the beginning of the year, orders were sent into the shires to gather all known male recusants to determine which of their number were 'obstinate' (to be imprisoned) and 'moderate' (to be committed variously into ecclesiastical custody, the parole of local gentlemen of good reputation or to voluntary incarceration at the responsibility of their non-dissenting relatives).[65] The former in particular were 'to be kepte from intelligence one with another', though predictably, the concentration of potential subversives in the same secure accommodation had quite the opposite effect. Some of the deputy Lords Lieutenant charged with implementing these restraints complained that what constituted obstinacy or moderation was beyond their wit to judge. The matter was referred back to Walsingham, who tried, and largely failed, to issue coherent guidelines.[66] Given this confusion, and the extremely variable performance of local authorities in enforcing orders against recusants (a problem that had exercised government for some years past), directions from the Council were applied with great inconsistency.[67] Some towns and shires confined even 'obstinate' male recusants very loosely, if at all; others exceeded their orders by detaining women also. The deputy Lords Lieutenant of Staffordshire received their orders and proceeded to do nothing about their own recusants until brusquely urged on by the Privy Council. The county's sheriff, William Bassett, was probably a Catholic himself, while Stafford town's clerk of the peace, Nicholas Blackwall, was later sacked for papist sympathies. By them and their friends, several leading recusants were given forewarning of their impending confinement and managed to flee the county.[68] Northamptonshire's authorities also dragged their feet, but, under the rigorous prompting of their own Lord Lieutenant, Sir Christopher Hatton, soon complied. At the other extreme, the widely cited but irresistible example of the appalling Godfrey Foljambe, deputy Lord Lieutenant of Derbyshire, who in February had locked up his own Catholic grandmother, does not appear to have been imitated widely.[69] Leading or influential recusants, however, were gathered and transferred by June to one of four castles – Maidstone, Leeds, Queenborough or Hertford – and thereafter to the Bishop of Ely's fortified Palace at Wisbech, where they formed a near-aristocracy of putative traitors.

Although dictated by the exigencies of a very dangerous moment, this policy of restraint was based upon the same fundamentally flawed assumptions that had fixed government policy for the past two decades. Elizabeth's councillors' fears had long mirrored Philip's hopes that a large proportion of dissenting Englishmen would rise up against their own rulers as a Spanish invasion force disembarked. As the armada arrived off English shores, however, all but a tiny minority of the nation's Catholics appear to have forgotten that they were such. When one of the more obtuse of their number, Ralph Langton, long the scourge of the Chester Bench, was asked of his fellow recusants 'do not thes fellowes in the castle and such like thinck that they shall taste of the enemyes handes as well as others?' he concurred heartily: 'No dowbte of that . . . if yt be King Phillip's quarel'.[70] The 'fellowes in the castle' at Wisbech, reputedly the most dangerous Catholics in England, were even more vociferous in their declarations of loyalty. Once the battle at sea commenced, many petitioned to be allowed to fight as common soldiers in the front line against the invaders. Their heartfelt offer was so embarrassing to government that its rebuff was worded almost graciously: 'It was replied that such our shutting up would more avail that behoof-ful service than the help of many more hands'.[71]

By the standards of the age, the ordeal of England's prisoners of conscience in 1588 was not harsh (though Burghley's later claim that they were 'altogether without any imprisonment' grotesquely understated the case).[72] Even leading recusants were treated, on the whole, as guests of the state, and protected from the occasional attentions of local patriotic mobs hoping to do their bit for the nation's defence. They were locked in their rooms at night and their correspondence was monitored, but these restrictions, and lack of access to their wives and families, were soothed by ample access to the substantial grounds of their prisons and a personal ration of a pint of wine per man per meal (this was for knighted recusants, mere squires enjoyed half the amount).[73] Nevertheless, the government took advantage of their incarceration to have each examined closely on the precise degree of their 'obstinacy' or 'moderation', and even following the departure of the armada and dispersal of levies, local officials were directed to continue to hold them as close prisoners.[74] Several were petitioning for their release as late as October, yet all declined the offer of their gaoler, Dr Pearne, Dean of Ely, to take a form of oath that managed to sneak in recognition of the Queen's absolute authority in spiritual matters. Some vainly offered their own, bespoke oaths in the unequivocal manner of Sir Thomas Tresham:

> I acknowledge myself her hignes natyf Lyoll subject wherby I am religiously bounden in christian duty ever to doe or humbly endure her sacred will . . . in all actions of defending her ryoall person from violence and preserving this realme and all other her highness dominions from invasion against all persons without exception be yt Prynce Poope, or Potentat whosoever . . .[75]

The sentiment was rarely expressed so explicitly, but patriotic fervour of this order made a mockery of government's witch-hunt (and of Lord Grey de Wilton's efforts in particular), as the fruits of its efforts confirmed. Soon after the armada campaign ended, an energetic enquiry conducted by the aldermen of twenty-five London wards into the activities of their imagined Catholic Underground would reveal a grand total of just thirty-six men sufficiently 'suspected in religion' to be worthy of identification (but not arrest) from a grand total of 21,665 citizens examined by them. If the seminarians' mission to England was a military one, as Elizabeth's councillors insisted, it had failed miserably.[76]

Curiously, measures to protect England from her domestic Catholics were not enforced strictly in the one place where a true subversive might have made his treacheries count – the fleet. It is hard to imagine Drake tolerating the presence, once discovered, of even the most supine 'church-papist' among his followers; elsewhere, there seems to have been little attempt either to determine or correct the confessional loyalties of the mariners. An early effort by Walsingham to inject something of the spirit of the Inquisition into the fleet almost cost Lord Sheffield his personal barber; but having been examined closely, the wretch convinced his less than rigorously Protestant commander that his possession of a proscribed papist tract had no treasonable motive.[77] The incident is notable in its isolation. Most of the English ships, even the major vessels, did not carry that indispensable instrument of spiritual discipline, a minister. Drake's *Revenge* did so of course, as did Howard's flagship; the men of Hawkins's *Victory*, however, were obliged to rely upon their captain's enthusiastic piety for succour. The irreligious Frobisher's *Triumph* was not only cleric-free but boasted an impeccably Catholic (and Iberian) boatswain, Simon Fernandez, a former pirate and veteran of the Carolina Banks navigation. In all, only some thirteen ministers were summoned to police the souls of more than 12,000 men, and this probably constituted an over-provision.[78] The common English mariner was not inclined to wanton acts of piety – hence the enduring, if optimistic, requirement for mandatory religious service in instructions for voyages of the period.[79] 'We holde it loste labor and offence to God, to minister Oathes vnto the generallitie of them' was the pithy observation of one group of commissioners, charged with examining the crews of several English vessels four years after the armada campaign.[80] This aversion to godliness (other than during tempests or when closing upon lee shores, when the seafaring Englishman became quite prayerful), and the difficulty with which deserters, the unfit or the dead could be replaced at shortnotice, necessarily inclined Howard and his subordinates to a degree of toleration of weak or even wrong beliefs. The silence from the fleet on this matter contrasted strongly with the clamour of Lords Lieutenant when weeding out evidence of 'seducement of the Pope's confederates' from their bands.[81]

The God of Battles was in any case less exercised by sectarian hair-splitting than his peacetime manifestation, an axiom that generals throughout history have recognized. By the morning of 23 July, the abilities and morale of every mariner in the English fleet – whether godly, cold-statute Protestant, church-papist, recusant, agnostic or outright 'derrydor of religion' – had assumed a far greater significance than his doctrinal tastes. In the previous evening, the English ships had reassembled following their inadvertent scattering and recommenced their pursuit of the armada. During the early hours of the morning a calm fell, leaving both fleets adrift. At dawn, however, the wind revived from the northeast, giving the weather gauge to the Spanish ships for the first time since the fleets met. Just a few miles separated them from the wide, inviting expanse of Chesil beach and Portland beyond. Lying to seaward, it seemed that the English fleet might be helpless to impede a landing there. The first crisis of the campaign had arrived.

THIRTEEN

Portland and Wight

Ther forse is wonderfull gret and strong. And yet we ploke Ther fethers by lyttel and littell.[1]

For Howard and his commanders, the armada's passage along the Dorset and Hampshire coasts from 23 to 25 July constituted the campaign's extended moment of potential disaster. Months earlier, a council of war chaired by Burghley had identified Portland, Portsmouth and the Isle of Wight as being among the 'places most to be suspected' as disembarkation points for the Spanish fleet's troops. As late as 23 July (as the armada lay off Portland), it was the opinion of captains in Seymour's squadron that Wight remained the more likely location for this attempt, being relatively lightly guarded but defensible once occupied in strength.[2] Alternatively, Lyme Bay – upon which the Spanish ships were closing that morning – could provide anchorage for all the vessels of the armada and gentle, sandy beaches upon which to set their expeditionary force, should Medina Sidonia have orders to seize his first available opportunity. The trained bands of Somerset, Devon, Wiltshire and Dorset were hurriedly converging on the armed camp below the ramparts of Portland Castle; but even had they been at full strength (they were not), these would have comprised just 10,000 foot and some 860 light horse, led by no more experienced leaders than their local captains – a force insufficient to impede a Spanish landing supported by the heavy guns of the armada, should the English fleet fail to intervene.[3] In fact, Medina Sidonia had no intention of attempting a landing as yet, but

Howard could not know his adversary's precise aims. On the morning of 23 July, he saw before him a very different enemy formation, which suggested that the Spanish Admiral intended something other than his stately eastward progress of the previous two days.

The armada's new deployment was Medina Sidonia's response to the experiences of the battle's first clash on 21 July, when his ships' *en lúnula* formation had proved unsatisfactory. It had deterred the enemy vessels from closing to grappling range within its interior curve but allowed them to pick at its edges almost unmolested. Moreover, its vast breadth – almost seven miles between extremities – made it difficult for the more effective Spanish fighting ships to move quickly to support their hard-pressed sisters. This vulnerability had brought occasional lapses in discipline. During their first exposure to the almost coordinated assault by Howard's *Ark Royal* and her consorts, a number of Spanish captains, regarding their vessels to be dangerously exposed, had hurriedly broken formation to move into the centre, where the main 'battle' offered greater protection. To prevent a recurrence of these potentially fatal episodes, Medina Sidonia used the lull in fighting on 22 July to alter radically his order of battle.[4]

Drifting athwart Portland the following morning, the English commanders had first sight of the new formation, in which a powerful rearguard comprising the former left and right *cuernos* screened and shepherded most of the slowest and least well-armed troop transports. Ahead of them, a smaller vanguard, led by Medina Sidonia's 'battle', could react in relatively short order, shielded from the enemy, to support those elements of the armada that came under heaviest assault – and, hopefully, close with their English assailants before they could withdraw. To Howard's preoccupied eye, however, it seemed that the large body of Spanish vessels closest to his own fleet – the new rearguard – was ideally placed to screen the landward formation should it attempt to disembark its troops during the following hours; a manoeuvre that might be achieved at relatively little risk if the English ships failed to re-capture the weather gauge.

The Lord Admiral responded swiftly to this potential danger – or as swiftly as the light, contrary wind allowed. Initially, trusting to the advantage of his ships' superior weatherly qualities, he attempted to overlap the most leeward Spanish vessels to regain the wind. This proved impossible. Observing the attempt, Medina Sidonia sent part of his vanguard, lying much further inshore, to intercept the thrust. Howard then made the bold decision to come entirely about, seeking to weather the opposite wing of the armada, and, by engaging from the south-east, draw it away from the shore. To achieve this objective, he had to lead his ships across the face of the Spanish rearguard – daring the enemy, in effect, to take its best shot as he passed.

The challenge was accepted. Coming about in turn, the Spanish rearguard advanced line abreast in a broad, shallow crescent towards the larboard flank of the English formation. Upon its extreme left wing, the ships of Don Alonso Martinez de Leiva's squadron closed upon Howard's *Ark Royal* and her consorts while Recalde's inshore division made for the rearmost vessels in the English line. As the two fleets converged, *Ark Royal, Victory, Elizabeth Jonas, Golden Lion, White Bear, Nonpareil* and their merchantmen consorts abandoned the attempt to outflank the Spanish formation in favour of an uncoordinated, close-range maul that drew in approximately half of the enemy's effective fighting ships. This has been interpreted by some commentators as a deliberate ploy to buy time for a group of English ships to the seaward (assumed to be led by Drake's *Revenge*) to outflank the left wing of the Spanish formation and push it back upon its centre.[5] More probably, Howard and Hawkins realized that they had no chance of outdistancing the approaching Spanish line and decided instead to engage it. What followed was perhaps the most confused sequence of the campaign, in which neither fleet exhibited much science or recognizable purpose. Once more, most of the Spanish commanders attempted single-mindedly to close to grappling range while disdaining to employ their ships' ordnance effectively; again, their intended victims used their superior gunnery skills and manoeuvrability to confound them. As the distance between the opposing ships closed (to half-musket range, according to Ubaldino's account), the rate of fire from the English vessels increased markedly. Spanish veterans of Lepanto present in the armada later claimed that the bombardment they endured this day was twenty times more intense than during that former battle; while even their English tormentors, pestered by a far lighter bombardment, likened the fire from the Spanish heavy guns to 'a hot skirmish of small shot'.[6] There remained a remarkable discrepancy, however, between the perception of this action and its reality. Few casualties were suffered in either fleet; Spanish losses for the entire day amounted to less than sixty fatalities from all causes, while England's sacrifice was said to be confined to the death of just one man, captain William Coxe of the bark *Delight* (though even this may have been a misreport of his demise at Gravelines a few days later).[7] The ordeal described by the protagonists may have been beyond their experience and fears, but it is clear that much, if not most, of the barrage of shot went wide of its intended targets, ricocheted or buried itself almost harmlessly in the ships' hulls.[8]

As this fray progressed, a more intimate encounter was taking place to the north. Earlier, when Howard came about to take his fleet southwards, its extreme leeward element – Frobisher's *Triumph* and her consort of ships, *Merchant Royal, Margaret and John, Centurion, Golden Lion* and *Mary Rose* – had anchored under Portland Bill.[9] Whether this was a matter of choice or necessity is unclear. The headland may have robbed the English vessels' sails of the wind as they attempted to weather the armada's inshore wing during the day's first manoeuvre. Conversely, the masters in this small squadron (if not their impulsive leader) would have been intimately familiar with the movements of the east and west Portland 'races' – fast moving eddies created by the confluence of southerly tides on either side of Portland Bill and the main west–east Channel current – which suggests that what appeared to be an anchorage of necessity may have been chosen deliberately.[10]

Medina Sidonia's vanguard lay directly to the east of Frobisher's vessels. As the rolling battle to the south developed, the Spanish admiral noticed the growing gap in the English order and detached the armada's four Neopolitan galleasses to deal with Frobisher's anchored squadron. These hybrid warships, carrying both oars and square-rigged sails, could manoeuvre more effectively in calm seas than any English ship. Commanded by the 'general of the galleasses', Hugo de Moncada, they were also the most heavily armed vessels in the Spanish fleet (absent the captured *Rosario* and *San Salvador*), with each carrying some fifty guns and 180–260 soldiers.[11] Having failed to enter the battle proper upon at least two occasions in the past twenty-four hours, Moncada responded promptly to his Admiral's orders.[12] His assault, however, provided yet another lesson in the limitations of contemporary sea warfare.

Frobisher's force was static, but his handling of the crisis was adept. Using his ship's boats to manoeuvre the *Triumph* almost as handily as the approaching galleasses, he directed the fire of his larger, lower-tier ordnance (which, in the morning's still waters, could finally be brought into play) into the hulls of the enemy vessels.[13] This was a common tactic employed by English warships seeking to damage an enemy at the waterline, but it seems that Frobisher had other motives. His first volleys were not of round but chain shot, largely ineffective against a ship's hull but devastating upon less robust surfaces. The galleasses' oars and oarsmen bore the brunt of this murderous assault, which not only spoiled the advantages of speed and manoeuvrability enjoyed by the Spanish vessels but discouraged them from presenting their broadside armament.[14] The encounter continued for almost ninety minutes. Unable to close with the enemy, Moncada was drawn into a slogging match in which the English guns enjoyed a decided advantage over his larger-calibre but shorter-range bow-chasers. Although he was criticized subsequently by his own men (and his admiral) for not seeking to force a boarding action with the enemy vessels, it is unlikely that the general of the galleasses could have done more. Portland's east race – to the larboard of Frobisher's ships – and the prevailing north-easterly breeze effectively prevented a flanking assault, leaving only a direct approach against a strong current and withering fire.

The episode graphically demonstrated the superior fighting qualities of the English ships even when not under sail. This was the only moment during the campaign when elements of the armada possessed a decisive local advantage in weight of ordnance, speed and freedom of manoeuvre; yet they were unable to make it count for anything. The English galleons under Portland Bill carried more and better gunners, and were commanded by men who had years of practise in the art of close ship-to-ship fighting.[15] With these advantages, the decision whether or not to grapple was always theirs to make, not the enemy's. The tactics of Terceira, the battle that had so hugely influenced Spanish plans for confrontation with the English fleet, had been rendered effectively useless within six years of their most devastating exposition.[16] Conversely, this same small but vicious encounter illustrates why the armada campaign was not to be the decisive military clash that Terceira – a land battle fought at sea – undoubtedly had been. When Moncada's own galleass *San Lorenzo* was driven aground at Calais several days later and examined by curious onlookers, it was said that not a single shot from this and subsequent engagements had entirely penetrated her hull.[17]

At approximately 10am the wind veered south-westerly, pushing to the east the Spanish rearguard's right wing and revealing to Howard the apparent predicament of the *Triumph* and her escort (by now, *San Martín* and a number of her escorts were moving towards Portland Bill to support their galleasses). Having been gifted the weather gauge, the Lord Admiral disengaged from his action against Leiva's squadron; bringing the *Ark Royal* about, he led the *Elizabeth Jonas, Galleon Leicester, Golden Lion, Victory, Mary Rose, Dreadnought* and *Swallow* northwards once more.[18] A running battle developed, involving the extreme right wing of the Spanish rearguard under Recalde, supported by elements of the vanguard moving to intercept the new English manoeuvre. Correctly identifying the Spanish flagship, the leading English vessels veered, closed and concentrated their fire accordingly. To anxious observers in her fleet, the *San Martín* seemed to disappear in smoke, though much of this was generated by her own ordnance, which, together with the deadly accurate fire from her musketeers and snipers, forced the English ships to stand off and deliver their shot from beyond effective range once more. Coming up to support their Admiral, vessels of both the Spanish rear- and vanguards engaged the English ships in piece-meal fashion. Thereafter, events are unclear. No extant account, English or Spanish, discusses in detail a diffuse and inchoate clash that continued until late afternoon or early evening, though the anonymous author of the *Relation of Proceedings* claimed that the fire of the English ships at one point forced their opponents to flock together like sheep.[19] If this was the case, no effort was made to exploit what would have been a potentially fatal confusion. What he or his sources may have witnessed, and derided, was rather the Spanish ships' close support and shielding of the *San Martín*, a manoeuvre that would be repeated with equal success some days later off Gravelines.[20] In the face of this coordinated defence, the principal English ships continued firing until their stocks of shot and powder fell dangerously low once more, at which point they broke off the action and withdrew. As night fell, the armada regrouped and continued its eastward passage. According to one Spanish calculation, approximately 5,000 rounds of heavy shot had been discharged by both fleets that day.[21] By far the greater proportion of that prodigious hail of iron and stone had been English fire, yet none of the Spanish vessels engaged had been seriously damaged, much less devastated, by its impact.

A curious omission from contemporary accounts of the day's fighting is any mention of Drake's contribution. Certainly, the Spanish rearguard was not 'rolled up' by any assault from seaward, as his admirers have speculated. The only action known to have developed from that direction occurred in the early evening, when the London merchantman *Mayflower* (commanded by Edward Bancks[22]) with several other, unnamed English vessels engaged and drove off a small group of Spanish ships that had detached from the southernmost flank of the armada's formation. This is the sole indication that there was in fact a group of English vessels to the south of the ships led by Howard and Hawkins that day.[23] It has since been inferred that the Lord Admiral, still piqued by Drake's abandonment of his station on the night of 21/22 July, deliberately excised his troublesome subordinate's contribution from subsequent reports of the battle's progress;[24] yet even Ubaldino's *Second Narrative*, a revised work intended to emphasize Drake's role in the battle, makes no mention of its hero's activities during this phase of the campaign. Until the wind veered south-westerly and then south-easterly that day, it would have been difficult for any English squadron to seaward to have beaten northwards once more into the Spanish flank. Thereafter, Drake's failure to engage the armada from the south to complement the Lord Admiral's assault would be inexplicable – that is, if the *Revenge* was indeed present in any southerly group of English ships. Possibly, she and her consorts were operating to the north of Howard's immediate formation as they would two days later, in which case his contribution there was equally obscure.[25] Having since been found by too many commentators who regard his absence as unacceptable, perhaps Drake should be allowed a rare moment of anonymity in the midst of a brawl about which, recalled Camden, every man had a different story.[26]

Once more, the English ships had suffered neither human nor material loss, but Howard could not have been happy with the day's work. There was little doubt that Medina Sidonia's tactics had given the armada the best of their latest encounter. One potential landing site had been denied to the would-be invaders, but the Solent – possibly the most tempting goal – was looming. The various elements of the armada had displayed far greater cohesion in battle than two days earlier, responded swiftly to threatening probes into their rearguard and preserved their formations, at little cost, in the face of a series of ferocious assaults. Spanish snipers and their fighting ships' heavy guns (most notably, those of the *San Martín*) had been sufficiently well handled to keep their English tormentors out of effective range. Most tellingly, their new deployment had allowed them to respond along interior lines that to an extent negated the superior handling and speed of the enemy vessels.

In contrast, the English ships had demonstrated once more that they could not be grappled, but otherwise their sound and fury had signified little. While the Spanish Admiral had made the best of his poor hand, Howard had squandered his advantages of gunnery and manoeuvrability in a series of barely coordinated attacks that seemed to lack any underlying strategy. He had led his fleet everywhere during the day – north, south and then north again – without once allowing initiative to his subordinates or seizing it from the enemy. The principal effect of the awesome discharge of the most powerful English ships' ordnance had been to render them almost toothless as the day closed. As his Spanish counterpart had found some twenty-four hours earlier, the Lord Admiral needed to give urgent thought to the manner in which he was fighting this battle.

*　　*　　*

Very little action occurred on 24 July. At dawn, the English fleet lay well
astern of the armada; however, the *Gran Grifon*, a hulk of the Levant
squadron, had drifted away from the Spanish rearguard and was set upon
by several English ships. One of these – usually identified as the *Revenge* –
gave her one broadside and then came about to deliver the other. It was a
fine display of the handiness of the best English ships, and achieved no more
than previously. Several men were killed upon the deck of the *Gran Grifon*;
their surviving comrades, angered and frustrated by the stand-off tactics of
their tormentors, dared them to close and fight like men, until Recalde's
San Juan and Medina Sidonia's *San Martín*, leading three of the four
Neopolitan galleasses, came to their aid. Outnumbered, peppered by some
of the heaviest Spanish gunnery to date (one vessel – again, possibly the
Revenge – had her main mast severely damaged by shot), the English ships
fell back once more towards their own formations. The disengagement
marked the end of fighting that day.[27]

The perfunctory nature of the encounter hints at the confusion of the
English response to Spanish tactics to date; not least the difficulty of maintaining adequate pressure upon the armada. It is likely that Drake, if it was
him, had been able to engage the *Gran Grifon* so fiercely only because he
had retained much of the *Rosario*'s munitions. The main business for the
remainder of the English fleet on 24 July was not to hinder the armada's
eastward progress but replenish its almost vanished powder and shot. This
was not easily done. Only now did the Privy Council at Whitehall order
the transfer to Portsmouth of a further seven lasts (16,800 pounds) of
powder and an unspecified quantity of shot from the Tower. None of this
would reach the fleet for several days, and some was still arriving in the
town on 30 July, long after Howard's ships had moved into the Narrow Seas
and North Sea.[28] The earl of Sussex managed to find and despatch ten
barrels of powder and 444 round shot from Portsmouth's stocks that afternoon (he also removed four and a half lasts of 'powder' from a group of
Stade merchantmen anchored in the port; but as this was sent to the Tower
rather than directly to the English fleet it was almost certainly unmixed salt-
petre).[29] With only this donation, the dwindling munitions from the captured *Rosario* and *San Salvador* and smaller contributions from other English
ports lying along the battle's path to date, Howard was content merely to
shadow the armada for the remainder of the day. In the meantime, he summoned his senior commanders for new orders.

So far, the absence of formal battle formations in the English fleet had
undermined the intrinsic advantages enjoyed by its individual elements. The

Lord Admiral's determination to lead most of his best ships personally into battle – much to his honour but little to his tactical insight – had ensured that the English onslaught had been delivered in an uncoordinated manner upon a relatively small proportion of the armada's vessels. It must have become clear by now that as long as the Spanish fleet maintained good order and was able to reorganize in time to support its hardest pressed elements, English ships would not be able to close sufficiently to do real damage with their guns without exposing themselves to the risk of being surrounded and grappled. Each day in which they failed to impose themselves decisively carried the armada closer to its feared rendezvous with Parma. Furthermore, communications within the English fleet – the only means by which any plan of battle could be directed at other than arm's length – were becoming progressively less satisfactory. As more vessels, principally levies but some voluntaries also, joined the fray, it was becoming difficult for the Lord Admiral to know what much of his fleet was doing at any point (if, indeed, it was doing anything at all).[30] Urged on, perhaps, by his senior commanders, he now proposed a new, very different order of battle. The English fleet was to be reorganized into four squadrons; not loose aggregations but autonomous groups intended to engage the armada's formations independently. Howard would take command of one of these, with Drake, Hawkins and Frobisher leading the others.

The precise allocation of ships within these squadrons is not clear, but it is probable that Drake continued to lead many of the vessels that had been with his element of the fleet since January. Among the ships assigned to his own squadron, Frobisher received Lord Sheffield's *White Bear* and Sir Robert Southwell's *Elizabeth Jonas*. Like his *Triumph*, these were relatively unwieldy but heavily armed 'great ships', capable both of giving and receiving much punishment. With their respective escort vessels, they were allocated, or assumed, the role of a 'hinge' intended to turn the inshore wing of the armada. In the following day's engagements, Drake's squadron would operate on the right flank of this force, with those of the Lord Admiral and Hawkins respectively to seaward.[31] Dividing the fleet's naval vessels in this manner would, ostensibly, dilute the impact of their firepower at any point; but the Lord Admiral also intended to make better use of his sparse munitions by drawing more of his armed merchantmen into action than had been engaged to date. That process would begin immediately. From each of the four new squadrons, Howard appointed six of them to move forward during the night of 24/25 July, firing randomly into the Spanish formations 'to keep the enemy waking'.[32] Unfortunately, a dead calm fell before midnight, holding the merchantmen within the fleet and allowing the less perturbable Spanish mariners their sleep.

At dawn on 25 July, three of the newly organized English squadrons lay becalmed to the west of the Spanish ships. Separated from the Spanish rear-guard, three vessels – *Doncella*, *San Luis* and *Duquesa Santa Ana* – offered tempting opportunities to enterprising English ships in the still waters between the two fleets. These were not strays, but deliberate lures, each carefully positioned to receive support from a squadron of the rearguard when the enemy closed. Medina Sidonia had reached a moment of decision regarding his objectives, and needed a diversion. He had not yet heard from Parma, despite having sent a number of *pataches* ahead of his fleet to discover the duke's state of readiness to attempt their rendezvous. Immediately prior to the commencement of the campaign, he had convened a council of war that interpreted – or, rather, misinterpreted – Philip's instructions regarding the option of occupying the Isle of Wight. Rather than await a definitive failure to meet with Parma before returning westward to secure a harbour on England's south coast (as his King, with a landsman's disregard for winds and currents, had directed[33]), Medina Sidonia seems informally to have agreed with his commanders (particularly supported by Recalde, who had visited the Solent previously and noted its potential) that they should make for St Helen's roads off Spithead, and, if feasible, force a landing on Wight *before* advancing further towards the Narrow Seas.[34] The plan had some merit, given that Parma's precise timetable was not known, but it was difficult to implement. The English fleet had to be neutralized – or at least kept sufficiently busy elsewhere – to allow the Spanish vanguard to enter and secure the eastern Solent unmolested. If this could be achieved, the entire Spanish fleet might then withdraw into its confined and defensible waters and ride in relative safety until word came that Parma was ready to embark his *tercios*.

The bait of the three stragglers was taken first by Hawkins, lying furthest to seaward. He had his ships' boats tow the *Victory* and her consorts towards the *Duquesa Santa Ana*, and opened fire as soon as the range closed sufficiently. Immediately, three of the four Neopolitan galleasses detached from the Spanish rearguard to relieve her. To the North, ships of Howard's squadron closed slowly upon the *San Luis* while Drake's squadron attempted to engage the *Doncella* (possibly without Drake, who appears to have withdrawn temporarily to make emergency repairs to the *Revenge*'s damaged mainmast). It may have escaped the notice of the eager English commanders, but each of these supposedly isolated vessels lay closest to some of the most powerful fighting ships of the armada.

Perhaps unwittingly, the fourth English squadron was ideally placed to deny Medina Sidonia his prize. Using the eastward push of the inshore current, Frobisher's ships had drifted past the leeward wing of the Spanish rearguard by first light. The *Triumph*, leading her consorts, lay furthest to the east. As two days earlier off Portland Bill, Medina Sidonia appears to have been the first Spanish commander to have noticed Frobisher's ship. There was little need now for sharp eyes, however; his own flagship was the *Triumph*'s intended prey, and began to take fire as the English broadside armament came to bear. Unfortunately for Frobisher, the other ships of his squadron lay too far astern to support him effectively, though several began to discharge their ordnance towards the Spanish Admiral's ship. Nevertheless, the *Triumph*'s guns were employed effectively, damaging the *San Martín*'s mainmast and killing several soldiers on her deck. Had the wind now arisen from the north or east as in the previous day, the English inshore squadron's manoeuvre might have seized a significant, perhaps decisive advantage by outflanking and forcing the enemy vanguard back upon its rearguard. Frustratingly, however, a light breeze rose from the south-west, allowing several Spanish galleons to move to support the *San Martín*. The remainder of Frobisher's squadron closed to assist the *Triumph*, but in doing so courted disaster.

To the south, Recalde, again leading the right wing of the Spanish rearguard, noticed this encounter and acted promptly. Disengaging and coming about after successfully repulsing elements of Drake's squadron, his ships formed a wedge, thrusting northwards, that threatened to separate much of Frobisher's squadron from the remainder of the English fleet. Frobisher himself lay too far to the east to withdraw. His immediate subordinates had a choice: to abandon him or risk envelopment and their own destruction. Most of the English inshore squadron's ships duly came about, but the *Bear* and *Elizabeth Jonas* bravely, if recklessly, continued to drift eastwards towards the *Triumph*, setting out their boats to tow her to safety.

On Recalde's larboard flank, Thomas Fenner's *Nonpareil* and Edward Fenton's *Mary Rose* took in their topsails and came to, hoping to tempt the Spanish ships to re-engage their own squadron. Their courageous challenge was ignored, and for the first time since the battle commenced, the wind appeared to favour Spanish ambitions to detach, close with and destroy a significant part of the enemy's strength. At this critical moment, however, Howard responded decisively. The Lord Admiral's squadron drove into the centre of the Spanish rearguard, which had been opened up by Recalde's move to the north. The manoeuvre entirely reversed the tide of battle.

Rather than deliver a decisive blow against a divided English fleet, the armada's formations were themselves threatened with dismemberment. Hastily reforming its right-centre (though without much of the enthusiastic Recalde's division, which continued to move against the leeward English ships), the rearguard came under furious close-range bombardment as the squadrons of Drake and Hawkins moved in to support Howard. Slowly, the entire Spanish formation was forced to fall back upon its vanguard.

As this action progressed the wind strengthened from the south-west, accelerating the armada's north-easterly drift. It also allowed Frobisher's *Triumph* to disengage from an increasingly parlous engagement in which she enjoyed the undivided attention of five or more major Spanish warships. Despite being one of the least weatherly of the English naval vessels, the speed of her flight – east and south in a great arc behind the armada to rejoin her fleet's opposite wing – astonished her pursuers, who were said by one Spanish observer to be standing still by comparison. As she performed this spectacular escape, English mariners in eleven ships' boats who had attempted to tow *Triumph* to safety used their oars to good effect and retreated rapidly to the east. The *Bear* and *Elizabeth Jonas* withdrew also, leaving Medina Sidonia with no potential prizes and a growing tumult approaching his rear. Its momentum brought a further, potentially fatal danger for the Spanish fleet.

Off Selsey Bill, north-east of Medina Sidonia's vanguard, lie the treacherous Outer Owers shoals. Though not on their charts, these disturbed waters must have been seen clearly by the Spanish Admiral and the captains of those ships that, with the *San Martín*, had drifted northward in the strengthening wind. As the English fleet pushed from the south-east, the bulk of the armada was slowly being squeezed towards its destruction. At about 3pm, with all thoughts of making Spithead (by now north-west of the Spanish ships) abandoned, Medina Sidonia fired a signal to have his fleet disengage the enemy and reform its sailing order. There was no question in which direction he must lead them: to seaward, away from the shoals but away also from any chance of making the last secure English haven west of the Narrow Seas.[35]

Howard could count this as his best day of battle to date. His fleet had fought to its last reserves of powder and shot, but the threat of a landing on England's south coast had been extinguished. With a precious breathing space in which to replenish his ships' munitions, and an imminent rendezvous with Seymour's Downs squadron that would give the English fleet a marked numerical advantage over the enemy, the most dangerous phase of the battle had passed. The conjunction of Medina Sidonia and Parma had of course to be prevented, or any independent attempt by the latter to carry his army into England, but there now seemed little likelihood that their invasion could proceed without interruption by the combined English fleet.

The Lord Admiral's relief mirrored that of the Privy Council, whose anxieties had tracked closely those apparent in despatches coming from the battle. Two days earlier, with Howard's admission of his thin success in their hands, the Queen's councillors had abandoned any pretence of a dual-threat strategy and sent orders to Seymour's squadron to move westwards to assist the main fleet. Only Sir Henry Palmer's *Antelope*, with twelve London merchantmen (still fitting out in the Thames), would support the coasters of Holland and Zeeland to cover the Low Countries' ports. A few hours later, even this drastic step seemed insufficient, and further orders directed that Palmer should go with Seymour also, leaving William Borough's near-useless galley *Bonovolia* to lead the replacement Narrow Seas squadron. On the evening of 25 July, however, news of Howard's successes off Wight changed everything. It was clear now that Medina Sidonia had only two realistic options: to seek a friendly French port on the Channel's southern coast or continue eastwards into the Narrow Seas. As soon as he received the Lord Admiral's good news, Walsingham anticipated the following morning's Council meeting and scribbled off a note to Seymour, rescinding his previous orders. His fellow councillors confirmed his action the next day, and the Narrow Seas squadron was directed instead to the 'river of Dunkirk' once more, to prevent Parma from communicating with, or coming out to join, the approaching armada. Wearily (and in some confusion, one suspects), both Seymour and his lieutenant Sir William Winter reminded the Council of the difficulty of maintaining station in the currents off Dunkirk, but agreed to do their best.[36]

In gratitude for his men's achievement, and to inspire further effort in the coming days, Howard convened an extraordinary council in the *Ark Royal* on the morning of Friday 26 July. There, he invoked his authority as Lord Admiral of England to knight several of his captains. His two junior squadron commanders, John Hawkins and Martin Frobisher, were obvious recipients, having exhibited great energy and commitment (if, in Frobisher's case, little common-sense) during the previous day's fighting. He also honoured his kinsmen Lord Thomas Howard and Lord Sheffield (both had distinguished themselves in action, though probably not more so than a

dozen other captains), a courtier-volunteer in the *Ark Royal*, Roger Townshend, and – surely the honour's most popular beneficiary among the fleet
– old George Beeston, summoned over from the *Dreadnought*.[37]

A dinner would have followed the ceremonies, not least to welcome the
earl of Cumberland, the most distinguished of a gaggle of volunteers who
joined the fleet that morning (many had already visited Tilbury and persuaded themselves that any prospect of glory lay elsewhere). The Lord
Admiral's tact and patience were tested when Cumberland insisted on having
suitable quarters prepared for him in the *Ark Royal*. However, being told
that the fleet's flagship was already 'much pestered, and scant of cabins', the
earl reluctantly agreed to bestow his august presence upon Raymond's *Elizabeth Bonaventure*.[38] These distractions settled, the remainder of the day was
consumed by urgent arrangements to make good the English ships' munitions and victuals. The tireless earl of Sussex sent out a further forty-eight
barrels of powder and 100 round shot from Portsmouth's fortifications'
dwindling but now unrequired allocation. During the next twenty-four
hours, he also collected and despatched a proportion of munitions previously distributed among Hampshire's trained bands.[39] Anticipating, for
once, the coming battles, the Privy Council had already authorized a further
fourteen lasts (33,600 pounds) of powder to be sent directly to the Downs,
to be available when the entire fleet combined in the Narrow Seas (though
at least five of these would not reach the English ships until all fighting had
ceased).[40]

The relatively short supply lines enjoyed by the English ships gave a
decided advantage, but it was a finite blessing. By 27 July, the nation's entire
accounted reserves of gunpowder were approaching exhaustion. At the
beginning of the year, the Tower had held in store some 131 lasts of mixed
powder. Distributions to the fleet, to the Low Countries, trained bands and
domestic fortifications had diminished this figure by two-thirds even before
the campaign commenced.[41] In the days since, a further twenty-one
lasts had been despatched to Howard's fleet or Seymour's squadron, while
Leicester's Tilbury camp had received ten. This quantity was more than
England's domestic industry could produce in a year. Even with the (probably unmixed) powder requisitioned from the Stade fleet, the Tower now
contained at most sixteen lasts, and no one knew what further clashes, at
sea or by land, would occur in the coming days. In desperation, the Privy
Council urged the Lord Mayor of London to scour his constituency for
merchants' private stocks of gunpowder. It has since been estimated that
the City, had it responded willingly and completely to this initiative,

might have provided a total of just seven-and-a-half further lasts.[42] In the absence of any surer supply, powder subsequently provided to her fleet would need to be stripped piecemeal from ports, garrisons, castles and trained bands' depots along the route of the coming sea battle, and not all would be provided unstintingly.[43] England, western Europe's foremost naval power, was testing the limits of her strategic reach after just three days' clashes at sea.

Victualling, another enduring matter for concern, was about to become more problematic still. The use made of musketeers and snipers in the Spanish ships had deterred English attempts to close to effective range almost as effectively as the threat of being grappled. To counter both of these dangers, the Privy Council now ordered the fleet's naval vessels to be 'double-manned' with their own sharpshooters. A group of approximately 100 soldiers was despatched to the *Ark Royal* from the Isle of Wight on 25 July by Lord Hunsdon's son, Sir George Carey, but they were immediately sent home by Howard, who saw no use for them. However, a thousand harquebusiers and musketeers from Kent's trained bands were put on notice to join the fleet when it came to the Downs.[44] These reinforcements would require more victuals than they carried with them, and there was little enough waiting for them at sea. Most of Seymour's squadron had by now only some four days' supplies remaining (though Sir William Winter and Sir Henry Palmer, currently sharing a roe deer carcass from Walsingham's estate, seem to have been comfortable enough), while the main fleet had little more.[45] The only immediate measure taken to alleviate the potential shortages that this significant reinforcement would generate was the Council's order of 26 July that beer be brewed in the Cinque Ports 'with all expedition' and carried to the fleet as it passed by. Two months earlier, Sir William Winter, surveying the construction work on Dover pier, had urged Burghley to establish a forward victualling depot in the town, allowing far more efficient and cost-effective distribution than the prevailing system, by which all supplies were sent down from London or Chatham (the carriage of materials constituted by far the greater part of their cost).[46] Now, as the battle approached the Narrow Seas, such a facility would have been ideally placed to serve the fleet, but no steps had been taken to act upon Winter's recommendation. Ships carrying three, two or even a single day's victuals were of course capable of operating effectively; but fighting to the last barrel of salt beef was a dangerous gamble, as any number of contemporary voyages had shown. The increasing scarcity of victuals in the English fleet was to determine the outcome of the campaign no less than shortages of powder

and shot; thereafter, failure to make good the deficiency would have consequences far more fatal than any sea battle.[47]

For the moment, however, morale and the fighting spirit of the English
fleet was improving rapidly as a two-knot breeze gently drove the enemy
further from the shores of southern England. In the two days following the
action off Wight, no further fighting took place.[48] On the afternoon of Sat-
urday 27 July, the armada came to Calais roads; at a signal from the *San
Martín*, the Spanish ships took in sail and dropped anchor. Medina Sidonia
had achieved the considerable feat of maintaining his fleet, virtually intact,
in the face of sustained assaults by the most powerful fighting fleet in
Europe. His battle casualties were said, improbably, to total fewer than 200
men (in addition to the unfortunates who died in the *San Salvador*'s magazine explosion), and although the armada had lost several vessels since
departing Corunna, the army and siege-train it transported had been largely
untouched by the previous days' clashes.[49]

Yet this success was fraught with unresolved dangers. No word had yet
been received from Parma as to when he would be ready to embark his
veterans. Until their rendezvous took place, the deep-draughted Spanish
ships might be obliged to remain at a perilously exposed anchorage, with
no safer haven in friendly hands along the coast before them. Most ominously, the English fleet was in sight to the west, and came to anchor as
Medina Sidonia's ships lowered their sails. Having held the initiative during
much of the previous week's confrontations, Philip's admiral had reached a
moment at which the fate of his armada passed decisively into the hands of
a friend before him and an enemy to the rear.

FOURTEEN

Gravelines and the North Sea

It's well; ambition's windy puff lies drown'd
By winds, and swelling hearts, by swelling waves.
It's well; the Spaniards, who the world's vast round
Devour'd, devouring sea most justly craves.[1]

Surveying the armada at anchor before him on the afternoon of 27 July,
Howard, like Medina Sidonia, had urgent decisions to make. While the
enemy had taken some punishment and lay exposed to more, the English
fleet had not significantly damaged its capacity to assist Parma's invasion
schedule. The latter, furthermore, had successfully disguised his movements
and intentions from rebel observers, who were unable, as yet, to pass on any
useful intelligence to their English allies. Howard was not aware that the
intended embarkation ports of the duke's army were already, if incompletely,
blockaded by Hollander and Zealander coasters (as he came to Calais he
was complaining in a despatch to Walsingham that the rebels were contributing nothing to the sea war[2]). Nor was the attitude of the authorities
in Calais towards their uninvited guests yet known, though a succession of
small boats plying between the town and anchored Spanish ships hinted at
some degree of local collaboration. All evidence available to the Lord
Admiral suggested that the feared rendezvous of armada and invasion army
might be within a few miles – and hours – of accomplishment. The
English fleet held the initiative, but exploiting it required speed and
decisiveness.

As Howard's ships anchored before Calais, Seymour's squadron was cruising somewhere between Dungeness and Folkestone on the southern Kent coast, searching vainly for its victualling ships. Summoned to join the main body of the fleet that afternoon, its arrival brought the combined English strength to some 140 sail. For the first time, the Lord Admiral enjoyed a potentially decisive advantage over the enemy, but even now there remained the problem of how to break the Spanish fleet's discipline. One man at least had strong views on how that might be accomplished. In the evening, Seymour's immediate subordinate, Sir William Winter, crossed from the *Vanguard* to the *Ark Royal*, and, by his own account, urged Howard to send fire-ships against the anchored Spanish fleet. This suggestion was well received (though perhaps momentarily forgotten as a tidal swell caused Lord Sheffield's *White Bear* and three other ships to run upon the *Ark*), and a council of war convened the following morning endorsed it.

Winter's claims for his apparently sole initiative cannot be tested, but the use of fire-ships against a fleet anchored off a lee shore had obvious attractions. After several days of enduring the best efforts of English gunners, Spanish morale could be expected to be extremely vulnerable to this most detested weapon of sea warfare. At best, several vessels might be consumed by fire or driven aground; at worst, their flight would be hasty and unco-ordinated, giving the English fleet its first opportunity to deal with a scattered enemy. In either case, Medina Sidonia's rendezvous with Parma would be at least delayed, and possibly foiled entirely. Agreement to the attempt by Howard's immediate subordinates appears to have been unanimous, and Sir Henry Palmer's *Antelope* was despatched to Dover to find suitable vessels to employ in the attack. In his absence, however, the necessity of acting before the Spanish Admiral could anticipate English intentions became apparent.[3] From within the fleet, eight vessels were chosen for an assault that evening. Drake's own *Thomas* of Plymouth (200 tons), *Bark Young* (sometimes identified as *Bear Young*, 140 tons) *Bark Talbot* (200 tons) Hawkins's *Bark Bond* (150 tons), *Hope* (40 tons), *Elizabeth* of Lowestoft (90 tons), *Angel* of Southampton and an unnamed vessel owned by one 'Cure' were hurriedly stripped out and packed with pitch and faggots.[4] Their ordnance was charged and double-shotted to increase the devastation among its intended victims as fire ignited the charges. Their skeleton crews – courageous men subsequently granted a shared bounty of £100 in addition to wages[5] – slipped cables at midnight and lit their fuses as they drifted, aided by a light westerly wind, toward the Spanish ships.

In fact, Medina Sidonia had foreseen the English employment of fire-ships and issued precise orders to deal with them. A screen of pinnaces was placed before his fleet that night to grapple and tow toward the beaches any drifting vessels. Those Spanish ships most closely threatened by fire were to weigh anchor (or buoy their cables if in imminent danger) and stand to seaward, but all were to reassemble at their former anchorages immediately thereafter. It was a sound plan, but rendered ineffectual by the anxieties that pervaded the Spanish fleet. Normal fire-ships were fearsome enough, but the legend of the 'hell-burners' – explosive-packed rebel barges that had destroyed Parma's bridging works at Antwerp three years earlier, killing hundreds of his men – greatly exercised the mariners and soldiers of the Spanish fleet, particularly as the inventor of these infernal devices was known since to have become an English pensioner.[6]

Medina Sidonia shared that fear and enjoyed several others not commonly appreciated by his men. Repeatedly frustrated during the previous days in his attempts to close with and grapple the enemy, he had sent on word to Parma to supply him with more manoeuvrable flyboats, which would allow his soldiers to chase and board the elusive English vessels. To date, the duke had not responded. As the armada arrived before Calais, however, it was met by one of its *pataches*, sent ahead some weeks earlier to make contact with Parma. Its captain brought no word of flyboats, only the unwelcome news that the army of Flanders would not be ready to put to sea and make their rendezvous for at least six days. Six days, if Philip's instructions were to be followed, during which the armada would lie at the mercy of an ever-strengthening foe and whatever stratagem he chose to adopt. Already, the Spanish admiral had been made aware that the authorities at Calais, while sympathetic to the Catholic League, would remain strictly neutral (the news came from the first boat-party of Spaniards to reach shore, who had found the governor of Calais and his wife taking the air in their coach along the sands, idly hoping to see a sea battle that day[7]). Water and victuals were provided from the town to make good some losses suffered at sea, but that was the limit of such assistance as the Spanish fleet should expect. If not yet doomed, Philip's hugely expensive enterprise of England required a greater coincidence of happy circumstances than even its most fatalistic critics had anticipated.

When, therefore, the glow of burning ships was first sighted to the west soon after midnight on 29 July, its psychological impact upon the men of the armada was immense. The two leading fire-ships were grappled as planned, and pulled clear. The remaining six, however, were not intercepted, and drifted among the anchored Spanish ships. As the fires took hold and the heated ordnance discharged or exploded, panic swept through the armada. Many ships' cables were slipped without being buoyed (most of the larger vessels had put out two or more to maintain their anchorage against strong local currents), and several vessels ran upon their neighbours as their mariners attempted frantically to get under way. The confusion generated was out of all proportion to the danger posed by the assault (none of the fire-ships struck or fired a Spanish vessel), a striking justification of Howard's decision to attempt it. The *San Martín* herself slipped anchor and then returned to her mooring once the fire-ships had passed by, but her example was hardly heeded, much less followed. At dawn, Medina Sidonia found himself surrounded by an 'armada' of just four ships – Recalde's *San Juan*, the marquis of Peñafiel's *San Marcos* and two (unidentified) Portuguese galleons. The remainder of the fleet lay strung out up to several miles to the north-east, towards the Bank of Flanders and Dunkirk. Despatching a pinnace, the Spanish admiral sent urgent word to his ships to stand off from the shoals and reassemble. Perhaps with a degree of relief at surrendering an impossible responsibility, he then prepared to buy time for them by dying gloriously. The sacrifice of eight minor English vessels, later valued at a paltry £5,100,[8] had delivered to Howard the greatest naval victory since Salamis – if he could seize it.

In fact, he and his commanders seem not to have anticipated the scale of their success, nor considered ways to exploit it. No attempt was made to follow up the fire-ships' assault during the night, when a string of fleeing ships with disoriented and panicked crews, many with their lights un-doused, drifted between the inshore shallows and the English fleet. All that had been determined at the previous day's council was that the Lord Admiral himself should lead the assault at daybreak, without provision to track the splintering enemy formation in the meantime. Though the scattered Spanish ships had little chance to re-group in darkness, this delay meant that much of the eventual English onslaught was made not upon individual vessels but a hastily re-assembling defensive formation that managed to shield (or divert attention from) most of its more vulnerable stragglers. That precious breath-ing-space preserved the greater part of the armada from early destruction – including, most importantly, the *San Martín* herself.

Howard then made what may be regarded as his second serious error of the campaign. At first light, rather than lead his squadrons personally against the scattered enemy, he disregarded his own orders and concentrated his efforts against the *San Lorenzo*, flagship of the Neopolitan galleasses, which had been sighted almost upon Calais sands. She had lost her tiller during the night in a collision with Leiva's *Santa Maria*; ironically, this seems have resulted from Moncada's refusal to panic at the approach of the fire-ships and his correspondingly tardy withdrawal. Now almost helpless, she presented an irresistible prize – one, furthermore, whose capture would diminish significantly a potential future threat to England's Dutch allies.[9] Nevertheless, that it should have been the English fleet's flagship that assumed responsibility for dealing with the galleass seems incredible, until one considers the probable state of Howard's mind that morning.

Two days later, he would receive from the Privy Council a memorial requesting information on spent supplies, casualties, the movement of prisoners and other matters 'her Majesty doth desire to be informed of'.[10] Within the various queries was a near-rebuke of his tactics: not in respect of his conduct on 29 July (for which the Council would have him know 'howe gratiouslie her Majestie did conceave of the great paines and dyscrecion his Lordship had used in this service in givinge continuewall annoyance to the Spanish Navye and weakninge theire forces'), but for his wider failure to board and capture more Spanish ships.[11] A breathtaking dismissal of the known dangers of such tactics, the query bore a heavier sting in being conveyed to Howard by Sir Francis Drake's cousin, Richard. It is not known whether this almost-public criticism was preceded by similarly querulous despatches in previous days, but for several months now the Lord Admiral had enjoyed almost daily reminders of his immediate subordinates' near-legendary exploits. During the previous week, he had led three hard-fought encounters with the greatest seaborne enemy England had yet seen, and had not a single prize to show for it. Drake, in stark contrast, had almost effortlessly added to an already glittering reputation and considerable wealth with his capture – more accurately, his gracious acceptance – of the *Rosario*. Howard cared for nothing more than his good name and honour; on the morning of 29 July, with the prospect of an outright victory before him, it seems that he chose instead to dispel reservations regarding his abilities as a fighting admiral by giving his Queen an indisputable trophy.[12]

Moncada had edged his shallow-draughted *San Lorenzo* into Calais haven, where *Ark Royal* could not follow. The Lord Admiral therefore despatched eleven pinnaces and ships' boats to take the stricken galleass, though she was aground before they could overwhelm her. Following a desperate small-arms fight she was boarded by the English mariners, who proceeded to slaughter those of her crew who had not fled the moment her keel touched sand. Moncada himself, shot through both eyes by a single musket ball, died defending his vessel. The victorious boarding party (led, according to Sir William Winter's account of the fight, by the as yet animate William Coxe) began to strip her of her coin and chapel fittings.[13] As they busied themselves, representatives of Calais's governor rode over the sands to congratulate them on their valour but remind them also of their employer's exclusive salvage rights over any vessel beached in his domains. Roughly handled by the Englishmen, they withdrew, at which the governor asserted his privileges with a brief volley from the town walls that killed several more English mariners. Without a prize to show for almost three wasted hours and dozens of casualties (the heaviest English losses of the campaign), Howard recalled his men and put about to rejoin the fleet.[14]

Drake, meanwhile, had emerged from several days' near-anonymity to lead the assault his Lord Admiral had temporarily abandoned. The *San Martín* and her few escorts lay nearest to the English ships; the *Revenge* came up with Fenner's *Nonpareil* and gave the Spanish flagship a single broadside before continuing north-eastwards to attempt to break into a slowly reforming body of Spanish ships. Hawkins's *Victory* and her escorts followed, each discharging their bow-chasers and broadsides at the *San Martín* as they passed (Beeston's *Dreadnought* gave a particularly ferocious close volley). Immediately behind them, Frobisher's ships came up to give their own bow-chasers and broadsides and then, typically, stayed to pound her and the galleons that attempted to shield her. The contrast between the tactics of Drake and Frobisher became a point of considerable contention between the two men after the battle, but whose was the more effective action is difficult to judge.[15] Drake's passage away from the *San Martín* was motivated neither by cowardice – as Frobisher furiously claimed – nor by a perceptive genius, betrayed by Howard's irresponsible assault upon the *San Lorenzo*, that otherwise would have resulted in a crushing victory for the English fleet (Corbett's interpretation[16]). It was of course vital to prevent the armada from regaining its defensive strength in formation, yet by far the most significant concentration was that coalescing around the Spanish flagship itself. Those vessels that had drifted the least distance from their Admiral during the previous night were slowly returning, largely unhindered by the *Revenge*, *Victory* or any of their consorts. They included the three surviving galleasses and several more of the armada's Portuguese galleons – the *San Martín*'s sister ships and probably the most effective fighting ships in the Spanish fleet. In the face of sustained fire from Frobisher's squadron and other, converging elements of the English fleet, they took up station around the *San Martín, San Juan* and *San Marcos* in a small-scale reprise of their *en lúnula* formation.

This was the nucleus about which the most of the 'troubleshooters' of the scattered armada gathered in the following hours, and to which the English ships subsequently gave their almost undivided attention (Drake and Hawkins appear to have returned to join the main thrust of English attacks with the advantage of the weather gauge, rather than attempt a flanking assault from the east). What followed was the hottest fight of the campaign, in which the hard-pressed Spanish crews exhibited considerable resolve and courage. Some vessels were pounced upon by English ships before they could find succour; others bore down deliberately upon their tormentors, drawing fire to divert the enemy from their Admiral. The *San Felipe* and *San Mateo*, both well-armed galleons, stood out before the main defensive formation and invited particularly heavy punishment in this manner. Their assailants appear to have included the *Ark Royal*, now returned from Calais haven, with *Vanguard*, *Rainbow* and *Antelope* – the three principal warships of Seymour's squadron, all of which came fresh to the battle with un-depleted munitions.

In contrast to the previous days' fighting, these close-range encounters were extremely bloody. Winter claimed that the heaviest guns of his *Vanguard* discharged 500 rounds of shot during the day's action, and most of that from within harquebus-range of the enemy. For the first time since the battle began, English fire began to inflict structural damage upon the most closely pressed Spanish ships, and human casualties were commensurately heavy. The *San Felipe* alone, her rigging shattered, top-deck smashed and ordnance dismounted, was said to have lost sixty men with a further 200 wounded; while from another, unnamed vessel's gunwales (possibly those of the *San Mateo*), blood was observed to be pouring with obscene vigour.[17] The near suicidal efforts of these ships had been goaded by days of frustration at failing to engage the enemy upon Spanish terms. The mariners of the *San Felipe* in particular, infuriated by what they regarded as the Englishmen's cowardly tactics, loudly taunted the 'Lutheran hens' even as English shot cut them down. A hopeful ensign in one of the English ships, calling upon the battered Spanish ship to yield with honour, took a fatal bullet for his pains – a rare English casualty.[18] Eventually, the *San Felipe* and *San Mateo*, both badly damaged, gained support from Recalde's *San Juan* and two galleons of the Levant squadron and were nursed back into the formation flanking the *San Martín*. Both, however, subsequently fell away as their sister ships drifted north, and were set upon once more. Closer in to the Flemish coast, *Maria Juan*, a Biscayan with fewer guns than the most effective of her sister ships, suffered a lonelier ordeal. She was surrounded and pounded to pieces by Robert Crosse's *Hope* and several other, unidentified English vessels.[19] Her surviving crew attempted to surrender, but before terms could be agreed she broke up in rising seas and sank with the loss of all but a handful of her 272 men – the only vessel of the 1588 armada to be destroyed by firepower alone.[20]

Other Spanish ships – *Santa Ana* and *Santa Maria de la Rosa* (respectively, the flag and vice-flag of the Guipúzcoan squadron), *San Pedro*, *Gran Grifon*, the Ragusan *San Juan de Sicilia* and the huge (but apparently lightly constructed) Venetian galleon *La Trinidad Valencera* – sustained serious lower hull damage and required emergency running repairs. Of these vessels, only the *Santa Ana* would survive the stormy passage around Scotland and western Ireland to return to Spain.[21] In contrast, the *San Martín*, whose gunners once more seem to have employed as gunners and not as extemporary (and superfluous) boarding parties, used her ordnance more effectively than did their compatriots; together with her musketeers, they kept her assailants from closing to deadly range for more than brief periods. She suffered only twelve fatalities that day, though several breaches at her waterline had to be patched hurriedly by divers.

Rightly, surviving accounts of the actions off Calais and Gravelines stress the devastating human effect of the English attacks; yet even of this most desperate fight, eyewitness perceptions outstripped the reality of the scale of the Spanish ordeal. Camden's later calculation that not above fifteen English ships were fully engaged in the action was surely an underestimation (an observer in the *San Martín* claimed that she was beset by twenty-four ships at one point); but Sir William Winter's comment on the English non-naval contingent's 'simple service' was telling.[22] As in previous clashes, a relatively small proportion of Howard's fleet – principally the Queen's larger ships, supported by a few of the most powerful London merchantmen – bore the brunt of fighting. The captains named in the English accounts of the day's fighting – Drake, Hawkins, Frobisher, Winter, Palmer, Beeston, Southwell, Crosse and Fenton – were conspicuous among many others only because they were doing their job. Their lesser escorts appear to have held what formation could be established in that overcrowded area of sea, but otherwise kept a prudent distance from the Spanish ordnance – 'making a show', in Winter's words. This was a display of common sense, not of cowardice. On the whole, the response of private English shipowners to the gathering threat of the armada campaign had been estimable, but it is hardly likely that their sense of duty was entirely undiluted by self-interest. Van Meteren later calculated that no more than twenty-two or twenty-three ships in the English fleet could 'conveniently assault' the ninety largest Spanish vessels owing to the latters' towering structures.[23] Again, this almost certainly over-stated the problem (the English crews intended no boarding actions in any case); but those ships that were clearly disadvantaged in superstructure and weight of ordnance probably did not test their luck too rigorously. Marine insurance was an innovation of later centuries, and reliance upon the Queen's sense of gratitude to make good private losses suffered in battle would have been unconscionably rash.[24] Many of the voluntary ships were commanded during the campaign by their owners, who must have been loath to risk a significant slice of their non-liquid capital in a fight that appeared to be going their way already. Other, waged captains doubtless had discreet orders from their employers to serve the Queen faithfully, defend themselves whenever necessary and charge headlong into the fray only as a last, desperate resort. The numerous levy ships, brought into the fleet under coercion and lightly armed at best, had even less incentive to sacrifice them-selves – and their ports' livelihoods – in what would have been little more than suicide assaults.

The true number of English 'fighting' ships in the action off Calais and Gravelines cannot be established with accuracy, but it was not nearly suffi-cient to seize that brilliant victory foreseen by Corbett and others, even had their attacks been coordinated more effectively. There was, simply, not enough to coordinate. If one assumes that approximately fifty of the better-armed English ships were fully engaged (probably a generous estimate), they remained too few to overwhelm an enemy whose scattering had provided dozens of potential objectives. Inevitably, any prior English strategy gave way to single-minded attempts to smash the most tempting targets. Those actions in which an individual Spanish vessel was cut out and pounded from within hailing distance brought dramatic success, but there were few such instances. The one significant Spanish formation – that which slowly coalesced about the *San Martín* – proved too strong to be broken by the most furious English attacks of the campaign. The attention it received, and the screen it provided, meant that no more than a quarter of the armada's ships were obliged to be engaged at all that day.[25] However closely the horror of war pressed upon the unfortunate crews in the most heavily assaulted vessels, it was a localized ordeal, often endured voluntarily to enable the greater part of the Spanish fleet to reform.

By mid-afternoon, squalls were building in the Narrow Seas, and visibility declined dramatically. The munitions in the most effective English vessels were by now almost spent, and Howard was readily persuaded – or persuaded himself – to disengage. Remarkably, Medina Sidonia appears to have been in fighting mood still, and wished to remain in the Narrow Seas and resume the engagement. But the battle between men and ships was drawing to a close. The *San Martín*'s pilots urgently reminded their admiral that the coming fight against unfamiliar currents, tides and shoals was the more immediate concern, that to attempt to hold station in the Narrow Seas against rising south-westerlies would be to risk placing the entire armada upon the beaches of Flanders. Northwards, away from its historic rendezvous with Parma's *tercios*, was the armada's only conceivable course. The day's losses had been heavy already; one ship sunk outright, one beached and stormed, two others (the redoubtable *San Felipe* and *San Mateo*) so badly damaged that they were obliged to make for the Flemish shore and probable capture. Most of the other vessels in the Spanish fleet were seaworthy still and even capable of further action, yet some 600 of their mariners and soldiers had died since daybreak, with a further 800 incapacitated by their wounds.[26] Outright defeat had been averted by the heroism of the fallen, but their ship-handling skills – vital in any waters – could not be replaced. Lacking cables and anchors, leaking and undermanned, the fleet of Spain was entering unknown and rising seas. Ahead of it lay a far more remorseless testing than anything Elizabeth's navy could provide.

In fact, the threat from the human enemy had now dissipated, though Medina Sidonia could not know this. The English fleet had suffered shortages of munitions several times in the previous days, but the barrel had been scraped – literally – and its dregs consumed in the battle off Calais and Gravelines. Scattered quantities of powder and shot were available still in England, but getting them to the ships that would have put them to the best use proved near impossible. The Privy Council, which had to manage its dwindling resources to meet a still-feared invasion attempt by Parma, sent out a stream of orders to the northern provinces to make good the losses urgently reported in the day's correspondences from Howard, Seymour, Winter and Thomas Fenner. At Newcastle, the earl of Huntingdon, President of the North, was directed to send to the fleet his available powder and shot of all sizes from demi-cannon to sacre (which, according to his letter to Burghley of 29 June, was little enough[27]); while the town's mayor was to send back to the fleet four armed vessels – *Daniel, Galleon Hutchin, Bark Lamb* and *Fancy* – previously ordered to escort the merchant adventurers' fleet to

Stade.[28] Berwick's Master of the Ordnance was instructed to despatch five lasts of powder from his stores (probably his entire reserves), and the garrison's victualler whatever supplies he could assemble to Holy Island, to be carried to Howard's ships as they passed by. These replenishments might have given the fleet a chance to re-engage the enemy once – if only once – more, but the orders that disposed them arrived much too late to be effective.

Not every resource that failed to find the fleet was a vital loss. Sir Walter Ralegh, helpfully despatched by the Council on 2 August to suggest to the Lord Admiral that he might wish to remove the munitions from his smaller, non-combatant vessels into the larger, fighting ships, met with the fleet only after its return southwards.[29] Far better use might have been made of the five lasts of powder that had sat in the holds of the ailing Nicholas Gorges's ships since 26 July, but they departed the North Foreland under Thomas Knyvet, their replacement commander, only on 1 August – again, too late to find the fleet before contact with the armada was lost. Another absentee was the *Roebuck*, carrying further, unspecified quantities of munitions. Since escorting the *Rosario* into Dartmouth on 22 July, she does not appear to have taken part in any fleet action; now, with her vital cargo, she went missing for almost three weeks, after which she was rumoured to have been commandeered by Lord Hunsdon for service in the north.[30]

With almost no remaining munitions, and little likelihood of early replenishment, the English fleet had made its final effort. In the evening of 29 July, after almost nine hours of furious engagement, Howard broke off his attack. The following morning, strengthening west-north-west winds pushed the armada ever closer to the shores of Flanders and possible destruction. To seaward, the English commanders watched without any inclination, or means, to assist its work. At 4pm with his fleet having drifted in rising seas as far north as Lowestoft, the Lord Admiral convened a council of his principal commanders in the *Ark Royal* to discuss their shrinking options.

The armada had been battered, but as long as its ships sat upon the waters rather than beneath them it was capable still of fulfilling its primary mission. Should it escape the Flemish shoals (which it did, gratefully seizing a change in wind direction even as the English commanders sat down to discuss their next moves), its further retreat had to be encouraged and monitored until it was irrevocably clear of English waters. Yet Parma's intact *tercios* needed to be watched also. Much to Lord Henry Seymour's voluble disgust, his squadron was ordered to detach from the fleet and resume its Narrow Seas station – a manoeuvre to be carried out at twilight to prevent its being noticed by the enemy.[31] This proved more difficult than expected, when a rush of voluntaries and levies, attempting to join the withdrawing ships, turned a discreet withdrawal into near-flight. However, Seymour's squadron had successfully departed by nightfall.[32] For the remaining vessels, all that remained of England's naval arsenal was Howard's immortal 'brag countey-naunce' with which to bluff out its lack of bite as it shadowed the armada.[33] Fortunately, the same change in wind direction to south-south-west that saved the Spanish fleet from the Flanders shore drove it quickly northwards, making a further close confrontation unlikely. Nevertheless, the superior sailing qualities of the English ships brought them close to embarrassment twice in the following days, when they began unwittingly to overtake the rearmost elements of the armada. On both occasions, several of the Spanish vessels took in sail to await the enemy and another chance to fight. They were disappointed, however; the English ships promptly did likewise to maintain a prudent distance.[34] It was not the noblest sequel to the great action of 29 July; but having made a supreme effort only to leave the armada seemingly capable of taking further punishment that they could no longer provide, the most aggressive of Howard's captains were content merely to shepherd the enemy away from English shores.

At midday on 2 August, as the English fleet lay some ninety miles east of the Northumbrian coast, contact with the armada was broken off. Two pinnaces were detached to follow in its wake, while Howard turned westwards to search for his promised munitions and victuals. Twenty-four hours later, his ships were still some forty miles from land when previously strong westerlies veered north-west. Making the coast of England at that latitude was clearly impossible for the moment, and the armada, should it choose to do so, could now retrace its path southwards through the North Sea and towards its longed-for rendezvous with Parma. In council, Howard and his officers decided to return to the Downs as quickly as possible to replenish their ships' stores before a new clash occurred.

The return passage proved difficult. The inconstant wind veered southwest on 4 August and grew to storm strength, effectively dissolving the English fleet's formations, though this also made the armada's recovery either of the Flanders or English coast almost impossible. Howard's *Ark Royal* had beaten south as far as Harwich by 7 August (she passed on directly to Margate), having last observed many of her sister vessels in danger of being cast onto the Norfolk shore. There were no English losses, however, and the following day nine of the Queen's ships (including Hawkins's *Victory*) and twenty-six London merchantmen crowded into Harwich harbour. Separated from them in the storm, the *Revenge, Elizabeth Jonas, Triumph* and *Mary Rose* continued to beat southwards towards the North Foreland. They joined their flagship at Margate later the same day.[35] The remaining vessels of the English fleet were driven into a dozen ports on the south-eastern English coast during the following twenty-four hours.

While the fabric of the fleet was largely intact, the implications of it having outrun its supplies were soon apparent. The ten days' battle, ranging across greater distances than any single naval encounter in history, had wreaked havoc upon the carefully financed victualling arrangements that Burghley summarized in optimistic detail on 9 August.[36] According to his calculations, all the ships of the English fleet had been fully victualled until 7 September or later. Yet as early as the day after the Lord Treasurer set down this comforting summary, the jeremiac Sir Thomas Heneage was reporting rumours from Margate that some of the ships' crews had been obliged to drink their own urine whilst at sea – and, worse, that the Lord Admiral himself was reduced to a diet of beans.[37] Doubtless these were sailors' stories, intended to impress the courtiers and other idlers who flocked to the quaysides to hear news of the late battle and its horrors; nevertheless, a large gap remained between victualling intentions and delivery. Sufficient funds appear to have been provided to Quarles and Darell to allow Burghley's planned schedule of supply (though the history of Leicester's Low Countries campaign illustrates how government accounting was often an exercise in wishful thinking). The journey from storehouse to mariners' mouths, however, proved far longer than that from Exchequer to Navy victualler.[38] Fifteen hoys had been appointed for the task of re-victualling the fleet, with two armed merchantmen assigned to their protection. On 7 August, these had been ordered northwards by the Privy Council to seek out Howard's ships. However, only three had managed to rendezvous at Harwich by the following day when a large proportion of the fleet dropped anchor there, with seven more said to be somewhere at sea.[39] Of the remaining five – if these existed other than in the Privy Council's plans – there was no sign.[40] The victuals assembled for the hoys, moreover, had been calculated to feed some 7,000 men, and Howard estimated that he now had almost 10,000 in his fleet (excluding the 2,000 mariners of Seymour's squadron).

Desperate to find his truant victuallers, Howard rested his flagship at Margate for only a few hours on 8 August before passing on to Dover. Shortages of foodstuffs affected all the English ships' crews, but there was particular reason for the Lord Admiral's anxiety. Though his fleet had not been seriously tested during the recent battle, the few wounded men it carried had the company of a far greater number who had begun to fall sick around them. As noted previously, an ague – possibly typhus – had swept through the fleet at Plymouth before the campaign commenced. Then, the *Elizabeth Jonas* had been the worst affected ship, losing some 200 men during the weeks of her enforced stay in Cattewater.[41] Her surviving crew had been set ashore while her ballast was removed and replaced, and carefully monitored fires lit between decks to clear the infection. Re-manned (with 'tall and able' mariners), she had put to sea with the fleet on 21 July, since when her undefeated pestilence had erupted once more and spread to other ships via the dozens of pinnaces that each day busily transmitted messages between its captains. Not surprisingly, the Queen's best, most heavily manned vessels bore the brunt of this pestilence as they had the fighting. Even the *Ark Royal* had been stricken (by 10 August, the commander of her complement of soldiers, Sir Roger Townsend, was said to have only a single surviving retainer from the group he had brought into the ship).[42] To add to the sick mariners' discomfort, many were clad only in sodden rags by now, having had little opportunity (and fewer funds) to make good the ravages of eight months of near-continuous service. Their heroic labours during the previous days, which had astonished Spanish observers, further weakened already vulnerable constitutions. In the immediate aftermath of the battle, Thomas Fenner, reporting from the *Nonpareil* on 4 August, had exulted that less than sixty Englishmen had lost their lives during the campaign: 'God make us and all her Majesty's good subjects to render hearty praise and thanks unto the Lord of Lords therefor.'[43] His calculation – and exhortation – was premature. As the Spanish armada began its greatest ordeal off the coasts of Scotland and Ireland, the disproportionately light casualty rate sustained by its enemy was about to be redressed.

FIFTEEN

A Contrary Success

O Noble England,
fall down upon thy knee!
And prayse thy GOD, with thankfull hart,
which still maintaineth thee![1]

Long before the outcome of the campaign could be determined, the armada's defeat was being advertised in a number of triumphalist blasts, hurriedly composed, printed and distributed throughout London. As early as 10 August, three ditties were registered at Stationers' Hall – Thomas Deloney's ballad on the seizure of the *San Lorenzo*, his 'The Quenes visitinge the camp at Tilberye' (which must have trotted from his quill in a single day, unless he had prior notice of the event), and 'A joyfull song of the Roiall Receaving of the quenes majestie, etc' by 'T.J.'. Six days later, John Aske's *Elizabetha Triumphans* joined them in circulation.[2] Effective propaganda, and the speed with which these works appeared indicates that they were little else, creates certainties from doubt. With the armada in British waters still and the best army in Europe poised just across the Narrow Seas, Englishmen needed reassurance that their bulwarks were not only intact, but likely to remain so.

The Queen's visit to Tilbury on 7/8 August was the defining act in that process of stiffening public resolve. Some days earlier, Leicester – hoping to have consecrated his role as a lynchpin of the nation's resistance to Spanish tyranny – had begged her to visit his 'poor lieutenantes cabyn' and stiffen the resolve of his (considerably less well-housed) army.[3] Elizabeth did not disappoint her waiting audience. Her descent upon Tilbury was the supreme iconic moment of her reign: a near-religious celebration of her embodiment of the nation. Taking water in the royal barge from Whitehall's Privy Stairs on the afternoon of 7 August, she was sent off by a vast crowd of Londoners, thoroughly swept and drenched by the same unseasonably foul weather that scattered the English fleet and brought its many elements to port that day. Their enthusiasm – and, presumably, their professional interest in how the royal barge would negotiate London Bridge in those difficult conditions – soothed that small ordeal.[4]

A few hours later, the Queen's small flotilla docked safely at a quay adjacent to the Tilbury – Gravesend boom (hastily repaired two days earlier following extensive damage when the boom parted and crashed down upon it[5]). Leicester's own entourage greeted her at the blockhouse on the northern shore, and most of his footmen and horse troopers lined the route between the river and camp on the hill as a vast honour guard. For contemporary descriptions of Elizabeth's progress past her army we have only the accounts of Deloney and Aske, neither of whose style tended to the blandly factual. Nevertheless, the scenes of near-adulation they described, if based on hearsay, were probably not exaggerated:

> Lord bless you all my friendes (she said)
> But doe not kneele so much to me:
> Then sent she warning to the rest,
> They should not let such reuerance be.

Leicester and his retainers escorted her through Tilbury camp and four miles further to Arderne Hall, requisitioned as the night's royal residence (its habitual tenant, Thomas Rich, retired graciously to alternative accommodation elsewhere).[6] The horsemen then withdrew, but as the Queen slept that night, 2,000 footmen formed a guard around Arderne's walls.[7] The following morning, dressed in a jewel-encrusted, faux-military ensemble and wielding a marshal's baton, Elizabeth abandoned her ladies-in-waiting and returned to the camp for the serious men's business of reviewing her forces. The bands paraded past her while Leicester and the Lord Marshall, Sir John Norreys, carrying tattered campaign banners from their Low Countries campaigns, introduced their formations (among whom proudly rode the sixty-year-old – and fearlessly Catholic – Viscount Montague, with his sons, infant grandson and 200 armed retainers[8]). A mock battle between two battalions was then staged for her edification 'in most warlik sort'. When all had been inspected, Elizabeth gave them her immortal peroration. It was a masterful exercise in crowd manipulation – concise, defiant, self-deprecating and marginally apocalyptic: 'I am come amongst you, as you see, at this time, not for my recreation, and disport, but being resolved in the midst, and heat of the battle to live, or die amongst you all, to lay down for my God, and for my kingdom, and for my people, my Honour, and my blood even in the dust.'[9] From those who heard her, she excited their unconditional loyalty, masculine ardour and, possibly unintentionally, something of the same confusion that she and her principal officers of state were experiencing regarding their 'victory'.

As Elizabeth dined in Leicester's tent following her speech, the earl of Cumberland arrived from Harwich with despatches from the fleet, reporting events of the days since the fight off Gravelines. Given the increasingly obvious difficulty in annihilating the armada (even had sufficient supplies of powder or shot been available), Cumberland's news was as good as the Queen might have expected. However, intelligence from the Low Countries arrived at Tilbury almost simultaneously, claiming that Parma would attempt to embark on the next spring tide with up to 50,000 men and 6,000 horse, and that the rebels' blockade before Dunkirk – one of his intended points of departure – had been scattered by the late storm.[10] The Queen seemed to dismiss this threat, refusing to halt orders, given two days earlier by the Council, for the disbandment of all but 6,000 foot at Tilbury to enable their home counties' harvests to be gathered.[11] 'Thus yor Lordship seeth that this place breedeth courage' wrote Walsingham to the absent Burghley.

Elizabeth's cool manner was not entirely ingenuous. An order for precisely the same partial disbandment of Leicester's bands was issued once more on 14 August, which indicates that the process had been quietly halted or countermanded in the meantime.[12] Courage was laudable; insouciance without an outright victory might yet be fatal. Though damaged, the Spanish fleet carried a considerable fighting force still, and no one in England knew its ultimate destination. There appeared to be several options available to Medina Sidonia: to return southwards through the North Sea to attempt to rendezvous with Parma on the next spring tide, to make for home immediately, or to put in at some friendly or neutral port to rest and repair damage to his ships before recommencing his King's great enterprise in the following year. The armada had been seen last off the coast of south-eastern Scotland, a nation composed of sufficient anti-English elements to provide at least a possibility of sanctuary there.[13] Another potential destination was western Ireland, where a powerful Spanish presence might provide the catalyst for widespread Catholic rebellion. In the meantime, there were few Englishmen who did not believe that Parma, even without assistance from Medina Sidonia, would take any opportunity to cross the Narrow Seas and settle his master's English 'problem' with the same industry he had applied to his task in the Low Countries (as if to draw the final, symbolic line beneath vestigial English hopes that the duke might, even now, prefer a diplomatic solution, the peace commissioners had been evacuated from Calais sands the previous day in Seymour's *Rainbow*).[14]

The remaining military threats facing the regime were therefore extremely difficult to assess accurately. Thomas Fenner and others may have allowed the prospect of an astonishingly one-sided battle to sway their judgement (though in hindsight we know theirs to have been the more accurate assessment), but their commanders were less sanguine. Howard, Drake and Hawkins, reporting separately, gave mixed opinions of their success. Hawkins, who seems to have been awestruck by his first sight of the enemy on 21 July and remained so ever since, reported the English successes accurately but still thought the armada 'the greatest and strongest combynacion, to my understandinge, that ever was gathered in Christendome'. His Lord Admiral lamented that the lack of victuals and munitions had cost England an outright victory, though with the English fleet concentrated in the Narrow Seas he thought it unlikely that Parma would attempt to put to sea without cover from the armada. Drake considered the Spanish fleet well-drubbed and probably incapable of returning south through the North Sea, but Parma, being as 'a beare robed of her whealpes' was likely to remain dangerous. All three urged that the main fleet should not be dispersed until Medina Sidonia's strategy could be divined: 'Sir, sure bynd, sure fynd. A kyngdom is a great wager', Howard warned Walsingham, attempting to dampen the Court's spirits sufficiently to extract money for his ships' and men's further service.[15]

Intelligences received in the days following the English fleet's loss of contact with the armada neither clarified the Spanish Admiral's intentions nor offered much support for any of the various opinions regarding his fate. As early as 6 August, Horatio Palavicino was confidently predicting that the armada was bound for Denmark, and suggested that a fleet under the earl of Cumberland (with Frobisher as his lieutenant) should pursue and destroy it there. Drake, too, thought Denmark a likely destination, having shrewdly observed that prevailing winds made a Scottish landing highly unlikely.

Nervously, the Privy Council sent Thomas Bodley to the fleet on 11 August, directing Howard to provide him with a ship to carry letters to the Danish Court and the Hanse towns, asking that aid be denied to the armada should it appear suddenly off their coasts.[16]

There was also other, conflicting evidence to indicate that the Spanish fleet might renew immediately its attempt to rendezvous with Parma's forces. On 18 August, a Yorkshire merchant, Richard Lewes, claimed to have sighted eighty sail off Flamborough Head. This received partial corroboration in one of a stream of contradictory reports from Seymour (who variously put the armada off Huisduinen at the mouth of the Texel, in the Moray Firth and somewhere athwart Orkney), and, on 22 August, Howard himself received apparently firm word from Sir Edward Norreys (brother of Sir John, presently commanding elements of the English forces in the Low Countries) that the Spanish fleet had been sighted returning southwards through the North Sea. To add to their confusion, letters from Sir George Carey and the Mayor of Southampton to the Council arrived separately the same day, passing on news from the crew of a Hampshire ship, returned from the north, of their sighting of a great number of ships between Orkney and Fair Isle fourteen days earlier.[17]

This uncertainty did much to keep government's spirits dampened. Walsingham fully shared Howard's regret that under-provisioning had robbed England of the outright victory that he, no less than his protégé Drake, had expected. 'Oure halfe doinges dothe breed dyshonor and leave the dysease uncured' he had observed gloomily to Burghley even as he exulted in the martial atmosphere at Tilbury.[18] Both men thereafter expressed support for Howard's demand that the English fleet be kept fully concentrated for some weeks to come. Predictably, however, their sense of urgency in providing the means to do this was considerably weaker than the Lord Admiral may have hoped. Whatever the implications of 'halfe doinges', neither man wished to be the one to make a decision on spending yet more of the Exchequer's disappearing funds. When the Lord treasurer suggested tentatively that they answer Howard's pleas in some practical manner, the usually forthright Walsingham became a model of circumspection: 'I thinke the same may be dyfurred untyll her Majesty's returne'.[19] Unfortunately, Elizabeth, having departed Tilbury on 9 August, crossed into Kent upon a mini-progress to bestow the gorgeous prospect of her entourage upon more of her fortunate subjects. She was at Erith two days later with Leicester, her ageing Galahad, and does not appear to have returned to London until 13 August at the earliest. Decisions on new expenditure were indeed 'dyfurred', therefore, and in the meantime the sinews of England's naval war-machine began to lose much of their tautness.

On 8 August, as the Queen had addressed her untested troops at Tilbury, some fifty campaign-battered ships joined the *Ark Royal* in Margate roads. Seymour commanded a further seventeen naval vessels and sixteen coasters at sea, while a third group, by now of some thirty-eight sail, lay at Harwich. In the fleet as a whole, approximately 12,000 men remained in service: all urgently required food, clothing and, if possible, pay. Burghley himself acknowledged the necessity of discharging the sick and the 'refuse' of the smaller vessels as soon as possible. The latter had proved of doubtful value in a fight, and 'to continew charges without nedeful cause, bryngeth repentance', as he observed sagely.[20] Yet until funds could be provided (and his unwilling sovereign had to be persuaded of the necessity), the unwanted and unusable men of the fleet remained the responsibility of the Lord Admiral and became a growing burden in dangerous proximity to the healthier men who, even now, might be needed to prevent Parma's *tercios* from descending upon England.

To his great credit, Howard did what he could. Having tried and failed to find adequate accommodation for his sick mariners in Margate, he was obliged to lodge them in farms, barns and even stables outside the town. As for the 'refuse', he took it upon himself to correspond directly with the Lord Lieutenants of counties in which the levy ships' home ports lay, asking them to provide funds for sufficient victuals to feed their crews on the homeward passage.[21] It was a hopeful initiative, answered, as far as extant records indicate, by not a single recipient of his pleas. To the contrary, many levy shipowners who had been so ill-advised as to fund the outfitting of their vessels personally in anticipation of reimbursement by their home ports were to find it extremely difficult to make good their losses, even when the Privy Council belatedly supported the Lord Admiral's initiative. A fortunate few – principally those with powerful connections at Court – appear to have received satisfaction. The burgesses of Exeter foolishly attempted to beard Walter Ralegh's half-brother George of monies due on his ship, hired by them as their levy contribution to the fleet. Walsingham's letter to them was a masterpiece of polite menace: 'I have staied him from acquaynting their Lordships with your slacknes herein upon the perswation I have that this my own letter shall sufficientlie prevaile with you without occasioning him to use any furthur sute, which would be to your molestacion.' A similar threat from the entire Privy Council appears to have persuaded the Devonshire towns of Torrington and Barnstaple, with their outlying hundreds of

Braunton and Fremington, to provide funds to discharge the Newfound-
lander *Seraphim* (one of the victualling barks that followed the fleet).[22] Elsewhere, however, local grudges nurtured by these unmet obligations seem to
have benefited only the provincial legal profession: at least one shipowner
was petitioning for satisfaction as late as 1595.[23]

Howard went to Whitehall on 11 August to present his report on the
battle and plead his men's case. He remained there, attending Privy Council
business, for nine days, during which time the situation at Margate deteriorated considerably.[24] At Dover once more on 21 August, he summoned his
senior commanders to report on the state of the ships. He was told that
most of those that lay in Margate roads were now infected, and that the
ague was growing more virulent. New men pressed in Essex, Suffolk,
Norfolk, Sussex and Southampton to replace the sick or dead, having no
previous exposure to the disease, appeared to be succumbing even more
quickly than those whose long service in the ships had bestowed a degree
of immunity.[25] The situation was so bad, claimed Howard in a letter to the
Council, that Sheffield and Lord Thomas Howard had been prevented from
attending his Dover meeting because the *White Bear* and *Golden Lion* lacked
sufficient fit men to weigh anchor.[26] Obviously, emergency measures would
be required to maintain even a reduced fleet at sea. As a first, necessary step,
the well-spring of plague, the *Elizabeth Jonas*, was ordered back to Chatham
for extensive fumigation carrying only a skeleton crew. It was decided that
the remainder of the fleet should be divided into two parts: the healthiest
elements to ride in the Downs, ready to intercept the returning armada or
any independent crossing by Parma, while the worst-infected vessels would
have their crews put ashore at Margate to rest, recover and, if necessary, be
replaced by a new press. If circumstance dictated that these ships should put
to sea at short notice to meet a returning armada, their shrunken complements were to be reinforced with soldiers currently billeted in the town. For
all his men, ill or hale, Howard urged immediate payment of their arrears
of wages, 'fynding it to com but this scantlie unto them, it breades a
marvailouse alteratione amongste them'.[27]

Yet Howard himself, in urging that the fighting core of the fleet be preserved, had unwittingly established priorities that would take from the
mouths of the neediest. Burghley's overwhelming concern was to find funds
to feed the Lord Admiral's still healthy mariners and discharge the voluntary ships whose crews were provisioned at government cost (as late as 21
November, the victualling bills for at least twenty-six of these vessels
remained outstanding[28]). Their sick comrades, being unable to contribute

further to England's defence, stood – or rather, lay – at the end of the queue, keeping company with the mariners of the uncompensated levy vessels to whom the government owed no obligation and therefore recognized none. Few of them would have misunderstood their predicament. Until 1593, when Elizabeth reluctantly sanctioned the provision of government funds for the relief of injured men, responsibility for mariners wounded in battle or otherwise incapacitated during naval service lay with their home parishes (to whom, after 1601, it devolved once more).[29] To be landed dozens or even hundreds of miles from home often constituted a death sentence to those unable to drag themselves from their sickbeds. For the men thus afflicted in 1588, only the Lord Admiral's personal efforts offered some hope of succour; and if he alone could not fully relieve their ordeal, he gave many at least a first hope of helping themselves.

Disappointed in his expectations of funds either from Whitehall or the levy ports, Howard resorted to creative methods of providing a bare minimum of comfort for his sick and wounded. By pawning his personal plate, he raised funds for victuals and slops for the worst-afflicted mariners. Then, with less than £3 remaining in his hands, he requisitioned 3,000 *pistoles* from Sir Francis Drake's *Rosario* haul. With this, the discharge of the walking sick began. Others were dismissed 'with faire words' and tickets to redeem against victuals, or with further private funds that Howard called upon with his diminishing credit. Many of the levy ships' crews, having not a single day's victuals remaining for their passage home, ate at the Lord Admiral's expense in this way. When his resources were exhausted once more, he pulled rank on Sir John Hawkins and reallocated a proportion of the victualling monies intended for the still-serving mariners (for which the Treasurer of the Navy was roundly berated by Burghley).[30] When all monies failed, Howard invoked a venerable tradition of his predecessors and issued licences to some of his convalescing wounded, permitting them to beg in churches along the route of their homeward journeys. His subsequent defence of his actions was uncharacteristically robust, even in the face of the Queen's ire: 'It were too pityfull to have men starve after such a sarvis . . . I had rather open the Queen's Majesty's purse somethyng to reliefe them . . . yf men shuld not be cared for better than to be let starve and dismyssed we shuld hardly get men to saile'.[31] Despite his almost frantic, and certainly heroic, efforts, the human cost of the state's inability to fully finance its wars was immense. One recent commentator has estimated that as many as half of the mariners who served in the fleet died within weeks of their finest hour, abandoned in rude lodgings around Margate or upon the road's verge as they tried desperately to reach their home parishes.[32]

This seemingly heartless neglect of sick and wounded mariners did not owe solely, or even predominantly, to indifference on the Queen's part (though one would search in vain for any occasion during the reign when her tenderness for 'other ranks' was much in evidence). The end of the sea battle – if it *had* ended – was not the last of government's extraordinary expenditure. The immediate threat to England began to clarify only from 17 August; on that day, Justin of Nassau's fleet of forty sail came into the Downs with news that Parma had only some seventy to eighty flat-bottomed, half-manned) barges with which to transport his army. Word came separately from Sir John Conway at Ostend and the States-General, that the Duke had in fact withdrawn most of his men from their coastal concentrations back into Brabant, prior to investing the English merchant-adventurers' former mart town of Bergen-op-Zoom. This triggered a definitive order the following day to break up the Tilbury camp. As Drake pointed out to Walsingham on 23 August, Medina Sidonia's support of any subsequent attempted invasion by Parma would require the coincidence not only of the two men's intentions on the same day, but of the brief spring tide and fair weather that would allow the barges to come out to the waiting fleet.[33] That conjunction, always fraught with potential mischance, was becoming increasingly implausible. The threat from Parma would remain a powerful one in English counsels (far stronger, in fact, than its reality); and as long as the duke commanded the Spanish forces in the Low Countries, the Narrow Seas would more than justify their name in the national consciousness. Fears that a brief period of prevailing easterlies might tempt him across their waters while the English fleet lay penned in the Downs ensured that the Channel squadron remained in being – and upon near-continuous active service – for months thereafter. But even the most fearful of Elizabeth's advisors were aware that lacking a friendly fleet to guarantee his *tercios'* safe passage, Parma's thrust would rely entirely upon chance, rather than grand design. And chance alone was not likely to seize the victory that Philip's strategy had so woefully failed to deliver.

The declining danger posed by the armada was not so easily tracked. As late as 1 September, a final, spurious rumour led the Privy Council to fear that it was returning through the North Sea, but other intelligence had already made this seem an unlikely manoeuvre.[34] A week earlier, one of the pinnaces despatched by Howard to shadow the armada had returned to Dover with news that the Spanish fleet had passed to the west of the

Orkneys, making its return eastwards extremely improbable. From that moment, Ireland or Spain became its only feasible goal. From 10 September, the first reports of sightings of Spanish ships off (and, in some cases, on) the north and western coasts of Ireland began to filter back into England. Preparations were made to reinforce English formations there, and Grenville and Ralegh, attempting once more to organize succour for their unfortunate Roanoke colonists, had yet another fleet commandeered – this time for patrol duties in the Irish Sea.[35] However, these measures were scaled down subsequently, and what remained was intended to intercept elements of the Spanish fleet that came to grief on Irish reefs, rather than to meet any substantial invasion of Ireland.[36]

Even now, however, there was little opportunity to address the plight of the fleet's sick or un-contracted mariners. At Dover on 26 August, Howard, in the midst of his desperate efforts to make good his widespread shortages of victuals and clothing, received a letter from Walsingham. It required his assessment of the time and preparations necessary to set out part of the fleet to intercept one of the incoming *flotas*. After conferring briefly with his lieutenant Drake (ill in bed in his lodgings), the Lord Admiral replied that none of his ships was fit to leave the Narrow Seas or Channel until they had been grounded for examination and repair at Chatham; a process that could not even commence until the next spring tide, some two weeks hence. He also pointedly expressed the opinion that some people seemed to believe that 'the islands' (the Azores) were but a jolly-boat's ride distant, and, to rub in the point, sent the ailing Drake to Court to explain to his inquisitors some basic facts regarding ocean voyaging.[37]

Howard's technical assessment of his ships' lack of seaworthiness was well-founded. On 3 September, Hawkins summarized the state of the Navy Royal for Burghley's benefit (perhaps the Lord Admiral's stark assessment had been considered too gloomy): 'Our ships (are) utterly unfytted, & unmette to follow any enterpryse from hence, without a thorrough new trymmynge, refreshynge & new furnyshyng with provycions, growndynge, & freshe men . . .'.[38] Three weeks later, the report of the shipwrights following twenty-three ships' grounding at Chatham (the Navy Royal's entire strength other than the Flanders squadron now commanded by Sir Henry Palmer) revealed widespread attrition to their fabrics. Only the *Elizabeth Jonas* (being pestilential still) and the *Mary Rose* ('very leaky') seem to have been entirely unemployable, but all except two others required early replacement of masts, spars, beams and even knees.[39] There could be no substantial naval expedition in the immediate aftermath of the armada campaign.

However, the query that so exasperated Howard was only the first foray in the regime's search for an early riposte to Philip's enterprise. With his fleet battered (if not destroyed), England had a rare opportunity to fatally wound Habsburg ambitions for European dominance. Predictably, the seizure of a plate fleet had been Elizabeth's first idea on how this might be achieved – a tempting solution to the Exchequer's emptying coffers and the death-knell to Philip's hopes of financing a swift reprise of the 1588 campaign. Without the comfort of that unlikely windfall, there was no question that England's public finances could be stretched to accommodate both the cost of future operations – whatever their ultimate form was to be – and the debts of past campaigns. Continuing economies were inevitable, and fell upon those least able to make any further contribution to the war effort.

Tensions created by this juggling of resources may have extended beyond the matter of who was to go hungry. Drake's visit to court on 27–8 August, during which he gave Walsingham the Lord Admiral's reply regarding the state of the fleet, was the first opportunity to involve him in discussions regarding the form of the coming project. It is hardly necessary to speculate that Drake himself took a lead in urging some form of strike against targets on the Iberian Peninsula. This, after all, had been his near-constant refrain for almost a year past. Little more than a month thereafter, he and Sir John Norreys would be named naval- and land-commander respectively of a vast English expedition to the Spanish mainland, which indicates that Drake had a principal role in discussions regarding the provision of men and ships.[40] Inevitably, as this process expanded it sequestered most available resources, further hampering the Lord Admiral's efforts to discharge his men.

Howard was privy to, but not part of, preparations for England's counter-offensive. It is not known if he wished or expected to command the coming expedition, only that he was not offered the opportunity. He had led the English fleet with distinction, but as the courtly reconciler, the manifestation of his sovereign's authority, pampering and soothing the widely dissimilar temperaments of her captains. England and the regime had been preserved, but it was not the victory imagined by those who had pushed hardest to see it fought. No less than some modern commentators, many contemporary Englishmen were coming to believe that Drake had been robbed of his – and, in reflection, their – glory by the Lord Admiral's cautious stewardship of the fleet (a process that Drake himself, busily creating the myth of his pre-campaign 'coast of Spain' initiative, did much to encourage[41]). Howard's place in the pantheon of England's heroes was assured, but it was not one that encouraged further faith in his circumspect nature.

Drake, in contrast, was the acknowledged master not only of offensive warfare but of warfare that paid for itself: a faculty that made his command of the fleet in the coming campaign almost mandatory. The counter-offensive against Spain was to be based upon very different assumptions than those that had met the threat from the armada and Parma. Elizabeth had risen decisively to their potentially fatal challenge, but with the immediate crisis passed, her expectations reverted immediately to those of the years in which the principal tools of English foreign policy had been the occasional subsidy and a heavily involved private sector. The present condition of the fleet and lack of funds to put right its faults at short notice would have made this inevitable in any case, but the Queen hardly required pretexts. She did not like fighting wars. She much preferred others to fight and she, sparingly, to support their efforts. Clearly, the new project required a firm royal hand upon its aims, objectives and implementation; but its provision, like that of the West Indies and Cadiz raids, could be borne substantially by those of her courtiers and merchants who recognized the opportunities on offer. The days of the English 'nation at arms' were coming to an end; what followed were projects that played less to duty and more to the instincts of the seafaring entrepreneurs who had done much to precipitate the war with Spain. Only one man – Drake – had a proven record of exciting (and controlling) the best efforts of such self-interested forces.

It is doubtful that Howard had been allowed to forget that Drake was, to most of his compatriots, England's premier fighting seaman – a man disqualified from supreme command only by his lowly birth. Whether the Lord Admiral's intense sensitivity to precedence (particularly his own) had been tested by his talented lieutenant's independence of spirit during the late campaign is unclear; certainly, any resentment he felt had been well-hidden. Similarly, Drake had not let the subordination of his genius to that of a professional courtier sour their working relationship. Both men maintained a correct and courteous demeanour in the weeks and months following the end of the campaign, though Drake's involvement in arrangements for the coming expedition to Spain and Portugal almost certainly kept them from more than occasional proximity. But this was a factious age. As soon as the commonplace of a routine freed from the threat of extinction reasserted itself, the qualities of England's two most senior naval commanders became the surrogate focus of other rivalries. Some of these clashes were hardly discreet. The smoke from the ships' ordnance had hardly cleared before Frobisher, a recent recipient of the Lord Admiral's favour, was threatening loudly to disembowel Drake for cowardice, desertion and, above all, the good fortune to make a profit from the campaign. Other spats, if quieter, were no less intense, and most were fuelled by loyalty to or antipathy for the fleet's vice admiral. Lord Sheffield and Lord Thomas Howard shared Frobisher's distaste for Drake (possibly resenting his low-born aspiration to greatness as much as his abandonment of the fleet on the night of 21/22 July), while the earl of Cumberland also joined the anti-Drake party, goaded by his loyalty to Howard and the contrast between Drake's glittering record as a privateer and his own disastrous showing to date.[42] Howard himself offered no overt criticism of his vice admiral at any point, but nor did he attempt to silence his supporters. Ironically, it was Drake, in refuting Frobisher's damaging accusations, who inadvertently confirmed his superior's ambiguous opinion of his conduct during the campaign by anxiously over-emphasizing the contrary in correspondence to Walsingham.[43] Above all of this petty bickering rose Lord Henry Seymour, who had devoted a large part of his own campaign to emulating Achilles in his tent. He finally stalked away from command of the Narrow Seas squadron sometime after 23 August, the day he asked Walsingham to relieve him rather than condemn him to another inglorious watch off Dunkirk. His parting blast, regretting the factions growing around his admiral, was somewhat shameless given his previously expressed poor opinion of almost all of his colleagues (including both Howard and Drake).[44]

Beyond the fleet, the matter briefly became a proxy cause amidst the habitual struggle for pre-eminence at Court. The sudden death of Leicester on 4 September removed the most adept practitioner of this semi-martial art, though his worst qualities were amply upheld in the person of his step-son, the Queen's rising favourite, Robert Devereux, earl of Essex. Essex, invited or otherwise, threw himself enthusiastically into support of Drake as a means of furthering his own, would-be glorious career, and took care to disseminate complaints of Howard's performance as Lord Admiral.[45] His chief rival for Elizabeth's affections, Sir Walter Ralegh, was, in contrast, a vociferous supporter of Howard's tactics during the campaign, and later excoriated the 'malignant fools' who criticized them.[46] Within three months of the battle, Essex and Ralegh had fought a duel, while Cumberland, the Queen's ceremonial 'Champion', had attempted to hack Essex to death during a supposedly friendly joust. If neither clash had its foundation in fleet rivalries (in the previous year Essex had boxed Ralegh's ears during a quarrel about which of them the Queen loved best), both exemplified the factiousness that a semblance – even the brief reality – of unity in adversity had disguised.[47]

*   *   *

As England's military leaders jostled to defend their posterity and trample upon that of their rivals, the pathetic remnants of their prey – the mariners and soldiers captured in the *Rosario* and the few survivors from the *San Salvador* – had begun to taste the fruits of defeat. Forty of her officers and gentlemen had been brought to London for interrogation in Bridewell gaol. Stripped of their fine clothes (which were carefully inventoried) and provided with more modest attire, they were questioned closely on the assumptions and orders that had set out the great armada. The answers they provided were enlightening, if divorced from reality. Their fleet orders had stipulated that any English ships taken at sea were be good prize of their captors, save for naval vessels, which would be requisitioned for the King's use. Between a third and a half of all Englishmen had been expected to rise up at word of the armada's approach and declare for pope and Philip. Once the invasion force(s) had landed in England, any remaining resistance was to be crushed mercilessly, but otherwise the armada's troops were to show no particular favour (or disfavour) to Catholic or Protestant Englishman. It was generally expected that Philip would allow the professionals in the Holy Office to commence that good work once the realm had been pacified.

Of more immediate interest to the English interrogators and their employers was the confirmation that a rendezvous with Parma had indeed been intended prior to a descent upon England (and that some separate, though vague accommodation had been made with the Guise regarding the eventual fate of Scotland). There was some doubt among the prisoners, however, as to whether Parma would govern the conquered nation thereafter in Philip's name or attempt to wield power independently of Madrid. During his own examination, Valdés angrily deflected English comments regarding the injustice of Philip's intentions, declaring that it was not his right, nor that of his interrogators, to judge a king's will. These broad strategic matters aside, the prisoners' examinations were curiously devoted to the minutiae of the *Rosario*'s fittings and cargoes. It seems that the Queen and her impoverished government wanted to know precisely what had been pillaged by Drake and his men before her officials performed their ship's inventory (which, incidentally, discovered no whips, either of standard or cruelly modified design).[48]

The Spaniards brought to London had been fortunate, notwithstanding the attentions of their interrogators. Most of their less exalted compatriots had been lodged in a gaol near Exeter under the charge of Sir John Gilbert (who referred fondly to the establishment as 'our Bridewell'). Receiving this unwanted intake, he had immediately apprised the Privy Council of his inability to feed them. The Council then proposed that those London and West Country merchants who had relatives or factors presently incarcerated in Spanish prisons might wish to assume the burden of their upkeep, thereby earning commensurate relief for their own hostages. This excellent suggestion – one that managed to be equally optimistic of mercantile altruism and the Holy Office's sense of fair play – was not well received. Wearying of its distracting burden, the Council then decided to allow 390 Spanish prisoners to buy their freedom at ten ducats – approximately £2 8s. – the man. As their senior officer, Valdés was obliged to write to Parma (his captors obligingly arranged postage and carriage for the letter), asking for the necessary funds and for boats to transport the freed men into the Low Countries. Initially, the duke was willing to oblige his petitioners, but he cavilled at a new, inflated ransom demanded by the Privy Council, which had changed its collective mind in the meantime and decided that prudence required the men be sent directly back to Spain. From Devon, meanwhile, Gilbert's fellow deputy Lord Lieutenant, George Carey, complained of Gilbert's abuse of his Spanish prisoners, who had been transferred to a hulk anchored in a creek beside Gilbert's estate, and used thereafter as slave labour to level his garden (the two men were engaged in a long and vicious local feud, and Carey's accusation may have been made more in envy than outrage). By 14 October, Carey claimed that the prisoners had been more or less abandoned to starvation by Gilbert, obliging himself to provide for them 'at the best and cheapest hand' – that is, at less than half the subsistence rate provided for by Council – from his own pocket.[49]

In November, this persistent inconvenience was aggravated by a new influx of prisoners of war – survivors from the hospital ship *San Pedro Mayor*, which, having survived a storm-tossed passage around Scotland and the western Irish coast, had almost made the coast of northern Spain before being blown back into the Channel and driven aground at Hope Cove, near Salcombe in Devon. Their fortunate landing place, ironically, lay within the estate of Sir William Courtenay, another deputy Lord Lieutenant of Devon, who, years later, would marry Francis Drake's widow Elizabeth. Courtenay immediately detained at his home eight of the 'better sort' of Spaniard, while George Carey took another two – the ship's apothecary and her sergeant – 'to make trial of what skill is in them' as he claimed to the Council. The remainder joined their compatriots from the *Rosario* and *San Salvador* in the West Country's 'Bridewell'.

By now, the Privy Council had lost all patience with its unwelcome guests. On 1 November, orders were sent to Gilbert and Carey to execute all the common Spanish-born mariners and soldiers, being 'most pernicious enemies to her Majesty'.[50] This ruthless decision, mirroring Sir Richard Bingham's concurrent treatment of shipwrecked Spanish prisoners in Ireland, was overturned three weeks later before being implemented.[51] The Flemings and Frenchmen among their number were freed on 27 November, to make their way home as best they might, while those who remained (including a considerable number of wounded or sick mariners, transferred into the *San Pedro Mayor* from other vessels of the armada during the campaign) were to be dispersed among 'barns and outhouses' near Exeter to prevent the spread of infection.[52]

Negotiations for the release of Spanish prisoners would continue for the remainder of 1588 and throughout 1589. The majority were set free only in November of the latter year after the Privy Council had told Parma to pay the full ransom or consider himself responsible for the prisoners' executions.[53] Fortunately, the duke's sense of honour prevailed. The more valuable Spanish officers, however, were allowed to enjoy a more protracted English hospitality. On his own behalf, the incorrigible Courtenay was to despatch a succession of ludicrously inflated demands for the release of his reluctant Spanish houseguests (his best effort was 25,000 ducats, or almost a quarter of the ransom Drake had accepted in 1586 to spare the entire city of Cartagena). He held some fifteen gentlemen still in mid-1590 and twelve two years later; eventually, it would require a curious alliance of the Privy Council and a Habsburg envoy, Pedro Cubiar (himself a former armada prisoner in England), to prise these unfortunates from their rapacious gaoler. The doubtful honour of most-welcome Spanish guest, however, fell to Lope Ruiz de la Pegna, apothecary of the *San Pedro Mayor*. Astonishingly, his skills were to remain on 'trial' by George Carey at his Cockington estate until at least March 1597, at which time the Council ordered his release in return for that of Carey's nephew, by then a prisoner of Spain (though treated there with considerably more tenderness, apparently, than the unfortunate Ruiz[54]).

*   *   *

The prolonged ordeal of England's prisoners of war reflected their status as an unwelcome distraction – the tail-end of a long manifest of priorities for the Privy Council. As it became clear that the battle was over, a new front opened in a war being fought as much for the soul as the entrails of western Europe. In Paris, Bernadino de Mendoza had hurriedly reconstructed an account of the recent campaign from several (supposedly) eyewitness accounts of Breton sailors which gave a clear victory to the Armada. Howard's *Ark Royal* and sixteen other naval vessels were said to have been sent to the seabed, while Drake allegedly had fled with the damaged remnants of the English fleet. Framing this heartening news as a letter from a disinterested merchant of Dieppe, the Spanish ambassador had it printed in pamphlet form and distributed on 29 August to stiffen the morale of Philip's Catholic League allies (though when he presented a copy personally to Henri III, he was told that the governor of Calais had already passed on a rather different account of the late fight). In turn, his English counterpart – and sometime employee – in Paris, Sir Edward Stafford, begged Walsingham to send some details to contradict this damaging version of events for his own French audience. Although deeply suspicious of Stafford's relationship with Mendoza, Walsingham responded swiftly with a brief journal of events for counter-publication in Paris (as early as 8 August, Howard, exhibiting an accomplished *politique*'s understanding of the importance of manipulating public impressions, had urged him to send news to 'my brouther Stafford' to rebut jibes previously circulated by Mendoza regarding England's lack of military prowess[55]). Once more, this was presented as the work of a third party with no special interest at heart. As a stopgap measure it was reasonably successful, but given the distance between European perceptions and reality more comprehensive assaults upon Spanish claims were required.

In the immediate aftermath of the campaign, an English translation of Medina Sidonia's report on his fleet, *La Felicissima Armada Que Rey Don Felipe Nuestro*, was published in London with a lengthy, mocking foreword by its translator, Daniel Archdeacon. Unabashedly triumphant, his piece portrayed a hubristic Goliath beaten down by the English David:

> For touching their folly, how ridiculous hath it bene, that . . . they shoulde come so long prouided against a land as it were unawares, so manie and mightie Monarchies against so . . . litle an Island: such huge ships against so small pinases, as it were, and of these to take (as the Lord bee praised they haue) so strange repulses . . . And therefore because they had raged against him, and their tumulte was come into his eares, did

put a hooke into their nostrilles, and a bridle into their lippes, and brought them back the same way they came . . .[56]

This was a first outing for the legend of plucky little English vessels overcoming great Spanish warships 'made like *Babel* towers'. However, in the fraught days immediately following the armada's retreat, Archdeacon's implication of a massive disparity of naval forces was not wholly helpful. Burghley, shrugging off the torments of gout (he had been incapacitated for weeks during and after the recent battle), composed several more useful ripostes to Spanish and Leaguer propaganda. The first of these, the most effective blast of the reign, was his *Copy of a letter sent out of England to Don Bernadin Mendoza, etc.*[57] Attributed to the pen of Richard Leigh, a recently executed seminary priest, it provided a detailed refutation of Mendoza's premature claims for a Spanish victory and, importantly, attempted to discourage thoughts of any further effort by Philip. Accordingly, and in contrast to Archdeacon's piece, the *Copy of a letter* vastly exaggerated the scale of England's military resources. The English shires were each said to be able and ready to provide a minimum of 25,000 trained men, and it was claimed that within a year the intact English fleet would be reinforced by an equal number of newly constructed warships. Spanish 'cowardice' during the late battle was lovingly emphasized, while the minutely observed adoration of Englishmen for their sovereign, and their bragging hope that Parma might arrive on English soil with thrice the expected number of Spaniards, hinted at the indomitable resistance his *tercios* might expect. From his traitor's grave, Leigh lamented:

> I may say, we have seen in the space of eight or nine days . . . all our hopes, all our buildings, as it now appeareth, but upon an imagined conquest, utterly overthrown, and, as it were, with an earthquake, all our castles of comfort brought to the ground, which now, it seemeth, were builded but in the air, or upon the waves of the sea; for they are all perished, all vanished away from our thoughts'.

The *Copy of a letter* was effective, but it was long and not easily digested. In the weeks following its imprinting in early September, the persistence of Spanish attempts to claim a victory required additional rebuttal, which Burghley duly provided in his far more accessible *A Packe of Spanish Lyes.*[58] In tabular (one might almost say tabloid) form, with lies propagated by several Spanish pamphlets reiterated on the left-hand side of the page and

Burghley's 'corrections' set exactly opposite, the pamphlet mocked estimates of English losses in ships, Drake's supposed capture by Medina Sidonia and James VI's apparent invasion of the border counties. Printed in English, French, German, Italian and Spanish by the end of December, it was distributed swiftly to reinforce intelligence, slowly reaching the courts of Europe, that Philip's enterprise of England – and the Counter-Reformation – had met with unmitigated disaster.

Lies, hyperbole and *schadenfreude* were of course the meat of any effective propaganda, but one feature both of the *Copy of a letter* and *Packe of Spanish Lyes*, poignant for its accuracy, was the admission that the fugitive seminary priests in England – 'manifest traytors' to a man – had failed utterly in their mission to subvert the political loyalties of English Catholics. The *Copy of a letter* mourned for a lost dream of deliverance:

> Such is our calamity, that it hath pleased God, as I think, for our sins, or else for confounding of our bold opinions, and presumptions, of our own strength, to put in the hearts of all persons here one like mind, and courage to withstand the intended invasion, as well in such as we accounted Catholicks, as also in the Hereticks; so has it appeared manifestly that for all our earnest proceeding for arming, and for contributions of money, and for all other warlike actions, there was no difference to be seen betwixt the Catholick and the Heretick. But in this case to withstand the threatened conquest, yea, to defend the person of the Queen, there appeared such a sympathy, concourse, and consent of all persons, without respect of religion, as they all appeared to be ready to fight, against all strangers, as it were with one heart and one body.

The *Packe of Spanish Lyes* put it more boldly (and mendaciously): 'If there were a mutinie of Catholikes, they should haue bene hanged or punished; but it was not knowen that one Catholicke did stir this summer, with hand or tongue, to mooue offence, neither was one imprisoned, or otherwise punished.'

In the bishop's palace at Wisbech, the leading members of Elizabeth's Catholic constituency must have been both comforted by this belated appreciation of their loyalty and startled by the revelation that none of them had in fact been confined. Neither official gratitude nor blatant revisionism brought their early release, however. On 22 October, commissioners appointed by the Council travelled to Ely to interrogate them closely on their understanding of the Queen's lawful dominion and defence of her person and regime.[59] Their answers (no longer extant) are unlikely to have been any less ardently expressed than previously. Nevertheless, they did not persuade their inquisitors, whose employers remained convinced that English Catholics, if quiescent, continued to represent a potential Trojan Horse for foreign military ambitions. That conviction, buttressed by the extreme dangers endured during the late national crisis, found expression in an untypically ruthless drive against the principal instruments of subversion.

As noted, arrests of seminary priests had accelerated as the threat from the armada grew during the spring months of 1588. In the aftermath of the campaign, the number of those who, with their abettors, were brought to trial and execution rose to a level unmatched at any other moment of Elizabeth's reign. Three died at Derby on 24 July, one at Stafford on 27 July (the latter suffering the full agony of a traitor's execution); in the three months thereafter to 28 November, a further twenty-seven priests and lay Catholics went to the scaffold. Fourteen perished in just three days, 28–30 August.[60] The fatal offence of one of these unfortunates, Margaret Ward, was to have provided a priest with a rope with which to escape from London's Bridewell gaol. In an exquisitely cruel refinement, she was stripped half-naked and scourged at the prison wall with the offending item immediately before her hanging.[61] This was a Marian intensity of persecution – though Ward's ordeal apparently revolted both the judge who was obliged to condemn her and the Queen herself, when apprised of it – and represented more than an understandable over-reaction to the dangers of invasion and insurrection. As a coldly judged matter of policy, Elizabeth's government was providing Philip, Sixtus v and William Allen with a timely reminder of what, irrevocably, they had lost.

Local sympathies were excited by these sanguinary episodes, but they were lost in the growing sense of euphoria at the defeat both of Philip's enterprise and the less tangible threat of insurrection that government had so industriously flagged. This mood intensified as news of Spanish losses filtered back from Ireland. As early as 20 August, Alexander Nowell, Dean of St Paul's, tempted fate by preaching a sermon lauding England's victory before the aldermen and livery companies of the City.[62] The first official thanksgiving day was appointed for 8 September, when banners from eleven Spanish ships were paraded at St Paul's Cross following a sermon upon the nation's deliverance. One of these, depicting Mary holding the infant Jesus, attracted particular derision, being draped over the pulpit throughout the proceedings. The spoils were then carried to London Bridge and hung among rotting traitors' heads on the Southwark gate.[63]

On 17 November, the anniversary of Elizabeth's accession, Thomas Cooper, bishop of Winchester, preached at St Paul's Cross before the livery companies in expectation of the Queen's presence (they were disappointed). On Tuesday 19 November a holiday was observed throughout the kingdom; the bells of the nation's great cathedrals pealed in triumph, and hundreds of improving sermons, followed more usefully by bonfire-illuminated feasts, celebrated a God-given victory. Finally, on 24 November, Elizabeth attended a magnificent thanksgiving service at St Paul's cathedral. From Somerset House in the Strand, she was carried along Fleet Street and up Ludgate Hill upon a canopied chariot-throne, its six pillars topped with imperial crowns and the lion and unicorn of England's arms. Behind her, the earl of Essex led a royal guard flanking her ladies-in-waiting, with other, lesser courtiers forming their rearguard. A song, apparently written by the Queen herself, was sung as the procession moved eastwards:

Lok and bowe downe thyne eare o Lorde
From thy bright spheare behould and see
Thy hand maide and Thy handy worke
Amongst thy pristes offeringe to thee
Zeale for incense reachinge the skyes
My self and septer sacryfyce

My sowle assend to holy place
Ascribe him strength and singe him prayse
For he refrayneth Prynces spyrits
And hathe done wonders in my daies
He made the wynds and waters rise
To scatter all myne enemyes

This Josephes Lorde and Israells god
The fyry pillar and dayes clowde
That saved his saincts from wicked men
And drenshet the honor of the prowde
And hathe preserved in tender love
The spirit of his Turtle dove[64]

Briefly, the cavalcade halted at Temple Bar in the Strand, the western extremity of the City, where the Lord Mayor and aldermen waited to greet their sovereign. Into her hands, the Mayor relinquished his sceptre of office and received it back with thanks for the City's late efforts on England's behalf. At St Paul's west door, the Bishop of London, John Aylmer, flanked by Dean Nowell and the cathedral's clergy, gathered to offer a similar welcome. All, to the dismay of the City's 'godly' and derision of its Catholics, wore their gold copes, hurriedly exhumed from long entombment in cupboards, chests and even outhouses (some were in tatters or bearing large scorch marks from previous mishandlings). Following prayers and a sung litany, Elizabeth sat in a specially constructed booth at the cathedral's crossing, where John Piers, bishop of Salisbury, gave a sermon of thanksgiving for his sovereign's late deliverance and appointed a prayer to be said throughout the kingdom's parishes:

> We cannot but confess, O Lord God, that the late terrible intended invasion of most cruel enemies was sent from thee, to the punishment of our sins, our pride, our covetousness, our excess in meat and drink, our security, our ingratitude, and our unthankfulness towards thee . . . and indeed our guilty consciences looked for, even at that time, the execution of that terrible justice upon us, so by us deserved . . . But thou, O Lord God, who knowest all things, knowing that our enemies came not of justice to punish us for our sins committed against thy Divine Majesty (whom they by their excessive wickedness have offended, and continually do offend, as much or more than we); but that they came with most cruel intent and purpose to destroy us, our cities, towns, countries, and people; and utterly to root out the memory of our nation from off the earth for ever; and withall wholly to suppress the Holy Word, and blessed Gospel of thy dear Son our Saviour Jesus Christ: which they, being drowned in idolatry and superstition, do hate most deadly . . . Wherefore it hath pleased thee, O Heavenly Father . . . to execute that dreadful execution which they intended towards us, to the amendment of our lives, and to execute justice upon our cruel enemies; turning the destruction that they intended against us upon their own heads . . .[65]

It was a pointed reminder of the covenant between God and Protestant England, one that though tested and bruised by Englishmen's manifold vices, had clearly surpassed and supplanted Israel's lost exemplar. With Piers's admonition regarding excesses of meat and drink echoing still, the Queen was escorted to Aylmer's palace for a long lunch with her host, and departed for Westminster only after dusk. The bishop's wife – who, like all clerics' spouses, Elizabeth regarded more as an abhorrent practice than a person in her own right – tactfully absented herself from the table.

Somewhere in the massive crowds lining the route of the royal procession that day stood the Jesuit Superior and future gunpowder-plotter, Henry Garnet. Like many other fugitive English priests, he welcomed the defeat of the armada as a harbinger of better times for the mass of loyal English Catholics. The enthusiasm in his report of the adulation that greeted the Queen at every step of her progress was entirely unfeigned, and his subsequent anguish at the ongoing persecution of his fellow priests did not reflect any sense that she had betrayed his hopes.[66] Garnet shared the belief, common among his co-religionists, that aggressive government policies had been enacted by radical Protestant ministers against the natural womanly instincts of their sovereign. To the extent that Elizabeth hardly ever intended legislation imposing religious conformity to be applied with its full, mandated severity (unlike many of her councillors and parliamentarians), they were correct.[67] It is remarkable, nevertheless, that the painstakingly constructed legend of Eliza's tenderness had found an equally receptive audience at both extremities of England's confessional divide.

Had they chosen to listen, however, Garnet and his flock were not being led into any false hopes of better times to come. Their quiescence during the armada campaign was acknowledged at the highest level of government, but it was almost universally considered to be the product of divine intervention, not individual conscience:

It was the worke of God, who shewed his Almightie power not onely in weakning the courage of the forreine enemies, but also in changing their hartes who are among ourselves most dangerous, and (had he not made them of wolves, for the time lambes) might more have perplexed us in a day, than could the out-enimies in a moneth . . . And they for al their proffered service then, are no whit the more to be favored & trusted now; Papistes being the solicitors, Papistes the prosecutors of this warre, Papistes the soldiers, and al attempted on the behalfe of the Pope and Papistes.[68]

This was a polemicist's blast, but no voice in the wilderness. On 4 February 1589, in the first session of parliament following the defeat of the armada, Sir Christopher Hatton rose to make the session's opening speech on behalf of the government. Though thankful for the nation's recent deliverance, he crushed any hopes that the regime's grip upon its subjects' consciences might loosen, whatever admissions of Catholic fealty to be found in Burghley's propaganda:

And here I maie not forget those vile wretches, those bloodie preists and false traiters, here in our bosomes . . . Thei have incorporated themselves into the bodie of all mischeif, and are accordinglie to be emploied by the heades of the same. But to make this thinge out of question, (Cardinal William) Allen himself hath set it doune as a pointe of the Romish religion that all preistes and catholickes are bound under paine of damnation . . . still to solicite the Pope and the Spaniarde, and never to geve over their former or the like attempts untill (yf it maie be) the before mentioned designmentes be fullie accomplished.[69]

No less than Burghley, Walsingham and their generation of Protestant polemicists, Allen had tied his putative flock to the prow of papal and Spanish ambitions for the recovery of England. The rocks that splintered those expectations left their binds intact.

SIXTEEN

England's Garland

Our English, either for fights, for discoveries, whether for tame ships, merchantmen, or wild ships, men-of-war, carry away the garland from all nations in the Christian world[1]

At approximately 4pm on Monday, 16 April 1605, a small English fleet commanded by Charles Howard – second Baron Effingham, earl of Nottingham and Lord Admiral of England still – came to anchor in the roads of Corunna. Immediately, the twenty great guns of Corunna fortress opened fire. Within minutes they were joined by twenty-six more, mounted in a second fortification recently constructed on the northern side of the town, and, from within Corunna itself, a third volley of thirty pieces, all of large calibre. Each English ship replied to this barrage with a single broadside volley, and prepared to receive boarders. From the harbour, a heavily decorated barge, crammed with the governor of Galicia, his retainers and other dignitaries, approached and lay alongside the fleet's flagship, the *White Bear* – no longer an ageing 'great ship', but newly rebuilt, one of the Navy Royal's most powerful vessels.[2] For the next hour these notables toured the ship, graciously accompanied by Nottingham and an entourage of his relatives, noblemen and courtiers. The Spaniards were apologetic; they had been told that the English fleet would make for Santander and had not themselves prepared adequate entertainment for their unexpected guests. Nevertheless, they invited Nottingham to be received ashore with formal honours the following day. At the governor's departure, the guns of the town and English fleet saluted each other once more with thunderous volleys from shotless ordnance.[3]

During the next few days, the representatives of each nation vied to outdo each other in high courtesies. Tuesday's feast in Corunna town was answered by a return bout in Nottingham's flagship on Wednesday. When not being officially entertained, the earl and his immediate followers, taking the air on horseback or in his coach around the town's hinterland, were chased and cheered relentlessly by the local peasantry (not least for the largesse Nottingham distributed prodigally from his deep purse). In turn, he acted ruthlessly to curb his men's innate rowdiness, which had threatened already to alienate their well-mannered hosts. An English mariner who, drunk while on shore leave in the port, expressed his religious partialities by thumping a priest was dragged before a drum-head tribunal in the *White Bear* and sentenced to be hanged. The governor of Corunna, his wife and his daughter were invited to the proceedings to witness the impartiality of English justice; distressed by the severity of the sentence, they begged Nottingham to commute it, excusing the offence on the grounds that the priest was well-known locally as 'a halfe lunaticke'. Offered the opportunity to hand down his own punishment, the governor directed that the mariner be committed instead to the *Bear*'s buttery for a square meal. It was all very agreeable.

For more than two weeks thereafter, the Englishmen enjoyed the hospitality of Corunna while preparations were made to carry them to the Spanish Court at Valladolid. Good lodgings were provided in the town for many of Nottingham's men, notwithstanding the widespread damage, still very much apparent, that Drake and Norreys had inflicted during their abortive raid fifteen years earlier. A minor disappointment arose when it became clear that the resources of the province as a whole could not support the locust-like passage of the earl's entourage (of some 650 courtiers, gentlemen, soldiers and their horses). A more modest party, of a mere 500 Englishmen, was assembled, while the frustrated expellees were ordered to remain with the fleet or return prematurely to England in its victualling boats. On 3 May, following a great festival, joust, pageant, fireworks display and banquet held in Nottingham's honour, a still-substantial convoy of carriages and horsemen departed Corunna, escorted by the Spanish King's chief commissioner in London during the previous year's peace negotiations, Juan Fernandez de Velasco y Tobar, duke of Frias and Constable of Castile ('Don Blasco' to his English companions).

Eleven days later, the English party arrived at Simancas, a few miles from Valladolid. The impact of Nottingham's first formal entry into the royal city on Thursday 16 May was spoiled when his entourage hastily broke rank in torrential rain and scattered to search out its many appointed lodgings. However, the earl's trampled dignity was salved two days later by the scale and grandeur of his first audience with Philip III, during which he presented formal letters of treaty from James I. With a further ceremony on 30 May, when Philip knelt to give his solemn oath to keep the terms of peace agreed between himself and his brother sovereign, the principal business of the earl's visit was concluded. All else during his three weeks' stay at Valladolid was delightful distraction, upon a scale not seen in Spain for years. The duke of Lerma, Philip's favourite and a man whose profligacy and corruption in office surpassed even Nottingham's, made it his particular duty to keep the earl and his followers entertained with pageants, religious festivals, military revues and bull-fights, all punctuated and complemented by lavish feasting. These occasions were attended by almost the entire corps of Spain's grandee families, none of whom tainted the atmosphere with anything but the most discreet reference to the late unpleasantness between their nation and that of their honoured guests. During these days, the French, Imperial and Venetian ambassadors to the Spanish Court came in turn to Nottingham's lodgings to pay their warm respects; he, conscious of the great benefits of collateral diplomacy, insisted upon leading each of them by the hand back to their coaches, an intimate gesture that further impressed his already besotted hosts.

The English embassy departed Valladolid on 8 June, many of its number enriched by a final shower of costly presents from the Spanish Royal Treasury. A diamond ring worth some £3,000 was placed upon Nottingham's finger by Philip himself; the pride of a considerable store of trinkets accumulated by the earl during the previous days. In the early evening, weighed down by booty and pursued by the acclaim of crowds that lined its route, the English convoy passed out of the city upon the road to Santander, where the English fleet now lay. Over the following eleven days, passing northwards in easy stages with ample rest-stops, Nottingham and his party were entertained by a succession of local dignitaries. Only once, as they passed through the wild Cantabrian Mountains on their final night in Spain, did they fail to find either warm welcome or adequate forage for a comfortable night's rest. This was a final hardship, however. In the morning they descended into Santander, and, following a final shipboard banquet in honour of the diligent 'Don Blasco', the English fleet set sail for England.

Robert Treswell, Somerset-Herald and chronicler of Nottingham's embassy, reported unequivocal delight among ordinary Spaniards that the long conflict with England was over:

Both in our going and return, we might well observe how joyful our coming seemed to the common people . . . who, for that they found by experience the ill reports made heretofore of our nation altogether untrue, admiring our civility and good behaviour . . . we received that kind congratulation and usage, that was possible for them to give, and us, as strangers and travellers, to receive.[4]

In England, his detailed account of the embassy and its success was published immediately to reconcile the public to the peace it marked and to foster a sense of reconciliation. It was largely a waste of paper. Even among Howard's own extended family, loyalties were torn. Lord Thomas Howard (now earl of Suffolk) wrote to Ralph Winwood, the English ambassador in Holland, lamenting the reputation his kin had acquired recently as lovers of Spain: 'For myself, I vow afore God, I have no inclination to the Spaniard more than the necessity of my master's service draws me too . . .'.[5] Sir Charles Cornwallis, political protégé of Nottingham's cousin Henry Howard, earl of Northampton, and the first official ambassador to Spain since Dr Man's departure thirty-seven years earlier, assiduously reported unfavourable gossip regarding Nottingham's behaviour during his Spanish visit, which Northampton promptly used to smear his kinsman's reputation at Court.[6] Elsewhere, the prospect of peace soothed few of the antipathies that had made conflict seem so necessary to many Englishmen. It became known, generally and contemptuously, as the 'Spanish peace'. In the previous year, disembarking at Calais following the conclusion of the London negotiations, the duke of Frias (who had bribed his English hosts with promethean energy) observed perceptively that 'the Queen was wholly theirs, the King indifferent, and the Council and Realme professed enemies'. The Venetian ambassador in London, Nicolo Molin, confirmed this shrewd assessment: 'There is a general disaffection . . . for no one can bear to see the Dutch abandoned; nor do they like this prohibition of the India Navigation'; and noted that Englishmen's new Scottish half-brethren, generally detested for their malevolent peace-mongering, were regarded as no better than Spaniards.[7] There was a popular prejudice that England had been duped by the terms of the treaty, and even several years later it was being denounced in pamphlets and from pulpits as a betrayal of the nation's strategic and spiritual interests. The courtier Anthony Weldon proclaimed furiously: 'The constable of Castile so plyed his Master's business (in which he spared for no cost) that he procured a peace so advantagious for *Spaine*, and so disadvantagious for *England*, that it and all Christendom have since both seen and felt the lamentable effect thereon'.[8] The opinion, if less articulately expressed, had been widespread since rumours first surfaced that England and Spain might be stumbling towards a treaty. On 27 October 1602, the diarist John Manningham had thought it worthwhile to report the words of a 'lusty cauallier', proclaiming loudly in a London ordinary that 'he would be hangd yf there were a peace with Spaine'.[9] As its inevitability became apparent, such blusters subsided to scorn, directed at those who worked most assiduously for an end to war. In the early months of 1605, as Nottingham's embassy prepared to embark upon its Spanish mission, one Stone, a wag, was overheard in another London ordinary, proclaiming that there were sixty fools going into Spain besides the Lord Admiral and his two sons. He was committed to the Bridewell and 'well whipt'.[10]

*   *   *

The conflict beneath which Nottingham's embassy to Spain drew a final line had endured some eighteen years, yet to characterize it as a 'war' requires a certain stretching of the modern understanding of the term. Even the grand clash of fleets during the 1588 armada campaign had been an indecisive confrontation. If Englishmen could count it as a victory, it was one bestowed largely by unseasonably foul weather and Spanish masters' inadequate understanding of the treacherous waters through which their battered ships were obliged to struggle home. In the years since that encounter there had been occasional thrusts by each side, intended to be fatal to the enemy's ability (or will) to continue the conflict, punctuated by much longer periods in which the protagonists waged war by proxy or private enterprise. Philip II's massively expensive imperial commitments ensured that he was unable, other than for brief periods, to gather naval forces sufficient to meet the Navy Royal upon remotely equal terms. For Elizabeth, the means to prosecute war – any war – upon other than a relatively modest scale remained equally elusive. If Goliath could not slay David, David had neither the reach nor resources to bring the giant to his knees.

In the period immediately following the failure of Drake and Norreys to destroy what remained of the Spanish fleet of 1588, or to detach Portugal from her unwilling marriage to Spain, the focus of the conflict switched to northern France. There, following the extinction of the Valois dynasty, the struggle between Henri of Navarre and the Catholic League promised to give either Spain or England a predominant advantage in their own conflict. For England, the greatest danger during these years lay in the possibility of Spanish forces establishing themselves on the southern shores of the English Channel, where, with the possession of a deep-water port, they might launch a seaborne invasion whose organization and passage could be effected while the Navy Royal was dispersed or committed elsewhere. Fortunately, Catholic League forces lost much heart and effectiveness following the assassination of the Guise brothers Henri and Louis in December 1588, though Philip's material assistance to his French allies had never been sufficient in any case to deliver decisive success. The threat posed to the Huguenot cause by the duke of Parma's relief of Paris in 1590 and his sweep into Normandy during 1591–2 evaporated with his retreat and death in the latter year (an event that narrowly forestalled his recall to Spain and disgrace); while the Anglo-French extermination of a Spanish expeditionary force outside Brest in 1594 removed a potential danger to England that even the Habsburg Archduke Albert's capture of Calais, two years later, could not quite resurrect. Henri IV converted to Catholicism in 1593, a decision that Burghley lamented as a huge loss to the reformed faith even as his Queen welcomed its political implications. Less than a year later Henri entered Paris; a year later still the Catholic League dissolved itself, and a viable French regime was re-established that owned few loyalties other than to itself (as Henri's prompt abandonment of his 'triple alliance' with Elizabeth and the States-General would prove). Meanwhile, the northern provinces of the Netherlands slipped irretrievably from their former overlord's grip following the death of Parma and the brilliant campaigns of Maurice of Nassau, which reversed most of the hard-won Habsburg gains of the previous decade. Fears of a Protestant apocalypse in north-western Europe, the crucial preoccupation of English foreign policy for a generation, were dissipating.

During this period, England's most substantial operations at sea (excepting the swarm of privateering voyages to the Iberian coast and the West Indies) were confined to a series of attempts, made annually during the years 1589–92, to intercept Philip's elusive plate fleets. In 1589 and 1590, squadrons commanded by Hawkins and Frobisher cast a double net off the Azores and the Portuguese coast that managed only to snare a number of minor prizes. In 1591, Lord Thomas Howard's squadron was chased away by a rejuvenated Spanish armada *del Mar-Océano*, which took Spain's only major English prize of the war: Grenville's *Revenge* (being lashed hard to the hulls of her tormentors, a vessel of the Navy Royal finally had the correct range to inflict serious damage, and sank two of them before surrendering).[11] Lacking the ability to remain on-station in the Azores for more than a month at most before their failing stores forced them home, these English expeditions had little more potential for success than single bayonet thrusts in a darkened room. The one substantial English consolation for a series of expensive efforts was the capture of the rich Goan carrack *Madre de Dios* during Frobisher's 1592 cruise – the richest prize taken by English ships during the sixteenth century. Unfortunately, she proved far more profitable to the light-fingered mariners who boarded her than to Elizabeth's increasingly bare Exchequer.[12]

The next phase of the conflict brought sporadic reversions to more direct confrontation. Twice, Anglo-Dutch forces attempted seaborne operations to destroy the resurgent Spanish naval threat. That of 1596, the sack of Cadiz, came close to securing a stunning profit; but the firing of every vessel of the *flota* trapped in Cadiz harbour transformed the campaign's ostensible victory into expensive failure and near-disgrace for its squabbling co-commanders, Essex and Howard (though the raid's major contribution to Philip's third bankruptcy provided some consolation). The second expedition, in 1597, was foiled by adverse winds and degenerated into yet another forlorn cruise around the Azores.

Meanwhile, the recovery of Spanish naval forces – albeit at crippling cost – and the humiliation of Cadiz tempted Philip II to repeat his enterprise of 1588 with the despatch of new armadas. In late 1596 a badly provisioned fleet departed Lisbon with the impossible task of disembarking an army in Brittany before seizing Brest as a base to facilitate an invasion of England in the following spring. It was scattered by storms off Finisterre with the loss of almost thirty ships and 2,000 men.[13] In 1597 an even larger expedition was despatched to seize Falmouth at a moment when Essex's huge fleet was cruising aimlessly in the Azores. Almost in sight of the Lizard, this, too, was scattered by storms and returned to Spain, though with fewer losses than the previous year's armada.[14] Thereafter, a 'war' that had six years yet to run saw no greater clashes than those that defeated Spanish assistance to the rebellions of Tyrone and O'Donnell in Ireland, though massive defensive preparations erupted in England once more during the summer of 1599 to meet the elusive threat of what became known subsequently, and with some embarrassment, as the 'invisible' armada.[15] With the surrogate conflict in France grinding to a halt, and the rebel Netherlanders now able to maintain themselves against Habsburg forces (despite their urgent claims to the contrary whenever the threat of peace negotiations between England and Spain loomed), the conflict's rationales were evaporating. Nevertheless, its protagonists continued to circle like exhausted prize-fighters who had neither the strength nor reach to finish the brawl.

Both nations increasingly needed a peace, with Spain's the more urgent case. The cost of continual conflict upon several fronts for more than thirty years had strained her resources to breaking point. Philip II defaulted upon his debts for a third time in November 1596; thereafter, his wars against England, France and the Netherlander rebels were financed wholly from the pockets of future generations. By 1598 his 'grand strategy' had constructed a national debt of some eighty-five million ducats, the equivalent of more than ten years' revenue of the entire Spanish empire. In June of that year, Richard Hawkins, writing to the Queen from a Seville gaol, observed perceptively: 'Of men there is no Kingdom that this day is so poor . . . the rent and rights of Spain amount to fourteen millions of ducats . . . but of this the King hath not free two hundred thousand ducats, for that the rest is at pawn for money taken and borrowed . . .'. [16] As the war entered its final years, Spain's domestic economy stagnated; abroad, after decades of under-provisioning by their mother country, the provinces of New Spain and Terra Firme were becoming self-sufficient in the production of wine, oil, grain and coarse cloths, the basic necessities of Spanish life overseas. As this formerly captive colonial market gradually disappeared, the principal outlet for Spanish manufactured goods in northern Europe – still, remarkably, the rebel provinces of the Low Countries – was closed off when the States-General retaliated against Philip's embargo of 1595. Fleets of Dutch raiders, formerly the scourge of coastlines between Ushant and the Baltic, joined their English brethren off Spain and in the Caribbean to seize by force what they could no longer purchase. The merchant marines of Spain and Portugal, vast at the beginning of the conflict, withered almost to extinction at the hands of the sea-rovers, the decay of their trade and the increasingly prohibitive cost of obtaining insurance upon cargoes. Those few vessels that survived were obliged clandestinely to hire English and Dutch mariners to supplement a near-vanished domestic pool of expertise. [17]

Reluctantly accepting his inability to wage war against the greater part of western Europe, Philip II finally loosened the reins of his inflexible policies. In May 1598 he came to terms with Bourbon France with the Treaty of Vervins. Having achieved this mirror image of the peace with which he commenced his kingship, and, three months later, bestowed qualified sovereignty of the loyal southern provinces of the Low Countries upon the Austrian branch of his family, he died. The accession of his son Philip III brought youthful optimism to the Spanish throne and some renewal of ambitions to force a resolution of the conflict with England (including the brief, ephemeral threat of the 'invisible' Armada), which, in the face of cold reality, subsided to attempts to influence the English succession to Habsburg advantage. More indicative of the growing appreciation of Spain's weakening position was his appointment, on 26 May 1599 (NS), of a first official ambassador to the government of the Low Countries – an acknowledgement both of the independence of the Archduke's authority and the failure of Spanish policy there for forty years past. It must have seemed poignant even then, that Don Balthasar de Zúñiga, to whom the role was entrusted, was the same man who had carried Medina Sidonia's first report of *La Gran Armada's* defeat to Philip II eleven years earlier.[18]

England's non-naval maritime strength had expanded as Spain's shrivelled. In home waters, the fishing and seaborne coal trades flourished during the war years. Further abroad, English penetration of the Mediterranean and Baltic had been both strengthened and regulated in the activities of the Turkey and Eastland companies, while the exemplar of future English imperial ambitions, the English East India Company, was founded as the new century commenced. All of these activities had complemented, and in turn been supplemented by, a vastly enhanced privateering industry that fed the English economy and its need for good ocean-going vessels and expert seamen. Even so, the Anglo-Spanish conflict had not been an unequivocally happy experience for Englishmen. The more substantial merchants of the City of London and the shrewder speculating nobility benefited greatly from the opportunities it had provided. Elsewhere, however, the cloth trade atrophied (the merchant adventurers lost their Stade mart in 1597 in retaliation for English interdiction of the Hanse Towns' Spanish trade), the outports' overseas traffic decayed, and a series of bad harvests from 1594 – disastrously so in 1597 and 1598, years in which plague returned to almost every major English town – hugely inflated the cost of subsistence as rural wages plummeted.[19] Had it not been for hurried imports of large quantities of Danzig rye to ease the plight of the poor (a cereal that even hungry Englishmen ate with strong reservations), an increasingly weary government would have faced widespread social unrest upon a scale not seen in half a century. Meanwhile, Englishmen watched with increasing irritation the rapid rise of Dutch seaborne power, particularly the burgeoning wealth the rebels derived, until 1595, from the vigorous exploitation of Spanish and Portuguese markets that England, in coming to the rebels' aid, had been denied for more than a decade.

The seemingly endless cost of maintaining large, often ineffectual armies in Ireland and the Low Countries exercised an enervating effect upon the nation. New subsidies were secured from parliament with greater difficulty than before; new men for service in the Netherlands and in the fleet were hardly secured at all.[20] Effectively bankrupted by its vast military commitments (and still awaiting repayment by the States-General of most of the funds committed to the Low Countries since 1585), Elizabeth's government went through the motions of waging a war from which it knew neither how to extract itself or steal a victory.[21] Tentative Anglo-Spanish peace negotiations, begun informally in 1598 in the cathartic (for Englishmen) aftermath of Vervins and resurrected by Archduke Albert in the following year, died ostensibly upon the insignificant matters of credentials, the precedence of its participants and mutual delusions regarding the extent of each other's war exhaustion.[22] From an English perspective, the nation had been in resistance to Spain for so long that the struggle had come to define the reign itself, making any proactive search for peace seem almost an assault upon the myth of the Queen's indomitability. Yet this was a myth that moved the hearts of her people much less now than it had a decade earlier. What was needed urgently was not further diplomatic initiative, but the death of the last human obstacle to envisaging a world without an Anglo-Spanish war.

That death, on 24 March 1603, closed the roll-call of the first rank of war casualties. Elizabeth's former brother-in-law, sometime-protector and eventual deadly enemy, Philip II, had been in his grave for more than four years, broken upon the wheel of a duty that no one man could ever have discharged adequately. By a month only, he had outlived William Cecil, first Lord Burghley – guiding political light of Elizabeth's regime and the only man with the authority to speak out for peace during the conflict's latter years. His sovereign, a woman who had treated him variously as an indispensable advisor, a trusted uncle and a dog during his long service to her, went to his bedside in his final days and spoon-fed him porridge. All his hawkish political colleagues had preceded him to the grave except the earl of Essex, who would soon fulfil Burghley's dire prophecy from the fifty-first psalm.[23] Walsingham and Leicester, the two most influential advocates of resistance to Philip's ambitions in the vital pre-war years, had fitted him with their indigestible bone and departed swiftly thereafter.[24] Francis Drake and John Hawkins, of all Elizabeth's common subjects the most adept confounders of the pretensions of *Inter Caetera* and Tordesillas, had been tempted back to the Panama Isthmus a last, fatal time in 1595. Their corpses remained there; grudging propitiations to the empire they had coveted in life.

Officially, the war ended on 19 August 1604 with the signing of the Treaty of London, though in fact the accession of James VI to the English throne a year earlier had brought an immediate suspension of official hostilities against Spanish territories and possessions. Philip III acknowledged the gesture promptly, allowing Catholic English merchants to trade openly in his ports once more. Some weeks later, even that confessional prerequisite was dropped, and an invitation lay open to the most vigorous persecutors of war against Spain to return to their former entrepôts and re-establish the venerable Anglo-Spanish trade.[25] Nottingham's 1605 embassy to Valladolid, to obtain the Spanish King's formal commitment to an already binding document, was the final, ceremonial act in closing the curtain upon a drama that had defined the history of a generation.

Like Medina Sidonia, his adversary during the 'War of 21 July', Nottingham had as yet many years of life before him, though recently he had suffered the triple bereavement of a wife, a queen and his main source of income: the tenth-share of proceeds from seized cargoes that, thanks to his new King's privateering prohibition, no longer poured into the Admiralty Court.[26] With his warrior's incentives gone, and the endemic corruption of the system over which he presided falling under increasing scrutiny, Nottingham had readily accepted the honour, and potential profit, of leading both the English peace commission during negotiations in London and the subsequent embassy to Spain. He did not, as far as is known, seek out or meet his old enemy during his latter employment.

To many, it seemed the peace that he and his fellow commissioners delivered after eighteen years of struggle and the occasional triumph offered little more than the *status quo ante* of the pre-war years. The Treaty of London, a product of months of painful negotiation, brought no major concessions from either side's now venerably entrenched positions. Spain, clinging to hopes of an unimaginable turn of fortune, would not, as yet, make peace with the Netherlander rebels, insisted that England's Catholics be given freedom of worship and demanded that her merchants and proto-colonists continue to be excluded from the New World markets over which Spain claimed exclusive rights of exploitation. The English response was that volunteers would continue to be allowed to serve in the States' armies (though direct English subsidies and military aid would cease, and Dutch forces be excluded from the 'cautionary towns'), that religious toleration was no more likely to be conceded in England than in Spain, and that no explicit commitment would be made regarding 'rights' granted by a bishop of Rome over a century earlier. Fears that the price of peace represented a betrayal either of England or Spain therefore proved empty, because the final treaty skirted almost every grievance that had brought them to war. Such undertakings that remained were treated by both parties as matters of aspiration rather than substance, and ignored accordingly. Depredations of English privateers sailing under Dutch commissions in the Caribbean (and, increasingly, the Mediterranean) continued to infuriate the Spanish government; but they could do little more than rely upon James's personal detestation of piracy to secure occasional redress. Englishmen, in turn, were angered by the Holy Office's renewed attentions to English merchants returning to Spain, and by retributions visited upon their compatriots in the Indies – precisely the same 'outrages' that had done much to fuel the Anglo-Spanish enmity.[27]

In the Netherlands, the recruitment of English volunteers into the States' armies was mirrored and exceeded by 'a strong and visible torrent' of English Catholics, now enjoying the legal right to flee their country's recusancy laws to serve Archduke Albert (an unanticipated corollary of James's attempt to find employment for his redundant troops).[28] Even the longed-for resumption of official trade proved disappointing. Antwerp, a shadow of its once-incomparable greatness, offered little temptation even to the more nostalgic English merchants; while those among their number hoping to resurrect the Anglo-Spanish trade as a profitable increment upon their burgeoning Mediterranean enterprises discovered that time had not stood still during the war years. The rise of a domestic cloth-making industry in wartime Spain had made English cloths much less attractive there than previously (ironically, the re-export of Spanish manufactured cloths would form a profitable element of England's overseas trade in the coming century), while Spaniards had come to regard French corn – at little more than half the price of its once-favoured English equivalent – as the logical supplement to their perennially inadequate harvests.[29]

*   *   *

Despite its inconclusive clashes, spluttering demise and unsatisfactory legacy, the Anglo-Spanish war was regarded as a defining episode by those who had lived beneath its shadow. To Englishmen, their nation's soul and identity – perhaps her very existence – had been preserved by their confounding of Philip II's strategy. Though the Spanish King had never quite seemed to decide whether he sought the compliance or obliteration of Elizabeth's regime, few in England – even among her Catholics – believed that anything other than their utter subjugation had been envisaged.[30] Without any sort of victory, larger ambitions to subordinate most of western Europe to Habsburg interests had been crushed by the appalling burden of financing at least one too many conflicts. In that sense, the late confrontation appeared not only to have been unavoidable but vital, and contemporary Englishmen's certainty on this point is readily understood. We need not wade too far into the mire of 'counter-history' to speculate that without the diversion of forces and resources demanded by his English war and the many irritations of its long prelude, Philip may have been able to gather sufficient resources to deal decisively with the Netherlander rebels. That victory, in turn, would have made the Catholic League's triumph in France significantly more likely. Without core political territories from which to resist the Counter-Reformation's onslaught, the formal organization of the Protestant faith in Europe west of the Rhine may have been extinguished in the longer term, or driven so far underground as to make any substantial recovery improbable. Upon that narrow logic alone, English resistance to Habsburg ambitions had achieved most of the principal objectives laid out by Cecil as long ago as 1569.

However, to identify a single strand of cause and effect in judging the merits of English strategy during the intervening years dismisses the complexity of the process that destroyed the old Anglo-Burgundian amity. All the above possibilities were seen by Englishmen to augur their own likely extinction; yet with equal relevance, one might ask to what extent the perceived dangers addressed by Cecil's objectives had been excited by English interventions. How far may many of Philip's 'aggressions' be regarded as defensive measures that spoke to his own fears? And how much did the worsening plight of England's Catholics – as legitimate a concern for the Spanish King as English fears for Protestant Netherlanders – provide a moral, even a humanitarian motive to buttress his more pragmatic objectives? All are fundamental questions that the victory of 1588 ensured would remain unasked by Englishmen. Their aims were just, their resistance vital; their victory was gifted by God as the manifest proof of His favour. Freedom – that curious, quasi-moral state appropriated by successive Anglo-Saxon regimes – had rung loudly at first peel. It was, and remains, a wilful perspective.

Philip II, to all but a handful of Englishmen, personified the evils of tyrannical rule. Yet unlike his father, Charles, who seemed to cast off the cares of government whenever he led an army, the Spanish King was not a natural warrior. Nor did he regard the physical extension of his power as necessarily desirable per se. Clearly, the remorseless, even pitiless manner in which he fulfilled often reluctant obligations would make that reluctance something of a moot point to his victims. But by the measure of his age, his actions in the Low Countries and France were largely legitimate responses to circumstance (as Elizabeth acknowledged, if tacitly, more than once). The first he initiated to restore civil order, his sovereign authority as overlord of the Seventeen Provinces and the 'true' religion whose sanctity he had sworn solemnly to uphold. He undertook the second to keep his most powerful enemy neutralized, to confine Protestant heresies north of the Pyrenees and to assist his co-religionists against opponents who were, at certain stages during the long French civil conflict, equally ready to contemplate the extermination of their enemy. Even his absorption of the Portuguese empire, which terrified Protestant and Catholic Europe almost equally, was hardly the manifestation of insatiable ambition proclaimed by his enemies. Philip's was certainly the strongest 'legitimate' claim to the throne of Portugal following the extinction of the native royal house; and if the wealth of her overseas possessions provided a baser lure, it was one at which every prince in Europe would have lunged, given the opportunity. These strategic commitments, moreover, brought costs as well as benefits. With the incremental drain upon resources they demanded, coupled with the distant but abiding prospect of a renewed confrontation with the Ottoman Empire, the Spanish King came to regard the opening of yet another front – against England – as necessary only after much equivocation. That process was driven largely by English ambitions, and the impact they had upon his patrimony.

These were not dynastic ambitions, however, which was Philip's enduring misapprehension. His diplomats and spies told him that the men who most vigorously assaulted his possessions and faith had powerful friends in the English Court, and this, undoubtedly, was true. But those 'friends' struggled to have their partialities enshrined in policy, until the increasing likelihood of a war with Spain (a peril for which they bore much responsibility) made prudent the adoption of more aggressive strategies. For many years, Elizabeth exercised a deadening influence upon any moves to encourage unnecessary confrontation. Her commitment to avoiding war was, in her mind, entirely consistent. When faced by the implications of Philip's outrage at English depredations at sea and subsidies to his rebellious subjects, she genuinely believed that her Habsburg cousin misjudged her own motives:

> The King of Spain doth challenge me to be the quarreller, and the beginner of all these wars; in which he doth me the greatest wrong that can be; for my conscience doth not accuse my thoughts, wherein I have

done him the least injury: but I am persuaded in my conscience, if he knew what I know, he himself would be sorry for the wrong that he hath done me.[31]

The Queen's misapprehension, in turn, was to believe that her sincerity in wishing to preserve peace was, or should have been, sufficient to absolve her complicity in those actions of her subjects that delivered anything but peace. Repeatedly, she lamented the passing of an ancient amity while turning a blind eye to events that largely ensured its passing, and her failure to appreciate this was bound up in a larger misconception. The Anglo-Spanish relationship had been built upon two mutual interests: containment of the threat from Valois France and the economic benefits derived from the 'Burgundian' trade. It may have survived the disappearance of both, but it could not withstand the collateral impact of the diffuse forces that extinguished them. Religion – the one issue upon which there could be no viable negotiation in the sixteenth century – provided the ground of contention upon which both parties staked their principal case and cause. Spiritual dissonances alone, however, may not have created sufficient momentum for war between England and Spain. Philip, unswerving in his personal orthodoxy (a 'personal' that encompassed the lives of all for whom his station made him responsible), nevertheless showed remarkably little appetite for ending England's apostasy until other factors intervened to justify a crusading enterprise. Absent the spiritual dimension (were that conceivable), the economic and political fluxes of the mid-sixteenth century would have made some degeneration of the Anglo-Spanish relationship almost inevitable. Yet the fatal element that turned non-amity into enmity is not so much to be found in the age's economic, political or even religious upheavals as in the inability of monarchs to understand the challenges they posed.

The revolt in the Low Countries – the most incendiary point of contact between the Elizabethan and Habsburg regimes – was nurtured in a confoundingly complex mix of spiritual ambitions and temporal grievances. Its resolution demanded either an overwhelming military victory by Philip (something Elizabeth seems to have hoped for at certain times prior to 1580, if only to rid the region of Spanish troops thereafter), or, impossibly, a mutual readiness to compromise on the part of its protagonists. The Spanish King's attempts to re-establish his authority over his Seventeen Provinces, hampered by English interventions, constituted the single most significant drain upon his resources, morale and personal health. Locked into a cycle of financial defaults and partial victories, the temptation to see a single, definable problem – England – as the key to unlocking his other shackles in north-western Europe became irresistible.

The English case is more convoluted. While Philip's autocratic hand lay upon every real or imagined Spanish provocation that brought war closer, Elizabeth was rarely able, or willing, to exercise a similar degree of initiative. The two unequivocally aggressive actions she authorized in 1585 – the West Indies raid and the despatch of an English army to the Netherlands – were immediate (perhaps hasty) responses to crises only partly of her making but wholly beyond her power to resolve. They were in no sense the first blows against the edifice of a power she wished to overthrow, much less replace. An English or British Empire was as yet the stuff of dreams of a very few of her subjects: dreams not shared in the least degree by their sovereign. As one whose very accession represented a minor miracle, Elizabeth had no strategic aims beyond dying in her bed and arranging the English succession to her own tastes. Indeed, she understood clearly that a strong Spain – strong enough, that is, to provide a continuing counter to French power – was very much in the interests of her regime and nation. Yet she was surrounded and advised by men whose sense of the inevitability of war with Spain predated by some years Philip's own determination to seek confrontation. The surrogate private resources that unavoidably supplemented those of Elizabeth's cash-strapped government also brought their own priorities, obliging policy to absorb, and sometimes even follow, agendas less pragmatic than her own. Effectively enfranchised, shifting coalitions of freebooters, would-be colonialists, mercantilist adventurers and militant Protestant radicals were indulged to a greater or lesser degree as the wider political temperature dictated. The implications of their actions often ensured that what Elizabeth intended as finesses upon more orthodox means of influencing the Spanish King proved fatally damaging to the policies she professed to follow.

With what they considered to be entirely defensive concerns, Elizabeth and Philip stumbled towards war, each regarding them self to be the innocent party. Neither realized – or, perhaps, was willing to accept – the extent to which circumstance and events, rather than policy, directed the other's actions. Partly, their blindness reflected the novelty of pressures to which they responded. Despite the strikingly dissimilar nature of their respective modes of government, both represented and upheld a late-medieval ideal of sovereignty in an age in which old ties of loyalty and self-interest were being splintered and reassembled in unfamiliar forms. The Spanish King's empire – its New World conquests apart – was a largely dynastic achievement whose disparate parochial bindings were unravelling. Stronger than purely social, economic and spiritual alignments (yet drawing strength from each), proto-nationalist pressures made Philip's efforts to preserve intact his portion of the Habsburg inheritance hugely problematic. The cost of his efforts fell most heavily upon the administrative cortex of that inheritance, Spain, a land whose increasingly atrophied economic processes and sparse natural resources were not nearly equal to the task. The foundations of her long decline, though not yet remotely discernible to contemporary Europeans, were laid during this enervating struggle to preserve dynastic glories.

Politically, Elizabeth governed a far more cohesive entity. During her long reign, however, it experienced a radical shift in how its individual elements regarded both themselves and the world around them. Obviously, while certain attitudes common to a majority of contemporary Englishmen can be identified, it would be futile to propose a single, all-inclusive template for the race. Even at the close of the reign, the Catholic 'old English' inhabitants of the Irish Pale would have considered themselves to share little of the experiences and attitudes of their Lancashire co-religionists; much less those of godly East Anglians, Welsh Marchers, West Country freebooters or the brashly self-conscious citizenry of London (who regarded anyone born outside her boundaries – Suffolker, Scot or Turk – as a 'stranger'). Then, as now, the minuscule physical geography of England harboured an astonishing diversity of social experience: sometimes receptive, but more often resistant, to outside influences. Travel could broaden both mind and experience for a peripatetic minority, but distances – physical and conceptual – were far greater in an age of bad roads, horse transport and no mass media of record. For every Englishman who stood upon the deck of a warship or marched towards Tilbury in 1588, intending to express his distaste for foreign tyranny in a practical manner, hundreds experienced the 'war' only in its collateral economic impact. Their villages and towns may never have entertained a Spaniard; their peculiar sense of self, of what was of concern to them, probably did not acquire more than a brief collective coherence in the face of successive invasion scares. Yet if the English experience was a vastly heterogeneous one, perceptions of what constituted the primary elements of 'Englishness' had been clarified significantly through the prism of a struggle that was thirty years in the making and required eighteen more thereafter to resolve. As the nature of that struggle was influenced by the evolution of social, economic and religious pressures, so they were etched in turn by the challenges it posed.

Some matters had affected almost all Englishmen, if in dissimilar ways. Elizabeth's reign commenced amid unprecedented expressions of self-doubt and vulnerability from a people who had only recently realized the full extent of their weakness. She, and they, inherited the still-unresolved problems of her father's political legacy – parlous finances, high inflation, an unfinished quasi-reformation and military exhaustion. She passed on much the same inheritance to her successor James, yet in the intervening half-century she had become Gloriana, the highest manifestation of her nation's will to greatness. That transformation was largely a psychological process, but some of its practical consequences were striking. Subsequent ages have marvelled at the half-century burst of creative genius that characterized the Elizabethan achievement, and how it propelled Englishmen to engage what, formerly, had been unfamiliar or feared:

> A thousand kingdoms will we seek from far,
> As many nations waste with civil war,
> Where the dishevel'd ghastly sea-nymph sings,
> Our well-rigg'd ships shall stretch their swelling wings,
> And drag their anchors through the sandy foam,
> About the world in ev'ry clime to roam.

Considered in themselves, the long-range voyages of merchants, raiders and would-be colonialists seeking to access, interlope upon or seize the traffic of exotic goods and treasure were the most palpable, and spectacular, tokens of advancement from the relatively insular preoccupations of the early Tudor age. In turn, however, they both influenced and were part of a wider expansion into unfamiliar worlds. At the turn of the century, burgeoning English interest and instruction in mathematics, astronomy and their applied disciplines – particularly the hydrographical sciences – were creating in London a 'school' to rival the venerable institutions of Seville and Lisbon. As John Davis boasted with justice in the preface of his (1607) *Seaman's Secrets*:

> I am fully perswaded that our Countrie is not inferiour to any for men of rare knowledge, singular explication, and exquisite execution of Artes Mathematicke, for what Strangers may be co(m)pared with M. Thomas Digges Esquire, our Countryman the great Archmastric, and for Theoreticall speculations to most cunning calculation, M. Dee and M. Thomas Heriotts are hardly to be matched: and for the mechanicall practises drawn from the Artes of Mathematicke, our Country doth yeelde man of principal excellencie, as M. Emery Mulleneux for the exquisite making of Globes bodies, and M. Nicholas Hellyar for the singularitie of portraiture haue the prayse of Europe, M. Baker for his skill and surpassing

grounded knowledge for the building of Ships advantageable to all purposes, hath not in any nation his equall.[32]

Davis might have noted also that English scientific instrument makers had come to produce some of the world's finest navigational and astronomical devices; that English metallurgists, considered to be third-rate in 1540, were by the closing years of the century so adept that many European states (including Spain) made great efforts to acquire ordnance forged in England.

The scientific representation of the widening English world had also been revolutionized. In 1540, the quayside rooms of Edward Gremell had been sacked at the Imperial envoy's request to preserve a Spanish chart of West Indian waters from the mischievous curiosity of Englishmen who knew little of the world's seas beyond their own 'Sleeve'. Three generations later, Iberian navigators who wished to broaden their own technical horizons sought out English charts. Gremell's compatriots now understood more regarding the effects of magnetic variation than any of their European neighbours, and one of them, Edward Wright, had recently solved the abiding problem of how to depict Mercator's projection upon a flat plot: a seminal development in the science of navigation.[33] That Englishmen should not under-esteem their own achievements, the literature of advancement had also expanded hugely in the latter years of Elizabeth's reign, culminating with the compendious second edition of Richard Hakluyt's *Principal Navigations . . . of the English Nation*. The world, laid newly bare, testified to English maritime vigour.

Yet the process had a darker side. Fuelling the engine that generated these many energies was an uncertainty regarding apparently timeless political, religious and economic norms that had mutated with bewildering speed. The anxieties encouraged by this flux were manifested, in their most extreme form, as a fear of extinction. A growing millenarian strand of English intellectual thought saw this as a final reckoning – 'the long day of mankind' approaching its evening.[34] To the less eschatologically minded, the darkness commenced somewhere across their Channel. Traditionally, the Englishman's distaste for foreigners had been little more than a symptom of his island parochialism, but growing engagement with a world from which his forefathers had retreated a century earlier awakened a more persistent, self-serving strand of chauvinism. What had been a self-conscious sense of otherness, of happy separation, became a precious, brittle object of increasingly malevolent foreign attention.

From the middle years of the sixteenth century, England – weakened by the long struggle to preserve a status it could not afford – had needed

Habsburg goodwill to neutralize the growing threat from Valois France. Yet the close engagement of Englishman and Spaniard during the period of Philip II's marriage to Mary Tudor excited rather than quelled fears that England's subjection was approaching. Once France, prostrated by her civil wars, ceased to provide a focus for English fears and antipathies, Spain stepped readily into the breach; wherever Englishmen looked for the means to attain some measure of parity with their more powerful neighbours, a Spaniard blocked the view. In the pursuit of lawful trade in Europe, English merchants increasingly fell foul of the Inquisition directly, or through the collateral impact of efforts to re-impose religious and civil conformity in Habsburg lands. In more distant regions, the barriers erected at Tordesillas more than half a century earlier denied their legitimate entry to the most promising alternative markets. As, in the early twentieth century, the German nation – strong, vital yet haunted by a nagging sense of inadequacy – would rationalize its own expansionary urges, many Elizabethan Englishmen convinced themselves that their nation could escape her humiliating role as a second-rank power only in confrontation.

Different preoccupations created different fears, and for many years this perception was not uniformly strong in English society. To its divines and their godly followers, the papacy remained the greater enemy: more consistently antagonistic to the Elizabethan regime than its mere instruments, the Valois and Habsburg dynasties. But England and Rome had no contiguous borders other than those of the soul. To the many Englishmen for whom the precise relationship of man and God was someone else's business to determine, the pope was a monster cast in the same die as the grotesqueries that adorned their cathedrals: malevolent, ill-willed, but the despoiler of the spiritual, not the physical self. Thus, as noted, their leaders' efforts to advertise the temporal threat of Catholicism per se were by no means immediately successful. Yet the theopathic nature of Philip II's kingship, and its implications for those whom Englishmen – however inaccurately – regarded as their fellow-travellers in God, increasingly made irrelevant the very real differences between papal and Spanish intentions.

This convergence of perceived threats to Englishmen's physical and spiritual safety did not in itself create 'identity', but its pressures helped to scour the channels into which their exceptionalism was already moving. Protected by the sea from the consequences of their actions upon and across it, they observed elsewhere the impact of extreme social, economic and religious disharmonies and comforted themselves that it was a peculiar fortune – God-given but enhanced by the innately superior qualities of their race –

to which they owed their preservation. One of the more striking products of this precarious detachment was the strengthening of a religious settlement that had often seemed likely to endure no longer than the regime that had conceived it. Vernacular gospels, prayer book and service gave the Englishman's relationship with God an insular, exclusive dimension; the possibility of a predestinate human fate rationalized and was seemingly validated by the earthly successes that popular prejudice – encouraged by government – held to be near-miraculous. With these happy underpinnings, a mass of contradictory form and practice, wedding pseudo-Catholic rites to aspirations of primitive purity, acquired a popular credibility. It did so not by reason of any intrinsic power to enthuse (like all compromises, it was intended to dampen immoderate feelings, not excite them), but because of its gradual identification as a central strand of the broader English resistance to alien mores. Few Englishmen could recite even one of the Thirty-Nine Articles that defined 'their' faith; almost all understood the innate superiority of their enlightened, superficially inclusive reformation to the doctrines propagated by inchoate anabaptistry or a degenerate Roman See.

Remarkably, English Catholics, their Coptic exile from an orthodox mainstream set in stone by the Anglo-Spanish enmity, were not entirely divorced from the same process. Bruised by the irreconcilable pressures of conscience and civic duty, and perennially burdened by the dark implications of their 'liberation' at foreign hands, their self-awareness as Catholics subtly modified in ways that pleased none of their tormentors. Even to those who managed to remain faithful to their rites, papal and Habsburg ambitions had become hardly less synonymous than to their Protestant compatriots: a revelation that accelerated the disengagement from a much-mourned but irrecoverable past. As Elizabeth came to the throne, re-connection with an ancient spiritual tradition seemed more than a possibility. When she departed it, leaders of the English Catholic community – the 'Appellants' – were attempting to rationalize a definitive separation of their political and spiritual loyalties in order to secure a sustainable future for Catholicism in Protestant England. In *extremis*, direct resistance to Roman diktat was regarded even by the most orthodox among the English Catholic hierarchy as a necessary evil if compliance required political dissent.[35]

The appropriation, or nationalization, of spiritual identity was not a peculiarly English phenomenon, but for Englishmen the process, coinciding with the period of Spain's seemingly remorseless advance towards European hegemony, provided ample moral justifications for expansionist impulses that were already pronounced. By the mid-1580s, they had come to regard themselves as the vanguard of resistance to the temporal and spiritual ambitions of Philip II. They defined their role as a righteous one: a struggle to preserve the integrity of the state, their legitimate interests, their own, true religion. When, on the eve of battle in 1588, Sir Henry Seymour spoke of 'lyttel [England's] great discovered strength', he referred ostensibly to her armed forces; yet in a deeper sense he spoke also of a consensus forged by this process. With the certainties it encouraged (and no matter how infinitely varied the 'English' perceptions that underlaid them), the conflict that ensued bore a modern face. This was a war for different ideals of civilization, for the preservation of the self.

In an autocratic age, Crown and Parliament established the bounds within which this process took place, but it was not one over which political authority presided. To draw a line beneath the Elizabethan age is difficult, therefore, notwithstanding the tidy near-coincidence of the death of the queen who gave it a name and the end of the conflict that defined it. Despite the vast expansion of overseas trade and the establishment of the first permanent English New World settlements in the following decades, the preoccupations of Englishmen reverted, with the end of the war, largely to introspective issues. The impact of redefinitions of community and obligation, the enduring question of where the English Reformation should draw its final line, and the fundamental implications of these matters for the relationship between monarch and people: these were to be the overwhelming 'political' concerns of the coming half-century, not a proto-imperial mission that the Anglo-Spanish conflict had seemed to presage.

This realignment of English perspectives occurred with notable swiftness. To a contemporary observer, Spain appeared to represent no less vital a threat to European Protestantism than before, and nothing in the individual Spaniard's nature or philosophy became noticeably more agreeable to Englishmen after 1605. Yet apparently fundamental passions were muted with a decisiveness that only overwhelming victory and extinction of an enemy should have delivered. Protestant polemicists continued to revile the intact Habsburg-papal world-conspiracy; their more secular countrymen ceased swiftly, on the whole, to detest Spaniards for more than their Spanishness. Was the wearying pall of a long, indecisive war alone sufficient to extinguish the fears that government had cultivated so strenuously, or were other, contrary pressures working upon English minds?

In 1586, Sir Walter Ralegh, a would-be builder of empires and England's most articulate loather of Spaniards, had boasted to the earl of Leicester: 'Your Lordshipe doth well vnderstand my affection towards Spayn, and how

I have consumed the best part of my fortune hating the tirrannus sprosperety of that estate'.[36] Most of his compatriots would have appreciated his sacrifice, but it had at its core a paradox. Ralegh's own contact with the Spanish empire, like that of his travelling countrymen, had been glancing, and almost entirely predatory. He was not yet born when his elder half-brothers began their brief careers pillaging Spanish cargoes; he was an infant in 1554 when his father conveyed Sir Peter Carew and his fellow failed anti-Spanish Marriage plotters out of Marian England.[37] His own, personal survey of the 'estate' of Spain – discounting the occasional palace corridor encounter with ambassador Mendoza and members of his small entourage prior to 1584 – had been confined to the narrow, bloody shore at Smerwick in 1581, where he had co-directed the slaughter of a handful of her soldiers among a far greater number of Italians. The threat posed to the reformed religion by Philip II's ambitions was more palpable, its spectre raised often by other men – Walsingham, Drake and Hawkins – in justifying their own fears and hatred. But Ralegh, a man whose keen intellectual curiosity notoriously probed the very nature of the soul (and who was more than once accused of atheism by his enemies) held at most a dispassionate regard for his own religion. There is no reason to doubt the sincerity of his feelings for Spain, only their foundation in an abhorrence of her 'tyranny'.

Leading officers of state, deeply exercised, even obsessed, by the state of religion in England and its implications for the safety of the regime, saw the exercise of Spanish power as unswervingly inimical to English interests. Their voices, loudly condemning the Spaniard's 'cruel immanitie, contrarie to all naturall humanitie', his treatment of heretics, rebels and the indigenous peoples of the New World, had unequivocally laid out England's moral case for confrontation. Yet the manifesto was partial in both senses of the word. The same voices had nothing to say regarding the butchery of English seminary priests and 'traitors' to their own commonwealth that was not entirely appreciative, and if they lamented England's own experiment in human trafficking – Hawkins's slaving voyages – it was only for its premature termination by Spaniards. In a fearful, sanguinary age, tormented by the perennial prospect of political and social chaos, the iron-handed policies of Habsburg government and institutions were not in themselves peculiarly objectionable. Spain's 'sprosperety', in contrast, whether of specie or political and military power, was something that Ralegh's countrymen resented in a nakedly covetous manner, whatever qualities tainted it. It was, for all its plundered provenance, the prize that most emphasized the divergent fortunes of England and Spain over the past century: it was the golden measure, to many Englishmen, of their own inadequacy.

Even at moments of extreme crisis, when expressing their contempt of perceived Spanish degeneracies most volubly, Elizabeth's subjects could not throw off the profound sense of inferiority they experienced when beholding the awesome Habsburg achievement. This was not merely a matter of temporal power per se – of colonies, armies or plate fleets. Their self-belief, however brash, was tested constantly by the knowledge that their society was as much in thrall to fashionable Spanish influences as Plantagenet England had been to those of France. As Ben Jonson would remind his compatriots in the new century:

> Aske from your Courtier, to your Innes of Court-man,
> To your mere Millaner; They will tell you all
> Your Spanish Iennet is the best Horse. Your Spanish
> Stoupe is the best Garbe. Your Spanish Beard
> Is the best Cut. Your Spanish Ruffes are the best
> Weare. Your Spanish Pauin the best Daunce.
> Your Spanish titillation in a Gloue
> The best Perfume. And, for your Spanish Pike,
> And Spanish Blade, let your poore Captaine speake.[38]

This cultural infection was not a collateral product of the new peace. It had survived and strengthened during a struggle spanning almost two generations: a struggle, in the opinion of many of its protagonists, for the very soul of England. To appreciate its pervasiveness one needs only to examine the portrait of the delegates to the Somerset House peace conference of 1604, in which six Habsburg notables face their five English counterparts (including Nottingham, Northampton and Sir Robert Cecil).[39] In the manner of their dress, ornament and deportment, we seem to be witnessing the deliberations of eleven high-born Spaniards.

As noted, frictions and prejudices persisted. The 'Black Legend' of alleged Spanish depravities did not die with peace; indeed, it re-grouped and even strengthened in the decades that followed, nurtured in part by continuing sources of Anglo-Spanish friction at a political level. Vitally, however, the victory of 1588 had cast the Habsburg colossus in a less fearful light. What Drake and his generation of freebooters already knew of the weaknesses in the fabric of Spanish power became evident, in the after-glow of that deliverance, to a nation that had absorbed years of scaremongering from its leaders. Thereafter, a seemingly invincible and remorseless enemy became palpably human once more; crises subsided, grievances became more habitually borne wounds and hatred of the apochryphal 'Spaniard' subsided to much the same scornful condescension that Englishmen bestowed upon any foreigner. As early as 1595, when the end of the war was not yet remotely in sight, Thomas Nashe's *Pierce Pennilesse* had discerned the gap between imperial pretensions and reality and dismissed this once-ogre as merely 'a Bragart in his mother's womb'. It seems hardly more damning an opinion than he held of the Frenchman ('wholly compact of deceiveable courtship, and for the most part loves none but himselfe and his pleasure'), Danes ('an arrogant asseheaded people, that naturally hate learning & all them that love it . . . burstenbellied sots') or the entire Italian peninsula ('the Academie of man-slaughter, the sporting place of Murther, the Apoticaries shop of poyson for all nations').[40] Meanwhile, his compatriots in the import trade, many of whom had been famously offended by the embargo of May 1585, quietly resurrected their highly profitable Anglo-Spanish businesses during the 1590s, adopting unconvincing Irish or Scottish accents and Celtic flags of convenience to safely visit their old haunts in Andalusia and Galicia. Some – the Catholics among them – had never left, nor ceased to traffic their wares northwards to a nation that loudly proclaimed its absolute resistance to Spain's 'tyranny' while eagerly absorbing all of its fruits.[41]

With fear of Hapsburg ambitions fading, and the benefits of engagement all too obvious, the only substantial motors of continuing English dislike of Spain in the following decades would be her perceived influence over the first two Stuart monarchs, her persistent but wishful assumption of the role of 'protector' of English Catholics via the diplomatic process (a tacit acknowledgement of the definitive victory of the Reformation in England) and the Spanish ambassador Gondomar's role in dragging Ralegh to the block – an episode that swiftly took its place in the pantheon of national grievances alongside the loss of Calais and 'betrayal' of San Juan de Ulúa. Sources of irritation, these intrusions were by no means sufficient to sustain the apocalyptic vision of England as a Habsburg vassal state. England and Spain would go to war again in 1625 and 1655, but these were little more than brief jostlings, entered into half-heartedly and prosecuted with similar vigour. By the early years of the restored Stuart monarchy, normal service had been resumed after a century-long hiatus, and Samuel Pepys could observe of himself and his fellow Londoners, if with great hyperbole, 'endeed, we do naturally all love the Spanish and hate the French'.[42] Nevertheless, in his journey from distant ally to epitome of human viciousness and prodigal return as the unwitting object of English 'love', the Spaniard had teased out at least one memorable characteristic of the English psyche. He had exposed the degree to which self-identity may be more about aversion than commonality.

Abbreviations

APC	*Acts of the Privy Council*
BL Add. MS	British Library, Additional Manuscripts
Cal. Patent Rolls	*Calendar of Patent Rolls*
Cal. SP Dom.	*Calendar of State Papers, Domestic series*
Cal. SP For.	*Calendar of State Papers, Foreign series*
Cal. SP Sp.	*Calendar of State Papers, Spanish series*
Cal. SP Venetian	*Calendar of State Papers, Venetian series*
EHR	*English Historical Review*
HMC	Historical Manuscripts Commission
LP Henry VIII	*Letters and Papers, Foreign and Domestic, of the reign of Henry VIII*
MM	*Mariners Mirror*
PRO SP	Public Record Office, State Papers

Notes

INTRODUCTION

1. The soldier-pope, formerly Giuliano della Revere. A declared enemy of the Borgias, he spent much of Alexander VI's pontificate in exile in France or in hiding in Italy. Their papacies were separated by the twenty-six-day reign of Pius III, Francesco Todeschini.
2. Sir Thomas Smith, *De Republica Anglorum* (1583), p. 85.

CHAPTER ONE

1. The (very probably apocryphal) encounter of delegates journeying to the treaty town of Tordesillas in 1494, recounted by Hakluyt, *Discourse of Western Planting*, pp. 106–7.
2. Robert Thorne to the English ambassador at Seville, Edward Lee (1527), on the commodities of the New World; Hakluyt, *Divers Voyages*, p. 27.
3. Details of the *Barbara's* voyage are derived from depositions made by three members of her crew (PRO HCA 1 (Oyer and Terminer) bundle 33). These were reproduced in Marsden, 'Voyage of the Barbara'.
4. Only two years earlier, Bristol merchants had been the first Englishmen granted rights to trade directly with the Canaries (Haring, *Trade and Navigation between Spain and the Indies*, p. 19).
5. Ewen, 'Organized Piracy', p. 31.
6. *LP Henry VIII*, XVI (ii), no. 487.
7. Ramsay, *Queen's Merchants*, p. 3; Ramsay, *City of London*, p. 3; Shillington and Chapman, *Commercial Relations of England and Portugal*, p. 130.
8. Compare Connell-Smith, *Forerunners of Drake*, pp. 104–126, *passim*. The claim that an Englishman was executed (PRO SP/1/124, 252) was made by Hugh Tipton, one of the more fortunate victims of the Inquisition, and cannot be substantiated.
9. Halle (*Union*, Henry VIII, f. 256) details the arraignment, condemnation and burning of three men at Windsor in 1539 for proposing that the sacrament of communion was no more than a commemorative symbol of the dissemination of God's Word. A fourth

man accused, John Marbecke ('a syngynge manne') recanted and was reprieved. On other persecutions, see Elton, *England under the Tudors*, p. 194.

10. An English voyage to Santo Domingo, Hispaniola in 1527 predated that of the *Barbara*, but details of its mission are few. In depositions subsequently given by local witnesses (who appear to have been 'led' blatantly by their examiners), it was said that some of the English crewmen had made a foray inland to steal food from an estate. This alleged incident apart, the Englishmen had been doing nothing more than attempting to barter a few English cloths for victuals to sustain them when the warden of the fortress at Santo Domingo opened fire upon their ship. Their technical infringement of the Spanish Crown's monopoly, though irrelevant in scale and intent, had counted for more than any overt act of brigandage (all extant references to the voyage reproduced in Wright, *English Voyages to the Caribbean*, pp. 1–5, 29–59, *passim*).

11. Evidence for all of these voyages is scanty. Hakluyt (*Principal Navigations*, XI, pp. 23–5) is the sole authority both for the Southampton adventurers and Hawkins's Brazil voyages, and, writing half a century later, must have utilized second- or third-hand sources. Documentary evidence for the *Paul's* 1540 voyage consists solely of ambiguous Plymouth customs records (reproduced in Williamson, *Sir John Hawkins*, pp. 13–14) relating to goods she shipped in that year.

CHAPTER TWO

1. Hakluyt, *Discourse of Western Planting*, p. 28.

2. These were the most common sixteenth-century terms for the breed. As in his previous discussions, the author would emphasize that the anachronistic term 'privateer' (in general use only from the seventeenth century) is employed for want of a universally understood contemporary equivalent.

3. Marsden, *Law and Custom of the Sea*, I, pp. 13, 19.

4. *Ibid.*, pp. 31–5. In fact, this amnesty provided that at least one of the malefactors should regard it as a stay of judgement only, and that 'if any wish to sue him for the death and robbery aforesaid', he would be obliged to face them upon his return from Gascony.

5. Compare the case of the ship *Mary Anne* (PRO HCA 13/5, 36 (25 November 1546)). Her Captain, William Rose, stopped a Spanish ship off Dursey Head and demanded 'whether the goodes laden in the sayde shippe were thers or Frenchemens'. Somewhat obligingly, the Spanish captain allegedly confessed immediately that half his cargo of wine (a favourite haul of English privateers) belonged to French owners, and was relieved of this. Half the spoils were sold off in Dingle, the remainder (some eight tuns of wine) retained for the comfort of their purloiners. The *Mary Anne*, presumably, was a happy vessel for some days thereafter.

6. English translation from French original reproduced in Marsden, *Law and Custom of the Sea*, I, pp. 54–5.

7. Ewen, 'Organized Piracy', p. 30.

8. Marsden, *Law and Custom of the Sea*, I, pp. 2, 136, 145; Wylie, *History of England under Henry IV*, I, pp. 379–9, *passim*; Pistono, 'Henry IV and the English Privateers', pp. 322–3.

9. Marsden, *Select Pleas*, I, p. xiv.

10. Oppenheim, *History of the Administration of the Royal Navy*, pp. 50–51.

11. F. C. Dietz, *English Public Finance*, 1485–1558, pp. 152–8 summarizes the parlous decay of royal finances between 1544 and 1547.

12. *LP Henry VIII*, XVII, no. 225; *LP Henry VIII*, XVIII, no. 276; *APC*, I, pp. 96, 123.

13. BL Harleian MS 424, f. 16. The manuscript's date has been incorrectly transcribed in Marsden (*Law and Custom of the Sea*, I, pp. 155) as the thirty-fifth (1543), rather than thirty-sixth regnal year.

14. Halle, *Union*, Henry VIII, f. 258.

15. Marsden, *Law and Custom of the Sea*, I, pp. 5, 35, 117; *Cal. Patent Rolls 1429–36*, pp. 511–12, 515.

16. In fact, the only previously issued general commission that came close to matching the indiscrimination of the 1544 proclamation was a policing action against a specified enemy. In 1398, Richard II authorized the inhabitants of all ports on the English east coast from Scarborough to Dover to equip vessels to chase and take pirates (*Cal. Patent Rolls 1396–9*, pp. 366–7).

17. F. C. Dietz, *English Public Finance, 1485–1558*, p. 155.

18. *LP Henry VIII*, xx (i), no. 922.

19. *Cal. SP Sp. 1545–6*, no. 2.

20. *Ibid.*, nos. 6, 8.

21. *Ibid.*, no. 7: 'The Flemings say that it would be more profitable for them if a state of open war existed than to continue long in this way; for in the case of war, either they would not sail at all, or they would provide for their protection: in any case they would escape this present miserable treatment' (modernized spelling).

22. Winchester, *Tudor Family Portrait*, p. 248 (modernized spelling).

23. A syndicate of Burgos merchants had shipped goods valued at 40,000 crowns to Southampton during 1543, where they had been stolen by local longboatmen. On 3 January 1545, three days before Charles's retaliatory embargo was declared, Chapuys and Van Der Delft informed the Emperor that the claims of the merchants had yet to reach an English court (*Cal. SP Sp. 1545–6*, no. 2).

24. On the Reneger 'incident', Connell-Smith (*Forerunners of Drake*, pp. 136–151, *passim*) is definitive.

25. *LP Henry VIII*, XVIII (i), 144.

26. *APC*, I, p. 212; *Cal. SP Sp. 1545–6*, nos 2, 48, 62, 83, 106.

27. *LP Henry VIII*, XXI (i), no. 563: 4 April 1546 (modernized spelling).

28. *APC*, I, pp. 383–4.

29. This raid, led by James Alday, James Logan and William Cooke, is discussed in detail in Connell-Smith, *Forerunners of Drake*, pp. 158–63.

30. *Cal. SP Sp. 1545–6*, nos 205, 231.

31. PRO HCA 24/13, 15: testimony of Martin Pérez Ubilla. See also p. 127.

32. *Cal. SP Sp. 1545–6*, nos. 220, 248; the report of impressments was made by the Imperial envoy Cornelius Scepperus to the President of the Flemish Council, Loys Scors, on 23 March 1546.

33. See *APC*, I, pp. 208, 244, 305. William Hawkins was perhaps the most famous of those ordered to make restitution of goods (in this case seized from the ships of a Spanish resident of Rouen), and suffered a brief term of imprisonment until he complied. Note, however, that Hawkin's seizure had contravened the terms of letters of marque secured by him early in 1543 which explicitly forbade assaults upon the possessions of the Emperor's Flemish and Spanish subjects (*LP Henry VIII*, XIX (ii), no. 340 (vi)). Had he sailed without bothering to secure a license, his offence presumably would have been lost within the grey, forgiving ambit of the (non-overriding) 1544 proclamation.

34. *APC*, I, pp. 436–7, 503–5, 529.
35. *Ibid.*, pp. 259–60.
36. *Cal. SP Sp. 1545–6*, nos 70, 106; *APC*, I, pp. 176, 211, 220, 233, 278, 307, 330, 352, 406, 434.
37. See *APC*, I, pp. 425, 540, 558–9: all are Council orders to English merchants to provide restitution to Spanish shipowners.
38. Howard to Burghley, 28 August 1588; PRO SP/12/215, 62.
39. See, for example, PRO HCA 24/13, 16: the case of the Spanish ship *Maria de Victoria*. She was intercepted off the coast of Flanders by eight English ships and ransacked. Testimony in the Admiralty Court from Sir Richard Roche, owner of part of the spoiled cargoes, indicated that the captains of two of the vessels – William Cooke and William Laggen – were themselves merchant factors.
40. Connell-Smith, *Forerunners of Drake*, p. 186.
41. PRO HCA 13/5, 3; PRO HCA 24/14, 34; *APC*, I, p. 265; *Cal. SP Sp. 1545–6*, no. 198: '. . . the cause of this is that the Lord Privy Seal has a share in the business, and stands in the way'. Willen (*John Russell*, p. 124) claims that Russell paid the money subsequently, but the sources she cites mention only the Council's judgement, not its implementation.
42. *APC*, I, p. 460; APC II, pp. 254–5. Items 27–31 of the articles of treason drawn up against Seymour relate to his various acts of piracy.
43. *Cal. SP Sp. 1545–6*, no. 301.

CHAPTER THREE

1. Hayward, *Life and Raigne of King Edward the Sixth*, p. 65.
2. The subject is vast and remains contentious. The author regards the following (in no particular order of merit, and setting aside many excellent articles and syntheses listed in the bibliography) to be among the more satisfying surveys of the period: Jordan, *Edward VI: The Young King* and *Edward VI: The Threshold of Power*; Beer, *Northumberland* and *Rebellion and Riot*; MacCulloch, *Tudor Church Militant*; Loach, *Parliament and the Crown in the Reign of Mary Tudor*; Loades, *The Reign of Mary Tudor*; and Mac-Caffrey, *The Shaping of the Elizabethan Regime*.
3. At her accession, Elizabeth inherited from her half-sister a relatively modest public finance debt of some £200,000, of which about £65,000 remained owing to lenders at Antwerp (F. C. Dietz, *English Public Finance, 1558–1641*, p. 7). The as-yet incalculable costs of final extraction from Mary's French war were not included in this figure.
4. See p. 28.
5. *APC*, II, p. 131.
6. PRO SP/10/4, 39; 7 August 1548.
7. *Cal. Patent Rolls, 1547–8*, p. 309; *1549–51*, p. 297.
8. PRO HCA 14/5, 288.
9. Stanford, 'The Raleghs take to the Sea', pp. 21, 23, 24–6. In 1547, John and George Ralegh, commanding two ships, had seized the *Concepcion* of Viana do Castelo, returning to Portugal from Ireland with a cargo of hides and Irish friezes. The *Concepcion*'s owners brought a case before the Admiralty Court to have the brothers' father Walter either produce his offspring (they were at sea, taking further prizes) or pay damages

towards a total claim of £1,100 (testimony reproduced in Marsden, *Select Pleas*, II, pp. 31–4).

10. *APC*, III, pp. 222, 230, 236, 245, 268, 361, 370; Marsden, *Law and Custom of the Sea*, I, p. 225; *Cal. SP Sp.*, *1550–52*, p. 269 (9 April 1557); *Cal. SP For. Edward VI*, pp. 615, 682. By the standards of his peers, Bethell appears to have been relatively incorrupt-ible, despite being imprisoned for some six weeks during 1554 upon suspicion of piracy (*APC*, V, pp. 99, 114). During a later conversation, William Hunnis, gentleman of the Chapel Royal, observed to him regarding a mooted voyage: 'I would be loath to spend my time fishing. I had rather go pirating'. Bethell (now a groom of the Wardrobe) retorted 'I will none such to go with me' (*Cal. SP Dom. Mary*, no. 340).

11. Pirates taken at Dover and Calais were executed there following a Council order of 26 August 1552, but many, if not all of these appear to have been Frenchmen. Another group from the West Country were executed in December of the same year (PRO SP/10/14, 66, 69; PRO SP/10/15, 72). These are the only known executions of pirates during Edward's reign.

12. *Cal. Patent Rolls 1548–9*, pp. 181–2.

13. *Cal. SP For. Edward VI*, pp. 270–1; *Cal. SP Sp. 1550–52* (3 July 1550).

14. Compare *Cal. Patent Rolls 1548–9*, p. 103; *Cal. Patent Rolls 1549–51*, pp. 296–8; *Cal. Patent Rolls 1550–53*, pp. 94–5, 103, 250–51.

15. Hakluyt, *Principal Navigations*, VI, pp. 136–7; Willian, *Studies*, pp. 95–101; Blake, *Europeans in West Africa, 1450–1560*, II, pp. 278–9.

16. Blake, *Europeans in West Africa*, II, pp. 311–14.

17. *APC*, V, pp. 162, 305, 315, 322, 348; Blake, *Europeans in West Africa*, II, pp. 354–5.

18. McDermott, *Martin Frobisher*, pp. 36–7. Even as Wyndham departed upon his first Guinea voyage, supplications were being made against him in the Admiralty Court by two Spaniards whose goods he had allegedly stolen (*APC*, IV, p. 328).

19. Rye, *England as Seen by Foreigners*, pp. 7, 78.

20. Not without reason, as he had little prior intention of accepting their limitations.

21. PRO SP/11/1, 20; PRO SP/11/2, 10. The query posed by Sir Ralph Horton to his workmen – of how they liked 'them [i.e., Spaniards] who will occupy their wives before their faces' (*Ibid.*, 2, 33) if facetious, nevertheless touched upon a widely shared concern.

22. The most detailed examinations of the English reaction to Mary's betrothal are those of Harbison (*Rival Ambassadors*, pp. 57–65) and Loades (*Reign of Mary Tudor*, pp. 110–39 *passim* and *Two Tudor Conspiracies*, pp. 12–19).

23. See Garrett, *Marian Exiles*, p. 33.

24. *Cal. SP For. Mary*, p. 244: Nicholas Wotton to Mary, 4 August 1556: 'these men brought nothing with them out of England, and were on such good credit with the people here that nobody would lend them one sous, and yet had they here found ships, which they had well manned and provisioned, and thus sail from French ports.' Peter Killigrew later admitted to his interrogators that his own vessel, the *Sacrett*, had been a reward for his energy and talents from the French King. He also testified that the Tremayne brothers (who fled to France following the collapse of Dudley's conspiracy) claimed to have six months' credit for board in Paris, but disliked the city and wished rather to go to the wars in Italy 'if there were anye' (PRO SP/11/9, 24). Another of the Dudley conspirators, 'Long John' Throckmorton, urged his fellows: 'We must flee the realm . . . I will find means that we have a house in France appointed us by the French King . . . where it shall be as safe as if we were at Jerusalem (*Cal. SP Dom. Mary*, no. 364).

25. *LP Henry VIII*, XXI (i), nos. 487, 591, 759, 783; PRO SP/10/9, 48.

26. *Cal. SP For. Mary*, p. 231; PRO SP/11/9, 13.

27. The first, dated 16 September 1556, was granted to a group of West Country mariners who had boarded and pillaged a French vessel at anchor in Falmouth harbour (*Cal. Patent Rolls 1555–7*, p. 517); the pardon was issued upon condition 'that they stand to right'.

28. PRO SP/11/9, 13, 25; *APC*, v, p. 308; Machyn, *Diary*, p. 111; *Cal. SP Venetian*, vi(i), 554. Killigrew's was one of four vessels that escaped initial capture, but was pursued and taken some days later.

29. PRO SP/11/11, 35; PRO SP/11/12, 70. In the case of Killigrew at least, an element of coercion may have encouraged his change of heart. Immediately following his capture, his brother Henry and several of his closest associates were imprisoned in the Tower and (reportedly) tortured. Killigrew's father offered compensation to all those who had suffered losses at his son's hands 'hoping thus more easily to obtain his pardon . . .' (*Cal. SP Venetian*, vi(i), 580).

30. Machyn, *Diary*, p. 131; Loades, *Reign of Queen Mary*, pp. 266–7; *Cal. SP. Venetian*, vi(i), 615. Upon at least one occasion during her reign, Elizabeth gave explicit instructions for captured pirates to be sorted into usable and expendable varieties (PRO SP/12/29, 23).

31. In 1554, for example, Flemish mariners in an Anglo-Imperial fleet patrolling the Channel in expectation of Philip's passage to England had been jostled by their English counterparts and openly mocked by England's new Lord Admiral, William Howard (Harbison, *Rival Ambassadors*, p. 187).

32. *Cal. SP Sp.*, xiii, 60.

33. Brigden, *London and the Reformation*, p. 556; PRO SP/11/2, 10(i). A 'cony' was a dupe, usually of the cuckolded variety.

34. Redworth, 'Matters Impertinent to Women', p. 601.

35. Nichols, *Chronicle of Queen Jane and . . . Mary*, pp. 81–2.

36. Harbison, *Rival Ambassadors*, pp. 197–8; *Cal. SP Sp. 1554–8*, p. 73 (Renard to Charles v, 13 October 1554): 'Since the King's return to town . . . the people of London have ceased to be as insolent as they formerly were . . . If the persistent rumour of the Queen's pregnancy is true, as it seems likely to be, there will be no more quarrels or disputes here . . .'

37. Hughes, *Reformation in England*, ii, p. 226.

38. *Cal. SP Sp. 1554–8*, p. 72.

39. Loades, *Two Tudor Conspiracies*, pp. 150–51.

40. On Stafford's project, see Loades, *Two Tudor Conspiracies*, pp. 186–7.

41. Compare the reports of the Venetian ambassador Michel Surian (*Cal. SP Venetian*, vi, pp. 1145–8; 8 June 1557: '. . . and what weighs more with them than anything else, is to see that all this is being done for benefit of aliens whom they detest, and most especially the Spaniards. They also perceive that these last are thus given an opportunity for making themselves absolute masters of the kingdom, as they seem to be doing, for the Queen is bent on nothing else, by reason of the great love she bears her husband . . .'

42. The seige and capture of the town of St Quentin by Philip's forces in July/August 1557; the war's only land campaign in which English forces participated.

43. Pollard, *Tudor Tracts*, p. 290. Only Hayward (*Annals*, p. 34), of all contemporary or near-contemporary commentators, offered a balanced view of Philip's efforts to recover Calais: 'King Phillip held himselfe obliged in honor to procure a restitutione of that towne, which, under his government, and principally in his cause and quarrell, was lost (but) the French were unwilling to receive that people to any footing in France whoe had soe roughly overtrampled all ther country before.'

44. PRO SP/12/266, 3.

45. Foxe, *Ecclesiastical History*, II, p. 2296 (reproduced in Pollard, *Tudor Tracts*, p. 332; modernized spelling): 'from the first beginning of Queen Mary's reign, wherein so many men, women, and children were burned; many imprisoned, and in prisons starved, divers exiled, some spoiled of goods and possessions, a great number driven from house and home, so many weeping eyes, so many sobbing hearts, so many children made fatherless, so many fathers bereft of their wives and children, so many vexed in conscience, and divers against conscience constrained to recant, and, in conclusion, never a good man in all the realm but suffered something during all this time of this bloody persecution'.

46. On the personal motives of Wyatt and his co-conspirator Robert Rudstone, see the deposition of Anthony Norton (PRO SP/11/3, 18(i)).

47. Garrett (*Marian Exiles*, p. 32) identified 788 named English men, women and children who fled to Germany or France. The figure is almost certainly incomplete, but there is no way of finding a more accurate figure. Foxe, who had no reason to understate his calculations, listed a total of 273 men and women who suffered death for their religious convictions during Mary's reign.

48. BL Add. MS 43827, f.14. The account is that of Rose Hickman, who managed to flee England some months after her husband and survived to live well into the seventeenth century. Before her own escape, she was obliged to have her new-born child baptised in the Catholic rite: 'but bicause I woulde avoide the popish stuff as much as I could, I did not put salt into the hankerchief that was to be delivered to the preist at the baptisme, but put sugar in it instead of salt'.

49. Hickman was and remained a leading importer of sugar from the Canaries; Lok and his siblings maintained a factor in Seville (during the Marian interlude this was their own, youngest brother, Michael).

50. See Kingsford, *Two London Chronicles*, pp. 40–41.

51. *APC*, VI, p. 179 (notice of an affray between Englishmen and Spaniards at Dartmouth), 303 ('touching a complaynte . . . by certain Spanyardes evyll intreated by the inhabytauntes of Plymouth').

CHAPTER FOUR

1. From the (somewhat overwrought) sermon of John Duport at St Paul's Cross, 17 November 1590; reproduced in Maclure, *St Paul's Cross Sermons*, pp. 70, 217.

2. It should be recalled of course that both Edward VI and Mary had introduced their own over-riding statutes to prevent their immediate, 'heretical' successor sibling from inheriting the throne. Neither instrument was regarded as legitimate by the vast majority of Englishmen; neither survived the reign of their respective authors by more than a few days.

3. Reproduced in Neale, *Elizabeth I and her Parliaments 1559–1581*, p. 35 (modernized spelling).

4. See *ibid.*, pp. 69–75, and MacCaffrey (*Shaping of the Elizabethan Regime*, pp. 59–61) for the traditionalist view that Elizabeth was obliged to follow, rather than lead, her more radical Protestant parliamentarians. More recently, it has been argued that the form of the Act was essentially that which the Queen had intended from the start, though with some compromises to the more conservative Lords to limit the powers of the newly provided Commission for Ecclesiastical Causes (Jones, 'Elizabeth's First Year', pp. 30–45, 52–3).

5. On the latter group, see Haigh's 'unthinking Christians' (*English Reformations*, p. 285).

6. Strype, *Ecclesiastical Memorials* (1822 ed.), II (ii), p. 464. During Henry VIII's declining years, Paget managed the considerable feat of maintaining the friendship of bishop Gardiner and his conservative colleagues even as he forged a close alliance with Hertford and Lisle. A relatively recent judgement on his spirituality (Gammon, *Statesman and Schemer*, p. 118) concludes: '(his) religious views were a mystery to many of his contemporaries, and are as difficult to define now as then'.

7. In 1550, John Burcher had simultaneously discerned both the revival of 'the simple truth' in England and a lack of true conviction (in other words, backsliding) among many of her gospellers (Robinson, *Zurich Letters*, II, p. 672)

8. Ramsey, *Tudor Economic Problems*, p. 116; Slack, *Impact of Plague*, p. 62. While more deaths occurred during the more famous 'Great Plague' of 1665, a greater percentage of London's population is thought to have died in the earlier outbreak.

9. Camden, *Annales*, p. 10.

10. Hayward, *Annals*, pp. 1–2: 'For every man's mynd was then travayled with a strange confusione of conceits, all things being immoderately eyther dreaded or desired. Every report was greedily both inquired and received, all truthes suspected, diverse tales beleeved, many improbable conjectures hatched and nourished. Invasione of straungeres, civill dissentione, the doubtfull dispositione of the succeeding Prince, were cast in every man's conceite as present perills; but noe man did buysy his witts in contriving remedyes . . . Generally, the rich were fearefull, the wise carefull, the honestly disposed doubtfull, the discontented and the desperate, and all such whose desires were both immoderate and evill, joyfull, as wishing trouble, the gate of spoyle.'

11. PRO SP/12/1/9; *Cal. SP For. 1558–9*, no. 422 (Mason to Cecil, 18 March 1559).

12. HMC Salisbury MSS, I, pp. 149–150.

13. *Ibid.*, p.151. Count Feria, the Spanish ambassador to England, put it slightly differently to Sir Thomas Chaloner, if no less effectively. Feria, reported Chaloner, predicted that England 'wold be another Millanne to sett the princes together by the eares', being 'without money, men, armor, fortresses, practise in warr, or good captaines' (BL Cotton MSS Galba C I, f. 39; 3 August 1559).

14. *Cal. SP Sp. 1558–1567*, nos 2, 5.

15. For Winter's (still under-valued) achievement, see Glasgow, 'The Navy in the First Elizabethan Undeclared War, 1559–1560', pp. 27–33, *passim*.

16. Glasgow, 'The Navy in the Le Havre Expedition, 1562–4', p. 281.

17. Elliott, *Imperial Spain*, pp. 222–5; Kamen, *Philip II*, p. 88.

18. See Cecil's frank comments to an unknown correspondent (the document is incomplete), dated 11 October 1562: '. . . you shall well understand the cawses of her Majestie's doings, as the same may be avowed to the world; and of all these two principally, – one to stay the Duke of Guise, as our sworne enemy, from his singular superioritie, th'other to procure us the restitution of Callice, or something to countervale it' (BL Cotton MSS Vespasian C VII, f. 224).

19. The origins of the 'Dutch' revolt have been examined exhaustively, and are mentioned only briefly here in setting the context of one element of subsequent Anglo-Spanish relations. Among the more useful English-language works on the subject are Parker, *The Dutch Revolt*; Wilson, *Queen Elizabeth and the Netherlands* (though this is strongly biased in favour of Wilson's hero, William of Orange); and Geyl, *Revolt of the Netherlands*.

20. Geyl, *Revolt of the Netherlands*, pp. 70, 75–6; Parker, *The Dutch Revolt*, pp. 53–6.

21. Her subjects were similarly unenthusiastic. In Colchester, for example, where a con-

scious policy of settling Calvinist refugees reinvigorated a moribund local economy, the godly elite eventually fell at odds with their less welcoming neighbours who regarded 'strangers' of whatever religious loyalties as undesirable aliens (Higgs, *Godliness and Governance*, pp. 279–80, 335).

22. *Cal. SP For. 1558–9*, no. 5: point four in Cecil's 'memorial of things to be done': 'Thomas Gresham's matters. Bonds'.

23. Ramsay, *City of London*, pp. 151, 153.

24. Hughes and Larkin, *Proclamations*, II, pp. 79, 100–01. The June 1557 proclamation required no prior legal examination to secure a commission, nor the subsequent payment of any portion of prize monies and wares to the Admiralty.

25. PRO SP/12/29, 23.

26. *Cal. SP Sp. 1558–1567*, nos 28–9, 39, 56; Machyn, *Diary*, p. 212 (22 September 1559).

27. Glasgow, 'The Navy in the Le Havre Expedition, 1562–4', pp. 284–5.

28. Hughes and Larkin, *Proclamations*, II, pp. 227–8.

29. BL Harleian MS 169, f. 12b; *Cal. SP For. 1558–9*, nos 185, 1203, 1404.

30. BL Cotton MSS Vespasian C VII, f. 133.

31. *Cal. SP For. 1561–2*, no. 877 (9 February 1562). On the same day Chaloner wrote to Sir John Mason, suggesting that the seven years he had previously spent in Flanders was lighter punishment than the seven months he had spent to date in Spain (*ibid.*, n. 878).

32. See, p. 10

33. Read, *Cecil and Elizabeth*, p. 289.

34. *Cal. SP. For. 1563*, nos 1465 (Hugh Tipton to Chaloner, 8 December), 1525 (Robert Hanley to Chaloner, 21 December). Both Tipton and Hanley commented upon the 'cruel usage' of the Englishmen.

35. *Cal. SP For. 1564–5*, no. 67: Chaloner to the Queen, 20 January 1564. He claimed that thirty English ships and a thousand mariners had been taken, and that he was attempting to have the latter conveyed to a 'more courteous prison'.

36. *APC*, VII, pp. 129–30.

37. Ramsay, *City of London*, p. 134.

38. BL Cotton MS Titus B XIII, f. 99.

39. Kervyn de Lettenhove and Gilliodts van Severen, *Relations Politiques*, III, pp. 297–9.

40. PRO SP/12/33, 21, 8 March 1564.

41. Ramsay, *City of London*, pp. 199, 201–3.

42. At the fall of Calais, the English Merchants of the Staple had transferred the seat of their business to Bruges, which further concentrated an already preponderant demand for their wool into Flemish hands.

43. For the proclamation (23 March 1564) imposing the embargo, see Hughes and Larkin, *Proclamations*, II, pp. 247–9. It noted that Antwerp merchants had attempted to bypass their own Regent's embargo by coming to London and lading English cloths in their own vessels.

44. Admittedly, there was an element of necessity in Elizabeth's direct representation to the Regent. Following the death of the unloved Quadra in summer 1563, the post of Spanish envoy to London remained vacant for almost a year, so the usual direct channel of communication with Spain was moribund. Nevertheless, the time required to communicate with Philip via the Low Countries made the Queen's demand pointless, as she must have been aware.

45. *Cal. SP For. 1564–5*, no. 630 (Chaloner to the English merchants of St Sebastian, 22 August 1564); Patent Rolls 6 Eliz. C. 66/1017, 1757. In the instructions appointing him ambassador to Elizabeth's Court (English copy in *Cal. SP Sp. 1558–1567*, no. 244, 19 January 1564) Guzman de Silva's first priority upon reaching England was to make urgent

representations to Elizabeth 'that the English shall cease this course of robbery and violence so alien to the peace and friendship that exist between the Queen and us'.

CHAPTER FIVE

1. The opening proposition of Cecil's 'state of the realm' memorial of January 1569; Haynes, *Cecil Papers*, p. 579.
2. See p. 36.
3. The preceding discussion is drawn from Haring, *Trade and Navigation*, pp. 3–11, 21–45; Elliott, *Imperial Spain*, pp. 182–3; Oppenheim, *Naval Tracts of Sir William Monson*, II, pp. 310–22. Elliot (*Imperial Spain*, p. 179) points out that a further brief period of liberalization occurred in the 1520s, when, under pressure from his German bankers, Charles v granted the right of trade with the Indies to specified foreign merchants and, subsequently, to all of his subjects. However, these concessions were swiftly, and successfully, challenged by Charles's Castilian subjects.
4. Haring, *Trade and Navigation*, p. 115.
5. The present author will use the term *flota* generically, and distinguish only occasionally between the Terra Firme *galeones* and *flotas* of New Spain.
6. Andrews, *The Spanish Caribbean*, pp. 83–4.
7. Hakluyt, *Divers Voyages*, pp. 79–98; *Principal Navigations*, IX, pp. 82–99; Williamson, *Sir John Hawkins*, pp. 96–7. The occasion of the Queen's unconvincing claim was de Silva's audience with her of 30 March 1566, at which he informed her of Menendez's eradication of the French colony: 'The Queen seemed greatly pleased at the success of the voyage and asked me to thank your Majesty warmly for having informed her of it, as she was always pleased to receive good news from your Majesty. She marvelled greatly, however, that I should say that Florida had been discovered and taken possession of by your Majesty's subjects . . . if that were the case, she asked your Majesty's pardon for having thought of conquering it . . .' (*Cal. SP Sp. 1553–1567*, no. 347).
8. These were a private resource, designed, built and owned by Don Albaro de Bazán (first Marquis of Santa Cruz, Philip II's future 'Captain General of the Ocean Sea') and hired to the Crown (Kirsch, *The Galleon*, p. 7).
9. Hawkins allegedly told a Spanish Pilot, Juanes de Urquiza, that he had been 'knighted' by Philip in 1554, at a banquet given by the notables of Plymouth to celebrate the future king-consort's arrival in England (Wright, *English Voyages to the Caribbean*, p. 79, n.1).
10. By far the most comprehensive analysis of Hawkins's slaving voyages remains that of Williamson (*Sir John Hawkins*, pp. 78–202; *Hawkins of Plymouth*, pp. 42–156), though his narrative is coloured by entirely uncritical interpretations of Hawkins's character and motives. The best 'modern' discussion (dating from 1984) is that of Andrews, *Trade, Plunder and Settlement*, pp. 116–28.
11. Provisional list of adventurers: BL Lansdowne MSS 6, ff. 48–9.
12. F. C. Dietz, *English Public Finance*, II, p. 17.
13. BL Cotton MSS Galba, C I, f. 218: '. . . it were better to abstaine for a while from the Indian voyages, being but the desire and gaine of three or four men, then still to continue, and so give cause of breach of amity . . .'
14. *Cal. SP Sp. 1558–1567*, nos 316 (27 August 1565), 330 (5 November 1565), 344 (23 March 1566). In his latter despatch, de Silva implicitly identified a potential conspiracy: 'These people (Hawkins and his men) are so greedy that if great care be not taken they may do us much harm, particularly if they join with the French out there, for I do not

know which are the worst. I cannot understand what the French Ambassador is negotiating with the Queen; he has been with her twice in the last 12 days'.

15. The figure was provided by de Silva, in his 5 November 1565 despatch to Philip.

16. Drake's presence in a 'Hawkins' expedition was noted for the first time in this year;
but Kelsey (*Sir Francis Drake*, pp. 17, 18–19) assumes his participation in the first two
slaving voyages also.

17. Wright, *English Voyages to the Caribbean*, pp. 102–3, 113–14. Bontemps, by now an
enthusiastic slave trader also, habitually threatened his intended customers' towns with
fire and sword unless they dealt with him. A few months later, he sacked and burned
the settlement of Puerto de Plata in response to its citizens' unenterprising attitude.

18. *Cal. SP Sp. 1558–1567*, nos 388, 423, 432.

19. *Ibid.*, no. 442; BL Cotton MSS Otho, E VIII, f. 17.

20. The quoted judgement is Corbett's (*Drake and the Tudor Navy*, I, p. 116). Note also
the similar view of Williamson (*Sir John Hawkins*, pp. 188–92), which has been adopted
by many subsequent Anglo-Saxon commentators.

21. Shillington and Chapman, *Commercial Relations of England and Portugal*, p. 140.

22. Parker, *Dutch Revolt*, pp. 82, 94–9.

23. See, for example, Kervyn de Lettenhove and Gilliodts van Severen, *Relations Politiques*,
IV, pp. 479, 488–9; *Cal. SP Sp. 1558–1567*, nos 433, 436–7, 441.

24. The phrase was Gresham's (Kervyn de Lettenhove and Gilliodts van Severen, *Relations
Politiques*, IV, p. 353).

25. Ramsay, *Queen's Merchants*, p. 124.

26. Richard Clough to Gresham, 2 September (*Cal. SP. For. 1566–8*, no. 1663). However,
another of Gresham's agents, Thomas Dutton, reported some days later that Alba was
ruthless in punishing those of his men who committed individual acts of violence or
robbery, and that the people of Antwerp were generally contented with the restitution
of order (*ibid.*, no. 1672).

27. Ramsay, *Queen's Merchants*, pp. 73–5.

28. Following a brief truce, the third phase of the French civil wars commenced in
September 1568.

29. BL Cotton MSS Caligula, C I, f. 97: 'A memoriall of things to be considered upon the
Queen of Scottes coming into the Realme'.

30. Man, also Dean of Gloucester, was, as a married Protestant cleric of common bloodstock, thrice unwelcome in Spain. It was alleged by his enemies there (though not
proven) that he had referred to the pope as a 'canting little monk' (Bell, 'John Man',
p. 88).

31. There remains some confusion as to the precise value of the bullion (various estimates
place it between £80,000 and £150,000). The figure given here is that calculated by the
most competent authority, Sir Thomas Gresham, in the financial summary he provided
to Cecil on 23 May 1572 (PRO SP/70/123, 178).

32. Many years after the incident, Richard Hawkins implausibly calculated his father's losses
at San Juan de Ulúa to have exceeded £100,000 (HMC Salisbury MSS, XVI, p. 145).

33. Word of Alba's embargo reached London on 3 January 1569, according to a memorandum drafted by Cecil two weeks later (BL Cotton MSS Galba, C III, f. 158).

34. Kervyn de Lettenhove and Gilliodts van Severen, *Relations Politiques*, V, pp. 96–102;
Hughes and Larkin, *Proclamations*, II, no. 556, pp. 301–5.

35. F. C. Dietz, *English Public Finance*, II, pp. 25–6; PRO SP/12/77, 30 (Gresham to Cecil,
7 March 1571).

36. Ramsay, *Queen's Merchants*, pp. 96–7. See also Read's now venerable but valuable discussion of the episode (*Cecil and Elizabeth*, pp. 433–5).
37. Haynes, *Cecil Papers*, pp. 579–88.
38. *Cal. SP For. 1566–8*, nos 1722 (Richard Clough to Gresham, 28 September 1567), 1864 (Sir Henry Norreys to the Queen, 15 December 1567)
39. HMC Salisbury MSS, II, p. 249.
40. In fact, the conference had been convened to coordinate efforts against the Huguenots and (on Philip's part) to detach France from her Turkish alliance (Kamen, *Philip of Spain*, pp. 102–3). The position of England was not touched upon. Nevertheless, Thomas Randolphe, describing it to Cecil six months later as a confederacy 'to maintayne papistry throughout Christendome' (BL Cotton MSS Caligula, B x, f. 369) of which Mary Stuart was a party, clearly expressed what was already in England a widespread anticipation of a Catholic counter-assault.
41. His correspondence confirming this is summarized in Read, *Cecil and Elizabeth*, p. 435.
42. F. C. Dietz, *English Public Finance*, II, p. 25. A petition to Philip from merchants affected by her seizures (*Cal. SP Sp. 1568–1579*, no. 94) claimed that seventy ships with cargoes valued at three and a half million ducats had been detained in English ports.
43. Philip had heard rumours of English negotiations for an alliance with Protestant German princes by the end of February 1569, at which time he ordered de Spes to discover the truth of it: 'it will be a decided proof that she is my enemy' (*Cal. SP Sp. 1568–1579*, no. 85).
44. Hawkins's personal testimony of his voyage – *A true declaration of the troublesome voyadge of M. J. Hawkins to the partyes of Guynea and the west-Indies* – was published by Thomas Purfoote in 1569 and later reproduced by Hakluyt, *Principal Navigations*, x, pp. 64–74. The (January 1569) proclamation ordering the seizure of Spanish ships provided a protracted justification of the Queen's actions by reference to the puzzling actions of 'the king her good brother'.
45. This is de Spes's claim, made in at least two relations of the history of his embassy in England (*Cal. SP Sp. 1568–1579*, nos 301, 325). Châtillon continued to work industriously as a recruitment agent for the Huguenot fleet. In March 1571 he asked Lord Cobham, Warden of the Cinque Ports, to stay the execution of several convicted English pirates, held at Dover Castle, until he could have his pick of them (PRO SP/12/77, 31).
46. PRO SP/12/48, 33, 37; *Cal. SP Sp. 1568–1579*, no. 125.
47. *Ibid.*, nos 84, 125, 134, 137, 229.
48. Parker, *Grand Strategy of Philip II*, pp. 156–7; *Cal. SP Sp. 1568–1579*, no. 70.
49. On this quality in general, and its impact specifically upon the Ridolfi plot, see Parker, 'Messianic Vision of Philip II', *passim*.
50. *Cal. SP Sp. 1568–1579*, no. 80.
51. Wernham, *Before the Armada*, p. 313.
52. Hawkins's 'treacheries' are most recently discussed in Parker, 'Messianic Vision of Philip II', pp. 198–203, 217–19, who questions the more traditional view (most robustly set out by Williamson) that Hawkins was being entirely disingenuous in his offer to assist Philip.
53. BL Harleian MS 260, f. 17; Elizabeth to Walsingham, 11 February 1570.
54. On the development of Cecil's belief in, and fear of, the 'conspyration', see also Thorpe, 'William Cecil and the Antichrist', pp. 290–94.
55. Haynes, *Cecil Papers*, pp. 585–6.
56. Hibbert, *Virgin Queen*, p. 174.

57. Ramsay, *Queen's Merchants*, pp. 167, 169.

58. On the fleets, see English intelligences from the Low Countries: Kervyn de Lettenhove and Gilliodts van Severen, *Relations Politiques*, v, pp. 667–8, 689–791; vi, pp. 115, 128–9.

59. *Cal. SP For. 1572–4*, nos 1, 103; Croft, *Spanish Company*, p. ix.

60. De Spes had been expelled from England in December of the previous year when his involvement in the Ridolfi plot became known (though it was March 1572 before the authorities could finally prise him from English soil). De Guaras acted as unofficial envoy between England and the Low Countries until a new envoy was appointed, though his main efforts seem to have been devoted to clandestinely recruiting disaffected Englishmen for Alba's army (McDermott, Martin *Frobisher*, pp. 86–9).

61. Quote from *APC*, VIII, p. 44 (20 September 1571).

62. The debate on Elizabeth's motives in expelling the Sea Beggars has been joined variously by Williamson (*Sir John Hawkins*, pp. 265–7), Black ('Elizabeth, the Sea Beggars, and the Capture of Brielle': *EHR*, XLVI (1931), pp. 30–47), Read ('Queen Elizabeth's seizures of the duke of Alba's pay ships', Wernham (*Before the Armada*, pp. 317–19), Wilson (*Queen Elizabeth and the Netherlands*, p. 27) and Sutherland ('Queen Elizabeth, the Sea Beggars and Brille'; in *Princes, Politics and Religion, 1547–1589*, pp. 183–206). On the available evidence (and despite the assistance given subsequently to the Sea Beggars' campaign by English volunteers already present in the Low Countries), the present author concurs with the two latter authors' dismissal of any deliberate stratagem on the part of Elizabeth or Burghley to use the expulsion to resurrect the rebels' cause.

63. Strype, *Annals*, II (i), pp. 253–4.

64. PRO SP/12/105, 68. Holstocke's flagship was the *Swallow*, his old command when, as vice admiral, he served in William Winter's Scottish campaign of 1559/60 (Glasgow, 'The Navy in the First Elizabethan Undeclared War, 1559–60', p. 37).

65. Marsden, *Law and Custom of the Sea*, I, pp. 196–7. Clowes, *Royal Navy*, I, p. 480. In 1551, while commanding one of the King's pinnaces in a sweep against pirates in the North Sea, Holstocke and his colleague William Tyrell had been admonished by the Privy Council for their over-robust interpretation of their commission: '... it is informed that their folkes have so serched the maryners of the hoyes by them lately stayed that they have taken awaye their clothes, stripped them and made havock of their biere, &c. ...' (*APC*, III, p. 361–2).

66. PRO SP/12/85, 57, 133–4; BL Lansdowne MS 13, ff. 129–30; McDermott, *Frobisher*, pp. 74–7.

67. Andrews, *Drake's Voyages*, p. 35.

68. Sir Roger Williams, *The Actions of the Low Countries*, p. 57; *Cal. SP Sp. 1568–1579*, nos 323, 339.

69. Murdin, *Cecil Papers*, II, p. 221.

70. Kervyn de Lettenhove and Gilliodts van Severen, *Relations Politiques*, vi, p. 485; *Cal. SP For., 1572–1574*, no. 491: The English troops arrived before Flushing on 10 July. Gilbert immediately charged the local governor with 'evil-meaning', claiming that he harboured 500–600 Frenchmen, and threatened to storm the town. Having been mollified by an agreement to garrison the town with an equal number of French and English troops, Gilbert marched off his remaining men to Ordenberg on 17 July.

71. Kervyn de Lettenhove and Gilliodts van Severen, *Relations Politiques*, vi, p. 421.

72. BL Lansdowne MS 15, f. 41. The question of a definitive solution to the problem of Mary Stuart had already been discussed at some length during the first session of Elizabeth's fourth Parliament (8 May–30 June 1572), when feelings regarding her com-

plicity in the Ridolfi plot were running high (speeches in Hartley, *Proceedings*, I, pp. 349–54, 393–4).

73. Read, *Walsingham*, I, pp. 221–2.
74. BL Add MS 48126, ff. 101–3.
75. English translation of Latin original (BL Stowe MS 177, ff. 64–80) reproduced in HMC, Salisbury MSS, II, p. 217. By its remarkably precise terms Philip's subjects were to be reimbursed to the amount of £100,076. 17s. 6d. (less expenses of £11,000) for losses suffered during the embargo; those of Elizabeth, £85,076 17s. 11d. (less £17,000).
76. Parker, *Grand Strategy of Philip II*, p. 164; MacCaffrey, *Queen Elizabeth and the Making of Policy*, pp. 193–4.
77. See below, p. 148. Two of the first 'raze-built' generation of galleons, the *Dreadnought* and *Swiftsure*, were constructed during 1573.

CHAPTER SIX

1. *England's Lamentation* (1584); a ballad on the late conspiracy of Francis Throckmorton; reproduced in Collier, *Broadside Black-letter Ballads*, pp. 21–8.
2. The author is aware that the following discussion largely ignores the entire left-wing of English dissent during these years. However, being only very rarely considered inimical to the security of the regime (though often criticized in the same breath as 'papists'), the activities of the more radical 'godly' or 'resolute' are not strictly relevant to this work.
3. William Fulke, chaplain to the earl of Leicester, quoted in Bauckham, *Tudor Apocalypse*, p. 133.
4. Rowlands, 'Hidden People', p. 10; Higgs, *Godliness and Governance*, p. 231; McGrath, 'Elizabethan Catholicism', pp. 415–28, *passim*; Palliser, 'Popular reactions to the Reformation', pp. 102–3.
5. The words were reported by a preacher complaining of the attitude of local (Lancashire) Catholics as late as 1602 (Haigh, *The English Reformation Revisited*, p. 183).
6. PRO SP/70/39, 60: 'The perills growing uppon (th)e overthrow of (th)e Prynce of Condees Cause' (20 July 1562).
7. *Cal. SP Dom. Eliz, addenda*, XV, 29. The earls of Northumberland and Westmorland (both of whom regarded themselves as effective monarchs in their lands) and the Dacre brothers had all suffered losses of authority or estate since Elizabeth's succession. All, as Catholics, hoped for better from Mary Stuart, should she be brought to the throne.
8. Sir George Bowes, who as Provost-Marshal took a leading role in suppressing the Rising, acknowledged that many present in the rebel army had been forcibly drafted (BL Cotton MSS Caligula, B IX, ff. 331–2: Bowes to Sussex, 17 November 1569).
9. HMC Salisbury MSS, I, pp. 450–51.
10. English translation of the bull in Hughes, *Reformation in England*, III, appendix V, pp. 418–20.
11. Strype, *Annals*, I (ii), pp. 371–2.
12. Hartley, *Proceedings*, I, p. 240. Aglionby argued not against the principle of compulsory attendance at prayer *per se*; but against the enforced taking of communion.
13. Trimble, *Catholic Laity*, p. 63; Sir Christopher Hatton to Parliament, 25 February 1587, quoted in Neale, *Elizabeth I and her Parliaments, 1584–1601*, p. 173.
14. Pollard (*Political History of England, 1547–1603*, p. 277) disagreed. He regarded the

Rising as a greater threat to the regime than the events of 1588. This may have been the perception of Elizabeth's government; but any comprehensive analysis of the events of 1569 – particularly regarding the likelihood or possibility of Alba's assistance to the rebels – must lead us to conclude that the Rising had no chance of success.

15. Hartley, *Proceedings*, ii, pp. 95, 97, 152–7. The deaths of fourteen of these unfortunates, executed on 28 and 30 August 1588, were recalled for general edification in the ballad *A warning to all false Traitors* (printed by Edward Allde 'at the long shop near vnto S. Mildred's Church'): Collier, *Broadside Black-letter Ballads*, pp. 57–62.

16. George Gifford published a diatribe in 1582 – *A Dialogue between a Papist and a Protestant* – which first named the breed of statutorily compliant Catholic in an apochryphal conversation between a 'Professor of the Gospel' and a 'Papist': '. . . there are Papists which will not come at the Churche: and there are Papistes which can keepe their conscience to themselves, and yet goe to Church: of ths latter sorte it seemeth you are: because ye goe to the Church' (reproduced in Walsham, *Church Papists*, p. 1).

17. On the failure of missionary activity to redirect Catholic loyalties, see Haigh, *The Reign of Elizabeth I*, pp. 202–4.

18. 'The Lord-Treasurer Burleigh's Advice to Queen Elisabeth in Matters of State and Religion', reproduced (with modernized spelling) in Malham, *Harleian Miscellany*, ii, p. 279.

19. Collinson, *Letters of Thomas Wood*, p. 16; Robinson, *Zurich Letters*, p. 5.

20. *Countrie Divinitie*, A2v–3r; quoted in Walsham, *Church Papists*, p. 106.

21. Wiener, 'Beleaguered Isle', p. 28.

22. The *Actes'* impact during the period of its earlier editions has, however, been much exaggerated by some commentators. See, for example, Haller, *Foxe's Book of Martyrs and the Elect Nation*, pp. 222–3; Wiener, 'Beleaguered Isle', p. 27. More recent commentaries have acknowledged among untutored contemporary Englishmen a persistent degree of indifference to Foxe's great work (see Loades, *John Foxe and the English Reformation*, p. 4; Felch, 'Shaping the Reader in the Acts and Monuments', p. 65; Usher, 'In a Time of Persecution', p. 250).

23. Arber, *Registers of the Company of Stationers*, i, p. xxxviii. On the linkage between printer and government, see Blagden, *Stationers' Company*, pp. 70–75.

24. Lilly, *Black-letter Ballads and Broadsides*, pp. 224–5.

25. *Ibid.*, p. 171.

26. *A dittie in the worthie praise of an high and mightie Prince* in *ibid.*, p. 236.

27. Malham, *Harleian Miscellany*, x, p. 272.

28. Lowers, *Mirror for Rebels*, pp. 36–7.

29. Metzger, 'Controversy and Correctness', p. 445.

30. *Ibid.*, pp. 38–9; Blayney, 'William Cecil and the Stationers', pp. 11–12, 27–30.

31. In 1571, Norton unsuccessfully attempted to append an addition to the Treasons Act which retrospectively excluded from the succession anyone who had ever challenged Elizabeth's right to the throne, and, moreover, to exclude their heirs also – a thinly veiled device intended to end any chance of a Stuart succession (Hartley, *Proceedings*, i, p. 212).

32. Some recent commentators have placed much emphasis on the 'mass' circulation of ballad sheets and other media, regarding the phenomenon as central to the growth of spiritual awareness. Watt (*Cheap Print and Popular Piety*, p. 12) suggests that some three to four million ballad sheets were in circulation in the second half of the sixteenth century, which would indeed constitute a profound penetration of an English society comprising only some four or five million people. The figure, however, is based not only upon the (reasonable) hypothesis that every one of the 3,000 or so ballads registered at Stationers' Hall over a fifty-year period received a print run of 1,000 to 1,500

copies, but also upon the (extremely unlikely) assumption that all or most subsequently survived the perils of natural wear and tear, fire, loss, indifferent reception and – the near-universal fate of cheap paper – sanitary usage.

33. *Anatomie of Abuses*, sig. T2r; Felch, 'Shaping the Reader in the Acts and Monuments', p. 65.

34. The words of the preacher Nicholas Robinson, quoted in Haweis, *Sketches*, pp. 161–2.

35. Haynes, *Cecil Papers*, p. 586. In its contemporary context, the term 'epicure' identified either a glutton, or, in this case, an agnostic or cynic.

36. See Thomas, *Religion and the Decline of Magic*, p. 191.

37. Higgs, *Godliness and Governance*, p. 220.

38. Thomas (*Religion and the Decline of Magic*, p. 204) refers to the period as 'the age of greatest religious indifference before the twentieth century', though perhaps he unfairly dismisses the competing claims of the eighteenth century.

39. Wiener ('Beleaguered Isle', pp. 37–8) disagrees, regarding the majority of contemporary Englishmen as already instinctively anti-Catholic. Yet all the voices she cites in support of this conclusion – Francis Hastings, John Fielde, Andrewe Willet, John Baxter and Robert Pricket – were virulently polemical Protestants who, with one exception, wrote at a time when England had been at war with Spain for more than a decade. That exception was John Fielde, whose (1581) *Caveat* knowingly repeated the lie that the papal bull of 1570 had been the engine for the Northern Rising that preceded it. Fielde himself was of course the exemplar of the group of extreme Protestant radicals whose beliefs and motives lay almost entirely outside the mainstream of contemporary English spiritual life.

40. Phillip Stubbes, *The Anatomie of Abuses*, sig. N3; John Audley, *A godly ditty or payer to be song vnto God for the preseruation of His Church, our Queene and Realme, against all traytours, Rebels, and papisticall enemies* (reproduced in Lilly, *Black-letter Ballads and Broadsides*, pp. 121–3).

41. BL Lansdowne MS 15, f. 48.

42. See Rowlands, 'Hidden People', p. 14; McClain, 'Without Church, Cathedral or Shrine', pp. 397–8; Leys, *Catholics in England*, pp. 33–4.

43. On 6 May 1586, Elizabeth regarded it necessary to issue a proclamation explaining the execution of two formerly reprieved priests, William Marsden and William Anderton (Hughes and Larkin, *Proclamations*, II, pp. 518–21). Having originally stressed that they would be prepared to die in the Queen's defence in the face of foreign invasion, and, moreover, promised not to proselytise but only keep to their own consciences, the Queen stayed their executions, 'her majesty minding nothing less than that any of her subjects, though disagreeing from her in religion, should die for the same.' Examined further, however, on what they would do or urge others to do if the pope invaded England, Anderton begged not to be asked to risk his life upon a hypothetical question (as 'in the meantime he may possibly be a Protestant and so then become of other opinion than he is now of'), while Marsden claimed that he would only pray 'that right may take place'. Both also denied that their former statements had included a promise not to attempt pastoral work. They were executed soon after.

44. 'Lord Treasurer Burleigh's advice to Queen Elisabeth in Matters of Religion and State', in Malham, *Harleian Miscellany*, II, p. 279.

45. Morey, *Catholic Subjects of Elizabeth I*, p. 194; Read, 'William Cecil and Elizabethan Public Relations', pp. 36–8; Malham, *Harleian Miscellany*, I, p. 515: 'that very Campion, I say, before the conference had with him by learned men in the Tower, wherein he was charitably vsed, was neuer so racked, but that he was presently able to walke, and

to write . . .'. The author of this short piece, entitled 'A Declaration of the favourable dealings of Her Majesty's Commissioners, etc' is not known. Read (*Lord Burghley*, p. 566 n. 75) suggests it was the work of Thomas Norton, who had provided an account of Campion's examination to Walsingham in March 1582 (following his own, brief imprisonment for speaking too forthrightly on Elizabeth's matrimonial manoeuvres) and another, unspecified document in the following month. It is equally likely that the man whom Burghley described as 'a very honest gentleman whom I knew to have good and sufficient means to deliver the truth against such forgers of lies and shameless slanders' was Walsingham himself.

46. See the regime's defence of proceedings against Throckmorton: *A discoverie of the treasons practised and attempted against the Queenes Majestie and the realme, by Francis Throckemorton* (1584); Bodleian Library, Malone MS 645, 8: 'Then, if these dangerous treasons be discovered by torture, (the onely meanes left unto Princes to discover treasons and attemptes against their States and Persons, where they finde apparent matter to induce suspition, as in the case of *Throckemorton*, upon sight of the plottes of hauens &c.) may the Law touch the traitour or not?'

47. Kingdon, *Execution of Justice*, p. 94 (modernized spelling).

48. See p. 298.

49. The English government long denied that any Catholics were imprisoned on a matter of conscience. However, it is clear that the concentration of leading Catholics in secure accommodation began as early as 1571 for no greater offence than 'maintaining' others in the practice of their religion – or, in the words of the Privy Council, 'as by theyr practyses abrode to corrupt others in stobbernes' (*APC*, VIII, p. 73). As all Christian sectarians define themselves as a part of a community, any degree of congregation would, by default, appear to constitute the 'maintenance' of others. Nevertheless, various legislation enacted during the 1580s removed the need for official *legerdemain* by making any practical expression of Catholic belief an offence.

50. Reported in BL Lansdowne MS 49, f. 4.

51. See Thomas Wilbraham's committee report to Parliament, 14 May 1572 (Hartley, *Proceedings*, I, pp. 322–3). In fact, Medinaceli's mission was to replace Alba as governor of the Low Countries and to re-supply the army there, as Elizabeth and her councillors knew perfectly well by mid-1572.

52. Maltby, *Black Legend*, p. 33.

53. Scottish edition reproduced in Malham, *Harleian Miscellany*, I, pp. 431–83.

54. All Souls, Oxford, Codrington Library MS 129; modern edition Caldecott-Baird, *The Expedition in Holland*, 1976.

55. Pollard, *Tudor Tracts*, pp. 420–49.

56. Churchyard, *A Lamentable Description, etc*, pp. 54, 60.

57. *Discourse of Western Planting* (Hakluyt Society facsimile ed. 1993), p. 52. The *Discourse* was intended as a briefing paper for the Queen, and was not published in any form until 1877. Nevertheless, its layout suggests that Hakluyt may have had a wider, if discreet, audience in mind than Elizabeth alone.

58. Quinn, *Roanoke*, I, p. 490.

59. Temple, *The World Encompassed by Sir Francis Drake*, p. 45; Foxe, *Actes*, IV, p. 450.

60. Mann, *Deloney's Works*, p. 480.

61. Quoted in Maclure, *Paul's Cross Sermons*, p. 67.

62. Percy managed (or was persuaded) to evade justice by committing suicide while awaiting trial in the Tower. He did so by the rather supple feat of putting a bullet into his own heart while lying in his bed.

63. 'A proper new ballad, breefly declaring the death and Execution of 14 most wicked Traitors, who suffered death in Lincolnes Inne Feelde neere London: the 20 and 21 of September, 1586'; reproduced in Collier, *Broadside Black-letter Ballads*, p. 37.

64. *The Intended Treason, of Doctor Parrie: and of his Complices, Against the Queenes moste Excellent Maiestie*; sig. A3v–A4r.

65. Strype, *Annals*, III (i), p. 625.

66. PRO SP/12/211, 50.

67. *A Prayer and also a thanksgiving* (1577), a ballad by 'I. Pitt, minister', reproduced in Collier, *Broadside Black-letter Ballads*, p. 19.

CHAPTER SEVEN

1. Excerpt from Elizabeth's speech to parliament, 1593, reproduced in Malham, *Harleian Miscellany*, II, p. 261. By this time of course, the Queen was aware that Philip's fleets were anything but 'invincible'.

2. 'Robert, Earl of Essex's Ghost, etc', in *The Harleian Miscellany*, III, p. 514.

3. As a young man, Wilson had been seized in Rome and sentenced to death for the content of tracts on rhetoric and logic he had published previously in England, but with his fellow prisoners was freed by a Roman mob when their gaol caught fire (Birch, *Memoirs*, I, p. 7).

4. *Cal. SP For. 1579–80*, no. 375 (modernized spelling).

5. Klarwill, *Fugger news letters*, II, p. 36.

6. Quoted in Parker, *Grand Strategy of Philip II*, p. 166.

7. Elliott, *Imperial Spain*, p. 181; the Spanish Crown's 'take' of silver realized 3,958,393 ducats in the period 1571–5; this rose to 9,060,725 ducats for the years 1581–5.

8. Englefield, formerly Sheriff of Oxfordshire and Berkshire and, at the age of thirty-one, one of Mary Tudor's Privy Councillors, had fled England soon after Elizabeth's accession. Since 1568 he had been a pensioner at Philip's Court (Loomie, *Spanish Elizabethans*, pp. 17–24).

9. *Cal. SP For. 1577–8*, no. 571.

10. HMC Salisbury MSS, III, p. 68.

11. *Cal. SP For. 1579–80*, no. 307 (1 June 1580).

12. *Cal. SP For. 1572–4*, no. 1452, 14 June 1574. Guaras had been acting as an unofficial agent in England since the ambassadorship of Quadra (*Cal. SP Sp. 1558–1567*, no. 241. 1 September 1563).

13. Philip was certainly considering such a diversion, though the logistical difficulties in despatching the 1574 fleet made it a small priority, and readily abandoned (Tazón, *Stukeley*, pp. 185–90).

14. PRO SP/12/95, 87(ii), 89; 12/97, 1, 2, 2(i), 3.

15. *Cal. SP For. 1581–2*, no. 278: 'Instructions for the treaty of a league offensive and defensive between us and the French King, and for other things depending thereon'. The note was drafted in Burghley's hand, but could hardly have expressed other than the Queen's intentions.

16. Wright, *English Voyages to the Spanish Main*, pp. xlvi–xlviii, 93, 96–9, 112–13, 234; Hakluyt, *Principal Navigations*, x, pp. 77–81, 82–8; Williamson, *Sir John Hawkins*, pp. 297–9.

17. See the deposition of John Oxenham (Wright, *English voyages to the Spanish Main*,

p. 174): 'Asked whether, to come thence, he had any command, order or licence from his sovereign; He said that (she) knew nothing of his coming'.

18. Andrews, *Spanish Caribbean*, p. 142; Andrews, *Drake's Voyages*, p. 34.

19. Hughes and Larkin, *Proclamations*, II, nos 450 (21 December 1558), 482 (21 July 1561), 499 (8 February 1563), 511 (2 August 1563), 519 (18 February 1564), 526 (31 July 1564), 562 (27 April 1569), 563 (3 August 1569), 573 (6 June 1570).

20. In 1572, the Privy Council had asked William of Orange to rescind letters of marque he had issued to Englishmen. Four years later, when ordering Henry Palmer to sweep the Channel clear of privateers, the Council specifically exempted from impeachment those who carried William's commission (PRO SP/12/70, 138; PRO SP/12/108, 28). On Habsburg 'commissions', note the claims of Alderman Pullison and a syndicate of merchants, complaining of the seizure of their ship *Thornback* 'by such persons as pretend to serve the Kinge of Spaine against the Prince of Orenge, the most parte being Englishemen . . .' (*APC*, IX, p. 28; 17 October 1575). These 'persons', apparently, were based in rebel-held Flushing.

21. Hughes and Larkin, *Proclamations*, II, p. 395.

22. On 29 June 1573, the Queen ordered Lord Admiral Lincoln to set out three or four ships to apprehend pirates infesting the mouth of the Thames (Haynes and Murdin, *Cecil Papers*, II, p. 257). The measure does not appear to have been successful. Exactly one year later, Burghley wrote to Walsingham suggesting that the English fleet of twenty-four vessels assembled to screen the anticipated armada from Santander (see p. 22) might be employed instead to clear the Thames, 'which is much haunted by pyrates' (PRO SP/12/97, 11).

23. Hughes and Larkin, *Proclamations*, II, p. 478. The only reference dating this piece (and which ensured its chronological placement in state papers) is a later endorsement – 'about 1580' – upon its reverse.

24. PRO SP/12/112, 5; PRO SP/12/113, 9; PRO SP/12/122, 6, 6(i), 16, 21, 24(i), 46, 59, 60; PRO SP/12/123, 2, 2(i), 3, 8, 10, 12, 12(i), 13, 13(i), 23, 24, 25, 38, 39.

25. Quoted in Hale and Fleetwood, *Admiralty Jurisdiction*, p. 351.

26. PRO SP/12/122, 58, 58(i), 58 (ii); Mathew, 'Cornish and Welsh Pirates', p. 346.

27. See the lists of convicted pirates and their 'maintainers', PRO SP/12/120, 83; PRO SP/12/125, 15; PRO SP/12/130, 41; individual cases cited in PRO HCA 1/2, 36–93 (3 May 1577–17 March 1578).

28. *APC*, IX, p. 366 (19 June 1577); PRO SP/12/135, 21.

29. HMC Salisbury MSS, V, p. 519; Gilbert, *Parochial History of Cornwall*, II, p. 6. However, as harbour master of the Duchy of Cornwall from April 1552 (Miller, *Killigrew*, p. 12), it is clear that Henry was unable (or unwilling) entirely to distance himself from the activities of his elder brothers Thomas and Peter, as his brief imprisonment for abetting piracy during Mary's reign indicates (see p. 335n29).

30. PRO SP/12/120, 83; PRO SP/12/125, 15; PRO SP/12/130, 41; PRO SP 68/11, 615.

31. Hamilton, *Book of Examinations and Depositions of Southampton, 1570–1594*, pp. 2–3, 7, 49.

32. Oppenheim, *Administration of the Royal Navy*, p. 178; Platt, *Medieval Southampton*, p. 222; *Cal. SP Sp. 1568–79*, no. 588 (15 August 1579).

33. PRO SP/12/144, 22, 25; PRO HCA 38/9 (22 September 1581); PRO HCA 3/18 (18 March 1582); *Cal. SP Scotland, 1581–3*, no. 380; Andrews, *Elizabethan Privateering*, p. 202.

34. Magdalene College, Cambridge, Pepys MS 2133, f. 73; *APC*, XIII, pp. 187–8.

35. PRO SP/12/123, 37; 12/138, 16(i); 12/144, 24; BL Lansdowne MS 142, f. 82. In 1569, Randall's ship *Salomon* had joined a small fleet of freebooters commanded by Martin

Frobisher. In 1571 he abetted the escape from custody of John Callice, one of the most persistent (and notorious) Elizabethan pirates. In 1578, during a brief legitimate phase, Randall sailed in the *Salomon* in Frobisher's third voyage to Baffin Island (McDermott, *Frobisher*, pp. 68, 214; Lloyd, *Dorset Elizabethans*, pp. 19, 38).

36. PRO SP/12/156, 19.

37. *Cal. SP Sp. 1568–79*, no. 588.

38. See his report of 8 May 1578 (*ibid.*, no. 495), regarding the voyage of one 'Stockwell' (identified tentatively by Quinn (*Gilbert*, I, p. 186 n. 2) as John Stukeley, who later sailed in Grenville's 1585 Virginia expedition): 'I have heard that the real intention is to rob ships on their way from your Majesty's Indies'. No such voyage took place.

39. *Cal. SP Sp. 1568–79*, nos 598 (13 September 1579), 611 (28 December 1579).

40. PRO SP/12/146, 7, 7(i), 13, 19, 32, 84; PRO SP/12/147, 15, 17–19, 25, 32, 36, 44, 48; PRO SP/12/148, 2–8; *APC*, XI, p. 381.

41. BL Harleian MS 6992, f. 59; 3 December 1579.

42. *Cal SP For. 1579–80*, nos. 336 (23 June), 401 (18 August), 428 (18 September: Thomas Stokes to Walsingham: '. . . and they say the soldiers have every one a white cross on their breast, naming themselves to be the Pope's men, though indeed they are all Spaniards').

43. Hartley, *Proceedings*, I, p. 503.

44. Greene, *Works*, V, p. 283.

45. The only extant subscribers' list for Drake's enterprise (BL Cotton MSS Otho, VIII, ff. 8–9) does not provide details of the Privy councillors' investments, but the return upon known subscriptions was estimated at some 4,700 per cent.

46. Mendoza to Philip II, 9 January 1581 (*Cal. SP Sp., 1580–86*, no. 60); 6 April 1581 (BL Add. MSS 26056.C, f. 138; contemporary English translation).

47. BL Sloane MS 326, ff. 20–21.

48. Text reproduced in Taylor, *Writings and Correspondence of the two Richard Hakluyts*, I, pp. 139–46.

49. PRO SP/12/144, 44.

50. *Cal. SP Sp. 1580–1586*, nos 58, 61, 82.

51. *Cal. SP For. 1580–81*, no. 168 (modernized spelling).

52. Hawkins had presented a substantial scheme for interrupting Spain's Atlantic trade in 1579 in a letter to Cecil (PRO SP/12/131, 64: 'A Provision for the Indies Fleet, drawn by Master Hawkins'), in which he argued for an Atlantic squadron that could intercept the plate ships and sack the coastal towns of the Caribbean thereafter.

53. PRO SP/12/148, 43–7.

54. Wernham, *Before the Armada*, pp. 360–62; MacCaffrey, *Queen Elizabeth and the making of policy*, pp. 273–4; *Cal. SP Sp. 1580–1586*, no. 124; Donno, *Madox*, p. 19; BL Lansdowne MS 31, f. 202r.

55. *Cal. SP For. 1562* (27 May), no. 103.

56. Hakluyt, *Principal Navigations*, p. 645.

57. The expedition's chief pilot, Thomas Hood, 'a wyse, diligent and vertuous man' according to Fenton, told the chaplain Richard Madox that 'he wil not geve a fart for al the cosmographers yn England, for he can tel more than al the cosmographers in the world' (Donno, *Madox*, p. 151). His record proved otherwise.

58. Wilson, *Queen Elizabeth and the Netherlands*, pp. 75–6. As a quid pro quo for the (1579) Union of Arras, by which the Walloon provinces affirmed their loyalties to Philip and his governor Farnese, Spanish troops had been withdrawn from their territory. The Union was a response to the earlier Union of Utrecht, by which the six northern

provinces had committed themselves to a common defence policy and, vitally, to allow each of their number to follow their preferred religious policies.

59. Donno, *Madox*, p. 20 n. 3.

60. Andrews, *Elizabethan Privateering*, p. 91.

61. PRO SP/12/142, 44; discussed in Williamson, *Sir John Hawkins*, p. 400.

62. Wright, *Further English Voyages*, p. XIX. This involvement was later 'confirmed' under torture by a mariner from one of Hawkin's ships who had been taken in ambush at Puerto Rico (ibid, p. 6).

63. *Ibid*, pp. 3–7; *Cal. SP For.*, XV, no. 277.

64. Reproduced from Hakluyt, *Principal Navigations* (1st ed.), p. 677.

65. Quinn, *Gilbert*, p. 59. Walsingham actively assisted Peckham, the leading Catholic investor, in his search for further shareholders, and was the dedicatee of Peckham's *True Reporte*.

66. See Quinn, *Gilbert*, pp. 50–51. Fernandez crossed the Atlantic in the *Squirrel*, a bark of some eight tons, crewed by just eleven men.

67. Barlowe's account of the voyage is reproduced in Quinn, *Roanoke*, I, pp. 91–115.

68. Quinn and Ryan, *England's Sea Empire*, p. 86.

69. *Cal. SP Sp., 1580–1586*, nos 59, 134,

70. Oxenham's alleged boast was reported by the council of the city of Panama in its deposition to Philip, 15 April 1577; reproduced in Wright, *English Voyages to the Spanish Main, 1569–1580*, p. 113.

71. *A True Reporte of the late discoveries, and possession of the newfound landes*, f. 4r.

72. *Discourse of Western Planting*, Cap.7, p. 44.

73. Taylor, *Writings and Correspondences*, II, p. 332.

74. In 1588, a Spanish expedition organized by Pedro Menendez Marques, governor of Florida, was set out to find and destroy the colony (in fact, the second colony), and to erect a Spanish fort upon its ruins. However, a preliminary reconnaissance, commanded by Captain Vicente Gonzalez, failed to discover traces of English settlement. (Quinn, *Roanoke*, II, pp. 816–22).

75. Parker, *Grand Strategy*, pp. 167, 169.

76. English translation in BL Add. MS 36315, f. 92; reproduced in Quinn, *Roanoke*, II, p. 717.

77. PRO SP/12/125, 70; Hakluyt, *Principal Navigations*, p. 3.

78. Digges, *Compleat Ambassador*, p. 128. See also p. 150 for Burghley's near-identical observation some thirteen years later.

CHAPTER EIGHT

1. Anthony Marten, 'An Exhortation to Her Majesty's Faithful Subjects', in Malham, *Harleian Miscellany*, II, p. 93.

2. The precise time of Drake's departure is given by Christopher Carleill's aide, Edward Powell, who sailed and kept a journal in the ship *Tiger*: BL Cotton MS Otho E VIII, f. 229; reproduced in Keeler, *Drake's West Indian Voyage, 1585–1586*, p. 70.

3. BL Harleian MS 285, f. 196.

4. Parker, *Grand Strategy*, p. 171.

5. PRO SP/12/168, 3; 3 February 1584: 'A memoryall of dyvers thinges necessary . . . to serve for martiall defence ageynst ether rebellion or invasion'.

6. Henry E. Huntington Library, Ellesmere MS 1694; all quotations taken from the transcription in Adams, 'New Light on the "Reformation" of John Hawkins, etc'.

7. PRO SP/12/2, 30; PRO SP/12/3, 44; discussed in Loades, *Tudor Navy*, p. 179.

8. The practice of paying 'bounties' to encourage private shipbuilding (either by way of customs allowances, quittances on duties for goods carried in the bounty ships or pro-rated cash awards) commenced in the fifteenth-century, though its application was extremely variable, with no bounties being paid in many years. The period 1572 to 1576, however, witnessed the greatest incidence of bounty ship constructions in the sixteenth century prior to the 1590s (all comments and data regarding the bounty are derived from B. Dietz, 'The Royal Bounty and English Merchant Shipping', *ad finem*).

9. Bodleian Library, Rawlinson MS C.846, 4, f. 61; discussed in Glasgow, 'Maturing of Naval Administration', pp. 14, 24–5.

10. The judgment is that of Andrews (*Drake's Voyages*, p. 92).

11. BL Lansdowne MSS 43, ff. 20–1; Strype, *Annals*, III, i, pp. 306–8.

12. See p. 134.

13. HMC Salisbury MSS, III, p. 67 (modernized spelling).

14. BL Lansdowne MSS 41, ff. 9–10. Adams ('The Outbreak of the Elizabethan Naval War', pp. 53–4) shows that the Queen intended to invest in this voyage as early as 29 July. What cannot be determined, however, is precisely what, at that time, she intended its ultimate purpose to be.

15. The suggestion was first made by Williamson (*Sir John Hawkins*, p. 411) and later repeated by Andrews (*Drake's Voyages*, p. 93).

16. Hartley, *Proceedings*, II, p. 77; Quinn, *Roanoke*, I, p. 125.

17. Wright, *Further English Voyages*, p. 9.

18. Quinn (*Roanoke*, I, p. 171 n.1) suggests this was approximately 50 per cent upon costs.

19. *Cal. SP. For. 1584–5*, pp. 370.

20. Correspondence containing these intelligences is summarized in Palmer, *Ireland in Tudor Foreign Policy*, pp. 116–17.

21. See Monson, *Tracts*, I, p. 121–2; Corbett, *Spanish War*, pp. xiii–ix; Corbett, *Drake and the Tudor Navy*, p. 12.

22. Respectively suggested by Parker (*Grand Strategy*, pp. 173–4) and Adams ('The Outbreak of the Elizabethan Naval War', pp. 56–7).

23. A compendium of grievances, drawn up many years later when negotiations for an Anglo-Spanish peace treaty were being discussed, alleged several appalling instances of persecution in the period prior to the 1585 embargo. It was claimed that 'Cutbeard' Tollarde, a gunner from the London ship *Emmanuel*, was seized in Sanlucar and later burned at the stake for refusing to kiss a religious picture touted through the streets by a beggar boy. A similar fate befell Walter Bett, a carpenter in a Saltash ship docked in the Guadalquivir at Seville, who inadvertently omitted to doff his cap and kneel as the sacrament was carried aloft in procession on the river's opposite bank. One John Jenkins was also taken and examined upon the accusation of a friar who had asked him if it were true that English 'priests' took wives. It is not known whether Jenkins's wit – he had replied that it was better they took their own than kept other men's – condemned him to a similar fate or redeemed him (all citations from BL Add. MS 48126: ff. 73–7). Another allegation, also made in the reign of James I by a Scottish shipowner in respect of the seizure of his vessel in the armada year, claimed that his crew had been arrested in Sanlucar for being 'protestantes and fleshe eatters on dayes prohibite'. Allegedly, though no formal trial proceedings took place, the master, master's mate and boatswain were burned at the stake and their shipmates condemned to the galleys thereafter (BL Lansdowne MS 142, f. 182).

24. Pierson, *Commander of the Armada*, p. 57.

25. Croft, *Spanish Company*, p. xxviii; Monson, *Tracts*, I, p. 125. BL Landsowne MS 115,

f. 196 provides a list of fifty individuals or syndicates to whom letters of reprisal were granted, to a total recovery value of £140,000.

26. PRO SP/12/180, 15; Monson, *Tracts*, I, p. 126 n. 8.

27. PRO HCA 24/53, f. 62r.

28. *Cal. SP For.*, xx, as dated. One of the vessels was a Venetian, three were French, three Biscayan, and the rest Guinea, Brazil and Madeira traders, valued in total at 294,500 crowns.

29. *Discourse of Western Planting*, p. 28.

30. Andrews, *Elizabethan Privateering*, p. 112.

31. The calculation of Hieronimo Lippomano, Venetian Ambassador at Madrid: *Cal. SP Ven. 1581–1591*, no. 616 (2 January 1588).

32. See cases cited in PRO SP 78/34, 609; PRO SP 84/42, 504; PRO HCA 24/66, 124; PRO HCA 24/68, 177 for examples of these trends.

33. On some repercussions of English depredations in European waters post-1585, see Dyer, 'Reprisals in the Sixteenth Century', pp. 192–7; McDermott, *Martin Frobisher*, pp. 372–5, 384–8.

34. Walsingham to Wotton, 11 June 1585; Bain, *Hamilton Papers*, II, pp. 650–51

35. PRO SP/12/179, 21; Quinn, *Roanoke*, I, pp. 171–2; 234–42. As recently as March, the proposal to seize the Spanish Newfoundland fleet had been rejected as likely (by Walsingham's own admission) to be regarded as a *casus belli* by Philip II (PRO SP/12/177, 58). Bernard Drake captured with seventeen Spanish fishing vessels, three Portuguese Brazilmen and a French Guinea trader.

36. PRO SP/46/17, 160. If a written commission to Drake was issued, it does not appear to have survived. The only documentary evidence of intent is the supremely ambiguous 'A discourse of Sir Francis Drake's voyage, which by God's Grace he shall well perform', the provenance, timing and purpose of which has yet to be established definitively (Lansdowne MSS 100/98; first reproduced in Corbett, *Spanish War*, pp. 69–74).

37. Keeler, *Drake's West Indian Voyage, 1585–1586*, pp. 15, 16, 282–9.

38. See Walsingham's interesting comment in a letter of 9 July 1586 to Leicester, regarding the earl's plea for a further commitment of men and materials to the Low Countries (Bruce, *Leycester Correspondence*, p. 341): '. . . yt shall in no sorte be fyt for her majestye to take a resolutyon in the cause until sir Francis Drake returne, at lest untyll the successe of his vyage be seene . . .'.

39. English version reproduced in Scott, *Somers Tracts*, I, 410–19. The 'restoration' of good government in the Low Countries had been a principal self-justifying (if wholly unrealistic) motive of the English government since 1572. In that year, the soldier Ralph Lane had presented the Queen's response to the magistrates of Nieuport's request for English protection: 'I gyve you t'understand that the Quenes Majestie my gracyous Soveraigne will by no meanes be enduced to take you from the subjection of your soveraigne lord the Kinges Majestie of Spayne, althoughe englishe garrysons be receyved emongst you; but this, by your humble request unto Her Majestie and the good endevour of your good freendes about Her Highnes personne, maye be broughte to passe that Her Majestie wil be contented to take the protection of your persons, your goodes and the auncient libertie of your countrye from tyrannycall governement of spannyshe garrysons uppon Her Majestie self, unto the use of the King of Spayne, to whose subjection Her Majestie is to delyver you agayne, when the said Kinge shall have taken awaye and throughlie cleared your countrye of all Spannyshe garrysons, and fullye eftsons restored you your auncient accustomed government of the nobilitie of your

countrue and your country lawes' (Kervyn de Lettenhove and Gilliodts van Severen, *Relations Politiques*, VI, pp. 490–91).

40. Various arguments for and against intervention, and assessments of Philip's likely reactions, are contained in BL Add. MS 48084, ff. 2–5, 6–9, 19–23.

41. *Ibid*, 48014 f. 202.

42. On Burghley's possible responsibility for this suggestion, see Read, *Lord Burghley and Queen Elizabeth*, pp. 308–9.

43. The surviving brothers Robert and Ambrose (later earl of Warwick) were restored in blood by statute following this campaign (Loades, *Reign of Mary Tudor*, p. 413).

44. Her response to Leicester's initiative (*ibid*, f. 257) was unequivocal regarding both the offence and its reward: '. . . our expresse pleasure and commaundement, all delayes and excuses layde a parte, you doe presentlie vpon the dutie of your allegiance, obaye and fullfill what soever the bearer hereof [i.e, Sir Thomas Heneage] shall direct you to doe in our name: whereof fayle you not as you will awnsware the contrarie at yo[u]r vttermost perrill.'

45. Neale, 'Elizabeth and the Netherlands', pp. 377, 380–83.

46. Sir Philip Sydney, Leicester's nephew and Walsingham's son-in-law, received a thigh wound that became gangrenous; he died twenty-five days later. Neither of the bereaved men fully recovered from the shock. In Walsingham's case, the pain was more acute for his being obliged to lay out some £6,000 from his own purse to satisfy Sydney's creditors (BL Cotton MSS Titus B VII, f. 65: Walsingham to Leicester, 5 November 1586).

47. See p. 174–5.

48. The concentration of a large fleet at Santander in 1574 (see p. 121) indicated that Philip had the ability, albeit with much effort, to gather significant naval resources in the Atlantic even prior to the Union of Crowns. However, this had been intended as an instrument to drive the Sea Beggars' fleet of relatively small vessels from the Narrow Seas and to destroy their on-shore sustainers thereafter. It was only with the acquisition of the navy of Portugal, and the construction of a new generation of Indies galleons between 1580 and 1584 (which the English government, as noted, believed to be an element of a putative Irish invasion), that the Spanish King gained the necessary means to prevent the Navy Royal slaughtering any Spanish invasion force in mid-Channel.

49. On Philip's change of heart, see Parker, *Grand Strategy*, pp. 179–81.

50. The words of Drake's chaplain Francis Fletcher ('The First Part of the Second Voiage about the World, etc', reproduced in *The World Encompassed by Sir Francis Drake*, p. 109.

51. BL Cotton MSS Galba, C VIII, f. 243.

52. Parker, *Grand Strategy*, pp. 209–10.

53. Pierson, *Commander of the Armada*, pp. 63–4.

54. Parker, *Grand Strategy*, pp. 186–8; *Fernandez-Armesto*, Spanish Armada, pp. 81–2; Jensen, 'The Spanish Armada: The Worst-Kept Secret in Europe', pp. 629–30.

55. Williamson, *Sir John Hawkins*, p. 414; see also Klarwill, *Fugger news letters*, II, p. 119. The government, mindful of Babington's claim of a French Catholic army preparing to invade England, misunderstood the purpose of the fleet, which had been assembled to assault the Huguenot stronghold La Rochelle.

56. Hartley, *Proceedings*, II, pp. 217, 227, 232.

57. *Ibid.*, pp. 244–58 for the petition and the Queen's response.

58. *Ibid.*, p. 229: the words, once more, of Job Throckmorton.

59. Mary was not named explicitly therein; the document referred to 'any person that shall or may pretend any title to the crown of this realm' (Malham, *Harleian Miscellany*, II, p. 9).

60. *Cal SP For. 1586–1588* (XXI, part I), pp. 123, 161 (items not numbered). Stafford's layman's opinion was that five English ships would be sufficient to break up the Lisbon concentration (PRO SP/78/16, 53).

61. The offer was conveyed by Henry Killigrew, whose instructions from Burghley are reproduced in Haynes and Murdin, *Cecil Papers*, pp. 224–5.

62. Paulet, who had repeatedly urged Mary's execution after due process of law, was outraged by this suggestion – 'God forbid that I should make so foul a shipwreck of my conscience, or leave so great a blot to my poor posterity, to shed blood without law or warrant' – and secretly had copies made both of Walsingham's letter (which he had been ordered to return promptly) and his own refusal (Morris, *Poulet*, pp. 362–3; modernized spelling).

63. Camden, *History*, p. 288; Mattingly, *Armada*, p. 35; *Cal. SP For. 1586–7*, nos 236, 239, 242, 276; *Cal. SP Ven. 1581–91*, no. 483.

64. *Ibid.*, no. 504. Ironically, Mary's will made no mention of her having relinquished her son's rights to the English throne in Philip's favour, despite her former promises.

65. BL Cotton MSS Caligula, C IX, f. 157.

66. The evidence for this is circumstantial but convincing. See Dickerman, 'A Neglected Phase of the Spanish Armada', *inter alia*.

67. Quoted in Parker, *Grand Strategy*, p. 195.

68. Andrews, *Elizabethan Privateering*, pp. 94, 113, 206.

69. Corbett, *Spanish War*, p. 106; *Cal. SP Sp., 1587–1603*, p. 257.

70. *Ibid* (modernized spelling), pp. 100–02.

71. Both Burghley and Walsingham subsequently used the evidence of this order to claim that Elizabeth had not wished Drake to mount his assault upon Cadiz: Burghley to Parma's unofficial envoy Andreas de Looe in July 1587 (PRO SP/77/1, 32), Walsingham to Sir Edward Stafford and, through him, to Henri III (PRO SP/78/17, 57).

72. PRO SP/12/198, 34.

73. The observation of Thomas Fenner, recalled in Haslop's *Newes Out of the Coast of Spaine*, sig. B1.

74. This was Mendoza's phrase, in a letter of 28 February 1587, interpreting Mary Stuart's execution as a divinely ordained prelude to Philip's assumption of the thrones of England and Scotland.

75. Parker, *Grand Strategy*, p. 194; Jensen, 'The Spanish Armada: The Worst-Kept Secret in Europe', p. 634 n. 62.

76. *Cal. SP For. 1586–1588* (vol. XXI, pt I), pp. 335, 365; *Cal SP Ven. 1581–91*, no. 510; *Cal. SP Sp. 1587–1603*, no. 131.

77. See his letters to Walsingham of 27 April: 'I assuer your honour the like preparation was never heard of nor known, as the King of Spayne hathe and daylye maketh to invade England' (PRO/SP/12/200, 46).

78. The phrase is Camden's (*History*, p. 308).

79. Pears, 'The Spanish Armada and the Ottoman Porte', p. 446 (modern translation of Latin text).

80. Parker, *Grand Strategy*, p. 192. On Harborne's efforts to have his expenses refunded, see BL Lansdowne MS 57, f. 23 (undated). According to his petition to the Queen, he received only £1,200 from the Turkey Company for six years in the ruinously expensive post as ambassador.

CHAPTER NINE

1.　Ralph Norris, *Fall of Antwerp*; reproduced in Firth; 'Ballad History of the Later Tudors', p. 98.

2.　Much has been made of the significance of losses of barrel hoops and staves, which undoubtedly made adequate provisioning of the armada problematical. However, the shortage can hardly be said to have influenced the tide of battle. Indeed, it may have assisted the Spanish cause, if indirectly. The early need to re-supply many of his ships because of faulty casking (for which the earlier losses were at least partly responsible) caused Medina Sidonia to put into Corunna harbour on 19 June (NS) during the armada's northward passage; a manoeuvre that preserved much of the fleet's fabric from the severe storms that swept in from the Atlantic a few hours later.

3.　Parker, *Grand Strategy*, p. 198.

4.　PRO SP/12/203, 33, 52; HMC Salisbury MSS, III, pp. 279, 288–90.

5.　BL Cotton MSS Galba, D I, f. 148; *Cal. SP For. 1587* (III), p. 372.

6.　BL Cotton MSS Galba, D II, f. 69.

7.　BL Lansdowne MS 53, f. 10.

8.　*Cal. SP For. 1586–8* XXI, (I), pp. 341–5.

9.　HMC, Foljambe MSS, ff. 101–10.

10.　Read, *Burghley*, p. 416; HMC Foljambe MSS, f. 127b; PRO SP/12/204, 2.

11.　Fissel, *English Warfare*, p. 142. On the difficulties encountered in financing the Netherlands campaign, see Neale, 'Elizabeth and the Netherlands', *passim*.

12.　HMC Salisbury MSS, III, p. 303. Estimate of Sir Thomas Shirley.

13.　Wernham, *Before the Armada*, p. 390.

14.　*Cal. SP For. 1587*d XXI, (III), pp. 120–23.

15.　HMC Salisbury MSS, III, p. 26: Leicester to Burghley, 15 June 1587.

16.　F. C. Dietz, *English Public Finance*, II, pp. 48, 55.

17.　Bruce, *Arrangements . . . for the Internal Defence of These Kingdoms*, App. XXXVI. The figure included expenditure upon internal defence, diplomatic activities and foreign subsidies.

18.　PRO SP/12/209, 14; F.C. Dietz, *English Public Finance*, II, p. 59.

19.　Bruce, *Leycester Correspondence*, p. 295.

20.　PRO SP/12/201, 45.

21.　Gould, 'The Crisis in the Export Trade 1586–1587', p. 216; Slack, *Impact of Plague*, p. 58; Fischer, *The Great Wave*, p. 92.

22.　Burghley to Walsingham, 24 October 1587 (Haynes and Murdin, *Cecil Papers*, p. 590): 'When her Majesty was informed from me by Mr Wolley of the Names of such, as should have been sent to the Lieutenants of the Maritym Countreys [sic], she changed her Mynd, resting upon Answer from the Lieutenants; as I thynk mislyking the Charge, which would not have been above 200 marks.'

23.　Crofts has received something of a drubbing from posterity. Undoubtedly a man of wavering religious convictions, and nervous of the implications of England's deteriorating relations with Spain, he had been granted a Spanish pension at some point prior to 1571 – possibly during Philip's brief reign as Mary Tudor's King-Consort (as had many impeccably Protestant Englishmen who managed to persuade the gullible Philip of their potential value to him). During 1579, Mendoza had apparently received some valuable 'inside' Court information from Crofts, though it is difficult to establish whether any of this was actually damaging to English interests. The Spanish ambassador repeatedly urged Philip to grant him a new pension, an initiative that the permanently impecunious Crofts appears to have encouraged. However, as Mendoza's other 'targets' for the Spanish King's bribes at this time included Burghley and the earl of Sussex, it would be unfair to take his advances alone as proof of Crofts's traitorous intent (*Cal. SP Sp. 1568–79*, nos 172, 524, 575, 591, 598). Following his return from the Low Countries in 1588, Crofts was briefly imprisoned in the Tower for having forged a suspiciously amiable relationship with Parma during their negotiations.

24. BL Cotton MSS Galba, D 1, f. 46.

25. Parker, *Grand Strategy*, p. 241.

26. Naval expenditure in 1586 (expenditure of the Treasurer of the Navy and victualling combined) had been £38,027 (Parker, 'Dreadnought Revolution', p. 289).

27. PRO SP/12/204, 2, 8: 206, 4; F .C. Dietz, *English Public Finance, 1558–1641*, p. 444. In fact, commissioners for the disposal of spoils taken during the West Indies raid had made their report in June 1587 (BL Lansdowne MS 3, f. 36; reproduced, with modern spelling, in Corbett, *Spanish War*, pp. 86–7). Presumably, its depressing conclusions – a return of 15s. upon every £1 invested – encouraged Burghley and the Queen to regard it as not quite definitive.

28. The most concentrated phase of construction had taken been undertaken in 1586, when ten new vessels had been built, including the *Vanguard* and *Rainbow*, both of some 500 tons (Oppenheim, *Administration of the Royal Navy*, pp. 120–21).

29. See Parker, 'Dreadnought Revolution', *passim*.

30. The *Foresight* has been included only provisionally in this list. Built in 1570 by Matthew Baker (possibly his first major commission), it may have been the first of the raze-built naval vessels, but this is not certain. The only extant data regarding her form seems to draw a strong distinction between hers and later designs. Richard Madox, in his diary of the 1582 Fenton voyage, observed that the *Galleon Oughtred* (later *Galleon Leicester*), built in 1578, was 'made lyke unto the Revenge but the Edward (*Edward Bonaventure*) was buylt at Rochester 8 years since & is lyke the forsyght' (Taylor, *Troublesome Voyage*, p. 154). Baker's cross-sectional mould for the Foresight survives in *Fragments of Ancient English Shipwrightry* (Pepys Library MS 2820; discussed in Barker, 'Fragments', *ad finem*), but this is insufficient to permit conclusions as to her overall dimensions. The little that is known of her proportions (Glasgow, 'Shape of Ships that defeated the Spanish Armada', p. 184), indicates that her ratios of keel to beam and depth to beam were not significantly different from those of *Dreadnought*; but it seems telling that she underwent what appears to have been significant modification to her fabric within eleven years of her construction (Adams, 'Ellesmere Survey', p. 104).

31. In this they have followed Williamson, who regarded the contribution to the process of the royal shipwrights and Hawkins's fellow officers of the Marine Causes as at best collateral, and at worst almost wholly obstructive to his genius (see his *Sir John Hawkins*, III, chapter 3).

32. PRO SP/12/215, 31.

33. The degree of standardization of naval design during these years remains obscure. The earliest evidence of official efforts to achieve consistency is found in the period immediately following the campaign, when Howard, Drake, George Winter, Hawkins, William Borough and Edward Fenton presented a 'device' recommending that four new ships be built for the Navy Royal: two in the form of the *Revenge* (though of greater burden), and two 'bastards betwixte a galleas and a galleon' (PRO SP/12/218, 31: 20 November 1588). Five months later, the same men formed a committee, with the ship-wrights Richard Chapman and Matthew and Christopher Baker, which established dimensions and form for the (1590) construction of three naval vessels, the *Merhonour*,

Garland and *Defiance* (PRO SP/12/223, 45). Note also Glasgow's detailed analysis showing significant variations in the proportions of post-1572 designs ('Ships that defeated the Spanish Armada', pp. 184–7) – again, an indication that considerable experimentation was being undertaken throughout the period.

34. PRO SP/12/244, 110; Salisbury and Anderson, *Treatise on Shipbuilding*, p. 4.

35. Glasgow, 'Ships that defeated the Spanish Armada', pp. 185–6.

36. Barker, 'Fragments', pp. 174–5; *Oxford Dictionary of National Bibliography*, Matthew Baker. On the variable quality of construction, note the opinion of the anonymous, near-contemporary author of a treatise on shipbuilding: 'But there are many good artificers that can draw a plot well and build a ship also, that if their work be compared with their plot you will find them very little to agree; and so many times good ships are spoiled in the building whose principal lines were well contrived in the plotting. The chiefest reason is want of skill in Arithmetic and Geometry to take all things truly of the plot' (Salisbury and Anderson, *A Treatise on Shipbuilding and a Treatise on Rigging Written about 1620–1625*, p. 32).

37. Adams, 'Ellesmere Survey', p. 108; Williamson, *Observations of Sir Richard Hawkins*, p. 8.

38. The four 'great ships' had been subjected to considerable repair work during 1578–9, but it is difficult to assess its effectiveness. Parker ('Dreadnought Revolution', p. 271) characterizes this as 're-building', but this may be overstating the magnitude of improvements to their fabric. In discussing work carried out upon the Queen's ships, the Ellesmere Survey of 1583 draws a clear distinction between 'new made' vessels (that is, re-built ships such as the *Nonpareil* and *Lion*) and 'new repaired'. The *Elizabeth Jonas*, *Triumph* and *Bear* fell into the latter category (probably having undergone modifications to reduce the height of their fore (and, possibly, aft) superstructures, but without any fundamental alteration of their hull design). Even the *Victory*, which underwent extensive work during 1586 (she was 'altered into the fourme of a gallion'), was modified at the relatively minor cost of £600 rather than re-built (Glasgow, 'Ships that defeated the Spanish Armada', p. 181). As Parker observes, these modifications did not result in any notable increase in the great ships' ordnance to tonnage ratios, which one might expect had radical hull re-working taken place. The survey explicitly forecast that all four vessels would come to the end of their effective lives between 1589 and 1592, at which time they were to be 'newe made'.

39. PRO SP/12/204, 20.

40. *APC*, xv, 22 October 1587, 7 December 1587.

41. PRO SP/12/209, 15; PRO E351/2224; *APC*, xv, 22 October 1587, 7 December 1587.

42. PRO SP/12/206, 15; reproduced in Corbett, *Spanish War*, pp. 240–41.

43. On the near-perennial disputes between the shipwrights and Hawkins, see Oppenheim, *Administration of the Royal Navy*, p. 396; Williamson, *Sir John Hawkins*, pp. 375–82 (a detailed but coloured account); and *Oxford Dictionary of National Biography* entries for Pett and Baker.

44. Oppenheim, *Monson*, I, pp. 134–5.

45. *Cal. SP Sp. 1587–1603*, no. 95.

46. In their October 1587 report, Pett and Baker stated that Frobisher's flagship, the *Foresight*, was weak in her timbers though serviceable in the short term. There is no indication that she was repaired between the end of her Narrow Seas service on 23 January 1588 and her conscription into Howard's fleet at Queenborough one week later (PRO E351/2225; PRO SP/12/208, 6). Of Frobisher's other ships, the *Rainbow*, *Scout*, *Charles*, *Moon* and *Tremontana* were less than five years old, *Achates* had bad timbers (the curse of unseasoned wood once more) but was serviceable, and the *Tiger* had been 'lately

well repaired'. Only the *Bull* had seriously decayed timbers, but 'being lately bound', was considered seaworthy.

47. Loades, *Tudor Navy*, p. 194.

48. Report of Pett and Baker, 22 January 1588; PRO SP/208, 18. A month later, when it appeared that the armada's departure from Lisbon was not imminent, the four 'great ships' were grounded, graved and re-masted during their Chatham stay. Similarly, ship-wrights at Plymouth took advantage of the January hiatus to ground the *Revenge*, *Hope* and *Nonpareil* (PRO SP/12/208, 72, 77).

49. PRO SP/12/208, 8.

50. Both vessels, with three other 'Levanters' returning from the eastern Mediterranean, had also taken part in an action in July 1586 against twenty Maltese galleys in Habs-burg service. After a sharp action lasting some five hours, the galleys had withdrawn (Hakluyt, *Principal Navigations*, VI, pp. 46–57). It was probably this encounter to which Thomas Fenner referred in the following year when commenting upon the limitations of galleys (see p. 168 and p. 354 n. 73).

51. See HMC Foljambe MSS, f. 61: 'Orders to be observed for the training of men by the several Captains to be continued in the Maritime Counties'.

52. As Boynton (*Elizabethan Militia*, pp. 90–93) has observed, there was little effective drilling of the bands between 1573 and 1577 owing to the widely varying estimates of available manpower and the cost of their training from county to county. Only in the latter year did government lay down stricter assessments of headcount and demand that training take place upon ten designated days each year.

53. The words of John Leveson, Deputy Lord Lieutenant of Kent (quoted in Mayer, *Prepa-rations of the County of Kent to Resist the Spanish Armada*, p. 6).

54. HMC Foljambe MSS, f. 96b.

55. Cruickshank, *Elizabeth's Army*, pp. 26–7, 54–5; Green, *Preparations in Somerset Against the Spanish Armada*, p. 101; Mayer, *Preparations of the County of Kent to Resist the Spanish Armada*, p. 8; PRO SP/12/212, 77.

56. See Walsingham's 1584 instructions for training of the bands (quoted in Mayer, *Prepa-rations of the County of Kent to Resist the Spanish Armada*, p. 18): 'And where the Cap-taine shalbe unskilful, beinge, as we wishe, the eldest sonne of a principall gentleman . . . then you cause some man skilfull in Martiall Profession, inhabiting thereabout, to assist him in such Trayning'.

57. See Boynton, *Elizabethan militia*, pp. 102–3; 178–81.

58. HMC Foljambe MSS, ff. 108b–109b; Boynton, *Elizabethan Militia*, pp. 62–70, 95–100, 130.

59. HMC Salisbury MSS, III, p. 293 (modernized spelling); *APC*, XX, as dated. Hunsdon was one of the more conscientious Lords Lieutenant, and strived to meet the ideal when manning his bands (see Boynton, *Elizabethan Militia*, pp. 17, 26).

60. Wake, *Musters, Beacons, Subsidies*, p. 123.

61. Goring and Wake, *Northamptonshire Lieutenancy Papers*, p. XXI.

62. Wake, *Musters, Beacons, Subsidies*, p. 17; Boynton, *Elizabethan Militia*, p. 81.

63. *APC*, XVI, pp. 216–17 (4 August 1588); HMC Salisbury MSS, V, pp. 357, 365.

64. F. C. Dietz, *English Public Finance*, II, pp. 57–8; *APC*, XV, 26 May 1588; HMC Fol-jambe MSS, f. 166.

65. Bruce, *Arrangements . . . for the Internal Defence of These Kingdoms*, App. V.

66. Nolan, *Sir John Norreys*, p. 109; Boynton, *Elizabethan Militia*, p. 128.

67. *Ibid*, pp. 128–9.

68. Lower, *Survey of the coast of Sussex*, p. 4. The raiders had attacked the port of Seaford, but were easily repulsed by local militiamen.

69. Read, *Walsingham*, III, p. 447 and n. 5. In his letter to Leicester of 9 October 1587 (BL Cotton MSS Galba, D 1, f. 46), Walsingham inferred that he had been near-incapacitated (by successive, though unrelated diseases) for several months.

70. Haynes and Murdin, *Cecil Papers*, II p. 590 (modernized spelling). In addition to Ralegh, Drake, Sir Richard Bingham and Sir Roger Williams had joined the commission by November, in which month they presented their preliminary report on vulnerable landing places and forces available to defend them (BL Add. MSS 48162, ff. 4r–5v).

71. *APC*, XVI, 1 April 1588.

72. Implementation of this order was suspended for financial reasons (see pp. 242–3).

73. *APC*, XV, 10 March 1588; Nolan, *Sir John Norreys*, pp. 108–15; HMC Foljambe MSS, f. 151b; Boynton, *Elizabethan Militia*, p. 154.

74. *APC*, XVI, 12 April 1588; PRO SP/12/186, 82 (quoted in Wark, *Elizabethan Recusancy in Cheshire*, p. 63).

75. HMC Foljambe MSS, ff. 142–3.

76. Rowse (*Grenville*, pp. 183–4), reproduces Grenville's glowing praise of one Captain Horde (probably Thomas Owrde, who previously had inspected the Somerset bands), whose example had fired his Cornish men to the point that none wished themselves excused their duties: 'Such' concludes Rowse, somewhat uncritically, 'was the spirit of the country in those golden days before the war'. Yet during those same golden days, Cornwall repeatedly failed to submit muster certificates – as required – to the Council: a strong indication that local muster-masters had difficulty in fully manning their bands (PRO SP/12/209, 42).

77. HMC Foljambe MSS, f. 172b.

78. Haynes and Murdin, *Cecil Papers*, II, pp. 608–9.

79. *APC*, XX, p. 229.

80. PRO SP/12/209, 50; HMC Foljambe MSS, f. 27.

81. PRO SP/12/213, 55 (28 July 1588): 'For your Londoners I se as the mattre stands, there servyce wyll be lytle except they haue their owne captains'.

82. *Ibid.*, ff. 176, 195. These latter allocations were not remotely realistic, and fiscal concerns ensured that only a fraction of the militia contingent assigned to protect the Queen's person was concentrated. Her bodyguard consisted almost entirely of voluntary contributions of lance and foot by Court officials and the nobility (see p. 243).

83. When summoning musters it had become almost habitual for the Privy Council to reassure their lieutenants that they would be utilized only in defence of their home counties (see *ibid.*, ff. 90, 106b).

84. Modern opinion variously gives Parma's army an early victory (Parker and Martin, *Spanish Armada*, pp. 249–58, *passim*) or, perhaps more realistically, a bitter struggle in which logistics (particularly regarding Parma's ability to re-supply his army from the Low Countries) would play a decisive role (Youings, 'State of Emergency', in *Royal Armada*, p. 203). The duke's may be the definitive judgement. He had considerable respect for the English soldier's staying power, based upon his experience in the Low Countries (Boynton, *Elizabethan Milita* p. 164).

CHAPTER TEN

1. Drake to Walsingham, 24 June 1588 (PRO SP/12/211, 53).

2. Stern, *Sir Stephen Powle*, pp. 24, 71.

3. In September, he had informed Burghley that there were already 15,000 Spanish troops in Ireland (HMC Salisbury MSS, III, p. 279).

4. *Cal. SP For. 1586–8* (xxi (i)), pp. 409, 445, 462, 493, 502.

5. On the suspiciously poor quality of Stafford's subsequent intelligences, however, see Liemon & Parker, 'Treason and Plot in Elizabethan Diplomacy', *passim*.

6. PRO SP/12/208, 22; 24 January 1588: 'I cannot tell what to thynk of my brouther Stafford's advertysments . . . but this I am suer of, yf her Majestie wolde have spent but a 1,000 crowns to have hade some intelygence, it wold have saved her Twenty tymse as muche'. On the uncharacteristic (though possibly disingenuous) peace-feelers put out by Walsingham as late as April 1588, see Read, *Walsingham*, III, pp. 276–8.

7. PRO SP/77/1, 365, 380, 388.

8. *Ibid.*, 367.

9. PRO SP/12/206, 42.

10. PRO SP/12/208, 6, 7. It has been variously suggested that the partial demobilization of January 1588 was utterly irresponsible (Froude, *History of England*, v, p. 12) or a reflection of the Queen's confidence that the fleet could be re-mobilized 'with ease and despatch' (Pollitt, *Bureacracy and the Armada*, p. 125). As the strategy was dictated above all by fiscal necessity in the face of widely conflicting reports regarding the armada's readiness to sail, both interpretations seem somewhat uncompromising.

11. *Cal. Plymouth Municipal Records*, p. 128 (Widey Court Book: 'It[e]m: p[ai]d. to Rob[er]te Scarlette for goinge out to discover the Spaynish Fleet – vj"'); Ubaldino, 'second narrative'; Naish, *History of the Spanish Armada*, pp. 83–4. Here as elsewhere, Drake's version of what these missing instructions proposed has often been accepted in lieu of the document itself – which, if it indeed existed, would directly have contradicted Howard's own instructions of 15 December 1587 (see p. 214). Evidence supporting Drake's claim that he had been ordered – at some point – to move to the coast of Spain arises in a margin note (in Burghley's hand) to the Privy Council's orders of 4 October 1587 to stay ships in English ports (PRO SP/12/204, 6): 'Yt was at the same time thowght meete that the L. Admirall should be set forthe into the Narrow Seas, and Sir Fra. Drake to be sent to the coast of Spaine, wherof the direction followeth'. Further evidence appears in a letter of 27 February 1588 from Walsingham to the earl of Shrewsbury (HMC Talbot Papers, p. 86), in which it is stated that the Queen had decided to send Drake there 'to withstand that nothing can be attempted either against Ireland or Scotland'. As to the first, the state of the Queen's ships in October 1587 made any further attempt on the Spanish coast that year unfeasible (though the option must have been discussed in light of the success of the Cadiz raid), so it is almost certain that Burghley's 'direction' was not made subsequently. The second refers to just one of several options arising from the strategic committee discussions that took place a few days before Walsingham wrote, rather than to any firm decision (there is no extant Council order authorizing Drake's removal from Plymouth for any purpose). Walsingham, a strong supporter of Drake's often-expressed intentions, may have read more into the Queen's vacillations than she intended. One other item of correspondence – Howard's note to Walsingham of 9 March (PRO SP/12/209, 10) – refers to the 'stay' upon Drake's ships at Plymouth, which infers an earlier order to the contrary (though without clarifying its precise context).

12. Howard to Walsingham, 27 January 1588 (PRO SP/12/208, 30): 'Towching Sir Francis Drake . . . yf you wold write a word or two unto him to Spare his pouder, yt wold doe well'.

13. PRO SP/12/208, 46, 47.

14. PRO SP/12/208, 64, 87; 12/209, 6, 12, 15(i).

15. *Cal. SP For. 1586–8* (xxi (i)), pp. 531–2, 556, 570.

16. PRO SP/12/208, 53.

17. From that date until 20 April, the four 'great ships' shared a complement of just 200 mariners (Bruce, *Arrangements . . . for the Internal Defence of these Kingdoms*, App. xxxix; Haynes and Murdin, *Cecil Papers*, ii, p. 620).

18. PRO SP/12/208, 70.

19. PRO SP/12/208, 79, 87.

20. PRO SP/12/208, 87; 12/209, 13. The only source of the story regarding Russell's intervention is Seymour's letter to Walsingham of 10 March.

21. PRO SP/12/209, 17.

22. PRO SP/12/209, 15, 27. The re-manning of Drake's squadron took place after 23 March, on which date Thomas Fenner reported that a sufficient soldiers, ensigns and gentlemen-volunteers had gathered for that purpose in Plymouth (PRO SP/209, 30). At this time he made no reference to mariners.

23. 'Preparations for resisting the Spanish Invasion, 1588'; in Nichols, *Progresses and Processions*, ii, A2v. The first English translation of this German prophecy appeared in John Securis's 1569 almanack (Bauckham, *Tudor Apocalypse*, p. 168).

24. BL Add. MS 48027, f. 691b; Read, 'William Cecil and Elizabethan Public Relations', pp. 24–5

25. F. C. Dietz, *English Public Finance*, ii, p. 55. The latter subsidies were collected with some difficulty. As late as 14 July 1588 the Privy Council was obliged to reprimand its commissioners in the shires for failing to apply themselves with sufficient industry (BL Lansdowne MS 57, 3).

26. F. C. Dietz, *English Public Finance*, ii, pp. 59–60.

27. BL Add. MS 6703, f. 31.

28. W. H. Noble, *Spanish Armada*, xvii, xxx; BL Lansdowne MS 56, 3; F. C. Dietz, *English Public Finance*, ii, p. 58.

29. It is extremely difficult to determine at which stage many ships joined the English fleet. The present author had assumed arbitrarily that the thirty-four ships listed as 'appointed to serve westwards under the charge of Sir Francis Drake' (as listed, post-campaign, in PRO SP/12/215, 76) were all at Plymouth by mid-March, and that about half of Seymour's eventual squadron strength of twenty-nine coasters were at sea by this time. However, it is by no means unlikely that some (or many) of these were later arrivals.

30. PRO SP/12/209, 15.

31. Pollitt, 'Bureacracy and the Armada: The Administrator's Battle' remains the most comprehensive (if occasionally over-sanguine) modern discussion of the bureaucratic organization behind England's military efforts in 1588.

32. Bruce, *Arrangements . . . for the Internal Defence of these Kingdoms*, App. xxxii; HMC Foljambe MS, ff. 296–7.

33. Andrews, *English Privateering Voyages*, pp. 40–49, *passim*. Andrews infers that Watts's ships were able to depart because the stay on ships had been relaxed since its imposition in the previous October and then re-applied prior to the detention of the Roanoke fleet. The present author cannot find extant evidence of any loosening of the original ruling during the intervening months.

34. See p. 156.

35. *APC*, xv, 31 March, 9 April 1588; Quinn, *Roanoke*, ii, p. 554. Two small vessels – a bark of thirty tons and a pinnace of five tons – were set out (carrying twelve new colonists) to relieve the colony in April; but their commander, Arthur Facy, decided instead to

wage war upon every merchantman he encountered. His bark was eventually mauled by two La Rochelle privateers and limped back to Bideford in May.

36. *APC*, xvi, 1 April 1588. The list given in PRO SP/12/237, 18 (reproduced in Lewis, *Elizabethan Ship Money*, appendix A), provided for forty-eight ships and twenty-nine pinnaces.

37. PRO SP/12/209, 70, 71, 75, 81, 84, 87, 88, 94–7, 101–2; Lewis, *Elizabethan Ship Money*, p. 22, appendix A; MacCaffrey, *Exeter, 1540–1640*, pp. 236–9.

38. PRO SP/12/215, 76.

39. *APC*, xv, 9 April 1588.

40. PRO SP/12/209, 93; BL Lansdowne MS 56, 61; Lewis, *Elizabethan Ship Money*, appendix C; *APC*, xv, 28 May 1588.

41. Jack, 'The Cinque Ports and the Spanish Armada', pp. 144, 146–7; Mayhew, *Rye and the Defence of the Narrow Seas*, p. 119.

42. See pp. 284–5.

43. *Cal. SP Sp. 1587–1603*, p. 261; reported by Mendoza to Philip, 5 April 1588.

44. PRO SP/12/209, 40, 89, 112. See also Williamson, *Age of Drake*, p. 308.

45. PRO SP/12/209, 112, Drake to the Queen, 28 April 1588.

46. For James VI's apparent (if insincere) vacillation between English and Spanish 'camps' within the Scottish nobility, see the voluminous correspondence between Archibald Douglas (the Scottish ambassador in London) and his brother Richard (HMC Salisbury MSS, III, *ad finem*).

47. Crofts and his colleagues appear to have been unconscionably gullible, if not traitorous as was later claimed. The report (or 'diary') of their visit to the Low Countries contained the remarkable preamble: 'You shall therefore understand that the Duke of Parma first and principally did laboure verie earnestlie . . . to enter into a coloquie for peace . . .' (BL Sloane MS 262, f. 41).

48. BL Harleian MS 6994, f. 120 (secretary's copy – with less idiosyncratic spelling – at f. 65); PRO SP/12/209, 99 (author's emphasis).

49. PRO SP/12/209, 113; 12/210, 11; HMC Talbot Papers, p. 90.

50. PRO E351/2225.

51. The number of vessels in Seymour's squadron would rise to some thirty-five to thirty-seven vessels as further levies joined him immediately prior to the campaign.

52. Howard's instructions to Seymour are contained in BL Cotton MS Otho, E IX, ff. 174v–175r. George Raymond had previously commanded one of the London merchantmen in the Cadiz raid. He was later lost with his ship during the 1591 East Indies expedition, of which he had been appointed admiral (Corbett, *Spanish War*, p. 141; Oppenheim, *Monson*, I, p. 152, IV, p. 180; Foster, *Lancaster*, p. 4).

53. PRO SP/12/210, 28.

54. The only detailed narrative of the meeting of fleets is Ubaldino's (Naish, *History of the Spanish Armada*, p. 87). The curious attention he devotes to describing Drake's lack of resentment at surrendering both his authority and his admiral's emoluments all but confirms the contrary.

55. PRO SP/12/210, 28, Howard to Burghley, 23 May.

56. HMC Bath MSS, II, p. 28, Drake to Burghley, 6 June 1588: 'the xxxth day we sette saile out of Plymouthe, having the winde easterlie . . . we endured a greate storme (consideringe the tyme of the yeare), that so muche as in keepinge sea we shoulde have bin putt to leaward of Plymouthe, ether for Porteland or Weighte . . .'.

57. PRO SP/12/209, 78.

58. PRO SP/12/210, 35. Pollitt ('Bureacracy and the Armada'), pp. 127–8) regards the vict-

ualling arrangements for the fleet as fundamentally successful: 'sufficient, at least in quantity, to carry the English force through and actually well beyond the battle in the Channel'. To the present author, this view appears to ascribe to the navy victuallers Quarles and Darell rather more foresight, resources and control over contrary winds than they would have admitted to enjoying. The evidence of Hawkins, Howard and others suggests that the arrangements came dangerously close to breakdown at several points, notwithstanding the victuallers' heroic efforts.

59. *APC*, xvi, 9 April 1588.
60. *Ibid.*, 29 March.
61. PRO SP/12/212, 61(i).
62. PRO SP/12/211, 70.
63. PRO SP/12/210, 35; PRO SP/12/211, 17, 18, 45, 51; PRO SP/12/213, 88. Howard's virtues stated in his commission of December 157 (Patent Rolls 30 Eliz. 17; m.7.d). Note also his comments to Walsingham, 15 June (*ibid.*, 26): '. . . the Spanishe forces, beinge for so long victualled as they are, mighte, in very good policie, detract time to drive us to consume oure victualles, which, for anything we [may see] is not to be supplied againe to serve the turne, by all the meanes that Her Majestie, and all you can doe'). Howard's only experience of 'war' prior to 1588 was in his role in 1569 as general of the horse of Warwick's army, charged with crushing the Northern Rising. The task had been completed before Howard and his troopers encountered any rebels.
64. *APC*, xvi, 3 June 1588, Privy Council to Seymour: '. . . yf the sayd Duke should have anie soche meaning you may have your Fleet in convenyent places to prevent and lett his attempt . . .'.
65. PRO SP/21/4, 453.
66. *APC*, xvi, 27 June 1588.
67. *APC*, xvi: orders for that day refer to the armada being 'abroad'.
68. PRO SP/12/211, 37, 47, 49, 50–53; PRO SP/12/212, 9, 10.
69. Walsingham's reminder to him of 6 June: PRO SP/12/211, 8.
70. Some confusion has arisen regarding the movements of the English fleet between 23 June and 12 July. It has been inferred that it returned to Plymouth within days of the earlier date and departed once more as late as 7 or 8 July (for example Rodger, *The Armada in the Public Records*, p. 10; Rodriguez-Salgado, *Armada*, p. 233). Yet the correspondence of Howard, Drake and Fenner (PRO SP/12/212, 9, 10, 18) clearly indicates that they remained at sea thoughout most, if not all, of this period. On 4 July, Drake recalled that his squadron had been off the French coast seeking word of the armada for almost two weeks, and urged that the fleet sail to the northern Spanish coast '*or at least more neerer then wee are now*' (author's emphasis). Fenner explicitly stated that on 7 July, as the decision was finally made to move southwards, the English fleet already lay fifteen leagues west-south-west off Ushant. This enduring misapprehension may have arisen from an original confusion of Julian and Gregorian dating in contemporary documents, repeated unwittingly thereafter; or by the vagueness of the 'Relation of Proceedings' on events during this period.
71. PRO SP/12/212, 18.
72. See his memorandum of 4 July (PRO SP/12/212, 9).
73. PRO SP/12/211, 38; PRO SP/12/212, 9; PRO/SP/12/211, 26.
74. PRO SP/12/212, 42.
75. The quotation is from Burghley's later parliamentary brief to Sir Christopher Hatton (4 February 1589), reproduced in Hartley, *Proceedings*, ii, p. 412.

CHAPTER ELEVEN

1. Sir Christopher Hatton to Parliament, 4 February 1589, Hartley, *Proceedings*, ii, p. 423.
2. In total, 197 vessels served in the various divisions of the English fleet during the armada campaign, but not simultaneously.
3. See Read, *Walsingham*, iii, p. 299; Lewis, *Armada*, pp. 101–2; Whiting, *Enterprise of England*, pp. 94–5; Kelsey, *Drake*, pp. 315–16.
4. This was the title of his chapter (*Drake*, ii, pp. 113–56) discussing English aims.
5. PRO SP/12/208, 47; PRO SP/12/209, 40.
6. BL Cotton MSS Otho, E ix, f. 164.
7. BL Cotton MSS Vespasian, C viii, f. 12; discussed in Read, *Burghley*, pp. 418–20. On the relatively widespread belief in aggressive strategies among Drake's contemporaries, see also the comments of Oppenheim (Monson, *Tracts*, i, pp. 63–4).
8. Drake himself acknowledged these hazards in detail; see Petruccio Ubaldino's 'second narrative' in Naish, *History of the Spanish Armada*, pp. 85–6.
9. Some commentators disagree. Fernandez-Armesto (*Spanish Armada*, p. 97) regards the English government's inability to interpret its intelligence with sufficient confidence as a missed opportunity. It is the present author's opinion, having reviewed the mass of information available in the months prior to the campaign, that it would have required acute percipience rather than confidence to have identified which of it was 'good' intelligence.
10. PRO SP/12/168, 3.
11. Read, *Walsingham*, iii, p. 294. The first broadly accurate assessment of the strength of the armada was provided from Spain by Walsingham's agent Nicholas Ousley as late as 17 April 1588 (BL Harleian MS 295, f. 182); two weeks later, intelligence from France (*ibid.*, ff. 186–7) provided more detailed figures. It reported an armada of 130 vessels, with a detailed breakdown of its manpower: 7,070 Spanish and 2,000 Portuguese soldiers, 160 'comon adventurers', 8,050 mariners, 160 boys, 238 gentlemen, 130 of their men, 137 commoners, 85 doctors, surgeons and apothecaries, 104 priests, friars and monks, 50 of their men, and, most worryingly, 90 hangmen and executioners. The recipients of this information had no way of testing its accuracy, however. Equally detailed, Thomas Fenner's report of 3 March (PRO SP/12/209, 6) had wildly overstated the armada's true strength.
12. Wooley, though not a leading voice in the formulation of policy, had assumed more responsibility within the Council as Walsingham's illnesses grew more debilitating. On 3 November 1586, during the debate upon Mary Stuart, it was he who had suggested to the Commons that a bill demanding Mary's execution be drawn up and presented to the Queen (Hartley, *Proceedings*, ii, pp. 197, 218).
13. Read, *Burghley*, p. 419.
14. Patent Roll 30 Eliz. 13: m.1; copy in HMC, Foljambe MSS, f. 307 (modernized spelling).
15. *Ibid.*, '. . . you should ply up and down, sometimes towards the north, and sometimes towards the south, as to you in your own discretion and judgement shall be thought may tend best to the impeaching of attempts and designs of the said Duke . . .'.
16. In fact, an early (undated) proposal for the defence of the Thames against a surprise descent by one or more galleys had envisaged the deployment of several of the Navy Royal's principal ships (under the overall command of Sir Henry Palmer) at several of the river's more vulnerable reaches – the *Victory*'s great bulk, for example, would block the passage between Tilbury and Gravesend forts, while the *Lion* would 'ryde about Greenehythe, there to receaue the Alarume from the Victory' (BL Cotton MSS Otho, E ix, ff. 181v–182r).

17. PRO SP/21/4, 425–6.

18. See Sir William Russell's comments to Walsingham, 26 March 1588; PRO SP/84/22, 178.

19. In June, twenty small Dutch vessels under the command of Cornelis Lonck van Roozendaal were appointed to join Seymour's squadron, but these were rejected as unsuitable and instead joined Nassau's coaster fleet (PRO/SP/12/211, 54; Schokkenbroek, 'Whither Serveth Justin . . . ?', p. 107). See also p. 265.

20. Froude, *History of England*, XII, pp. 415–16.

21. Seizures of Danish vessels by English pirates had resulted, in March 1588, in a stay of all English Eastland ships in Danish harbours. An English envoy, Daniel Rogers, was despatched hurriedly to Denmark with conciliatory messages from the Queen. Even as his 'chested treasure' vanished, Burghley quickly found the £331 19s. necessary for Rogers's passage (*APC*, XVI, 1 April 1588; HMC Salisbury MSS, III, p. 329; Bruce, *Arrangements . . . for the Internal Defence of these Kingdoms*, app. XXXVI).

22. PRO SP/12/212, 80; Howard to Walsingham: 'the southerly wynde brought us back from the cost of Spayne, then our God blessed us, with torninge us back'.

23. It has recently been suggested (Martin and Parker, *Spanish Armada*, p. 146) that the armada had a 'golden opportunity' to trap the English ships in Plymouth harbour. As with other speculative scenarios, hindsight supplies intelligence that Medina Sidonia had no way of obtaining. It should be noted, however, that his vice admiral, Juan Martínez de Recalde, later criticized the decision not to attempt to trap the English fleet in Plymouth Sound (Parker, 'Anatomy of Defeat', p. 329).

24. Perhaps the only man with appropriate recent experience of commanding a fleet action at sea – Edward Wilkinson, 'admiral' of the five levanters that had fought off twenty Maltese galleys at Pantalarea in 1586 – was not present in the 1588 English fleet.

25. That is, three days' passage from the Downs to Plymouth and the period 23 June to 12 July when the entire fleet patrolled the western approaches and northern Biscay.

26. '. . . I dare assure your Honour, if you had seen that which I had seen, of the simple sarvis that hath bin done by the marchaunte & coast shippes, you woulde have saide that we had byne little holpen by them, otherwise then they did make a shew' (Winter to Walsingham, 1 August 1588, PRO SP/214, 7). Camden's later comments regarding the final stages of the campaign (*History*, p. 415) are even more uncompromising: 'And now there were in the English Fleet 140 Sail, all of them Ships for Fight, good Sailers, and nimble and tight for tacking about which way they would: yet there were not above fifteen of them which did in a manner sustain and repell the whole brunt of the Fight.'

27. 'If we chance to meete with any enemies, that foure ships shall attend upon the Admirall, viz. the Francis of Foy, the Moone, the Barke Dennis, and the Gabriel: and foure upon my Lieutenant generall in the Judith, viz. the Hopewel, the Armenal, the Beare, and the Salomon: and the other foure upon the Vizadmirall, the Anne Francis, the Thomas of Ipswich, the Emmanuel, and the Michael' (Best, *True Discourse*, in Hakluyt, *Principal Navigations*, VII, pp. 324–5).

28. On this potentially disastrous disadvantage, see the later experience of the Four Days Battle (Pepys, *Diary*, VII, pp. 161 n.3, 194 n.2.

29. See Article 29 of Ralegh's (1617) *Orders to be observed by the commanders of the fleet, etc* (after Gorges's 'Observations and overtures for a seafight, etc': BL Lansdowne MS 213): 'But if we find an enemy to the leewards of us, the whole fleet shall follow the admiral, vice-admiral, or other leading ship within musket shot of the enemy; giving so much

liberty to the leading ship as after her broadside delivered she may stay and trim her sails' (quoted in Corbett, *Fighting Instructions, 1530–1816*, p. 42). This, certainly, was what Howard and his officers attempted, if not often successfully, during the armada battle. However, both Ralegh and Gorges continue: 'This you must do upon the windermost ship or ships of an enemy, which you shall either batter in pieces, or force him or them to bear up and so entangle them, and drive them foul one of another to their utter confusion'. Corbett (*ibid.*, p. 32) believed that Gorges's original 'Observations' (particularly their acknowledgment of the benefits of line-ahead fighting) may have predated the armada campaign by ten years; inferring that the employment of line-ahead attacks to drive enemy ships back upon each other was already a practiced tactic of English commanders in 1588. This seems doubtful. In arguing his case, Corbett suggested that the genesis of this section of the 'Observations' lay in Gorges's experiences in the brief (1578) naval campaign in Irish waters. In fact, no significant engagement took place during the operation. The present author considers it far more likely that the armada battle itself provided the first substantial confirmation of the benefit of line-ahead fighting in large-scale engagements which the 'Observations', and Ralegh, subsequently noted.

30. Parker, 'Dreadnought Revolution', p. 269.
31. BL Sloane MS 2177, f. 15b: 'A discription of what order our Fleet shall keepe togeather in Fight and yt is to be vnderstood that the first in every frontier are her Maiesties shipps'.
32. Several years later, John Young, captain of the fireship *Bark Young* during the armada campaign, wrote: '. . . the strongest in battling of a navy is to fight in breast with the best of her Majesty's ships, and the best of the merchants ships divided amongst them.' (PRO SP/12/259, 48).
33. For a discussion of Lisle's fighting instructions, see Loades, *Tudor Navy*, pp. 132–3.
34. See Gorgas's *Observations*: '. . . to set down precisely the particular division of battles and alterations of fights that must be acted in the field or on the seas according to time or place, is of all other councils and proscription the most fruitless and frivolous and especially in sea-service when the wind and waves, two so inconstant elements and powerful commanders, do chiefle predominate.' (Quoted, with modernized spelling, in Glasgow, 'Gorgas' Seafight', p. 183).
35. PRO SP/12/96, 257; PRO SP/12/186, 8.
36. One of the first recognizable 'tarpaulins' was Sir Henry Palmer, third-in-command in Seymour's squadron during the armada battle. Of a long-established though modest Rochester family, he appears to have gone to sea as a child. Following his first known senior appointment as commander of a Channel squadron in 1574, he was repeatedly employed on Crown service (in 1580 he also became one of the commissioners responsible for the repair and maintenance of Dover harbour). Almost every year from 1587 until he replaced William Borough as Comptroller of the Ships in 1598 (a post he held until his own death in 1611, and the reversion of which passed to his son Henry), Palmer commanded naval squadrons in the Channel (all details from the *Oxford Dictionary of National Biography*, entry for Sir Henry Palmer).
37. Parker (*Grand Strategy*, p. 254) observes that 'Elizabeth's warships . . . had been served by the same officers and crews for years, patrolling the Narrow Seas, showing the flag of the coast of Ireland, and (in the case of several ships) cruising in Spanish waters'. This continuity should not be overstated. Certainly, many such operations had provided invaluable experience for their participants; but each new campaign required the hiring or pressing, from scratch, of new ships' complements. Many officers and

mariners had served in several of these campaigns, but in a number of vessels. None, as far as we know, returned to the same ship in successive voyages except as a matter of coincidence. The armed merchantmen were far more likely to have enjoyed some continuity of command (Flicke in the *Merchant Royal* is an obvious case), but again, not necessarily of manning. Prior to the armada campaign, only the men in the Narrow Seas squadron, being almost constantly employed since autumn 1587, may be said to have been intimately familiar with their vessels.

38. See Edward Hellowes's fulsome praise in the respect in his dedication to Howard of his (1578) *A Booke of the Invention of the Art of Navigation, etc*: '. . . respecting your . . . experience of the sea and sea matters, with shippes and shipping . . . your readines and aptnes in all weathers, to manure not only the meanest matters, as all maner of cordage and tackle within boord, namely sheat, halliard, bowline, tacke and helme, with such other, as also the vse and practice of the *Astrolobe, Balistilio, Carde*, and Compasse, but also the diligent search in knowledge, of allcapes, forelands, shores, ports, creeks, hauens, races, tides, bankes and rocks: all which things although not usual to noble men, and yet most necessarie vnto all manner persons that haunteth the seas . . .' (reproduced by Waters, 'Lord Howard as a Seaman, 1578', *MM*, vol. 41, p. 337).

39. PRO SP/12/237, 62. Gorges had previously (1576) commanded a Channel squadron.

40. For brief biographies of the Fenners, see Andrews, *Elizabethan Privateering*, pp. 89, 90–91.

41. Corbett, *Spanish War*, p. 47 n. 1; *Oxford Dictionary of National Biography*, entry for Sir Robert Crosse.

42. Corbett, *Spanish War*, pp. XII, 186–7; Laughton, *Defeat of the Spanish Armada*, II, pp. 324–6.

43. *LP Henry VIII*, XXI (i), p. 358. William Borough's patent to succeed Holstocke as Comptroller was issued before the end of the year. It seems, however, that he had been acting Comptroller for some months prior to this, as Benjamin Gonson had in turn replaced Borough as Clerk of the Ships by the time of the armada campaign.

44. The mutiny of the *Golden Lion* has since clouded the reputation of a man whose contribution to England's naval tradition was as significant as Drake's, if less spectacular. Borough was one of the first generation of English masters to be taught by Sebastian Cabot, and had both commanded and supervised the despatch of Muscovy Company voyages for more than a quarter of a century. Even in the 1580s he remained one of England's few authorities on navigation, and was the author of a seminal work on magnetic variation of the compass.

45. Corbett, *Spanish War*, p. 295; Glasgow, 'The Navy in the Le Havre expedition, 1562–4', pp. 283, 294–5. Details of Beeston's early career and doubtful age are taken from biographical notes prepared by John Elsworth, church warden of St Boniface church in Bunbury, Cheshire, where Beeston is buried.

46. The reference is that of Seymour, in a letter to Walsingham, 12 July 1588: 'And to heape on braveryes for conquering lyttel England, yt hath alwayes ben renowned, and now most famous by the great discovered strength, as well by sea as by land, the same also united with thousandes resolute cyvill myndes, how can the [Spaniards] enter into any conceit they should any wayes prevayle?' (PRO SP/12/212, 34).

47. The phrase was Sir Christopher Hatton's, from his opening speech to the 1589 parliament (Hartley, *Proceedings*, II, p. 417).

48. Marten, 'An Exhortation to Stir up the Minds of all Her Majesty's Faithful Subjects, etc'; Maliham, *Harleian Miscellany*, II, p. 104.

CHAPTER TWELVE

1. Thomas Deloney, *A joyfull new Ballad Declaring the happy obtaining of the great Galleazzo,* etc; reproduced in Collier, *Broadside Black-letter Ballads,* p. 81.

2. See Howard to Walsingham, 17 July (PRO SP/12/212, 60): 'Some 4 or 5 ships we have discharged [because the] sickness in some is very greate, so we are faine to discharge some of the ships to have there men to furnish others.'

3. The only reference to the order in which the English ships emerged from Plymouth Harbour is that of van Meteran's 'Miraculous Victory, etc' (English translation, Hakluyt, *Principal Navigations,* IV, p. 211). This was not an eyewitness account.

4. All information on weather during the armada campaign is drawn from Daultrey, 'The Weather of Northwest Europe during the Armada Campaign'; and Douglas and Lamb, *Weather Observations and a tentative Meteorological analysis of the Period May to July 1588.*

5. Duro, *La armada invencible,* II, p. 274.

6. The most detailed (if necessarily speculative) discussion of the Spanish formation is that of Pierson, *Commander of the Armada,* pp. 133–5.

7. Whyte to Walsingham, 8 August (PRO SP/12/214, 43). White commanded the *Bark Talbot,* later employed at Calais as a fire-ship.

8. At his most optimistic, Philip hoped, but did not necessarily aim, for total victory against England. He seems to have believed that Elizabeth might swiftly seek terms following Parma's successful landing in England. Those conditions of an armistice that the Spanish King regarded as mandatory were the total withdrawal of English forces from the Low Countries and surrender of the 'cautionary towns', and full freedom of worship allowed to English Catholics. The payment of compensation for English depredations during the previous four years was a further, though negotiable matter (Parker, *Grand Strategy,* p. 196; Jensen, 'The Spanish Armada: The Worst-Kept Secret in Europe', pp. 638, 640).

9. To luff: to bring or maintain a vessel as close to the wind as possible in order to prevent her from falling away to leeward.

10. Recalde to Medina Sidonia, 31 July 1588 (NS); Parker, 'Anatomy of Defeat', p. 323.

11. Thompson, 'Spanish Armada Guns', p. 370 n. 4.

12. See Parker, 'Dreadnought Revolution', p. 270. On the types and numbers of guns carried in the Spanish fleet comparative to those of the English ships, see Thompson, 'Spanish Armada Guns', *ad finem.*

13. Calvar, 'Summary Report', p. 190, 15c; Waters, 'Armada', Appendix C. Waters calculates that the average weight of shot fired by the English ships during the battle was just 11.65 pounds.

14. See Parker, 'Dreadnought Revolution', *ad finem.*

15. It is impossible to determine the exact number and type of guns carried by individual ships in the English fleet in 1588. We have accurate data for those carried in the Queen's ships at the time of Sir William Winter's survey of 1585 (PRO SP/12/185, 34; reproduced in Corbett, *Spanish War,* pp. 300–08), and the 'proportion' (invariably more than the numbers then surveyed) that he regarded as optimum. We also have details of ordnance provided to naval vessels on active service in 1595 and 1596 (PRO WO55 (War Office Misc. Entry Books) piece 1627: 'A view and survey of all her Majestie's ordnance'). There are extant, if incomplete, figures for ordnance supplied from the Tower to Drake's squadron at Plymouth in the early months of 1588 (PRO E351/2607), though not for the pieces carried already in his ships. From all of this we may make only partly

informed guesses. Given that the figures for ordnance provided in 1595/6 to ships that had been built before 1586 (and not since rebuilt) are broadly similar to Winter's recommendations (though with some variations between types of gun) the author's comments are based on the arbitrary assumption that they were armed in 1588 broadly according to his 'proportion'.

16. Kirsch, *The Galleon*, pp. 55–6.

17. On shot provision, see the indenture for delivery of ordnance and munitions for the *Elizabeth Bonaventure* and *Ayde* for Drake's 1585/6 West Indies raid (PRO EKR/64, 9, reproduced in Corbett, *Spanish War*, pp. 27–32). This shows a provision for most types of gun in the range of twenty-five to thirty rounds per piece. Only culverin shot for the *Elizabeth Bonaventure* is given at a proportion of almost fifty rounds per gun. Significantly, however, the *Elizabeth*, was an older, broad-beamed, deep-draughted design with much greater storage space than her more modern sister ships.

18. Stewart, *English Ordnance Office*, p. 92.

19. Report of the Council of War, 27 November 1587 (Monson, *Tracts*, II, p. 268): '. . . it is unlikely that the King of Spain will engage his fleet too far within the Sleeve before he has mastered some one [*sic*] good harbour . . .'.

20. PRO SP/12/212, 80. In the same despatch, Howard was frank about his tactics that day: 'we durste not adventure to put in amongste them theire fleete beinge soe stronge'.

21. For Sussex's turbulent relations with the Privy Council, the Marquis of Winchester (his co-Lord Lieutenant), his immediate subordinates and almost everyone tasked with providing armour and weapons to his trained bands, see Boynton, *Elizabethan Militia*, pp. 101, 142–4, 187.

22. *APC*, XVI, 24 July 1588. The *Prudence* and *Bark Clifford* were stripped (PRO SP/12/214, 28), while a third vessel belonging to Cumberland, the *Sampson*, subsequently joined the fleet, though too late to see service (Spence, *Privateering Earl*, p. 78). On 6 August, she was listed as 'absent' from Seymour's squadron, to which she had been assigned (PRO SP/12/214, 39(i)).

23. PRO SP/12/214, 56.

24. PRO SP/12/213, 71.

25. See the comments of Giovanni Mocenigo, Venetian ambassador in Paris (*Cal. SP Venice 1581–9*, no. 706; 11 August 1588 (NS)): '. . . they would consider themselves victorious, even if they died to a man along with the enemy, provided they could save the Kingdom, as they propose to do by one bloody battle, which shall so weaken the Spanish forces that they dare not venture on a landing'.

26. PRO SP/12/212, 82.

27. Discussed in McDermott, *Martin Frobisher*, pp. 364–5.

28. Of the two Englishmen discovered in the *Rosario*, one, the remarkable Tristram Winslade, was later brought to the Tower, where officers were ordered to interrogate him robustly: 'using torture to hym at their pleasure'. He not only survived the experience but managed to rejoin his Habsburg employers; in 1600 he was one of the regiment of 'pensioners' serving in the Low Countries under Sir William Stanley (*APC*, XVI, 8 September 1588; Loomie, *Spanish Elizabethans*, p. 263). A Spanish report on the pensioners referred to Winslade as 'a well-born gentleman . . . loyal and has endured much suffering'.

29. It has been assumed by some commentators that munitions from the *San Salvador* were immediately distributed around the English fleet, but this was not the case. She was taken into Weymouth where Sir John Gilbert conducted a detailed inventory of her

armaments. He then sent her powder and shot back to the fleet, though the bark carrying this vital cargo did not depart Weymouth until 26 July (PRO SP/12/213, 59; PRO SP/12/215, 49(i–iii)).

30. Details of the events of 22 July are largely drawn from the *Relation of Proceedings*: BL Cotton MSS Julius, F x, ff. 111–17, and the testimony of the captain, master and lieutenant of the *Margaret and John*: PRO SP/12/213, 89. In describing the episode, Ubaldino (in Naish, *History of the Spanish Armada*, p. 89) typically ascribed Drake's seizure of the *Rosario* to dutifulness and Howard's unwitting pursuit of the Spanish ships to over-eagerness.

31. *APC*, xvi, 23 July 1588.

32. All figures from Burghley's 'Memorandum of Charges': PRO SP/12/213, 3 (22 July 1588).

33. PRO SP/12/212, 66.

34. Bruce, *Arrangements . . . for the Internal Defence of these Kingdoms*, App. xxix; Nolan, *Sir John Norreys*, p. 119.

35. It is difficult to know how many men certified as available to the maritime counties' trained bands actually marched during July 1588. Bruce (*Arrangements . . . for the Internal Defence of these Kingdoms*, App. xxix) and Haynes and Murdin (*Cecil Papers*, ii, p. 611) give a potential (that is, certified) maximum of 27,000 foot and horse, but see p. 371 n. 53.

36. See p. 159.

37. Nolan, *Sir John Norreys*, p. 120

38. *Ibid.*, p. 111.

39. See the poor opinion of certain captains in Kent regarding plans for a fighting retreat: McGurk, 'Armada Preparations in Kent', p. 85.

40. The best contemporary pictorial representation of the Tilbury/Gravesend defences is that of Robert Adams.

41. *APC*, xvi, 24, 26 July.

42. HMC Foljambe MSS, f. 180.

43. All 5,000 foot from the Essex trained bands had been assigned to Tilbury, rather than to 'forward' concentrations that might have provided cover for their beaches and ports at short notice (*ibid.*).

44. Bruce, *Arrangements . . . for the Internal Defence of these Kingdoms*, App. xxx.

45. BL Cotton MSS Galba, D iii, f. 221. See also p. 353 n. 44 for Heneage's record with Leicester.

46. PRO SP/12/213, 27.

47. John Stow, *Annals*, quoted in 'Preparations for resisting the Spanish Invasion, 1588': Nichols, *Progresses and Processions*, ii, A2r. Their dancing and leaping should have been hampered by the burden of each day's official marching rations: 1 lb of dried biscuit, 1 1/2 lbs of bread, 2 1/2 lbs of beef, 1 lb of cheese, 1/2 lb of butter, and, most vitally, 2 quarts of beer and a quart of wine (Bruce, *Arrangements . . . for the Internal Defence of these Kingdoms*, App. xxxvi). However, as Leicester's subsequent complaints to Walsingham indicate, few received more than a fraction of this generous provision before departing their homes, and most arrived at Tilbury almost famished.

48. PRO SP/12/213, 38, 55; PRO SP/12/214, 1. The first of these references, a letter from Leicester to Walsingham on 26 July, provides a catalogue of the earl's woes. The shipwrights Peter Pett, Matthew Baker and Richard Chapman had spent some £315 on the bulwark and bridge by 12 August, of which they had been reimbursed just £20 (*APC*, xvi, as dated).

49. See the similar opinion of Nolan (*Sir John Norreys*, p. 116).

50. In April 1586, Norreys had given a bloody (though inconclusive) repulse to Count Mansfelt's besieging force at Grave.

51. HMC Foljambe MSS, f. 196b; Nolan, *Sir John Norreys*, p. 122; Boynton, *Elizabethan Militia*, p. 160.

52. See the provisional instructions sent to the deputy Lords Lieutenant of Norfolk (Bruce, *Arrangements . . . for the Internal Defence of these Kingdoms*, App. x): 'And to prevent the expectation of the enemye, for victuall and carriages in this countye, upon his invasion, there must bee greater care used, the rather the corne may be burned and spoyled, then lefte unto their use. And all cataill, whatsoever, upon such extremitie, may be conveyed into Marsheland . . . and, lykwise, that noe carts or cart-horses be left behinde, for the ayde of the enemye.'

53. Aske's references to Tilbury camp as the 'Camp Royal' (*Elizabetha Triumphans*, pp. 16–17) has since caused some commentators to assume that there was no third, distinct military concentration around London besides those commanded by Leicester and Norreys. However, the context of numerous specific references by the Privy Council to the Queen's bodyguard (and the re-assignment of several leading figures from Tilbury to St James's Palace) indicates that the forces at Tilbury remained wholly distinct from those assigned to the Queen's defence. For what appears to be (though cannot be confirmed as) the definitive allocation of forces between Hunsdon and Leicester, see HMC Foljambe MSS, f. 194b (document dated 29 July 1588).

54. The 27,000 men of the maritime counties' trained bands were never intended to concentrate in their entirety as part of the 'grosse army'. As the composite host shadowed the armada passed eastwards along the English coast, 'old' formations – those that had come furthest from the west – dropped out and returned home as the bands of the counties into which they advanced joined it. The bands of each county were allocated with some precision to join with those of one or more of their neighbours to cover specific sites thought vulnerable to landing attempts (PRO/SP/12/211/72).

55. *APC*, xvi, as dated.

56. HMC Foljambe MSS, f. 194b.

57. Goring and Wake, *Northamptonshire Lieutenancy Papers*, p. 66.

58. On the day the sea-campaign commenced, Lord Chandos wrote to Walsingham complaining that his trained bands were being depleted by the withdrawal of the retainers of the earls Worcester and Pembroke to protect the Queen (PRO SP/12/212, 74).

59. On 23 July, Hatton was ordered by the Council to bring his 400 picked Northamptonshire men to Court 'with all convenyent speid that may be vsed' (Goring and Wake, *Northamptonshire Lieutenancy Papers*, pp. 60–61. Three days later, it was estimated that of 17,600 men from eleven named shires appointed to guard the Queen, 11,009 remained at home still (Bruce, *Arrangements . . . for the Internal Defence of these Kingdoms*, App. xxxi).

60. HMC Foljambe MSS, f. 193 (modernized spelling).

61. *Ibid.*, ff. 195–6.

62. HMC Rutland MSS, p. 594. Reporting in June 1588, Sir Edward Stanley informed Burghley that the bands of both Lancashire and Cheshire had not undertaken a single day's drilling in the previous two years (PRO SP/12/208, 86). Nevertheless, when it appeared that the armada might seek to land its troops in nothern England or Scotland, 500 foot and 25 horse were subsequently required from both counties to join Huntingdon's forces at Newcastle (*APC*, xvi, 13 August). The modesty of this requisition (the city of Lincoln alone was asked to provide 700 foot and 30 horse) indicates that fears of their poor quality, or of local dissenters, remained strong.

63. Knappen, *Two Elizabethan Puritan Diaries*, pp. 79–80.

64. Council to Sir Christopher Hatton, 4 January 1588 (Goring and Wake, *Northamptonshire Lieutenancy Papers*, p. 47); Wark, *Elizabethan Recusancy in Cheshire*, p. 74; HMC Salisbury MSS, III, p. 96. Two days before the armada appeared off the English coast, the Privy Council congratulated the earl of Shrewsbury on his capture of two seminary priests. The justices of York assizes were put on notice to proceed (rather less than impartially) with the 'conviction, condemnation and execution' of these unfortunates (HMC Talbot MSS, p. 92). Their recusant followers – by definition, 'seditious and traitorous persons' – were to be held in prison pending examination.

65. See the case of the Suffolk recusant Edward Sulyard, who was committed to the care of his London-resident brother-in-law, Thomas Tyrrell (MacCulloch, 'Catholic and Puritan in Elizabethan Suffolk', p. 260.

66. PRO SP/12/208, 15, 16, 19, 37; BL Harleian MS 703/51–2.

67. See the Privy Council's complaint of June 1582 (*APC*, XII, p. 451) to all the kingdom's sheriffs and justices of the peace: 'Having perused the late certificats of the recusants sent from the severall counties within the realme, & findinge, that, in divers of the said counties, some are presented & not indicted, & but a few indicted, & convicted according to the late statute made for the retaininge of her majesties subjects in there due obedience . . .'.

68. Petti, *Roman Catholicism in Elizabethan and Jacobean Staffordshire*, pp. 26, 28, 30 n. 2.

69. Goring and Wake, *Northamptonshire Lieutenancy Papers*, p. 46; HMC Shrewsbury Papers, N, f. 121.

70. Wark, *Elizabethan Recusancy in Cheshire*, pp. 70–71.

71. PRO SP/12/211, 22; HMC, Various Collections, III, p. 53 (Sir Thomas Tresham to the Archbishop of Canterbury, 25 March 1590). Having refused this and similar offers, Burghley nevertheless put great emphasis upon them in his later *Copy of a letter sent out of England* (see p. 297).

72. *Copy of a letter sent out of England, etc*; in Malham, *Harleian Miscellany*, II, p. 68.

73. Anstruther, *Vaux of Harrowden*, p. 175.

74. *APC*, XVI, 17 August; HMC Rutland MSS, p. 256.

75. Quoted in Noble, *Huntingdonshire and the Spanish Armada*, p. 60. Tresham, a devout and often wilfully confrontational Catholic, had almost certainly given shelter to Edmund Campion in his Hoxton home when the priest fled London (Anstruther, *Vaux of Harrowden*, p. 82).

76. Bruce, *Arrangements . . . for the Internal Defence of these Kingdoms*, App. LXVII. Langbourne, Bridge Within and Cripplegate wards were the hotbeds of dissent, with nine, seven and six reported 'suspects' respectively.

77. PRO SP/12/208, 64.

78. BL Cotton MSS Otho, E IX, f. 192. Hawkins usually supervised prayers himself in his vessels, and prescribed harsh penalties for those absenting themselves (Williamson, *Hawkins of Plymouth*, pp. 71–2).

79. Instructions for Frobisher's 1578 northwest voyage (reproduced in George Best's *True Discourse*) and for Ralegh's (1617) Guiana expedition (PRO SP/13/92, 9) required divine service to be celebrated twice each day at sea.

80. BL Lansdowne MS 70, f. 183.

81. Lord Hunsdon's phrase, from his exhortation to his captains to keep the taint of Catholicism out of their bands (BL Lansdowne MS 40, 8; reproduced in Boynton, *Elizabethan Militia*, p. 101).

CHAPTER THIRTEEN

1. Howard to Walsingham, 29 July 1588, PRO SP/12/213, 64.

2. PRO SP/12/213, 12. Howard had also previously received intelligence that at least a proportion of Parma's *tercios* might be directed to seize Wight (BL Cotton MSS Otho, E IX, f. 168; February 1588).

3. Bruce, *Arrangements . . . for the Internal Defence of these Kingdoms*, App. XXIX; Haynes and Murdin, *Cecil Papers*, p. 611; Lloyd, *Dorset Elizabethans*, p. 190; PRO SP/12/211, 72. It is very unlikely that the contingents from Somerset and Wiltshire, which had consistently failed to provide adequate certificates of their musters – were up to full complement (Boynton, *Elizabethan Militia*, pp. 173–4).

4. *Cal. SP Sp. 1587–1603*, no. 362; Medina Sidonia to Moncada, 2 August 1588 (NS).

5. See McKee, *From Merciless Invaders*, pp. 145–7, which portrays the English action on 23 July as an almost preternaturally brilliant exhibition of the art of sea warfare. The only evidence that Drake's *Revenge* led the forward, southernmost vessels of the English fleet at this point is Ubaldino's oblique reference to the *Nonpareil* as the leading vessel of the named group of English ships as they moved southwards (*Second Narrative*, in Naish, *History of the Spanish Armada*, p. 92). An original element of Drake's squadron at Plymouth, she was usually in close proximity to the *Revenge* during the campaign.

6. *Relation of the Proceedings*, f. 114r. The opinion, however, appears to have been at least third-hand. From Carisbrooke Castle on the Isle of Wight, Sir George Carey (Lord Hunsdon's son) used a near-identical form of words in his letter of 25 July to the earl of Sussex (PRO SP/12/213, 43).

7. See William Winter's report of 1 August (PRO SP/12/214, 7; Laughton, *Defeat of the Spanish Armada*, II, p. 9), in which he inferred that Coxe died after 29 July ('who sithen that time is slayne'). The *Delight* was owned by Winter, who probably knew her unfortunate captain personally.

8. There is much Spanish comment regarding the weight (and, by inference, the rate) of English fire compared with that of the Spanish ships. The author can find no contemporary opinion, however, upon the accuracy of its delivery.

9. The latter two vessels, commanded by Robert Wilcox and Francis Burnell respectively, are not to be confused with the naval ships of the same names.

10. Referring to Frobisher's decision to anchor under Portland Bill, a recent commentator (Hanson, *Confident Hope of a Miracle*, p. 318) has stated that he 'knew every inch of the coast, every cove and headland, every rock and shoal, and every quirk of the tides and currents'. While there is little firm evidence to support or contradict this confident assertion, the record of Frobisher's repeated technical clashes with his ships' masters during the three Baffin Island expeditions of 1576–8 (in which he emerged as the mistaken party with awesome consistency) suggests that he did not enjoy – or particularly seek – an intimate understanding of tides, currents and the other minutiae of the pilot's art. He was rather an inspirational (if often divisive) leader of men possessing these skills.

11. Pierson, *Commander of the Armada*, p. 238.

12. It was later reported that on the morning of 22 July, Moncada had seen Howard's *Ark Royal* almost unattended (having outrun the rest of the English fleet during the previous night), and unsuccessfully sought Medina Sidonia's permission to engage her (account of Van Meteren in Hakluyt, *Principal Navigations*, IV, pp. 215–16). In the early hours of the morning of his assault upon Frobisher's ships, Moncada had been ordered

to attack a number of English vessels detached from their fleet, but had either ignored the order or been prevented from discharging it by adverse weather (Pierson, *Commander of the Armada*, pp. 145–6).

13. Frobisher's use of ships' boats to manoeuvre the *Triumph* was first noted in Gorges's *Observations and Overtures for a Seafight*, discussed in Glasgow, 'Gorgas' Seafight', pp. 183–4.

14. The galleasses had a bank of twenty-five oars on either side, with each oar wielded by up to seven slaves (BL Sloane MS 262, f. 66v).

15. The *Triumph* carried at least twenty heavy guns (cannon, cannon-perrier, culverin and demi-culverin) and perhaps as many as thirty-three (PRO SP/12/185, 34), while the *Merchant Royal* was possibly the most powerful merchantman in the English fleet (see Lewis, 'Armada Guns', *MM*, xxviii, pp. 272–3). The *Centurion* and *Margaret and John*, of 250 and 200 tons respectively, were among the larger vessels supplied by the City and were likely to have been well-armed. In 1590, both vessels were part of a Levanter squadron that drubbed a fleet of Spanish galleys commanded by the famous Andrea Doria. In an action off Marseilles in the following year, the *Centurion* single-handedly fought off several Spanish galleys (Hakluyt, *Principal Navigations*, vii, pp. 31–8, *passim*). Of the vessels in Frobisher's squadron at Portland Bill, only the *Mary Rose* (70 tons) carried insignificant ordnance.

16. On criticism of Moncada, see Martin and Parker, *Armada*, p. 155. Spanish eyewitness accounts infer that during this skirmish one of the *Triumph*'s consorts was on the point of surrendering; but they appear to have misunderstood why the English ships' boats were being set out.

17. *Cal. SP Sp. 1587–1603*, no. 385. See also the comments of the anonymous member of the English peace commissioners' party who examined the beached *San Lorenzo* on 3 August (BL Sloane MS 262, ff. 67v): 'In the side also of the shipp, were to be seene, which did sticke in the bourdes, sondrie pellettes of Saker & demi culverin shott & Muskett.'

18. All details of individual ships from the *Relation of Proceedings*.

19. *Ibid.*, f. 114r.

20. See pp. 270–71. Recalde expressed disgust at the behaviour of some of the Spanish ships in this action, accusing their crews of attempting to take refuge behind each other during the most heavily pressed English assaults (quoted in Martin and Parker, *Armada*, p. 155; Parker, 'Anatomy of Defeat', p. 329). This, however, was an habitual complaint of the most energetic fighters in both fleets of compatriots who did not match their own efforts (see the comments of William Winter, p. 365 n. 26), and may be an exaggeration – certainly, Recalde also referred to every English course-change or withdrawal as some form of 'flight'. Again, if there was panic among the Spanish crews, it was not exploited in any significant manner by English commanders who were desperate to break up the Spanish formations.

21. Pierson, *Commander of the Armada*, p. 151. This was the testimony of Alonso de Vanegas, a gunnery captain in the *San Martín*.

22. Possibly a relative of the haberdasher, alderman (1560–1565) and sheriff of the same name (Ramsay, *John Isham's Accounts*, p. 42; Beaven, *Aldermen of the City of London*, i, p. 346).

23. Ubaldino, *Second Narrative*, in Naish, *History of the Spanish Armada*, p. 93.

24. Corbett, *Drake and the Tudor Navy*, ii, p. 239.

25. Corbett (*ibid.*, pp. 239–40) believed that Drake was indeed to the north of Howard's ships, and in Nelsonian manner (his comparison) led the assault upon the right (leeward) wing of the Spanish rearguard while Howard was 'uselessly' engaging its oppo-

site wing. This theory relies upon the *Relation of Proceedings'* reference to 'a troop of her Majesty's ships and sundry merchants' that assaulted the Spanish fleet 'to the west-ward' prior to Howard's return northwards. Without corroborating evidence, Corbett concludes peremptorily that their leader 'must . . . have been the *Revenge*'. However, it is more likely that the wind, rather than any significant action, drove back the right wing of the Spanish rearguard that morning. Had Drake's entire squadron been in that vicinity and pressing its attack effectively, it is unlikely that Recalde's division would have had the freedom to come about to intercept Howard's vessels as they returned. For an even less likely interpretation of the day's actions, see McKee, *From Merciless Invaders* (pp. 149–50), in which it is suggested that the Spanish fleet actually was rolled up from the south by Drake's squadron (surely the decisive moment of the campaign, had it occurred), but then – rather lamely – that the day's battle came to an end thereafter.

26. *History*, Book III, p. 414: 'Thus as to the Account and Particulars of the Engagements they who were present at them do not report the same thing, whilst on both Sides every man relates what he himself observed.'

27. Evidence that the vessel was the *Revenge* is circumstantial. A survey carried out by Hawkins two months later concluded that she needed a new mainmast, her present one being 'decayed and perished with shot' (PRO SP/12/216, 40; Laughton, *Defeat of the Spanish Armada*, II, p. 252). The intensity of the day's fighting in general appears to have been much exaggerated by contemporaries. Vanegas claimed that a further 5,000 rounds of shot were expended during this action (Martin and Parker, *Armada*, p. 158). This seems very unlikely. The English fleet (which was depleting its munitions far more quickly than the Spanish ships) had not been re-supplied significantly since the previous day, and simply did not have the means to continue as before. Nor is there any indication that more than a few vessels from either fleet were involved in the action against the *Gran Grifon*, making the claimed discharge of shot an impossible tally both for their gunners and individual ships' stores.

28. On that day, 120 barrels of powder and 120 shot, despatched from the Tower, were received by the Earl of Sussex (PRO SP/12/214, 28).

29. *Ibid.*, 29. Stade, at the mouth of the Elbe, had been chosen as the English cloth mer-chants' staple in 1587 after Hamburg's city council, angered at the loss of the Hanse's privileges in England and increasingly anxious at the deterioration of Anglo-Spanish relations, refused to renew their mart privileges for more than a year's duration at a time (Gould, 'Crisis in the Export Trade', pp. 217–18).

30. Medina Sidonia, viewing his enemy from a distance, thought that the English fleet (which departed from Plymouth comprising some sixty-five vessels) had swelled to include a hundred ships during the battle's first twenty-four hours (*Cal SP Sp. 1587–1603*, no. 361).

31. Clearly, the allocation of ships within the four squadrons was not immutable. During the action on 25 July, for example, Fenton's *Mary Rose* was operating in Drake's squadron. Several days later, however, in the fighting off Gravelines, he had rejoined his brother-in-law Hawkins (*Relation of Proceedings*).

32. *Ibid.*

33. Parker, *Grand Strategy of Philip II*, p. 196.

34. In 1575, Recalde had commanded a fleet of forty-eight troop-ships bound for Dunkirk. This had anchored in the Solent for a week, during which Recalde must have observed its tides, currents and accessibility.

35. The campaign diary of an anonymous Spanish 'soldier' (possibly the work of Recalde,

whose views it reflected closely and in whose ship the soldier claimed to sail) criticizes Medina Sidonia's decision to break off that day's engagement, but Recalde himself was perhaps too single-mindedly concentrating on Frobisher's squadron to notice the Owers (Parker, 'Anatomy of Defeat', p. 329).

36. *APC*, xvi, as dated; PRO SP/12/213, 49–50.

37. Townshend held no naval command during the campaign (he may have served as a commander of the soldiers posted in the *Ark Royal*); however, his had been one of the names of captains 'that have charge of her Majesty's ships particularly sent to the seas' in a document of 22 December 1587 (PRO SP/12/206, 43).

38. Carey, *Memoirs*, p. 18.

39. *APC*, xvi, 26 July 1588. The threat to the Solent now passed, the earl of Sussex was ordered to send home all but 400 men of the trained bands appointed to protect Portsmouth.

40. Nicholas Gorges's merchantmen, in which this quantity was carried, were kept in the Thames by adverse winds until after the battle had passed on to the north (Gorges's report to Walsingham, 31 July: PRO SP/12/213, 70). A few days later, Gorges fell ill (of 'his old infirmitie of bleeding': PRO SP/12/214, 4) and had to be replaced, which further delayed the ships' passage to the fleet.

41. PRO SP/12/206, 44.

42. BL Add. MS 48162, f. 8v; *APC*, xvi, 27 July 1588; Stewart, *English Ordnance Office*, p. 86.

43. Lewes, for example, held forty-two barrels of powder in store, but sent only twenty to the fleet as it passed by. At least two of those retained were consumed subsequently in the vital purpose of celebrating England's victory over the armada (Salzman, *Town Book of Lewes*, ff. 27r–v, 28v).

44. *APC*, xvi, 26 July 1588; BL Add. MS 33740, f. 2.

45. PRO SP/12/213, 49, 50. Ostensibly victualled until 10 August (PRO SP/12/213, 2), many of Howard's ships had departed from Plymouth with only part of their allocations. They do not appear to have been re-supplied between 21 July and 27 July, when the main fleet came to anchor before Calais (see n. 45 below). By 29 July, Howard was claiming that many of his vessels were victualled 'but for a very short time', and Seymour's 'not for one day'. On 1 August, Seymour himself complained to Walsingham 'we arr in manner famyshed for lakk of victuals . . . yet by encrease of soldiars the same is all wasted'; and, on 4 August, Thomas Fenner confirmed that 'There were many ships in our Fleete, not possessed with three dayes victuall' (PRO SP/12/213, 64; PRO SP/12/214, 3, 27).

46. PRO SP/12/210, 32.

47. Pollitt ('Bureaucracy and the Armada', p. 129), maintaining that victualling arrangements during the campaign were largely satisfactory, cites an apparent *surplus* of victuals in the fleet's victualling ships, subsequently spoiled and sold off at Dover early in November. These vessels – *Elizabeth* of Lyme, *Seraphim*, *Gift of God*, *Sparrowhawk*, *Pelican*, *True Dealing*, *Jonas* of Topsham and *Mayflower* – were paid for serving the fleet from 25 July until 5 September (AO1/1788/324/12: post-campaign accounts of Marmaduke Darell). However, having departed Plymouth four days *after* the fleet, and followed in its wake as far north as Newcastle, it is likely that a significant proportion of their lading was not so much unrequired as undelivered. All extant correspondence from the would-be recipients of these victuals contradicts Pollitt's claim.

48. One modern analysis of the campaign (Martin and Parker, *Armada*, pp. 201–3) theorises that Drake, with his capture and examination of the *Rosario* on 22 July, his assault upon

the *Gran Grifon* on the morning of 24 July, and his breaking of the Spanish rearguard's right wing on the following day had by now identified the profound limitations of Spanish guns and gunnery tactics. From this, it is posited that a conscious decision was made by Howard and his lieutenants to avoid further action 'to conserve their ammunition stocks for an all-out attack on the Armada when it reached its vulnerable station off Flanders . . . having divined the essential outlines of Philip's Grand Design.' This is an ingenious hypothesis; however, it attributes to the senior English commanders (and to Drake in particular) a degree of prescience that their surviving correspondence singularly fails to confirm. Drake's role in the above actions – the capture of the *Rosario* aside – is by no means clear; nor, indeed, can it be said that the Spanish right-wing, though pestered, *was* broken on 25 July. Given that English understanding of Spanish intentions remained extremely diffuse even after the battle, it seems more probable that Howard, knowing the English South coast now to be safe from a potential landing but unaware of what was yet to come, held off further attacks upon the armada until 29 July because he needed desperately to replace his munitions and to reinforce the fleet with Seymour's squadron. As Martin and Parker point out, English attacks off Gravelines and Calais were pressed far more closely than previously; but as shall be discussed, they were principally directed against vulnerable (that is, unsupported) targets. Wherever the Spanish ships kept or recovered their *en lúnula* formation or its *en arco* variant, English assaults were delivered with the same circumspection as in earlier clashes, however perceptions of Spanish gunnery tactics had modified in the meantime.

49. Again, the statistics were provided by Alonso de Vanegas.

CHAPTER FOURTEEN

1. 'Robert, Earl of Essex's Ghost', in Malham, *Harleian Miscellany*, III, p. 517.
2. PRO SP/12/213, 64 (29 July 1588): 'Ther is not on[e] Flushynger nor Holonder at The sees'. For the most comprehensive recent examination of the rebels' naval campaign (and English perceptions thereof) see Schokkenbroek, 'Whither Serveth Justin . . . ?' (*God's Obvious Design*, pp. 101–11).
3. Palmer returned from Dover in the early hours of 29 July with nineteen boats filled with pitch and brushwood, but these were sent back (PRO SP/12/213, 72).
4. The latter two vessels are not mentioned in any fleet list, which suggests that they were victualling boats, both probably of less than 100 tons.
5. Haynes and Murdin, *Cecil Papers*, II, p. 626.
6. The Mantuan Federico Giambelli, currently advising on the construction of the Gravesend Tilbury boom (which separated upon being raised for the first time).
7. *Cal. SP Sp. 1587–1603*, no. 439.
8. Hawkins's estimate 'For the burnt ships', Haynes and Murdin, *Cecil Papers*, II, p. 627.
9. Martin and Parker (*Armada*, p. 176) note the possibility that the powerful *San Lorenzo*, if allowed to escape capture or destruction, might have been requisitioned and repaired thereafter by Parma to clear the shoal-ridden Flemish coast of his Dutch blockaders.
10. PRO SP/12/213, 69.
11. *APC*, XVI, as dated.
12. Corbett (*Drake and the Tudor Navy*, II, p. 274) attributes the Lord Admiral's actions to his 'mediaeval instincts'. Following the fight for the *San Lorenzo*, Howard's mood may be gauged from a short note he appended to an earlier, unsent letter, urging his cor-

respondent (probably Burghley) to inform the Queen that he had 'spoyled one of their greatest shipps' (BL Cotton MSS Otho, E ix, f. 189v).

13. See the comments of the anonymous Englishman who examined the beached *San Lorenzo* six days later (BL Sloane MS 262, f. 66v): 'At [th]e sterne of the galeas in the verie top was the Chapple for there Idolatrouse service, much battered w[i]th great shott.' The identification of Coxe as the leader of the boarding parties was Winter's alone; two other accounts – the anonymous 'declaration of the proceedings of the two fleets' and van Meteren's 'Miraculous Victory, etc' (PRO SP/12/214, 42(i) and Hakluyt, *Principal Navigations*, IV, p. 223 respectively), state that its leader was the *Ark Royal*'s lieutenant, Amyas Preston. According to Howard (PRO SP/12/213, 64), Preston was 'sore hurte' during the action.

14. Henry Whyte's commentary on the day's fighting (PRO/SP/12/214, 43) suggests that Howard did not rejoin the fleet until some three hours following Drake's first assault upon the *San Martín*. Richard Tomson's detailed account of the fight for the galleass (PRO SP/12/213, 67) states that the English 'were masters of her above two houres'. Winter claims that Howard's *Ark Royal* had returned to engage the reforming Spanish fleet by 9am.

15. The present author, having previously given Drake credit for his tactics (McDermott, *Martin Frobisher*, p. 363), has come to consider that available evidence casts their efficacy in a more equivocal light.

16. Corbett, *Drake and the Tudor Navy*, II, p. 279.

17. *Cal. SP Sp. 1587–1603*, no. 439. Figures for the *San Felipe*'s complement from Pierson, *Commander of the Armada*, p. 242.

18. Reported by the purser of the *San Salvador*, Pedro Coco Calderon; English translation in *Cal. SP Sp. 1587–1603*, no. 439.

19. The identification of the *Hope* is made by Van Meteren alone (Hakluyt, *Principal Navigations*, IV, p. 226)

20. According to the Venetian ambassador at Seville (*Cal. SP Venetian, 1581–91*, no. 746), the *Maria Juan*'s captain was rescued.

21. On *La Trinidad*'s construction, see Martin, 'The Ships of the Spanish Armada', p. 60.

22. See p. 365 n. 26. The (almost certainly exaggerated) estimate of English ships assaulting *San Martín* was that of Vanegas.

23. Hakluyt, *Principal Navigations*, IV, p. 224.

24. Those who surrendered their vessels to be fire-ships were luckier in obtaining full recompense, though the hopeful hint to Walsingham of Henry Whyte, captain and owner of the *Bark Talbot*, might have spoken for many: 'but this cumfort I have, her highness, with your honour's furtheraunce, may easely remedy my greefe' (PRO SP/12/214, 43).

25. Sir William Winter described the Spanish formation that bore the brunt of English attacks as being in the shape of a wing of sixteen ships (that is, sixteen on each side of the formation's centre), though stragglers that attempted to join it were also caught up in the fighting.

26. The estimate of casualties is that of Vanegas.

27. BL Harleian MS 6994, f. 66: 'In Tynemouthe, I thinke there is little or nothing at all, and in the store-house at Newcastle, there is as little to supply'.

28. These had been detached from Seymour's squadron for the purpose on 10 July (PRO SP/12/212, 34(i)).

29. *APC*, xvi, 2 August.

30. PRO SP/12/214, 56; PRO SP/12/215, 41. On 8 August, the Council ordered Sir Robert Constable to despatch five lasts of powder to the earl of Huntingdon and to Berwick

castle to make good their losses (*APC*, XVI, as dated). Possibly, this late supply had been secured after pleas for private stocks held in City warehouses (see pp. 262–3).

31. Seymour was assiduous in expressing his frustrations in correspondence to the Court; yet only days later he was providing the Council with reasons of why he should not abandon the Narrow Seas station to join with Howard once more (PRO SP/214, 3–4, 39; *APC*, XVI, 7 August 1588).

32. Winter's is the only reference to this attempted mass desertion (PRO SP/12/214, 7).

33. PRO SP/12/214, 42.

34. Sir Horatio Palavicino's 'Relation' of the battle (PRO SP/12/215, 77) preferred to explain the distance maintained between the two fleets as an attempt by the Spanish ships to flee from their advancing enemy. Corbett (*Drake and the Tudor Navy*, II, p. 297) recalls English plans to dislodge the armada from any anchorage it might have attempted to make during these days with more fire-ships. However, vessels, pitch and brimstone assembled for this task remained at Dover, to be provided to Howard only when he returned south once more (*APC*, XVI, 12 August).

35. They immediately lost her company again. Howard took the *Ark Royal* to Dover the same day to search for his victualling boats.

36. PRO SP/12/214, 56

37. *Ibid.*, 53.

38. See Neale, 'Elizabeth and the Netherlands', pp. 385–7.

39. *APC*, XVI, as dated; PRO SP/12/214, 54; the earl of Cumberland, who with despatches had transferred out of the *Ark Royal* into a pinnace bound for Harwich on 7 August, confirmed to Burghley that at least some hoys lay in the port that day.

40. Figures provided by Hawkins (PRO SP/12/214, 46). The Council's calculations may have included the eight victualling boats which had followed the fleet – albeit at a great distance – from Plymouth.

41. See p. 204.

42. PRO SP/12/214, 66, Howard to Walsingham, 10 August: 'The Elizabeth Jonas, which hath don as well as eaver anie ship did in any service hathe had a greate infectione in her from the begininge, soe as of the 500 men which she caried oute, by the time we had bin in Plimmouthe three weekes or a month, there were ded of them 200 and above . . .'.

43. PRO SP/12/214, 27.

CHAPTER FIFTEEN

1. Thomas Deloney, *A joyfull new Ballad Declaring the happy obtaining of the great Galleazzo*, etc; reproduced in Collier, *Broadside Black-letter Ballads*, p. 79. The title of this chapter derives from Maurice Kyffin's mocking of prognostications for the year 1588: 'Whereby appears, Men's prophecies be vain, when God decreeth a contrary success . . .', appended to his (1587) *The Blessednes of Brytaine* in a hurriedly revised second edition published almost immediately following the campaign.

2. Aske, *Elizabetha Triumphans, with a Declaration of the Manner how her Excellency was entertained by her Souldyers into her Campe Royall, At Tilbery, in Essex.*

3. PRO SP/12/213, 46, 27 July 1588.

4. Since the beginning of the sixteenth century the central drawbridge of London Bridge had been inoperable, making the alternative passage between its dangerously confining starlings obligatory.

5. PRO SP/12/215, 34 (Leicester to Elizabeth, 5 August): '. . . only we had a myshapp of

a landing place, whear hoys and boates had somewhat broken the bridge; but all to be repared by tomorrow nyght erly, agenst the next day, to doe you servyce.'

6. Christy, 'Queen Elizabeth's visit to Tilbury in 1588', pp. 52–3.

7. Deloney, *Works*, p. 476, Aske, *Elizabetha Triumphans*, p. 21.

8. Burghley's was the only recollection of Montague's presence at Tilbury (Malham, *Harleian Miscellany*, II, p. 76). Montague had previously voted in Parliament against the bills for restoration of the Royal Supremacy and Uniformity (his particularly eloquent speech against the former is reproduced in Hartley, *Proceedings*, I, pp. 7–11). Notwithstanding this pedigree, Elizabeth was upon more than one occasion a welcome (and appreciative) guest at his Cowdray Park estate.

9. *Cabala*, p. 260.

10. This inflated estimate of the strength of Parma's forces was repeated on 11 August by Leicester's aide, Thomas Fowler (HMC Dudley Papers, p. 213).

11. *APC*, XVI, as dated. Priority of discharge was given to those who lived nearest the camp, should they need to be summoned once more.

12. Both orders refer to the reduction of Tilbury strength to 6,000 men, though the Horse were to remain at the camp.

13. The Privy Council certainly believed this to be a strong possibility; see their orders of 13 August to the earl of Shrewsbury (APC, XVI, as dated; HMC Talbot Papers, p. 93).

14. BL Harleian MS 6994, ff. 136; Sloane MS 262, f. 67v; PRO SP/12/214, 44. The rumours of Parma's movements were brought by the soldier Thomas Morgan, who had arrived at Margate with 800 musketeers as Howard's ships came to anchor there. In fact, Parma had lost any confidence that the goals of his element of the 'enterprise of England' could be achieved (see O'Donnell, 'The Requirements of the Duke of Parma for the Conquest of England', pp. 90–91, 95–6).

15. PRO SP/12/213, 71; PRO SP/12/214, 50, 65.

16. *APC*, XVI, as dated.

17. PRO SP/12/215, 6, 8, 9, 22, 28, 37, 39.

18. BL Harleian MS 6994, f. 138.

19. *Ibid.*, f. 142; PRO SP/12/214, 54.

20. PRO SP/12/215, 3.

21. PRO SP/12/20, 20(i).

22. *APC*, XVI, 8 September 1588. No further correspondence occurs in respect of the vessel, suggesting that the matter was settled soon after.

23. See *APC*, XVI, 10, 13, 18, 21, 22 September; HMC City of Exeter papers, pp. 63–4; BL Harleian MS 703, ff. 76–7, 80. The suit was that of John Young, owner of *Bark Young*, whose charges were to have been borne by the towns of Arundel, Chichester, Shoreham, Brighthelmstowe and Lewes (*APC*, XVI, pp. 61, 66–7).

24. *APC*, XVI, 9 August. Howard attended a Privy Council meeting on 16 August that authorized the payment of victualling monies (though not relief monies for the sick).

25. Approximately 600 pressed men were ordered by the Council to be at Dover or Sandwich by 6 August, to make good anticipated losses in battle (*APC*, XVI, 14 August).

26. PRO SP/12/215, 40, 41.

27. PRO SP/12/215, 41.

28. PRO SP/12/218, 34.

29. Oppenheim, *Administration of the Royal Navy*, p. 135. In 1590, Hawkins and Drake founded the Chatham Chest, a fund supplied by mandatory contributions deducted

from mariners' pay, to provide for their disabled comrades. However, its resources were never remotely adequate to supply the needs of its petitioners, nor safe from the embezzlements of many, if not most of its subsequent treasurers in the seventeenth century.

30. PRO SP/12/215, 59, 63.
31. PRO SP/12/215, 66.
32. The suggestion is that of Loades, *Tudor Navy*, p. 253.
33. PRO SP/12/215, 24–5, 46; *Cal. SP For.*, XXII, p. 142.
34. *APC*, XVI, as dated.
35. PRO SP/63/136, 34, 41–3; *APC*, XVI, 15 September.
36. PRO SP/215, 47; PRO SP/12/217, 39–44, 46–50.
37. PRO SP/12/215, 59.
38. PRO SP/12/216, 3.
39. PRO SP/12/216, 40.
40. However, as Wernham has indicated (*Expedition of Sir John Norris and Sir Francis Drake*, p. xiv), very little documentary evidence survives regarding the genesis of this project, and the identity of its early movers remains a matter for speculation.
41. Drake's extensive conversations with Ubaldino, during which his claims for sole (or predominant) ownership of the strategy were made, took place in the months prior to April 1589, when the latter presented Burghley with his completed *Narrative* (Naish, *History of the Spanish Armada*, p. 69).
42. Stone, *Sir Horatio Palavicino*, p. 24; Spence, *Privateering Earl*, pp. 67–8, 72.
43. In a letter of 11 August to Walsingham (PRO SP/12/214, 70), Drake asked the Queen's secretary to emphasize to Elizabeth the Lord Admiral's 'honorable using' of him. The coincidence of this strange request with Frobisher's accusations (as reported by one of Drake's men, Matthew Starke, on the same day) seems significant.
44. PRO SP12/215, 45.
45. HMC Molyneaux papers, p. 645 (Lady Lincoln to Sir William Moore, 30 July 1588): 'Upon Sunday night late my L. of Essex and Sir Tho. Gorges came to the court from Dover . . . whereat there is much grief conceyued in the Court that my Ld. Admirall that suffered them to passe so farre without fight, and that he prevented not the opportunity they haue now gotten of refreshing their men'. On Essex's forceful (and, possibly, unwanted) involvement in the 1589 Peninsular campaign, see Cummins, *Drake*, pp. 199–201, 211–2, 214, 216.
46. *History of the World*, book v, cap. ii, vi. Note also Ralegh's affecting dedication to Howard and Sir Robert Cecil in the preamble to his (1596) *Discoverie of the large, rich, and beautifull Empire of Guiana, etc*: 'In my more happy times as I did especially Honour You both, so I found that your loves sought mee out in the darkest shadow of adversitie, and the same affection which accompanied my better fortune, sored not away from me in my many miseries: al which though I can not requite, yet I shal ever acknowledge . . .' (reproduced in Hakluyt, *Principal Navigations*, x, p. 339).
47. The fracas was reported in a Spanish intelligence letter of 22 August 1587 (*Cal. SP Sp. 1587–1603*, no. 132: 'The new Confidant's Advices from England').
48. PRO SP/12/214, 16–17, 19–22; PRO SP/12/215, 67(i).
49. *APC*, XVI, 1 August; PRO SP/12/216, 25; PRO SP/12/217, 10, 21; Boynton, *Elizabethan Militia*, p. 179. Carey (of Cockington, Devon) is not to be confused with Sir George Carey, son of Lord Hunsdon and Captain of the Isle of Wight in 1588.

50. *APC*, XVI, pp. 328–9, 1 November 1588.

51. PRO SP/12/218, 14, letter of Anthony Ashley, agent for the salvage of the *San Pedro Mayor*, to the Privy Council, 22 November (reproduced in Laughton, *Defeat of the Spanish Armada*, II, pp. 292–4) .

52. *APC*, XVI, pp. 373–4.

53. PRO SP/78/19, 234.

54. The fate of the 'better sort' of prisoner from the *Rosario* and *San Pedro Mayor* is discussed comprehensively in Martin, *Spanish Armada Prisoners*, pp. 58–9.

55. PRO SP/12/214, 50.

56. Archdeacon, *A true Discourse of the armie which the King of Spaine caused to be assembled in the Haven of Lisbon, in the kingdome of Portugall, in the Yeare 1588, against England*, pp. 11–12.

57. *The Copy of a Letter Sent Out of England To Don Bernadin Mendoza, Ambassador In France For The King Of Spain, Declaring The State Of England; Contrary to the Opinion of Don Bernadin, and of all his Partisans, Spaniards and Others, etc*; printed by J. Vautrollier: reproduced in Malham, *Harleian Miscellany*, II, pp. 60–85.

58. *A Packe of Spanish Lyes, sent Abroad in the World, First Printed in Spaine, in the Spanish Tongue, and Translated out of the Originall*, printed by Christopher Barker: reproduced in *Malham, Harleian Miscellany*, II, pp. 117–29.

59. Caraman, *Henry Garnet*, p. 76.

60. Pollen, *English Martyrs*, pp. 12–14.

61. Caraman, *Henry Garnet*, p. 72; Trimble, *Catholic Laity*, p. 136.

62. Aske, *Elizabetha Triumphans*, p. 63.

63. Strype, *Annals*, III (ii), p. 27.

64. Reproduced in Naish, *History of the Spanish Armada*, pp. 101–2.

65. Aske, *Elizabetha Triumphans*, p. 66; Strype, *Annals*, III (ii), pp. 28–9.

66. Caraman, *Henry Garnet*, pp. 78, 81–2.

67. Read, *Walsingham*, II, p. 294.

68. Rogers, *An Historical Dialogue*, pp. 84–5.

69. Hartley, *Proceedings*, II, p. 420.

CHAPTER SIXTEEN

1. Fuller, *Worthies*, I, p. 31.

2. She was rebuilt in 1598–9.

3. All details of Nottingham's embassy to Spain are drawn from Robert Treswell's 'Relation', reproduced in Malham, *Harleian Miscellany*, II, pp. 535–66.

4. *Ibid.*, p. 566 (modernized spelling).

5. HMC Buccleuch MSS, I, p. 58.

6. Winwood, *Memorials*, II, p. 92.

7. *Ibid.*, p. 31; *Cal. SP Venetian*, X, nos 69, 242, 278.

8. *The Court and Character of King James*, pp. 26–7. The revenge of a spurned man, the work is extremely vituperative.

9. Bruce, *Diary of John Manningham*, p. 74: 'for which words he was sent for to the Court, and charged as a busie medler, and a seditious fellowe . . .'. Implausibly, the cavalier's defence in Court was that he had meant that peace would render him unemployable and obliged him to turn to crime; therefore, he would almost certainly be hanged. The 'ordinary' in which he made his imprudent statement was a form of ale-house serving set-price two-course meals.

10. HMC Buccleuch MSS, I, p. 53, *Cal. SP. Venetian*, XI, no. 10; Sir Dudley Carleton to Ralph Winwood (10 March 1605): Winwood, *Memorials*, II, p. 217.

11. Ralegh, 'Last Fight of the Revenge'; in Hakluyt, *Principal Navigations*, VII, p. 43.

12. McDermott, *Martin Frobisher*, pp. 394–9.

13. With typical indecision, Philip had redefined the armada's mission at the last moment, it having been assembled originally to assist Tyrone's Irish rebellion. The most comprehensive (and recent) analysis of the Spanish enterprises of 1596–7 is Tenace, 'A Strategy of Reaction, etc'.

14. The objectives of the 1597 expedition suffered from Philip's confused strategic vision even more than its predecessor. At various times in the months prior to its despatch, it had been intended to seize Milford Haven and Bristol, re-allocated to another attempt on Brest, and, finally, to its definitive Falmouth operation (*ibid.*, pp. 873–6).

15. On the 1599 'armada' preparations in England, see Wernham, *Return of the Armadas*, pp. 263–72, *passim*.

16. Allen, *Philip III*, p. 2; HMC Salisbury MSS, VIII, pp. 210–11.

17. Croft, 'English Mariners Trading to Spain and Portugal, 1558–1625', p. 264.

18. Allen, *Philip III*, pp. 17–18, 24–5.

19. Slack, *Impact of Plague in Tudor and Stuart England*, p. 62. Note also the diary observation of Samuel Ward (Knappen, *Two Elizabethan Puritan Diaries*, p. 116), lamenting 'My want of grief and sorrow in respect of the plague now raging in so much of our Contrey'.

20. On the growing difficulty in pressing soldiers and mariners, see Wernham, *Return of the Armadas*, pp. 203–4.

21. For the government's financial situation in the final years of Elizabeth's reign, see F. C. Dietz, *English Public Finance*, II, pp. 86–99.

22. HMC Shrewsbury and Talbot Papers, II, f. KII (Thomas Edmonds to the earl of Shrewsbury, 12 June 1600).

23. 'Blood-thirsty men shall not live out half their days'. According to Camden (*Annales*, p. 218), Burghley admonished Essex with these words during a heated argument regarding peace negotiations.

24. Naunton, *Fragmentia Regalia*, p. 61: 'Madame', saith he [Walsingham], 'I beseech you to be content and fear not. The Spaniard hath a great appetite and an excellent digestion, but I have fitted him with a bone for these twenty years that Your Majesty shall have no cause to doubt him, provided that if the fire chance to slake which I have kindled, you will be ruled by me and now and then cast in some of your English fuel, which will then revive the flame'. After a long illness (probably testicular cancer, exacerbated by mercury poisoning from his 'medicine'), Walsingham died on 6 April 1590 (Halliwell, *Diary of John Dee*, p. 33; Camden, *Annales*, p. 394).

25. PRO SP/94/9, 20; HMC Salisbury MSS, XV, p. 73.

26. This halt in the privateers' trade was brief. Predictably, many of them immediately offered their services to the States-General (*Cal SP Venetian*, X, no. 292).

27. One unlucky group of (alleged) English pirates seized by Spanish colonists had their hands, feet, ears and noses cut off before being tied to trees and smeared with honey for the sustenance of the local insect population (*Cal. SP Venetian*, X, no. 307).

28. Loomie, *Spanish Elizabethans*, p. 177; 'Sir Robert Cecil and the Spanish Embassy', p. 33; Winwood, *Memorials*, II, p. 28 (Cranborne to Winwood, 4 September 1604) 'I understand that the *Archduke* beginneth to frame companies of *English* . . .'. The emigration of militarily effective Catholic males so worried the government that legislation was enacted hurriedly, obliging Englishmen to swear an oath of loyalty to the Crown

before departing to take up service overseas. It was reported by the Venetian ambassador in London that Dutch mariners had a policy of drowning any Englishman intercepted at sea on his way to serve the Archduke.

29. Winwood, *Memorials*, II, p. 38.
30. On Philip's motives, see Tenance, 'Strategy of Reaction', p. 880.
31. Excerpt from Elizabeth's address to parliament, 1593; reproduced in Malham, *Harleian Miscellany*, II, p. 261.
32. Markham, *Voyages and Works of John Davis*, pp. 235–6.
33. On Wright's achievement (and every other aspect of contemporary English hydrographical developments), Waters, *The Art of Navigation*, remains unsurpassed.
34. Ralegh, *History*, I, p. 204.
35. For the appellant movement's philosophy upon church and state, see Pritchard, *Catholic Loyalism in England*, pp. 146–74, *passim*. The most striking example of disobedience occurred in 1603, when the senior Catholic cleric resident in England, the arch-priest George Blackwell (appointed by the pope against the wishes of the appellants, who had sought to establish an English episcopalian structure in-parallel with its Protestant equivalent), was directed by Rome to ensure that none of his flock took the oath of allegiance to James I. Blackwell not only refused to publish the pope's ban but ostentatiously took the oath himself and loudly urged his fellow Catholics to do likewise (Bouwsma, *The Waning of the Renaissance*, p. 110).
36. BL Harleian MS 6994, f. 2; 29 March 1586.
37. Rowse, *Tudor Cornwall*, p. 306.
38. *The Alchemist*, IV, ii.
39. National Portrait Gallery, NPG 665, plate 3. For doubts concerning the provenance of the piece, see Brown and Elliot, *Sale of the Century*, pp. 145–6.
40. Nashe, *Pierce Pennilesse, His Supplication to the Divell*, sigs. C2–3, D2.
41. On the illicit wartime traffic between England and Spain, see Croft, 'Trading with the Enemy, 1585–1604', pp. 285–302, *passim*.
42. Pepys, *Diary*, II, p. 188; 30 September 1661. The observation was made following a fracas in Cheapside between the entourages of the French and Spanish ambassadors which resulted in several fatalities – all, to the delight of Londoners, Frenchmen.

Bibliography

Place of publication London unless stated otherwise

MANUSCRIPT SOURCES

Bodleian Library: Malone MS 645
British Library:
——, Additional MSS: 6703, 26056, 33740, 36315, 48014, 48027, 48084, 48126, 48162.
——, Cotton MSS: Caligula, B IX–X, C I, IX; Galba, C I, III, VIII, D I–II; Julius, F x; Otho, E VII–IX; Titus, B VII, XIII; Vespasian, C VII–VIII.
——, Harleian MSS: 169, 295, 424, 703, 6994.
——, Lansdowne MSS: 6, 13, 15, 16, 41, 43, 49, 56, 57, 70, 100, 115, 142, 213.
——, Sloane MSS: 262, 326, 2177.
——, Stow MSS 177.
Magdalene College, Cambridge: Pepys MS 2133.
Public Record Office:
——, E351/AO1 (Declared accounts of the Navy)
——, High Court of Admiralty Records (HCA): Oyer & Terminer 1/2; Acts 3/18, Examinations 13/5–8; Exemplars 14/5; Libels 24/13–14; Warrants 38/9.
——, Patent Rolls: 6 Eliz. C 66; 30 Eliz. M7.
——, State Papers Domestic series SP 1 (Henry VIII), SP10 (Edward VI), SP 11 (Mary), SP12 (Elizabeth), SP 13 (James I): these are too numerous to reproduce here (refer to footnote references). J. K. Laughton (see entry below) reproduced most of the relevant English state papers relating to naval matters during the period of the armada campaign. However, his occasionally idiosyncratic transcriptions, and late-Victorian practice of 'correcting' contemporary grammar and sentence structure, have inclined the present author to refer to the original manuscripts for quotations.
——, WO55 (War Office Misc. Entry Books)/1627.

PRIMARY PRINTED SOURCES

Calendars:

Acts of the Privy Council, 1542–1604 (32 vols, 1890–1907).

Calendar of Letters and Papers (Foreign and Domestic) Henry VIII (22 vols, 1862–1932).

Calendar of State Papers, Edward VI, Domestic (1992), *Foreign* (1861).

Calendar of State Papers, Elizabeth, Foreign, 1558–9 (23 vols, 1863–1950).

Calendar of State Papers, Mary, Domestic (1998), *Foreign* (1861).

List and Analysis of State Papers, Elizabeth, Foreign, 1589–93 (4 vols, 1964–84).

Calendar of Patent Rolls: 1396–9 (1909), *1429–36* (1903), *1547–8* (1924), *1548–9* (1925), *1549–51* (1927), *1555–7* (1937).

Calendar of Plymouth Municipal Records (1893).

Calendar of State Papers, Spanish, 1544–58 (7 vols, 1890–1954).

Calendar of State Papers relating to English affairs . . . in the archives of Simancas, 1558–1603 (4 vols, 1892–9).

Calendar of State Papers and Manuscripts relating to English affairs existing in . . . Venice: 1556–7 (1873), *1581–91* (1894), *1604* (1903), *1605* (1904).

Historical Manuscript Commission Reports:

——, Bath Longleat MSS, vol. v (Talbot, Dudley & Devereux Papers, 1980)

——, Buccleuch MSS, vol. 1 (1899)

——, City of Exeter Papers (1916).

——, Foljambe MSS (15th Report, App. v, 1897)

——, Molyneaux MSS (7th Report, 1879)

——, Rutland MSS (12th Report, Apps IV, 1888)

——, Salisbury MSS, vols. II–XVI (1883–1933)

——, Shrewsbury and Talbot Papers (2 vols, 1966, 1971)

——, Various Collections, vol. III (1904)

Other Primary Sources:

Adam, W., *Chronicle of Bristol* (facsimile edition, Bristol, 1910).

Andrews, K. R. (ed.), *English Privateering Voyages to the West Indies 1588–1595* (Hakluyt Society, 1959).

Andrewes, L., *The Copie of the Sermon (on Lam. I, 12) preached on Good Friday Last before the kings maiestie* (1610).

Arber, E., *A Transcript of the Registers of the Company of Stationers of London 1554–1640* (5 vols, 1875–94).

Aske, J., *Elizabetha Triumphans, with a Declaration of the Manner how her Excellency was entertained by her Souldyers into her Campe Royall, At Tilbery, in Essex* (1588).

Bain, J. (ed.), *The Hamilton Papers, letters and papers illustrating the political relations of England and Scotland in the sixteenth century* (2 vols, Edinburgh, 1890, 1892).

Birch, T., *Memoirs of the Reign of Queen Elizabeth From the Year 1581 until her Death . . . From the Original Papers of his intimate Friend, Anthony Bacon, Esquire, etc.* (ed. 1754).

Blake, J. W. (ed.), *Europeans in West Africa 1450–1560* (2 vols, Hakluyt Society, 1941–2).

Bruce, J., *The Cabala, Mysteries of State, in Letters of the Great Ministers of K. James and K. Charles: Wherein Much of the Publique Manage of Affaires is Related* (1654).

Bruce, J., *Report on the Arrangements which were made, for the Internal Defence of these Kingdoms, when Spain, by its Armada, Projected the Invasion and Conquest of England, etc.* (printed for the Cabinet Office, 1798).

Bruce, J., (ed.), *Correspondence of Robert Dudley, Earl of Leycester, During his Government of the Low Countries in the Years 1585 and 1586* (Camden Society, 1844).

——, *Diary of John Manningham, 1602–3* (Camden Society, 1868).

Caldecott-Baird, D. (ed.), *The Expedition in Holland 1572–1574 . . . from the Manuscript of Thomas Morgan* (1976).

Camden, W., *Annales, or the Historie of the Life and Reigne of that Famous Princesse, Elizabeth, etc.* (4th ed., 1688).

Carey, R., *Memoirs of the Life of Robert Carey, Baron of Leppington and Earl of Monmouth, Written by Himself* (ed. 1759).

Churchyard, T., *A Lamentable, and pitifull Description, of the wofull warres in Flaunders, since the foure last yeares of the Emperor Charles the fifth his raigne* (1578).

Collier, J. P. (ed.), *Broadside Black-letter Ballads, printed in the Sixteenth and Seventeenth Centuries* (New York, 1868).

Collinson, P. (ed.), *Letters of Thomas Wood, Puritan, 1566–1577* (Special Bulletin of the Institute of Historical Research no. 5, 1960).

Corbett, J. S. (ed.), *The Spanish War 1585–1587* (Navy Records Society, 1898).

——, *Fighting Instructions 1530–1816* (1971).

Croft, P. (ed.), *The Spanish Company* (London Record Society, 1973).

Davies, D. W. (ed.), *The Actions of the Low Countries, by Sir Roger Williams* (Ithaca, N.Y., 1964).

Digges, D., *The Compleat Ambassador: or two treaties of the intended marriage of Queen Elizabeth, etc.* (1655).

Donno, E. S. (ed.), *An Elizabethan in 1582: The Diary of Richard Madox, Fellow of All Souls* (Hakluyt Society, 1976).

Duro, C. Fernández (ed.), *La armada invencible* (2 vols, Madrid, 1884, 1885).

Foster, Sir W. (ed.), *The Voyages of James Lancaster, 1591–1603* (Hakluyt Society, second series, LXXXV, 1940).

Foxe, J., *Actes and Monuments* (8 vols, ed. 1870).

Fuller, T., *The Worthies of England* (3 vols, ed. 1840).

Gilbert, D. (ed.), *The Parochial History of Cornwall: Founded on the Manuscript of Mr Hals and Mr Tonkin, with additions and various appendices* (4 vols, 1838).

Goring, J., and J. Wake (eds), *Northamptonshire Lieutenancy Papers and other Documents, 1580–1614* (Northants Record Society, 1974).

Greene, R., *Life and Complete Works* (15 vols, Huth Library, 1881–6).

Hakluyt, R., *Discourse of Western Planting* (Hakluyt Society facsimile edition, 1993).

—— (ed.), *The Principal Navigations, Voyages, Traffiques and Discoveries of the English Nation, etc.* (12 vols, MacLehose edition, Glasgow, 1903–5).

——, *Divers Voyages touching the discouerie of America, and the Ilands adiacent vnto the same, etc.* (Hakluyt Society facsimile edition, Amsterdam, 1967).

Halle, E., *The Union of the Two Noble Houses of Lancaster and York* (Scolar facsimile edition, Menston, 1970).

Hamilton, G. H. (ed.), *Book of Examinations and Depositions of Southampton, 1570–1594* (Southampton Record Society, 1914).

Hartley, T. E. (ed.), *Proceedings in the Parliaments of Elizabeth I*, vol. I, 1558–81 (1981); vol. II, 1584–9 and vol. III, 1593–1601 (1995).

Haslop, H., *Newes Out of the Coast of Spaine. The True Report of the honourable service for England, perfourmed by Sir FRAVNCIS DRAKE, in the months of Aprill and May last past 1587, etc.* (1587).

Hattendorf, J. B., R. J. B. Knight, A. W. H. Pearsall, N. A. M. Rodger and G. Till (eds),

British Naval Documents 1204–1960 (Aldershot, 1993).

Haynes, S., and W. Murdin (eds), *Collection of State Papers relating to affairs in the reigns of Henry VIII, Edward VI, Queen Mary and Queen Elizabeth, Left by William Cecil, Lord Burghley* (2 vols, 1759).

Hayward, J., *The Life and Raigne of King Edward VI* (1630).

——, *Annals of the First Four Years of the Reign of Queen Elizabeth* (Camden Society, 1840).

Huth, H. (ed.), *Fugitive Tracts Written in Verse, which illustrate the Condition of Religious and Political Feeling in England and the State of Society there during Two Centuries* (1875).

Keeler, M. F., *Sir Francis Drake's West Indian Voyage 1585–1586* (Hakluyt Society, 1975).

Kempe, A. J. (ed.), *The Loseley Manuscripts. Manuscripts and other rare documents, illustrative of some of the more minute particulars of English history, biography, and manners, from the reign of Henry VIII, to that of James I* (1835).

Kervyn de Lettenhove, J. M. B. C., and L. Gilliodts van Severen (eds), *Relations Politiques des Pays-Bas et de l'Angleterre, sous le règne de Phillipe II* (11 vols, Brussels, 1888–1900).

Kingdon, R. M. (ed.), *The Execution of Justice in England by William Cecil* and *A True, Sincere, and Modest Defense of English Catholics by William Allen* (Ithaca, N.Y., 1965).

Kingsford, C. L. (ed.), *Two London Chronicles from the collections of John Stow* (Camden Society, 1910).

Klarwill, V. von (ed.) *The Fugger news letters. Being a selection of unpublished letters from the correspondents of the House of Fugger* (2 vols, 1924, 1926).

Knappen, M. M., *Two Elizabethan Tudoe Diaries* (Chicago, 1933).

Knighton, C. S., and D. M. Loades (eds), *The Anthony Roll of Henry VIII's Navy* (Aldershot, 2000).

Kyffin, M., *The Blessednes of Brytaine* (ed. 1588).

Laughton, J. K. (ed.), *State Papers relating to the Defeat of the Spanish Armada, Anno 1588* (Navy Records Society, 2 vols, 1894).

Lilly, J. (ed.), *Black-letter Ballads and Broadsides, Printed in the Reign of Queen Elizabeth, Between the Years 1559 and 1597* (1870).

Lower, M. A. (ed.), *A survey of the Coast of Sussex, made in 1587, with a view to its defence against Foreign Invaders, and especially the Spanish Armada* (Lewes, 1870).

Malham, J. (ed.), *The Harleian Miscellany* (12 vols, 1808–11).

Mann, F. O. (ed.), *The Works of Thomas Deloney* (Oxford, 1912).

Markham, A. H. (ed.), *The Voyages and Works of John Davis the Navigator* (Hakluyt Society, 1878).

Marsden, R. G. (ed.), *Select Pleas in the Court of Admiralty* (2 vols, 1892, 1897).

——, 'Voyage of the Barbara', in Laughton, J. K. (ed.), *Naval Miscellany*, vol. II (1912), pp. 3–66.

——, *Law and Custom of the Sea*, vol. I (1915).

Mayer, J. (ed.), *On the Preparations of the County of Kent to Resist the Spanish Armada* (Liverpool, 1868).

McCann, T. J. (ed.), *Recusants in the Exchequer Pipe Rolls, 1581–1592* (Catholic Record Society, 1986).

Morris, J. (ed.), *The Letter-Books of Sir Amias Poulet, Keeper of Mary Queen of Scots* (1874).

Naish, G. B. (ed.), *Documents Illustrating the History of the Spanish Armada* (National Maritime Museum, Maritime Monographs & Reports no. 17, 1975).

Naunton, R., *Fragmenta Regalia* (1641).

Nichols, J., *The progresses and public processions of Queen Elizabeth* (4 vols, 1788–1821).

Nicols, J. G. (ed.), *Diary of Henry Machyn, Citizen of London, 1550–1563* (Camden Society,

1848).

——, *The Chronicle of Queen Jane, and of Two Years of Queen Mary, etc.* (Camden Society, 1849).

——, *Narratives of the Days of the Reformation, etc.* (Camden Society, 1859).

Noble, T. C. (ed.), *The Names of those Persons who subscribed towards the Defence of this Country at the time of the SPANISH ARMADA, 1588, and the amounts each contributed* (1886).

Noble, W. M. (ed.), *Huntingdonshire and the Spanish Armada, edited from Original Manuscripts* (1896).

Oppenheim, M. (ed.), *The Naval Tracts of Sir William Monson* (Navy Record Society, 5 vols, 1902–1914).

Peckham, G., *A True Reporte, of the late discoveries, and possession, taken in the right of the Crowne of Englande, of the Newfound Landes: By that valiaunt and worthye Gentleman, Sir Humfrey Gilbert Knight* (1583).

Petti, A. G. (ed.), *Roman Catholicism in Elizabethan and Jacobean Staffordshire: Documents from the Bagot Papers* (Staffordshire Record Society, fourth series, vol. IX, 1979).

Pollard, A. F., *Tudor Tracts 1532–1588* (1903).

Pollen, J. H., *Unpublished Documents Relating to the English Martyrs*, vol. 1 (Catholic Records Society, 1908).

Prichard, M. J., and D. E. C. Yale (eds), *Hale and Fleetwood on Admiralty Jurisdiction* (1993).

Quinn, D. B., *The Roanoke Voyages 1584–1590* (2 vols, Hakluyt Society, 1952).

——, (ed.), *The Voyages and Colonising Enterprises of Sir Humphrey Gilbert* (2 vols, Hakluyt Society, 1938).

Ralegh, Sir W., *Excellent Observations and Notes, Concerning the Royall Navy and Sea Service* (1650).

——, *A History of the World in Five Books* (11th ed., 1736).

Ramsay, G. D. (ed.), *John Isham's Accounts, 1558–1572* (Northants Record Society, 1962).

Robinson, H. (ed.), *The Zurich Letters*, second series, 1558–1602 (Parker Society, 1845).

Rodger, N. A. M. (ed.), *The Armada in the Public Records* (HMSO, 1988).

Rogers, T., *An Historical Dialogue Touching Antichrist and Poperie, Drawen and Published for the common benefit and comfort of our Church in these dangerous daies, etc.* (1589).

Rye, W. B., *England as Seen by Foreigners in the days of Elizabeth and James I* (1865).

Salisbury, W., and R. C. Anderson, *A Treatise on Shipbuilding and a Treatise on Rigging Written about 1620–1625* (Society for Nautical Research Occasional Publications no. 6, 1958).

Salzman, L. F. (ed.), *The Town Book of Lewes, 1542–1701* (Sussex Record Society, 1945–6).

Scott, W. (ed.), *A collection of scarce and valuable tracts . . . particularly that of the Late Lord Somers* (13 vols, 1809–15).

Smith, Sir T., *De Republica Anglorum* (1583).

Strype, J., *Ecclesiastical Memorials, relating chiefly to Religion, etc.* (ed. 1822, 3 vols).

——, *Annals of the Reformation and Establishment of Religion, etc.* (ed. 1824, 3 vols).

Stubbes, P., *The Anatomie of Abuses* (1583).

——, *The Intended Treason, of Doctor Parrie: and of his Complices, Against the Queenes moste Excellent Maiestie* (c. 1585–6).

Taylor, E. G. R., *The Original Writings and Correspondence of the two Richard Hakluyts* (Hakluyt Society, 1935).

——, *The Troublesome Voyage of Captain Edward Fenton, 1582–1583* (Hakluyt Society, 1959).

Tawney, R. H., and E. Power, *Tudor Economic Documents* (3 vols, 1924).

Temple, R. C., *The World Encompassed by Sir Francis Drake* (1926).

Wake, J. (ed.), *A Copy of Papers Relating to Musters, Beacons, Subsidies, etc. in the County of*

Northampton, A.D. 1586–1623 (Northants Record Society, 1926).

Walden, A., *The Court and Character of King James* (1650).

Williamson, J. A. (ed.), *The Observations of Sir Richard Hawkins* (1933).

Winwood, R., *Memorials of affairs of state in the reigns of Queen Elizabeth and King James I, etc.* (3 vols, 1725).

Wright, I., *English Voyages to the Caribbean, 1527–1568* (Hakluyt Society, 1929).

——, *English Voyages to the Spanish Main, 1569–1580* (Hakluyt Society, 1932).

——, *Further English Voyages to Spanish America, 1583–1594* (Hakluyt Society, 1949).

Wriothesley, Charles, *Chronicle of England* (ed. W. D. Hamilton), 2 vols, 1875, 1877.

SECONDARY SOURCES

Adams, S., 'The Outbreak of the Elizabethan Naval War against the Spanish Empire: The Embargo of May 1585 and Sir Francis Drake's West Indies Voyage', in Rodriguez-Salgado and Adams, *England, Spain and the Gran Armada*, pp. 45–69.

——, 'New Light on the 'Reformation' of John Hawkins: the Ellesmere Survey of January 1584', *EHR*, CV (1990), pp. 96–111.

Allen, P. C., *Philip III and the Pax Hispanica, 1598–1621* (New Haven, 2000).

Andrews, K. R., *Elizabethan Privateering* (Cambridge, 1964).

——, *Drake's Voyages* (1967).

——, *The Spanish Caribbean: Trade and Plunder, 1530–1630* (New Haven, 1978).

——, 'The Elizabethan Seaman', *MM*, LXVIII (1982), pp. 245–62.

——, *Trade, Plunder and Settlement: Maritime enterprise and the genesis of the British Empire, 1480–1630* (Cambridge, 1984).

Anstruther, G., *Vaux of Harrowden, a recusant family* (1953).

Barker, R., 'Fragments from the Pepysian Library', *Revista da Universidade de Coimbra*, XXXII (1986), pp. 161–78.

Bauckham, R., *Tudor Apocalypse* (Abingdon, 1978).

Beaven, A. B., *The Aldermen of the City of London* (vol. I, 1908).

Beer, B. L., *Northumberland: The Political Career of John Dudley, Earl of Warwick and Duke of Northumberland* (Kent, Ohio, 1973).

——, *Rebellion and Riot: Popular Discord in England in the Reign of Edward VI* (Kent, Ohio, 1982).

Bell, G. M., 'John Man: The Last Resident Ambassador in Spain', *The Sixteenth Century Journal*, VII (1976), pp. 75–93.

Black, J. B., 'Elizabeth, the Sea Beggars, and the Capture of Brille', *EHR*, XLVI (1931), pp. 30–47.

Blagden, C., *The Stationers' Company: A History, 1403–1959* (1960).

Blayney, P., 'William Cecil and the Stationers', in R. Myers and M. Harris (eds), *The Stationers' Company and the Book Trade 1550–1990* (Winchester, 1997), pp. 11–34.

Bossy, J., *The English Catholic Community, 1570–1850* (1975).

Boulind, R., 'Tudor Captains: the Beestons and the Tyrells', *MM*, LIX (1973), pp. 171–8.

Bouwsma, W. J., *The Waning of the Renaissance* (2000).

Boynton, L., *The Elizabethan Militia 1558–1638* (1967).

Brigden, S., *London and the Reformation* (Oxford, 1989).

Brown, J., and J. Elliot (eds), *The Sale of the Century: Artistic Relations Between Spain and Great Britain, 1604–1655* (2003).

Calvar, J., 'Summary Report on the Nueva collección documental de las hostiladades entre

España e Inglaterra (1568–1604)', in Gallagher and Cruickshank, *God's Obvious Design*, pp. 187–91.

Caraman, P., *Henry Garnet, 1555–1606, and the Gunpowder Plot* (1964).

Christy, M., 'Queen Elizabeth's visit to Tilbury in 1588', *EHR*, XXXIV (1919), pp. 43–61.

Clowes, W. L., *The Royal Navy: A History from the Earliest Times to the present* (vol. 1, 1897).

Collinson, P., 'The Elizabethan Exclusion crisis and the Elizabethan Polity', *Proceedings of the British Academy*, LXXXIV (1993).

Connell-Smith, G., *Forerunners of Drake* (Plymouth, 1954).

Corbett, J. S., *Drake and the Tudor Navy, with a History of the Rise of England as a Maritime Power* (2 vols, 1898).

Cressy, D., 'The Spanish Armada: Celebration, Myth and Memory', in J. Doyle and B. Moore (eds), *England and the Spanish Armada: Papers arising from the 1988 Conference, University College, University of New South Wales, Australian Defence Force Academy, Canberra, Australia* (Sydney, 1988).

Croft, P., 'English Mariners Trading to Spain and Portugal, 1558–1625', *MM*, LXIX (1983), pp. 251–66.

——, 'Trading with the Enemy, 1585–1604', *Historical Journal*, XXXII (1989), pp. 281–302.

Cruickshank, C. G., *Elizabeth's Army* (Oxford, 1966).

Cummins, J., *Francis Drake: The Lives of a Hero* (1995).

Daultrey, S., 'The Weather of Northwest Europe during the Armada Campaign', in Gallagher and Cruickshank, *God's Obvious Design*, pp. 113–41.

De Beer, E. S., 'The Lord High Admiral and the Administration of the Navy', *MM*, XIII (1927), pp. 45–50.

Dickerman, E. H., 'A Neglected Phase of the Spanish Armada: The Catholic League's Picard Offensive of 1587'; *Canadian Journal of History*, XI (1976), pp. 19–23.

Dietz, B., 'The Royal Bounty and English Merchant Shipping in the Sixteenth and Seventeenth Centuries', *MM*, LXXVII (1991), pp. 5–20.

Dietz, F. C., *English Public Finance 1485–1641* (2 vols, 1964).

Douglas, K. S., and H. H. Lamb, *Weather Observations and a tentative Meteorological analysis of the Period May to July 1588* (Norwich, 1979).

Duffy, M. (ed.), *The New Maritime History of Devon*, vol. 1 (1992).

Elliott, J. H., *Imperial Spain, 1469–1716* (1963).

Elton, G. R., *England under the Tudors* (1955).

Ewen, C. L'Estrange, 'Organized Piracy round England in the sixteenth-century', *MM*, XXV (1949), pp. 29–42.

Felch, S., 'Shaping the Reader in the Acts and Monuments', in Loades, *John Foxe and the English Reformation*, pp. 52–65.

Fernández-Armesto, F., *The Spanish Armada: The Experience of War in 1588* (Oxford, 1988).

Firth, C. H., 'The Ballad History of the Reigns of the Later Tudors,' Transactions of the Royal Historical Society, third series, III (1909), pp. 51–124.

Fischer, D. H., *The Great Wave: Price Revolutions and the Rhythm of History* (Oxford, 1996).

Fisher, H. A. L., *The Political History of England*, vol. V, 1485–1547 (1906).

Fissel, M. C., *English Warfare 1511–1642* (2001).

Froude, J. A., *History of England from the Fall of Wolsey to the death of Elizabeth* (12 vols, ed. 1969).

Gallagher, P., and D. W. Cruickshank, *God's Obvious Design* (1988).

Gammon, S. R., *Statesman and Schemer: William, First Lord Paget – Tudor Minister* (Newton

Abbot, 1973).

Garrett, C., *The Marian Exiles* (Cambridge, 1938).

Gerson, A. J., 'The English Recusants and the Spanish Armada', *American Historical Review*, XXII (1917).

Geyl, P., *The Revolt of the Netherlands* (1945).

Glasgow, T., 'The Shape of the Ships that Defeated the Spanish Armada', *MM*, L (1964), pp. 177–87.

———, 'The Royal Navy at the start of the Reign of Elizabeth I', *MM*, LI (1965), pp. 73–6, 298.

———, 'The Navy in Philip and Mary's War, 1557–1558', *MM*, LIII (1967), pp. 321–42.

———, 'The Navy in the First Elizabethan Undeclared War, 1559–1560', *MM*, LIV (1968), pp. 23–37.

———, 'The Navy in the Le Havre Expedition, 1562–1564', *MM*, LIV (1968), pp. 281–96.

———, 'Maturing of Naval Administration', *MM*, LVI (1970), pp. 3–25.

———, 'Gorgas' Seafight', *MM*, LIX (1973), pp. 179–85.

Gould, J. D., 'The Crisis in the Export Trade 1586–1587', *EHR*, LXXI (1956), pp. 212–22.

Green, E., *The Preparations in Somerset Against the Spanish Armada* (1888).

Haigh C., *English Reformations* (Oxford, 1993).

———, *The English Reformation Revisited* (Cambridge, 1987).

———, (ed.), *The Reign of Elizabeth I* (Athens, Ga, 1987).

Haller, W., *The Rise of Puritanism* (Columbia, N.Y., 1938).

———, *Foxe's Book of Martyrs and the Elect Nation* (1963).

Harbison, E. H., *Rival Ambassadors at the Court of Queen Mary* (Princeton, N.J., 1940).

Haring, C. H., *Trade and Navigation between Spain and the Indies in the time of the Hapsburgs* (Gloucester, Mass., 1964).

Haweis, J. O. W., *Sketches of the Reformation and Elizabethan Age Taken from the Contemporary Pulpit* (1844).

Haynes, A., *Robert Cecil, 1st Earl of Salisbury: Servant of Two Sovereigns* (1989).

Hibbert, C., *The Virgin Queen* (1992).

Higgs, L. M., *Godliness and Governance in Tudor Colchester* (Ann Arbor, 1998).

Holt, M. P., *The French Wars of Religion, 1562–1629* (Cambridge, 1995).

Hughes, P., *The Reformation in England* (1963).

Hughes, P. L., and J. F. Larkin, *Tudor Royal Proclamations*, vols 2 and 3 (New Haven, 1969).

Jack, S., 'The Cinque Ports and the Spanish Armada', in J. Doyle and B. Moore (eds), *England and the Spanish Armada: Papers arising from the 1988 Conference, University College, University of New South Wales, Australian Defence Force Academy, Canberra, Australia* (Sydney, 1988).

Jensen, J. De Lamar, *Diplomacy and Dogmatism: Bernadino de Mendoza and the French Catholic League* (Cambridge, Mass., 1964).

———, 'The Spanish Armada: The Worst-Kept Secret in Europe'; *The Sixteenth Century Journal*, XIX (1988).

Jones, N. L., 'Elizabeth's First Year: The Conception and Birth of the Elizabethan Political World', in Haigh, *The Reign of Elizabeth I*, pp. 27–53.

Jordan, W. K., *Edward VI: The Young King* (Cambridge, Mass., 1968).

———, *Edward VI: The Threshold of Power* (Cambridge, Mass., 1970).

Kamen, H., *Philip of Spain* (1997).

Kelsey, H., *Sir Francis Drake: The Queen's Pirate* (1998).

Kenny, R. W., *Elizabeth's Admiral: The Political Career of Charles Howard, Earl of Nottingham 1536–1624* (Baltimore and London, 1970).

Kirsch, P., *The Galleon of the Armada Period* (1990).

Leimon, M., and G. Parker, 'Treason and Plot in Elizabethan Diplomacy: the "Fame of Sir Edward Stafford" Reconsidered', *EHR*, CXI (1996).

Lewis, A. H., *A Study of Elizabethan Ship Money, 1588–1603* (Philadelphia, 1928).

Lewis, M., 'Armada Guns: A Comparative Study of English and Spanish Armaments', *MM*, XXVIII (1942), pp. 41–73, 104–47, 231–45, 259–90; XXIX (1943), pp. 3–39, 100–21, 163–78, 203–31.

Leys, M. D. R., *Catholics in England, 1559–1829: A Social History* (1961).

Loach, J., *Parliament and the Crown in the Reign of Mary Tudor* (Oxford, 1986).

——, (ed.), *The Mid-Tudor Polity c.1540–1560* (1980).

Loades, D. M., *Two Tudor Conspiracies* (Cambridge, 1965).

——, *The Reign of Mary Tudor* (1979).

——, *The Tudor Navy* (Aldershot, 1992).

——, *The Mid-Tudor Crisis, 1545–1565* (Basingstoke, 1992).

——, (ed.), *John Foxe and the English Reformation* (Aldershot, 1997).

Lloyd, R., *Dorset Elizabethans at Home and Abroad* (1967).

Loomie, A. J., The Spanish Elizabethans (New York, 1963).

——, 'Philip III and the Stuart Succession in England', *Revue belge de Philologie et d'Histoire*, XLIII (Brussels, 1965), pp. 492–514.

——, 'Sir Robert Cecil and the Spanish Succession'; *Bulletin of the Institute of Historical Research*, XLII (1969), pp. 30–57.

Lowers, J. K., *Mirrors for Rebels: A Study of Polemic Literature Relating to the Northern Rebellion, 1569* (Berkeley, 1953).

MacCaffrey, W., *The Shaping of the Elizabethan Regime* (Princeton, N.J., 1968).

——, *Exeter 1540–1640* (Cambridge, Mass., 1975).

——, *Queen Elizabeth and the Making of Policy 1572–1588* (Princeton, N.J., 1981).

——, *Elizabeth I: War and Politics, 1588–1603* (Princeton, N.J., 1992).

MacCulloch, D., 'Catholic and Puritan in Elizabethan Suffolk', *Archive for Reformation History*, LXXII (1981), pp. 232–90.

——, *Tudor Church Militant* (1999).

Maclure, M., *The St Paul's Cross Sermons, 1534–1642* (Toronto, 1958).

Maltby, W. S., *The Black Legend in England: The development of Anti-Spanish sentiment, 1558–1660* (Durham, N.C., 1971).

——, *Alba: A Biography of Fernando Alvarez de Toledo, Third Duke of Alba 1507–1583* (Berkeley, 1983).

Martin, C., 'The Ships of the Spanish Armada', in Gallagher and Cruickshank, *God's Obvious Design*, pp. 41–68.

Martin, C., and G. Parker, *The Spanish Armada* (1999).

Martin, P., *The story of the* Nuestra Señora del Rosario *and her crew, and of other prisoners in England, 1587–97* (Exeter, 1988).

Mathew, D., 'The Cornish and Welsh Pirates in the Reign of Elizabeth', *EHR*, XXXIX (1924), pp. 337–48.

Mattingly, G., *The Armada* (1959).

Mayhew, G. J., *Rye and the defence of the Narrow Seas: a 16th Century Town at War*, (Sussex Archaeological Collections, CXXII, 1984).

McBride, G. K., 'Elizabethan foreign policy in microcosm: the Portuguese pretender, 1580–9'; *Albion*, V (1973).

McClain, L., 'Without Church, Cathedral, or Shrine: The Search for Religious Space among Catholics in England, 1559–1625'; *The Sixteenth Century Journal*, XXXIII (2002), pp. 381–99.

McDermott, J., *Martin Frobisher: Elizabethan Privateer* (2001).

McGrath, P., 'Elizabethan Catholicism: a Reconsideration'; *Journal of Ecclesiastical History*, xxxv (1984), pp. 414–28.

McGurk, J., 'Armada Preparations in Kent and Arrangements made after the Defeat (1587–1589)', *Archaeologia Cantiana*, lxxxv (1970).

McKee, A., *From Merciless Invaders* (1963).

Metzger, M. L., 'Controversy and Correctness': English Chronicles and the Chroniclers, 1553–1568'; *The Sixteenth Century Journal*, xxvii (1996), pp. 437–51.

Meyer, A. O., *England and the Catholic Church under Queen Elizabeth* (English edition, 1915).

Miller, A. C., *Sir Henry Killigrew: Elizabethan Soldier and Diplomat* (Leicester, 1963).

Morey, A., *The Catholic Subjects of Elizabeth I* (1978).

Neale, J. E., 'Elizabeth and the Netherlands, 1586–7', *EHR*, xlv (1930), pp. 373–96.

——, *The Elizabethan House of Commons* (1949).

——, *Elizabeth I and her Parliaments, 1559–1581* (1953), *1584–1601* (1957).

Nolan, J. S., *Sir John Norreys and the Elizabethan Military World* (Exeter, 1997).

O'Donnell, H., 'The Requirements of the Duke of Parma for the Conquest of England', in Gallagher and Cruickshank, *God's Obvious Design*, pp. 85–99.

Oppenheim, M., *A History of the Administration of the Royal Navy and of Merchant Shipping in Relation to the Navy from 1509–1660* (1896).

Palliser, D. M., 'Popular Reactions to the Reformation', in Haigh, *The English Reformation Revised*, pp. 94–113.

Palmer, W., *The Problem of Ireland in Tudor Foreign Policy, 1485–1603* (Woodbridge, 1994).

Parker, G., *The Dutch Revolt* (1977).

——, 'The Dreadnought Revolution of Tudor England', *MM*, lxxxii (1996), pp. 269–300.

——, *The Grand Strategy of Philip II* (1998).

——, 'The Place of Tudor England in the Messianic Vision of Philip II', *Transactions of the Royal Historical Society*, sixth series, xii (2002), pp. 167–221.

——, 'Anatomy of Defeat: The Testimony of Juan Martínez de Recalde and Don Alonso Martínez de Leyva on the failure of the Spanish Armada in 1588', *MM*, xc (2004), pp. 314–48.

Pears, E. A., 'The Spanish Armada and the Ottoman Porte', *EHR*, viii (1893), pp. 439–66, p. 446.

Pierson, P., *Commander of the Armada: The Seventh Duke of Medina Sidonia* (1989).

——, 'The Development of Spanish Naval Strategy and Tactics in the Sixteenth Century'; in M. R. Thorpe and A. J. Slavin (eds), *Politics, Religion & Diplomacy in Early Modern Europe* (Kirksville, Mo., 1994).

Pistono, S. P., 'Henry IV and the English Privateers', *EHR*, xc (1975), pp. 322–30.

Platt, C., *Medieval Southampton* (1973).

Pollitt, R., 'Bureacracy and the Armada: The Administrator's Battle', *MM*, lx (1974), pp. 119–32.

Quinn, D. B., and A. N. Ryan, *England's Sea Empire* (1983).

Ramsay, G. D., *The City of London in International Politics at the accession of Elizabeth Tudor* (Manchester, 1975).

——, *The Queen's Merchants and the Revolt of the Netherlands* (Manchester, 1986).

Ramsey, P., *Tudor Economic Problems* (1966).

Rasor, E. L., *The Spanish Armada of 1588: Historiography and Annotated Biography* (Westport, Conn., 1993).

Rawlinson, H. G., 'The Embassy of William Harborne to Constantinople, 1583–88', *Transactions of the Royal Historical Society*, fourth series, v, (1922) pp. 1–27.

Read, C., *Sir Francis Walsingham* (3 vols, Cambridge, 1925).

——, 'Queen Elizabeth's seizures of the duke of Alva's pay ships'. *Journal of Modern History*, 1 (1933), pp. 443–64.

——, *Mr Secretary Cecil and Queen Elizabeth* (1955).

——, *Lord Burghley and Queen Elizabeth* (New York, 1960).

——, 'William Cecil and Elizabethan Public Relations', in S. T. Bindoff, J. Hurstfield, and C. H. Williams (eds), *Elizabethan Government and Society: Essays presented to Sir John Neale* (1961).

Redworth, G., 'Matters Impertinent to Women': Male and Female Monarchy under Philip and Mary', *EHR*, CXII (1997), pp. 597–613.

Richards, J., 'Before the "Mountaynes Mouse": Propaganda and Public Defence Before the Spanish Armada'; in J. Doyle and B. Moore (eds), *England and the Spanish Armada: Papers arising from the 1988 Conference, University College, University of New South Wales, Australian Defence Force Academy, Canberra, Australia* (Sydney, 1988).

Roberts, J. C. de V., *Devon and the Armada* (1988).

Rodger, N. A. M., *The Safeguard of the Sea: A Naval History of Britain*, vol. 1, 660–1649 (1997).

Rodriguez-Salgado, M. J. (ed.), *Armada, 1588–1988* (National Maritime Museum, 1988).

Rodriguez-Salgado, M. J., and S. Adams (eds), *England, Spain and the Gran Armada, 1585–1604* (Savage, Maryland, 1991).

——, 'The Count of Feria's Dispatch to Philip II of 14 November 1558'; *Camden Society Miscellany*, XXVIII (1984).

Rowlands, M. B., 'Hidden People: Catholic Commoners 1558–1625', in M. B. Rowlands (ed.), *English Catholics of Parish and Town, 1558–1778* (Catholic Record Society, 1999).

Rowse, A. L., *Tudor Cornwall* (1941).

Scarisbrick, J. J., *Henry VIII* (Berkeley, 1968).

Schokkenbroek, J. C. A., 'Whither Serveth Justin . . .?', in Gallagher and Cruickshank, *God's Obvious Design*, pp. 101–11.

Shillington, V. M., and A. B. W. Chapman, *Commercial Relations of England and Portugal* (New York, 1970).

Slack, P., *The Impact of Plague in Tudor and Stuart England* (Oxford, 1985).

Spence, R. T., *The Privateering Earl: George Clifford, 3rd Earl of Cumberland, 1558–1605* (Stroud, 1995).

Stanford, 'The Raleghs take to the Sea', *MM*, XLVIII (1962), pp. 18–34.

Stebbing, W., *Sir Walter Ralegh* (1899).

Stern, V. F., *Sir Stephen Powle of Court and Country* (1992).

Stewart, R.W., *The English Ordnance Office: A Case-Study in Bureaucracy* (1996).

Stone, L., *An Elizabethan: Sir Horatio Palavicino* (Oxford, 1956).

Sutherland, N. M., *Princes, Politics and Religion 1547–1589* (1984).

Tazón, J. E., *The Life and Times of Thomas Stukeley (c. 1525–78)* (Aldershot, 2003).

Tenace, E., 'A Strategy of Reaction: The Armadas of 1596 and 1597 and the Spanish Struggle for European Hegemony', *EHR*, CXVIII (2003), pp. 855–82.

Thomas, K., *Religion and the Decline of Magic: Studies in Popular Beliefs in Sixteenth and Seventeenth-Century England* (1971).

Thorpe, M. R., 'William Cecil and the Antichrist: a Study in Anti-Catholic Ideology'; in M. R. Thorpe and A. J. Slavin (eds), *Politics, Religion & Diplomacy in Early Modern Europe* (Kirksville, Mo., 1994).

Trimble, W. R., *The Catholic Laity in Elizabethan England 1558–1603* (Cambridge, Mass., 1964).

Usher, B., ' "In a Time of Persecution": New Light on the Secret Protestant Congregation in Marian London', in Loades, *John Foxe and the English Reformation*, pp. 233–51.

Walsham, A., *Church Papists: Catholicism, Conformity and Confessional Polemic in Early Modern England* (1993).

Ward, S., *A True and Full Narrative of those two never to be forgotten Deliverances, the Spanish Invasion in 88, and the Hellish Powder Plot, 1605, etc.* (1671).

Wark, K. R., *Elizabethan Recusancy in Cheshire* (Manchester, 1971).

Waters, D. W., *The Art of Navigation In England in Elizabethan and Early Stuart Times* (1958).

——, *The Elizabethan Navy and the Armada of Spain* (National Maritime Museum, Maritime Monographs and Reports no. 17, 1975).

——, 'Lord Howard as a Seaman, 1578', *MM*, xli (1955), pp. 336–7.

Watt, T., *Cheap Print and Popular Piety, 1550–1640* (Cambridge, 1991).

Webb, H. J., *Elizabethan military Science: The Books and the Practice* (Madison, Wisc., 1965).

Webb, J., 'Elizabethan Piracy: The evidence of the Ipswich Deposition Books', *Suffolk Review*, li, no. 3 (Ipswich, 1960).

Wernham, R. B., *Before the Armada: The Growth of English Foreign Policy, 1485–1588* (1966).

——, *The Making of Elizabethan Foreign Policy, 1558–1603* (1980).

——, *After the Armada: Elizabethan England and the Struggle for Western Europe, 1588–1595* (Oxford, 1984).

——, *The Return of the Armadas: The Last Years of the Elizabethan War against Spain, 1595–1608* (Oxford, 1994).

Whiting, R., *The Enterprise of England* (1988).

Wiener, C. Z., 'The Beleaguered Isle: A study of Elizabethan and early Jacobean anti-Catholicism'; *Past and Present*, li (1971), pp. 27–62.

Whitehead, B. T., *Brags and Boasts: Propaganda in the Year of the Armada* (Stroud, 1994).

Willan, T. S., *Studies in Elizabethan Foreign Trade* (Manchester, 1959).

Willen, D., *John Russell, First Earl of Bedford* (1981).

Williamson, J. A., *Sir John Hawkins, the Time and the Man* (Oxford, 1927).

——, *The Age of Drake* (1938).

——, *Hawkins of Plymouth* (1949).

Wilson, C., *Queen Elizabeth and the Netherlands* (1970).

Winchester, B., *Tudor Family Portrait* (1955).

Wylie, J. H., *History of England under Henry IV* (4 vols, 1884–98).

Index

Admiralty, Court and officers of, 6, 14, 17, 23–4,
  26–7, 39, 58–9, 61, 122, 125, 127, 153–5, 167,
  198, 313, 334n18
Aglionby, Edward, 96–7, 343n12
Álava, Don Francés de, Spanish ambassador to
  Paris, 81
Alba, Don Fernando Álvarez de Toldeo, Duke
  of, x, 73–80, 82, 84–89, 91, 93, 95, 108, 118–9,
  340nn26, 33, 342n60, 343n14, 346n51
Albert of Austria, Archduke of the Netherlands,
  308, 311, 314, 383n28
Albigensian Crusade, 90
Alcazar, Seville, 65
Alday, James, 332n29
Alençon/Anjou, Francis Hercule, Duke of, 87,
  136, 144
Alexander VI (Rodrigo de Borja y Borja), pope,
  xi, 330n1
Algiers, 194
Allde, John, 102
Allen, William, 106–7, 112, 166, 197, 298, 302
Amboise, 'Tumult' of (1560), 53
Anderton, William, 345n43
Anglesey, 189, 244
Anglo–Imperial Treaty (1543), 18, 23, 43
Angra, port of Terceira, 133
Annebaut, admiral Claude d', 187
Anne of Austria, Queen of Spain, 86
António of Avis, Prior of Cato, Dom, 118, 128,
  133–8, 143, 149–50, 157, 167, 213
Antwerp, 8, 79–8, 91, 121, 136, 151, 159, 267, 314;
  English cloth mart at, 35, 56, 72, 82, 86, 91;
  merchants of, 338n43; money markets at, 56,
  60, 74, 77, 197; sack of (1576), 109–110; 'hell-
  burners' of, 266

Aragon, xii
Archdeacon, Daniel, 295–6
Arderne Hall, 280
Ardres, Treaty of (1546), 28, 30
Armada of Spain (1588), xiv, 97, 162, 168, 191,
  365n23; preparations at Lisbon, 171–2, 358n48;
  intelligence of obtained by English agents,
  172–3, 191–4, 196, 364nn9, 11; at sea, 206;
  driven into Corunna, 206–8, 355n2; sighted in
  Channel, 228; first clash with English fleet,
  229–231; engaged off Portland, 250–5,
  374nn20, 25, 375n27; fight off Wight, 258–6;
  routed by English fire-ships at Calais, 266–8;
  rumoured to be returning through the North
  Sea, 281–3, 287; fate off Ireland, 288;
  squadrons of: Andalusian, 231; Biscayan, 208,
  230, 272; Guipúzcoan, 231; Levant, 256, 271
Arnemuiden, 195–6
Arras, Union of, 349n58
Artois, 54
Arundel, 380n23
Arwennack, Falmouth, 126
Ashley, Anthony, 382n51
Aske, John, 279–80, 371n53
Assize, Court of, 6
Assonleville, Christophe d', Imperial envoy, 60
Ataranzanas, arsenal of Seville, 65
Atkinson, Clinton, 127–8
Atlantic Ocean, 66, 69, 91, 161, 350n66
Audley, John, 104
Aumale, Claude, Duke of, 166
Auneau, battle of (1587), 169
Avilés, Pedro Menéndez de, 67, 339n7
Avis, Portuguese Royal House of, 80, 117–8
Azores, 136, 213, 224, 288, 309

Babington, Anthony, conspiracy of, 111–12, 163, 353n55

Baffin Island, 128, 140, 220, 348n35, 373n10

Bahia, Brazil, 10

Baker, Christopher, 225, 356n33

Baker, Matthew, 177–80, 320, 356nn30, 33, 357n46, 358n48, 370n48

Bale, John, 99

Ballard, John, 112

Baltic, naval supplies from, 215

Baltimore, Ireland, 25

Bancks, Edward, 253

Bancks, Edward, alderman, 374n22

Barker, Andrew, 122

Barn Elms, 165

Barnstaple, 284

Bassett, William, 245

Baxter, John, 345n39

Bayonne, 13

Bedford, Francis Russell, Earl of, 48, 125

Beeston, George, 225, 262, 270, 272, 367n45

Belém, fortress of, 211

Benin, 36

Bergen-op-Zoom, 192, 287

Bermuda, 151

Berwick, 182, 275, 378n30

Bethell, Richard, 34, 334n10

Bett, Walter, 351n23

Bideford, 361n35

Bingham, Sir Richard, 133, 359n70

Black Raven, Paternoster Row, 111

Blackwall, Nicholas, 245

Blackwell, George, 384n35

Blackwell Hall, 175

Bletchington Hill, 187

Bodenham, Roger, 117, 120

Bond of Association (1584), 114, 164

Bontemps, Jean, 70, 340n17

Book of Common Prayer, 113

Borough, William, 177, 223, 225, 261, 356n33, 366n36, 367nn43, 44

Boste, John, 105

Boulogne, 19, 30, 32, 87, 215, 225

Bourbon, House of, 53, 144

Bowes, Sir George, 343n8

Boyte, Philip, 128

Brabant, 75, 287

Brabant, John, 105

Bradford, John, 99

Braunton, 285

Brazil, 3, 10, 67, 137, 331n11

Brazil wood, 4

Brest, 34, 40, 308–9, 383n14

Bridewell, gaol, 292, 307

Brielle, 87, 150, 173

Brighthelmstowe (Brighton), 187, 380n23

Bristol, 7, 27, 58, 126, 200, 383n14; merchants of, 330n4

Bristol, Treaty of (1574), 91, 118, 121–2, 148

Brittany, 34, 309

Bronkhorst, House of, 55

Bruges, 338n42

Bruse, Robert, 28

Brussels, 50

Burburata, Tierra Firme, 69–71

Burcher, Johm, 337n7

Burgos, prior and merchants of, 24, 332n23

Burnell, Francis, 373n9

Cabot, Sebastian, 367n44

Cadiz, 65, 162, 167–9, 171, 173, 176, 179, 181, 210, 218, 309, 360n11, 362n52

Caesar, Gaius Julius, 189

Calais, xv, 19, 32, 40, 43–4, 50–1, 253, 264–7, 269–73, 282, 295, 306, 308, 327, 334n11, 335n43, 337n18, 338n42, 354n71, 376nn45, 48

Calderon, Pedro Coco, 378n18

Calicut, 135

Callice, John

Calshot Castle, 126

Calshot Point, 3

Camden, William, 50, 255, 272, 365n26

Campion, Edmund, 106, 345n45, 372n75

Campvere, 195–6

Canary Islands, 3, 67, 330n4, 336n49

Canterbury, 242

Canterbury, John Whitgift, Archbishop of, 237, 372n71

Cape Finesterre, 167, 309

Cape Gris-Nez, 195

Cape Palos, 127

Cape Roque, 4

Cape St Vincent, 3, 22

Cape Verde, 87, 137, 224

Cardiff, 124

Carew, Sir Peter, 40, 325

Carey, Sir George, 263, 283, 373n6, 381n49

Carey, George, of Cockington, 293–4, 381n49

Caribbean, 5, 66, 68, 72, 121–3, 129, 146, 224, 310, 314, 349n52

Carisbrooke Castle, Isle of Wight, 373n6

Carleill, Christopher, 138, 143, 156, 350n2; *Discourse* of, 138, 143

Carleton, Sir Dudley, 383n10

Carolina Banks, 139, 247

Cartagena, Tierra Firme, 66, 162, 218, 294

Casa de Contratación, Seville, 65–7, 132

Castile, xi, xii, 65

Castillo, Hernando de, 118

Catalonia, 54

Cateau–Cambrésis, conference and treaty of, 43

Catherine de'Medici, Queen–Dowager and Regent of France, 53, 79, 89, 147, 169

Catholic League, 129, 144, 215, 267, 295, 307–8, 315, 353n55

Catholics, English (see also Church Papists and

Recusants, recusancy), 48, 76, 83, 92–9, 104–8, 111–14, 164, 243–8, 297–8, 301–2, 313–5, 319, 322–3, 343n5, 344, nn16, 17, 346n49, 368n8, 383n28, 384n35

Catholics, Irish, xv, 83, 319

Cattewater, Plymouth, 70, 208, 278

Cavendish, Thomas, 139

Cecil, Sir Robert, 243, 326, 381n46; as Viscount Cranborne, 383n28

Cecil, Sir William, 1st Baron Burghley, 44, 50–1, 59–60, 70, 76–9, 81–91, 93, 95, 98, 100–2, 104–6, 113, 120, 126, 131, 135, 143, 147, 149, 157–8, 164–5, 167, 173–6, 180, 186–7, 189, 193, 195–7, 202–3, 209–10, 212–3, 238, 242–3, 249, 263, 277, 281, 283–6, 288, 301–2, 308, 312, 315, 337n18, 338n22, 340nn31, 33, 341n40, 342n62, 348n22, 349n52, 350n78, 353n42, 354nn61, 71, 355nn15, 21, 23, 356n27, 359n3, 360n11, 362n56, 363n75, 365n21, 377n12, 379n39, 380n8, 381n41, 383n23; survey of the nation and threats thereto (1569), 78–9, 82, 93, 339n1, 341n54; on dangers from domestic Catholics, 95, 345n45; on the state of English Protestantism, 98–9, 344n18; involved in state censorship of printed matter, 101–2; pamphlets and tracts of: *Execution of Justice in England* (1583), 106; *Copy of a letter sent out of England to Don Bernadin Mendoza* (1588), 296–7, 372n71; *A Packe of Spanish Lyes* (1588), 296–7; early proposal for a strategy against a Spanish invasion (1584), 212

Cercamp, peace negotiations of, 51, 56

Chaloner, Sir Thomas, English ambassador to Spain, 58–9, 69, 337n13, 338nn31, 34, 35, 45

Chamberlayn, Sir Thomas, 58

Chancellor, Richard, 36

Chancery, Court of, 14

Chandos, William Brydges, Lord, 371n58

Chapman, Richard, 178, 356n33, 370n48

Chapuys, Eustace, Imperial envoy, 6, 23, 332n23

Charles v, Emperor, xiii, 6–11, 18–28, 32–3, 37–8, 55, 93, 109, 315, 332n23, 339n3

Charles IX, King of France, 89

Chatham, 195, 198, 202, 225, 263, 285, 288, 358n48

Chatham Chest, 381n29

Chaundelor, John, 3, 12

Cheapside, 384n42

Chesil, 248

Chester, 245

Chichester, 380n23

Churchill, Winston, 243

'Church Papists', 104

Churchyard, Thomas, 109

Cimarrones, escaped Negro slaves, 122, 132, 149

Cinque Ports, 13, 15, 20, 200, 263, 341n45

Clement VII, pope, 7

Clere, Sir John, 41

Clinton and Saye, Edward de Fiennes, Edward de, Baron (later Earl of Lincoln), Lord Admiral, 34, 50, 68, 125, 135, 198, 348n22

Clough, Richard, 340n26, 341n38

Clowter, Thomas, 26

Cobham, Lord Thomas, 109, 133, 341n45

Coggeshall, 200

Colchester, 104, 200, 337n21

Cole, Richard, 40

Coligny, Gaspard de, admiral, 66, 89

Coligny, Odet de, Cardinal de Châtillon, 81, 137, 341n45

Colonial projects, English (*see also* Roanoke Island), 138–143, 151, 155

Commission for Ecclesiastical Causes, 336n4

Common Bench, court, 6

Common Prayer, Book of, 53

Contaduría Mayor, junta of, 142

Constable, Sir Robert, 243, 378n30

Conway, Sir John, 287

Cooke, William, 332n29

Corbett, Julius, 209–10, 270, 365n29, 374n25, 377n12, 379n34

Cordell family, merchants, 154

Cordell, Thomas, 181

Cornwall, 34, 125, 348n29

Cornwallis, Sir Charles, 306

Corunna, 205–6, 208, 216, 264, 303–4, 355n2; governor of, and family, 304

Council of Trent, 33, 78

Council of Troubles, 74

Courteney, Edward, Earl of Devon, 39

Courteney, Sir William, 293–4

Coventry, diocese of, 186

Cowdray Park, 380n8

Coxe, William, 251, 270, 373n7

Cranmer, Thomas, 102

Creake, Alexander, 128

Crépy, Treaty of (1544), 19, 21, 59

Crofts, Sir James, 175, 210, 355n23, 362n47

Cromwell, Thomas, 7

Crosse, Robert, 218, 224, 272, 367n41

Cuba, 65

Cubiar, Pedro, 294

Cumberland, George Clifford, Earl of, 234, 262, 281–2, 291, 369n22, 379n39

Cure, shipowner, 266

Dacre, Leonard, 343n7

Dacre, Lord Thomas, 343n7

Danzig, 311

Darell, Marmaduke, 204, 238, 277, 362n58, 376n47

Dartmouth, 5, 26, 126, 237, 275, 336n51

Davis, John, *Seaman's Secrets* of, 320–1

Davison, William, 165

'Day of the Barricades', 215

Dedham, 200

Dee, John, 320
Delft, Francis Van Der, Imperial envoy, 21, 28, 332n23
Deloney, Thomas, 110–11, 279–80
Denbighshire, 125
Denmark, 154, 172, 215, 282, 365n21
Deptford, 180
Derby, 298
Desmond, Gerald Fitzgerald, Earl of, 121
Deventer, 160, 244
Devon, xv, 34, 125, 128, 198, 204, 293
Dieppe, 194, 215, 295
Digges, Thomas, 320
Dingle, 331n5
Domesday Book, 13
Doria, Gian Andrea, 374n15
Dorset, 125
Douai, English seminary at, 91, 98
Douglas, Archibald, Scottish ambassador, 362n46
Douglas, Richard, 362n46
Dover, 147, 182, 187, 263, 266, 277, 285, 287–8, 332n16, 334n11, 341n45, 366n36, 376n47, 377n3, 379nn34, 35, 380n25
Downs, 195, 204–6, 214, 262, 276, 285, 287, 365n25
Drake family, of Littleham, 34, 154
Drake, Bernard, 156, 198, 352n35
Drake, Elizabeth, 294
Drake, Francis, 12, 70–1, 88, 122–3, 132–7, 140, 195, 207, 218, 222–5, 228, 230, 251, 254–60, 266, 269–72, 282–3, 286, 289–91, 293, 295, 312, 325–6, 340n16, 356n33, 359n1, 362n45, 363n70, 367n44, 370n30, 373n5, 374n25, 375n31, 376n48, 381nn29, 43; circumnavigation, 123, 128–9, 131, 150, 224, 349n45, 353n50, 359n70; West Indies raid of, 146–7, 150–2, 156–7, 160–3, 176, 180, 212, 224, 294, 350n2, 352nn36, 38, 369n17; at Cadiz, 167–9, 173, 176, 180, 212, 224, 354n71; with squadron at Plymouth, 181, 193, 196, 199, 204, 213–4, 360n12, 361nn22, 29, 362nn54, 56, 368n15, 373n5; urges more aggressive strategy against Spain, 194, 200, 216, 360n11; appointed vice-admiral of the English fleet, 202–3; alleged role in planning the English campaign strategy, 209–11, 364nn7, 8, 381n41; capture of the *Rosario*, 235–7, 256, 292–3; expedition to Spain and Portugal (1589), 289–91, 304, 307, 381n40
Drake, Richard, 269
Drenthe, 74
Dudley, Sir Henry, conspiracy of, 40–1, 334n24
Dudley, Lord Henry, 158
Dungeness, 266
Dunkirk, 155, 194, 261, 268, 281, 291, 375n34
Duport, John, 336n1
Dursey Head, 331n5
Dutton, Thomas, 340n26
Dye, John, 126

East Bergholt, 200
'Easterlings', Baltic merchantmen, 167
East India Company, 132, 311
Eastland Company, 311, 365n21
Eastwater, Plymouth, 70
Edgar, King of England, 217
Edinburgh, Treaty of (1560), 52
Edward I, King of England, 15
Edward III, King of England, 16
Edward IV, King of England, 15
Edward VI, King of England, xii, 31–3, 36, 37–8, 100, 148; religious policy, 32, 45, 334n11, 336n2
Egmont, House of, 55
Elbe, river, 375n29
Elderton, William, 100–1
Eleanor of Burgundy, xii
Elizabeth I, Queen of England, xi, xiii, xiv, xv, 31–2, 41, 47–52, 54–63, 68–91, 109, 111–12, 114, 118, 120, 122–3, 128–9, 131–7, 143–5, 186, 188, 193–5, 197, 211, 223, 239, 273, 297–8, 311, 314, 316–20, 333n3, 335n30, 338nn44, 45, 339n7, 342nn62, 72, 343n7, 344n31, 346nn51, 57, 347nn1, 8, 15, 348n22, 351n14, 352n39, 353n44, 354nn71, 80, 356n27, 360n11, 362n45, 364n12, 365n21, 377n12, 379n5, 380n8, 381n43, 384n31; character, 48, 147; marriage plans of, 48, 87; religious policies, 49, 92–107, 301–2, 336n4, 345nn43, 45, 346n49; attitude towards English colonial projects, 138–142; Spanish policy 146–7, 149–50, 156–61; reliance upon private resources, 148–9, 290, 318; reluctance to execute Mary Stuart, 164–5; subsidies to German Protestant armies, 169; seeks negotiations with Parma, 175–6, 192–3, 197; guard for the protection of, 188–90, 205, 219, 243–4, 359n82, 371nn53, 58; resists early re-manning and concentration of fleet, 195, 201–2; refuses to allow fleet to seek out the armada, 206–8, 214; visit to Tilbury, 240, 279–81, 283–4; reluctance to pay off fleet, 286–7; celebrates armada victory, 299–300; post–armada foreign policy, 307, 311–2; death, 312
Elizabeth of Valois, 5, 79
Ellesmere Survey, 148
Elsinore, 172
Ely, 297
Emden, 61, 175
Ems, river, 61, 175
Englefield, Sir Francis, 119, 347n8
English Channel (also 'Sleeve'), 13, 27, 34, 40, 44, 61, 81, 88, 93, 110, 124, 162, 168, 171–2, 195, 201, 203, 205, 207, 216–7, 219, 229, 240, 288, 293, 308, 321, 353n48, 362n58
English fleet, combined, 193, 195–6; victualling, 193, 203–6, 211, 263–4, 277–8, 362n58, 363n63, 376nn45, 47; manning, 193–5, 204; innovative nature of, 217–8; problems in discharging mariners, 284–7

Englishmen, antipathy towards foreigners, 38–9, 327, 337n21; towards Spaniards, 38–46, 108, 315–6, 322, 324–8, 334n21, 335nn 31, 36, 41; Spanish visitors' opinions of, 43; awareness of 'self', 319–24

Enriquez, Don Martin, Viceroy of New Spain, 71–2

Erisey, James, 224

Erith, 283

Escorial, monastery and palace, 166, 170

Essex, 240, 285

Essex, Robert Devereaux, Earl of, 243, 291, 299, 309, 312, 380n45, 383n23

Exeter, 127–8, 199–200, 284

Everton, Richard, 5

'Evil May Day', riots of, 38, 107

Facy, Arthur, 361n35

Fair Isle, 283

Falmouth, 189, 309, 335n27, 383n14

Fenner family, 153–4, 218, 367n40

Fenner, Edward, 224

Fenner, George, 224

Fenner, Thomas, 194, 210, 220, 259, 274, 278, 282, 354n73, 358n50, 361n22, 363n70, 364n11, 376n45

Fenner, William, 224

Fenton, Edward, 128, 135–6, 140, 150, 225, 259, 272, 349n57, 356n33, 375n31

Ferdinand, King of Aragon, xi, 8

Feria, Gómez Suárez de Figueroa, Count, 57, 337n13

Fernandez, Simon, 139, 143, 247, 350n66

Fernando de Noronha, island of, 4

Ferrers, George, 43

Fielde, John, 345n39

First Enterprise, the, 134–5

Fisher, William, 111

Fitzmaurice, James, 130

Flamborough Head, 283

Flanders, 54, 78, 163, 169–70, 174–5, 207, 214, 267–8, 273, 275–6, 338n31, 376n48

Fleet Street, 102, 299

Fleming, Thomas, 228, 238

Fletcher, Francis, 353n50

Flicke, Robert, 224, 366n37

Florence, 168

Florida, 66, 69–70, 138–9, 141, 339n7

flotas (also *galleones*, plate fleets, Goan carracks), 66, 71, 91, 133, 137, 151, 162, 169, 171– 2, 174, 288, 308–9, 339n5

Flushing, 87–9, 150, 173, 195–6, 342n70

Foljambe, Godfrey, 245

Folkestone, 266

Fotheringay Castle, 165

Fowler, Thomas, 380n10

Foxe, John, 99, 103, 107–8; *Actes and Monuments* of, 103, 108, 336nn45, 47, 344n22

Four Days' Battle, 365n28

France, xii, 18–20, 28, 30, 32, 44, 50–2, 79, 81, 83, 87, 91, 109, 129, 154, 215, 310, 316–7, 322, 327, 341n40; war with England, (1543) 18–20; (1557/8) 43–4; (1562/3) 57–9, 78; Wars of Religion, 53–5, 60, 73, 78, 123, 130, 134, 157, 165, 322, 334n24, 335n43, 363n70

Franch–Compté, 73

Francis I, King of France, 7, 18–19, 93, 218

Francis II, King of France, 52–3

Frederick II, King of Denmark, 215

Fremington, 285

Frias, Don Juan Fernandez de Velasco y Tobar, Duke of, 304–6

Friesland, 74

Frobisher, Martin, 88, 128, 135, 140, 156, 179, 193–4, 202, 218, 220, 223, 230, 247, 252–3, 257, 259–60, 270, 272, 282, 348n35, 357n46, 372n79, 373nn10, 12, 374nn13, 15, 375n36, 381n43; threatens Drake's life, 235, 237, 291; knighted, 261; capture of the *Madre de Dios*, 309

Fuggers of Augsburg, bankers, correspondence, 118

Fulke, William, 343n3

Galicia, governor of, 302

Gardiner, Stephen, bishop of Winchester, 7, 337n6

Garnet, Henry, 301,

Gascoigne, George, 109–110,

Gelderland, 74,

Gembloux, battle of, 120.

Geneva, 45, 165, .

Genoa, explorations of, xi; pay-ships from (1568), 76–7; reported participation in papal crusade against England, 119

George, the, Westminster, 175

Giambelli, Federico, 377n6

Gibraltar, 59

Gifford, George, 98–9, 344n16

Gilbert, Sir Humphrey, 89, 138–9, 155, 342n70

Gilbert, Sir John, 293, 369n29

Glasgow, bishop of, 133.

Glasier, Richard, 3, 12

Gloucester, 200

Gomera, island of, 4

Gondomar, Diego Sarmiento de Acuña, 327

Gonson, Benjamin, 225, 367n43

Gonzales, Vicente, 350n74

Gorcum, 109

Gorges, Arthur, 224, 365n29, 366n34

Gorges, Nicholas, 224, 275, 367n39, 376n40

Gorges, Sir Thomas, 380n45

Granvelle, Antoine Perronot de, bishop of Arras, cardinal, 28, 55, 59–60

Gravelines, 251, 272–3, 281, 375n31, 376n48

Gravesend, 239–40, 280, 364n16

Great Yarmouth, 15, 187, 189

Greenhithe, 364n16

Greenwich, 88

Gregory XIII (Ugo Boncompagni), pope, 119

Gremell, Edward, 6, 321

Grenville, Sir Richard, 139, 151–2, 188, 198, 204, 288, 308, 349n38

Gresham, Sir Thomas, 60, 74, 77, 338n22, 340nn24, 26, 31

Grey, Lady Jane, 38

Grindall, Edmund, bishop of London, 90

Guadalquivir, river, 65, 351n23

Guaras, Antonio de, 87, 121, 342n60, 247n12

'Guard of the Indies', Spanish fleet, 67

Guatemala, 123

Guernsey, 172

Guinea (see also Sierra Leone), 36–7, 67, 224, 334n18; slaves acquired in, 68–71

Guise, Charles, Cardinal, 52

Guise, François, Duke of, 52, 337n18

Guise, Henry, Duke of, 89, 165, 215; assassination of, 308

Guise, Louis, Cardinal, 165; assassination of, 308

Guise forces, 53–4, 73, 76, 78, 89, 111, 129, 131, 142, 144, 147, 166, 170, 194, 207, 292

Guisnes, 44

Gulf of Mexico, 71

Haarlem, 108

Habsburg, Dynasty of, xiii, xv, 4, 7, 10, 17, 30, 38–9, 43, 46, 56, 66, 73, 78, 289, 319, 322

Hainault, 54

Hakluyt, Richard, the elder, 141

Hakluyt, Richard, the younger, 110, 132, 140, 153, 155; *Divers Voyages* of (1582), 138; *Discourse of Western Planting* of, (1584), 110, 139–141, 346n57; *Principal Navigations* of (1589) 143; (1598–1600), 321

Halfpenny, Thomas, 128

Halle, Edward, 20

Hamburg, 74, 77, 82, 375n29

Hammes, 44

Hanley, Robert, 338n34

Hanseatic League, 58, 154, 283, 311, 375n29

Harborne, William, 170, 192, 354n80

Hariot, Thomas, 320

Harwich, 189, 240–1, 276–7, 281, 284, 379n39

Hastings, 27, 45

Hastings, Francis, 345n39

Hatton, Sir Christopher, 131, 135, 150, 161, 185, 197, 213, 244, 301, 343n13, 363n75, 364n1, 367n47, 371n59, 372n64

Havana, 66

Havre, Le (also 'Newhaven'), 59–60

Hawkins family, 154

Hawkins, John, xv, 12, 88, 122–3, 133, 148–50, 228, 282, 312, 325, 341n52, 349n52, 372n78; slaving voyages, 67–72, 77, 80, 82, 108, 218, 325, 339nn9, 10, 14, 340nn16, 32, 341n44, 350n62; Treasurer of the Navy, 156, 177–8,

180, 214, 238, 286, 288, 356n33, 377n8, 381n29; urges pre-emptive strike against Spain, 194, 210; commands the *Victory* as rear-admiral of the English fleet, 202–3, 207, 212, 218, 223–5, 230, 232, 247, 251, 253, 257–8, 260, 266, 270, 272, 362n59, 375n31; knighted, 261

Hawkins, Richard, 178, 224, 310, 340n32

Hawkins, William, brother of John, 77, 137–8, 225

Hawkins, William, father of John, 10, 26, 67–8, 137, 331n11, 332n33

Hawkins, William, the younger, 224

Hellier, Nicholas, 320

Hellowes, Edward, 367n38

Heneage, Sir Thomas, 135, 241, 243, 277, 353n44

Henri II, King of France, 39, 41–3, 51–3, 334n24; as Dauphin, 19

Henri III, King of France, 87, 134, 144, 157, 165, 176, 215, 295, 354n71; as Duke of Anjou, 87

Henri IV, King of France, 308; as King of Navarre, 89, 144, 215, 307–8

Henri, Prince of Condé, 80, 137, 343n6

Henry VI, King of England, 20

Henry VII, King of England, xii, 15, 56

Henry VIII, King of England, xii, xiii, 6–9, 11, 13, 18–25, 28–33, 47, 93, 95, 97, 185, 225, 239, 337n6; as prince, xii,

Henry of Avis, cardinal, King of Portugal, 117

Hertford Castle, 245

Hickman, Anthony, 45, 336nn48, 49

Hickman, Rose, 45, 336n48

Hispaniola (Haiti), 5, 22, 65–6, 68–9, 151, 331n10

Holland, 74–5, 81, 91, 121, 150, 157, 175, 215

Holbrooke, Richard, 35

Holstocke, William, 34, 87, 179–80, 225, 342nn64, 65, 367n43

Holy Island, 275

Hood, Thomas, 349n57

Hooker, John, 110

Hope Cove, Salcombe, 293

Hopton, Sir Hugh, 240

Horsey, Sir Edward, 88, 135

Horsley, Gilbert, 122

Horton, Sir Ralph, 334n21

Howard, Charles, 2nd Baron Effingham, Lord Admiral, 114, 154, 156, 162, 167, 180–1, 192–6, 198, 216–7, 219–20, 222–4, 228–31, 234–8, 247, 249–257, 259–263, 265–6, 268–70, 272, 274–7, 282–91, 295, 356n33, 357n46, 360nn6, 11, 12, 362n58, 363nn63, 70, 365nn22, 29, 367n38, 368n2, 369n20, 370n30, 373nn1, 2, 12, 374n25, 376nn45, 48, 377n12, 378n14, 379nn31, 34, 42, 381nn43, 45, 46; urges concentration of the English fleet, 201–2; at Plymouth, 203–8; fears English fleet may be defeated for lack of provisions, 205; advised by informal council, 205, 210; embassy to Spain (1605), 303–7, 313, 382n3; Cadiz expedition (1596), 309; as Earl of Nottingham, 325

Howard, Charles the younger, 224
Howard, Lord Thomas, 220, 261, 285, 291, 308;
  as Earl of Suffolk, 306
Howard, William, 1st Lord Effingham, 51, 335n31
Howe, William, 102
Huguenots, 53, 73, 75–6, 89, 91, 107; privateers,
  66–7, 76, 122, 149, 155; armies, 54, 59, 80,
  174, 341n40
Huisduinen, 283
Humber River, 19
Hunnis, William, 334n10
Hunsdon, Sir Henry Carey, Lord, 185, 242–3,
  263, 275, 358n59, 371n53, 372n81, 373n6,
  381n49
Huntingdon, Henry Hastings, Earl of, 274,
  371n62, 378n30

'Iconoclastic Fury' (1566), 73
Idiáquez, Don Juan de, 166,
Inquisition, the (also Holy Office), 9–10, 29, 53,
  58, 64, 107–8, 152–3, 167, 292–3, 314, 351n23
Ireland, 32, 63, 129–30, 182, 214, 272, 288, 311;
  English campaigns in, 130–2, 182; Spanish
  involvement in, 130–1, 152, 309, 359n3
Irish Sea, 27
Isabella, Queen of Castile and León, xi, 8, 65
Isabella, Hispaniola, 151
Islas Lucayas (Bahamas), 65
Islington, 243
Italy, 51, 157

James VI/I, King of Scotland and England, 166,
  297, 305–6, 312, 314, 351n23, 354n64, 362n46,
  384n35
James, Thomas, 26
Jemmigen, battle of (1568), 76
Jenkins, John, 351n23
Jewel, John, 99
John of Austria, Don, Governor-General of the
  Low Countries, 109, 119–20
Johnson, Ben, 326
Johnson, Otwell, 22
Joinville, Treaty of, 144, 152, 155, 157, 160
Julius II (Giuliano della Rovere), pope, xii, 330n1
Justin of Nassau, 287, 365n19

Katherine of Aragon, Queen of England, xii, 7
Kent, 125, 240, 283
Kent, Henry Grey, Earl of, 165
Killigrew family, 154
Killigrew, Elizabeth, 126
Killigrew, Sir Henry, 126, 335,n29, 348n29, 354n61
Killigrew, John, 335n29
Killigrew, Peter, 34, 40, 126, 334n24, 335nn28, 29,
  348n29
Killigrew, Thomas, 40, 348n29
King's Bench, court, 6
Knollis, Sir Francis,

Knollis, Sir Francis the younger, 156, 187, 243
Knollis, Henry, 133
Knyvet, Thomas, 224, 275
Kyffin, Maurice, *Blessednes of Brytaine* of, 379n1

La Goleta, fortress of Tunis, 119
La Margarita, Tierra Firme, 69–71, 137
La Rochelle, 89, 207, 353n55, 361n35
Lacy, Alexander, 102
Lane, Ralph, 352n39
Las Casas, Bartolomé de, 108
Lane, Ralph, 352n39
Lannoy, House of, 55
Laudonnière, Réne de, 67, 69
Lee, Edward, 330n2
Leeds Castle, 245
Le Havre, 226
Leicester, Robert Dudley, Earl of, 51, 68, 84–5,
  90, 106, 120, 122, 131, 133–5, 137, 150, 156, 161,
  167, 189, 213, 324, 343n3, 353nn43, 44, 46,
  355n15, 359n69; as Captain-General of English
  forces in the Low Countries (1585/6), 158–60,
  162, 169, 277, 352n38; (1587), 174–5, 215; Lieu-
  tenant and Captain-General of English land
  forces, (1588), 239–243, 262, 279–81, 283,
  370nn47, 48, 371n53, 379n5, 380n10; death of,
  291, 312
Leigh, Richard, 296
Leighton, Sir Thomas, 172, 187–8
Leiva, Don Alonso Martinez de, 251, 253, 269
Lemnius, Levinus, 38
León, 65
Lepanto, sea-battle of, 119, 217, 251
Lerma, Don Francisco Gomez de Sandoval y
  Rojas, Duke of, 305
'Levanters', English Turkey Company vessels,
  168, 231, 358n50
Leveson, John, 358n53
Leveson, Richard, 224
Lewes, 376n43, 380n23
Lewes, Richard, 283
Lichfield, diocese of, 186
Ligne, House of, 55
Lima, 123
Limehouse, 240
Lincoln, Earl of, *see* Clinton and Saye
Lincoln, Elizabeth de Fiennes, Countess of,
  380n45
Lippomano, Hieronimo, 352n31
Lisbon, 162, 165–8, 171–2, 178, 192, 194–6, 198,
  210–11, 309, 354n60
Little Britain, 102
Lizard Peninsula, 238, 309
Logan, James, 332n29
Lok, Mary, 45
Lok, Michael, 336n49
Lok, Thomas, 45, 336n49
Lollards, laws against reactivated, 43

London, 6, 41–2, 45, 56, 60, 87, 108–9, 124, 129,
139, 152, 166, 172, 188, 190, 204, 263, 292, 311,
320, 335n36, 338n43; merchants of, 36, 56, 68,
77, 127, 143, 153–4, 166, 181, 239–40, 242, 292;
apprentices, 107; diocese of, 186; loans to gov-
ernment from, 198; merchantmen of, sent to
the fleet, 199; Common Council of, 199; sup-
plies of gunpowder in, 262–3; wards of:
Bridge Within, 372n76; Cripplegate, 372n76;
Langbourne, 372n76
London Bridge, 239, 280, 298, 379n4
London, John Aylmer, bishop of, 300
London, Treaty of (1604), 312–3
Looe, Andreas de, 192, 354n71
Lords Lieutenancies, English, 173, 185, 189–90,
199, 247–8, 358n59; of Staffordshire, 244; of
Northamptonshire, 244
Lords of the Congregation, 51–2, 55
Lorraine, 73
Lovell, John, 70
Lowestoft, 275
Low Countries (also Seventeen Provinces,
Netherlands), x, xiv, 8, 18, 41, 43–4, 79, 81,
109, 179, 281–2, 287, 311, 338n44, 342n60;
merchants of, 21–2, 58–9, 154, 169, 198, 214,
262; commercial disputes with England, 32,
36, 55–7, 60–3, 68, 72, 152–153; revolt in, 54,
56, 62, 73–6, 79–80, 83–9, 91, 108–110,
119–121, 123, 129, 131, 136, 142, 144–5, 152,
169–70, 213, 308–9, 315–8, 346n51, 349n58,
362n47; Protestant refugees from, 56, 75, 107;
English troops in, 88, 91, 108–9, 118, 146–7,
149, 157–61, 173–4, 182–3, 239, 283, 311–2, 316,
342n70, 368n8; withdrawn from, 169, 188;
English Catholic volunteers in, 314, 383n28
Ludgate Hill, 299
Lyme Regis, 199, 234
Lime Regis Bay, 237, 249
Lynn, 26

Machyn, Henry, 58
Madeira, 57
Madox, Richard, 349n57, 356n30
Madrid, 91, 129, 152, 176, 192, 292
Magnus Intercursus, Anglo–Burgundian trade
agreement, 8, 56, 60
Maidstone Castle, 245
Man, John, 76, 306, 340n30
Manington, Ambrose, 224
Manningham, John, 307
Mar, John Earskine, Earl of, 165
Marbecke, John, 330n9
Margate, 196, 202, 276–7, 284–5, 380n14
Margaret of Parma, Regent of the Netherlands,
55, 60–1, 73, 119, 338nn43, 44
Margaret of Valois, 89
Marian exiles, 45, 48, 56
Marine Causes, Office and officers of, English

naval administration, 68, 179–80, 209, 223,
225, 357n43, 367n43
Marques, Pedro Menendez, 350n74
Marshalsea prison, Southwark, 127
Marsden, William, 345n43
Marseilles, 374n15
Mary, Queen Dowager of Hungary, Regent of
the Netherlands, 35
Mary of Guise, Regent of Scotland, 50–2
Mary Stuart, Queen of Scotland and France, xi,
51–2, 75–6, 81, 84, 90, 96, 111–12, 144, 341n40,
342n72, 343n7, 354n59; trial and execution of,
163–66, 169, 173, 354nn62, 64, 74, 364n12
Mary Tudor, Queen of England, xiii, 31–2, 36,
38–49, 322, 333n3, 334n21, 335nn36, 41, 336n2,
347n8, 348n29; religious policy, 42–6, 48–9,
60, 100–1, 336nn45, 47, 48, 355n23
Mason, Sir John, 50, 338n31
Maurice of Nassau, Prince of Orange, 195, 308
Medinaceli, Don Juan de la Cerda, Duke of,
108, 346n51
Medina Sidonia, Don Alonso Pérez de Guzmán
el bueno, Duke of, 166, 168, 172, 201, 207,
211, 216, 220, 223, 229–30, 233, 249–50, 252,
255–6, 258–61, 264–8, 274, 281–2, 287, 295,
297, 313, 355n2, 365n23, 368n10, 373n12,
375nn30, 33
Mediterranean, 8, 54, 181, 314
Medway, river, 225
Melcombe Regis, 124
Mendoza, Bernardino de, Spanish ambassador,
111, 127–8, 131, 133–4, 137, 139, 144, 153, 166,
169, 295–6, 325, 349nn38, 46, 354n74, 355n23,
362n43
Mendoza, Lope Hurtado de, 24
Mercator, Gerard, projection of, 321
Mercenaries, German, 74, 174
Mercers, guild (also 'company') of, 41–2
Merchant Adventurers, 'company' of, 61, 63,
74–5, 77, 174, 375n29
Merchants, Anglo–Spanish (see also Spanish
Company), 7–12, 18, 28–9, 58, 81, 117, 128,
152, 154, 162, 166, 313–4, 327
Meteren, Emanuel Van, 273, 368n3, 378n19
Metz, 51
Middelburg, 150–1, 159, 161, 173–4, 196
Mildmay, Sir Walter, 130–2, 164
Milford Haven, 189, 383n14
Missionaries, Catholic, in England, 105–7, 194,
345nn43, 45, 372n64
Mocenigo, Giovanni, Venetian ambassador,
369n25
Mokkesand, John, 26
Molin, Nicolo, Venetian ambassador, 306
Moluccas (also 'Spice Islands'), 133, 137, 140, 150,
156, 225
Molyneaux, Emeric, 320
Moncada, Hugh de, 252–3, 269–70, 373n12, 374, 16

Montague, Anthony Browne, Viscount, 280, 380n8

Montanus, Reginaldus Gonsalvius, 108

Montauban, 89

Montmorency, Anne de, Constable of France, 58

Moore, Sir William, 380n45

Moray Firth, 283

Morgan, Sir Thomas, 188, 380n14

Morgan, Walter, 108–9

Morisco Rebellion, 84

Morocco (also 'Barbary Coast'), 36–7

Mostaganem, battle of, 54

Mousehole, Cornwall, 206

Munguia, 24

Munster, 121

Muscovy, 36–7

Muscovy Company (also Russia Company), 135, 367n44

Musselburgh, battle of, 226

Musters, General, 78, 130, 173, 182, 238; Particular (Trained Bands), 173, 181–91, 213, 358nn52, 56, 59, 359nn82, 83, 84; of Cheshire, 183, 371n62; Cornwall, 238, 359n76; Derbyshire, 183; Devon, 238, 249; Dorset, 239, 249; Essex, 240, 370n43; Hampshire and Isle of Wight, 183, 262; Hertfordshire, 240; Kent, 183, 239, 242, 263, 370n39; Lancashire, 183, 244, 371n62; Leicestershire, 243; Lincolnshire, 371n62; London, 188–9, 242, 359n81; Norfolk, 239; Northamptonshire, 185, 243, 371n59; Somerset, 183, 238, 249, 373n3; Staffordshire, 183; Sussex, 183; Wiltshire, 249, 373n3; Worcestershire, 243; provision of weapons for, 184–6; provision of horses for, 185–6; ordered to be ready to march, 206; deployments in 1588, 238, 242–4, 359n82, 370nn35, 47, 371nn 53, 54, 58, 62; measures to exclude Catholics from, 244, 247–8, 372n81

Naarden, 108

Namur, 120

Naples, 168

Narrow Seas, 59, 61, 73–4, 83, 121, 131, 166, 177, 193, 214, 232, 234, 242, 256, 258, 260–3, 274–5, 282, 287–8, 353n48, 357n46, 360n11, 379n31

Nashe, Thomas, *Pierce Pennilesse* of, 327

Naval forces, Dutch, due under Treaty of Nonsuch, 212, 261, 265, 365n19, 377n2

Naval operations, English, (1543–4) 19; (1545), 218; (1546), 25; (1559/60), 52, 88, 342n64; (1562/3), 226; (1573) 88; (1574) 121; (1580) 130; West Indies Raid (1585), 146–7, 150–2, 156–7, 160–2, 318, 356n27; Cadiz raid (1587), 166–9; Narrow Seas squadrons, 179, 287–8, 291, 366nn36, 37; Portugal (1586), 180; Atlantic raids (1589–92), 308–9; Cadiz (1596), 309; Azores (1597), 309

Naval operations, Spanish, (1570), 86, 342n58; (1571) 86, 342n58; (1574) 121, 347n13; Brest (1593/4), 308; armadas of 1596–7, 309, 383nn13, 14

Navy Royal, English, nature, strength and condition of, improvements to, 148, 162, 176–81; mobilization to meet the armada, 179–81; condition following campaign, 288–9,

Netherlands, the, *see* Low Countries.

Newcastle, 19, 97, 274, 371n62, 376n47, 378n27

Newfoundland fishing fleets, French, 33

Newport, Isle of Wight, 26

Nicaragua, 122

Nieuport, 352n39

Nijmegen, 175

Nimes, 89

Noailles, François de, bishop of Dax, French ambassador, 42

Noble, John, 122

Nombre de Dios, 122, 131

Nonsuch, Treaty of, 146, 157–8

Norfolk, 276, 285

Norfolk, Thomas Howard, 3rd Duke of, 7

Norfolk, Thomas Howard, 4th Duke of, 82, 84–86

Normandy, 308

Norreys, Sir Henry, 283, 341n38

Norreys, Sir John, 159, 187–9, 205, 239, 241–2, 280, 289, 304, 307

Northampton, Henry Howard, Earl of, 306, 326

Northern Rising, 85, 95–7, 105, 108, 111, 113, 343n14, 345n39, 363n63

North Foreland, 275, 277

North Sea, 256, 276, 281–3, 287, 342n65

Northumberland, John Dudley, Viscount L'Isle, Earl of Warwick, Duke of, 24, 27–8, 33, 36, 38, 337n6, 363n63; commands English fleet (1545), 222

Northumberland, Sir Henry Percy, 8th Earl of, 111, 346n62

Northumberland, Sir Thomas Percy, 7th Earl of, 82, 111, 343n7

Norton, Thomas, 102, 344n31, 345n45

Norwich, 32

Notre Dame, Paris, 165

Nowell, Alexander, 298, 300

O'Donnell, Hugh Roe, 309

Oleron, Isle d', 20

Ommelanden, 74

Orange–Nassau, House of, 55

Ordenberg, 342n70

Ordnance, English tactical innovations, 217–8 ; supplied to English fleet, 368n15, 369n17; limitations of technology, 231–2, 251, 253, 368n13; Spanish limitations in employment, 217–8, 231

Ordnance, munitions, English shortages, 233–4, 256–7, 260, 262–3, 274–5, 282–3, 369n29, 375n27, 376n43

Ordnance, types discussed: Demi–cannon, 231, 233; Culverin, 231–3; Demi–culverin, 231–3; Falcon, 184; Minion, 184; Sacre, 184

Øresund, 215,

Orkney Islands, 283, 288

Ostend, 205, 287

Ostriche, William, 9

Ottoman Porte and Empire, 54, 84, 119, 161, 170, 192, 316, 341n40; naval truce with Spain (1577), 170

Oughtred, Henry, 135

Ousley, 364n11

Owers, shoals, 260

Owrde ('Horde'), Thomas, 359n76

Oxenham, John, 122, 137, 140, 347n17, 350n70

Oxford, Ann de Vere, Countess of, 241

Oxford, Edward de Vere, Earl of, 241

Pacific Ocean, 123, 136

Pacification of Ghent, 119

Paget, William, Lord, 23, 49, 51, 337n6

Palavicino, Sir Horatio, 186, 282, 379n34

Palmer, Sir Henry, 193, 261, 263, 266, 272, 288, 348n20, 364n16, 366n36, 377n3

Palmer, Henry the younger, 366n36

Panama, 88, 122–3, 132, 140, 218, 312, 350n70

Pantalarea, 365n24

Papacy, 51, 79, 93, 113–4, 119, 130, 322–3; bulls: *Inter Caetera* (1493), xi, xii, 8, 11, 37, 132, 312–3; *Regnans in Excelsis* (1571), 96, 100; schemes to recover England for Catholicism, 93, 130–1, 147, 349n42

Paris, 89, 108, 133, 139, 165–6, 168–9, 172, 194, 215, 295, 308, 334n24

Parliament, English, 6, 43, 96–7, 106–7, 147, 163–4, 197, 311, 324, 336n4, 342n72, 343n13, 347n1, 364n11, 12, 380n8, 384n31

Parma, Alexander Farnese, Duke of, 119–20, 136, 142, 144, 149, 151–2, 158–60, 162–3, 170–6, 179, 189–90, 192, 194, 196–7, 201, 205, 208, 212–7, 219–20, 224, 233, 238–42, 244, 256–8, 261, 264–7, 274–6, 281–5, 287, 292–4, 296, 308, 349n58, 354n71, 362n47, 363n64, 368n8, 373n2, 377n9, 380nn10, 14

Paston, Clement, 225.

Paternoster Row, 111.

Paulet, Sir Amias, 165, 354n62

Pearne, Dr, Dean of Ely, 246.

Peckham, Sir George, 138–9, 143, 350n65; *True Reporte* of, 138, 140, 350n65

Peere, William, pirate, 26

Pegna, Lope Ruiz de la, 294

Pelham, Sir William, 140

Pembroke, William Herbert, Earl of, 68, 135, 371n58

Peñafiel, Don Juan Téllez Girón, Marquis of, 268

Peppit, Gilbert, 125

Pepys, Samuel, 103, 327

Pernambuco, Brazil, 3

Pett, Peter, 177–80, 240, 357n46, 358n48, 370n48

Philip of Burgundy, father of Charles v, 8, 56

Philip II, King of Spain, xi, xii, xiii, xiv, xv, 37, 50–63, 67–91, 95, 109, 113–4, 117, 119, 128–134, 136–145, 147, 179, 195, 210, 212–3, 220, 223, 244–5, 298, 311, 315–8, 322, 324–5, 335nn36,41, 42, 43, 338n44, 339nn8, 9, 341nn40, 42, 43, 347nn8, 13, 348n20, 349nn46, 58, 350n70, 352nn35, 39, 353nn40, 48, 49, 354nn64, 74, 77, 355n23, 362n43; as Charles V's regent in Spain, 23–4, 28; as King–Consort of England, 32, 36, 41–6, 108; as King of Portugal (see also Union of the Crowns), 117–8; begins to consider military measures against England, 139–42, 152–8, 161–3; authorizes support of Throckmorton plot, 144, 212; reaction to Mary Stuart's execution, 166; begins assembly of ships at Lisbon, 167–9, 180, 192; authorizes peace negotiations between Elizabeth and Parma, 176; strategy for the armada (1587), 214; (1588), 216–7, 233, 258, 267, 287, 289, 369n19; strategy for later armadas, 383nn13, 14; intentions for England following victory, 292, 314, 368n8; bankruptcies, 309–10; makes peace with France and relinquishes direct rule of Low Countries, 310; death, 310, 312

Philip III, King of Spain, 305, 310–11, 313

Phillips, John, 3–5, 12

Picardy, 54, 166

Pilgrimage of Grace, 95

Pillars of Hercules, 168

Pinkie, battle of, 225

Piracy, 11, 15–30 *passim*, 33–5, 37, 40–1, 57, 59, 61, 63–4, 87–8, 123–9, 314, 333n2, 334nn10, 11, 18, 335nn27, 30, 342n65, 348nn22, 27, 29, 35, 365n21, 383n27

Pius III (Francesco Todeschini), pope, 330n1

Pius v (Michele Ghislieri), pope, 85–6, 96, 100

Plague, in England, 45, 175, 311, 337n8, 383n19

Plate, river, 195

Plomleigh, John, 126

Plymouth, 26, 40, 76, 131, 146, 151–2, 156, 167, 189, 193, 201–9, 214, 216, 222, 225, 228–9, 234, 238, 278, 336n51, 339n9, 358n48, 360n11, 361nn22, 29, 362n56, 363n70, 365n23, 25, 368n3, 375n30, 376n47, 379n40

Plymouth Hoe, 193, 228

Plymouth Sound, 208–9, 229

Poole, 26, 189, 199

Poole, William, 224

Port courts, 6

Portland, 234, 248–50, 252–3, 362n56

Portland Bill, 252, 259, 374n15

Portland Castle, 249

Portsmouth, 3, 40, 186, 189, 249, 256, 262, 376n39

Portugal, xi, 24, 87, 117–8, 131–2, 138, 167, 193, 210, 213, 307, 310; New World Possessions of, xi; West African trade, 36–7, 68, 72, 87, 135, 137; Far East trade, 132, 135–6; northern European entrepôt at Antwerp, 8; interlopers trading in Spanish Caribbean, 66; naval resources of, 118; union off with Spain (1580), 121, 130, 135–8, 148, 168, 179, 316, 353n48
Portugalete, 152
Potosí, silver mines of, 118
Poultry, London, 102
Powell, Edward, 350n2
Powle, Stephen, 192, 194
Presbyterianism, 98
Preston, Amyas, 378n13
Pricket, Robert, 345n39
Privateers, English (also likedealers, voluntaries), 11, 13–30 *passim*, 33–5, 57–61, 81, 86, 136–8, 142, 153–5, 162, 181, 310, 314, 331nn2, 3, 332nn16, 21, 23, 29, 33, 333nn 3, 37, 39, 41, 352nn28, 33, 35, 383n26
Privateers, Dutch (see also Sea–Beggars), 66, 149, 310, 314
Privateers, Flemish, 17
Privateers, French (*see also* Huguenot), 17, 40, 44, 60, 66–8, 72, 81, 122, 361n35
Privateers, Scottish, 18, 60
Privy Council, 6, 22, 26–8, 33–7, 47, 58, 84, 87, 90, 124–6, 130, 142–3 , 149–50, 153, 161, 163–4, 167, 173, 176, 179, 183, 185–8, 198–202, 204–5, 234, 237, 239–47, 256, 261–3, 269, 274–5, 277, 281, 283–7, 295, 297, 342n65, 346n49, 348n20, 349n45, 359n83, 360n11, 361n25, 363n64, 371n53, 372nn64, 67, 379nn31, 40, 380nn13, 24, 25, 382n51; plans war strategy, 209–16, 222; attitudes towards prisoners of war, 293–4
Proclamations, on restraint of piracy, (1398), 332n16; (1547), 33; (1558), 57; (1569), 87; (1575), 124; (1577), 124; authorizing privateers, (1544), 20–2, 28, 57, 332nn16, 33; (1557), 57, 338n24; (1563), 58; (1585), 153–5
Propaganda, 99–103, 107–11, 295–7, 344n32
Protestantism, state of, in England, 49, 85, 92–3, 98–9
Public finances and expenditure, English, 14, 21, 69, 77, 86, 159–60, 173–5, 184, 289, 331n11, 333n3, 383n21; foreign subsidies, 157, 173, 169, 174, 215, 355n11; on the Navy Royal, 176, 197, 356n26; levies and public loans, 197–8
Pudsey, Southampton merchant, 10, 11
Puerto de Plata, 340n17
Puerto Real, 168
Puerto Rico, 138, 151, 350n62
Puerto Santa Maria, 168
Pullison family, merchants, 154
Pullison, Thomas, alderman, 348n20
Purfoote, Thomas, 341n44
Puritans, 85

Quadra, Alonso de la, Spanish ambassador, 57, 338n44, 347n12
Quarles, James, 195–6, 204, 238, 277, 362n58
Queenborough, 193–5, 357n46
Queensborough Castle, 245

Ralegh family, 34
Ralegh, Carew, 150
Ralegh, George, 284, 333n9
Ralegh, John, 333n9
Ralegh, Walter, the elder, 34, 325, 333n9
Ralegh, Sir Walter, 110, 150–1, 155, 187, 192, 275, 288, 292, 324–5, 327, 359n70, 365n29, 372n79, 380n46
Rame Head, 229
Randall, Hugh, 128, 348n35
Randolphe, Thomas, 341n40
Ratcliffe, 240
Raymond, George, 202, 262, 362n52
Recalde, Juan Martínez de, 230, 232, 256, 258–60, 271, 365n23, 374nn20, 25, 375nn34, 35
Recessions, English, (1555–6), 32; (1586–7), 175; (1594–8), 311–2
Recusants, recusancy (*see also* Catholics, English), 98, 104, 139, 142, 175, 188, 244–5, 355n22, 372nn64, 65, 67, 71, 75, 76
Relation of Proceedings, 254, 363n70, 370n30, 374n25
Renard, Simon, Imperial envoy, 41
Reneger, Robert, 10, 22–3, 27, 58, 332n24
Rheims, English seminary at, 98
Rhine, 175, 315
Ribault, Jean, 67, 69, 138
Rich, Thomas, 280
Richard II, King of England, 332n16
Richard III, King of England, 16
Ridolfi, Roberto, conspiracy of, 85, 105, 108, 111, 165, 342nn60, 72
Rio de la Hacha, Tierra Firme, 69–71,
Rio Grande, 65.
Roanoke Island (also 'Virginia'), English colony at, 139, 141, 151, 155–6, 199, 204, 288, 349n38, 350n74, 361nn33, 35
Robinson, Nicholas, 345n34
Rochester, 356n30
Rogers, Daniel, 365n21
Rogers, Richard, vicar of Westerfield, 244
Rome, 7, 8, 91, 104, 130, 133, 165–6, 192, 322, 347n3
Roozendaal, Cornelis Lonck van, 365n19
Rose, William, 331n5
Rotterdam, 108
Rouen, 58, 165, 332n33
Rowse, A. L., 359n76
Rudstone, Robert, 336n46
Runnymede, 45
Russell, Lord John, 6, 27–8
Russell, Sir William, 195, 361n20, 365n18
Rye, 26–7, 35, 200

St Bartholemew's Day, massacre of, 89–90, 108, 142

St James's Palace, Westminster, 243

St Julian, fortress of, 211

St Katherine's Dock, London, 6

St Paul's, Cathedral and Cross, 111, 298–300

St Quentin, seige and capture of (1557), 41, 44, 158, 335n42

St Sebastian, English merchants at, 338n45

St Valéry, battle of (1568), 76

Sackville, Thomas, Lord Buckhurst, 159

Sagres, 168

Salamanca, 43

Salamis, sea–battle of, 268

Salisbury, diocese, of, 186

Salisbury, John Piers, bishop of, 300

Saltash, 351n23

San Augustin, Florida, 162, 218

Sancerre, 89

Sandwich, Kent, 242, 380n25

San Juan de Ulúa, roadstead of Vera Cruz, xv, 71, 76, 80, 108, 218, 327, 340n32

Sanlucar de Barrameda, 117, 351n23

San Miguel, Azorean Island of, 134

Santa Cruz, Albaro de Bazán, Marquis of, 59, 134, 142–3, 339n8; proposes plan to invade England, 162–3, 168; commands gathering armada, 166–8, 171–2, 174, 192, 211

Santa Marta, Tierra Firme, 71

Santander, 121, 305, 348n22, 353n48

Santiago, 123, 137

Santiago de Cuba, 66

Santo Domingo, 162, 218, 331n10

San Vicente, Brazil, 132

Savoy, 73

Scarborough, 332n16

Scarborough Castle, 43

Scarlette, Robert, 360n11

Scepperus, Cornelius, 332n32

Scheldt, river, 91, 173–4, 195, 205

Scheyfve, Jehan, Imperial ambassador, 35

Schmalkalden League, 8

Scillies, 28, 199, 206–7, 214

Scors, Loys, 332n32

Scotland, 20, 32, 50, 52, 87, 108, 144, 166, 172, 201, 214, 226, 272, 281–2, 292–3, 371n62

Sea-Beggars, 18, 75, 77, 81–3, 86– 9, 91, 108–9, 121, 155, 342n62, 353n48

Seaford, 358n68

Second Enterprise, the, 134

Securis, John, 361n23

Seine, 58

Selsey Bill, 260

Seres, William, 100–1

Seventeen Provinces, the, *see* Low Countries

Seville, 28, 58, 65, 68–9, 169, 310, 320, 330n2, 336n49, 351n23, 378n20

Seymour, Lord Henry, 177, 194; commands

Downs squadron, 200–2, 205–6, 214, 216, 224, 238, 249, 260–3, 266, 271, 274–7, 282–4, 291, 324, 361nn20, 29, 362nn51, 52, 363n64, 365n19, 367n46, 369n22, 376n45, 378n28, 379n31

Seymour, Lord Thomas, 28, 33–5, 154, 333n42

Shaftesbury, 139

Sheffield, Edmund, Lord, 202, 220, 247, 257, 261, 285, 289

Sheppey, Isle of, 189, 205

Ship bounties, 148, 351n8

Ship levies, 198–201, 212, 273, 362n36

Shipping, merchant, as auxiliary naval resource, 11, 13–14, 147, 154, 156, 166–7, 181, 198, 212

Ships, named English, *Achates*, 179, 357n46; *Advice*, 221; *Angel of Southampton*, 266; *Anne Frances*, 365n27; *Antelope*, 177, 261, 266, 271; *Ark Royal* (formerly *Ark Ralegh*), 177–8, 221–2, 224, 229–30, 236, 250–1, 253, 261, 266, 269, 271, 275–6, 278, 284, 376n37, 378nn 13, 14, 379nn35, 39; *Ascension of London*, 221; *Ayde*, 221, 224; *Barbara* (London), 3–6, 11, 27, 136; *Bark Bond*, 224, 266; *Bark Burr*, 221; *Bark Clifford*, 369n22; *Bark Denys*, 365n27; *Bark Fenner*, 181; *Bark Lamb*, 274; *Bark Manington*, 224; *Bark St Leger*, 221; *Bark Talbot*, 156, 221, 224, 229, 266, 378n24; *Bark Young*, 221, 266, 366n32, 380n23; *Bartholemew*, 221; *Beare Leicester*, 365n27; *Bonavolia*, 225, 261; *Brave of London*, 221; *Bull*, 179, 357n46; *Centurion of London*, 221, 252, 374n15; *Chance*, 221; *Charles*, 179, 221, 357n46; *Daniel*, 274; *Defiance*, 356n33; *Delight*, 221, 251, 373n7; *Diamond*, 221; *Disdain*, 221, 229; *Dreadnought*, 177–8, 221, 225, 253, 270, 343n77, 356n30; *Edward Bonaventure*, 181, 221, 356n30; *Elizabeth Bonaventure*, 156, 180, 202, 221, 262, 369n17; *Elizabeth Drake*, 221; *Elizabeth Jonas*, 178, 202, 221, 224, 251, 253, 257, 259–60, 277, 285, 288, 357n38, 379n42; *Elizabeth of Lowestoft*, 266; *Elizabeth of Lyme*, 376n47; *Emmanuel of Bridgewater*, 365n27; *Emmanuel of Exeter* ('Armenal'), 365n27; *Emmanuel*, 351n23; *Fancy*, 274; *Fleur de Luce*, 58; *Foresight*, 177, 179, 221, 225, 356n30, 357n46; *Frances of Foy*, 365n27; *Frances of London*, 221; *Gabriel*, 365n27; *Galleon Dudley*, 199, 221, 224; *Galleon Fenner*, 153; *Galleon Hutchin*, 274; *Galleon Leicester* (formerly *Galleon Oughtred*), 135, 137, 156, 181, 221, 224, 253, 356n30; *Garland*, 356n33; *Gift of God*, 376n47; *Golden Hind* (1580) 131; *Golden Hind* (1588), 221, 228, 238; *Golden Lion*, 177, 179, 221, 224, 251, 253, 285, 357n38, 364n16, 367n44; *Golden Lion* (merchantman), 252; *Golden Noble*, 221; *Golden Ryall*, 221; *Greyhound*, 41; *Griffin*, 224; *Hart of Dartmouth*, 221; *Hercules of London*, 221; *Hind of Exeter*, 221; *Hope*, 221, 224, 272, 358n48, 378n19;

Hope of Plymouth, 221; *Hopewell* (1578), 365n27; *Hopewell of London*, 221; *Jesus of Lubeck*, 69, 71; *Jonas of Topsham*, 376n47; *Judith* (1568), 71; *Judith* (1578), 128, 365n27; *Larke*, 221; *Leonard*, 33; *Magdelene Russell*, 27; *Makeshift*, 193; *Margaret and John*, 221, 235–6, 252, 370n30, 374n15; *Mary Anne*, 331n15; *Mary Rose* (1545), 217; *Mary Rose* (1588), 221, 225, 236, 253, 259, 277, 288, 375n31; *Mary Rose* (merchantman), 252, 374n15; *Mayflower* (victualling hoy), 376n47; *Mayflower of London*, 221, 253; *Merchant Royal*, 181, 221, 224, 366n37, 374n15; *Merhonour*, 356n33; *Michael*, 365n27; *Minion*, 71, 80; *Minion of Bristol*, 221; *Minion of London*, 221, 225; *Minion of Plymouth*, 221; *Moon*, 179, 221, 357n46; *Moon* (1578), 365n27; *Nonpareil* (formerly *Philip and Mary*), 177, 221, 224, 251, 259, 270, 278, 357n38, 358n48, 373n5; *Passport*, 221; *Paul*, 331n11; *Pelican*, 376n47; *Primrose*, 152–3, 156; *Prudence*, 369n22; *Rainbow*, 177, 179, 202, 271, 282, 356n28, 357n46; *Red Lion of London*, 221; *Revenge*, 177–8, 221, 230, 236, 251, 255–6, 258, 270, 277, 308, 356nn30, 33, 358n48, 373n5, 374n25, 375n7; *Roebuck*, 181, 236–7, 275; *Rose of Harwich*, 15; *Royal Defence*, 221; *Sacrett*, 334n24; *Salamander*, 41; *Salomon*, 348n35, 365n27; *Sampson*, 369n22; *Scout*, 179, 357n46; *Sea Dragon*, 156; *Seraphim*, 285, 376n47; *Spark of Plymouth*, 221; *Sparrowhawk*, 376n47; *Spy*, 193; *Squirrel*, 350n66; *Susan Parnell*, 224; *Swallow*, 221, 225, 253, 342n64; *Swiftsure*, 177–8, 221, 224, 343n77; *Tiger*, 179, 357n46; *Tiger* (1585 merchantman), 350n2; *Tiger of London*, 221; *Tiger of Plymouth*, 221; *Thomas Drake*, 224; *Thomas of Ipswich*, 365n27; *Thomas of Plymouth*, 221, 266; *Thornback*, 348n20; *Toby of London*, 221; *Tremontana*, 179, 357n46; *Trinity of Totnes*, 26; *Triumph*, 177, 202, 221, 230, 252–3, 257, 259–60, 277, 357n38, 374nn13, 15, 16; *True Dealing*, 376n47; *Unity*, 221, 224; *Vanguard*, 177, 225, 232, 266, 271, 356n28; *Victory*, 178–9, 202, 221, 230, 251, 253, 258, 270, 276, 357n38, 364n16; *Virgin God Save Her*, 199; *Warspite*, 232; *White Bear*, 178, 202, 221, 224, 236, 251, 257, 259–60, 266, 285, 303–4, 357n38; *White Lion*, 156, 167, 224;

Ships, named French, *Guillaume*, 200

Ships, named Spanish and Portuguese, *Barbara of Lequetia*, 24; *Doncella*, 258; *Duquesa Santa Ana*, 258; *Gran Grifon*, 256, 272, 375n27, 376n48; *La Trinidad Valencera*, 272, 378n21; *Madre de Dios*, 309; *Maria Juan*, 272, 378n20; *Nuestra Señora del Rosario*, xv, 235–7, 252, 256, 269, 275, 286, 292, 294, 368n28, 376n48, 382n54; *San Catalina*, 231; *San Felipe*, 271–2, 274, 378n17; *San Juan de Portugal*, 230, 233,
256, 268, 271; *San Juan de Sicilia*, 272; *San Lorenzo*, 253, 269–70, 374n17, 377nn9, 12, 378nn13, 14; *San Luis*, 258; *San Marcos*, 268, 271; *San Martín*, 230–1, 252–3, 255–6, 259–60, 264, 268, 270–4, 374n21, 378n22; *San Mateo*, 271, 274; *San Pedro Mayor*, xv, 272, 293–4, 382nn51, 54; *San Salvador* (1545), 22–3; *San Salvador* (1588), xv, 231, 237, 252, 256, 264, 292, 294, 369n29, 378n18; *Santa Ana* (Biscayan squadron), 208; *Santa Ana* (Guipúzcoan squadron), 272; *Santa Barbara*, 5–6, 11; *Santa Maria*, 269; *Santa Maria de la Rosa*, 272; *São Felipe*, 169, 176; *Trinity*, 25–6

Ships, types: Cromsters, Dutch, 215; Galleasses, 226, 252–3, 256, 374n14; Galleons, 168; development of English raze (or 'race') built design, 176–8, 343n77, 356nn30, 33; limitations of, 232–3; Galleys, 168, 208, 231, 358n50, 364n16, 365n24, 374n15; Pataches, 208, 267; Zabras, 208

Shirley, Sir Thomas, 355n12

Shoreham, 26, 187, 380n23

Shornecliff, 242

Shrewsbury, George Talbot, Earl of, 135, 156, 165, 360n11, 372n64, 380n13

Sicily, 168

Sierra Leone, 68–9

Silva, Don Guzman de, Spanish envoy, 63, 69–70, 338n45, 339nn7, 14, 340n15

Simancas, xiv, 304

Sixtus v (Felice Peretti), pope, 161, 166, 169, 298

Sluys, 173–4, 176, 196, 241

Smerwick, 130–2, 325

Smith family, merchants, 154

Smithfield, 108

Solent, the, 3, 217, 255, 258, 375n34, 376n39

Somerset, Edward Seymour, Earl of Hertford, Duke of, 32, 337n6

Somerset House, 299; peace conference at (1604), 304, 306, 313, 326

Sonoy, Dirck, 196

Sores, Jacques de, 66

Soundings, the, 27

Sousa, Antonio Lopes de, Portuguese ambassador, 36

Southampton, 3, 10, 22, 26–7, 36, 126–7, 134, 283, 285

Southwell, Sir Robert, 202, 224, 257, 272

Spain, x, xi, 9, 18, 27, 44, 51, 60, 64, 68, 72, 81, 83, 86, 89–90, 93, 117, 124, 130, 145, 147, 154–5, 161, 169, 192–3, 195, 207, 210, 212–6, 272, 288, 293–4, 303–10, 319, 321–2, 324, 327, 338nn31, 44, 360n11, 364n11, 365n22; New World possessions and commodities of, xi, 9–10, 37, 64–72, 112, 118, 121–3, 128, 130, 133, 137, 142, 147–9, 156–7, 165, 169, 313, 339n3, 347n7, 349n52; merchants and merchant shipping of, 21, 25–6, 29, 59, 152–4, 179; Newfoundland fishing fleet of, 156, 352n35; state of, at end of Anglo–Spanish war, 310

Spanish Company, the, 9, 127

Spes, Don Guerau de, Spanish envoy, 76–7, 81, 341n43, 342n60

Spindelow, Henry, 224

Spithead, 258, 260

Stade, 256, 262, 275, 311, 375n29

Stafford, 244, 298

Stafford, Sir Edward, 153, 165, 168, 172, 192, 194, 295, 354nn60, 71, 360nn5, 6

Stafford, Thomas, 43, 335n40

Standen, Sir Anthony, 162

Stanley, Sir Edward, 371n62

Stanley, Sir William, 160, 244, 369n28

Staple, English merchants of the, 338n42

Star Chamber, 96

Starke, Matthew, 380n43

States–General, 134, 144–5, 150, 157, 173–4, 188, 215, 287, 308, 310, 312, 383n26

Stationers' Company, 102

Stationer's Hall, 102, 279, 344n32

Statutes and other legislative instruments: Act of Supremacy (1534), xii, 49; Six Articles (1539), 9, 49; Restraint of Appeals (1533), 49; Dispensations Act (1534), 49; Treason Act (1534), 49; Restraint of Annates (1534), 49; Submission of the Clergy (1534), 49; Ten Articles (1536), 49; Dissolution of the Monasteries (1536 &1539), 49; Dissolution of the Chantries (1545), 49; Acts of Uniformity (1549 & 1552), 49; Forty-Two Articles (1553), 49; Act of Uniformity (559), 49, 53, 85, 94, 114, 380n8; Thirty-Nine Articles (1563), 53; Treasons Act (1572), 97, 344n31

Stokes family, merchants, 154

Stone, a wag, 307

Straits of Magellan, 132

Strand, London, 299

Stranguishe, Henry, 34, 40, 57–8

Stokes, Thomas, 349n42

Stubbes, Philip, 103–4, 112

Stukely ('Stockwell'), John, 349n38

Stukely, Sir Thomas, 83

Suffolk, 285

Sulyard, Edward, 372n65

Surian, Michel, 335n41

Sussex, 285

Sussex, Sir Henry, 4th Earl of (from 1583), 88, 186, 234, 256, 262, 369n21, 373n6, 375n28, 376n39

Sussex, Sir Thomas Radcliffe, 3rd Earl of, 60, 355n23

Sweveghem, François de Halewynd, Sieur de, 87

Sydenham, Humphrey, 224

Sydney, Sir Philip, 90, 353n46

Tactics, fleet, English, 217–8, lack of mass manoeuvre experience, 218–9; lack of adequate signalling techniques, 219; little formal command structure at outset of campaign, 219–20; rudimentary line–ahead formation employed, 220, 230, 365n29; provisional fleet deployment, 221–2; absence of standing naval officer corps, 222–3

Tactics, fleet, Spanish, 229–30; *en lúnula* defensive formation, 271, 229, 376n48; *en arco*, 376n48, 378n25; reorganized after first clash, 250

Tagus, river, 167, 169, 211

Temple Bar, London, 299

Terceira, Azorean Island of, 133–4; sea battle off (1582), 134, 142, 212, 217, 253

Tewkesbury, 200

Texel, river, 283

Thames, river, 60, 124, 167, 199, 214, 216, 225, 238–40, 348n22; bulwark across, 239–40, 264n16, 370nn40, 48, 376n40, 377n6

Thanet, Isle of, 205

Thompson, Humphrey, 40–1

Thompson, John, 40–1

Thorne, Robert, 330n2

Throckmorton, Francis, conspiracy of, 111, 144, 160, 343n1, 346n46

Throckmorton, Job, 164–5, 353n58

Throckmorton, 'Long John', 334n24

Throckmorton, Sir Nicholas, 49

Tilbury, 128, 364n16; armed encampment at (1588), 238–41, 262, 279–81, 283–4, 287, 319, 370nn43, 47, 48, 371n53, 380nn11, 12

Tilbury Ness, 239

Tipton, Hugh, 330n8, 338n34

Tollarde, 'Cutbeard', 351n23

Tomson, Richard, 378n14

Topsham, Devon, 25

Torbay, 234

Tordesillas, Treaty of (1494), 8, 9, 11, 37, 64, 132, 138, 312, 322, 330n1

Torres Viejo, fortress of, 211

Torrington, 284

Totnes, 26

Tower of London (also Ordnance Office), 77, 335n29, 346n62, 355n23, 368n28; ordnance and munitions issued from, 173, 234, 238, 256, 262, 368n15, 375n28

Townshend, Sir Roger, 261, 278, 376n37

Tremayne, Andrew, 334n24

Tremayne, Nicholas, 334n24

Tresham, Sir Thomas, 246, 372nn71, 75

Treswell, Robert, 305–6, 382n3

Tripoli, 54

Tudor, Dynasty of, xiii, 56, 95

Tuncker, Thomas, 172

Tunis, 119

Turkey Company, 170, 311, 354n80

Tuscany, Grand Duke of, 162

Tynemouth, 378n27

Typhus, in the Spanish fleet, 172; in the English fleet, 204, 228, 278, 284–7, 368n2, 379n42
Tyrell, Sir William, 34, 40, 342n65
Tyrone, Hugh, Earl of, 309, 383n13

Ubaldino, Petruccio, 203, 210, 251, 253, 360n11, 362n54, 364n8, 370n30, 373n5, 381n41
Ubilla, Martin Pérez, 332n31
Upnor Castle, 240,
Urquiza, Juanes de, 339n9
Ushant, 207, 214, 310, 363n70
Utrecht, 74; union of, 349n58

Valdés, Don Diego Flores de, 236
Valdés, Don Pedro de, 236, 292–3
Valladolid, 304–5, 313
Valois, Dynasty of, xii, xiii, 4, 7, 17, 30, 33, 44, 51, 56, 66, 73, 78, 144; extinction, 307, 322
Vanegas, Alonso de, 374n21, 375n27, 377n49, 378nn22, 26
Varamund, Ernest, 108
Vassy, massacre at, 53
Vaughan, John, 154
Vendôme, Duke of, 50
Venezuela, 69, 71
Venice, 165, 191, 194; Doge and Senate of, 169, 191
Vervins, Treaty of, 310
Vienna, 22
Villa Nova, Pedro de, 25–6

Wachen, Baron de, admiral, 70
Wadsworth, James, 99
Wales, 189
Walsingham, Sir Francis, ambassador in Paris, 90; Privy Councillor, 91, 8, 102, 109, 120, 131–5, 139–40, 142–4, 149, 152, 155, 161–2, 165, 167, 172, 187, 189, 191–4, 196, 205–6, 210, 213, 234, 238, 245, 247, 261, 265, 281–4, 287–9, 291, 295, 302, 312, 325, 345n45, 348n22, 349n42, 350n65, 352nn34, 35, 38, 353n46, 354nn62, 71, 77, 355n22, 358n56, 359nn1, 69, 360nn6, 11, 12, 361n20, 363nn63, 69, 364nn11, 12, 365nn18, 22, 26, 367n46, 368n2, 370nn47, 48, 371n58, 376nn40, 45, 378n24, 379n42, 381n43, 383n24
Wapping Stairs, 40–1, 128
Ward, Margaret, 298
Ward, Samuel, 383n19
Wareham, 124
Warwick, 96, 164
Warwick, Ambrose Dudley, Earl of, 353n43
Wash, the, 189
Watson, William, 172
Watts family, merchants, 154
Watts, John, 198, 361n33
Weldon, Anthony, 306
Western Risings, 95

West Indies, 72
Westmorland, Charles Neville, Earl of, 82, 343n7
West Sussex, 125
Wetherby, Yorks, 97
Weymouth, 124, 128, 199, 369n29
Whitehall, 76, 93, 184, 190, 197, 243, 280, 285–6
Whyte, Henry, 224, 229, 378nn14, 24
Wight, Isle of, 26, 189, 249, 258, 261, 263, 362n56, 373n2
Wilbraham, Thomas, 346n51
Wilcox, Robert, 373n9
Wilkinson, Edward, 365n24
Willet, Andrewe, 345n39
Willoughby, Bertie Peregrine de Eresby, Lord, 159
William of Nassau, Prince of Orange and the Netherlands, 75, 81, 120, 123, 137, 144–5, 147, 149, 160, 348n20
Williams, Sir Roger, 220, 359n70
Willoughby, Sir Hugh, 36
Wilson, Thomas, 117, 130, 347n3
Wilton, Arthur, Lord Grey de, 187, 243, 246
Winchester, William Paulet, Marquis of, 369n21
Winchester, Thomas Cooper, bishop of, 299
Winchester, Robert Horn, bishop of, 105
Windsor, 330n9
Winslade, Tristram, 369n28
Winter, George, 88, 356n33
Winter, John, 133
Winter, Sir William, 52, 88, 156, 179–80, 219, 223, 225, 261, 263, 266, 270–2, 274, 337n15, 342n64, 365n26, 368n15, 373n7, 374n20, 378nn13, 25, 379n32
Winter, William, the younger, 156, 225
Winwood, Ralph, 306, 383nn10, 28
Wisbech, bishop of Ely's palace at, 245–6, 297
Wood, John, 6
Woodhouse, Sir William, 41, 57
Wooley, John, 213, 355n22, 364n12
Woolwich, 180
Worcester, William Somerset, Earl of, 87, 371n58
Worseley, Sir Richard, 26
Wotton, Nicholas, 334n24, 352n34
Wright, Edward, 321, 384n33
Wriothesley, Thomas, Earl of Southampton, 27
Wroth, John, 192
Wurtemberg, Duke of,
Wyatt, Sir Thomas, rebellion of, 39, 41, 44, 336n46
Wyndham, Thomas, 27, 37, 334n18

York, assizes at, 372n64
Yorke, Rowland, 160
Young, John, 366n32, 380n23

Zeeland, 74–5, 81, 91, 121, 150, 157, 215
Zuñiga, Don Balthasar de, 311
Zutphen, seige of, 159–60